THE SOLZHENITSYN READER

THE SOLZHENITSYN READER

New and Essential Writings

1947–2005

EDITED BY

Edward E. Ericson, Jr., and Daniel J. Mahoney

ISI BOOKS

Solzhenitsyn, Aleksandr Isaevich, 1918–2008

The Solzhenitsyn reader : new and essential writings, 1947–2005 /
edited by Edward E. Ericson, Jr., and Daniel J. Mahoney. —1st
paperback ed. —Wilmington, DE : ISI Books, c2009.

p. ; cm.

ISBN: 978-1-935191-55-1
First published in hardcover, c2006.

1. Solzhenitsyn, Aleksandr Isaevich, 1918-2008—Translations
into English. 2. Russian literature—20th century—Translations into
English. I. Ericson, Edward E. II. Mahoney, Daniel J., 1960–
III. Title.

PG3488.O4 A2 2009   2008939036
891.78/44—dc22   0903

Published in the United States by:
ISI Books
Intercollegiate Studies Institute
3901 Centerville Road
Wilmington, DE 19807
www.isibooks.org

Interior design by Beer Editorial and Design

Manufactured in the United States of America

Contents

Preface to the Paperback Edition

With the death of Aleksandr Isaevich Solzhenitsyn on August 3, 2008, the world has lost one of the great souls of this or any age, a writer of skill and grace and a true friend of human liberty and dignity. The numerous articles written about his life and legacy in the weeks that followed were for the most part respectful. With a few notable exceptions, commentators paid tribute to the extraordinary facts of Solzhenitsyn's life as well as to the singular role that he played in undermining the moral and political legitimacy of the entire Communist enterprise. After decades of ignoring Solzhenitsyn—or relegating him to a past with little relevance to the present or future—Anglophone elites found themselves needing to come to terms with the human and historical significance of a writer who had changed the course of history through his refusal to bow before the violence and lies that were the hallmark of ideological despotism.

Yet there was something rather dated about many of the judgments put forward by foes and friends alike. This should not have come as a surprise since the English-speaking world had not, truth be told, paid adequate attention to Solzhenitsyn since at least the early 1980's. Alas, a campaign of disinformation and distortion that suggested that the author of *The Gulag Archipelago* was not a friend of human liberty had done its work in some quarters. Many people's judgments were based on old prejudices rather than on the totality of Solzhenitsyn's writings and the remarkable consistency of his thought over a 60-year period. Others had just stopped paying attention (publishers had largely ceased to make new—and old—books by Solzhenitsyn available to the public). One also witnessed a lamentable tendency to reduce Solzhenitsyn to the level of a commentator on current events, an approach that is now almost habitual among journalistic commentators on his work. In our view, a very different approach is necessary if we are to render justice to Solzhenitsyn's achievement. Now that Solzhenitsyn's life and work are completed we are called to engage him openly, honestly, and critically for what he is: a writer, historian, and moral and political philosopher (in the highest, non-academic sense of that term) of the first rank.

The editors first conceived this *Reader* to address a lacuna in North American publishing and commentary regarding Solzhenitsyn. Readers can confront for the first time a wide range of the genres that make up Solzhenitsyn's immense and varied *oeuvre* from the remarkable poems from prison, camp, and exile that help illuminate how Solzhenitsyn became Solzhenitsyn to the movingly elegiac "Miniatures," or "prose poems," that Solzhenitsyn began writing again upon his return to Russia in 1994. For the first time in English, one can read significant excerpts from *March 1917* and *April 1917,* the concluding "knots" of *The Red Wheel,* excerpts from the unexpurgated original 96-chapter version of *The First Circle,* one of the eight two-part short stories that Solzhenitsyn wrote in the 1990s ("No Matter What"), and significant excerpts from 1998's *Russia in Collapse* and from the two-volume historical work on Russia's "Jewish Question," *Two Hundred Years Together* (a work much commented on but little read). In addition the *Reader* includes the fullest range of Solzhenitsyn's essays and speeches available in English, some for the first time or in new translations. In our judgment, this volume allows readers to have access to a splendid belletrist, a political analyst and historian who defends moderation against the extremes, and a principled advocate of justice, conscience, and self-limitation. A perusal of its pages also makes clear that Solzhenitsyn is an original theorist of *self-government* rather than the "authoritarian" of legend.

We have been deeply moved by the response of so many readers to the opportunity that *The Solzhenitsyn Reader* has given them to discover—or rediscover—the merits of Solzhenitsyn as a writer, a historian, and a thinker of enduring relevance. Our hope is that this new paperback edition will provide yet another opportunity for general readers and scholars, as well as for teachers and students, to encounter the humane art and moral wisdom of Aleksandr Solzhenitsyn.

Edward E. Ericson, Jr.
Daniel J. Mahoney

September 6, 2008

Acknowledgments

This book was conceived in the winter and spring of 2003, in the months leading up to a conference that was held at Harvard University to commemorate the twenty-fifth anniversary of Aleksandr Solzhenitsyn's much-discussed Harvard commencement address. Prior to participating in that exhilarating conference, we coeditors had, in solo performances, shared our knowledge of and appreciation for Solzhenitsyn in many classrooms, at scholarly conventions, to various public gatherings large and small, via radio and television, and through numerous publications. We repeatedly encountered, to our deep satisfaction, a high level of interest and engagement among our audiences. When an auditor would ask what to do next, however, we found ourselves resorting to book lists too bulky and diffuse to be immediately useful. If only, we would sigh to ourselves, there were a single volume that brought together a wide range of the variegated output of "our" prolific writer. This book answers that felt need.

Our collaboration is rooted in a personal friendship of more than a dozen years. It began with a shared intellectual interest in Solzhenitsyn. Then, as a stone dropped in water sends circles of little waves rippling out, we discovered countless other mutual affinities and loyalties, and our friendship broadened and deepened. Even so, Solzhenitsyn has remained our core interest. Working together closely has brought surprisingly little tension into the alliance of two independent-minded men. Instead, the predominant mood has been—as improbable as it may sound—one of joy. We were working eagerly and contentedly on a project in which we believed deeply. Furthermore, our initial high hopes for the project have been greatly exceeded by the result.

This happy outcome owes much to others. We offer sincere thanks to Carmella Murphy and Janet Truscott of Assumption College for their generous interventions on the computer and for helping with various clerical matters. We are similarly indebted to student assistant Leslie Harkema of Calvin College, who, among her tasks, worked what her "boss" considered computer magic as she put hard-copy texts through the scanner and brought them forth in electronic type. Our faithful friend Alexis Klimoff of Vassar College put his superior translation skills at our disposal for parts of *Two Hundred Years Together*, and his points of advice and encouragement are too numerous to list. Various other translations by Alex are noted in the section of credits below. Michael Nicholson of the University College at Oxford University, another exceptionally gifted translator, prepared the English texts of those parts of *March 1917* and *April 1917* that appear in this volume. We pay special homage to the primary English-language translator of Solzhenitsyn's literary works, Harry Willetts, who, shortly before he died in 2005 at the age of eighty-two, finished his work on the complete ninety-six-chapter version of *The First Circle*, parts of which are first reaching English readers through this volume. Other Willetts translations are mentioned in the subsequent list of credits. And Yermolai Solzhenitsyn, firstborn son of Aleksandr and Natalia Solzhenitsyn, took time from his hectic schedule to render a new translation of *Live Not by Lies!* As the credits indicate, he also translated "We have ceased to see the Purpose," his father's address to the International Academy of Philosophy in Liechtenstein.

For the contributions of the other two sons, Ignat and Stephan Solzhenitsyn, it is next to impossible to express adequately our heartfelt gratitude. Initially, they volunteered, despite their demanding careers, to translate a considerable number of items for the *Reader*. Ignat took on the taxing task of translating some poetry: a chapter from the long narrative poem, *The Trail*, and the three lyric poems appearing under the rubric "Poems: Prison, Camp, and Exile." In addition (and in order of their placement in the volume), he translated a new version of the "Open Letter to the Secretariat of the RSFSR Writers' Union"; also, from *Miniatures, 1958–60*, a new version of "A Prayer," the hitherto-untranslated "Means of Locomotion," and a substantial revision of "The Old Bucket" (originally translated by Michael Glenny); and, from *Miniatures, 1996–99*, the hitherto-untranslated miniatures "In Twilight," "Rooster Song," "Nocturnal Thoughts," and "A Prayer for Russia." Stephan's translating burden was similarly substantial: in order of appearance in the volume, the not-so-short story "No Matter What"; selections from *Russia in Collapse*; parts of *Two Hundred Years Together*; the "Cavendish Farewell"; the "Greeting at Vladivostok"; the "Message at the Opening of the Center for Russian Culture Abroad"; and, to complete the *Miniatures, 1996–99*, "Remembrance of the Departed." The two brothers combined their efforts to translate "Playing Upon the Strings of Emptiness" and the "Reflection on the Vendée Uprising." In addition, the pair cleaned up many translations by others, usually for accuracy, sometimes for elegance.

Then, as if the great loving care and keen attention to detail with which Ignat and Stephan performed these onerous labors were not enough, we coeditors found ourselves unable to resist tapping their encyclopedic grasp of their father's *oeuvre* and began peppering them with questions. A four-sided friendship that had been firmed up at the Harvard celebration of 2003 blossomed into a collegial working relationship that we two academics could only wish were characteristic of the academy at large. Even as Ignat and Stephan assiduously avoided usurping any prerogatives of the editors, we editors kept soliciting their counsel because it was uniformly wise. To us, if not necessarily to them, it felt as if decisions were growing organically out of four-way conversations. (And we all learned what an astonishingly supple medium e-mail can be!) It is not false humility to say that the editors alone are responsible for any and all faults in this volume; it is simply true to say that for the volume's virtues credit goes to four friends with one shared purpose.

The editors' greatest indebtedness is to two people with whom they never spoke directly: the author and his wife. Every item in this *Reader* appears with the Solzhenitsyns' explicit permission. The editors proposed the contents; the author said yes or no (rarely no, and then with compelling reason). Solzhenitsyn and his wife never saw—and Ignat and Stephan saw only a relatively small part of—the editors' commentary. Nor did the Solzhenitsyns exercise control over the project. Rather, they willingly and generously supported the editors' work. For their help and for the trust they freely demonstrated the editors are profoundly grateful.

We would be remiss if we failed to thank Solzhenitsyn's literary agent Claude Durand of Editions Fayard in Paris. At a crucial moment he acted as an intermediary with "Moscow" and provided helpful information along the way. His support and encouragement are much appreciated.

As the volume made its way through press, the editors incurred one more major debt, to Jeremy Beer, editor in chief of ISI Books, as well as to his staff. Jeremy fully shared our enthusiasm for this project and brought his considerable intellectual and editorial talents to bear on the final shape of the *Reader*. For that partnership, too, we are very grateful.

Daniel Mahoney would also like to thank *First Things*, *Society*, and *National Review* for permission to use small segments from pieces of his that originally appeared in those magazines. He is also grateful to the Earhart Foundation for the generous support it provided for work on the *Reader* during the summer of 2004.

The editors wish to thank several publishers and copyright holders for permission to reprint their materials; they also wish to acknowledge the translators of those works. Thanks for previously published material follows:

- "Harvard Address," which begins on p. 561, is reproduced from pages 1–61 of *A World Split Apart: Commencement Address Delivered at Harvard University*, by Aleksandr I. Solzhenitsyn, copyright © 1978 by The Russian Social Fund for Persecuted Persons and Their Families, translated by Irina Alberti. English-language translation copyright © 1978 by Harper & Row, Publishers, Inc. Reprinted by permission of HarperCollins Publishers.

• The selection from *The Oak and the Calf* beginning on p. 87 is from pages 1–17 of *The Oak and the Calf*, by Aleksandr I. Solzhenitsyn, copyright © 1975 by Aleksandr I. Solzhenitsyn, translated by Harry Willetts. English-translation copyright © 1979, 1980 by Harper & Row Publishers, Inc. Reprinted by permission of HarperCollins Publishers.

• The selections from *The Gulag Archipelago* that appear beginning on p. 216 are from *The Gulag Archipelago 1918–1956*, by Aleksandr I. Solzhenitsyn, authorized abridgment with a new introduction by Edward E. Ericson, Jr., copyright © 1985 by The Russian Social Fund. Reprinted by permission of HarperCollins Publishers. Selections from parts I–IV were translated by Thomas P. Whitney. Selections from parts V–VII were translated by Harry Willetts.

• "Repentance and Self-Limitation in the Life of Nations" (page 527ff.) is taken from *From Under the Rubble*, by Alexander Solzhenitsyn, copyright © 1974 by YMCA Press, translated by a team under the direction of Michael Scammell. It is reprinted by permission of Little, Brown and Company.

• "Playing Upon the Strings of Emptiness," which starts on p. 585, first appeared in the *New York Times Book Review* and is reprinted by permission of the *New York Times*.

• The short story "What a Pity," which begins on p. 62, was translated by Robert Chandler and is reprinted here by permission. It first appeared in *Russian Short Stories from Pushkin to Buida*, edited by Robert Chandler.

• The English-language translations of the "Nobel Lecture" and the "Templeton Lecture" are reproduced with the permission of their translator, Alexis Klimoff.

• "The Larch," "Lightning," "The Bell at Uglich," "The Belltower," "Growing Old," "Shame," "Ill Weeds," "Morning," and "The Curtain," all from *Miniatures, 1996–99*, are reproduced with the permission of their translators, Michael Nicholson and Alexis Klimoff, as well as Editions Arthème Fayard. They originally appeared as an appendix to Joseph Pearce, *Solzhenitsyn: A Soul in Exile* (London: Harper Collins, 1999).

• Harry Willetts's translations of the *Miniatures, 1958–60*, originally appeared in *Encounter* magazine in 1963.

• Excerpts from *August 1914,* by Aleksandr Solzhenitsyn, translated by H. T. Willetts, are reprinted by permission of Farrar, Straus and Giroux, LLC. Translation copyright © 1989 by H. T. Willetts.

• Excerpts from *Cancer Ward,* by Aleksandr Solzhenitsyn, translated by Nicholas Bethell and David Burg, are reprinted by permission of Farrar, Straus and Giroux, LLC. Copyright © 1968, 1969 by The Bodley Head Ltd.

• Excerpts from *November 1916,* by Aleksandr Solzhenitsyn, translated by H. T. Willetts, are reprinted by permission of Farrar, Straus and Giroux, LLC. Translation copyright © 1999 by H. T. Willetts.

• "We have ceased to see the Purpose" is taken from *"The Russian Question" at the End of the Twentieth Century,* by Aleksandr Solzhenitsyn, translated by Yermolai Solzhenitsyn. It is reprinted by permission of Farrar, Straus and Giroux, LLC. Translation copyright © 1995 by Farrar, Straus & Giroux, Inc.

• "The Easter Procession" and "The Old Bucket" are from *Stories and Prose Poems,* by Aleksandr Solzhenitsyn, translated by Michael Glenny. They are reprinted by permission of Farrar, Straus and Giroux, LLC. Translation copyright © 1971 by Michael Glenny.

• "Matryona's Home," translated by H. T. Willetts, is reprinted by permission of Farrar, Straus and Giroux, LLC.

The editors are also grateful to Editions Arthème-Fayard for permission to publish the following material that is appearing in English for the first time in this volume:

• The short story "No Matter What," and "In Twilight," "Rooster Song," "Nocturnal Thoughts," "Remembrance of the Departed," and "A Prayer for Russia" from *Miniatures, 1996–99.*

• "Besed," the excerpts from *March 1917* and *April 1917,* the excerpts from *Russia in Collapse,* and the excerpts from *Two Hundred Years Together,* as well as Ignat Solzhenitsyn's new translation of "A Prayer."

• "A Reflection on the Vendée Uprising," "Cavendish Farewell," "Greeting at Vladivostok," and "Message at the Opening of the Center for Russian Culture Abroad," in addition to Yermolai Solzhenitsyn's new translation of "Live Not By Lies!"

Finally, the Solzhenitsyn family has kindly allowed us to reproduce the following material, which also appears here for the first time in English:

• The three selections included in "Poems: Prison, Camp, and Exile."

- The early miniature "Means of Locomotion."

- The excerpts from the ninety-six-chapter version of *The First Circle.*

- Ignat Solzhenitsyn's new translation of the "Open Letter to the Secretariat of the RSFSR Writers' Union."

A full list of translation credits follows: 1. *The Trail*—Ignat Solzhenitsyn; 2. Poems: Prison, Camp, and Exile—Ignat Solzhenitsyn; 3. Stories. *Matryona's Home*—H. T. Willetts. *The Easter Procession*—Michael Glenny. *What a Pity*—Robert Chandler. *No Matter What*—Stephan Solzhenitsyn; 4. *The Oak and the Calf*—H. T. Willetts; 5. *The First Circle*—H. T. Willetts; 6. *Cancer Ward*—Nicholas Bethell and David Burg; 7. *The Gulag Archipelago*—Thomas P. Whitney (Parts I-IV) and H. T. Willetts (Parts V-VII); 8. *The Red Wheel*—H. T. Willetts (*August 1914, November 1916*) and Michael Nicholson (*March 1917, April 1917*); 9. *Russia in Collapse*—Stephan Solzhenitsyn; 10. *Two Hundred Years Together*—Alexis Klimoff and Stephan Solzhenitsyn; 11. Essays and Speeches. *Open Letter to the Secretariat of the RSFRS Writers' Union*—Ignat Solzhenitsyn. *Nobel Lecture*—Alexis Klimoff. *Repentance and Self-Limitation in the Life of Nations*—translated by a team under the direction of Michael Scammell. *Live Not by Lies!*—Yermolai Solzhenitsyn. *Harvard Address*—Irina Alberti. *Templeton Lecture*—Alexis Klimoff. *Playing Upon the Strings of Emptiness*—Ignat Solzhenitsyn and Stephan Solzhenitsyn. *We have ceased to see the Purpose*—Yermolai Solzhenitsyn. *A Reflection on the Vendèe Uprising*— Stephan Solzhenitsyn and Ignat Solzhenitsyn. *Cavendish Farewell*—Stephan Solzhenitsyn. *Greeting at Vladivostok*—Stephan Solzhenitsyn. *Message at the Opening of the Center for Russian Culture Abroad*—Stephan Solzhenitsyn; 12. Miniatures. *Breathing, Lake Segden, The Duckling, A Poet's Ashes, The Elm Log, Reflection in Water, A Storm in the Mountains, The City on the Neva, Sharik, Yesenin's Birthplace, The Kolkhoz Rucksack, The Fire and the Ants, We Shall Never Die, Approaching the Day, Along the Oka*—H. T. Willetts. *The Larch, Lightning, The Bell at Uglich, The Belltower, Growing Old, Shame, Ill Weeds, Morning, The Curtain*—Michael Nicholson and Alexis Klimoff. *Means of Locomotion, A Prayer, In Twilight, Rooster Song, Nocturnal Thoughts, A Prayer for Russia*—Ignat Solzhenitsyn. *The Old Bucket*—Michael Glenny and Ignat Solzhenitsyn. *Remembrance of the Departed*—Stephan Solzhenitsyn.

Edward E. Ericson, Jr.
Daniel J. Mahoney

August 18, 2006

Editors' Introduction

By all Soviet standards, the life of Aleksandr Isaevich Solzhenitsyn should never have happened. By any standard, it is a sensational life—action-packed and dramatic. At its core were thoughts that strayed outside officially established boundaries, thoughts that led to words which placed him in direct conflict with state authority.

The purpose of this book is to make the broad sweep of Solzhenitsyn's remarkable *oeuvre* available to English-speaking readers, most of whom are at best only vaguely familiar with his personal story and various works. The purpose of this introduction is to present enough of Solzhenitsyn's life and thought to support a knowledgeable reading of the texts that follow. Misstatements about his life abound. Accurate information is plentiful, however, and much of it comes from the author himself. Many of his literary works are autobiographical in inspiration. In addition, he has written a long narrative poem about his youth and two books of memoirs, covering roughly two decades apiece. (An autobiography covering 1918–74 remains unpublished.) The many misrepresentations of Solzhenitsyn's thought have been even more problematic. The second half of this introduction provides a summary of his basic convictions. After this groundwork the volume is devoted to Solzhenitsyn's own texts, accompanied by editors' introductions.

Writing without letup for more than a half century, no matter how dire his circumstances, Solzhenitsyn has produced a prodigious corpus comprising an extraordinarily wide range of genres. All phases of the author's career and almost all of his genres are represented in this volume. Its sampling includes early poems (though not the plays), early and late short stories, early and late "miniatures" (or prose poems), essays and speeches, and selections from long works: novels, memoirs, books of political analysis and historical scholarship, and long literary masterpieces that defy generic classification (namely, *The Gulag Archipelago* and *The Red Wheel*). This volume gathers together well-known and little-known texts, some of which have not until now appeared within any book. Of special interest are the previously untranslated materials; more than a quarter of this volume is given over to writings that make their English-language debut here. In addition, some previously available texts appear in new translations done specifically for this volume. Although the editors do not try to camouflage their respectful admiration of the man and his writings, their main burden is to let Solzhenitsyn speak for himself.

✢ LIFE ✢

Solzhenitsyn's life is rich with paradoxes. A small-town high-school teacher, Solzhenitsyn reached the pinnacle of world fame. He earned enthusiastic acclaim worldwide for the power of his literature, kudos for his courage in standing up to a criminally unjust regime, and recognition for his vital role in changing the course of history. He also was viciously attacked, at home and abroad, as few writers of any time have been. He passed many of his prime years caught up in a whirlwind of controversial activity that deprived him of the quiet solitude necessary for a writer and threatened his very survival. Amid the exceptional flux of his life, one thing remained constant: He remained committed to exploring the subject he had chosen in youth as the topic of his magnum opus, namely, the Bolshevik Revolution and its causes. Yet here, too, paradox reigned, for his attitude toward the revolution took a 180-degree turn.

LIFE IN THE SOVIET UNION

Solzhenitsyn was born on December 11, 1918, in Kislovodsk, a resort town in southern Russia, to parents of peasant stock who had nevertheless obtained university educations. The timing of his birth made him a virtual son of the revolution, a member of the generation known as October's children, in whom the Bolsheviks invested their highest hopes for advancing their cause. His father, Isaaki Semyonovich Solzhenitsyn, a decorated artillery officer during World War I, died as a result of a hunting accident six months before his son was born. The author's mother, née Taissia Zakharovna Shcherbak, was the daughter of an enterprising Ukrainian farmer whose extensive holdings were expropriated by the Bolsheviks. When the impoverished woman went to Rostov-on-Don to seek work as a stenographer, little Aleksandr was cared for by his maternal grandparents, with help from two of his aunts, his mother's sister Maria and sister-in-law Irina Shcherbak. The growing boy was strongly influenced by his Aunt Irina, a feisty woman who shared with him her love of Russian literature and devotion to Russian Orthodoxy. From age six, the boy lived with his mother in Rostov in a tumbledown building, within which their living quarters measured twelve feet by nine and included no plumbing. He passed several summers with Aunt Irina.

At the tender age of ten, Solzhenitsyn began keeping a journal containing his literary writings, to which he affixed the grandiose title *The Twentieth Century*, with a subtitle to match: "On the Meaning of the Twentieth Century." Although the collection contained a good share of ephemeral juvenilia, the high ambition that framed his boyish exercises was destined to be enduring. By age eighteen, he began to turn this vision into reality by writing on the run-up to the Bolshevik Revolution of 1917, which he considered the most earth-shaking event of modern world history. Only when he was in his seventies would he stop working on this mammoth literary project, by then named *The Red Wheel*.

At school Solzhenitsyn inevitably experienced conflicts between his extended family's Christian values and his teachers' ideological indoctrination. He gradually acquiesced to Marxism-Leninism and joined the standard Communist youth organizations. His increasingly heartfelt ideological commitment shaped his youthful literary interpretation of the revolution. Nevertheless, the battle for his heart and mind waged by two competing worldviews was in only its early stages and would become the central inner drama of his life. In adulthood his firsthand experience of Soviet reality would eventually cause an about-face in his attitude toward the revolution. He remained convinced that the totalitarian experiment inaugurated by the Bolsheviks gave the twentieth century its distinctive character, but he came to believe that it must be resisted on behalf of the human spirit. He returned with adult thoughtfulness to the Christian worldview of his rearing. Solzhenitsyn's mature articulation of Christian truths was deeply informed by his experience in the prison camps. There he witnessed human nature *in extremis* and learned about the heights and depths of the human soul. His was a faith rooted in experience and severed from every form of sectarianism. With a similar reliance on experience, he described the dehumanizing consequences of the revolution by using his own life narrative as a microcosm of his people's tumultuous story. Indeed, the turmoil of his life served as a simulacrum of the turbulence not only of Russia but of the twentieth century as a whole.

The normal adolescent process of loosening the bonds of parental control was complicated in Solzhenitsyn's case by the poor health of his mother, who had contracted tuberculosis in the early 1930s and would die prematurely in 1944. So, instead of following his dream of studying literature at a university in Moscow, he stayed at home to care for her and in 1936 enrolled in a standard five-year curriculum at Rostov University, where, for lack of a literature program, he majored in mathematics and physics. This curricular second choice would later seem to him providential, for his science background would help him draw better assignments in the army and in prison. He developed his literary interests by registering in 1939 for a correspondence course offered by the prestigious Moscow Institute of Philosophy, Literature, and History (MIFLI). Also while at the university, he met Natalia Reshetovskaya, a chemistry major whom he married in 1940. His plan to move to Moscow for advanced study at MIFLI fell through when the Nazis invaded the Soviet Union in 1941.

Solzhenitsyn's first military posting was to a horse-drawn transport unit, where his ineptitude with horses gave other soldiers much mirth. Then he was switched to artillery, soon was leading a front-line battery, and, like his father before him, became decorated for heroism and promoted to captain. Wartime brought Solzhenitsyn many observations of the Soviet regime's viciousness that shook but did not demolish his faith in Marxism. His long narrative poem *The Trail* records some of these occasions for doubt. His career as a soldier ended disastrously in 1945 when military censors inspected letters he was exchanging with a boyhood friend in which they wrote disparagingly of Stalin and speculated about how to reform the Soviet state. Thus commenced Solzhenitsyn's own procession through the stages of arrest, interrogation, and incarceration that he was later to reveal to the world through *The Gulag Archipelago*. He was sentenced to eight years in forced-labor camps, to be followed by "perpetual exile" far from home.

The first prison camps to which Solzhenitsyn was assigned were located in the Moscow area. His health deteriorated seriously, but worse were his psychological bewilderment and the mortifying moral compromises that he could not withstand. As he gained hitherto unimaginable insights into the Soviets' systematic brutalization of innocent people, his faith in Marxist dogma, which wartime had undermined, now crumbled completely. By contrast, he encountered personal nobility in many of the so-called "enemies of the people." Serene, radiant Christians particularly impressed him. This first, perplexing phase of his imprisonment provided materials for two early plays, *Prisoners* and *The Republic of Labor*.

The next stage, which lasted from 1946 to 1950, found Solzhenitsyn in one or another *sharashka*—first for a year at Rybinsk on the Upper Volga, and then for three years at Marfino, located in suburban Moscow and formerly a seminary complex. The term *sharashka* refers to a prison research institute, at which incarcerated scientists and engineers were brought together to work on technical projects for the government and in turn were allowed relaxed conditions and generous amenities by gulag standards. Solzhenitsyn took advantage of the relative leisure and the presence of other well-educated *zeks* (prisoners) to ponder his recent experiences and their larger implications. *The First Circle* is based on his Marfino years. As the novel makes clear, by the time Solzhenitsyn left Marfino he had definitively rejected his youthful Marxism and was moving toward, though not quite to, a renewed embrace of Christianity. He assigned to his alter ego, Gleb Nerzhin, his own Socratic quest for a principled point of view that would do justice to his desire "to temper, to cut, to polish one's soul so as to become *a human being.*"

In 1950 a conflict with the authorities caused Solzhenitsyn to be reassigned to hard labor at a large new prison camp at Ekibastuz in Kazakhstan, a camp that housed political prisoners exclusively. This location provided the materials for *One Day in the Life of Ivan Denisovich.* At this site Solzhenitsyn witnessed increasingly rebellious *zeks* systematically assassinating camp informers and participated in a general strike in 1952. *The Gulag Archipelago* recounts this uprising, as well as a much more serious one in 1954 at the nearby Kengir camp.

Solzhenitsyn eluded punishment for striking because he had to undergo surgery for abdominal cancer. In the recovery room the still-groggy patient listened to Dr. Boris Kornfeld's fervent account of his own recent conversion to Christianity. Later that very night, Kornfeld was killed by persons unknown for reasons unknown. This unforgettable episode, recounted in "The Ascent," a crucial chapter in *Gulag,* was a key event in reigniting Solzhenitsyn's Christian faith.

Solzhenitsyn's sentence ended on February 9, 1953, the precise eight-year anniversary of his arrest. He was exiled to Kok-Terek, a village in Kazakhstan, and was forbidden any contact with persons from his past. His wife had earlier (with her husband's permission) filed for divorce in order to escape the unbearable discrimination that accompanied being a prisoner's spouse; by 1952 she had married another man. Solzhenitsyn survived in exile by teaching high school students mathematics and physics. In every spare moment he wrote, first putting onto paper what he had mentally composed while incarcerated. Later in 1953 his cancer recurred, and soon it was diagnosed as terminal. Given only a few weeks to live, unable to eat or sleep, he received permission to travel three hundred miles to Tashkent, Uzbekistan, for treatment. Before the trip he jammed his manuscripts into a bottle and— in a unique twist on the Soviet-era concept of "writing for the drawer"— buried it. The treatment at the clinic was successful, and he resumed his routines at Kok-Terek. His time at Tashkent formed the basis for another novel, *Cancer Ward.*

In 1956 Soviet leader Nikita Khrushchev, in an effort to consolidate his hold on power, gave a now-famous secret speech to the Twentieth Congress of the Communist Party of the Soviet Union denouncing Stalin for deviating from Leninist principles. This wide-ranging attack rocked both the Soviet leadership and Communists abroad. It called into question the Soviet

Union's monolithic impregnability. Soviet citizens experienced the after-effects in an unpredictably changeable cultural liberalization known as the "Thaw." The somewhat relaxed atmosphere benefited Solzhenitsyn directly. Shortly after the government ended the practice of "perpetual exile" in April 1956, he moved to a village in Russia named Miltsevo, where he continued to teach school and write, finishing the first draft of *The First Circle*. His much-praised story "Matryona's Home" is set in Miltsevo. In early 1957 he was officially "rehabilitated," with the 1945 charges expunged from his record. Then he remarried Natalia Reshetovskaya and moved with her to the provincial city of Ryazan, where again he taught and wrote.

Addressing another Congress of the Communist Party in 1961, Khrushchev vigorously urged the intensifying of liberal reform. Also speaking on behalf of reform was Aleksandr Tvardovsky, the editor of *Novy Mir*, who implied that his prestigious journal would accept submissions previously deemed too controversial. Seeing his opening, Solzhenitsyn decided to try to pursue publication, choosing the manuscript now known as *One Day in the Life of Ivan Denisovich*. The manuscript made its way through intermediaries to Tvardovsky, who, as was his custom, took it home to read. He put on his robe, sat on his bed with pillows propping him up, and started reading. Having barely begun, he got up, put on his office clothes, and resumed reading. He knew he was in the presence of a masterpiece; the occasion required dignified attire. He read it through twice. Solzhenitsyn, despite having second thoughts, had irreversibly entered a long period of conflict pitting a lone unshielded citizen against untrammeled state power.

Tvardovsky approached Khrushchev personally for approval to publish the new work, arguing that its anti-Stalinism would buttress the leader's initiatives. Khrushchev, in turn, gave copies to the members of the Party presidium and called a meeting at which each one had to speak for or against publishing. Solzhenitsyn had no doubt whatsoever that *One Day* was laden with political significance. But Khrushchev had his own ideas of how to appropriate the book for political purposes: The responses of the presidium members allowed him to determine who was with him in his de-Stalinization campaign and who was not. Thus, before a word of Solzhenitsyn's had ever been published, his writing was misused, or abused, for extraneous political purposes—in this case, to distinguish the sheep from the goats, Khrushchev style. Having his work treated in narrowly ideological terms has been the bane of Solzhenitsyn's reception everywhere ever since.

Novy Mir published *One Day in the Life of Ivan Denisovich* in November 1962. Establishment writers followed Khrushchev's lead in praising the little book and politicizing its significance. The depiction of prison-camp life, a prohibited subject that was nonetheless known by myriad Soviets through their family members' experiences, created a sensation among ordinary citizens. Millions of copies circulated from hand to hand. The work was a bombshell abroad, as well. The West hailed the author as a truth-telling freedom fighter and the text as great art. At a stroke, an unknown provincial schoolteacher became famous worldwide. This fame protected Solzhenitsyn somewhat through the long struggle to come. One unexpected but particularly welcome consequence was the flood of letters that ex-*zeks* sent to Solzhenitsyn. These eyewitness accounts were just what he needed to resurrect his plans to write *The Gulag Archipelago.*

Solzhenitsyn was inducted into the Soviet Writers' Union, but his efforts to follow up *One Day* with other publications resulted in the appearance of only a few stories and an essay on language. Official favor was soon transformed into open hostility. Harassment by the KGB became ever more intense. Solzhenitsyn fought back by publicizing the KGB's maneuvers, often through Western media. His handling of the conflicts during the 1960s established his reputation as a tough, effective infighter with a courageous spirit. His climactic battle to be published came at meetings with establishment writers over *Cancer Ward.* A 1966 meeting was amicable and encouraging; but when nothing happened, in May 1967 he poured his frustration into a scalding letter that sternly attacked censorship and the literary establishment's craven complicity in it. Four months later, the writers' union refused to recommend *Cancer Ward* for publication. During this intense period Solzhenitsyn began keeping notes on events, and these were the raw materials that went into his memoir, *The Oak and the Calf.*

While the public skirmishes proceeded in one dizzying round after another, Solzhenitsyn was living virtually a second life in private. As an "underground" writer he was working on *The Gulag Archipelago.* Only when *Invisible Allies* appeared in 1991 did readers learn the spellbinding story of how he composed this immense work in the face of seemingly unbearable constraints, all the while keeping so occupied with other work that the authorities could never guess he was managing this project, too. Although his intermittent labors on *Gulag* ran from 1958 to 1968, during the mid-sixties he made four visits to a "Hiding Place" in Estonia provided by old gulag mates of his and their friends; and there, he reports, he worked as he never had before. He sent a microfilm of *Gulag* to the West in 1968, the same year in which *The First Circle* and *Cancer Ward* were published in the West.

In 1969 Solzhenitsyn was finally expelled from the Writers' Union, an action that left him formally unemployed and thus vulnerable to legal sanctions for "social parasitism." This action drew fresh protests from Western writers, whose support had repeatedly helped restrain his persecution by the state. Also in 1969 Solzhenitsyn turned his attention to the intended masterwork that he had envisioned and commenced in his youth, *The Red Wheel.* The first installment, or "knot," entitled *August 1914,* appeared in Paris in 1971 and in an unacceptable English translation in 1972. The considerably expanded final version appeared in 1983 and in an excellent English translation in 1989. Further "knots" were to dominate his writing time throughout his exile in the West.

Solzhenitsyn returned to world headlines in 1970 when he was awarded the Nobel Prize in Literature. The West cheered the announcement, but uniform howls of umbrage filled the Soviet press. He did not travel to Stockholm to participate in the public celebration, because the Soviet government would not guarantee that he could return home. His *Nobel Lecture* did not appear until two years later, and only in 1974, after he had been exiled, did he receive the Nobel insignia in person.

The conflict between author and authorities that persisted through the 1960s reached its highest pitch in the early 1970s. Libraries followed orders to destroy their copies of *One Day* and the few other published works by Solzhenitsyn. KGB actions against him included ransacking his cottage and severely beating a friend of his who happened to be there, mailing him and his wife threatening letters, and—the topper—attempting to kill him by poisoning. With no reason left to conceal his personal opinions and attitudes, in 1972 he publicized a letter to Patriarch Pimen criticizing the Russian Orthodox hierarchy for its accommodations with the energetically atheistic Soviet regime.

In 1970 Father Alexander Schmemann, an American Orthodox theologian, had written an insightful essay on Christian themes in Solzhenitsyn's writings, which, had it been heeded, could have forestalled much of the critical confusion that was soon to envelop Solzhenitsyn. This puzzlement surfaced in the West when the first version of *August 1914* appeared. Some reviews were favorable or ambivalent, but disappointment was the prevailing mood. Solzhenitsyn noticed among Russians, as well, a "schism among my readers." In *August 1914* the signs of Solzhenitsyn's patriotic and Christian commitments were too clear to be ignored and bothered some reviewers. Plainspoken critic Mary McCarthy encapsulated the rising qualms in her complaint that Solzhenitsyn was "rude and unfair" toward the liberal "advanced circles" of 1914: "He has it in for those people, just as he would have it in for you and me, if he could overhear us talking." Thus were the terms set for a major defection from Solzhenitsyn.

Meanwhile, Solzhenitsyn's remarriage to Reshetovskaya was coming apart. He entered a relationship with Natalia Svetlova, a Moscow mathematician who was one of his "invisible allies." Reshetovskaya attempted suicide. A divorce petition was first rejected by the authorities but then accepted in early 1973. Afterward, aided by Novosti, the KGB-related press agency, Reshetovskaya wrote a memoir that cast Solzhenitsyn in an unflattering light. Solzhenitsyn has never tried to absolve himself of all guilt for the divorce.

Nevertheless, his second wife became, with respect to their family life and his mission as a writer, a partner in every sense of the word.

In mid-1973 the KGB, having gotten wind of *The Gulag Archipelago* and hunting for a copy, hauled in for interrogation Elizaveta Voronyanskaya, a Leningrad woman who had served Solzhenitsyn as an amanuensis. Against Solzhenitsyn's instructions, she had not destroyed her copy, lest all others be confiscated and the work lost to posterity. After five days and nights of nonstop questioning, she cracked. The KGB got its manuscript. Shortly thereafter, she died, either by suicide or (as Solzhenitsyn thinks more likely) by murder. Knowing the KGB's skill at quoting out of context to reverse intended meanings, Solzhenitsyn signaled his Swiss lawyer to publish *Gulag* in the West. His decade-long war with the authorities was entering its final battle. The publication of *Gulag* led directly to his expulsion from his homeland.

On February 12, 1974, came the knock on the door. Such had been his consistent success in outfoxing the authorities that even an attempted delivery the day before of a summons from the prosecutor's office did not set off Solzhenitsyn's mental alarm bells. So on the fateful day of his arrest, he found himself in a state of "witless shock." He was about to lose his Soviet citizenship and be charged with treason, a crime that could draw a sentence of capital punishment. At Lefortovo prison he again went through the ignominies accompanying arrest and wondered what would happen next. Another prison sentence or an execution, even one staged to look like an accident, probably would have made him a martyr figure in perpetuity. Shrewdly, then, the authorities packed him onto an airplane and sent him West, where the prickly fellow could soon enough become a burr under the West's saddle. Moreover, as he knew, being cut off from his homeland could not possibly be good for his ongoing work as a Russian writer. He did not know where his plane was headed until, upon landing, he saw the sign for Frankfurt-am-Main in West Germany. The world press avidly relayed all the developments of his unfolding saga. In virtual unison, Western commentators, including Western Communists, condemned the Soviet action against Solzhenitsyn and praised his personal courage and literary achievement. He left behind for the Russian public a brief exhortation entitled "Live Not by Lies!"

LIFE IN EXILE

The West welcomed Solzhenitsyn warmly and enthusiastically. Well-wishing crowds surrounded him wherever he went. Telegrams of encouragement and invitations to speak poured in. So did messages from numerous countries offering him residence. *The Times* of London declared him "the man who is for the moment the most famous person in the western world." He relished the prospect of speaking without constraint to audiences clamoring to hear him. The first sour note to mar the good feelings came within days of his arrival in the West, as journalists began to irritate him with their incessant badgering and errors in reportage. The earliest interviews did not help. A 1974 interview conducted by the American TV fixture Walter Cronkite was notable for its ill-informed, uncomprehending questions. Sometimes Solzhenitsyn divulged political attitudes that caught his interlocutors off guard and discomfited them. Nagging second thoughts about this exile started spreading among Westerners.

Solzhenitsyn made Zurich, Switzerland, his first Western residence. His wife and sons joined him there. Their house, close to the street, offered no cushion from noise and well-meaning tourists. One of his various favorable impressions of Switzerland came when he observed direct democracy in action in the canton of Appenzell. He saw a connection between the localism of Swiss-style politics and the grassroots democracy of Russia's nineteenth-century *zemstvos*, and the town-hall meetings he later witnessed in Vermont would further reinforce his sympathy for democracy from the bottom up. Years later, these various models would guide his specific democratic proposals for post-Soviet Russia in *Rebuilding Russia*. While in Switzerland, Solzhenitsyn also set up the Russian Social Fund to hold all royalties earned worldwide from *The Gulag Archipelago* and to disburse the money covertly to political prisoners and prisoners of conscience, along with their families. Later, former *zeks* were included among the beneficiaries.

By 1974 the reservations about Solzhenitsyn among Western elites were congealing into a negative consensus. As the monumental *Gulag Archipelago* was appearing, so was *Letter to the Soviet Leaders*, initially sent privately to its intended audience in 1973 but released to the public when it received no acknowledgment. Oddly, Western opinion about him was affected less by the big book than by the little letter. This brief proto-programmatic statement urged the Soviet leaders, who could hardly be asked to relinquish power, simply to drop their pretenses of truly believing in Marxism anymore and, for starters, to embrace moderate reforms. Westerners commonly interpreted his gradualist proposals as evidence of his "authoritarianism." This charge was to become an endlessly repeated staple in the solidifying caricature of Solzhenitsyn. Journalist Jeri Laber, who in 1972 had praised Solzhenitsyn as a person and a writer, in 1974 declared his art dull and his politics reactionary. Her memorable generalization, "he is not the 'liberal' we would like him to be," was echoed in other commentaries, often with eerily similar wording.

After having gotten settled into the West, Solzhenitsyn fulfilled a sense of obligation by hitting the lecture circuit. In 1975 he delivered addresses in

New York and Washington to the AFL-CIO, America's leading labor organization; he also spoke to an appreciative group of US senators. These discourses, along with two presentations he made in England in 1976, are available in the collection entitled *Warning to the West*. By this time, the press's coverage of Solzhenitsyn had become decidedly chilly. President Gerald Ford, prompted by Secretary of State Henry Kissinger, refused to invite Solzhenitsyn to the White House, privately calling him "a goddam horse's ass." Ford's snub was universally condemned, and the Republican Party's platform of 1976 included a Solzhenitsyn-inspired plank called "Morality in Foreign Policy." The one Western country where Solzhenitsyn had a profound and enduring influence was France, where the revelations in *The Gulag Archipelago* led a whole generation of young intellectuals to abandon Marxism.

By early 1975 Solzhenitsyn was hunting for a new home in North America. After searching fruitlessly in Ontario, he accepted, sight unseen, a friend's recommendation of a fifty-acre wooded hillside property above the village of Cavendish, Vermont, and took occupancy in 1976. Alongside its ample but not extravagant chalet, he ordered built a three-story library, including a small chapel. This location provided quiet for writing, access to America's extensive interlibrary loan service, and education in a major language for his three sons, Yermolai, Ignat, and Stephan. (Mrs. Solzhenitsyn's son by a previous marriage and her mother also were part of the household.) Solzhenitsyn had a simple chain-link fence put up around the property to keep out hunters and snowmobilers—and, Mrs. Solzhenitsyn smilingly added later, journalists. The modest fence led some journalists to speculate wildly—and from a distance—about why the ex-prisoner felt he needed it. The sons went to American public schools. The family went to the Orthodox church in nearby Claremont, New Hampshire. Mr. and Mrs. Solzhenitsyn attended a Cavendish town meeting to introduce themselves and explain their situation, were welcomed by a warm ovation, and established easy relations with the locals, who casually but carefully guarded the newcomers' privacy. Solzhenitsyn had finally attained optimum conditions for his life as a writer, and he took full advantage of them.

In 1978 Solzhenitsyn agreed to deliver the commencement address at Harvard University. The speech itemized the West's current failings, located their genesis in Enlightenment thought, and cast its proposed remedies in philosophical and religious terms that extended even to the proper relationship between body and soul. Before the well-represented press and intelligentsia, he spoke of journalists' hasty and superficial judgments and intellectuals' loss of will and decline of courage. This address immediately became Solzhenitsyn's best-known utterance; and, although it elicited numerous appreciative responses, they were overshadowed by the many vociferous objections. This address confirmed the media's negative view of Solzhenitsyn. More importantly, press coverage of the event implanted wariness about him in the public consciousness.

Solzhenitsyn returned to his seclusion and his writing. But he was not as withdrawn as he may have seemed. *The Little Grain Managed to Land Between the Millstones*, memoirs about his two decades in exile, chronicles many experiences he had and persons he dealt with. Quite a few events took place in public but drew little press attention. In 1982 he presented speeches in Japan and Taiwan. Somewhat greater notice attended his 1983 visit to England to receive the Templeton Prize for Progress in Religion. While there, he also met with many luminaries: Prime Minister Margaret Thatcher for a substantive conversation, the archbishop of Canterbury for a dinner, Prince Charles and Princess Diana for a luncheon. Also, he sat for a television interview with Malcolm Muggeridge. Later in 1983 he gave an interview to Bernard Pivot for a highly regarded French television program. In all, Pivot interviewed him four times; these appearances responded to French interest in the Russian author and fueled it further.

In the second half of the 1980s, Solzhenitsyn followed closely the momentous events unfolding in the Soviet Union. For twenty years he had been predicting, as few had been, that Soviet communism was on its way to dying. He had also been anticipating that during his lifetime he would return home in the flesh—which, all things considered, was essentially the same forecast. Not even his close friends could bring themselves to believe him, but now it seemed increasingly possible that his prophecies would be fulfilled. In 1988 a Moscow periodical tested Mikhail Gorbachev's announced new policy of *glasnost* ("openness," or "publicity") by advocating that Solzhenitsyn's citizenship be restored and the treason charge dropped. The third of his three requirements for returning home—the domestic publication of all his writings—also seemed to be in the works. He granted *Novy Mir* permission to publish parts of *The Gulag Archipelago* in 1989, with other books to follow. At this point, the Communist Party's chief ideologist intervened, declaring that to publish these works would be "to undermine the foundations on which our present [Soviet] life rests." But the powers proved powerless to stop the appearance of some Solzhenitsyn texts, first in obscure outlets and soon in mainstream ones. These publishing events snowballed to the point that *Novy Mir* declared 1990 to be "the year of Solzhenitsyn." Public events moved with apparent inexorability, from the fall of the Berlin Wall in November 1989 to the death of the Soviet Union on December 25, 1991, when the red flag over the Kremlin was lowered for the last time. The foreshortened twentieth century that began in 1914–17 ended in 1989–91. Solzhenitsyn was ready, and in July 1990 he dispatched a long essay known in English as *Rebuilding Russia*, which sketched practical short-term and long-term proposals for Russia as it emerged from under the Soviet rubble. This essay can be considered a sequel to his 1973 *Letter to the Soviet Leaders*, but this time he addressed not the leaders fading from power but the Russian citizenry on the verge of coming into its own.

Solzhenitsyn also was making plans to move back to Russia. The family contracted for a house to be built just outside Moscow, and his wife made three trips to Russia to prepare for the move. Meanwhile, the media, eager to see what political role he might play, impatiently asked why he was dallying in Vermont. One reason was that, before he could allow himself to be caught up in the public life of Russia, he had to tie up loose ends on *The Red Wheel*. Only in 1994 could he refer to his intended masterpiece as "this huge beast now felled." In addition, as he eventually explained, he thought that entering the arena of practical politics was not the best way for him to help Russia, that his greatest power would continue to reside in his words.

Solzhenitsyn said his farewells to the West in some speeches in Europe. His largest audience gathered at a ceremony in France observing the two-hundredth anniversary of the massacres of opponents of the French Revolution. His most important address, which rehearses some themes in his "Harvard Address" in a more subdued way, was presented at the International Academy of Philosophy, a Roman Catholic institution in Liechtenstein. In the United States he gave a few interviews and showed up to say thanks and farewell at a Cavendish town meeting, where the locals bookended his sojourn among them with a hearty ovation that matched the one he had received seventeen years earlier.

Life in Russia

Solzhenitsyn landed on Russian soil on May 27, 1994. The euphoria prompted by the collapse of the Soviet Union had subsided. An assessment of the recent world-transforming events was underway, but few Western Sovietologists showed interest in revisiting their erroneous analyses. Nor were Solzhenitsyn's detractors inclined to reassess either his prescience regarding the death of the Soviet Union or his role in bringing it about. Nevertheless, journalists did take notice of his return to Russia. And they were immediately startled by his decision to enter not through a Moscow airport but through the back door, as it were, of the Pacific coast, an entry that was not only dramatic but symbolic. His plane touched down at Magadan, the capital of the region of Kolyma, where the harshest gulag camps had been located, and thus the symbolic capital of the gulag as a whole. He flew next to Vladivostok, Russia's main Pacific port of entry, where four thousand citizens stood in the rain for hours to give him a hero's welcome. Then commenced a train trip, filmed by a BBC-TV crew, that took two months and ended at Moscow. At whistle stops all along the way, crowds were on hand to greet him. These stops featured lively give-and-take sessions rather than lectures. The purpose of the trip—as well as of a subsequent one-month tour to revisit old haunts and follow-up journeys in 1995, 1996, and 1997—was to meet ordinary citizens and jot down their descriptions of current conditions, so that later he could represent this "other" Russia to Moscow's ruling elites.

Solzhenitsyn was greatly disappointed to learn how little his fellow Russians had read him, even after his works had been published. The practice of the Russians' great indoor sport of reading had declined precipitously—as had magazine circulation numbers—in the roiling early 1990s. Furthermore, many Russians wanted simply to forget the tragedy of the Soviet past, in which almost all of them were to some degree implicated. Some had taken him as their moral guide, and others were ready to learn from him. But, broadly speaking, Russians were equally eager to acclaim him for his heroism and to consign him to the sealed-off past. The pattern of reception was generally similar among Western commentators: The man formerly dismissed as wrongheaded was now dismissed as irrelevant.

During his first year in Moscow, Solzhenitsyn made almost a hundred public appearances. He addressed the Duma, Russia's legislature, and endured jeering disdain from some members. He met privately with President Boris Yeltsin for two hours and met with other politicians at their request. Probably his greatest direct influence on the rebuilding of Russia came through a couple of conferences on local government, at which participants from the provinces were particularly receptive auditors. Whether the issues were political or cultural, his coolest reception came from Moscow's elites. His highest visibility came through the regular television program that he was granted in early 1995. This program, in which he did not hesitate to criticize certain government policies, was canceled after about eight months, allegedly for low ratings.

Within a year's time, the novelty of Solzhenitsyn's presence wore off, and he faded from public view, a process abetted by a certain decline in his health. Although he continued to make sporadic public appearances, much of his time went into producing an impressively large and varied body of old-age writing. He discovered that, now that he was back home, he could again write miniatures. He wrote experimental short fiction that he called "binary tales." He wrote *Russia in Collapse*, a sequel of sorts to *Rebuilding Russia*. He wrote a two-volume study of the thorny relationship between Russians and Jews, entitled *Two Hundred Years Together*, exerting every effort to treat the controversial subject matter evenhandedly. He prepared for publication the extensive memoirs of his life in exile, *The Little Grain*. And he added to *Literary Miscellany*, his commentaries on Russian writers.

A surprising development in 2006, however, is a reminder that, since the future is unpredictable, Solzhenitsyn's reputation is subject to change. A Russian television network carried a ten-part series of Solzhenitsyn's novel *The First Circle*, for which the author served as the screenwriter, consulted on the production, and provided the voiceover. The first installment racked up the largest audience share of the week, and the series attracted roughly 15 million viewers per show.

Furthermore, the television screening of *The First Circle* did not arrive out of the blue. Solzhenitsyn's social and political ideas are finally gaining influence among the Russian public and are helping to shape a new consensus in society and government. In the years immediately after the fall of communism, Solzhenitsyn was nearly alone in drawing attention to Russia's demographic crisis and to the lamentable neglect of the 25 million Russians in the "near abroad." All that has now changed. His notion of a strong, traditional, yet noncommunist and nonimperial Russia is no longer subject to derision, as it was during the 1990s. At the same time, Solzhenitsyn has in no way succumbed to the temptation of normalizing the Soviet past by treating it as a defective but legitimate expression of the Russian national tradition.

The sheer drama of Solzhenitsyn's life cannot be overstated. The story he has lived is on a par with those which he has put down on paper. His courage is legendary. Through many ordeals he has remained steadfastly faithful to his sense of mission. This dedication has given his life an exceptional coherence; seldom has a human life had such a seamless quality. He has earned every bit of fame he has received. The future will cast its own judgment about his writings. But he is indubitably that uncommon man whom common men struggle to fathom.

✦ THOUGHT ✦

Aleksandr Solzhenitsyn understands himself to be, above all, a writer and artist. But the remarkable range of his intellectual concerns and the dramatic impact of his work go far beyond anything that is typically associated with "art" in the Western world today. In fact, it is hard to think of another belletrist who has had a comparable impact on the politics of the twentieth century. No other writer could plausibly claim to have brought down an "evil empire" built upon the twin pillars of violence and "the lie." Solzhenitsyn is a "living classic" in the tradition of Dostoevsky and Tolstoy. He is also a moralist who defends the age-old distinctions between good and evil and truth and falsehood, and a historian whose writings have done much to illumine the complex sources of the Soviet tragedy. He has wisely eschewed any direct political role for himself and has pointedly warned against reductively political readings of his texts. At the same time, he has been a subtle and effective practitioner of "great politics." He can be described as a writer who, in the words of one of his characters, assumed the role of a "second government" by guarding his people's memory, language, and soul when they were in mortal danger from an unprecedented form of despotism. If it is a mistake to judge Solzhenitsyn by narrowly political criteria, it is also inadvisable to understate the political dimensions of his work, especially if we understand politics in the most capacious sense of the term.

The contemporary West increasingly takes for granted a subjectivist understanding of the writer's calling. It is enamored of the "creative artist" who follows his genius where it leads and who "creates" imaginary worlds that transport and titillate his readers. This identification of the literary vocation with creativity and "authenticity" as ends in themselves makes it difficult for readers to understand Solzhenitsyn's own literary practice, in which he combines the multiple and complementary roles of writer, historian, and moralist. He self-consciously adheres to a Russian literary tradition that recognizes no essential distinction between the concerns of art, morality, and politics. The distinguished Solzhenitsyn scholar Alexis Klimoff has ably captured the difference between these two approaches: "in contrast to the Western tendency to draw a sharp distinction between fiction and nonfiction, the great Russian prose writers of the [nineteenth] century took pride in the way that their works addressed and reflected the actual historical, social, or moral conditions of their homeland. Literary achievement was not seen in the ability of a powerful imagination to create a vivid fictional world ex nihilo, but rather in the writer's skill in selecting, shaping, and ordering the data of reality, in this sense re-creating it in aesthetically compelling ways." Like his great nineteenth-century predecessors, Solzhenitsyn forgoes inventing fictive worlds and, instead, depicts Reality in its grandeur and misery. In particular, he presents the tragic dislocations of a century overrun by Dostoevsky's "Devils," those architects of a "progressive" future who tore the world asunder and scattered salt on its wounds. Solzhenitsyn's art is deeply rooted in personal experience but is never solipsistic or narrowly self-referential.

Of all his writings, the *Nobel Lecture* (1972) best conveys the unity of Solzhenitsyn's "social" and "artistic" concerns. (All references to the *Nobel Lecture* are to Klimoff's authoritative translation, which appeared in Solzhenitsyn's *East and West* [1980] and is reprinted in this Reader). As Solzhenitsyn explains in an absorbing chapter of his autobiographical *The Oak and the Calf* entitled "Nobeliana," he labored long and hard to achieve a judicious balance between his theory of art and his view of the moral and political responsibilities of the writer. His initial attempts to combine "the two themes—society and art" failed, since "the two overstrained shafts sprang apart again and would not be bent into line." He did not release the lecture to the public until two years after he was awarded the Nobel Prize, for only then was he satisfied that he had successfully fused these two themes. Thus, a close examination of this carefully wrought text serves effectively as an introduction to the author's thought and work as a whole.

The *Nobel Lecture* provides a near-perfect encapsulation of Solzhenitsyn's artistic and moral-political concerns and their essential harmony. It does justice to both without politicizing art or ignoring the duty that the writer owes to society out of both gratitude and self-respect. It also provides a limpid statement of Solzhenitsyn's theory of art, which reaffirms the traditional notion of the essential unity of truth, goodness, and beauty, and provides an original reflection on the relations between the universal and the particular, between the universal moral law and the distinctive national cultures within which human beings live. He brilliantly articulates the social responsibility of the artist and highlights the salutary role that "world literature" can play in providing a "common scale of values" for a world that is for the first time experiencing "universal history," the sense of belonging to *one* history and *one* world. The speech concludes with a particularly memorable and prophetic discussion of the power of the word to overcome and "to defeat" violence and the lie.

TWO UNDERSTANDINGS OF THE ARTIST'S VOCATION

The *Nobel Lecture* is divided into seven discrete parts. The first two sections introduce Solzhenitsyn's conception of art as a gift that finally resists every human effort to master it. Human beings have repeatedly attempted to use it for low or trivial purposes and to "adapt it . . . toward transient political or limited needs." But art transcends such self-serving efforts: "each time and in every usage it bestows upon us a portion of its mysterious inner light." There is something mysterious and transcendent about this gift, so much so that it resists all efforts at definition. Rather than attempting to define art or to enumerate its various facets, Solzhenitsyn begins by sketching two competing self-understandings of the artist. (It should be noted that when Solzhenitsyn speaks about art in the *Nobel Lecture* he almost always has the written word in mind.)

The first kind of artist, taking what may be called the "modern" view of his role, "imagines himself the creator of an autonomous spiritual world; he hoists upon his shoulders the act of creating the world and of populating it, together with the total responsibility for it." But this heady articulation of the artist's task expects too much of mortal men. No human being, not even a "mortal genius," can build a "balanced spiritual system" upon the illusion that man is "the center of existence." The *Nobel Lecture* thus begins with a rejection of that "anthropocentric humanism" that Solzhenitsyn would later argue (in his Harvard Address of 1978) was responsible for the fateful turn that Western humanity took at the beginning of the modern era. This willful confusion of man with God is the characteristic spiritual perversion at the heart of distinctively modern and postmodern reflection.

Solzhenitsyn openly identifies with the second understanding of the artist's vocation. In this view, the "artist recognizes above himself a higher power and joyfully works as a humble apprentice under God's heaven." Remarkably, his responsibility is "graver and more demanding" than the first sort, because he takes "responsibility for all he writes and paints—and for the souls which apprehend it." But the second sort of artist rejects every form of subjectivism and self-assertion. He knows that he did not create the world and rejects any hubristic claim that he can "control it." Above all, he has "no doubts about its foundations." To be sure, this artist recognizes that the world is shrouded in mystery. But he also understands that the created world nonetheless has an order and structure, an underlying harmony, that he must aim to "vividly communicate" to others. This "apprentice under God's heaven" is acutely aware of "the beauty and ugliness of man's role" in the world and has no illusions about the persistence of evil or imperfection in the human heart. One of the principal themes of Solzhenitsyn's art (in the famous words of *The Gulag Archipelago*) is that the line between good and evil "passes not through states, nor between classes, nor between political parties either—but right through every human heart—and through all human hearts." But "even amid failure and at the lower depths of existence—in poverty, in prison, and in illness," an artist with this second kind of self-understanding experiences "a sense of enduring harmony" that "cannot abandon him." Rather than attempting to impose his will on reality, he responds with receptivity and gratitude to the mystery of God's creation.

As the *Nobel Lecture* makes clear, Solzhenitsyn is a realist who affirms the underlying intelligibility of the world. In his view, speech and reason can make sense of personal experience and relate it to benevolent "foundations" that finally elude all human manipulation and control. Solzhenitsyn accepts the validity of a classical Christian cosmology and anthropology, one that has nothing in common with the facile modern (and postmodern) belief that the universe is indifferent or even hostile to human purposes. If Solzhenitsyn is a "realist" who believes in the objective character of Reality, he never confuses Art with some didactic or rationalistic articulation of the nature of things. Through reason and experience human beings have access to unchanging human nature and to a moral order that transcends cultural and historical relativity. But Solzhenitsyn acknowledges the important respects in which art transcends discursive reasoning. It is through its "dazzling convolutions" and "unforeseeable discoveries" that art has such a "powerful impact on men." Its "magical" qualities cannot be "wholly accounted for by the artist's view of the world, by his intention, or by the work of his unworthy fingers." The artist-as-"apprentice" comes to appreciate that he is a care-taker of a truly ineffable gift. Art allows us to see that "not everything can be named. Some things draw us beyond words." However "indistinctly" or "briefly," art gives human beings access to "revelations the likes of which cannot be achieved by rational thought." At its most sublime, art provides human beings with a momentary glimpse of the "Inaccessible" without in any way undermining the intelligibility of the created order. Solzhenitsyn's model artist thus draws upon the best resources of reason and revelation. He remains in touch with the underlying harmony of the world and attempts to make sense of its "givenness." This view of art is far from the vain and plati-tudinous emphasis on autonomy or self-creation that dominates contempo-rary discussions of art and literature.

Solzhenitsyn is not a dogmatic thinker. But his major writings demon-strate that he has no doubts about the ultimate goodness or intelligibility of the world. For Solzhenitsyn, every authentic understanding of the artist's responsibility moves toward such an affirmation. There can be no humane or humanizing art without confidence in the ultimate integrity of the natu-ral order of things. Otherwise, art collapses underneath its own pretenses, even if the modern artist is tempted to blame his failure to sustain a project of human autonomy on "the chronic disharmony of the world . . . the com-plexity of modern man's divided soul, or . . . the public's lack of understand-ing."

The insights of section one are the bedrock of the *Nobel Lecture* as a whole. Thus, they necessarily resurface in various subsequent sections.

"Beauty Will Save the World"

The second section of the lecture provides a remarkably suggestive discus-sion of Dostoevsky's "enigmatic remark" that "Beauty will save the world" (words that are attributed to Prince Myshkin by Ippolit in Dostoevsky's *The Idiot*). Solzhenitsyn admits that these words puzzled him for the longest time, since beauty has surely "ennobled" and "elevated" human beings without in any way saving them from themselves. But on further consideration, Solzhenitsyn came to appreciate the profound depth of insight of Dostoevsky, a man to whom "it was given to . . . see many things."

In a particularly eloquent formulation, Solzhenitsyn evokes "the old trinity of Truth, Goodness, and Beauty," which "is not simply the decorous and antiquated formula it seemed to us at the time of our self-confident materi-alistic youth." Solzhenitsyn is by no means a naïve thinker who *conflates* beauty with truth and goodness or closes his eyes to the manifold tensions inherent in the human condition. But in no small part because of his experience in the camps, Solzhenitsyn came to appreciate that art can complete the work of Truth and Goodness by restoring the lost unity of life and truth. He suggestively compares the old trinity of Truth, Goodness, and Beauty to trees no longer allowed to flourish in our modern and postmodern worlds. When "the overly straight sprouts of Truth and Goodness have been crushed, cut down, or not permitted to grow," then perhaps the "whimsical, unpredictable, and ever surprising shoots of Beauty will force their way through and soar up to *that very spot*, thereby fulfilling the task of all three." The modern conceit is to reduce art to a mere product of human making or to discern in it an epiphenomenal reflection of underlying historical or socioeconomic determinants. The radically modern theorist reduces beauty to one idiosyncratic "value" among others and denies its capacity to give human beings access to an order of goodness and truth.

In Solzhenitsyn's view, there is too much self-indulgence and willful despair in this attempt to define the world as an inexpiable struggle among irreconcilable values. The modernist fails to appreciate the ways in which beauty provides an existential verification of the natural order, or at least allows truth and goodness to retain a tenuous foothold in the human world. Moreover, Solzhenitsyn's own life and witness serve to vindicate the Dostoevskyan insight about the capacity of beauty to save the world. From the early 1920s through the late 1960s, there had been no shortage of books written about totalitarianism or the Soviet camp system. But none had come close to moving hearts and minds the way *The Gulag Archipelago* did upon its publication. *The Gulag Archipelago* is faithful to the facts and contains many instructive discussions of historical, legal, and philosophical matters related to the rise of the Soviet "sewage disposal system." But it is first and foremost a work of art, "an experiment in literary investigation." Its often sardonic authorial voice, as well as its artful weaving together of Solzhenitsyn's personal experience and the testimony of 256 *zeks* with historical research and profound spiritual reflection, allowed it to capture precisely what was entailed in the ideological deformation of reality.

There is every reason to welcome new works of historical scholarship that draw upon previously inaccessible material from the archives of the Soviet state, party, and secret police. Solzhenitsyn has certainly done everything to encourage and support such endeavors. But an excellent work of recent scholarship such as Anne Applebaum's *Gulag: A History* (2003) will never displace *The Gulag Archipelago* because it serves different, if ultimately complementary, purposes. Because Solzhenitsyn brought beauty as well as philosophical reflection to bear upon the truth, *The Gulag Archipelago* was able to convey magisterially the sheer monstrousness of the ideological Lie. It illumined the truth about "the soul and barbed wire" precisely because it transcended the concerns of historical scholarship, narrowly understood. To his great credit, Solzhenitsyn understood that the elaborate ideological fictions that defined Soviet communism would collapse once they were confronted by a truly artful rendering of "the soul of man under socialism" (in conjunction, that is, with a critical mass of citizens who had opted for "nonparticipation in lies"). With the publication of *The Gulag Archipelago* on December 30, 1973, Solzhenitsyn could plausibly maintain that this was the moment foretold by the "foul midnight hags" of *Macbeth*, the fateful moment "when Birnham Wood shall walk."

BRIDGING THE DIFFERENT "SCALES OF VALUES"

The central sections of the *Nobel Lecture* are dedicated to an exploration of the indispensable role that literature can play in bridging the "yawning chasm" that separates peoples and cultures in the contemporary world. Solzhenitsyn's "theoretical" exploration of the problem is clearly inspired by the great practical difficulty that people in the Communist bloc had in making the totalitarian experience "visible and understandable" to an uncomprehending Western world. Solzhenitsyn sets out to explain this insensitivity, this inability of people who address each other to make out "distinct speech." The fact that words of warning "ring out and fade away . . . leaving no taste, no color, no smell" is not simply the fault of a West that has succumbed to "the spirit of Munich," which is "a malady of the will of affluent people." More fundamentally, it reflects the way human beings come to comprehend the world and to forge their "scale of values," the "actions and intentions" that shape them as individuals and peoples. Human beings are so constituted to be most attentive to what is closest to home, to see the world through their experience as individuals and as "members of groups." For millennia, humanity was dispersed within particular communities whose contact with the rest of the world was intermittent at best. Human beings lived within "the scattered nations" and formed "scale[s] of values" and moral judgments based upon their particular individual and collective experiences. They were rarely cognizant of the rest of the world or of fundamental disjunctions between cultures and values.

Solzhenitsyn is not a relativist who believes that something is "true on this side of the Pyrenees, false on the other." Along with speaking confidently about the unchanging features of human nature, he derides fashionable denials of the existence of moral law. But he also knows that human beings are constituted to live within specific nations and traditions whose disappearance "would impoverish us not less than if all men should become alike, with one personality and one face." In a profoundly unfashionable discussion, Solzhenitsyn articulates the crucial place of nations in God's providential design: They are "the wealth of mankind, its generalized personalities; the least among them has its own unique coloration and harbors within itself a unique facet of God's design." Solzhenitsyn does justice to both our common humanity and the dignity of a world constituted by a variety of national forms and cultural traditions. He rejects facile cosmopolitanism, even as he acknowledges the crucial necessity of rectifying the dangerous myopia that prevents peoples from judging reality according to a common scale of values.

In the fifth section of the *Nobel Lecture* Solzhenitsyn places great—perhaps inordinate—hope in the ability of "world literature" to reconcile the various scales of values and to provide humankind with a "single system of evaluation for evil deeds and good ones." Literature alone is able to "direct man's power toward that which is more fearsome rather than that which is closer at hand." It alone has the spiritual density to "impress upon a sluggish and obstinate human being someone else's far-off sorrows or joys." Solzhenitsyn insists that "propaganda, coercion, and scientific proofs," the chosen tools of a deformed modernity, "are all equally powerless here." Art, in contrast, can reach into the depths of men's souls and can facilitate and transmit experiences that were previously unavailable to them. Solzhenitsyn does not hesitate to call "miraculous" this ability of literature to convey collective experiences despite "differences in language, custom, and social structure." In this regard, Solzhenitsyn makes clear that his "dissident" opposition to censorship and the repression of national literature had nothing to do with a libertarian commitment to "freedom of expression." Rather, it was rooted in his recognition of the crucial role that literature plays in conveying memories and experiences across generations and among peoples. Literature has a unique capacity to conserve the *soul* of a people and to allow lived experiences to become comprehensible across the bounds of time and space. The destruction of a free, high-minded, and morally serious national literature is nothing less than an affront to the common cause of humanity.

World literature builds upon "well-established traditions of national literatures" and allows the "peaks" of that literature to speak to the whole of humanity in a way that was unthinkable even two or three generations ago. It is by no means an "abstraction" invented by literary critics but rather a concrete manifestation of the "growing spiritual unity of mankind." Solzhenitsyn welcomes the interest that people all over the world evince for the "internal affairs" of faraway nations, for "the salvation of mankind lies only in making everything the concern of all." But as Solzhenitsyn makes clear elsewhere, this is a far cry from inviting one nation to impose its political system, even a democratic one, by force.

THE RESPONSIBILITY OF THE WRITER

In the sixth section of the *Nobel Lecture*, Solzhenitsyn addresses the moral and political responsibility of the artist. Solzhenitsyn does not question "the *right* of an artist" to "express nothing but his personal experience" or to withdraw into "self-created worlds or into the realms of subjective whim." But this refusal on the part of the self-absorbed artist to come to terms with the responsibilities inherent in his vocation reflects a profound absence of self-knowledge. In withdrawing into himself, this sort of artist forgets that the "greater part" of his gift "has been breathed into him ready-made at birth." With his God-given talent comes a "responsibility" that "has been imposed upon his free will." The artist thus misinterprets the nature of his gift and derogates his weighty responsibility for shaping a truly common or public world. His abdication of responsibility is all the more troubling in an ideological age when "the same old atavistic urges—greed, envy, unrestrained passion, and mutual hostility"—tear apart the common world under the guise of "respectable pseudonyms like class, race, mass or trade union struggle."

In an anticipation of the principal themes of his 1978 Harvard Address, Solzhenitsyn takes aim at the mendacities of the Communist East, where "a primitive rejection of all compromise is given the status of a theoretical principle," and at the erosion of self-restraint and authoritative institutions that threatens the integrity of Western rule-of-law societies. In a discussion that won him few friends in left-liberal intellectual quarters, Solzhenitsyn expresses nothing but contempt for what Dostoevsky called the "subservience to progressive little notions," which has widely characterized intellectual life in the modern democratic world. Solzhenitsyn laments a civilizational crisis marked by indulgence toward revolutionary violence, an excessive deference to the most irresponsible demands of the young, and contempt for anything that smacks of "conservatism."

As the great Polish poet and Nobel Laureate Czeslaw Milosz observed in a penetrating commentary on Solzhenitsyn's *Nobel Lecture*, the Russian writer's harsh evaluation of the New Left and the cultural dislocations of the 1960s has more in common with the "commonsensical" judgments of the typical blue-collar worker than it does with the "progressivism" of Western intellectual elites. In Solzhenitsyn's view, the writer's engagement with society entails something much more demanding than deference to the liberationist and antinomian currents at work in contemporary culture.

In a manner reminiscent of Burke's *Reflections* or Dostoevsky's *Devils*, Solzhenitsyn defends the civilized inheritance that is a precondition for the responsible exercise of human freedom. If art is a gift from on high that tests the free will of the artist, so liberty provides a spiritual challenge for free men and women to find a principled mean between coercion and license.

The public-spirited writer must resist the ideological deformation of reality in both its totalitarian and its Western "progressivist" forms. The writer must answer for "the evils of today's world" even if they did not enter the world as a result of his own efforts. He takes responsibility for the world by speaking the truth and calling "good and evil" by their names.

DEFEATING THE LIE

Despite what appears to be a deeply pessimistic evaluation of the course of modern civilization, Solzhenitsyn ends the *Nobel Lecture* on a characteristically hopeful note. He concludes his text by invoking the capacity of literature to undermine a totalitarian world built upon the twin pillars of violence and lies. Unlike the conventional analysis of academic political scientists and historians, Solzhenitsyn never understood the Soviet Union to be one tyranny among others. Rather, it was an *ideological regime* built upon lies that could only be maintained through the most hyperbolic violence. At the beginning of an ideological adventure flush with revolutionary fervor for the creation of a new man and society, violence "act[ed] openly and even [took] pride in itself." But as revolutionary expectations became routinized, the regime increasingly lost its ideological self-confidence. It relied less upon repeated displays of physical violence and more upon the coerced and voluntary participation of its subjects in a phantasmagoric world of lies.

At the end of the *Nobel Lecture*, Solzhenitsyn sketches a path to the comprehensive de-totalitarianization of the Communist world. He places his hopes not in armed revolution but in the self-conscious refusal of decent men and women to "participate in lies." This is the path of civic salvation. Solzhenitsyn would reiterate this claim even more emphatically in his 1973 *Letter to the Soviet Leaders* and in the manifesto "Live Not by Lies!" that was released to the Western press and in *samizdat* on the eve of his involuntary exile from the Soviet Union in February 1974. All these texts demonstrate that Solzhenitsyn was among the first to appreciate the terrible vulnerability of an "empire of lies" to "ordinary brave" men and women who would opt for "spiritual integrity" over "spiritual slavery." His insight would be developed with considerable theoretical sophistication by the Czech dissident playwright Václav Havel in his 1979 essay "The Power of the Powerless." Havel freely acknowledged that his analysis was fundamentally indebted to Solzhenitsyn's original insight.

If Solzhenitsyn exposed the intrinsic vulnerability of a regime based upon lies, he also highlighted literature's unique capacity "to defeat the lie," to expose its violence for what it really was. Solzhenitsyn's life and work amply confirm the wisdom of the Russian proverb that he cites at the conclusion of his *Nobel Lecture*:

One word of truth shall outweigh the whole world.

For Solzhenitsyn, this proverb is no literary flight of fancy. The ideocratic regime was based upon something far more destructive of the human soul than mere violence or physical coercion. It *spiritualized* despotism through its requirement that its subjects lie about a whole range of matters great and small. These lies were rooted in the more fundamental "illusion that men and social organizations can be transformed at a stroke" (Raymond Aron). Art—with its words of truth—exposes this lie in all its sordid reality and thus allows human beings to come to terms with the common human world of freedom and responsibility.

THE CONTINUING RELEVANCE OF SOLZHENITSYN

Today most informed observers appreciate the central role that Solzhenitsyn played in the defeat of communism. More than any other figure in the twentieth century, he exposed the ideological "lie" at the heart of Communist totalitarianism. The French historian Alain Besançon has suggestively compared the Solzhenitsyn of *Gulag* to St. George, the semi-mythological spiritual warrior and slayer of dragons. This image undoubtedly captures the courage and intensity of Solzhenitsyn's efforts to delegitimize a regime that killed tens of millions of its own citizens in a misguided effort to create a "socialist" utopia, freed of conflict and human imperfection. Thanks to Solzhenitsyn, far fewer people today defend the good intentions of the original Bolshevik Revolution of 1917 or blame the Soviet tragedy primarily on the depravity and will-to-power of Joseph Stalin. With unmistakable genius, Solzhenitsyn has put ideology—and ideological terror—on the cognitive map of contemporary man. Martin Malia is right to suggest that *The Gulag Archipelago* is the closest we are going to come to a Nuremberg trial for the other great totalitarian regime of the twentieth century.

Yet a legend persists that Solzhenitsyn is somehow not a true friend of human liberty. Nothing could be further from the truth. In fact, he is a political moderate and a strong proponent of conservative constitutionalism. In a series of writings, beginning with his *Letter to the Soviet Leaders* (1973) and culminating in *Russia in Collapse* (1998), he has been a consistent advocate of the rule of law, economic development fueled by human-scale technology, and revived local self-government in Russia along the lines of the prerevolutionary *zemstvos* (local and provincial councils). But, with some admirable exceptions, journalists and academics have failed to make the requisite effort needed to understand Solzhenitsyn's judicious melding of the best of Western thought and Russia's native cultural and intellectual traditions.

Solzhenitsyn is ritualistically dismissed as a Slavophile, romantic, agrarian, monarchist, theocrat, even anti-Semite. There are few major intellectual figures who have been so systematically misunderstood or have been the subject of as many willful distortions. It is an axiom among progressive-minded cultural elites in both Russia and the West that he has little or nothing to say to or about the "modern world." Yet Solzhenitsyn has never called for the restoration of monarchy and explicitly denies being a "Slavophile." He does not share the nineteenth-century Slavophiles' indulgence toward autocracy (however liberal-minded), their excessive sense of Russian national exclusiveness, or their romantic support for the peasant commune instead of a system of individual land ownership. Solzhenitsyn is better understood as the latest in a distinguished line of what the intellectual historian of Russia Donald Treadgold has called "syncretistic" thinkers. These thinkers have tried to combine "ideas from the West with ideas coming from the indigenous tradition." Solzhenitsyn's true forebears and inspirations include Russian Christian liberal thinkers of the late nineteenth and early twentieth centuries such as Vladimir Soloviev and Sergei Bulgakov. Like them, Solzhenitsyn admires and draws upon the spiritual and intellectual resources of the wider Western tradition while rejecting those currents of scientism, atheism, and subjectivism that identify human progress with the triumph of secular humanitarianism.

What accounts for the widespread hostility to Solzhenitsyn in both Russia and the West? To begin with, some on the Left undoubtedly refuse to forgive Solzhenitsyn for his pivotal role in defeating the Communist behemoth. In addition, Solzhenitsyn is one of a series of conservative-minded thinkers who brings together a measured critique of philosophical modernity, of what he has termed "anthropocentric humanism," with an appreciation of the liberty that is the centerpiece of Western civic life. But it is difficult for either the demi-educated or progressive-minded to understand the politics of prudence. Others, including many Western journalists and secular-minded Russian intellectuals, reflexively identify patriotism and religion with reaction, with insular attitudes that are incompatible with a forward-looking society. In *November 1916*, Solzhenitsyn writes appreciatively about the leader of the *zemstvo* movement, D. M. Shipov, who combined support for self-government with a deep respect for Russia's spiritual traditions. He was a partisan of liberty who did not want Russia slavishly to imitate the secular West. But Solzhenitsyn notes that the pernicious habit had already developed of dismissing such men as "Slavophiles," reactionaries. Solzhenitsyn's comments about the distorted reception of Shipov's ideas apply equally well to the standard characterizations of Solzhenitsyn's own position:

> Shipov was trying to show the majority that making rights and
> guarantees the basis of reform meant destroying, frittering away
> the religious and moral idea which was still intact in the mind of
> the people. In return, his opponents in the majority called him a
> Slavophile, although he did not recognize either the divine ori-
> gin of absolutism or the superiority of Orthodoxy to other forms
> of Christianity—but it had become the custom half a century
> earlier (and remained so a half a century later) to call anyone
> who chooses to deviate from direct imitation of Western models,
> anyone who assumes that Russia's path . . . might be peculiar to
> itself—a reactionary, a Slavophile.

How does one begin to break out of the interminable recycling of distortions and misrepresentations that are relentlessly directed at Solzhenitsyn?
To begin with, it is necessary to recognize that the defense of human liberty
and dignity is not exhausted by the categories or assumptions of late modernity. Solzhenitsyn is a liberal in the sense that he is acutely aware of the
myriad moral and cultural prerequisites of human liberty. As a careful reading of his Harvard and Liechtenstein addresses makes clear, Solzhenitsyn's
alternative to the "calamity of an autonomous, irreligious humanistic consciousness" has never been a romantic communal or theocratic society, but
rather a free one where individual rights are limited by "the moral heritage
of Christian centuries with their great reserves of mercy and sacrifice."
Solzhenitsyn's real target in those speeches was never democratic liberty (he
has been an indefatigable advocate of local self-government and a critic of
"oligarchy" in the new Russia) but rather the diminution of "man's responsibility to God and society." In Solzhenitsyn's striking formulation from his
1983 "Templeton Lecture," the terrible calamities of the twentieth century
all derive from the fact that "men have forgotten God." Solzhenitsyn is a
partisan of "liberty under God" against the pernicious illusion that men can
build a world that defers to no limits above the autonomous human will.

Solzhenitsyn has meditated on the problem of conjugating liberty and
the moral contents of life with great penetration and finesse in the various
volumes of *The Red Wheel*. These books include profound reflections on the
character of political moderation and the requirements of a statesmanship
that would unite Christian attentiveness to the spiritual dignity of man with
an appreciation of the need to respect the unceasing evolution of society.
Solzhenitsyn takes aim at reactionaries who ignore the inexorability of human "progress," at revolutionaries who take nihilistic delight in destroying
the existing order, and at "false liberals" who refuse to explore prudently the
necessarily difficult relations between order and liberty, tradition and
progress.

In nearly all of his major writings, Solzhenitsyn appeals to the indispensability of the spiritual qualities of "repentance" and "self-limitation" for a truly balanced individual and collective life. But he never turns the classical or Christian virtues into an antimodern ideology that would reject the necessity of living with the tensions inherent in a dynamic, modern society. He is not, however, unduly sanguine about the prospects for these virtues in the contemporary scene. As he writes in *November 1916*, "In the life of nations, even more than in private life, the rule is that concessions and self-limitation are ridiculed as naïve and stupid." Solzhenitsyn thus has no illusions about repentance and self-limitation becoming the explicit and unchallenged foundation of free political life. His more modest hope is to obtain a hearing for the Good amidst the cacophony of claims that vie for public notice. Neither genuflecting before progress nor irresponsibly rejecting it, Solzhenitsyn insists, as he put it in the 1993 Liechtenstein address, that we must "seek and expand ways of directing its might towards the perpetration of good." Solzhenitsyn's moral vision has too often been politicized in ways that mistake his rejection of progressivist illusions for a reactionary refusal to admit the possibility of authentic progress.

Solzhenitsyn is, in truth, a liberal conservative who wants to temper the one-sided modern preoccupation with individual freedom with a salutary reminder of the moral ends that ought to inform responsible human choice. Like the best classical and Christian thinkers of the past, he believes (as he put it in *November 1916*) that human beings should not "neglect their spiritual essence" or "show an exaggerated concern for man's material needs." Thus, while he displays a rich appreciation of the limits of politics, he also recognizes that "a Christian must . . . actively endeavor to improve the holders of power and the state system." And when Solzhenitsyn addresses specifically political questions, he does so as a principled advocate of political moderation. His portrait in *August 1914* of Prime Minister Pyotr Stolypin's efforts to establish a constitutional order that would be consistent with Russia's spiritual traditions and that would keep Russia from falling into the revolutionary abyss contains some of the wisest pages ever written about statesmanship. Solzhenitsyn self-consciously writes as a defender of the "middle line" of social development and in the service of human liberty and dignity.

Contrary to legend, then, Solzhenitsyn is no cranky reactionary who rejects the modern world *tout court*—he would have no difficulty appreciating the wisdom of Nietzsche's rebuke to conservatives: "whisper to the Conservatives . . . only a crab can crawl backwards." Nor is he a brooding pessimist who is given over to apocalyptic speculations and cynical despair. The final note in his work is in fact one of hope—precisely because he believes that the givenness of reality is the most fundamental fact about the world we human beings are privileged to inhabit. Life is a gift to be cherished despite the reality of evil, which can never be wholly extinguished from the world or from the human soul. The struggle between good and evil in every human heart should not be seen as a reason for despair but rather as evidence of a "trial of our free will" that allows for both intellectual and moral virtue to emerge.

Solzhenitsyn told his most recent biographer, Joseph Pearce, that contrary to common opinion he understands himself to be first and foremost an optimist. Despite everything, he has never lost faith in the Providence of God or in the decency and courage of ordinary human beings. It is important to remember that *The Gulag Archipelago* ends on a note of both hope and catharsis. The dramatic third volume pays eloquent tribute to the spirited resistance of many of his fellow citizens to the evils of Soviet totalitarianism. Even *Russia in Collapse*, despite its undeniably bleak description of contemporary Russia, acknowledges those myriad decent souls who refuse to accommodate themselves to post-Communist corruption or to succumb to a pernicious nostalgia for the monstrous Communist past. Solzhenitsyn reminds us that, even after seventy years of totalitarianism and more than ten years of misguided reforms, Russia still has its fair share of patriotic citizens, public-spirited entrepreneurs, and morally upright people of faith. There is still time to chart an alternative path toward self-government and self-limitation. Time and again, then, Solzhenitsyn has refused to despair, because he knows that the future is open and that evil can never triumph once and for all. This salutary emphasis on free human agency is at the heart of Solzhenitsyn's magnum opus, *The Red Wheel.* The tragedy of nihilistic revolution could have been averted if more Russians had chosen the path of moral and political responsibility. There was thus nothing inevitable about the success of the Bolshevik revolution of 1917.

Solzhenitsyn was the most eloquent scourge of ideology in the twentieth century. His work makes abundantly clear why we should not wish the calamity of a "great revolution" on any nation or people. As Solzhenitsyn puts it in his moving Vendée address of September 29, 1993, "we have all lived through the twentieth century, a century of terror, the chilling culmination of Progress about which so many dreamed in the eighteenth century." But Solzhenitsyn's critique of ideological revolution, his assault on the politics of that Progress, is ultimately at the service of restoring hope to acting man. Only by freeing ourselves from a false confidence in the inevitability of Progress will we "be able to improve, patiently, that which we have in any given 'today.'" Solzhenitsyn's work and witness teach us that the true alternative to revolutionary utopianism is not postmodern nihilism but gratitude for the givenness of the world and a determined but patient effort to correct injustices within it. It is certainly "vain" to hope that revolution can change human nature, but it is by no means presumptuous to believe that "the social improvements which we all so passionately desire can be achieved through normal evolutionary development."

That said, Solzhenitsyn rightly insists that we must never forget the ultimate limits of the political realm. The search for truth and the moral self-development of the individual finally transcend the scope of politics. While recognizing its central place for human freedom and dignity, Solzhenitsyn never gives politics the last word.

I

THE TRAIL

The dramatic publication in 1962 of *One Day in the Life of Ivan Denisovich* catapulted an obscure Russian schoolteacher and writer into the international spotlight. That work, however, marks not the beginning but the continuation of a long period of secretive literary activity that had begun in prison, camp, and exile and that intensified after Solzhenitsyn's return to "freedom" in 1956. It is to these early writings that one must turn to appreciate the genesis of his remarkably multifaceted intellectual and literary project. Of these, the narrative poem *Dorozhen'ka* (*The Trail, The Road, The Way*) most fully conveys the arduous path that eventually led to Solzhenitsyn's radical and definitive break with communism.

The Trail is an autobiographical poem of more than 7,000 lines published in Russian in 1999. Its author composed the poem between 1947 and 1952 under the worst of circumstances: as a prisoner of the Soviet state and without the benefit of pen and paper. As he composed the poem, he memorized it using techniques so unforgettably described in the third volume of *The Gulag Archipelago*. Utilizing a specially devised rosary as a mnemonic device, Solzhenitsyn was able to accumulate no fewer than 12,000 lines of verse during his time in a Special (Labor) Camp. This remarkable feat of memorization was a heroic effort on Solzhenitsyn's part to hold on to those experiences that crucially shaped him in the six years leading up to his arrest and incarceration in February 1945.

The autobiographical main character Sergei Nerzhin begins his odyssey as a true believer of such intensity that he awakens early on each day of his honeymoon to read Karl Marx. Nerzhin's rigid convictions largely blind him to the perversities of the ideological world that envelops the lives of every Soviet citizen. But in *The Trail* Solzhenitsyn mightily struggles to come to terms with his past. He forthrightly confronts those intimations of reality that somehow managed to break into his youthful world of illusions. In the opening chapter, Solzhenitsyn describes a canoe journey that he and a friend took along the Volga River in 1939. These two "Boys from the Moon" were oblivious to the evidence of inhuman forced labor and collectivization that was all around them. In the second chapter ("Honeymoon"), Nerzhin and his new bride come across a trainload of condemned zeks, an encounter that has a powerful, if temporary, impact on this committed Marxist. In later chapters, Solzhenitsyn describes encounters with Vlasovites, Russian soldiers who out of desperation and despair chose to fight with the dreaded German enemy rather than to help sustain a monstrous Soviet regime. Gradually these experiences left their cumulative mark on Solzhenitsyn/Nerzhin, although they did not lead to any immediate break with Sovietism. What Solzhenitsyn needed was a dramatic catalyst to open his eyes fully to the surreal world around him. This catalyst finally arrived in the form of his arrest at the front and his dazed return to Russia as a prisoner (events described in detail in chapters ten and eleven of *The Trail*).

The excerpt that follows is chapter five ("Besed") of *The Trail*. Together with chapter nine ("Prussian Nights"), it is the only part of *The Trail* to have been translated into English. It takes its name from a river and village in Belarus where Solzhenitsyn saw action during his military service in World War II. Everything in this chapter happened exactly as described. A hauntingly lyrical description of the austere Belarusian countryside ("this infertile and forsaken land") begins this chapter. The countryside's peaceful "silence" contrasts quite strikingly with the noise and clamor of the advancing Red Army. The poem as a whole is marked by a startlingly complex rhyme/meter scheme and varying line lengths that create a true polyphony among themselves. With a remarkably dense and energetic style, Solzhenitsyn captures the tense drama of the front, where his artillery unit was pounded day and night from the air and ground by German forces.

There's no log, no stump, no rounded scrap of wood
To close up the trench, above your head.

Called in for consultations with his commanders, Lieutenant Nerzhin witnesses a rear thoroughly disconnected from the
harsh realities of the front. This sempiternal disconnect between
front and rear is reinforced and amplified by the lies and propaganda that define "official" Soviet reality. Nerzhin is then invited
to witness the execution of an alleged collaborator. He is revolted
by the almost mirthful atmosphere that surrounds the execution,
one worthy of some victory celebration. His reaction to the execution is a *moral* one, that of a decent, civilized human being and
not that of an ideologue who relishes the destruction of an "enemy of the people." The grotesque, hideous suffering of the hanged
man made a deep impression on Solzhenitsyn. So, too, did the
extraordinary undulating of the German "Frame" bomber—
would she bomb or not bomb those gathered for the execution?
These experiences reinforced Solzhenitsyn's growing sense that
there is a higher Meaning, or Fate, above us. Invited to stay the
night for the revelries that were to follow the execution, a disil-
lusioned Nerzhin instead opts "to trek into the hell of bridgehead
night." His final cry of solidarity with the executed Nikolayev
reveals that Solzhenitsyn/Nerzhin's capacity for moral evaluation has not been wholly obliterated by Marxist dogmatism.

Solzhenitsyn did not have the opportunity to write down
the immense mass of *The Trail* until the summer of 1953, when
he was in exile in Central Asia. His herculean efforts to confront
his past, to defy his totalitarian masters through critical self-
examination, and to preserve the memories that risked being lost
forever can only compel admiration. *The Trail* describes the path
of suffering and enlightenment that allowed Solzhenitsyn to become the mature and self-aware writer that we know. The same
indomitable will that allowed Solzhenitsyn to survive imprisonment, cancer, and years of persecution is evident in this powerful
testimony to a key stage in a great writer's spiritual evolution.

Chapter 5
"Besed"[1]

. . . to reinstate hard labor, and capital
punishment through hanging.
(From a decree of the Presidium of the
Supreme Soviet, April 1943.)

Was not born there, nor had called it home.
And will never visit there again.
Yet my heart adopted as its own
This infertile and forsaken land. . . .
Swamps. And woods. No way for wheat to grow.   5
Fields—nowhere. Hard to raise tomatoes.
Sands and silt and wetlands cold and low,
Only rye and taters.
On the hillocks—gray, unmoving, still, and silent windmills,
In the pastures—yellow flowers shorn of all sweet scent,   10
Churches all beheaded . . . sorry shacks' foundations dismal . . .
Brushwood crossings . . . bridges rotten, wasted, bent. . . .
Tursk, Chechersk, and Zhlobin, and Sviatoye . . .

---

[1] Besed [pronounced "BAY-set"]: The name of both a river and a village in
Belarus, where Solzhenitsyn's sound-ranging battery unit fought during autumn
1943, and where the action of this chapter takes place.

Rogachiov ... Madory[2] ...
There's a piece of me I know I left there—   15
Something that will come again to me no more.
Ever for a long march on the ready,
Service I compelled, and service did I give.
So light-headed, thoughtless, free, in future
    I would never live.   20
We retreat—I'm sullen; we attack—I'm happy;
From my flask I draw, and fight with soul.
Vishenki. Shiparnia. Rudnia-Shliagi.
Besed. Zabolotye. Sverzhen. Ola.
Fear, and laughter, and a soldier's simple death ...   25
Dnepr and Sozh. Berezina and Drut.
There's a something there I know I left—
    Now it's moot. . . .

Flowing toward the rapid, murky Sozh,
'Tween the aspen saplings on its banks,   30
During autumntime both cold and fine,
Slowly-running Besed cools without a ripple,
As a placid lake without a current.
Yellow-crimson trees that line its shores
Lean their branches half the way across. . . .   35
    During quiet weather,
    Lightly, as a feather,
One can hear the leaves swoon down and drop. . . .
It is well to sneak here, to the realm of silence,
To espy a squirrel, hear a mouse's rustle;   40

---

[2] Tursk, Chechersk, etc.: Names of other towns, villages, and rivers in the same area of Belarus.

Also well to burst in here upon a steed,
Branches biting, hooves in yellow leaves,
To scare out a long-eared frightened hare,
"Hey-hey-hey!" to holler in pursuit.
We, however, plowed into these dozing woods   45
With the rowdy, reckless brandishing of army axes,
With the snakelike hissing of *katyushas*,[3]
With the din of cannons, with our engines' roar.
From Desna we thrust some hundred miles,
Setting up a bridgehead past the river Sozh,   50
Having crossed, we handed over Besed village
To the staffers, writers, commissars.

Rough, that bridgehead at Yurkovichi-Sherstin.
Many boys we left there in its wake,
Near its aspen saplings quickly felled,   55
Near its houses, laid to utter waste.
Mines would rip our only bridge, our only flimsy
Artery. . . .
Every day we straightened and attacked full-bore
Only to dank burrows to retreat.   60
In the dark of autumn night, cut off from our army,
We were beaten, pushed, and pressured into that black river—
Operation to expand the bridgehead!—
Who can understand your anguish and your fear?
All the land lies open, dead, disfigured, torn in craters . . .   65
All's dug up, all, all that can be dug,
There's no log, no stump, no rounded scrap of wood

---

[3] *Katyusha*: a multi-barreled vehicle-mounted rocket launcher widely used by the Soviet Army in World War II.

To close up the trench, above your head.
Day and night they pound, they pound, they pound
Our human mass,   70
And not one stray missile will lie down and
Pass. . . .
Ashen, pallid faces in red clay;
Ground's too wet—our shovels cannot shape it.
Trapped here! What a sorry, wretched piece of turf,   75
Little more than one square mile of earth.
We are pecked and pecked from planes above,
We're cut down, cut down by heavy mortars,
When the *sixes*[4] hiss and hiss, the *squeakers*[5] bark and bark—
Hug the ground! These, too, are aimed at us! . . .   80
Day and night our sappers[6] patch the bridge,
And our signalmen in water catch their cables
While the Germans pour it, pour it on the bridge,
And there trickles from the bridge a pinkish water. . . .
Once the lines are patched, then from the Mainland[7]   85
Pour and pour all cuss words known to man:
"Are ya stuck, ya
No-good mucking sacks?
Every single officer and every soldier
MUST! A!!—TTACK!!!"   90

---

[4] *Six*: a six-barreled German mortar.
[5] *Squeaker*: a heavy German mortar with a highly distinctive sound.
[6] Sapper: A military engineer who specializes in sapping and other field fortification activities, or who lays, detects, and disarms mines.
[7] Mainland: soldier slang for a land area temporarily secure from the enemy.

One time, I was in a slit,[8] on drenched wet straw,

Chewing mindlessly upon a stem of stalk,

Was it even I, who lost all train of thought,

Could not hear the shelling: soft? or loud?

Could not see; what was it: dark? or light?   95

My whole being was a hollow,

And I knew I couldn't change a thing.

I went numb, and neither past nor home could I recall,

Just I chewed and chewed and chewed upon this tube-like stalk of

Straw,   100

Suffocated, drowsy, overcome.

Suddenly, a soldier leaning over:

Comrade senior battery commander! You are

Summoned. To battalion H.Q."[9]

What H.Q.? H.Q.? ... Ah, yes, H.Q., gosh darn it!   105

Somewhere there are people living? Let them live, but

Let us be as well. Devil take you, BatCom:[10]

Want me to climb out and drive right to the shelling? ...

Hey, how goes our bridge? It can't be

Whole?!   110

Look'ee here! *The Russian fights with style.*

Just a year ago you never saw

Such an orderly efficient crossing:

Horses—Hey! and drivers—Go! No crowding.

From the right bank to the left, from left to right,   115

Soldiers we still have in Mother Russia!

To the left bank like the wind now take us

Up and out.

---

[8] Slit: a tiny, narrow trench just big enough to hold one person.
[9] H.Q.: headquarters.
[10] BatCom: battalion commander.

Now I'm glad to go, if only for an hour

To be summoned from that blackened pit of wrath;   120

Breathing deeply the true air of life,

Quietly I rode along a forest path.

All moved freely here; the forest bubbled.

Just in case, the dugouts were protected doubly,

Trebly, even by six tiers of timber decking.   125

Drivers were the first, as always, to grow hasty—

Parked their trucks but slightly down the ramps for safety,

Leaving their rear wheels exposed to shrapnel.

R.A.P.'s,[11] stores, stables—every inch is taken!

Thinning out the forest, trees were cut and felled,   130

Tractors dragged them to the dugout excavations,

Soldiers fired up their field kitchens,

Started to heat up a field bath,

Battery of cannons took its firing position,

Battery of howitzers shot full-blast from a meadow,   135

Vodka was passed out amongst a giddy bevy—

There peeped out, and hid again from battle,

Only the brave generals' O.P.[12]

It's amazing, how it is: you come here from the rear—

Seems like frontlines here,   140

Look how close, how near!

There's no life worth living,

There's no light worth seeing.

Should you come here from the front, however—

What deep   145

Rear!

------

[11] R.A.P.: regimental aid post.
[12] O.P.: observation post.

Besed's buried under drifts of sand so gray.

People, horses, trucks—no house, no hut has vacancy to stay.

Radio stations and repair shops—bombings can't dislodge them!—

Jammed into the baths and jammed into the barns.   150

White-coat girls, from the medical battalion,

Flit along the street, no dallying:

She is rarely modest (tasting willingly—

Or unwillingly?—a soldier's true and bitter plight),

Rather—vulgar, sassy, spoiled by caresses,   155

On her head a modish hat cocked to the side.

From beyond the Sozh—the din of battle,

As the tired cannons pounded, rattled.

Meek and dim and faint and low above the earth

Slid the autumn sun and gave no warmth.   160

Once inside H.Q., I see the drapes are starched;

Coarse cloth runners lying on the floors; a clock that strikes;

On the wall—four placards: two of Stalin. Also:

"Daddy! Kill a German!"; "Don't forgive and don't forget!"

Clerks were writing softly, squeaky-neat.   165

When I entered, someone muttered: "Welcome . . . health . . ."

"So, how goes it, eagles?"—"Poorly."—"Why?"—"S.U. gun.[13]

Every night it *hurls*, and we know no rest."

. . . As prescribed, the BatCom chewed me out:

"Here's the thing . . . before . . . I didn't . . . call you out . . .   170

Thought, with your experience . . . laid my hopes . . . that you'd make out. . . .

Nighttime brought a hit! the corps itself!! H.Q.!!!

Who??—don't know?!—at least make up a lie or two. . . .

Now I can't name any targets for the higher ranks. . . .

What in heck you doing there, up on that river bank?   175

---

[13] S.U. gun: self-propelled gun.

Somehow I don't see a keen *artillery style*.
You may go." I'm through the door, but there's the J.P.O.:[14]
"*Oberleutenant*,[15] good health! Why aren't you shaven clean?
Take some papers, brochures, pass them round, explain.
Oh, and did you run the propaganda chat,   180
'Death for death and blood for blood'?
These citations are no good,
Some are long, and some are cut too short,
You had best re-do them, I am sorry:
Get them back to me by dinnertime tomorrow.   185
Rybakov's heroics you too clearly indicate,
Ivanov's heroics are too standard-boilerplate."
One more step, but here's the J.L.O.:[16] "I want some proof!
How'd you lose three carbines in the river? What'd they,
Vanish—poof?   190
And your petrol?
Did you not use up five times your weekly ration?!
A precise accounting you'd best fashion!
You think Moscow brooks excuses? What, your pay's too high?
We'll withhold times twelve-point-five, and hang you dry!"   195
Then the *partorg*[17] grabs me by the arm: "Inform me,
Are your men *applying*?[18] By the way, how come now
Don't I see your name?
What a poor exemplar!
Shame, you   200
Officer!"
Junior chief of staff says, "Take these Army orders. Get to

---

[14] J.P.O.: junior political officer.
[15] *Oberleutenant*: a playful use of the German term for Senior Lieutenant.
[16] J.L.O.: junior logistics officer.
[17] *Partorg*: Communist Party organizer.
[18] Applying: i.e., to join the Communist Party.

Know them—they're important. Very. Take your time."
S.C.O.[19] asks, "What about your gas masks? Better?"
And the doctor, "Baths? Lice? Hygiene? Grime?"   205
I've served long enough—what's asked of me is clear:
I salute, I listen—but don't hear.
Anyway, I'll do it how I think I ought,
While they'll write it up the way they want.
Not my first day in the army—well I know the deal.   210
If you dispatch me to heaven, I'll just click my heel:
"Shall I leave straightway?" Says the chief of staff,
"Tarry, spend the night; why rush? There's straw-stalk in your hair. . . .
Halt, unwind—or have you got a fine young lass,
In your soldier's lair?"   215
On my shoulder placed his hand, and asked with pleasure:
"To a proper execution, Nerzhin, have you ever
Been? . . ."

———————————

Where the village street came to an end,
Where the fir-grove clustered—there, hard by the fresh-felled post   220
There now waded through the deep sand to attend, an
Idle watchers' host.
Corporals, lieutenant-colonels, captains, majors,
Privates, sergeants—girls and boys not much beyond teenagers,
SMERSH men,[20] doctors, staffers from H.Q.,   225
Local women in their headscarves; passing guardsmen watching too.

———————————

[19] S.C.O.: senior chemical warfare officer.
[20] SMERSH: the Soviets' frightening abbreviation for their dread World-War-II–
era military intelligence: SMERt SHpionam (Death to Spies).

Simple, basic is the high place that's made ready,

All is steady:

Roughly hewn, still brown-striped, stands the post of virgin pine,

At its top—a beam, a hook, some twine.   230

Right at five there drove up from the rear

By the brushwood road a nimble "Willys,"[21]

Carrying two colonels; coming near,

They walked out and stood right in the middle.

Both displayed on epaulettes the thin stripes of the law: 235

One—a shortish Jew, and one—a blunt-nosed Slav.

Playing with the holster of his pistol,

"Bring him over here!"—the short one squealed shrilly.

From the retinue emerged two gunners nimbly,

And they flung the massive barn door open widely, briskly.   240

Brought him. Dressed at random, in civilian clothes.

Half-asleep still. There is straw in his disheveled hair, all tousled.

Hands are tightly tied behind his back. He looks perplexed and puzzled.

People whisper: "German?" No—our own.

Fixed his gaze upon the throng; then, hobbling past the guards on show,

He drew near on even, languid feet.

"No one's read his sentence. . . ." "He knows nothing. . . ." "*Does not know!. . .*"

Then unfurled the short colonel a small sheet,

Rearranged with caution the matte shoulder-belt

Of his foppish purse.   250

Then a sergeant with a thick red neck

Fetched a stool, and set it underneath the post.

In unnatural pose, with hands behind his back,

Having hung his head, cast down his drooping eyes,

The accused assumed that stance of shabby actors,   255

Which shouts "guilty" to the gallery's greedy eyes.

---

[21] Willys was the brand name used by Willys-Overland Motors, best known for their production of Jeeps.

Torn-up trousers, and a grimy sullied shirt;
Did he hear? not hear? the judge's mumbled burring—
"By the verdict of the Soviet Union
Quorum . . . judge . . . divisional . . . tribunal . . ."   260
Could they find no other, better, reader?!
Quickly he spat out some words like seeds,
Trapping other words behind his lips:
"Nikolayev . . . traitor . . . to his country . . .
Having . . . by the German occupiers . . ."   265
Timid women, reckless brave lieutenants
Huddled, hung on every word, as taut as wire.
Gilding the red death-post with its final rays,
Sank the setting yellow sun behind the Sozh.
Thundering not two miles away, beyond the forest,   270
Solo-engine Junkers[22] dove and bombed in shuddering waves,
Taking turns, they dashed to blast the river crossing.
Higher up, above them all—sure and swift and light—
Yakovlevs[23] and Messerschmitts[24] did
Fight,   275
And, in searing smoke and smouldering ruin downed,
Wounded planes fell to the ground.
Anti-aircraft guns shot from the river,
Pounding at the Junkers, missing badly,
Flakes of white explosions blazing, flaring upward madly.   280
. . . Heck, right now our sappers, drenched to bone, in shivers,
Try to stop the fallen, drifting beams as best they can.
And yet no one, no one bends his mind to them.
"By decree of April . . . section number . . . put to death . . ."

---

[22] Junkers was a famous German aircraft manufacturer.
[23] Yakovlev (Yak) was a famed line of Russian fighter aircraft.
[24] Messerschmitt was another famous German aircraft manufacturer, known primarily for its World-War-II-era fighter aircraft.

No one looks above, where, gliding to the zenith,   285
    Through the blinding, light-drenched sunset sky,
    Paused and froze above us (whence she came?)
    Focke-Wulf One Hundred Eighty-Nine—the
                    Frame.[25]
No, the guards do see her. Now she's noticed by a   290
    Staffer. Then a second, third, a fifth, a sixth
Throws his head back, listening no longer; and another,
    More, and more—and now the whole big crowd.
Someone shifted from the center to the side for cover,
    Someone else instinctively ducked down.   295
    Silence fell, no further was the sentence read.
Tense with hope, the one who'll die raised up his head,
    Bidding that his judges die with him together. . . .
She's a thorough watchman. Effortlessly could she
Scrutinize our herd, to whom her eye was tethered,   300
            Scoping every speck.
                Would she
            Bomb us to a wreck?
And there was, there was a soundless minute:
    Scales swayed in judgment: who shall die?—   305
As if this were settled not by men, not here, but
                In the sky.
Was it that its payload was inopportune then?
    Or it saved its bombs for use another day?
Leaving in effect "By verdict of the Union,"   310
    That Frame shifted, budged—and slid away.
    All exhaled. Then softly started moaning
    The accused, and lowered down his gaze,

---

[25] The Focke-Wulf FW-189 was a twin-engine, three-seat tactical reconnaissance aircraft. It came to be known as the "Frame" because of its distinctive open-frame design, clearly visible even from the ground.

The dark colonel finished, muffing up the reading
      Of the phrase.   315
Then the other, blunt-nosed, colonel roared out: "Is it clear?!"
    Clamor by the river . . . Silence here. . . .
    Straightway, and without a jolt or jerk, the
      Able sergeant-major set to work.
    No unneeded movement; there's a trick to all: 320
  Nudged him in the back, not rudely guiding forward,
    By the post he stood him near himself, withal,
    Climbed up to ensure the gear was all in order.
      Finding satisfactory the hook,
        And the rope quite stout,   325
    Hoisted up the man with no big effort,
  Nimbly pushed his head up through the noose,
    Tightened it, examined it all round—
    That it aptly lie nor low nor high—
    Then jumped down and swiftly with his foot   330
      Booted out the stool.
  Silent till his death, the hanged man started writhing,
    Groaning, jerking, wheezing in distressed dismay.
     Maybe he imagined he was shouting?
  Was he looking round for help nearby arrayed,   335
    When he slowly started swinging circles,
  Turning this way, that way? Back and forth he swayed,
    Like, as if, he sought some friendly human faces:
    Finding none—forlornly turned away.
    His ten fingers—singly!—bended   340
      And unbended
    Tight behind his back, and wouldn't close,
    As if cataloguing every torment,
    As if tallying up every moment

That he lived through on that post.   345
His unclosing eyes filmed over and stopped shifting lively—
His mouth froze in spasming, trembling state,
Then—there was no more to Nikolayev,
Nothing but a rigid dorsal plate.
Right side, left side—each without a rudder,   350
Now a leg would jolt, and now a shoulder shudder,
Like a puppet on invisibly pulled strings,
Like a lifeless frog on voltage springs,
An unheard-of dance, a wild dance he
Danced away, and—done. . . .   355

"What's the matter, Nerzhin, what's the haste? . . .
Spend the night here with us!" — "I must go. It's six."
Sinking in the sticky sandy gluey marsh,
People scattered noiselessly, in utter hush.

Stay the night here? Takes some getting used to.   360
Best to trek into the hell of bridgehead night.
Nikolayev! Why do you stay silent?!?
Why won't you cry out? . . .

2

POEMS: PRISON, CAMP, AND EXILE

Solzhenitsyn's arrest on February 9, 1945, began an intellectual and spiritual odyssey that culminated in his definitive break with communism and his return to the patriotic and religious convictions of his youth. The autobiographical *First Circle* describes Gleb Nerzhin's turn away from the world of ideology toward love of country, as well as his determined search fueled by philosophical idealism for the underlying purpose of things; but the authorial alter ego Nerzhin represents a Solzhenitsyn in transition. For their part, the luminous poems from prison, camp, and exile illustrate not the end of the journey but rather the attainment of that settled "point of view" that would henceforth inform all of Solzhenitsyn's subsequent writings.

The first of the three poems in this section, "Prisoner's Right," was written in the labor camp at Ekibastuz in 1951. It summarizes some general thoughts about camp arguments that Solzhenitsyn heard and participated in. This poem is Solzhenitsyn's own contribution to these arguments about Russia's future. The voice is recognizably that of the "mature" Solzhenitsyn. He rejects the claim that prisoners have any special "rights" as victims or any special claim on the attention of others. Instead, he calls on them to cultivate the "illumined interior suffering core" that allows for spiritual growth and moral self-development. Solzhenitsyn does not lose sight of the "endlessly long" number of Russians and Chinese who have perished at the hands of Communist totalitarianism. His poem beautifully evokes the one "right" that belongs to every *zek*: the right to be "rancorless sons / Of our luckless and sad Russian land."

"Acathistus" was written in February 1952, when Solzhenitsyn lay in the camp clinic at Ekibastuz, recovering from surgery. The operation appeared to be successful (although a biopsy was sent to Omsk for routine examination), and this poem expresses Solzhenitsyn's gratitude for his new lease on life. Only much later, in response to a written query, did Omsk reply that the tests showed a seminoma. This deeply moving poem describes Solzhenitsyn's loss of faith under the influence of "bookish wisdom" (primarily Marxist-Leninist dogma) and his ultimate return to the faith of his fathers as a result of "purpose-from-High's steady fire." This "song of praise" concludes with Solzhenitsyn's magnificent proclamation of his faith in the Providence of the living God. "Acathistus" first appeared as part of *The Gulag Archipelago*, part IV, chapter 1, "The Ascent," perhaps the richest and most studied chapter of that magisterial work.

The last poem in this section, "Death—not as chasm," was written on December 2, 1953, in Dzhambul, a regional center in southern Kazakhstan. Solzhenitsyn's doctors had just told him that he had two weeks to live. Leaving the clinic, he composed this poem as he walked down the street. The poem conveys the pathos of a dying man grieving less for himself than for a still "crucified" Russia. The Russian writer approaches death stoically but with deep love of country informing his "otherworldly gaze." Although he would live for another fifty years and more, this would turn out to be the final poem which he would write.

Prisoner's Right

Yoke of years that we lived in a prison
Grants no rights: we're entitled to naught.
Not to pulpits. Nor lecterns. Nor glory.
Nor power. Nor halos of saints.
Nor in memoirs to mix with fatigue
Our colorless ashen complaints,
Nor: that armies of youths should now run astride life
By the path that we treaded for them.
All will go as 't will go. There's no point
To pound out the wheel's rut in advance.
An illumined interior suffering core:
May, for everything, this be our one recompense.
It's the loftiest gem of all earthly gemstones.
And, to carry it home undefiled,
Let of our phantom rights, then, the very least be:
Our secreted right to an equal revenge.
There's a number. So endlessly long,
Comprehensible just to Chinese and to Russians,
All those fallen, extinguished, without guilt or trace:
In that number we're nil upon nil upon nil. . . .
Our right is but one:
To be rancorless sons
Of our luckless and sad Russian land.
Let our grievances burn, rot, decay deep inside
To the outside we'll spring living shoots: only then,
Looking up, will our Russia's fatigued countryside
See the Sun it awaited so long.

Acathistus[1]

When, oh when did I scatter so madly
All the goodness, the God-given grains?
Was my youth not spent with those who gladly
Sang to You in the glow of Your shrines?

Bookish wisdom, though, sparkled and beckoned,
And it rushed through my arrogant mind,
The world's mysteries seemed within reckon,
My life's lot like warm wax in the hand.

My blood seethed, and it spilled and it trickled,
Gleamed ahead with a multihued trace,
Without clamor there quietly crumbled
In my breast the great building of faith.

Then I passed betwixt being and dying,
I fell off and now cling to the edge,
And I gaze back with gratitude, trembling,
On the meaningless life I have led.

Not my reason, nor will, nor desire
Blazed the twists and the turns of its road,
It was purpose-from-High's steady fire
Not made plain to me till afterward.

Now regaining the measure that's true,
Having drawn with it water of being,
Oh great God! I believe now anew!
Though denied, You were always with me. . . .

---

[1] *Acathistus*: in the Orthodox Church, a reading or song of praise.

["Death—not as chasm"]

Death—not as chasm, but death as a crest,
A ridge onto which has ascended the road.
Up in the black sky that shrouds my deathbed
Gleams the White Sun of God.

Turning about I see in its white rays
Russia, my Russia, to her polar wreaths;
View her with that otherworldly gaze
Carved out on stelae[1] by wise ancient Greeks.

I see you clearly, no rancor or spite:
Your lows. And your glory. And daily life's fight.

No more shall I see you thus: crucified;
No more shall call Resurrection t'your side. . . .

---

[1] stela \Ste´la\, n.; pl. Stel[ae]. (Gr. Antiq.) A small upright stone slab, used as a graveside monument by the ancient Greeks. It typically had a vertical line dividing the slab in half. On one side were depicted the dead person's loved ones, while on the other was shown the dead man himself, gazing immutably, powerlessly, across the line he could not cross.

3

STORIES

When Solzhenitsyn began writing at the tender age of nine, he started with stories. By his teenage years, he was producing short fiction, drama, and poetry and was planning long fiction. From his apprenticeship on, his dedication to literary art manifests itself in versatility and experimentation. As he was settling into his adult writing career in the late 1940s and early 1950s, short stories were part of his varied output. And short stories were among the genres to which he returned after he moved back to Russia in the 1990s. In the late stories he experimented with a new format that he called the "binary tale," in which two moments widely separated in time are narrated in distinct parts, then are tied together by a common thematic thread.

Although Solzhenitsyn's literary reputation rests largely on his long works of fiction and nonfiction, his short fiction meets high standards as well, from the celebrated *One Day in the Life of Ivan Denisovich* to the acclaimed "Matryona's Home" to many shorter stories. Concise form and a delicate touch are part of his repertoire. Only the formal dictates of genre distinguish the stories from his other writings. All of the works participate in a single moral vision and draw upon a common fund of raw materials. For example, two of the late stories expand upon notes left over from *The Red Wheel,* and two others are based on the author's wartime experiences.

Matryona's Home

"Matryona's Home," written in 1959, is Solzhenitsyn's best-known—and arguably his best—short story. As befits Solzhenitsyn's fidelity to the realism of nineteenth-century Russian literature, the story's characters and events are not invented but come from real life. The artistry lies in patterning the particulars so that thematic meaning emerges. Ignatich, the narrator, closely parallels Solzhenitsyn as an ex-prisoner who, after serving a prison term in the gulag, is now released from his subsequent sentence of "perpetual exile" in Kazakhstan and moves back to Russia, taking lodging with the real-life Matryona in the actual village of Miltsevo.

The plot moves inexorably toward its fatal climax. Toward the petty and tawdry villagers who instigate the tragic events, Solzhenitsyn is unsparing, despite his love of the Russian people. Characterization is typically his greatest strength as a writer of fiction, and in Matryona he rises to the demanding challenge of creating a character who is both good and credible. A life filled with suffering has not beaten her down. She consistently exhibits moral nobility as she overcomes adversity, takes joy from work well done, lives in harmony with nature, helps even unappreciative neighbors, and harms no one. The first syllable of Matryona's name is the Russian word for "mother," and in her life readers may glimpse symbolic aspects of long-suffering Mother Russia. The conclusion alludes to Abraham's prayer for the city of Sodom in Genesis 18 and suggests that Matryona, though not formally religious, embodies a God-pleasing righteousness.

A hundred and eighty-four kilometers from Moscow trains were still slowing down to a crawl a good six months after it happened. Passengers stood glued to the windows or went out to stand by the doors. Was the line under repair, or what? Would the train be late?

It was all right. Past the crossing the train picked up speed again and the passengers went back to their seats.

Only the engine-drivers knew what it was all about.

The engine-drivers and I.

In the summer of 1956 I was coming back from the hot and dusty desert, just following my nose—so long as it led me back to Russia. Nobody waited or wanted me at any particular place, because I was a little matter of ten years overdue. I just wanted to get to the central belt, away from the great heats, close to the leafy muttering of forests. I wanted to efface myself, to lose myself in deepest Russia . . . if it was still anywhere to be found.

A year earlier I should have been lucky to get a job carrying a hod this side of the Urals. They wouldn't have taken me as an electrician on a decent construction job. And I had an itch to teach. Those who knew told me that it was a waste of money buying a ticket, that I should have a journey for nothing.

But things were beginning to move. When I went up the stairs of the N— Oblast Education Department and asked for the Personnel Section, I was surprised to find Personnel sitting behind a glass partition, like in a chemist's shop, instead of the usual black leather-padded door. I went timidly up to the window, bowed, and asked, "Please, do you need any mathematicians somewhere where the trains don't run? I should like to settle there for good."

They passed every dot and comma in my documents through a fine comb, went from one room to another, made telephone calls. It was something out of the ordinary for them too—people always wanted the towns, the bigger the better. And lo and behold, they found just the place for me—Vysokoe Polye. The very sound of it gladdened my heart.

Vysokoe Polye did not belie its name. It stood on rising ground, with gentle hollows and other little hills around it. It was enclosed by an unbroken ring of forest. There was a pool behind a weir. Just the place where I wouldn't mind living and dying. I spent a long time sitting on a stump in a coppice and wishing with all my heart that I didn't need breakfast and dinner every day but could just stay here and listen to the branches brushing against the roof in the night, with not a wireless anywhere to be heard and the whole world silent.

Alas, nobody baked bread in Vysokoe Polye. There was nothing edible on sale. The whole village lugged its victuals in sacks from the big town.

I went back to Personnel Section and raised my voice in prayer at the little window. At first they wouldn't even talk to me. But then they started going from one room to another, made a telephone call, scratched with their pens, and stamped on my orders the word "*Torfoprodukt.*"

Torfoprodukt? Turgenev never knew that you can put words like that together in Russian.

On the station building at Torfoprodukt, an antiquated temporary hut of gray wood, hung a stern notice, BOARD TRAINS ONLY FROM THE PASSENGERS' HALL. A further message had been scratched on the boards with a nail, *And Without Tickets.* And by the booking-office, with the same melancholy wit, somebody had carved for all time the words, *No Tickets.* It was only later that I fully appreciated the meaning of these addenda. Getting to Torfoprodukt was easy. But not getting away.

Here too, deep and trackless forests had once stood, and were still standing after the Revolution. Then they were chopped down by the peat-cutters and the neighboring kolkhoz.[1] Its chairman, Shashkov, had razed quite a few hectares of timber and sold it at a good profit down in Odessa oblast.

The workers' settlement sprawled untidily among the peat bogs—monotonous shacks from the thirties, and little houses with carved façades and glass verandas, put up in the fifties. But inside these houses I could see no partitions reaching up to the ceilings, so there was no hope of renting a room with four real walls.

Over the settlement hung smoke from the factory chimney. Little locomotives ran this way and that along narrow-gauge railway lines, giving out more thick smoke and piercing whistles, pulling loads of dirty brown peat in slabs and briquettes. I could safely assume that in the evening a loudspeaker would be crying its heart out over the door of the club and there would be drunks roaming the streets and, sooner or later, sticking knives in each other.

This was what my dream about a quiet corner of Russia had brought me to … when I could have stayed where I was and lived in an adobe hut looking out on the desert, with a fresh breeze at night and only the starry dome of the sky overhead.

I couldn't sleep on the station bench, and as soon as it started getting light I went for another stroll round the settlement. This time I saw a tiny marketplace. Only one woman stood there at that early hour, selling milk, and I took a bottle and started drinking it on the spot.

---

[1] kolkhoz: A Soviet collective farm.

I was struck by the way she talked. Instead of a normal speaking voice she used an ingratiating sing-song, and her words were the ones I was longing to hear when I left Asia for this place.

"Drink, and God bless you. You must be a stranger round here?"

"And where are you from?" I asked, feeling more cheerful.

I learned that the peat workings weren't the only thing, that over the railway lines there was a hill, and over the hill a village, that this village was Talnovo, and it had been there ages ago, when the "gypsy woman" lived in the big house and the wild woods stood all round. And further on there was a whole countryside full of villages—Chaslitsy, Ovintsy, Spudni, Shevertni, Shestimirovo, deeper and deeper into the woods, farther and farther from the railway, up towards the lakes.

The names were like a soothing breeze to me. They held a promise of backwoods Russia. I asked my new acquaintance to take me to Talnovo after the market was over, and find a house for me to lodge in.

It appeared that I was a lodger worth having: In addition to my rent, the school offered a truckload of peat for the winter to whoever took me. The woman's ingratiating smile gave way to a thoughtful frown. She had no room herself, because she and her husband were "keeping" her aged mother, so she took me first to one lot of relatives then to another. But there wasn't a separate room to be had and both places were crowded and noisy.

We had come to a dammed-up stream that was short of water and had a little bridge over it. No other place in all the village took my fancy as this did: There were two or three willows, a lopsided house, ducks swimming on the pond, geese shaking themselves as they stepped out of the water.

"Well, perhaps we might just call on Matryona," said my guide, who was getting tired of me by now. "Only it isn't so neat and cozy-like in her house, neglects things she does. She's unwell."

Matryona's house stood quite nearby. Its row of four windows looked out on the cold backs, the two slopes of the roof were covered with shingles, and a little attic window was decorated in the old Russian style. But the shingles were rotting, the beam-ends of the house and the once mighty gates had turned gray with age, and there were gaps in the little shelter over the gate.

The small door let into the gate was fastened, but instead of knocking my companion just put her hand under and turned the catch, a simple device to prevent animals from straying. The yard was not covered, but there was a lot under the roof of the house. As you went through the outer door a short flight of steps rose to a roomy landing, which was open to the roof high overhead. To the left, other steps led up to the top room, which was a separate structure with no stove, and yet another flight down to the basement. To the right lay the house proper, with its attic and its cellar.

It had been built a long time ago, built sturdily, to house a big family, and now one lonely woman of nearly sixty lived in it.

When I went into the cottage she was lying on the Russian stove under a heap of those indeterminate dingy rags which are so precious to a working man or woman.

The spacious room, and especially the best part near the windows, was full of rubber plants in pots and tubs standing on stools and benches. They peopled the householder's loneliness like a speechless but living crowd. They had been allowed to run wild, and they took up all the scanty light on the north side. In what was left of the light, and half-hidden by the stovepipe, the mistress of the house looked yellow and weak. You could see from her clouded eyes that illness had drained all the strength out of her.

While we talked she lay on the stove face downwards, without a pillow, her head towards the door, and I stood looking up at her. She showed no pleasure at getting a lodger, just complained about the wicked disease she had. She was just getting over an attack; it didn't come upon her every month, but when it did, "It hangs on two or three days so as I shan't manage to get up and wait on you. I've room and to spare, you can live here if you like."

Then she went over the list of other housewives with whom I should be quieter and cozier, and wanted me to make the round of them. But I had already seen that I was destined to settle in this dimly lit house with the tarnished mirror in which you couldn't see yourself, and the two garish posters (one advertising books, the other about the harvest), bought for a ruble each to brighten up the walls.

Matryona Vasilyevna made me go off round the village again, and when I called on her the second time she kept trying to put me off, "We're not clever, we can't cook, I don't know how we shall suit. . . ." But this time she was on her feet when I got there, and I thought I saw a glimmer of pleasure in her eyes to see me back. We reached agreement about the rent and the load of peat which the school would deliver.

Later on I found out that, year in year out, it was a long time since Matryona Vasilyevna had earned a single ruble. She didn't get a pension. Her relatives gave her very little help. In the kolkhoz she had worked not for money but for credits, the marks recording her labor-days in her well-thumbed workbook.

So I moved in with Matryona Vasilyevna. We didn't divide the room. Her bed was in the corner between the door and the stove, and I unfolded my camp-bed by one window and pushed Matryona's beloved rubber plants out of the light to make room for a little table by another. The village had electric light, laid on back in the twenties, from Shatury. The newspapers were writing about "Ilyich's little lamps," but the peasants talked wide-eyed about "Tsar Fire."

Some of the better-off people in the village might not have thought Matryona's house much of a home, but it kept us snug enough that autumn and winter. The roof still held the rain out, and the freezing winds could not blow the warmth of the stove away all at once, though it was cold by morning, especially when the wind blew on the shabby side.

In addition to Matryona and myself, a cat, some mice, and some cockroaches lived in the house.

The cat was no longer young, and gammy-legged as well. Matryona had taken her in out of pity, and she had stayed. She walked on all four feet but with a heavy limp: One of her feet was sore and she favored it. When she jumped from the stove she didn't land with the soft sound a cat usually makes, but with a heavy thud as three of her feet struck the floor at once—such a heavy thud that until I got used to it, it gave me a start. This was because she stuck three feet out together to save the fourth.

It wasn't because the cat couldn't deal with them that there were mice in the cottage: She would pounce into the corner like lightning, and come back with a mouse between her teeth. But the mice were usually out of reach because somebody, back in the good old days, had stuck embossed wallpaper of a greenish color on Matryona's walls, and not just one layer of it but five. The layers held together all right, but in many places the whole lot had come away from the wall, giving the room a sort of inner skin. Between the timber of the walls and the skin of wallpaper the mice had made themselves runs where they impudently scampered about, running at times right up to the ceiling. The cat followed their scamperings with angry eyes, but couldn't get at them.

Sometimes the cat ate cockroaches as well, but they made her sick. The only thing the cockroaches respected was the partition which screened the mouth of the Russian stove and the kitchen from the best part of the room.

They did not creep into the best room. But the kitchen at night swarmed with them, and if I went in late in the evening for a drink of water and switched on the light the whole floor, the big bench, and even the wall would be one rustling brown mass. From time to time I brought home some borax from the school laboratory and we mixed it with dough to poison them. There would be fewer cockroaches for a while, but Matryona was afraid that we might poison the cat as well. We stopped putting down poison and the cockroaches multiplied anew.

At night, when Matryona was already asleep and I was working at my table, the occasional rapid scamper of mice behind the wallpaper would be drowned in the sustained and ceaseless rustling of cockroaches behind the screen, like the sound of the sea in the distance. But I got used to it because there was nothing evil in it, nothing dishonest. Rustling was life to them.

I even got used to the crude beauty on the poster, forever reaching out from the wall to offer me Belinsky, Panferov, and a pile of other books—but never saying a word. I got used to everything in Matryona's cottage.

Matryona got up at four or five in the morning. Her wall-clock was twenty-seven years old, and had been bought in the village shop. It was always fast, but Matryona didn't worry about that—just so long as it didn't lose and make her late in the morning. She switched on the light behind the kitchen screen and moving quietly, considerately, doing her best not to make a noise, she lit the stove, went to milk the goat (all the livestock she had was this one dirty-white goat with twisted horns), fetched water and boiled it in three iron pots: one for me, one for herself, and one for the goat. She fetched potatoes from the cellar, picking out the littlest for the goat, little ones for herself and egg-sized ones for me. There were no big ones, because her garden was sandy, had not been manured since the war and was always planted with potatoes, potatoes, and potatoes again, so that it wouldn't grow big ones.

I scarcely heard her about her morning tasks. I slept late, woke up in the wintry daylight, stretched a bit, and stuck my head out from under my blanket and my sheepskin. These, together with the prisoner's jerkin round my legs and a sack stuffed with straw underneath me, kept me warm in bed even on nights when the cold wind rattled our wobbly windows from the north. When I heard the discreet noises on the other side of the screen I spoke to her, slowly and deliberately.

"Good morning, Matryona Vasilyevna!"

And every time the same good-natured words came to me from behind the screen. They began with a warm, throaty gurgle, the sort of sound grandmothers make in fairy tales.

"M-m-m . . . same to you too!"

And after a little while, "Your breakfast's ready for you now."

She didn't announce what was for breakfast, but it was easy to guess: taters in their jackets or tatty soup (as everybody in the village called it), or barley gruel (no other grain could be bought in Torfoprodukt that year, and even the barley you had to fight for, because it was the cheapest and people bought it up by the sack to fatten their pigs on it). It wasn't always salted as it should be, it was often slightly burnt, it furred the palate and the gums, and it gave me heartburn.

But Matryona wasn't to blame: There was no butter in Torfoprodukt either, margarine was desperately short, and only mixed cooking fat was plentiful, and when I got to know it I saw that the Russian stove was not convenient for cooking: The cook cannot see the pots and they are not heated evenly all round. I suppose the stove came down to our ancestors from the Stone Age because you can stoke it up once before daylight, and food and water, mash and swill, will keep warm in it all day long. And it keeps you warm while you sleep.

I ate everything that was cooked for me without demur, patiently putting aside anything uncalled-for that I came across: a hair, a bit of peat, a cockroach's leg. I hadn't the heart to find fault with Matryona. After all, she had warned me herself,

"We aren't clever, we can't cook—I don't know how we shall suit. . . ."

"Thank you," I said quite sincerely.

"What for? For what is your own?" she answered, disarming me with a radiant smile. And, with a guileless look of her faded blue eyes, she would ask, "And what shall I cook you for just now?"

For just now meant for supper. I ate twice a day, like at the front. What could I order for just now? It would have to be one of the same old things, taters or tatty soup.

I resigned myself to it, because I had learned by now not to look for the meaning of life in food. More important to me was the smile on her roundish face, which I tried in vain to catch when at last I had earned enough to buy a camera. As soon as she saw the cold eye of the lens upon her, Matryona assumed a strained or else an exaggeratedly severe expression.

Just once I did manage to get a snap of her looking through the window into the street and smiling at something.

Matryona had a lot of worries that winter. Her neighbors put it into her head to try and get a pension. She was all alone in the world, and when she began to be seriously ill she had been dismissed from the kolkhoz as well. Injustices had piled up, one on top of another. She was ill, but not regarded as a disabled person. She had worked for a quarter of a century in the kolkhoz,[1] but it was a kolkhoz and not a factory, so she was not entitled to a pension for herself. She could only try and get one for her husband, for the loss of her breadwinner. But she had had no husband for twelve years now, not since the beginning of the war, and it wasn't easy to obtain all the particulars from different places about his length of service and how much he had earned. What a bother it was getting those forms through! Getting somebody to certify that he'd earned, say, 300 rubles a month; that she lived alone and nobody helped her; what year she was born in. Then all this had to be taken to the pensions office. And taken somewhere else to get all the mistakes corrected. And taken back again. Then you had to find out whether they would give you a pension.

To make it all more difficult the Pensions Office was twenty kilometers east of Talnovo, the Rural Council Offices ten kilometers to the west, the Factory District Council an hour's walk to the north. They made her run around from office to office for two months on end, to get an *i* dotted or a *t* crossed. Every trip took a day. She goes down to the rural district council— and the secretary isn't there today. Secretaries of rural councils often aren't here today. So come again tomorrow. Tomorrow the secretary is in, but he hasn't got his rubber stamp. So come again the next day. And the day after that back she goes yet again, because all her papers are pinned together and some cock-eyed clerk has signed the wrong one.

"They shove me around, Ignatich," she used to complain to me after these fruitless excursions. "Worn out with it I am."

But she soon brightened up. I found that she had a sure means of putting herself in a good humor. She worked. She would grab a shovel and go off to lift potatoes. Or she would tuck a sack under her arm and go after peat. Or take a wicker basket and look for berries deep in the woods. When she'd been bending her back to bushes instead of office desks for a while, and her shoulders were aching from a heavy load, Matryona would come back cheerful, at peace with the world and smiling her nice smile.

"I'm on to a good thing now, Ignatich. I know where to go for it (peat she meant), a lovely place it is."

"But surely my peat is enough, Matryona Vasilyevna? There's a whole truckload of it."

"Pooh! Your peat! As much again, and then as much again, that might be enough. When the winter gets really stiff and the wind's battling at the windows, it blows the heat out of the house faster than you can make the stove up. Last year we got heaps and heaps of it. I'd have had three loads in by now. But they're out to catch us. They've summoned one woman from our village already."

That's how it was. The frightening breath of winter was already in the air. There were forests all round, and no fuel to be had anywhere. Excavators roared away in the bogs, but there was no peat on sale to the villagers. It was delivered, free, to the bosses and to the people round the bosses, and teachers, doctors, and workers got a load each. The people of Talnovo were not supposed to get any peat, and they weren't supposed to ask about it. The chairman of the kolkhoz walked about the village looking people in the eye while he gave his orders or stood chatting, and talked about anything you liked except fuel. He was stocked-up. Who said anything about winter coming?

So just as in the old days they used to steal the squire's wood, now they pinched peat from the trust. The women went in parties of five or ten so that they would be less frightened. They went in the daytime. The peat cut during the summer had been stacked up all over the place to dry. That's the good thing about peat, it can't be carted off as soon as it's cut. It lies around drying till autumn, or, if the roads are bad, till the snow starts falling. This was when the women used to come and take it. They could get six peats in a sack if it was damp, or ten if it was dry. A sackful weighed about two poods[2] and it sometimes had to be carried over three kilometers. This was enough to make the stove up once. There were two hundred days in the winter. The Russian stove had to be lit in the mornings, and the "Dutch" stove in the evenings.

"Why beat about the bush?" said Matryona angrily to someone invisible. "Since there've been no more horses, what you can't heave around yourself you haven't got. My back never heals up. Winter you're pulling sledges, summer it's bundles on your back, it's God's truth I'm telling you."

The women went more than once in a day. On good days Matryona brought six sacks home. She piled my peat up where it could be seen, and hid her own under the passageway, boarding up the hole every night.

"If they don't just happen to think of it, the devils will never find it in their born days," said Matryona smiling and wiping the sweat from her brow.

What could the peat trust do? Its establishment didn't run to a watchman for every bog. I suppose they had to show a rich haul in their returns, and then write off so much for crumbling, so much washed away by the rain. . . . Sometimes they would take it into their heads to put out patrols and try to catch the women as they came into the village. The women would drop their sacks and scatter. Or somebody would inform and there would be a house-to-house search. They would draw up a report on the stolen peat, and threaten a court action. The women would stop fetching it for a while, but the approach of winter drove them out with sledges in the middle of the night.

When I had seen a little more of Matryona I noticed that apart from cooking and looking after the house, she had quite a lot of other jobs to do every day.

---

[2] pood: 36.11 pounds

She kept all her jobs, and the proper times for them, in her head and always knew when she woke up in the morning how her day would be occupied. Apart from fetching peat, and stumps which the tractors unearthed in the bogs, apart from the cranberries which she put to soak in big jars for the winter ("Give your teeth an edge, Ignatich," she used to say when she offered me some), apart from digging potatoes and all the coming and going to do with her pension, she had to get hay from somewhere for her one and only dirty-white goat.

"Why don't you keep a cow, Matryona?"

Matryona stood there in her grubby apron, by the opening in the kitchen screen, facing my table, and explained to me.

"Oh, Ignatich, there's enough milk from the goat for me. And if I started keeping a cow she'd eat me out of house and home in no time. You can't cut the grass by the railway track, because it belongs to the railway, and you can't cut any in the woods, because it belongs to the foresters, and they won't let me have any at the kolkhoz because I'm not a member any more, they reckon. And those who are members have to work there every day till the white flies swarm, and make their own hay when there's snow on the ground—what's the good of grass like that? In the old days they used to be sweating to get the hay in at midsummer, between the end of June and the end of July, while the grass was sweet and juicy. . . ."

So it meant a lot of work for Matryona to gather enough hay for one skinny little goat. She took her sickle and a sack and went off early in the morning to places where she knew there was grass growing—round the edges of fields, on the roadside, on hummocks in the bog. When she had stuffed her sack with heavy fresh grass she dragged it home and spread it out in her yard to dry. From a sackful of grass she got one forkload of dry hay.

The farm had a new chairman, sent down from the town not long ago, and the first thing he did was to cut down the garden-plots for those who were not fit to work. He left Matryona fifteen hundredths of sand—when there were ten hundredths just lying idle on the other side of the fence. Yet when they were short of working hands, when the women dug in their heels and wouldn't budge, the chairman's wife would come to see Matryona. She was from the town as well, a determined woman whose short gray overcoat and intimidating glare gave her a somewhat military appearance. She walked into the house without so much as a good morning and looked sternly at Matryona. Matryona was uneasy.

"Well now, Comrade Vasilyevna," said the chairman's wife, drawing out her words. "You will have to help the kolkhoz! You will have to go and help cart muck out tomorrow!"

A little smile of forgiveness wrinkled Matryona's face—as though she understood the embarrassment which the chairman's wife must feel not being able to pay her for her work.

"Well—er," she droned, "I'm not well, of course, and I'm not attached to you any more . . . ," then she hurried to correct herself, "what time should I come then?"

"And bring your own fork!" the chairman's wife instructed her. Her stiff skirt crackled as she walked away.

"Think of that!" grumbled Matryona as the door closed. "Bring your own fork! They've got neither forks nor shovels on the kolkhoz. And I don't have a man who'll put a handle on for me!"

She went on thinking about it out loud all evening.

"What's the good of talking, Ignatich. I must help, of course. Only the way they work it's all a waste of time—don't know whether they're coming or going. The women stand propped up on their shovels and waiting for the factory hooter to blow twelve o'clock. Or else they get on to adding up who's earned what and who's turned up for work and who hasn't. Now what I call work, there isn't a sound out of anybody, only . . . oh dear, dear—dinner time's soon rolled round—what, getting dark already. . . ."

In the morning she went off with her fork.

But it wasn't just the kolkhoz—any distant relative, or just a neighbor, could come to Matryona of an evening and say, "Come and give me a hand tomorrow, Matryona. We'll finish lifting the potatoes."

Matryona couldn't say no. She gave up what she should be doing next and went to help her neighbor, and when she came back she would say without a trace of envy, "Ah, you should see the size of her potatoes, Ignatich! It was a joy to dig them up. I didn't want to leave the allotment, God's truth I didn't."

Needless to say, not a garden could be plowed without Matryona's help. The women of Talnovo had got it neatly worked out that it was a longer and harder job for one woman to dig her garden with a spade than for six of them to put themselves in harness and plow six gardens. So they sent for Matryona to help them.

"Well—did you pay her?" I asked sometimes.

"She won't take money. You have to try and hide it on her when she's not looking."

Matryona had yet another troublesome chore when her turn came to feed the herdsmen. One of them was a hefty deaf mute, the other a boy who was never without a cigarette in his drooling mouth. Matryona's turn only came round every six weeks, but it put her to great expense. She went to the shop to buy tinned fish, and was lavish with sugar and butter, things she never ate herself. It seems that the housewives showed off in this way, trying to outdo each other in feeding the herdsmen.

"You've got to be careful with tailors and herdsmen," Matryona explained. "They'll spread your name all round the village if something doesn't suit them."

And every now and then attacks of serious illness broke in on this life that was already crammed with troubles. Matryona would be off her feet for a day or two, lying flat out on the stove. She didn't complain, and didn't groan, but she hardly stirred either. On these days, Masha, Matryona's closest friend from her earliest years, would come to look after the goat and light the stove. Matryona herself ate nothing, drank nothing, asked for nothing. To call in the doctor from the clinic at the settlement would have seemed strange in Talnovo, and would have given the neighbors something to talk about—what does she think she is, a lady? They did call her in once, and she arrived in a real temper and told Matryona to come down to the clinic when she was on her feet again. Matryona went, although she didn't really want to; they took specimens and sent them off to the district hospital—and that's the last anybody heard about it. Matryona was partly to blame herself.

But there was work waiting to be done, and Matryona soon started getting up again, moving slowly at first and then as briskly as ever.

"You never saw me in the old days, Ignatich. I'd lift any sack you liked, I didn't think five poods was too heavy. My father-in-law used to say, 'Matryona, you'll break your back.' And my brother-in-law didn't have to come and help me lift on the cart. Our horse was a warhorse, a big strong one. . . ."

"What do you mean, a warhorse?"

"They took ours for the war and gave us this one instead—he'd been wounded. But he turned out a bit spirited. Once he bolted with the sledge right into the lake, the menfolk hopped out of the way, but I grabbed the bridle, as true as I'm here, and stopped him. . . . Full of oats that horse was. They liked to feed their horses well in our village. If a horse feels his oats he doesn't know what heavy means."

But Matryona was a long way from being fearless. She was afraid of fire, afraid of "the lightning," and most of all she was for some reason afraid of trains.

"When I had to go to Cherusti the train came up from Nechaevka way with its great big eyes popping out and the rails humming away—put me in a proper fever. My knees started knocking. God's truth I'm telling you!" Matryona raised her shoulders as though she surprised herself.

"Maybe it's because they won't give people tickets, Matryona Vasilyevna?"

"At the window? They try to shove first-class tickets on to you. And the train was starting to move. We dashed about all over the place, 'Give us tickets for pity's sake.'

"The menfolk had climbed on top of the carriages. Then we found a door that wasn't locked and shoved straight in without tickets . . . and all the carriages were empty, they were all empty, you could stretch out on the seat if you wanted to. Why they wouldn't give us tickets, the hard-hearted parasites, I don't know. . . ."

Still, before winter came Matryona's affairs were in a better state than ever before. They started paying her at last a pension of eighty rubles. Besides this she got just over a hundred from the school and me.

Some of her neighbors began to be envious.

"Hm! Matryona can live forever now! If she had any more money she wouldn't know what to do with it at her age."

Matryona had herself some new felt boots made. She bought a new jerkin. And she had an overcoat made out of the worn-out railway-man's greatcoat given to her by the engine-driver from Cherusti who had married Kira, her foster-daughter. The humpbacked village tailor put a padded lining under the cloth and it made a marvelous coat, such as Matryona had never worn before in all her sixty years.

In the middle of winter Matryona sewed two hundred rubles into the lining of this coat for her funeral. This made her quite cheerful.

"Now my mind's a bit easier, Ignatich."

December went by, January went by—and in those two months Matryona's illness held off. She started going over to Masha's house more often in the evening, to sit chewing sunflower seeds with her. She didn't invite guests herself in the evening out of consideration for my work. Once, on the feast of the Epiphany, I came back from school and found a party going on and was introduced to Matryona's three sisters who called her "nan-nan" or "nanny" because she was the oldest. Until then not much had been heard of the sisters in our cottage—perhaps they were afraid that Matryona might ask them for help.

But one ominous event cast a shadow on the holiday for Matryona. She went to the church five versts[3] away for the blessing of the water, and put her pot down among the others. When the blessing was over the women went rushing and jostling to get their pots back again. There were a lot of women

---

[3] verst: 0.6629 miles.

in front of Matryona and when she got there her pot was missing, and no other vessel had been left behind. The pot had vanished as though the devil had run off with it.

Matryona went around the worshippers asking them, "Has any of you girls accidentally mistook somebody else's holy water? In a pot?"

Nobody owned up. There had been some boys there, and boys got up to mischief sometimes. Matryona came home sad.

No one could say that Matryona was a devout believer. If anything, she was a heathen, and her strongest beliefs were superstitious. You mustn't go into the garden on the feast of St. John or there would be no harvest next year. A blizzard meant that somebody had hanged himself. If you pinched your foot in the door you could expect a guest. All the time I lived with her I didn't once see her say her prayers or even cross herself. But, whatever job she was doing, she began with a "God bless us," and she never failed to say "God bless you," when I set out for school. Perhaps she did say her prayers, but on the quiet, either because she was shy or because she didn't want to embarrass me. There were icons on the walls. Ordinary days they were left in darkness, but for the vigil of a great feast, or on the morning of a holiday, Matryona would light the little lamp.

She had fewer sins on her conscience than her gammy-legged cat. The cat did kill mice. . . .

Now that her life was running more smoothly, Matryona started listening more carefully to my radio. (I had, of course, installed a speaker, or as Matryona called it, a peeker.)

When they announced on the radio that some new machine had been invented, I heard Matryona grumbling out in the kitchen, "New ones all the time, nothing but new ones. People don't want to work with the old ones any more, where are we going to store them all?"

There was a program about the seeding of clouds from airplanes. Matryona, listening up on the stove, shook her head, "Oh dear, dear, dear, they'll do away with one of the two—summer or winter."

Once Chaliapin was singing Russian folk songs. Matryona stood listening for a long time before she gave her emphatic verdict, "Queer singing, not our sort of singing."

"You can't mean that, Matryona Vasilyevna . . . just listen to him."

She listened a bit longer, and pursed her lips, "No, it's wrong. It isn't our sort of tune, and he's tricky with his voice."

She made up for this another time. They were broadcasting some of Glinka's songs. After half a dozen of these drawing-room ballads, Matryona suddenly came from behind the screen clutching her apron, with a flush on her face and a film of tears over her dim eyes.

"That's our sort of singing," she said in a whisper.

So Matryona and I got used to each other and took each other for granted. She never pestered me with questions about myself. I don't know whether she was lacking in normal female curiosity or just tactful, but she never once asked if I had been married. All the Talnovo women kept at her to find out about me. Her answer was, "You want to know—you ask him. All I know is he's from distant parts."

And when I got round to telling her that I had spent a lot of time in prison she said nothing but just nodded, as though she had already suspected it.

And I thought of Matryona only as the helpless old woman she was now, and didn't try to rake up her past, didn't even suspect that there was anything to be found there.

I knew that Matryona had got married before the Revolution and come to live in the house I now shared with her, that she had gone "to the stove" immediately. (She had no mother-in-law and no older sister-in-law, so it was her job to put the pots in the oven on the very first morning of her married life.) I knew that she had had six children and that they had all died very young, so that there were never two of them alive at once. Then there was a sort of foster-daughter, Kira. Matryona's husband had not come back from the last war. She received no notification of his death. Men from the village who had served in the same company said that he might have been taken prisoner, or he might have been killed and his body not found. In the eight years that had gone by since the war Matryona had decided that he was not alive. It was a good thing that she thought so. If he was still alive he was probably in Brazil or Australia, and married again. The village of Talnovo, and the Russian language, would be fading from his memory.

One day, when I got back from school, I found a guest in the house. A tall, dark man, with his hat on his lap, was sitting on a chair which Matryona had moved up to the Dutch stove in the middle of the room. His face was completely surrounded by bushy black hair with hardly a trace of gray in it. His thick black mustaches ran into his full black beard, so that his mouth could hardly be seen. Black side-whiskers merged with the black locks which hung down from his crown, leaving only the tips of his ears visible; and broad black eyebrows met in a wide double span. But the front of his head as far as the crown was a spacious bald dome. His whole appearance made an impression of wisdom and dignity. He sat squarely on his chair, with his hands folded on his stick, and his stick resting vertically on the floor, in an attitude of patient expectation, and he obviously hadn't much to say to Matryona who was busy behind the screen.

When I came in he eased his majestic head round towards me and suddenly addressed me, "Master, I can't see you very well. My son goes to your school. Grigoriev, Antoshka. . . .

There was no need for him to say any more. . . . However strongly inclined I felt to help this worthy old man I knew and dismissed in advance all the pointless things he was going to say. Antoshka Grigoriev was a plump, red-faced lad in 8-D who looked like a cat that's swallowed the cream. He seemed to think that he came to school for a rest and sat at his desk with a lazy smile on his face. Needless to say, he never did his homework. But the worst of it was that he had been put up into the next class from year to year because our district, and indeed the whole oblast and the neighboring oblasts, were famous for the high percentage of passes they obtained, and the school had to make an effort to keep its record up. So Antoshka had got it clear in his mind that however much the teachers threatened him they would put him up in the end, and there was no need for him to learn anything. He just laughed at us. There he sat in the eighth class, and he hadn't even mastered his decimals and didn't know one triangle from another. In the first two terms of the school year I had kept him firmly below the pass line and the same treatment awaited him in the third.

But now this half-blind old man, who should have been Antoshka's grandfather rather than his father, had come to humble himself before me—how could I tell him that the school had been deceiving him for years, and that I couldn't go on deceiving him, because I didn't want to ruin the whole class, to become a liar and a fake, to start despising my work and my profession.

For the time being I patiently explained that his son had been very slack, that he told lies at school and at home, that his mark-book must be checked frequently, and that we must both take him severely in hand.

"Severe as you like, master," he assured me, "I beat him every week now. And I've got a heavy hand."

While we were talking I remembered that Matryona had once interceded for Antoshka Grigoriev, but I hadn't asked what relation of hers he was and I had refused to do what she wanted. Matryona was standing in the kitchen doorway like a mute suppliant on this occasion too. When Faddei Mironovich left saying that he would call on me to see how things were going, I asked her, "I can't make out what relation this Antoshka is to you, Matryona Vasilyevna."

"My brother-in-law's son," said Matryona shortly, and went out to milk the goat.

When I'd worked it out I realized that this determined old man with the black hair was the brother of the missing husband.

The long evening went by, and Matryona didn't bring up the subject again. But late at night, when I had stopped thinking about the old man and was working in a silence broken only by the rustling of the cockroaches and the heavy tick of the wall-clock, Matryona suddenly spoke from her dark corner, "You know, Ignatich, I nearly married him once."

I had forgotten that Matryona was in the room. I hadn't heard a sound from her—and suddenly her voice came out of the darkness, as agitated as if the old man were still trying to win her.

I could see that Matryona had been thinking about nothing else all evening.

She got up from her wretched rag bed and walked slowly towards me, as though she were following her own words. I sat back in my chair and caught my first glimpse of a quite different Matryona.

There was no overhead light in our big room with its forest of rubber plants. The table lamp cast a ring of light round my exercise books, and when I tore my eyes away from it the rest of the room seemed to be half-dark and faintly tinged with pink. I thought I could see the same pinkish glow in her usually sallow cheeks.

"He was the first one who came courting me, before Yefim did ... he was his brother ... the older one.... I was nineteen and Faddei was twenty-three.... They lived in this very same house. Their house it was. Their father built it."

I looked round the room automatically. Instead of the old gray house rotting under the faded green skin of wallpaper where the mice had their playground, I suddenly saw new timbers, freshly trimmed, and not yet discolored, and caught the cheerful smell of pine-tar.

"Well, and what happened then?"

"That summer we went to sit in the coppice together," she whispered. "There used to be a coppice where the stable-yard is now. They chopped it down. . . . I was just going to marry him, Ignatich. Then the German war started. They took Faddei in the army."

She let fall these few words—and suddenly the blue and white and yellow July of the year 1914 burst into flower before my eyes: the sky still peaceful, the floating clouds, the people sweating to get the ripe corn in. I imagined them side by side, the black-haired Hercules with a scythe over his shoulder, and the red-faced girl clasping a sheaf. And there was singing out under the open sky, such songs as nobody can sing nowadays, with all the machines in the fields.

"He went to the war—and vanished. For three years I kept to myself and waited. Never a sign of life did he give. . . ."

Matryona's round face looked out at me from an elderly threadbare headscarf. As she stood there in the gentle reflected light from my lamp her face seemed to lose its slovenly workaday covering of wrinkles, and she was a scared young girl again with a frightening decision to make.

Yes. . . . I could see it. . . . The trees shed their leaves, the snow fell and melted. They plowed and sowed and reaped again. Again the trees shed their leaves, and snow fell. There was a revolution. Then another revolution. And the whole world was turned upside down.

"Their mother died and Yefim came to court me. You wanted to come to our house, he says, so come. He was a year younger than me, Yefim was. It's a saying with us—sensible girls get married after Michaelmas, and silly ones at midsummer. They were short-handed. I got married. . . . The wedding was on St. Peter's day, and then about St. Nicholas' day in the winter he came back. . . . Faddei, I mean, from being a prisoner in Hungary."

Matryona covered her eyes.

I said nothing.

She turned towards the door as though somebody were standing there. "He stood there at the door. What a scream I let out! I wanted to throw myself at his feet! . . . but I couldn't. If it wasn't my own brother, he says, I'd take my axe to the both of you."

I shuddered. Matryona's despair, or her terror, conjured up a vivid picture of him standing in the dark doorway and raising his axe to her.

But she quieted down and went on with her story in a singsong voice, leaning on a chair-back, "Oh dear, dear me, the poor dear man! There were so many girls in the village—but he wouldn't marry. I'll look for one with the same name as you, a second Matryona, he said. And that's what he did— fetched himself a Matryona from Lipovka. They built themselves a house of their own and they're still living in it. You pass their place every day on your way to school."

So that was it. I realized that I had seen the other Matryona quite often. I didn't like her. She was always coming to my Matryona to complain about her husband—he beat her, he was stingy, he was working her to death. She would weep and weep, and her voice always had a tearful note in it. As it turned out, my Matryona had nothing to regret, with Faddei beating his Matryona every day of his life and being so tightfisted.

"Mine never beat me once," said Matryona of Yefim. "He'd pitch into another man in the street, but me he never hit once. . . . Well, there was one time . . . I quarreled with my sister-in-law and he cracked me on the fore-head with a spoon. I jumped up from the table and shouted at them, 'Hope it sticks in your gullets, you idle lot of beggars, hope you choke!' I said. And off I went into the woods. He never touched me any more."

Faddei didn't seem to have any cause for regret either. The other Matryona had borne him six children (my Antoshka was one of them, the littlest, the runt) and they had all lived, whereas the children of Matryona and Yefim had died, every one of them, before they reached the age of three months, without any illness.

"One daughter, Elena, was born and was alive when they washed her, and then she died right after. . . . My wedding was on St. Peter's day, and it was St. Peter's day I buried my sixth, Alexander."

The whole village decided that there was a curse on Matryona.

Matryona still nodded emphatic belief when she talked about it. "There was a *course* on me. They took me to a woman as used to be a nun to get cured, she set me off coughing and waited for the *course* to jump out of me like a frog. Only nothing jumped out. . . ."

And the years had run by like running water. . . . In 1941 they didn't take Faddei into the army because of his poor sight, but they took Yefim. And what had happened to the elder brother in the first war happened to the younger in the second . . . he vanished without trace. Only he never came back at all. The once noisy cottage was deserted, it became old and rotten, and Matryona, all alone in the world, grew old in it.

So she begged from the other Matryona, the cruelly beaten Matryona, a child of her womb (or was it a spot of Faddei's blood?), the youngest daughter, Kira.

For ten years she brought the girl up in her own house, in place of the children who had not lived. Then, not long before I arrived, she had married her off to a young engine-driver from Cherusti. The only help she got from anywhere came in dribs and drabs from Cherusti: a bit of sugar from time to time, or some of the fat when they killed a pig.

Sick and suffering, and feeling that death was not far off, Matryona had made known her will: The top room, which was a separate frame joined by tie-beams to the rest of the house, should go to Kira when she died. She said nothing about the house itself. Her three sisters had their eyes on it too.

That evening Matryona opened her heart to me. And, as often happens, no sooner were the hidden springs of her life revealed to me than I saw them in motion.

Kira arrived from Cherusti. Old Faddei was very worried. To get and keep a plot of land in Cherusti the young couple had to put up some sort of building. Matryona's top room would do very well. There was nothing else they could put up, because there was no timber to be had anywhere. It wasn't Kira herself so much, and it wasn't her husband, but old Faddei who was consumed with eagerness for them to get their hands on the plot at Cherusti.

He became a frequent visitor, laying down the law to Matryona and insisting that she should hand over the top room right away, before she died. On these occasions I saw a different Faddei. He was no longer an old man propped up by a stick, whom a push or a harsh word would bowl over. Although he was slightly bent by backache, he was still a fine figure; he had kept the vigorous black hair of a young man in his sixties; he was hot and urgent.

Matryona had not slept for two nights. It wasn't easy for her to make up her mind. She didn't grudge them the top room, which was standing there idle, any more than she ever grudged her labor or her belongings. And the top room was willed to Kira in any case. But the thought of breaking up the roof she had lived under for forty years was torture to her. Even I, a mere lodger, found it painful to think of them stripping away boards and wrenching out beams. For Matryona it was the end of everything.

But the people who were so insistent knew that she would let them break up her house before she died.

So Faddei and his sons and sons-in-law came along one February morning, the blows of five axes were heard and boards creaked and cracked as they were wrenched out. Faddei's eyes twinkled busily. Although his back wasn't quite straight yet he scrambled nimbly up under the rafters and bustled about down below, shouting at his assistants. He and his father had built this house when he was a lad, a long time ago. The top room had been put up for him, the oldest son, to move in with his bride. And now he was furiously taking it apart, board by board, to carry it out of somebody else's yard.

After numbering the beam-ends and the ceiling boards they dismantled the top room and the storeroom underneath it. The living room, and what was left of the landing, they boarded up with a thin wall of deal. They did nothing about the cracks in the wall. It was plain to see that they were wreckers, not builders, and that they did not expect Matryona to be living there very long.

While the men were busy wrecking, the women were getting the drink ready for moving day—vodka would cost a lot too much. Kira brought a pood of sugar from Moscow oblast, and Matryona carried the sugar and some bottles to the distiller under cover of night.

The timbers were carried out and stacked in front of the gates, and the engine-driver son-in-law went off to Cherusti for the tractor.

But the very same day a blizzard, or "a blower" as Matryona called it, began. It howled and whirled for two days and nights and buried the road under enormous drifts. Then, no sooner had they made the road passable and a couple of trucks gone by, than it got suddenly warmer. Within a day everything was thawing out, damp mist hung in the air and rivulets gurgled as they burrowed into the snow, and you could get stuck up to the top of your knee-boots.

Two weeks passed before the tractor could get at the dismantled top room. All this time Matryona went around like someone lost. What particularly upset her was that her three sisters came and with one voice called her a fool for giving the top room away, said they didn't want to see her any more, and went off. At about the same time the lame cat strayed and was seen no more. It was just one thing after another. This was another blow to Matryona.

At last the frost got a grip on the slushy road. A sunny day came along and everybody felt more cheerful. Matryona had had a lucky dream the night before. In the morning she heard that I wanted to take a photograph of somebody at an old-fashioned hand-loom. (There were looms still standing in two cottages in the village; they wove coarse rugs on them.) She smiled shyly and said, "You just wait a day or two, Ignatich, I'll just send the top room there off and I'll put my loom up, I've still got it, you know, and then you can snap me. Honest to God!"

She was obviously attracted by the idea of posing in an old-fashioned setting. The red, frosty sun tinged the window of the curtailed passageway with a faint pink, and this reflected light warmed Matryona's face. People who are at ease with their consciences always have nice faces.

Coming back from school before dusk I saw some movement near our house. A big new tractor-drawn sledge was already fully loaded, and there was no room for a lot of the timbers, so old Faddei's family and the helpers they had called in had nearly finished knocking together another homemade sledge. They were all working like madmen, in the frenzy that comes upon people when there is a smell of good money in the air or when they are looking forward to some treat. They were shouting at one another and arguing.

They could not agree whether the sledges should be hauled separately or both together. One of Faddei's sons (the lame one) and the engine-driver son-in-law reasoned that the sledges couldn't both be taken at once because the tractor wouldn't be able to pull them. The man in charge of the tractor, a hefty fat-faced fellow who was very sure of himself, said hoarsely that he knew best, he was the driver, and he would take both at once. His motives were obvious: According to the agreement the engine-driver was paying him for the removal of the upper room not for the number of trips he had to make. He could never have made two trips in a night—twenty-five kilometers each way, and one return journey. And by morning he had to get the tractor back in the garage from which he had sneaked it out for this job on the side.

Old Faddei was impatient to get the top room moved that day, and at a nod from him his lads gave in. To the stout sledge in front they hitched the one which they had knocked together in such a hurry.

Matryona was running about amongst the men, fussing and helping them to heave the beams on to the sledge. Suddenly I noticed that she was wearing my jerkin and had dirtied the sleeves on the frozen mud round the beams. I was annoyed, and told her so. That jerkin held memories for me: It had kept me warm in the bad years.

This was the first time that I was ever angry with Matryona Vasilyevna.

Matryona was taken aback. "Oh dear, dear me," she said. "My poor head, I picked it up in a rush, you see, and never thought about it being yours. I'm sorry, Ignatich."

And she took it off and hung it up to dry.

The loading was finished, and all the men who had been working, about ten of them, clattered past my table and dived under the curtain into the kitchen. I could hear the muffled rattle of glasses and, from time to time, the clink of a bottle, the voices got louder and louder, the boasting more reckless. The biggest braggart was the tractor-driver. The stench of hooch floated in to me. But they didn't go on drinking long. It was getting dark and they had to hurry. They began to leave. The tractor-driver came out first, looking pleased with himself and fierce. The engine-driver son-in-law, Faddei's lame son, and one of his nephews were going to Cherusti. The others went off home. Faddei was flourishing his stick, trying to overtake somebody and put him right about something. The lame son paused at my table to light up and suddenly started telling me how he loved Aunt Matryona, and that he had got married not long ago, and his wife had just had a son. Then they shouted for him and he went out. The tractor set up a roar outside.

After all the others had gone Matryona dashed out from behind the screen. She looked after them, anxiously shaking her head. She had put on her jerkin and her headscarf. As she was going through the door she said to me, "Why ever couldn't they hire two? If one tractor had cracked up the other would have pulled them. What'll happen now, God only knows!"

She ran out after the others.

After the booze-up and the arguments and all the coming and going it was quieter than ever in the deserted cottage, and very chilly because the door had been opened so many times. I got into my jerkin and sat down to mark exercise books. The noise of the tractor died away in the distance.

An hour went by. And another. And a third. Matryona still hadn't come back, but I wasn't surprised. When she had seen the sledge off she must have gone round to her friend Masha.

Another hour went by. And yet another. Darkness and with it a deep silence had descended on the village. I couldn't understand at the time why it was so quiet. Later I found out that it was because all evening not a single train had gone along the line half a verst from the house. No sound was coming from my radio and I noticed that the mice were wilder than ever. Their scampering and scratching and squeaking behind the wallpaper was getting noisier and more defiant all the time.

I woke up. It was one o'clock in the morning and Matryona still hadn't come home.

Suddenly I heard several people talking loudly. They were still a long way off, but something told me that they were coming to our house. And sure enough I heard soon afterwards a heavy knock at the gate. A commanding voice, strange to me, yelled out an order to open up. I went out into the thick darkness with a torch. The whole village was asleep, there was no light in the windows, and the snow had started melting in the last week so that it gave no reflected light. I turned the catch and let them in. Four men in greatcoats went on towards the house. It's a very unpleasant thing to be visited at night by noisy people in greatcoats.

When we got into the light though, I saw that two of them were wearing railway uniforms. The older of the two, a fat man with the same sort of face as the tractor-driver, asked, "Where's the woman of the house?"

"I don't know."

"This is the place the tractor with a sledge came from?"

"This is it."

"Had they been drinking before they left?" All four of them were looking around them, screwing up their eyes in the dim light from the table-lamp. I realized that they had either made an arrest or wanted to make one.

"What's happened then?"

"Answer the question!"

"But . . ."

"Were they drunk when they went?"

"Were they drinking here?"

Had there been a murder? Or hadn't they been able to move the top room? The men in greatcoats had me off balance. But one thing was certain: Matryona could do time for making hooch.

I stepped back to stand between them and the kitchen door. "I honestly didn't notice. I didn't see anything." (I really hadn't seen anything—only heard.) I made what was supposed to be a helpless gesture, drawing attention to the state of the cottage: a table-lamp shining peacefully on books and exercises, a crowd of frightened rubber plants, the austere couch of a recluse, not a sign of debauchery.

They had already seen for themselves, to their annoyance, that there had been no drinking in that room. They turned to leave, telling each other this wasn't where the drinking had been then, but it would be a good thing to put in that it was. I saw them out and tried to discover what had happened. It was only at the gate that one of them growled, "They've all been cut to bits. Can't find all the pieces."

"That's a detail. The express at 21.00 hours nearly went off the rails. That would have been something." And they walked briskly away.

I went back to the hut in a daze. Who were "they"? What did "all of them" mean? And where was Matryona?

I moved the curtain aside and went into the kitchen. The stink of hooch rose and hit me. It was a deserted battlefield: a huddle of stools and benches, empty bottles lying around, one bottle half-full, glasses, the remains of pickled herring, onion, and sliced fat pork.

Everything was deathly still. Just cockroaches creeping unperturbed about the field of battle.

They had said something about the express at 21.00. Why? Perhaps I should have shown them all this? I began to wonder whether I had done right. But what a damnable way to behave—keeping their explanations for official persons only.

Suddenly the small gate creaked. I hurried out on to the landing, "Matryona Vasilyevna?"

The yard door opened, and Matryona's friend Masha came in, swaying and wringing her hands. "Matryona . . . our Matryona, Ignatich. . . ."

I sat her down and through her tears she told me the story.

The approach to the crossing was a steep rise. There was no barrier. The tractor and the first sledge went over, but the towrope broke and the second sledge, the homemade one, got stuck on the crossing and started falling apart—the wood Faddei had given them to make the second sledge was no good. They towed the first sledge out of the way and went back for the second. They were fixing the towrope—the tractor-driver and Faddei's lame son, and Matryona, heaven knows what brought her there, was with them, between the tractor and the sledge. What help did she think she could be to the men? She was forever meddling in men's work. Hadn't a bolting horse nearly tipped her into the lake once, through a hole in the ice?

Why did she have to go to the damned crossing? She had handed over the top room, and owed nothing to anybody. . . . The engine-driver kept a look-out in case the train from Cherusti rushed up on them. Its headlamps would be visible a long way off. But two engines coupled together came from the other direction, from our station, backing without lights. Why they were without lights nobody knows. When an engine is backing, coal-dust blows into the driver's eyes from the tender and he can't see very well. The two engines flew into them and crushed the three people between the tractor and the sledge to pulp. The tractor was wrecked, the sledge was matchwood, the rails were buckled, and both engines turned over.

"But how was it they didn't hear the engines coming?"

"The tractor engine was making such a din."

"What about the bodies?"

"They won't let anybody in. They've roped them off."

"What was that somebody was telling me about the express?"

The nine o'clock express goes through our station at a good speed and on to the crossing. But the two drivers weren't hurt when their engines crashed, they jumped out and ran back along the line waving their hands and they managed to stop the train. . . . The nephew was hurt by a beam as well. He's hiding at Klavka's now so that they won't know he was at the crossing. If they find out they'll drag him in as a witness. . . . "Don't know lies up, and do know gets tied up. Kira's husband didn't get a scratch. He tried to hang himself, they had to cut him down. It's all because of me, he says, my aunty's killed and my brother. Now he's gone and given himself up. But the madhouse is where he'll be going, not prison. Oh, Matryona, my dearest Matryona. . . ."

Matryona was gone. Someone close to me had been killed. And on her last day I had scolded her for wearing my jerkin.

The lovingly drawn red and yellow woman in the book advertisement smiled happily on.

Old Masha sat there weeping a little longer. Then she got up to go. And suddenly she asked me, "Ignatich, you remember, Matryona had a gray shawl. She meant it to go to my Tanya when she died, didn't she?"

She looked at me hopefully in the half-darkness . . . surely I hadn't forgotten?

No, I remembered. "She said so, yes."

"Well, listen, maybe you could let me take it with me now. The family will be swarming in tomorrow and I'll never get it then." And she gave me another hopeful, imploring look. She had been Matryona's friend for half a century, the only one in the village who truly loved her.

No doubt she was right.

"Of course . . . take it."

She opened the chest, took out the shawl, tucked it under her coat and went out.

The mice had gone mad. They were running furiously up and down the walls, and you could almost see the green wallpaper rippling and rolling over their backs.

In the morning I had to go to school. The time was three o'clock. The only thing to do was to lock up and go to bed.

Lock up, because Matryona would not be coming.

I lay down, leaving the light on. The mice were squeaking, almost moaning, racing and running. My mind was weary and wandering, and I couldn't rid myself of an uneasy feeling that an invisible Matryona was flitting about and saying good-bye to her home.

And suddenly I imagined Faddei standing there, young and black-haired, in the dark patch by the door, with his axe uplifted. "If it wasn't my own brother I'd chop the both of you to bits."

The threat had lain around for forty years, like an old broadsword in a corner, and in the end it had struck its blow.

When it was light the women went to the crossing and brought back all that was left of Matryona on a hand-sledge with a dirty sack over it. They threw off the sack to wash her. There was just a mess . . . no feet, only half a body, no left hand. One woman said, "The Lord has left her her right hand. She'll be able to say her prayers where she's going. . . ."

Then the whole crowd of rubber plants was carried out of the cottage . . . these plants that Matryona had loved so much that once when smoke woke her up in the night she didn't rush to save her house but to tip the plants on to the floor in case they were suffocated. The women swept the floor clean. They hung a wide towel of old homespun over Matryona's dim mirror. They took down the jolly posters. They moved my table out of the way. Under the icons, near the windows, they stood a rough unadorned coffin on a row of stools.

In the coffin lay Matryona. Her body, mangled and lifeless, was covered with a clean sheet. Her head was swathed in a white kerchief. Her face was almost undamaged, peaceful, more alive than dead.

The villagers came to pay their last respects. The women even brought their small children to take a look at the dead. And if anyone raised a lament, all the women, even those who had looked in out of idle curiosity, always joined in, wailing where they stood by the door or the wall, as though they were providing a choral accompaniment. The men stood stiff and silent with their caps off.

The formal lamentation had to be performed by the women of Matryona's family. I observed that the lament followed a coldly calculated age-old ritual. The more distant relatives went up to the coffin for a short while and made low wailing noises over it. Those who considered themselves closer kin to the dead woman began their lament in the doorway and when they got as far as the coffin, bowed down and roared out their grief right in the face of the departed. Every lamenter made up her own melody. And expressed her own thoughts and feelings.

I realized that a lament for the dead is not just a lament, but a kind of politics. Matryona's three sisters swooped, took possession of the cottage, the goat, and the stove, locked up the chest, ripped the two hundred rubles for the funeral out of the coat lining, and drummed it into everybody who came that only they were near relatives. Their lament over the coffin went like this, "*Oh nanny, nanny! Oh nan-nan!* All we had in the world was you! You could have lived in peace and quiet, you could. And we should always have been kind and loving to you. Now your top room's been the death of you. Finished you off it has, the cursed thing! Oh why did you have to take it down? Why didn't you listen to us?"

Thus the sisters' laments were indictments of Matryona's husband's family: They shouldn't have made her take the top room down. (There was an underlying meaning too: You've taken the top room all right but we won't let you have the house itself!)

Matryona's husband's family, her sisters-in-law, Yefim and Faddei's sisters, and various nieces lamented like this, "*Oh poor auntie, poor auntie! Why* didn't you take better care of yourself! Now they're angry with us for sure. Our own dear Matryona you were, and it's your own fault! The top room is nothing to do with it. Oh why did you go where death was waiting for you? Nobody asked you to go there. And what a way to die! Oh why didn't you listen to us?" (Their answer to the others showed through these laments: We are not to blame for her death, and the house we'll talk about later.)

But the "second" Matryona, a coarse, broad-faced woman, the substitute Matryona whom Faddei had married so long ago for the sake of her name, got out of step with family policy, wailing and sobbing over the coffin in her simplicity, "*Oh my poor dear sister! You* won't be angry with me, will you now? Oh-oh-oh! How we used to talk and talk, you and me! Forgive a poor miserable woman! You've gone to be with your dear mother, and you'll come for me some day for sure! Oh-oh-oh-oh! . . ."

At every "oh-oh-oh" it was as though she were giving up the ghost. She writhed and gasped, with her breast against the side of the coffin. When her lament went beyond the ritual prescription the women, as though acknowledging its success, all started saying, "come away now, come away."

Matryona came away, but back she went again, sobbing with even greater abandon. Then an ancient woman came out of a corner, put her hand on Matryona's shoulder, and said, "There are two riddles in this world: How I was born I don't remember, how I shall die I don't know."

And Matryona fell silent at once, and all the others were silent, so that there was an unbroken hush.

But the old woman herself, who was much older than all the other old women there and didn't seem to belong to Matryona at all, after a while started wailing, "Oh my poor sick Matryona! Oh my poor Vasilyevna! Oh what a weary thing it is to be seeing you into your grave!"

There was one who didn't follow the ritual, but wept straightforwardly, in the fashion of our age, which has had plenty of practice at it. This was Matryona's unfortunate foster-daughter, Kira, from Cherusti, for whom the top room had been taken down and moved. Her ringlets were pitifully out of curl. Her eyes looked red and bloodshot. She didn't notice that her headscarf was slipping off out in the frosty air and that her arm hadn't found the sleeve of her coat. She walked in a stupor from her foster-mother's coffin in one house to her brother's in another. They were afraid she would lose her mind, because her husband had to go for trial as well.

It looked as if her husband was doubly at fault: Not only was he moving the top room, but as an engine-driver he knew the regulations about unprotected crossings, and should have gone down to the station to warn them about the tractor. There were a thousand people on the Urals express that night, peacefully sleeping in the upper and lower berths of their dimly lit carriages, and all those lives were nearly cut short. All because of a few greedy people, wanting to get their hands on a plot of land, or not wanting to make a second trip with a tractor.

All because of the top room, which had been under a curse ever since Faddei's hands had started itching to take it down.

The tractor-driver was already beyond human justice. And the railway authorities were also at fault, both because a busy crossing was unguarded and because the coupled engines were traveling without lights. That was why they had tried at first to blame it all on the drink, and then to keep the case out of court.

The rails and the track were so twisted and torn that for three days, while the coffins were still in the house, no trains ran—they were diverted on to another line. All Friday, Saturday, and Sunday, from the end of the investigation until the funeral, the work of repairing the line went on day and night. The repair gang was frozen, and they made fires to warm themselves and to light their work at night, using the boards and beams from the second sledge which were there for the taking, scattered around the crossing.

The first sledge just stood there, undamaged and still loaded, a little way beyond the crossing.

One sledge, tantalizingly ready to be towed away, and the other perhaps still to be plucked from the flames—that was what harrowed the soul of black-bearded Faddei all day Friday and all day Saturday. His daughter was going out of her mind, his son-in-law had a criminal charge hanging over him, in his own house lay the son he had killed, and along the street the woman he had killed and whom he had once loved. But Faddei stood by the coffins clutching his beard only for a short time, and went away again. His tall brow was clouded by painful thoughts, but what he was thinking about was how to save the timbers of the top room from the flames and from Matryona's scheming sisters.

Going over the people of Talnovo in my mind I realized that Faddei was not the only one like that.

Property, the people's property, or my property, is strangely called our "goods." If you lose your goods, people think you disgrace yourself and make yourself look foolish.

Faddei dashed about, never stopping for a sit-down, from the settlement to the station, from one official to another, stood there with his bent back, leaning heavily on his stick, and begged them all to take pity on an old man and give him permission to recover the top room.

Somebody gave permission. And Faddei gathered together his surviving sons, sons-in-law, and nephews, got horses from the kolkhoz and from the other side of the wrecked crossing, by a roundabout way that led through three villages, brought the remnants of the top room home to his yard. He finished the job in the early hours of Sunday morning.

On Sunday afternoon they were buried. The two coffins met in the middle of the village, and the relatives argued about which of them should go first. Then they put them side by side on an open sledge, the aunt and the nephew, and carried the dead over the damp snow, with a gloomy February sky above, to the churchyard two villages away. There was an unkind wind, so the priest and the deacon waited inside the church and didn't come out to Talnovo to meet them.

A crowd of people walked slowly behind the coffins, singing in chorus. Outside the village they fell back.

When Sunday came the women were still fussing around the house. An old woman mumbled psalms by the coffin, Matryona's sisters flitted about, popping things into the oven, and the air round the mouth of the stove trembled with the heat of red-hot peats, those which Matryona had carried in a sack from a distant bog. They were making unappetizing pies with poor flour.

When the funeral was over and it was already getting on towards evening, they gathered for the wake. Tables were put together to make a long one, which hid the place where the coffin had stood in the morning. To start with they all stood round the table, and an old man, the husband of a sister-in-law, said the Lord's prayer. Then they poured everybody a little honey and warm water, just enough to cover the bottom of the bowl. We spooned it up without bread or anything, in memory of the dead. Then we ate something and drank vodka and the conversation became more animated. Before the jelly they all stood up and sang "*Eternal remembrance*" (they explained to me that it had to be sung before the jelly). There was more drinking. By now they *were* talking louder than ever, and not about Matryona at all. The sister-in-law's husband started boasting, "Did you notice, brother Christians, that they took the funeral service slowly today? That's because Father Mikhail noticed me. He knows I know the service. Other times it's saints defend us, homeward wend us, and that's all."

At last the supper was over. They all rose again. They sang "*Worthy is she.*" Then again, with a triple repetition of "*Eternal remembrance.*" But the voices were hoarse and out of tune, their faces drunken, and nobody put any feeling into this "eternal memory."

Then the main guests went away, and only the near relatives were left. They pulled out their cigarettes and lit up, there were jokes and laughter. There was some mention of Matryona's husband and his disappearance. The sister-in-law's husband, striking himself on the chest, assured me and the cobbler who was married to one of Matryona's sisters, "He was dead, Yefim was dead! What could stop him coming back if he wasn't? If I knew they were going to hang me when I got to the old country I'd come back just the same!"

The cobbler nodded in agreement. He was a deserter and had never left the old country. All through the war he was hiding in his mother's cellar.

The stern and silent old woman who was more ancient than all the ancients was staying the night and sat high up on the stove. She looked down in mute disapproval on the indecently animated youngsters of fifty and sixty.

But the unhappy foster-daughter, who had grown up within these walls, went away behind the kitchen screen to cry.

Faddei didn't come to Matryona's wake—perhaps because he was holding a wake for his son. But twice in the next few days he walked angrily into the house for discussions with Matryona's sisters and the deserting cobbler.

The argument was about the house. Should it go to one of the sisters or to the foster-daughter? They were on the verge of taking it to court, but they made peace because they realized that the court would hand over the house to neither side, but to the rural district council. A bargain was struck. One sister took the goat, the cobbler and his wife got the house, and to make up Faddei's share, since he had "nursed every bit of timber here in his arms," in addition to the top room which had already been carried away, they let him have the shed which had housed the goat, and the whole of the inner fence between the yard and the garden.

Once again the insatiable old man got the better of sickness and pain and became young and active. Once again he gathered together his surviving sons and sons-in-law, and they dismantled the shed and the fence, and he hauled the timbers himself, sledge by sledge, and only towards the end did he have Antoshka of 8-D, who didn't slack this time, to help him.

They boarded Matryona's house up till the spring, and I moved in with one of her sisters-in-law, not far away. This sister-in-law on several occasions came out with some recollection of Matryona, and made me see the dead woman in a new light. "Yefim didn't love her. He used to say, 'I like to dress in an educated way, but she dresses any old way, like they do in the country.' Well then, he thinks, if she doesn't want anything, he might as well drink whatever's to spare. One time I went with him to the town to work, and he got himself a madam there and never wanted to come back to Matryona."

Everything she said about Matryona was disapproving. She was slovenly, she made no effort to get a few things about her. She wasn't the saving kind. She didn't even keep a pig, because she didn't like fattening them up for some reason. And the silly woman helped other people without payment. (What brought Matryona to mind this time was that the garden needed plowing and she couldn't find enough helpers to pull the plow.)

Matryona's sister-in-law admitted that she was warm-hearted and straightforward, but pitied and despised her for it.

It was only then, after these disapproving comments from her sister-in-law, that a true likeness of Matryona formed itself before my eyes, and I understood her as I never had when I lived side by side with her.

Of course! Every house in the village kept a pig. But she didn't. What can be easier than fattening a greedy piglet that cares for nothing in the world but food! You warm his swill three times a day, you live for him—then you cut his throat and you have some fat.

But she had none. . . .

She made no effort to get things round her. . . . She didn't struggle and strain to buy things and then care for them more than life itself.

She didn't go all out after fine clothes. Clothes, that beautify what is ugly and evil.

She was misunderstood and abandoned even by her husband. She had lost six children, but not her sociable ways. She was a stranger to her sisters and sisters-in-law, a ridiculous creature who stupidly worked for others without pay. She didn't accumulate property against the day she died. A dirty-white goat, a gammy-legged cat, some rubber plants. . . .

We had all lived side by side with her and never understood that she was that righteous one without whom, as the proverb says, no village can stand.

Nor any city.

Nor our whole land.

The Easter Procession

At age six, Solzhenitsyn witnessed a midnight Easter celebration in Novocherkassk at which young rowdies jeered the faithful. "The Easter Procession" describes a reprise of that ugly scene, this time at Peredelkino a half century into the Soviet era. This work is listed among his stories but is almost devoid of characterization and plot. Though longer than his prose poems, it is like them in its descriptive-reflective method. As the text explains, this is an effort to transpose a visual picture into prose.

That picture features sharp contrast. Authentic believers, mostly old women, assemble to worship on the holiest day of the Orthodox church calendar. Young toughs, excited by mere spectacle, gather around menacingly. Old Russia and the new Soviet order collide. Yet this year's occasion is judged "one of the better years," an understatement of the kind employed when Ivan Denisovich characterizes his day as almost a good one, whereas readers consider it almost unbearable. But the narrator wonders what Russia will reap from sowing atheism in youthful hearts.

Connoisseurs tell us that an artist should not paint everything exactly as it is. They say that color photography does this and that by means of curved lines and combinations of triangles and squares we should convey the essence of a thing rather than the thing itself. But I do not see how color photography could pick out what is significant among the faces in an Easter procession at the patriarchal church of Peredelkino half a century after the Revolution and compose them meaningfully into a single picture. Depicted in conventional terms (even without the aid of triangles), a present-day Easter procession can tell us a great deal.

Half an hour before the bells start ringing, the forecourt of the patriarchal Church of the Transfiguration looks as gay as a Saturday-night hop in the recreation hall of some remote industrial town. Girls in bright scarves and ski pants (true, some of them are wearing skirts) are walking around in noisy groups of threes and fours; they jostle to get into the church, but it is very crowded in the porch, as the old women have been in their places since early evening, so the girls start yapping at them from the doorway. Then they stroll around the churchyard, shrieking uninhibitedly and calling out to each other, staring at the green, pink, and white lights hanging in front of icons on the church walls and beside the graves of bishops and archpriests. The boys, ranging from hulking great toughs to scrawny weaklings, all have the same arrogant look on their faces. (What, one wonders, have these teen-agers got to feel superior about? The fact that they're good at ice hockey?) Almost all of them are wearing caps, and if some of them are bareheaded it has nothing to do with the fact that they are on consecrated ground. About one in four has been drinking, one in ten is drunk, and half of them are smoking—in that repulsive way with the cigarette stuck to the lower lip. There is no incense yet; instead of it, swathes of gray-blue cigarette smoke rise towards the Easter sky under the electric light of the churchyard in dense, hovering clouds. They spit on the asphalt path, jostle each other in fun, and whistle loudly. Some are using obscene language, and a bunch are jigging to dance music from transistor radios. Some of them kiss their girlfriends, who are then pulled from one boy to another, staring aggressively around as though the knives may come out at any minute. Once they start flashing their knives at each other, they may easily turn them on the members of the congregation, because the attitude of these youths to churchgoers is not the usual attitude of the young to the old or of guests to a host; they regard them as a housewife regards flies.

However, the knives are not brought out, as three or four policemen are strolling up and down nearby, just to keep an eye on things. The boys are not swearing noisily but simply as part of their normal conversation, so the police fail to notice that they are breaking the law, and smile amiably at the rising generation. And the police are not going to snatch the cigarettes out of their mouths or pull the caps off their heads, because this is a public place and the right not to believe in God is safeguarded by the constitution.

Huddling close to the cemetery fence and the church walls, the believers dare not protest but just keep glancing around, hoping that no one will jab them with a knife or force them to hand over their watches, which they need to check the last minutes before Christ's resurrection. Here, outside the church, the grinning, swirling mob far outnumbers the Orthodox. They are even more intimidated and suppressed than in the days of Tartar rule; the Tartars at least did not come to crowd out the faithful at the Easter morning service.

These youths are not breaking the law; although they are doing violence, it is bloodless. Their lips twisted into a gangsterish leer, their brazen talk, their loud laughter, their flirting and snide jokes, their smoking and spitting—it all amounts to an insult to the Passion of Christ, which is being celebrated a few yards away from them. It is expressed in the arrogant, derisory look worn by these snotty hooligans as they come to watch how the old folk still practice the rites of their forefathers.

Among the believers I catch a glimpse of one or two Jewish faces. Perhaps they are converts, or perhaps they are just onlookers. Glancing around warily, they too are waiting for the Easter procession. We all curse the Jews, but it would be worthwhile having a look around us to see what kind of Russians we have bred at the same time. These are not the militant atheists of the thirties, who snatched the consecrated Easter cakes out of people's hands, dancing and caterwauling and pretending to be devils. This generation is just idly inquisitive: The ice-hockey season on television is over, the football season has not started yet, and what brings them to church is sheer boredom. They push the churchgoers aside like so many sacks of straw; they curse the church for its commercialism, yet for some reason they buy candles.

One thing is odd: They are all outsiders, yet they all know each other—and by their first names. How is it they are such good friends? Do they all come from the same factory? Or is it that these occasions unite them in a kind of freemasonry?

The bell tolls loudly above our heads, but there is something false about it; the chimes sound somehow tinny instead of deep and sonorous. The bell is ringing to announce the procession. Now things really get going, although it is not the believers who are on the move but the crowd of shrieking youngsters, as they mill around in the churchyard in twos and threes. They are hurrying, even though they have no idea what they are looking for, which way to go, or where the procession will come from. They light red Easter candles, then show off by using them to light their cigarettes. They crowd together as if waiting for a foxtrot to begin; all it needs is a beer stall for these tall, curly-headed lads (at least our race gets no shorter) to start blowing white froth onto the graves.

The head of the procession has already left the porch and is turning in this direction, to the accompaniment of a gentle peal of bells. Two laymen are walking ahead asking the comrades to leave as much space as possible. Three paces behind them comes an elderly, balding churchwarden, carrying a heavy cut-glass lantern fixed to a pole. He looks up cautiously at the lamp as he tries to keep it steady, and glances from side to side with equal apprehension. . . . And this is the start of the picture which I would so like to paint, if only I could: the churchwarden's terror that the builders of the new society may close in, jump on him, and beat him up. The spectators can sense his fear.

Girls in trousers, holding candles, and boys with cigarettes stuck in their mouths, in caps and unbuttoned coats—some with immature, moronic expressions of totally unfounded self-confidence; others with simple, credulous faces: A lot of these must be in the picture—tightly packed, watching a spectacle which cannot be seen elsewhere for any money. Behind the lantern come two men carrying a religious banner, and they too, instead of walking apart, are huddling together from fear.

After them come ten women in pairs, holding thick lighted candles. They must also be in the picture, elderly women with faces set in an unworldly gaze, prepared for death if they are attacked. Two out of the ten are young girls of the same age as those crowding round with the boys, yet how pure and bright their faces are. The ten women, walking in close formation, are singing and looking as solemn as though the people around them were crossing themselves, praying, and falling to their knees in repentance. They do not breathe the cigarette smoke; their ears are deaf to the vile language; the soles of their feet do not feel how the churchyard has been turned into a dance floor.

And so the real procession begins. A slight tremor runs through the crowd on both sides and the noise has died down a little.

The women are followed by seven men, priests and deacons in bright copes. As they are walking out of step and bunched together, they get in each other's way, and there is almost no room to swing their censers or to raise the ends of their stoles in blessing. Yet this is the procession in which, had he not been dissuaded from taking part, the Patriarch of All Russia should have walked and conducted the service. . . .

The tightly packed little party hurries by—and that is all there is of the procession. No one else. There are evidently no worshipers in the procession, for if there were they would by now have left the church. No worshipers, yet this bunch of rowdies swarms along behind as though they were bursting through the broken doors of a warehouse to loot, tear open packets of food, brushing against the doorposts, spinning around in a whirlpool, crowding together, shoving their way through —and for what? They do not even know themselves. To see the priests making fools of themselves? Or are they just pushing for the sake of pushing?

It is extraordinary—a religious procession without worshipers, without people crossing themselves, a religious procession of people with caps on, smoking cigarettes, with transistors in their breast pockets. The front row of the crowd as it squeezes its way into the churchyard must also be in the picture; then it will be complete.

An old woman turns aside to cross herself and says to another:
"It's better this year, there's no rowdiness. There are so many police."
Ah, so that's it. This is one of the better years. . . .

These millions we have bred and reared—what will become of them? Where have the enlightened efforts and the inspiring visions of great thinkers led us? What good can we expect of our future generations?

The truth is that one day they will turn and trample on us all. And as for those who urged them on to this, they will trample on them too.

Easter Day
April 10, 1966

What a Pity

"What a Pity" was finished in 1965, published in 1978, and translated into English in 2003. In *The Gulag Archipelago* (vol. 3, pp. 409–14), Solzhenitsyn describes meeting an impressive old man who before the Bolshevik Revolution had started developing a hydroelectric plant and irrigation system deep in Central Asia. After serving a term in the gulag, the man is consigned to perpetual internal exile, his whereabouts unknown to his family. Then his adult daughter in Moscow notices a newspaper article describing her father's engineering feat and mentioning his location.

In "What a Pity," Solzhenitsyn transmutes this factual material into fiction. The main change is to make the daughter, Anna, the central consciousness. While trying to take the newspaper for her mother, she is approached by a suspicious policeman, who represents the oppressive Soviet regime. He relents when he learns that the article praises her father. This story, while entirely realistic, has a hint of symbolism. As Anna sees in raindrops her image in miniature, the story reveals in microcosm the tragedy of Soviet life. "What a pity," the journalist writes, that the engineer "did not live to see the triumph of his brilliant ideas." The real pity is that, though the man lives on, the regime keeps him confined and claims the credit due him.

The institution Anna Modestovna had to go to for the document was closed for lunch. This was annoying but it made sense to wait: It would only be fifteen minutes, and she could get everything finished before her own lunch break was over.

Anna Modestovna didn't want to wait on the staircase, so she went back outside.

It was a late October day, damp but not cold. There'd been some fine drizzle during the night, but it had stopped now. Trucks roared by along the tarmac, sometimes sparing the passers-by but more often spraying them with thin mud. There was something appealing about the gray, raised boulevard between the carriageways, and Anna crossed onto it.

There was hardly anyone on the boulevard, even in the distance. Here, if you avoided the puddles, you could walk over the coarse sand without getting your shoes wet. Under the trees lay a dark layer of wet leaves and, if you went close, a faint smell seemed to waft up from them—perhaps left over from when the leaves were alive, or maybe the beginning of decay; between the two carriageways of exhaust fumes, this boulevard was a rest for your lungs.

Anna stopped. There was no wind and the whole thick network of branches, little twigs, and next year's buds was strung with countless drops of water, all silvery-white in the gloom. There being no wind, the moisture had collected and formed into hanging drops. Taking her folded umbrella in the same hand as her handbag, and pulling off her glove, Anna began running her fingers underneath the drops, sliding them off. When she did this carefully the drop would transfer intact onto her finger, not breaking up but just slightly flattening. The wavy patterns on her finger showed up more clearly through the drop, which acted like a magnifying glass.

Each drop was also a convex mirror. In this mirror, against a light background of cloudy sky, she could see dark shoulders in a coat, and a head in a woollen hat, and even the interwoven branches above her head.

Anna forgot herself and began hunting for bigger and bigger drops, sometimes slipping them onto a fingernail and sometimes onto the fleshy part of her finger. Then, right beside her, she heard firm footsteps and she let her hand drop, ashamed to be behaving in a way more appropriate to her youngest son.

The passer-by, however, had seen neither the game she was playing nor Anna Modestovna herself—he was the kind of person who notices nothing on a street except a free taxi or a tobacco kiosk. He was a young man with the unmistakable stamp of a higher education, carrying a bulging bright-yellow briefcase and wearing a bright overcoat of soft worsted and a fur hat with a crease down the middle. Only in the capital do you encounter men with such expressions—self-assured, victorious. Anna knew people like this and she was afraid of them.

On guard now, she walked on and came across a newspaper display board standing on pale blue posts. Behind the glass lay the inside and outside pages of *Labor*. The glass had been chipped in one corner, water had got inside, and one sheet of newspaper was soaked. But at the bottom of this sheet, Anna saw a headline above two columns of print: "The New Life of the Chu River."

This was somewhere she knew: She had been born there, in the Seven Rivers region. Wiping the pane with her glove, Anna Modestovna began to skim through the article.

The writer of the article was no miser with words. He began at the Moscow aerodrome: how he had taken his seat in the aeroplane and, as if in contrast with the dismal weather, how everyone had been in a joyful mood. Then he described his fellow-travelers: who was flying with him and why. He even said a word about the stewardess. After that he described the aerodrome at Frunze and how, as if in harmony with the sunny weather, everyone was still in a joyful mood. Then he recounted his journey along the Chu valley. Using a rich variety of technical terms, he described the hydraulic works, the hydroelectric power station, and the irrigation canals; he enthused at the sight of desert lands that were now irrigated and fruitful, and he expressed astonishment at the harvest statistics of the collective farms.

At the end he wrote: "But few know that this grandiose and majestic transformation of an entire region of nature was first conceived a long time ago. Our engineers did not have to carry out detailed surveys of the valley, its geological strata and water systems. The whole of the central project was completed on the basis of laborious calculations carried out in 1912, forty years ago, by the talented Russian hydrographer and hydraulic engineer, Modest Aleksandrovich V.,[1] who then, in the same year, began the initial works, risking his own capital."

Anna Modestovna was neither shocked nor overcome with joy; it was rather that she had begun to tremble, both inside and outside, as if at the start of an illness. She bent down, to see the final paragraphs right in the corner, and she again tried to wipe the glass clean. With difficulty she read: "But under the bigoted Tsarist regime, indifferent as it was to the interests of the people, his plans could not be realized. They ended up gathering dust in the Department of Land Amelioration, and the excavations he had already completed were abandoned."

"What a pity!" the journalist exclaimed in conclusion. "What a pity that the young enthusiast did not live to see the triumph of his brilliant ideas! That he is unable to gaze upon the now transformed valley!"

Anna felt a sudden fear, surging up like boiling water, because she knew what she was going to do now: She was going to steal this newspaper! Like a thief, she looked around, first to her right, then to her left. There was

---

[1] Modest is an uncommon name and the heroine's patronymic is Modestovna. It is clear that he is her father.

nobody on the boulevard, just someone's back in the distance. What she was doing was unseemly, quite disgraceful, but. . . .

The newspaper was held in place by three drawing pins across the top. Anna put her hand through the break in the glass. Where the newspaper was wet in the corner, it crumpled at once into a lithe damp ball and came off the pin. Standing on tiptoe, Anna managed to reach across to the middle pin, loosen it, and pull it out. But the third, furthest pin was beyond her reach—and Anna just pulled on the newspaper. It tore—and the whole sheet came away in her hand.

Immediately, behind her back, she heard the piercing staccato of a policeman's whistle.

As if scorched (there was little she didn't know about fear, and a policeman's whistle was frightening enough at any time), Anna withdrew her now empty hand and turned around.

It was too late to run away, and it would have made things worse. Coming towards her—not down the boulevard, but through a gap in the boulevard fence, which Anna had not noticed before—was a tall policeman, looking all the bigger because of the wet raincoat he was wearing with the hood thrown back.

He did not call out. He came up to her, in no hurry. He looked down at Anna Modestovna, then at the newspaper—which had dropped down, somewhat crumpled, behind the glass—then at Anna again. He towered over her, strict and severe. It was clear from his hands and from his pink, broad-nosed face that he was someone fit and strong—the kind of man to drag people out of a blaze or carry out an arrest without using firearms.

Without raising his voice, the policeman asked: "What's all this, citizen? Do we want to be fined twenty-five rubles?" (Oh, please, let it just be a fine! She was afraid of some harsher interpretation of her behavior.)

"Or do you not like people reading newspapers?"

"What do you mean? No, no! Forgive me!" said Anna, somehow almost wriggling. "I'll put it back straight away . . . if you'll allow me. . . ."

No, hardly. Even if he did allow her, a sheet of newspaper with one wet corner and one torn corner would not be so very easy to put back.

The policeman continued to look down at her, giving no indication of his decision.

He'd been on duty a long time and it had been raining. It would be nice to take the woman back to the station, along with her newspaper. While he filed his report, he'd dry out a little. But he wanted to understand. A respectably dressed woman, middle-aged, not drunk. She looked at him, waiting for her punishment. "What have you got against the newspaper?"

"There's something about my father!" All apology, she was clasping to her chest the handle of her umbrella, her handbag, and the glove she had taken off. She had not noticed that she had cut her finger against the glass.

Now the policeman understood. Pitying her because of her bleeding finger, he nodded. "Being criticized, is he? But what difference is one copy going to make?"

"No-o! No, no! The opposite—he's being praised!"

At this point she saw the blood on her finger and began to suck it. And she kept on looking at the policeman's large, simple face.

His lips barely parted. "But why? Couldn't you have bought it in a kiosk?"

"But look at the date!" She quickly took her finger from her lips and pointed to the undamaged sheet of newspaper beneath the other half of the glass. "It's been there three days. Where am I going to find another copy now?"

The policeman looked at the date. Again at the woman. And again at the crumpled sheet of newspaper. He sighed: "I should file a report. And fine you. . . . All right then, but don't do it again. Take it quickly, before anyone sees."

"Oh thank you! Thank you! How kind you are! Thank you!" Anna Modestovna said the words over and over again, at the same time as repeating some kind of wriggle or bow. Instead of putting her handkerchief to her finger, she quickly slipped the hand with the pink finger under the glass, seized the edge of the newspaper and pulled it out. "Thank you!"

The newspaper opened out. Anna, as best she could with one edge being soaked and having only one free hand, folded it. With one more polite little wriggle, she said: "I'm very grateful to you. You can't imagine what a joy this will be to my mother and father! May I go?"

Standing alongside her, he nodded.

And she walked quickly away, quite forgetting why she had come to this street, clutching the newspaper, which she had folded askew, and sucking now and again on her finger.

She must hurry back to her mother. So the two of them could read this together! Once her father's place of exile had been determined, mother would go and visit him. She could take the newspaper with her.

The journalist hadn't known! He hadn't known—or he would never have written that! And the editorial board didn't know—or they'd never have let it through. The young enthusiast had lived to see the day. He had lived to see the triumph of his brilliant ideas, because his death sentence had been commuted and he had instead spent twenty years in prisons and camps. And then, while on his way, under guard, to some remote place of eternal exile, he had petitioned Beria himself, asking to be sent to the Chu valley. But in the end he had been sent somewhere else, and the local internal affairs office had no idea what to do with the useless old man: there was no suitable job for him—and as for a pension, he had not yet put in enough years of work.

No Matter What

"No Matter What," completed after Solzhenitsyn returned to Russia in 1994, is one of several late stories written in the experimental form that he labels "binary" tales. These two-part stories are linked by character and plot tenuously or, as in this case, not at all. Instead, they are linked on the level of theme.

In part one, set during World War II, five Soviet soldiers commit the peccadillo of filching a few potatoes. The lieutenant who reports them represents a familiar Solzhenitsyn type: a moral man whose rectitude is misdirected by ideology. His realistic superior opts for soldiers' full stomachs over rigid rules. "No matter what," this major explains, stating the theme that connects the story's two parts, "you cannot change human nature even under socialism."

Part two, set in post-Soviet Russia and considerably more involved, grew directly out of a side-trip Solzhenitsyn made while traversing Siberia on his journey home from exile abroad. In these hinterlands he observed the desolation wrought by ostensibly benevolent central planners and used this raw material to show one particular set of consequences of disregarding reality, whether natural or social. A settled old way of life in which villagers sustained themselves in harmony with nature was turned topsy-turvy by never-completed Soviet development projects that produced only ecological devastation and human impoverishment. A smooth-talking bureaucrat visiting from Moscow shows only that the "democratic" new administration is "not going to reverse anything, no matter what." Among the many forlorn villagers, the presence of citizens with experience, wisdom, and gumption gives hope that vigorous local self-government could flourish if Moscow authorized it.

In real life, Solzhenitsyn gave voice to these voiceless in the halls of power. *Russia in Collapse* is a clear textual example.

❧

- I -

Supper for the reserve regiment was served at six in the evening, even though lights-out did not come until ten. Someone had correctly figured that the men would get by without any more food that way, and would sleep through until morning.

Lights-out may have been at ten, but no amount of political reading could match up against the long, dark November evenings, and the lights in the barracks were dim besides. So the soldiers were allowed to hit the sack earlier; and night inspection was done earlier, too.

Lieutenant Pozushan was company commander, a straight arrow not so much from service (they had been hurried through military school), but from his internal sense of duty, and the present dread moment for the Soviet Union. Bitterly he swallowed the radio news accounts from Stalingrad. We were barely holding them back, it seemed, and the lieutenant even wished their regiment were sent there. He could find no peace on these dull evenings, could not even sleep. And tonight, as the hours dragged on to midnight, he up and went to inspect company quarters.

All quiet with the first and second platoon—only the dim blue light of the tinted bulbs. The stoves were already dark and had cooled. (The rooms were heated with tin stoves, with makeshift ducts leading out the windows. The old basement furnace had long stood dormant.)

At the third platoon, not only was the stove still hot, but five of the men sat huddled around it, bundled in their dark padded jackets and pants, butts right on the floor.

The lieutenant entered—they flinched. And jumped up.

The lieutenant attached no meaning to this at first, but let them sit, just scolded them quietly, so as not to wake the others: Why weren't they asleep? And where did they get the firewood?

Private Harlashin answered right away: "Woodchips, comrade lieutenant. Picked them up over at the target range."

Well, all right.

"And why aren't you sleeping? Got too much strength? You better save it for the front."

They hemmed and hawed; nothing clear.

Ah, it's their business, after all. Probably telling each other stories about girls, or such like.

He was already turning to leave, but suspected something. Up *this* late? And they certainly hadn't been expecting him. And the fire in the stove was weak—it could hardly warm them.

"Oderkov, open the door."

Oderkov sat right by the door of the stove, but gave a blank look: what door?

"Oderkov!"

Among them the lieutenant discerned junior sergeant Timonov, their section commander.

The soldiers froze. No one moved.

"What is this? Open it, I said."

Oderkov lifted his arm as though it were made of lead. Took the turn-handle, strained to lift it.

All the way to the end.

And with no less strain he pulled on the door, and pulled some more.

Inside the stove, amidst the glowing coals, was a round, soot-stained standard-issue mess-pot. A steam odor poured into the room, cutting through the foul air of drying stockings.

"What are you boiling?" asked lieutenant Pozushan, still just as quietly, not to wake the platoon, but very strictly.

It became clear to the five of them that he would not drop it. No avoiding an answer.

Timonov got up. Not very firmly. Arms at his side, but squirming. One step closer to the lieutenant, to be all the quieter: "Sorry, comrade lieutenant. We were on mess hall duty today. Grabbed us a few raw potatoes."

Of course! Pozushan only now realized it: Their battalion was on duty today and tomorrow. He had forgotten that the supply sergeant ordered a team to work the mess hall. And so they went.

A darkness slid, not over the lieutenant's eyes, but into his breast. Like silt muddying the water. Like dirt.

Not swearing at them outright but with a pained voice, he let out a plea to the fighting men, all of them now on their feet: "Are you nuts? Do you have any idea what you are doing? The Germans are in Stalingrad. The country is starving. Every grain gets counted! And you?"

What else to say to them, so mindless, ignorant, unconscientious? What else to infuse into their backward heads?

"Timonov, take out the pot."

With the mitten that lay nearby, Timonov took the red-hot handle and, trying not to nick the coals, carefully lifted and pulled out the pot.

The bottom of the black pot was still covered with spots of glowing ember. The embers burned out. Timonov held on.

The other four awaited their demise.

"An offense like this, why, this is grounds for court-martial!" said the lieutenant. "Very simple and easy: Just hand your names to the Political Department."

Something else unpleasant now tugged at him. Oh yes, that's it: Timonov was the one who had come to the lieutenant to ask if the regiment would write to his collective farm in Kazakhstan in defense of his family; they were being hounded for something. Pozushan couldn't remember what for, but it was clear he couldn't help; the regiment commanders would never sign a paper like that.

It came together oddly somehow. Either it made Timonov all the guiltier, or maybe less so.

The potatoes were boiling in their skins. Looked like about twenty of them, small ones.

And they gave off a teasing smell.

"Go pour out the water in the sink and bring the pot back. Quickly."

Timonov went, but not quickly.

In the dim light, the lieutenant scanned the faces of his silent fighting men. Their expressions were gloomy, complex. Biting their lips. Eyes down, or to the side. But outright repentance—no, he couldn't read it on any of their faces.

Heavens, what is this coming to?

"If we go off stealing government property, how are we going to win the war? Just think about it!"

Dull and impenetrable they stood.

Yet this is with whom we march. To victory. Or to defeat.

Timonov returned with the pot. One could not even tell if all the potatoes were still in it.

Those undercooked potatoes.

"Tomorrow we sort this out with the commissar," said the lieutenant to the other four. "To bed." But to Timonov: "Come with me."

In the hallway he ordered him: "Wake the supply sergeant, and put the pot in his custody."

He himself could hardly get to sleep afterward: a horrible episode, and in his own company! And he had almost missed it. Maybe this had occurred before? Lawlessness, theft are all around, and he didn't even suspect it, just learned of it by chance.

In the morning he closely interrogated supply sergeant Guskov. The latter swore that he knew nothing. Why, nothing even remotely similar had ever happened in the company.

Looking into Guskov's perceptive countenance, his little mobile eyes, Pozushan for the first time wondered: That trait, which he so liked in Guskov—his organizational capacity, prudence, and quick resolution of any difficulties that arose, all of which greatly eased the job of a company commander—could cheating also be a part of that trait?

Still early, before breakfast, the lieutenant went to battalion commissar Fatianov. This was a crystal soul, remarkably pleasant, straightforward, with big clear eyes. He conducted excellent political instruction with the men, not by rote, not in a mechanical voice.

Their battalion staff were assigned to two little rooms in a small house, across the wide square, which was used to place the entire reserve regiment in general formation, when necessary, or for marching drills.

It was a cold, dank November morning, foggy with drizzle. (And what is it like today in Stalingrad? The morning reports gave no clear picture.)

In the first room sat two middle-aged clerks, who hardly noticed the lieutenant's entry. Is the commissar in? They nodded toward the second room.

Knocked on the door. And opened it.

"Permission to enter." He crisply brought his hand to his temple (he was getting good at saluting). "Permission to address you, comrade major."

Major Fatianov sat at the battalion commander's table, but along the side. The commander was not in. At a second larger table by the window, all covered in papers, sat the quiet, mild-mannered captain Krayegorsky, the chief of staff. The major was without his overcoat, but in a cap. The captain was dressed for indoors, his carefully trimmed graying hair exposed neatly on his head.

"What's new, lieutenant?" asked the major, as ever both kindly and with a hint of a laugh, while leaning back in his chair.

Pozushan with trepidation reported everything. Four or five pounds of potatoes carried off from the kitchen and pocketed. There is suspicion that this could have occurred during other times when his company was on kitchen duty. It is possible that this occurred in other companies, as well. The episode is directly suited for court-martial, but how can we go that far? (Not only out of pity for them, the fools; but heading for the front, it is also unwise to thin one's own ranks.) What measures, then? What punishment? Should the episode be made public within the company? Or within the battalion? Or not public at all?

The major narrowed his wide clear eyes. He gazed attentively at the lieutenant. He was thinking it over.

Or was he?

He very much took his time with an answer. First he sighed. Clutched the back of his head—and here his cap shifted forward, its peak toward his forehead. Sighed once more.

"An exemplary case," he uttered with great strictness.

And sat silent.

Was the next step forming inside him? Some punishment?

"You know, lieutenant, you weren't with us the summer of '41. You didn't see what huge warehouses were burned. And what looting went on as it happened. Both in the cities and in the army itself. Good heavens, what a hauling-off!"

"True, I did not see that, comrade major. But even from military school I know: People steal. From the quartermasters to the kitchen-hands to the supply sergeants. We students were always like hungry dogs, always getting the short end. It's all the more reason to fight it! If everyone is going to steal, we will collapse the army's own supports."

The major yawned slightly.

"Ye-e-s. You have the right perspective on it. Educate your men that way; your company has a weak political officer as it is."

The lieutenant stood, a bit disheartened. He expected a firm and immediate decision from the commissar—and instead all was adrift. This was nothing like the commissar's own words during their political instruction.

The door now opened wide, and the battalion supply sergeant entered with dispatch, wearing a brand new padded jacket. In his left hand he carried by the handle an identical round mess-pot, without a lid, except that it was a pure, clean olive green.

"Comrade commissar!" with a swing of his right hand to touch his ear-flapped hat. "The sample! Be so good as to taste it."

Taking the *sample* was indeed the job of the commissar of the battalion on duty. But this sample was over half a pot of creamy hot millet, enough to serve four, and heavily buttered, too, like nothing ever seen in the regiment's mess hall.

"Ye-e-s," prolonged the commissar once more, took off his cap, and laid it on the table. This revealed his wavy, slightly curled dirty blond hair, which always kept his appearance agreeable and well-disposed.

The supply sergeant carefully placed the pot on an unoccupied corner of the table. Next to it he set out three wooden spoons, still freshly painted.

"Have a seat, captain," the commissar invited the chief of staff. And Krayegorsky started shifting over, together with his chair.

The sergeant saluted and left.

The pot was steaming and giving off a delicious smell.

"The battalion commander is not here, why don't you join us, lieutenant," kindly offered the commissar, with a glint in his bright eyes, as if he was having a laugh. But not at lieutenant Pozushan's expense, no. . . .

No!!

"Thank . . . you," Pozushan struggled to pronounce. His throat seized, as if choking.

Hand to cap in salute, with bitterness like never before:

"Permission to leave."

But major Fatianov looked on—open, approving, friendly, understanding.

"Life marches on," he said quietly. "You cannot turn it on a dime anyway, no matter what. You cannot change human nature even under socialism."

And with a playful squint: "Let them finish cooking those potatoes. No sense letting them rot."

The lieutenant saluted crisply one more time, turned himself to the left, and pushed open the door.

- 2 -

Hard to believe, but just before the war, men were still hauling bargeloads of salt from the mouth of the Angara up to the mouth of the Ilim. They did it in teams, harnessed to a tow-rope. In places they would take horses along for a boost, and waited on some stretches until help came from a tailwind. They managed all right, three runs a season.

In time, a fleet of small motorboats plied up and down the Angara, and for another twelve years after technical school Anatoly piloted different craft down to the Yenisey. But in '74 they started impounding the river near Boguchany, and motorboats were finished. No hydro station, either: just a mess. Further upstream, the Bratsk and Ust-Ilim dams had already been put up, leaving fewer than three hundred navigable miles, and little more than a hundred of them, up to Kezhma, that weren't dead, that still had any life. On this remnant, the boy who once went by Tolik—himself now fifty—would pilot what turned up.

So it was today. Both captain and steersman, he sat in the cabin behind the wheel, dressed in a heavily worn blue jacket, and guided a jet-propelled cutter, with a salon full of guests below deck. His soul was all in knots. He ached for this last reach of the river—in her true, undefiled banks—as though the pain were his own: Can we convince them? Could it work?

The side window was slid open, and the familiar fresh breath of river air flowed in.

Over on the River Lena, lit buoys and markers were still intact. You could make as many runs as you can manage, and soon you would earn enough for an apartment. But here all the buoys had disappeared over the past twenty years, despite a guaranteed depth of just two feet. So you guide by memory, by wit, by a sharp eye. You must see every whirlpool ahead of time and note where it spins. Forward, and you read the river: all fifteen of the rocky shallows until Kezhma, with their slight elevation drops. But then no bankside slope, no rock, no cliff face, no little cape, no estuary could be confused with any other. It is only to the untrained eye that it appears all the same, like sheep in a herd, or like moose.

Moose and bears, for their part, had stopped swimming across the Angara: The water had grown much colder because of the Ilim hydro station. The waters of the Lena are so much warmer.

But the captain loved the Angara like his wife, and he would not trade her in for another.

Over the stately river, a sunny day was slowly breaking out. A glitter evenly covered the surface.

A line of white clouds stretched far beyond the right bank. But it would melt away.

The waters of the Angara are always quiet in June. From mid-August, the northerly wind will churn up hefty waves. August is also when the Sayan Mountains thaw and the big waters come rolling.

The low narrow door from the interior stairs opened. The mechanic Khripkin squeezed through—head like a ball, body like a ball—and sat on the side bench. You couldn't fit a third into the cabin without blocking the door.

"What's going on down there, Semyon?"

Semyon may have been an unkempt fellow, with black, ungroomed hair and a face as if it was poured cast iron, but he had quick and perceptive eyes.

"Who wants anything to do with work, Anatol Dmitrich? Valentina Filippovna barely got started, but Scepura is already serving up drinks, right from early morning. The minister has his eyes on the appetizers, too, I think."

The captain took a course to the right bank, with a barren gradual slope in the distance.

It hadn't always been barren. Time was—an evergreen taiga stood here. Then a timbering camp was thrown up. The land was not part of the flooding zone, but adjacent, and the timber was valuable. So they clear-cut it. But once pine is cleared, it does not grow back; only aspen does, eventually.

Since pine logs do not sink, they were floated downriver. "All the local pine," he sighed, "just got jammed up senselessly near Boguchany, while in other places, look what great larch they took down! What birch! Except those logs sink, and there were no barges to carry them, so the trees still lie up there, rotting." He fell silent. "You try lying around like that."

"When was this?" asked Khripkin in his impatient tone.

"Ten years ago. Then seven."

"During perestroika, already?"

"Then too. One shipment after another. They threw up twenty-seven camps along this stretch, down to Boguchany."

Yet how much healthy forest stood even now, higher up in the hills.

He made his way to the left bank, since he could see a swirl gathering over the rocky shallows to the right.

Going with the current, the bow does not stir up the water.

A water not yet entirely robbed of its blues.

The repetitive rumbles of the motor could be felt all the way up in the cabin.

"If only he asked me," Khripkin figured aloud, "I would give him my piece."

The captain thought about it, without turning.

"Well, maybe go, liven things up a bit; just don't ruin it. We all know you have a . . ."

"I don't believe any of those bosses, whether the old ones or the new ones."

The captain turned around, by no means agreeing, but answering softly still.

"No, how come? You can talk sense with the new ones."

The mechanic sat a bit longer, glancing at the water.

He thumped his way down the stairs.

And came out into the front of the hall. Facing him were a few people on leather chairs that were bolted to the floor. Next to the minister—a hale and hearty fellow in a bright-colored summer suit—sat Valentina Filippovna. She kept a stack of papers on her knees, but carried on without looking down, without pause, with conviction. Behind them sat two from the entourage: one an athletic, broad-shouldered bull of a man; the other—with a big open notebook. Across the aisle was regional head Zdeshnev and a dried-up-looking fellow from Irkutsk, wearing a black suit.

Back yet farther, behind the seats, was a similarly bolted table, already fitted with a white tablecloth, two servers in white aprons carrying and setting down on it plates, bottles, glasses. Here too was the fat man Scepura, his graying hair in a crew cut, in a bright multicolor American sweatshirt underneath an unbuttoned sportcoat. He gave orders quietly, but with quick, sure motions of his hands.

The mechanic would have been happy to stand by and listen, but he was not endowed with a mug that belonged here. And he would have been even happier to have his say, but there was no butting in.

So he went—slowly, one steep step after another—down to the motor room.

Valentina Filippovna was chairman of the regional committee for environmental protection and rational use of natural resources. Although she was still very young, no one called her by the diminutive "Valya." She had an open face, a head-on look without any flirting mannerism, and she was chiseling away at the high-placed guest that had flown in.

"They started building the Boguchan hydro station two years before the project was even ready, such was the hurry. But it has been twenty years now, and the whole project has become outdated. Even at the intermediate level to which the water has been raised, the entire sturgeon hatch is dying. Musquash are dying by the tens of thousands. Nearer the dam, algae blooms are turning the Angara into a swamp."

The minister listened on—not just attentively but sympathetically. He shook his head in disbelief. Once or twice he signaled his aide, a slender man with an elongated, intelligent face, and the latter took notes down quickly.

She spoke with such passion, fingers touching her throat, as if it were about her own fate.

"And now, if the latest decree of the government is acted upon, completing the station to its maximum project height, it would mean flooding another half-million square miles. Underneath that land are more than 120 million cubic feet of peat. And a magnesium ore deposit, several hundred million tons. . . ."

"Ore, too!" tossed the minister over his shoulder to the aide.

He was in middle age, naturally vibrant, alert. His tie, according to some new fashion, was lowered; and the collar was unbuttoned at the top. Leg over leg, even swinging back and forth at times.

To either side, behind the wide clean windowpanes of the salon, the bluish-gray river water rushed by; while farther off the banks passed by, now hill, now meadow.

The waterjet motor did not impede their conversation.

Valentina Filippovna, herself an applied chemist, a graduate of the Forestry Academy and with work experience at her back, did not stumble and did not tire in explaining to the high-placed guest—with an increasing hope—what troubles had already piled up; how the treatment systems at Bratsk and Ust-Ilimsk and the Baikalsk pulp and paper plant were unwisely applying chemicals that killed nature's own capacity for biological treatment.

The minister, one could sense, was calm, firm in his accomplishments, sure of himself. If someone like that takes up an issue—how could he not succeed?

. . . But there is more: All the timber that was hastily felled and is now decomposing at the bottom of the Angara—it is giving off phenols and turpentine, so that the once legendary pristine waters of the Angara have degraded down to Class V, now even Class VI, the worst level of ecological hazard. But if one were to stop the completion of the Boguchan hydro station, more than a hundred miles of running river could be saved, and in those reaches the Angara can cleanse itself. Otherwise, the whole of the Angara dies; all of it will be stagnant water. . . .

Even in her rather short service, Valentina Filippovna had seen her fill of bosses who were endlessly calm, even if matters were falling apart in front of their eyes. They were groomed to be that way; and they were all large, too, following some rule of selection different from the rest of us. But this one—no, he is different. And he is so highly placed besides! If this one speaks. . . . His youthful, perhaps cheerful look also gave her comfort for some reason.

The resourceful Scepura, having arranged everything back at the table, walked up and, to ease the possible fatigue of the guest, invited everyone, if not to break off the conversation completely, then to continue it at table. (Once or twice he looked askance: What is this activist doing here, meddling about, breaking the rhythm?)

But the minister wouldn't bite on the offer. He wanted to hear other voices, too.

That dried-up fellow in the black suit, the governor's representative, kept silent the whole time, but looked on a bit sardonically.

Then Ivan Ivanovich Zdeshnev hastened to speak up. He was the manager of the expansive district surrounding the river. He did not look like much of an administrator. He had a simple snub-nosed face, a jacket that wasn't formal and didn't match the color of his slacks. Still, he forced himself to remember the importance of his own position, and the whole confluence of troubles, and the high estate of his guest.

"You understand, I am sure, that I, as the *mayor* of these parts, am under significant *pressing* from the population. We have all become hostages of the Boguchan hydro station here, of whether or not it will happen. If it does, our livelihood will come to a poor end indeed."

He glanced at the minister's face to check if he had crossed the line and spoken too boldly.

But the minister's eyes were filled with comprehension and a business-like significance. No, they exhibited no anger whatsoever.

What's more, the secretary in the back had written it all down in his notebook.

Ivan Ivanych knew well that there is a limit to permissible debate, that one must not argue too hotly. And yet. . . .

"Look how Old Keul was relocated from the zone of flooding. . . . It did not turn out overly well. The village is three hundred years old. The villagers wouldn't go, and that was that. So then they took to burning down the villagers' cottages. The villagers fought back with pitchforks and axes. All right, then, they left the cemetery alone for the time being. But they still resettled the villagers to New Keul. Turned out that place sat atop quick ground: no building cellars there."

No, even now the boss showed no displeasure. Why, he seems . . . like an understanding sort of person. So Ivan Ivanych came out with another example, having no shortage of them.

"In the hamlet of Kata—Kata stream is right opposite Iodorma, where we are headed—one old lady never did let them tear down her cottage: 'Kill me here, on the spot.' They left her alone. . . . And so she catches burbot in wintertime, and piles it up frozen in the barn. They bring her bread by helicopter, in exchange for the fish."

He now caught himself, for he had gotten carried away, and laid out well too much.

"Be so kind as to pardon me, but the *imidzh* of a *mayor* does not permit me to be silent, either. . . ."

In reality, the visiting boss was no minister, but only a deputy—the deputy, however, of a very highly placed minister indeed. He came here to sort out the privatization of the huge, clumsy local timber processing complex, which needed a rapid and sure exit out of the hands of the state—rapid, because privatization had not only many friends but likewise many opponents. A monster like that no one could buy, and no one would want it all anyway, so the solution was to break it up into forty-two enterprises. That had all been passed during the past few months, and the deputy minister came just to close the deal as soon as possible. This he had done successfully, and knew he would make his superiors happy. Now, these past few days, he kept being asked to take a ride down the Angara, so why not indeed? And today, in his last day here, they took off in the cutter. But who was this woman? Who got her in here? She is so hot and bothered about all this! Must be she's not married. He hadn't ever heard of this problem of a downstream power station, so now what? . . .

The cutter went onward, but they had not reached Iodorma as yet, and Scepura, in full frontal assault, persuaded the company to sit down at the table. He bustled about warmly, all cheerful, as if on a big holiday, even though the day was as common as they come. Shall we start off with some champagne?

Corks popped from two bottles, glasses filled with foam. Valentina Filippovna wouldn't even take a seat at the table, somberly refusing for a long time.

The whole of Ust-Ilim had known Scepura—the round-headed little fat man, energetic despite being on the wrong side of fifty, and quick with words—even as far back as twenty years ago, when he was an electrician hanging on ropes above the Angara, erecting the dam. Here they assembled the best from the whole Union, and he made the cut. After that, he took law classes by correspondence course, then was promoted to the prosecutor's office, then returned to the pulp plant. Here he managed worker life, then made personnel decisions, then headed up the administration, signing permission slips for people to return back to Russia, and was even nominated for deputy director of the whole timber processing complex. When everything turned upside down, he became merely a hotel manager, and here he was: catering, pouring champagne, entertaining, his assistants at the ready.

Before the good cheer settled in, the taciturn representative of the governor had occasion to tell the visiting leadership of a few more gloomy items, leaving it to the guests how to report the issue further. So many power stations were built in Irkutsk province that up to fifty percent of the electric capacity has stood idle for the past three years. It was planned that aluminum smelters would consume it, but those wouldn't be built even in another twenty years. So if one were to complete the Boguchan project now, where would one send the electricity? China seems like the only option, but a high-voltage line halfway across the Siberian taiga is a more expensive proposition than completing Boguchan station itself.

The minister was amazed. It was all hard to believe, yet a real government official was reporting it. The situation was only getting more complex.

"Yes, to be sure," he resonated in a weighty bass. "These solid arguments need to be taken into account."

Then the governor's representative added that the Boguchan completion was being egged on by the Krasnoyarsk authorities. They settled over 25 thousand people down by Boguchany to build the dam, and now they have no jobs.

The minister raised his brow. "Egged on" sure did not sound like a government term, but then, but then even this breaks through sometimes, it's only human. . . .

The promontories receded, first on the right bank, now also on the left.

What breadth!

The men had started on the vodka.

The minister's cheeks acquired a bit of rose.

He glanced toward the windows on the right, glanced toward the left, then pronounced thoughtfully: "Didn't Pushkin make some mention of the Angara?"

But no one offered to take him up on it.

In the meantime, the cutter approached the left bank.

The whole company left the table and went ashore to stretch their legs.

The shy captain descended from the cabin, too. And the mechanic popped out of the motor room. Scepura's assistants, in their white aprons, scurried and scurried to set up right onshore, next to the water, to prepare a barbecue and soup from the fish they had brought.

In single file, they ascended the pockmarked bankside hillock.

. . . There, a village street ran parallel to the river with houses on one side, and deep behind it, another—much shorter—set of houses. The street was comprised of something like a road—but no wagon could make it through here; its axle would break in the ruts and potholes formed of dried mud.

Besides, it wouldn't have anywhere to go, in any direction.

Nor was it much of a place to walk or stretch: You could break your legs here.

With the motor off, silence stood over the entire Angara, on both shores, and for several miles beyond. Only the ring of mosquitoes by one's ears.

The houses, still undestroyed, stood in a row. One of them even had freshly painted light blue decorations at the roof-end. In front of it, the sides of a turned-over flat-bottom boat were painted with the same blue color. Along the row of cottages, not a single door, not a single window was open. On one house was a sign: "Everyday wares." The bolt on the door had rusted, but not yet the sign.

No one. No chickens to peck at the ground here, no cat to sneak by. Only the grass grows on, oblivious to tragedy. And the peaceful green treetops in the front yards.

Life had been here. . . .

Then again, here was a tall pile of freshly cut thick branches, just the size for splitting into firewood. So people live here even now.

It grew warm; the day had heated up.

Suddenly a cuckoo. From across the Angara—how far that must be, yet how audible.

That is breadth. That is stillness. . . .

All stood around in silence.

Then Zdeshnev called out lustily: "Za-bo-lot-nov! Niki-forych! Zabolotnov!

Meanwhile, he explained to the leadership. This was the hamlet of Iodorma, twenty-two households in all. It had a clinic once, and a school through fourth grade, but now it has all been cleared out for flooding. Here, too, Irkutsk province ends, and Krasnoyarsk lies beyond. But Zabolotnov, sixty-three himself and with an old sick wife, wouldn't go anywhere. "Here lie my father and mother," he said, "and I am not leaving." Well, they let him alone for now. And so, in the new times, with collective farms disbanded, he has taken up farming on his own. What you see on the other side of the Angara isn't the bank, but two islands, with a sleeve of the river behind them.

On the rocky island he keeps his calves, and on the fertile grassy one—the dairy cows. The milk is transported downriver by cutter. His wife cannot move about anymore, so he rows across the river at dawn and does the milking himself. He has plowed and planted there, too.

"He does all this alone?"

"No, he has his two sons with him. One of them painted these roof decorations. Their wives live in New Keul. They will be coming in summertime, bringing his seven grandchildren. Why, there he is."

He was walking from somewhere, a long rein hanging in his hand. Wearing sackcloth pants, a cheap color-drawn jersey and a black short-wool cap, he made a so-so impression, a nondescript, ragged little man, yet with a firm step. He looked over the whole scene from afar and understood it was the leadership.

He approached.

"Good health and greetings!"—his voice was not that of an old man.

No beard, and keeps up with his shaving. Face and neck look brown, with a wart on his cheek.

Only Ivan Ivanych extended him a hand, and shook it.

"So tell us, Nikiforych, how many head do you have?"

"Oh, used to raise three hundred. Nowadays, if we're not counting the leased-out cattle, seventy are left. And a score of horses."

Hard to believe he could run all this.

"So how do you manage?"

"Oh, I'd be managing a lot better if not for the scoundrel speculators. The regional co-ops fell apart. The meat plant cheats you. The milk plant cheats you. An honest buyer is what we need, but where do you get one? We can't get to market without our own engines, either."

Ivan Ivanych put his questions to Nikiforych, but set his eyes on the visiting boss.

"So how do you get your bread?"

"I can get up to twelve hundred pounds off an acre sometimes, after it's been fallow; that's enough for us. We grind it; and we bake it."

"Where are your sons?"

"Over on those islands."

"Two sons?"

"There were three. One drowned. Age sixteen," he sighed. "His boat capsized," he sighed again. His eyes, not wide to begin with, compressed further. "God gave him. God took him away."

He fell silent—and everyone stayed silent out of politeness.

Nikiforych, as if none of these arrivals was present, as if not seeing anything, faded out and quietly concluded, persuading himself: "I do love God."

Everyone became uncomfortable and awkward. They stayed silent again.

And now hobbled over his old lady, in a dark skirt and warm, brown knit sweater. She was carrying a clay pitcher, careful not to trip, and two mugs. These she placed on a wide log.

She bowed: "Fresh hot milk. Care to sample it?"

Valentina Filippovna: "Do I ever, missus. Thank you."

She poured, and began to drink, even closing her eyes: "Can't get this in the city anymore."

No one seemed to be drawn to the second cup, and so the quiet captain walked up from the back row, with an innocent look.

Yet he exchanged a conspiratorial glance with Valentina Filippovna.

He poured in silence, and began to drink.

Ivan Ivanych, meanwhile, had found a way to continue: "So, say, Vasily Nikiforych: how do you view the new life?"

Eyes alive again, he answered: "Seems it's taken a turn for the better. They never dispossessed my father, but they sent him, age seventy-five, to work under some kid. 'I am a landholder,' my father would say, 'and they stuck me under that pipsqueak.' He died of the bitterness."

Even while answering, Zabolotnov realized that these guests had not come to listen to his stories. In that case, it was obvious what brought them. So he continued: "Such a merry folk we had here, a working village. Fields were sown on every bank. A place full of life. Rye stood two meters tall. Every island in green. Hayfields. Cropfields. Potatoes sprout here—thirteen-fold. Now, all have quit. Hopeless. You break your back not knowing what comes next."

This boss seemed to be a listening one; he understands it all, nodding his head. What's not to understand here? Such a land of plenty—and to abandon it, put it under shallow standing water. . . . But he answered cautiously:

"The government in Moscow has its reasons. One can't see them from here."

Zabolotnov didn't lose his nerve.

"So what about Moscow? I've been to Moscow once. The sky there is low. And people walk about in a herd."

Thus they stood, in a cluster on a random slope, some higher, some lower, beside two pits. The odor of smoke beckoned from the bank below, where the barbecue and fish soup were coming along well.

Zabolotnov finished his thought: "What course has been set—for river or for man—is the one to follow."

The untidy mechanic reared up from behind, walked around the others and fired off, looking straight at the minister: "And do we have any say?"

The boss readily turned with a receptive look: "Of course you have a say. We have democracy now. That is what campaigns are for."

It seemed the mosquitoes avoided the cast-iron figure of the mechanic—was it because of his smell? But then they flew past Nikiforych, too, like one of their own.

"And when there's no campaign? When a bear tears a cow to death, he doesn't just eat it; he lets it lie around, so it has an aroma."

The minister didn't understand, and crossed his brows: "What question are you talking about?"

The unkempt portly mechanic stared familiarly at the equally portly, albeit taller and carefully coiffed, minister.

"We have questions piled up taller than that rye, which used to grow here. You want a question: How about the timber complex, why did they rip it into forty enterprises? Now they have all stopped. For every man there are three foremen, and all are out of work. Meanwhile, those who broke it up lined their pockets with millions. And not in rubles, either. They steal in a big way, not like us—and they know how to hide it and not get caught."

The modest captain looked at the mechanic with reproach, but the latter didn't see him. He had been afraid of his getting wound up and rabid, ruining everything. All was coming together, and the boss seemed amenable: So speak gently to him. And not about everything all in one go.

The minister's lips grew willfully curled. And for the first time he said in a scolding voice: "Without direct proof, you have no right to make such statements."

But Khripkin was not a bit fazed: "Make statements or not, no one will hear us. Now then—all that is left of the Angara is this middle stretch, so let it go to rot, too? Whoever had a brain could produce electricity just by turning wheels in the current, without any dams. Instead they put up a whole series of them. And now we're going to finish it off? The water is not even warm enough for the fish any longer."

Valentina Filippovna fixed her gaze on the minister. No, he wouldn't just ignore this, would he? Hadn't it touched him? How could he not be inspired by the doomed breadth of this proud river, standing here over this reach? He must be feeling something.

He was sure to be feeling the bites of the mosquitoes, because he kept slapping at them, but even then his arm didn't twitch nervously, as if sure that it would reach and crush its target.

As for this greasy troublemaker, you cannot explain everything to him—and why talk specifically to him, anyway?

The mosquitoes were getting the better of the others too, just when the ever-present Scepura quietly reported that the food was ready. But—with the mosquitoes, and not to invite extra people—why not repair to the salon?

They descended to the bank.

Nikiforych stood as he had stood, legs apart. No motion. No surprise.

Zdeshnev found a moment to say to him: "Maybe, old man, we will get somewhere with this."

The mechanic walked alongside the captain. They had not been invited to the salon.

"This tourist? No-o, Anatol Dmitrich, you need to know their type. They are not going to reverse anything, no matter what."

But the melancholy captain kept hope.

Valentina Filippovna walked uncertainly, head bent down, trying also not to trip on her heels.

Down by the bank the boss caught up with her and said quietly, with sympathy: "Don't be downcast. All your arguments have been noted. They are going to be taken into account."

She threw up her head toward the minister joyfully: "Thank you!"

The cutter reversed course and started upstream.

The bluffs along the bank reappeared in the distance, then drew closer. Later, a crag passed by.

Back in the salon, the men boisterously savored their fish soup, with vodka.

Scepura held court the loudest: "Oh yes, I was, you might say, a manager with a future. But now, they broke me under."

Who doesn't let loose a bit with vodka, served with soup and a barbecue? The minister's face grew softer, redder, even more youthful. In a high position, you simply have to comport yourself with dignity. But here, we're all people; and there is a hot meal, too.

"I had more troubles at work than you'd expect, for my age," roared Scepura, "but I don't skulk about it. And I hate to hear how people say now that *all that* was unnecessary, the wrong path. What do you mean, wrong path? What about all our victories? What about Bratsk and Ust-Ilimsk?!"

It made for a good riverboat tour, all in all. That evening, board the plane and fly to Moscow. Then, in a couple days, a trip abroad. All these arguments, these doubts—they make sense, too, of course. But he remembered, quite suddenly he recalled, the words of that woman: "the *latest* decree of the government." . . .

"When was that?" he asked of the Irkutsk fellow.

"Three months ago, in confirmation of the previous one."

We-e-l-l, what was the purpose, then, of lunging toward the top, contesting the point: You would only harm yourself.

After all, he knew the lay of the land in the halls of power. If a decision is adopted, and even reconfirmed, there is no changing it anyway, no matter what. All will proceed according to plan.

1993, 1995

4

THE OAK AND THE CALF

The *Oak and the Calf* is Solzhenitsyn's account of the predicament of a writer dedicated to telling the truth while harried by a totalitarian regime based on the ideological lie. Beyond fulfilling the informative purpose of memoirs, he shapes the sensational material of his most dramatic years into a work of art. Solzhenitsyn is the weak little calf of the title, butting its head against the immovable oak of state power—futilely, it would seem. But Solzhenitsyn, a self-styled "unshakable optimist," believed that in the end truth is stronger than falsehood. The Soviet Union did in fact collapse, and the calf's nudging helped.

Solzhenitsyn broke through the censors' filter with the appearance in 1962 of *One Day in the Life of Ivan Denisovich*, but soon thereafter he found his publishing window shut and official harassment of him increasing. So in 1967, he began keeping a record of his conflict with the authorities. As he surmised, they were keeping a record, too, which became public in 1995 under the title *The Solzhenitsyn Files*. The first installment of *Oak*, covering the events from 1961 on, ran to four chapters, of which "The Writer Underground" is the first. He added supplements in 1967, 1971, 1973, and 1974, then published the resulting "agglomeration of lean-tos and annexes" in 1975. Once the Soviet Union expired, Solzhenitsyn published *Invisible Allies*, which he had long withheld to protect those of his helpers who were identified by name. In the Russian edition, this work is now folded into *Oak* as the fifth and final supplement. To *Oak* are appended eighty pages of invaluable documents.

"The Writer Underground" establishes themes that run throughout the volume. An oppressive regime could deprive

Solzhenitsyn of the colleagueship on which a writer thrives and cause him to bury his words in a bottle in the ground. But he could retain his inner freedom and, transcending tit-for-tat combat, faithfully "try to see the present in the light of eternity." The chapter features the manifold thoughts that tumble through the underground writer's mind, carrying the plot only up to his dangerous decision to come "Out of Hiding" (the title of the second chapter).

The narrative pace picks up in subsequent chapters. They tell the stories of his breakthrough into print with *One Day*, confrontations with the Soviet Writers' Union that ended with his failure to get longer works published, battles with the regime over his controversial receipt of the Nobel Prize in Literature, increasingly ugly vilifications in the press and menacing actions by the secret police, and the capstone event of his arrest and exile in 1974. Aleksandr Tvardovsky, editor of the prominent literary journal *Novy Mir* and Solzhenitsyn's publisher, is richly characterized as tragically divided by his competing loyalties to Russian literature and the Communist Party. The friendship between him and Solzhenitsyn was genuine but complicated; the editor's pusillanimity and alcoholism frustrated the author.

Solzhenitsyn demonstrates a military strategist's boldness and cunning as he plays a life-or-death high-stakes game with monolithic state power. When he outfoxes the authorities, as he often does, he shows a boyish delight in winning against great odds. With equal candor he unsparingly chronicles his blunders. He remains amazingly productive throughout stress-filled years. A sense of invulnerability stemming from repeatedly outmaneuvering his foes cracks when the KGB finally moves in to arrest and deport him, and in this memorably narrated climactic episode, he admits to being "in a state of witless shock." But he quickly regains his emotional equilibrium, judges the calf's exertions to have been "worthwhile," and contentedly concludes, "I praised God for what I had been able to achieve."

The Oak and the Calf: Chapter I

The Writer Underground

Underground is where you expect to find revolutionaries. But not writers.

For the writer intent on truth, life never was, never is (and never will be!), easy: His like have suffered every imaginable harassment—defamation, duels, a shattered family life, financial ruin or lifelong unrelieved poverty, the madhouse, jail. While those who wanted for nothing, like Lev Tolstoy, have suffered worse torments in the claws of conscience.

All the same, to plunge underground, to make it your concern not to win the world's recognition—Heaven forbid!—but on the contrary to shun it: This variant of the writer's lot is peculiarly our own, purely Russian, Russian and Soviet! It is now certain that Radishchev[1] was writing something important in the last years of his life, and that he prudently kept it well hidden—hidden so well that we won't find it now and will never know what it was. Pushkin, too, cleverly enciphered the tenth chapter of *Eugene Onegin,* as everyone knows. That Chaadayev practiced cryptography for years is not so generally known. He distributed his manuscript sheet by sheet among a number of books in his large library. Of course, this is no way of hiding things if the Lubyanka comes looking; however many books there may be, it can always muster enough operatives to take every book by its spine and patiently worry it. (Never hide things in books, my friends!) But the Tsar's gendarmes had no eyes for such things. Chaadayev died, but his library remained intact into the postrevolutionary era, and the disjoined pages which no one knew of languished within it. In the twenties they were discovered, assembled, and studied, and in the thirties prepared at last for publication, by D. I. Shakhovskoy. But then Shakhovskoy was *put inside* (never to emerge) and Chaadayev's manuscripts are to this day kept secret in

---

[1] Founder of the Russian revolutionary tradition.

Pushkin House: Publication is now forbidden because of their *reactionary character!*

And so Chaadayev holds an unbeaten record—110 years after his death!—as the longest-suppressed Russian writer! What a piece of writing this must have been!

Much freer times followed. Russian writers no longer wrote "for the desk drawer" but could publish whatever they liked (and only critics and publicists used carefully chosen Aesopian language). So freely did they write, so free were they to rock the framework of the state, that Russian literature, no other, nurtured all those young people who conceived a hatred for the Tsar and the gendarmes, took up revolution, and carried it through.

But once across the threshold of the revolutions it had summoned into being, literature stopped short; it found itself not in the sparkling daylight beneath the open sky, but under a sloping ceiling, in the narrowing space between converging walls. Soviet writers very quickly discovered that not every book can *get through.* Ten years or so later, they had discovered that royalties may take the form of barred windows and barbed wire. Once more writers started concealing what they had written, although they did not utterly despair of seeing their books in print before they died.

Before I was arrested, I knew very little about such things. I drifted into literature unthinkingly, without really knowing what I needed from it, or what I could do for it. I just felt depressed because it was so difficult, I thought, to find fresh subjects for stories. I hate to think what sort of writer I would have become (for I would have gone on writing) if I had not been *put inside.*

Once arrested, once I had spent two years in prisons and camps, depressed now by the mountainous overabundance of subjects, I accepted as effortlessly as the air I breathed, accepted with all the other unchallengeable realities before my eyes, the knowledge that not only would no one ever publish me, but a single line could cost me my life. Without hesitation, without inner debate, I entered into the inheritance of every modern Russian writer intent on the truth: I must write simply to ensure that it was not all forgotten, that posterity might someday come to know of it. Publication in my own lifetime I must shut out of my mind, out of my dreams.

I put away my idle dream. And in its place there was only the surety that my work would not be in vain, that it would someday smite the heads I had in my sights, and that those who received its invisible emanations would understand. I no more rebelled against lifelong silence than against the lifelong impossibility of freeing my feet from the pull of gravity. As I finished one piece after another, at first in the camps, then in exile, then after rehabilitation, first verses, then plays, and later prose works too, I had only one desire: to keep all these things out of sight and myself with them.

In the camp this meant committing my verse—many thousands of lines—to memory. To help me with this I improvised decimal counting beads and, in transit prisons, broke up matchsticks and used the fragments as tallies. As I approached the end of my sentence I grew more confident of my powers of memory, and began writing down and memorizing prose—dialogue at first, but then, bit by bit, whole densely written passages. My memory found room for them! It worked. But more and more of my time—in the end as much as one week every month—went into the regular repetition of all I had memorized.

Then came exile, and right at the beginning of my exile, cancer. In autumn 1953 it looked very much as though I had only a few months to live. In December the doctors—comrades in exile—confirmed that I had at most three weeks left.

All that I had memorized in the camps ran the risk of extinction together with the head that held it.

This was a dreadful moment in my life: to die on the threshold of freedom, to see all I had written, all that gave meaning to my life thus far, about to perish with me. The peculiarities of the Soviet postal censorship made it impossible for me to cry out for help: Come quickly, take what I have written, save it! You can't very well appeal to strangers anyway. My friends were all in camps themselves. My mother was dead. My wife had married again. All the same, I sent for her to say goodbye, thinking that she might take my manuscripts away with her, but she did not come.

In those last few weeks that the doctors had promised me, I could not escape from my work in school, but in the evening and at night, kept awake by pain, I hurriedly copied things out in tiny handwriting, rolled them, several pages at a time, into tight cylinders, and squeezed these into a champagne bottle. I buried the bottle in my garden—and set off for Tashkent to meet the new year (1954) and to die.

I did not die, however. (With a hopelessly neglected and acutely malignant tumor, this was a divine miracle; I could see no other explanation. Since then, all the life that has been given back to me has not been mine in the full sense: It is built around a purpose.) That spring as I deliriously took possession of the life restored to me (perhaps only for two or three years?), in the first flush of my happiness I wrote *The Republic of Labor*. This I did not try to memorize: For the first time I knew the joy of not having to burn a work piecemeal as I learned it by heart; the joy of writing *Finis* with the beginning still undestroyed, of being able to survey the play as a whole, of making a fair copy of each successive draft, correcting it and copying it again.

But when I had destroyed the rough copies, how was I to preserve the final draft? A fortuitous suggestion, and some timely help from outside, took me along a new path: It appeared that I must master a new trade, must learn to make *hidey holes*, some farther away, some near to hand, where my papers, finished or in production, would be safe not only from a casual thief but from the perfunctory inspections to which exiles were subjected. As though I had too little to do, with my thirty hours of teaching, and my administrative duties at school, and my bachelor cookery (my secret life as a writer made it impossible for me to marry)— as though writing underground were not difficult enough in itself, I must now learn a new skill: that of hiding what I had written.

One new skill led to another: that of microfilming my manuscripts for myself (without a single electric light bulb and under a sun that hardly ever retired behind the clouds). The microfilms were then fitted into the covers of a book, in two envelopes addressed to Aleksandra Lvovna Tolstoy, at her farm in the USA. I knew nobody else in the West, not a single publisher, but I felt sure that Tolstoy's daughter would not deny me her help.

You read about the front line, or about the underground, when you are a boy and you wonder where people found such desperate courage. You cannot imagine yourself enduring so much. That was what I thought as I read Remarque *(All Quiet on the Western Front)* in the thirties, but when I got to the front myself I came to the conclusion that it is all much less difficult, that you gradually begin to feel at home even there, and that writers make it seem much more frightening than it really is.

It is the same with the underground. If you are plunged into it suddenly and find yourself wearing a black mask and taking a solemn oath or signing your name in blood by the light of a red lantern, it is no doubt very frightening. But a man whom family life has long ago rejected, who lacks foundations on which to build a solid existence (even if he still wanted to), who has only his inner life, can learn one new shift after another, find hiding place after hiding place, make contacts which lead to new contacts, get used to code words in letters or at rendezvous, know some people only by nicknames and communicate with others through a chain of intermediaries, until he wakes up one morning and thinks: Well, I'll be damned! I've been underground all this time without realizing it!

It is mortifying, of course, to have to go underground not for the revolution but merely for the sake of literature.

The years went by, I was released from my place of exile, I moved to Central Russia, married, was rehabilitated and permitted to lead a life of modest comfort and degrading conformity—but I was by now just as accustomed to the cryptoliterary underworld as to the smooth surface of my life as a teacher. Whatever problems arose—which draft to consider final, what completion date to aim at, how many copies to type, what size paper to choose, how to squeeze more lines on the page, what typewriter to use, where to put the copies afterward—I could not breathe freely while they answered themselves, like the writer who has only to complete his work, feast his eyes on it, and move on. No, for the underground writer all these problems meant hard and anxious calculation: where and how the work is to be kept, under what cover it will be transported, what new hiding places must be devised as the volume of writings and of copies steadily grows.

Volume indeed was the most important thing—not creative output measured in thousands of words, but bulk in cubic centimeters.

My still unimpaired eyesight, my naturally minute "onion seed" handwriting, and the especially thin paper which I sometimes managed to bring back from Moscow were all a great help. I made things still easier for myself by destroying outright all rough drafts, outlines, and superseded versions; by typing as tightly as possible, leaving no space between lines and using both sides of the paper; and by burning the fair copy of the manuscript as soon as the copying was finished (since I first began writing in jail, I had put my trust in fire alone). This method was followed for my novel *The First Circle*, my story *Shch-854*,[2] and my film script *Tanks Know the Truth*, to mention nothing earlier.[3]

Some of these precautions, of course, proved not to have been strictly necessary, but God helps those who help themselves. It was statistically almost unthinkable that the Cheka-KGB might suddenly come crashing into my apartment for no better reason than that I was an ex-zek; there were millions of ex-zeks around, after all.[4] But I was guided by the proverb "The woodpecker could hide in the forest but for his beak."

I had to adapt my whole life to the need for tight security; make no friends or acquaintances at all in Ryazan, where I had recently gone to live; invite nobody to my home and accept no invitations—because if I did, it would be impossible to claim later on that I never had a single hour free, not one in a month or even in a year, not even on public holidays, or when I was on vacation. I could not afford to let any scrap of what I had hidden escape from the apartment, or allow an observant eye inside for a moment. My wife observed my rules strictly, and I greatly appreciated this. Among my colleagues at work I took care never to reveal any broader interests, and always to make a show of indifference to literature ("hostile" literary activity had been one of the charges brought against me at the time of my arrest in 1945, and KGB agents might be keeping me

---

[2] Original title of *One Day in the Life of Ivan Denisovich*. It refers to the prison identification number of the protagonist.

[3] I could have wept when I destroyed the original of my film script. It had been written in very special circumstances. But one anxious evening I had to burn it. The job was made much easier by the fact that my Ryazan apartment was heated by a stove. With central heating, burning a manuscript would have given me much more trouble. [Author's note.]

[4] But if they had descended, death, and nothing less, is what I could have expected, unknown and defenseless as I then was. The reader will be able to convince himself of this when, someday, he reads the complete original text of *The First Circle* (in ninety-six chapters). [Author's note.]

under observation to see whether or not I had cooled off in this respect). And finally, though at every step in my daily life I collided with conceited, rude, stupid, and greedy bureaucrats of every degree and in every institution, and though I sometimes saw a chance to crash through a barrier and sweep away the rubbish with a well-aimed complaint or a determined protest, I could never allow myself to do so, never take half a step out of line in the direction of rebellion, of resistance, but had always to be a model Soviet citizen, always to submit to every bully and acquiesce in any stupidity.

The pig that keeps its head down grubs up the deepest root.

It was not at all easy! I might as well be in exile still, or back in the camp wearing the same old number patches, still unable to hold my head up or straighten my back, owing obedience to every pair of epaulets.

My indignation could safely boil over in the book I was writing at the time—but I would not allow that either, because the laws of poetry command us to rise above our anger and try to see the present in the light of eternity.

But all this tribute I paid without a murmur: Even under these conditions I was working solidly and well, though I had little enough spare time and no genuine peace and quiet. It was a strange experience for me to hear prosperous, leisured, famous writers on the radio, instructing listeners on methods of achieving concentration at the beginning of a working day, telling them that it is most important to eliminate all distractions, and especially important to surround yourself with congenial objects. I myself had learned long ago in the camp to compose and to write as I marched in a column under escort; out on the frozen steppe; in an iron foundry; in the hubbub of a prison hut. A soldier can squat on the ground and fall asleep immediately, a dog in freezing weather is as snug in his own shaggy coat as he would be by a stove, and I was equipped by nature to write anywhere.

Now that I was free I had become fussier (the human spirit is subject to the law of compression and decompression). I was disturbed by the radio and by people talking, but even so, even to the accompaniment of the constant roar of trucks hurtling toward my window in Ryazan, I acquired the knack of writing a screenplay. All I needed was an hour or two of continuous free time! God had spared me creative crises, fits of despair, and impotence.

Throughout these years as an underground writer—five years in the camp before my illness, seven years of exile and then of freedom, my "second life" after my astounding recovery—my mood, my state of mind, which I would almost call one of exultant happiness, hardly varied. The shrill, vainglorious literature of the establishment—with its dozen fat magazines, its two literary newspapers, its innumerable anthologies, its novels between hard covers, its collected works, its annual prizes, its adaptations for radio of impossibly tedious originals—I had once and for all recognized as unreal, and I did not waste my time or exasperate myself by trying to keep up with it. I knew without looking that there could be nothing of merit in all this. Not because no talent could emerge there—no doubt it sometimes did, but there it perished too. For it was a barren field, that which they sowed. I knew that in such a field nothing could grow to maturity. When they first came to literature they had, all of them—the social novelists, the bombastic playwrights, the civic poets, and needless to say the journalists and critics joined in an undertaking never, whatever the subject, whatever the issue, to mention the essential truth, the truth that leaps to the eye with no help from literature. This solemn pledge to abstain from truth was called socialist realism. Even writers of love poems, even those lyric poets who had sought sanctuary in nature or in elegant romanticism, were all fatally flawed because they dared not touch the important truths.

Moreover, I lived through those years as an underground writer in the conviction that I was not the only aloof and cunning one. That there were dozens of stubborn, self-contained individuals like me—each of us writing, with honor and conscience as his guides, all that he knew about our age, the essential truth about it, which is not entirely made up of prisons, executions, camps, and places of exile, but which cannot be told in full if you overlook them. Yes, dozens and dozens of us, all suffering from lack of air—but for the present it was impossible for us to come out into the open and reveal ourselves even to each other. When the time came we should all emerge simultaneously from the depths of the sea, like the Three and Thirty Heroes of Pushkin's tale *Tsar Saltan*—and this was how the great literature that we had scuttled at the time of the Great Break, or earlier, would rise again.

A third belief of mine was that we, the host in gleaming casques, would rise from the sea only posthumously and figuratively. Our books, preserved by faithful and ingenious friends, would rise and not our bodies: We ourselves should be long dead. I had not as yet come to believe that an upheaval in our society might be caused by literature, might begin in literature (though this was surely the very lesson that Russian literature should have taught us). I thought that society would be shaken and even renewed for other reasons, that when a fissure appeared, a breach opening onto freedom, our underground literature would at once push its way through to explain to perplexed and troubled minds why things could not have been otherwise, to trace the tangled threads back to 1917.

The years went by, and it began to look as though I had been mistaken in all three of my beliefs.

The field of literature proved not quite so barren as I had thought. Try as they might to leach all nutriment out of the soil, all moisture, everything that sustains life—life still broke through. Who can deny the vitality of Tvardovsky's "Tyorkin in the Next World" or of the peasants in Zalygin's "Krutye Luchiny"? How can we deny that there is life in the names of Shukshin, Mozhayev, Yevgeny Nosov, Tendryakov, Belov, Maksimov, and even Soloukhin? Or that Yuri Kazakov would be a powerful writer of lasting worth if he would look the great truths in the face? There are other names I could list, but this is not the place. And there are bold young poets besides. But in my too general view, the Writers' Union, which in its day had refused membership to Tsvetayeva, anathematized Zamyatin, treated Bulgakov with contempt, ostracized Akhmatova and Pasternak, seen from the underground was a veritable Sodom and Gomorrah, or a rabble of hucksters and moneychangers littering and defiling the temple, whose stalls must be overturned and they themselves scourged and driven into the outer porch. I was surprised and overjoyed to find myself mistaken.

I was mistaken in my second prophecy too, but this time to my sorrow. We were after all rather few—secret and stubborn, yes, and fortunate men. We should never add up to a whole literature. The Cheka had swept with a stiffer broom than I had thought. How many fine minds, perhaps even geniuses, had been ground into the earth, as though they had never been, with nothing to show for their lives? (Or are there some still more obstinate and cunning than we were? Are they still, today, writing away in silence, keeping their heads down, because they know that the hour of freedom is not yet at hand? It may be so. If my story had been told in the Prose Section a year or two earlier, who would have believed it?)

Varlam Shalamov put out his leaves at the very first sign of spring: He believed in the promise of the Twentieth Congress and dispatched his verses along the pioneer trails that samizdat was blazing. I read them in summer 1956, trembling as I recognized a brother! One of the secret brothers of whose existence I knew beyond doubt. I had a chance, through some intermediaries, to confide in him there and then, but I was less trusting than he was, and besides, I had still a great deal to get on paper and my health and my age allowed me to be patient —so I kept silent and went on writing.

I was mistaken in my third belief too. We began to emerge from the black, bottomless waters much sooner than I had expected, to emerge in our own lifetime. I lived to enjoy the happiness of peeping out and shying the first pebbles at Goliath's stupid brow. The brow was undamaged, the pebbles bounced off, but as they fell to the ground they blossomed into break-herb,[5] and people greeted them with joy or hatred; none passed by heedlessly.

Later, by contrast, the pace slackened. Life dragged on like a lingering cold spring. History began to cast loop after nooselike loop of complications, hoping to lasso every one of us, and strangle as many as possible. Things moved so sluggishly (just as we should have expected) that we no longer had any choice: There was nothing for it but to hurl a few last stones, with our last remaining strength, at that impenetrable brow.

Yes, yes, of course—we all know that you cannot poke a stick through the walls of a concrete tower, but here's something to think about: What if those walls are only a painted backdrop?

---

[5] Magical plant in Russian folklore with the power to burst open locks and thus to unseal otherwise inaccessible passages.

Looking back, even a fool would be able to predict it today: The Soviet regime could certainly have been breached only by literature. The regime has been reinforced with concrete to such an extent that neither a military coup nor a political organization nor a picket line of strikers can knock it over or run it through. Only the solitary writer would be able to do this. And the Russian younger generation would move on into the breach.

Obvious? Yet no one foresaw it, either in the thirties or in the fifties. That's the trouble with the future: It slips away and eludes us.

For twelve years I quietly wrote and wrote. Only in the thirteenth did I falter. This was in spring 1960. I had written so many things, all quite unpublishable, all doomed to complete obscurity, that I felt clogged and supersaturated, and began to lose my buoyancy of mind and movement. I was beginning to suffer from lack of air in the literary underground.

The underground writer's enormous advantage is freedom to write as he likes: He needs to keep neither censors nor editors in his mind's eye, nothing confronts him except his material, nothing hovers anxiously over him except the truth. But there is in his position one inevitable drawback: lack of readers, and above all exacting readers of refined literary sensitivity. The underground writer chooses his readers (I had about a dozen of them, mostly former zeks, and I did not manage to show all my work to any one of them: We lived in different towns, none of us had time or money to spend on travel, nor spare rooms to put up visitors) by quite different criteria: political reliability and ability to keep quiet. These two qualities rarely keep company with refined artistic taste. So that the underground writer hears no rigorous criticism based on a knowledge of the best in contemporary literature. It seems, however, that every writer sorely needs such criticism, needs sober assistance in plotting the position of his work in the universe of art, even if it is only at intervals of five or even ten years. Pushkin's advice to the "exacting artist"—to be content if he himself is satisfied with his work—is very sound, but not the last word on the subject. When you have been writing for ten or twelve years in impenetrable solitude, you begin without realizing it to let yourself go, to indulge yourself, or simply to lose your eye for jarring invective, for bombast, for banal conventional joints where you should have found a firmer fastening.

Later, when I popped up from underground and began *lightening* my works for the outside world, lightening them of all that my fellow countrymen could hardly be expected to accept at once, I discovered to my surprise that a piece only gained, that its effect was heightened, as the harsher tones were softened; and I began to discover the places where I had let myself off too easily, putting in a chipped and crumbling brick instead of an intact and fireproof one. From my first contact with the professional literary milieu I knew that I must pull myself together!

In my complete ignorance I had fallen particularly short of the mark in my plays. When I took to writing plays in the camp, then in exile, I had in mind the only theatrical productions I had ever seen—in provincial Rostov in the thirties—which even then were on a level that world theater had long left behind. Convinced as I was that what matters most in creative art is truthfulness and experience of life, I did not appreciate that *forms* become obsolete, that tastes in the twentieth century change abruptly and cannot be ignored by any author. Now, after visiting Moscow theaters in the sixties (no longer, alas, theaters for actors or even playwrights, but theaters in which directors are almost the sole creators of the performance), I regret having written plays.[6]

In 1960 I could not have diagnosed or explained all this precisely, but I felt myself growing stale while my already sizable bundle of writing was going to waste—and I began to feel a sort of fidgety need to stretch and move around. Since there could be no movement, since I dared not stir an inch in any direction, I began to pine: My cleverly planned, soundless, and invisible literary enterprise had fetched up in a blind alley.

Shortly before his death Tolstoy wrote that it is always immoral for a writer to publish in his own lifetime. We should, he thinks, write only for the future, and let our works be published "posthumously." Tolstoy reached his pious conclusions on this as on all else only after making the full round of sins and passions, but in any case, what he says is untrue even for slower epochs, and still more so for our swift-moving times. He is right that the thirst for repeated successes with the public spoils a writer's work. But it is even more damaging to be denied readers for years on end—demanding readers, hostile readers, delighted readers—to be denied all opportunity to influence the world about you, to influence the rising generation, with your pen. Quiescence means purity—but also irresponsibility. Tolstoy's judgment is ill-considered.

The new works being printed, which till then had merely amused me, now began to irritate me. It was just then that Ehrenburg's and Paustovsky's memoirs appeared, and I sent a sharp review to various journals—rejected, of course, by all of them, because nobody had ever heard of me. In form, my article looked like an attack on memoir literature generally, but its real purpose was to express my exasperation with writers who had seen the great dark epoch, and yet were forever trying to sidle round it, ignoring the things that mattered most, telling us nothing but trivialities, sealing our eyes with emollients till we no longer saw the truth. Why should they be so afraid, these established writers whom nothing threatens?

That autumn, pacing my den, with the strength going out of me, I applied my mind to the problem of writing something that, even if it could not be pub-

---

[6] Shalamov's prose has also, in my opinion, suffered from the fact that he worked for many years in seclusion. It could have been much improved, with no change in the range of material or the author's viewpoint. [Author's note.]

lished, could at least be shown to people! at least not be hidden! So I had the idea of writing *Candle in the Wind,* a play about today, but set in no particular country: a play about any prosperous society, East or West, in our decade.

This play, the least successful thing I ever wrote, was also the most difficult. More precisely, I realized for the first time how a piece of work may stubbornly refuse to come right, even after four or five rewritings: You can throw out whole scenes and replace them with others—and it still looks hopelessly artificial. I spent a great deal of labor on it and thought I had finished—but no, it was still no good. I had based it on the true story of a particular Moscow family; I had not cheated once; I had expressed only ideas I sincerely held, many of which I had long cherished, refusing right from the first act to humor the censors—why, then, was it such a failure? Could it possibly be because I had avoided a specifically Russian setting—not at all for purposes of camouflage, and not merely to ensure that it need not be hidden, but to give it a more general significance: It was even more relevant to the fat, complacent West than to us—and that off Russian ground I am doomed to lose my feel for the Russian language? But others write easily in this faceless, tongueless style and it comes off, so why can't I? Obviously, some writers have no gift for generalization, just as others have no talent for the specific. You can't take abstraction just so far, and from then on write concretely. (But perhaps the main reason for failure was the insubstantiality of the female character.)

I made another attempt in 1961, without clearly realizing what I was doing. For no particular reason, I simply took *Shch-854* and copied it out in a "lightened" version, leaving out the roughest episodes and expressions of opinion, and also the long story that the captain second class tells Tsezar about the way Americans were taken in by our faked prosperity at Sebastopol in 1945. I did it for no clear reason—and put it aside. But I let it lie without concealment. What a happy state to be in, what a feeling of freedom it gave me—not racking my brains to find a hiding place for a newly finished work, but simply keeping it in my desk drawer: a reason for happiness that writers do not sufficiently appreciate. I had never once gone to bed without making sure that everything was hidden, and rehearsing my behavior in case there was a knock in the night.

All my secrecy was beginning to wear me out, and it created problems more head-splitting than any that arose from my writing. But there was no relief in sight from any quarter, and the Western radio, which I always listened to in spite of jamming, as yet knew nothing of the deep subterranean shifts and fissures which were soon to produce a quake on the surface. No one knew anything, and I had nothing good to look forward to, when I began polishing and revising *The First Circle.* After the drab Twenty-First Congress, which damped and muted the splendid promise of the Twentieth, there was no way of foreseeing the sudden fury, the reckless eloquence of the attack on Stalin which Khrushchev would decide upon for the Twenty-Second! Nor, try as we might, could we, the uninitiated, ever explain it! But there it was—and not even a secret attack, as at the

Twentieth Congress, but a public one! I could not remember when I had read anything as interesting as the speeches at the Twenty-Second Congress. In my little room in a decaying wooden house where one unlucky match might send all my manuscripts, years and years of work, up in smoke, I read and reread those speeches, and the walls of my secret world swayed like curtains in the theater, wavered, expanded, and carried me queasily with them: Had it arrived, then, the long-awaited moment of terrible joy, the moment when my head must break water?

I must make no mistake! I must not thrust out my head too soon. But equally, I must not let this rare moment pass me by!

There was also a good speech at the Twenty-Second Congress from Tvardovsky, and one theme he touched on was that although it had long since been possible to publish more freely and boldly, "we do not take advantage of the opportunity." *Novy Mir*, he hinted, might publish bolder and more polemical things, if only it had them.

I did not distinguish the Tvardovsky who had written *Muravia* from the general run of poets who swung the censers of falsehood. And I knew none of his memorable individual poems: I had discovered none when I looked through his 1954 two-volume collected works in my place of exile. But long ago, at the front, I had taken note of *Vasily Tyorkin* as a remarkable feat: Long before the appearance of the first truthful books about the war (since Nekrasov's *In the Trenches of Stalingrad*, not so many of them have succeeded—perhaps half a dozen in all), amid the fume and crackle of gibbering propaganda which always accompanied our bombardments, Tvardovsky had succeeded in writing something timeless, courageous, and unsullied, helped by a rare sense of proportion, all his own, or perhaps by a sensitive tact not uncommon among peasants. (This sensitivity beneath the coarsened and uncouth peasant exterior, and in spite of the hardships of peasant life, never ceases to astonish me.) Though he was not free to tell the whole truth about the war, Tvardovsky nevertheless always stopped just one millimeter short of falsehood, and nowhere did he ever overstep the one-millimeter mark. The result was a miracle. I am not speaking only for myself; I had excellent opportunities to observe its effects on soldiers in my battery during the war. It was the peculiarity of our job as a sound-ranging unit that they had a great deal of time, even in combat conditions, to listen to readings (at night, at field signal posts, while someone would read from the communications center). Of the many things offered them, they obviously had a special preference for *War and Peace* and *Vasily Tyorkin*.

But lack of leisure in the camp, in exile, as a teacher, and underground had prevented me from reading "The House by the Roadside" or any of his other work. (I did read "Tyorkin in the Next World," in manuscript copies, in 1956. Samizdat always had first claim on my attention.) I did not even know that a chapter of *New Horizons* had been published in *Pravda*, and that the poem had received a Lenin Prize that year. I read the poem as a whole much later, the chapter "Thus It Was" when I came across it in *Novy Mir*. As things then were, in the atmosphere of general timidity, it looked daring: Auntie Darya's night work; "Hurrah, he'll get it right again"; and even "Like some strange fairground fantasy, skyscraping Moscow rose before me. . . ." As long ago as that, I had felt my first impulse to show some of my writing to Tvardovsky. Should I risk it? But leafing through the same chapter and reflecting on it, I also encountered the "stern father," who was "unjust" yet "just," and found that to him, too, we "owed our victory"; learned of Stalin's affinity with "martial steel," and that

> In history's golden book of fame
> No doubtful comma, not a crooked line
> Shall cast a shadow on our name.
> What's done is done. . . .

This was a little too bland: Had forty shameful years of camps cast no shadow on our honor? A little too smooth: "What's done is done"; "there's nothing we can do, or undo." The same could be said about fascism in all its forms. Perhaps Nuremberg was unnecessary? What's done is done. . . ? An impotent philosophy, that does not venture to pronounce judgment on history.[7] The poet's foot cautiously explored the ground beside the paved highway, but he dared not step off it.

What would he do if I struggled out of the quagmire, hand outstretched: Step down and help me! Would he come—or would he hang back?

Nor was *Novy Mir* clearly distinguished in my mind from other journals: Judging by the content of its main pages, I saw little difference between it and them. (The contrasts among the magazines that they themselves discerned were trivial in my eyes and are still more so in historical perspective—whether you look backward or forward.) All these magazines used the same terminology, the same oaths and adjurations, and none of this could I take even by the teaspoonful.

---

[7] Lydia Chukovskaya, in her *Notes on Anna Akhmatova*, recalls how angry Tvardovsky's chapter "Childhood Friend" had made Akhmatova five years earlier: "New lies for old!" she exclaimed.

> "Our country? Why bring the country into it?
> The people? The people had no part in it."

Ah, but the poet was one with the zek—

> "Had sampled it all, and eaten the same bread"—

while the zek

> "With an invitation card like mine
> Was the Kremlin's no less welcome guest!"

Yes, a useful escape ladder of lies for 1956. [Author's note.]

But the muffled rumble of subterranean strata, which broke through into the Twenty-Second Congress, must have had some meaning. I made up my mind to it. I had never known what prompted me to "lighten" *Shch-854,* or what purpose it could serve, but this was where it proved useful. I decided to submit it to *Novy Mir.* (But for this, something worse would have happened. A whole year of claustrophobic nausea had worn me down to the point at which I must break out.)

I did not go to *Novy Mir* myself. My legs simply would not carry me, since I foresaw no success. I was already forty-three, and I had knocked about the world too much to call on an editor like a boy with his first story. My prison friend Lev Kopelev undertook to hand the manuscript in. Although there were six author's sheets of it, it made quite a slim packet: typed, of course, on both sides, with no margins, and no spaces at all between lines.

I handed it over—and was gripped by the agitation, not of an ambitious young author, but of a hard-bitten camp veteran who has been incautious enough to leave a trail.

This was at the beginning of November 1961. I had never been near a Moscow hotel, but on this occasion I took advantage of the slack season just before the holiday and obtained a bed. There I lived through days of last-minute waverings and indecision—and I still had time to stop the story, to ask for it back. (I stayed on not because of my indecision, but to read a samizdat copy of *For Whom the Bell Tolls,* lent to me for three days. Until then I had not read a single line of Hemingway.)

The hotel, as it happened, was in Ostankino, right next to the *sharashka* in which the action of *The First Circle* takes place, and where, with my first experience of prison, I began writing seriously. In the intervals of reading Hemingway I went out and strolled along the fence around my old *sharashka.* It stood just as it had then, its unchanged perimeter enclosing the same tiny space in which so many outstandingly able people were once squeezed to-gether, and which had seethed with our debates and our ingenious schemes.

I strolled about now some ten meters from the bishop's arklike house, and those old linden trees, those immortal lindens under which I had paced back and forth, back and forth, back and forth, morning, noon, and night, for three years on end, dreaming of freedom's bright distant dawn in other and brighter years, and in a brighter Russia.

Now, on a clammy overcast day, in the sloppy November snow, I walked on the other side of the fence, along a path by which only guards on their way to relieve comrades on the watchtower had trudged in the old days, and I thought: What have I done? I have put myself in their hands again.

How could I, with no one forcing me, have come to inform against my-self? . . .

THE FIRST CIRCLE

Solzhenitsyn's autobiographical and much-admired *The First Circle* is his first full-length novel. Although the complete Russian text has been available for years, the only version available in English since its publication in 1968 has been an eighty-seven chapter version, which Solzhenitsyn had "lightened" in the vain hope that it would pass muster with the Soviet censors. Only in 2005 did Harry Willetts, shortly before he died, complete the authorized English translation of the full ninety-six chapter version. Excerpts from this text appear here for the first time. With these selections it is now possible for English-language readers to begin considering how the newly available material changes the novel.

Of the nine chapters presented below, three (2, 47, and 61) are entirely new in English, and two others (1 and 26) are significantly amplified. Six of the nine are presented uncut, and three (47, 60, and 61) are excerpted. The hitherto-missing parts substantially revise three characters—Volodin, Sologdin, and Nerzhin—who are indubitably among the novel's principal figures. Also included here are three other significant figures—Rubin, Spiridon, and Avenir. Sticking to chapters about this limited cast is designed to facilitate a coherent reading experience.

The novel is set during December 24–27, 1949, and the main action occurs on prison grounds near Moscow that originally encompassed a seminary. The religious overtones of these time and place settings, along with the title (drawn from Dante's *Inferno*), provide the groundwork for a novel about conflicting sets of beliefs. Soviet authorities had turned the ecclesiastical site into a *sharashka*, an institution where incarcerated scientists and technologists were required to work on secret state projects in exchange for better provisions and gentler treatment than others received in the gulag system. The large cast comprises a cross section of society, including persons inside and outside the *sharashka* and historical personages (such as Stalin) alongside fictional characters.

The novel's structure is polyphonic. Thus, various major and minor characters take turns as the central consciousness for a chapter or more and, though retaining the third-person narration of the novel as a whole, are able to impart their points of view. This technique facilitates the presentation of clashing worldviews. Gleb Nerzhin, the author's alter ego, embodies Solzhenitsyn's own intellectual grapplings during his four years in the Marfino *sharashka*. Fellow *zeks* Lev Rubin and Dmitri Sologdin—based on the real-life Lev Kopelev and Dimitri Panin, respectively—provide foils for Gleb. Both Kopelev and Panin, in books of their own, vouch for the accuracy of Solzhenitsyn's self-portrait in the character of Nerzhin.

The intense but respectful conversations among these three intellectual inmates advance the central theme of the novel, namely, what it means to become a truly human being. Rubin remains an unreconstructed Communist, whereas Sologdin is an iconoclastic contrarian. Nerzhin skeptically resists all ready-made worldviews; his characterization features his quest for a point of view of his own, a process that emphasizes actively cultivating one's own soul. Innokentii Volodin, a Soviet diplomat and the most important fictional character outside the *sharashka*, similarly finds his settled beliefs failing and in need of replacement. Every other personage, as well, from Stalin on down, is responsible above all else for developing his innate humanity within the intrinsically dehumanizing setting of the Soviet system. In keeping with the moral principle that ideas and actions have consequences, each character's thoughts and deeds push toward one side or the other the line dividing good and evil that cuts through every human heart; some characters spiritually blossom but more shrivel.

The characterization that suffered the most from the "lightening" process is that of Volodin. His recorded telephone call in chapter 1 becomes the test case in the task assigned to some prisoners of developing technology to identify callers by voice-prints; this assignment sets in motion the "detective-story" plot line linking characters inside and outside the *sharashka*. In the "lightened" version Innokentii tries to caution a doctor acquaintance against imperiling himself by sharing an experimental drug with Westerners he is about to visit. In the undistorted version, however, Innokentii has learned that a Soviet spy in New York is about to pick up classified information on atomic technology. The comfortable insider, no longer able to suppress his awareness that he operates within a criminal, totalitarian regime, now faces a stark moral dilemma: Should he act on this news? He decides to place a telephone call of warning to the US Embassy. Acting out of a sense of the highest responsibility imaginable causes him to commit the highest crime imaginable: nothing less than treason. Chapter 2 shows what he is up against. Spiritless, mindless functionaries who ceaselessly monitor phone calls are cogs in the fail-safe machinery of ruthless oppression, which now begins to grind him up.

Volodin's role as the opening chapter's central consciousness establishes his status as a major character, and subsequent, previously suppressed chapters supply new insights into his moral development that raise his profile further. Called an Epicurean by friends, he decides to brush up on the old master but is distracted when he stumbles upon letters written by his now-dead mother. He had admired his absent father because of the man's storied exploits on the Bolshevik side of the Civil War. His mother had seemed, by comparison, anxious and weak. Yet her letters now reveal her independent life and thoughts. She cherished—and capitalized—ideas rendered archaic by the Revolution: "Truth, Goodness, Beauty, Good and Evil, the Ethical Imperative." Innokentii's newly attained frame of mind opens him to receiving from her a posthumous message bespeaking the traditional outlook of prerevolutionary Russia.

Eager to learn more, Volodin seeks out his mother's brother, Uncle Avenir (who does not appear in the shortened text of *The First Circle*). A man of simple habits and free mind, Avenir imparts a heretical assessment of the Bolshevik Revolution. Innokentii comes to see that his father has done to his mother, in microcosm, what the Bolsheviks had done to Mother Russia. Avenir concludes by invoking the biblical concept (also used elsewhere by Solzhenitsyn) that the sins of the parents are visited on the children and exhorting Innokentii to "cleanse yourself of them." As the novel ebbs, Innokentii scrambles to find resources beyond Epicureanism that will allow him to face his imminent descent into the hell of the gulag with equanimity.

Sologdin is second only to Volodin in the alterations of character effected by the complete version. No longer can Sologdin be considered merely an eccentric advocate of extreme individualism. Rather, his critique of collectivism is grounded in his hearty commitment to Christianity. As he watches Nerzhin moving away from Marxism, he confidently predicts that Nerzhin "will come to God"—not God in a general sense but "a concrete Christian God"—and to an acceptance of every Christian dogma, including the Trinity and the Immaculate Conception.

The main change in Gleb Nerzhin comes with the delineation in chapter 47 of a key step in his intellectual odyssey. A brief excerpt suffices to shows how definitively he has broken with Marxism. Initially reduced to skepticism, Nerzhin now denies that justice is relative or merely class-based and asserts, instead, that justice is "the foundation of the universe" and that we are "born with a sense of justice in our souls." Although giving thought to absolutes and universals suggests some movement in Sologdin's direction, Nerzhin stops short of embracing Christianity. This vital excerpt becomes part of the context for Nerzhin's subsequent reflections about his intellectual odyssey in chapter 66. The erstwhile Marxist examines the appeal of the longstanding Russian idea that wisdom resides in the peasantry, who in this view are the purest repositories of the Russian spirit. Yet he has learned from observation that the peasants are not in all ways morally superior, and so he decides that his only path to becoming a fully actualized human being is to think for himself and in that way to fashion his own soul. Nerzhin's odyssey holds promise of further growth; it also remains open-ended.

Although Spiridon and Rubin remain the same in the "lightened" and the complete texts, they are intrinsically important characters whose presence gives novelistic context to the changes in Sologdin and Nerzhin. Spiridon embodies, just as Ivan Denisovich and Matryona do in their eponymous stories, "the people" to whom Nerzhin considers going for wisdom. Rubin, far from being a stick-figure representation of a viewpoint, is a fully realized character who receives about as much space as Nerzhin. Despite his blind fidelity to Marxism, Rubin is a man of conscience. He cares deeply about humanity and is a true friend to Nerzhin. Rubin's presence underlines the moral appeal of Marxism. Not to recognize this appeal is to underplay the drama of Nerzhin's change of heart.

The selections provided below fill in some gaps. Only when the entire Willetts translation is published will English readers be able to appreciate *The First Circle* properly.

The First Circle: Chapter 1

Torpedo

The filigreed hands pointed to five minutes past four.

The bronze of the clock was lusterless in the dying light of a December day.

A high window, beginning at floor level, looked down on bustling Kuznetsky Most. Maintenance men trudged doggedly to and fro, scraping up fresh snow which was already caking and turning brown under the feet of pedestrians.

State Counselor Grade Two Innokentii Volodin surveyed all this unseeingly, lolling against the edge of the embrasure, and whistling something long drawn out and elusive. His fingertips flipped over the pages of a glossy foreign magazine, but he had no eyes for it.

Volodin State Counselor Grade Two—the diplomatic-service equivalent of lieutenant-colonel—was tall, narrow-shouldered, and wore a suit of some silky material instead of his uniform, looking more like a well-off young drone than an official of some importance in the Ministry of Foreign Affairs.

It was time to switch the lights on or go home, but he stayed where he was.

Four o'clock was not the end of the working day, but only of its daytime part. Everyone would now go home, have something to eat, and take a nap; then at 10 p.m. the thousands and thousands of windows in forty-five All-Union and twenty Union-Republican ministries would light up again. A single individual ringed by a dozen fortress walls could not sleep at nights, and he had trained the whole of official Moscow to stay awake with him until 3 or 4 in the morning. Knowing the peculiar nocturnal habits of their lord and master, all sixty-odd ministers kept vigil, like schoolboys awaiting a summons from the headmaster. To fight off sleep they would summon their deputies, then deputy ministers would rouse heads of department, research officers would erect ladders and swarm over card-indexes, clerks would charge along corridors, and stenographers would break the points of their pencils.

Today was no exception. It was Christmas Eve in Western calendars, and all the embassies had fallen silent and given up calling two days ago, but the Ministry would be sitting up through the night just the same.

They—the Western diplomats—had two weeks of holiday ahead of them. Trusting babes! Stupid donkeys!

The young man's nervous fingers leafed through the magazine hastily, mechanically, while hot waves of terror welled up inside him, then subsided, leaving him cold.

Innokentii flung the magazine away and began pacing the room, shuddering.

Should he call or shouldn't he? Must it be now? Would Thursday or Friday be too late over there?

Too late. . . . There was so little time to think about it, and absolutely nobody to ask for advice!

Surely there was no way of finding out who had made a call from a phone box? If he spoke only in Russian? If he didn't hang around but walked away quickly? Surely they couldn't identify a muffled voice over the telephone? It must be a technical impossibility.

In three or four days' time he would be flying there himself. It would be more logical to wait. More sensible.

But it would be too late.

Oh, hell! His shoulders, unused to such burdens, hunched in a shiver. It would be better if he had never found out. Better not to know.

He scooped up all the papers on his desk and carried them to the safe. His agitation grew and grew. Innokentii lowered his brow onto the dull-red painted iron of the safe and rested there with closed eyes.

Then suddenly, as though he felt his last chance slipping away from him, withoutcalling for a car, without so much as closing his inkwell, Innokentii rushed for the door, locked it, handed in his key to the guard at the end of the corridor, almost ran down the stairs, overtaking the usual gold-braided personages, dived into his overcoat, planted his hat on his head, and ran out into the damp twilight.

Rapid motion brought him some relief.

His low-heeled French shoes, worn fashionably without galoshes, sank into the slush.

As he passed the Vorovsky monument in the ministry courtyard, Innokentii looked up and shuddered. The new building of the Great Lubyanka, which looked out on Furkasov Passage, suddenly acquired a new significance for him. This gray-black nine-storied hulk was a battleship, and the eighteen pilasters loomed like eighteen gun turrets on its starboard side. And Innokentii's tiny craft was being helplessly sucked into its path, under the bows of the swift, heavy vessel.

Or no—he wasn't a helpless, captive canoe—he was deliberately heading towards the battleship like a torpedo!

He could hold out no longer! He turned right along Kuznetsky Most. A taxi was about to pull away from the curb. Innokentii grabbed it, hurried the driver downhill, then told him to turn left, under the newly lit street lamps of the Petrovka.

He still couldn't decide where to make his call—where he could be sure that no one would be hovering impatiently, distracting him, peering through the door. But if he looked for a single phone booth in some quiet spot, he would make himself more conspicuous. Wouldn't it be better to pick one in the thick of it all, as long as it had soundproof brick or stone walls? And how stupid he had been to chase around in a taxi and make the driver a witness. He dug into his pocket, hoping not to find the fifteen kopecks for the call. If he didn't he could obviously put it off.

At the traffic lights on Okhotny Ryad his fingers felt and drew out two fifteen-kopeck pieces simultaneously. So that was that.

It seemed to calm him down. Dangerous or not, he had no alternative.

If we live in a constant state of fear, can we remain human?

Without intending it, Innokentii now found himself riding along the Mokhovaya past the embassy. Fate was taking a hand. He pressed his face against the window, craning his neck, trying unsuccessfully to make out which windows were lit up.

They passed the University, and Innokentii motioned to the right. It was as though he was circling his target in order to position his torpedo correctly.

They sped up to the Arbat; Innokentii gave the driver two notes and stepped out, and crossed the square, trying to moderate his pace.

His throat and his mouth were dry with the dryness which no drink can relieve.

By now the Arbat was all lit up. Before the "Khudozhestvenny" Cinema there was a big queue for "The Ballerina's Romance." A faint bluish mist clouded the red "M" over the metro station. A woman with a dark Southern complexion was selling little yellow flowers. The doomed man could no longer see his battleship, but his breast was bursting with desperate resolve.

Remember, though; not a word in English. Let alone French. Mustn't leave the smallest clue for the tracker dogs.

Innokentii walked on, erect and no longer hurrying. A girl eyed him as he passed.

And another one. Very pretty too. Wish me well out of it!

How big the world is, and how full of opportunities! But all that's left for you is this narrow passage.

One of the wooden booths outside the station was empty, but seemed to have a broken window. Innokentii walked on, into the station.

Here the four booths set in the wall were all occupied. But in the one to the left a rough-looking character, not quite sober, was finishing his call and hanging up the receiver. He smiled at Innokentii and started saying something. Innokentii took his place in the booth, carefully pulled the thick-paned door to, and held it shut with one hand: The other, still gloved, trembled as it dropped a coin into the slot and dialed a number.

After several prolonged buzzes the receiver was lifted at the other end.

"Is that the secretariat?" Innokentii asked, trying to disguise his voice.

"Yes."

"Please put me through to the Ambassador immediately."

The answer came in very good Russian.

"I can't ring the Ambassador. What is your business?"

"Give me the chargé then! Or the military attaché! Please be quick!"

There was a pause for thought at the other end. Innokentii put himself in fate's hands: If they refused—let it go at that, don't try a second time.

"Very well, I'm connecting you with the attaché."

He heard them making the connection.

Through the thick glass he saw people passing, within inches of the row of phone booths, hurrying, overtaking one another. One person peeled off and stood impatiently waiting his turn outside Innokentii's booth.

Somebody with a thick accent and a well-fed, indolent voice spoke into the telephone:

"Hallo. What did you want?"

"Is that the military attaché?" Innokentii asked brusquely.

"Yes, air attaché," drawled the voice at the other end.

What next? Screening the receiver with his hand Innokentii spoke in a low voice but urgently:

"Mr. Air Attaché! Please write this down and pass it to the Ambassador immediately."

"Just a moment," the leisurely voice answered, "I'll call an interpreter."

"I can't wait!" Innokentii was seething. And he had dropped his attempt to disguise his voice. "And I will not talk to any Soviet person! Do not put the receiver down! This is a life-and-death matter for your country! And not only your country! Listen! Within the next few days a Soviet agent called Georgii Koval will pick something up at a shop selling radio parts, the address is. . . ."

"I don't quite understand," the attaché calmly replied, in halting Russian. He, of course, was sitting on a comfortable sofa, and no one was on his trail. Animated female voices could be heard in the room around him. "Call the Canadian Embassy. They have good Russian speakers there."

The phone booth floor was burning under Innokentii's feet, and the black receiver with its heavy steel chain melting in his hand. But a single foreign word could destroy him!

"Listen! Listen!" he cried in despair. "In a few days' time the Soviet agent Koval will be given important technological information about the production of the atomic bomb, at a radio shop. . . ."

"What? Which avenue?" The attaché sounded surprised. He paused a moment. "Who are you anyway? How do I know you're speaking the truth?"

"Do you know what a risk I'm taking?" Innokentii rapped back. Somebody seemed to be knocking on the glass behind him. The attaché was silent. Perhaps taking a long puff at his cigarette.

"The atomic bomb?" he repeated dubiously. "But who are you? Tell me your name."

There was a muffled click and dead silence followed, unbroken by rustling or buzzing.

They had been cut off.

The First Circle: Chapter 2

A Blunder

There are establishments in which you suddenly come across a dull red lamp over a door marked—"Staff only." Or, more recently, it may be an imposing plate-glass sign: "Strictly no entrance to unauthorized persons." There may even be a grim security guard sitting at a little table and inspecting passes. As always, confronted with the forbidden, your imagination runs away with you.

In reality, the door opens onto another unremarkable corridor, perhaps a bit cleaner. A streak of cheap red carpet, standard government issue, runs down the middle. The parquet floor has been more or less polished. Spittoons are stationed at fairly frequent intervals.

But there are no people. There is no movement out of one door and into another. And these doors are all covered with black leather, black leather distended by padding, pinned down by white studs and bearing shiny oval numberplates.

Even those who work in one such room know less about what goes on in the room next door than they do about the gossip of the day on the island of Madagascar.

On the same gloomy frost-free December evening, in the building of the Moscow Central Automatic Telephone Exchange, on one of those forbidden corridors and in one of those inaccessible rooms, known to the superintendent of the building as Room 194 and to Department XI of the 6th Administration of the Ministry of State Security as Post A-1, two lieutenants were on duty. Not in uniform, however: They could enter and leave the telephone exchange with greater propriety in civilian dress. One wall was occupied by a switchboard and acoustic apparatus—black plastic and shiny metal. A long schedule of instructions, on dingy paper, hung on the other.

These instructions anticipated and warned against every imaginable breach of or departure from routine in monitoring and recording calls to and from the US Embassy, stipulating that two persons should be on duty at all times, one listening in continuously, never removing the earphones, while the other should never leave the room except to go to the lavatory, and that they should alternate duties at half-hour intervals.

If you followed these instructions, mistakes were impossible.

But such is the fatal incompatibility of officialdom's perfectionism with man's pitiful imperfection that these instructions had for once been disobeyed. Not because the men on duty were novices, but because they were experienced enough to know that nothing special ever happened, least of all on the Western Christmas Eve.

One of them, the flat-nosed Lieutenant Tyukin, was certain to be asked in next Monday's politics class "who are 'the friends of the people' and how do they fight against the social democrats," why we had to break with the Mensheviks at the Second Congress, and had been right to do so, why we had reunited at the Fifth Congress, again acting correctly, then at the Sixth Congress again gone our separate ways, and yet again had been right to do so.

Tyukin wouldn't have dreamed of starting his reading on Saturday, with little hope of memorizing anything, except that after duty on Sunday he and his sister's husband intended to do some serious drinking. He would never be able to take any of that crap in with a hangover on Monday morning, and the Party organizer had already rebuked him and threatened to bring him before the Party bureau. The important thing was not answering in class but being able to present a written summary. Tyukin hadn't been able to find time all that week, and had been putting it off all day, but now he had asked his colleague to carry on working for a while, made himself comfortable in a corner by the light of a desk lamp, and started copying into his exercise book selected passages from the "Short Course."

They hadn't yet got round to switching on the overhead light. The auxiliary lamp by the tape recorders was on. Kuleshov, the curly-haired lieutenant with the chubby chin, sat with his earphones on, feeling bored. The Embassy had phoned in its shopping orders in the morning, and from lunchtime onward seemed to have fallen asleep. There hadn't been a single call.

After sitting like this for some time, Kuleshov decided to take a look at the sores on his left leg. They kept breaking out again and again for unknown reasons. They had been dressed with "brilliant green," zinc ointment and a streptocidal preparation, but instead of healing, the sores had spread under the scabs. The pain had begun to make walking uncomfortable. The MGB clinic had made an appointment for him with a professor. Kuleshov had recently been given a new flat, and his wife was expecting a child. And now these ulcers were poisoning what should have been a comfortable life.

Kuleshov removed the tight earphones, which pressed on his ears, moved to a lighter spot, rolled up the left leg of his trousers and his long underwear, and began cautiously feeling and picking at the edges of the scabs. Dark pus oozed out under the pressure of his fingers. The pain made his head spin and blotted out all other thoughts. For the first time the thought shot through his mind that perhaps these were not just sores but . . . he tried to remember a terrible word he had heard somewhere: gangrene? . . . and . . . what was that other thing?

So he did not immediately notice the bobbins start noiselessly spinning as the tape recorder automatically switched itself on. Without taking his bare leg from its support, Kuleshov reached for the earphones, put one ear to them and heard:

"How do I know you're speaking the truth?"

"Do you know what a risk I'm taking?"

"The atomic bomb? But who are you? Tell me your name."

THE ATOMIC BOMB!!! Obeying an impulse as instinctive as that of a man who grabs the nearest object to break his fall, Kuleshov tore out the plug from the switchboard, disconnecting the two telephones—and only then realizing that, contrary to instructions, he had not intercepted the caller's number.

The first thing he did was to look over his shoulder. Tyukin was scribbling his summary and had eyes for nothing else. Tyukin was a friend, but Kuleshov had been warned to keep an eye on him, which meant that he had received similar instructions. As he turned the rewind knob of the recorder, and plugged in the spare recorder to the Embassy loop, Kuleshov thought at first of erasing the recorded message to conceal his blunder. But he remembered at once—his chief had often said that the work of their post was duplicated by automatic recording in another place—and he dropped that silly idea. Of course the recording was duplicated, and for suppressing a conversation like that you'd be shot!

The tape had rewound itself. He turned the replay knob. The criminal was in a great hurry and very agitated. Where could he have been speaking from? Obviously not from a private apartment. And hardly from his place of work. It was always from public phone booths that people tried to get through to embassies.

Opening his directory of phone booth numbers, Kuleshov hurriedly dialed a telephone on the steps at the entrance to the Sokolniki underground station.

"Genka! Genka!" he croaked. "Emergency! Call the operations room! They may still be able to catch him!"

The First Circle: Chapter 26

Sawing Wood

It was getting light.

Thick frost had trimmed with white the fence posts of the prison area and the outer security zone, the barbed wire in tangles of twenty strands at a time, bristling with thousands of spiky asterisks, the sloping roof of the watchtower, and the weed running wild on the wasteland beyond the wire.

Dmitri Sologdin admired this miracle with unshaded eyes. He was standing near the sawhorse. He was wearing a padded jacket, prison camp issue over blue overalls, and his head, on which the first traces of gray could be seen, was uncovered. He was a nonentity, a slave without rights. He had been inside for twelve years, but because he had been sentenced to a second term, there was no knowing when, if ever, his imprisonment would end. His wife had wasted her youth waiting in vain for him. To avoid dismissal from her present job, as from so many others, she had pretended that she had no husband, and had stopped writing to him. Sologdin had never seen his only son—his wife had been pregnant when he was arrested. Sologdin had gone through the forests of Cherdynsk, the mines of Vorkuta, two periods under investigation, one of six months, one of a year, tormented by lack of sleep, drained of his strength, wasting away. His name and his future had long ago been trampled into the mud. All he possessed was a pair of well-worn padded trousers and a tarpaulin work jacket, kept at present in the storeroom in expectation of worse times to come. He was paid thirty rubles a month—enough for three kilos of sugar—but not in cash. He could breathe fresh air only at stated times, authorized by the prison authorities.

And in his soul there was a peace that nothing could destroy. His eyes sparkled like those of a young man. His chest, bared to the frost, heaved as though he was experiencing life to the full.

Long ago, when he had been under interrogation, his muscles were shriveled ropes, but they had expanded and grown firm again, and they demanded exercise. That was why, quite voluntarily and for no reward, he went out every morning to chop and saw wood for the prison kitchen.

But axe and saw can be terrible weapons in a convict's hands, and they were not readily entrusted to him. The prison authorities were paid to suspect that the convict's most innocent act is a treacherous ruse; they judged others by themselves, refused to believe that a man would volunteer to work for nothing, stubbornly suspected Sologdin of planning his escape, or armed mutiny, especially as there were hints of both in his record. Standing orders therefore provided that a warder should stand five paces away from Sologdin while he worked, out of range of his axe, but watching every movement. There were warders willing to perform this dangerous duty, and the prison authorities, reared in the admirable ways of Gulag, did not think one watcher to one worker a waste of manpower. But Sologdin turned obstinate, and aggravated their suspicions by declaring that he would not work in the presence of a "screw." That was the end of his woodchopping for a time. (The prison governor could not coerce prisoners. This was not a prison camp. The inmates here were engaged in intellectual labor and did not come under his ministry.) The real trouble was that the planners and accountants had made no provision for this work, and the women who came from outside to cook the prisoners' food refused to chop wood because they were not paid extra for it. The authorities tried detailing off-duty warders to do the job, tearing them away from their dominoes in the orderly room. The warders were all blockheads, hand-picked as young men for their physical fitness. But during their years of service in prisons, they seemed to have lost the habit of work—their backs soon started aching, and the pull of the dominoes was strong. They just couldn't produce enough firewood, so the governor had to give in and authorize Sologdin and any other prisoners who turned up (it was usually Nerzhin and Rubin) to chop and saw without additional surveillance. The sentry on the watchtower could in any case see them clearly, and the duty officers too were told to keep an eye on them.

As darkness retreated and the waning lamplight merged with the light of day the rotund figure of Spiridon the yardman appeared from round the corner of the building. He was wearing a fur hat with earflaps—no other prisoner had been given one—and a quilted jacket. The yardman was also a convict, but subordinate to the commandant of the Institute, not to the prison authorities. To keep the peace, he sharpened the axes and the saw for the prison too. As he got nearer, Sologdin could see the missing saw in his hands.

Spiridon Yegorov walked around the yard, which was guarded by machine guns, at all hours from reveille to lights out, without escort. One reason why the authorities felt able to relax the rules was that Spiridon was blind in one eye and had only thirty percent vision in the other. The sharashka's budget provided for three yardmen because the yard was really several yards joined together, two hectares in area, but Spiridon, unaware of this, did the work of all three and felt none the worse for it. What mattered was that here he could "eat his bellyful," at least a kilo and a half of black bread, because there was plenty of bread and to spare, and the lads let him have some of their gruel. Spiridon was conspicuously fitter, and plumper, than he had been in Sev-Ural-Lag, where he had acted as nanny to many thousands of logs.

"Hey, Spiridon!" Sologdin called out impatiently.

His face, with its graying ginger moustache, and graying ginger eyebrows, was very mobile and, when he was answering someone, often expressed eagerness to oblige. As it did now, Sologdin did not know that this exaggerated show of helpfulness was often derisive.

"What d'you mean what's the matter? The saw won't cut!"

"I can't think why," Spiridon said, sounding surprised. "You've complained about it I don't know how many times this winter. Let's have a little go."

He held the saw by one handle.

They began sawing. The saw jumped out once or twice, trying to change its place because it wasn't lying comfortably, but then it sank its teeth in and was away.

"You grip it awful hard," Spiridon cautiously advised him. "Just get three fingers round the handle like round a pen and move nice and easy, smooth like . . . that's it . . . you've got it! Only when you pull it towards you, don't tug at it."

Each man believed himself superior to the other: Sologdin because he knew all about mechanics, the resistance of metals, and other scientific matters, and also because of his broad grasp of social issues, Spiridon because material objects always obeyed him. Sologdin, however, patronized the yardman openly, while Spiridon hid his feelings.

Even halfway through the thick log, the saw never looked like sticking; it cut away with a thin whine, spluttering pine shavings onto the two men's overall trousers.

Sologdin burst out laughing.

"You're a wizard. Spiridon! You had me fooled. You sharpened the saw and set it yesterday."

Spiridon complacently chanted in time to the saw. "She chews and chews and never swallows, but all her sawdust gives to others."

And before the saw was through, the butt of the log fell off under the pressure of his hand.

"I didn't sharpen it at all," he said, turning the saw over so that Sologdin could see the cutting edge. "You can see the teeth are just the same today as they were yesterday."

Sologdin bent down to look at the saw and could see no file marks. But the rascal had certainly done something to it.

"Come on, Spiridon, let's cut another length."

Spiridon held his back. "No, I can't. I'm all worn out. All the work my grandfathers and great-grandfathers didn't do has landed on me. Anyway, your pals will be here soon."

Sologdin's friends, however, were in no hurry.

It was now broad daylight. A morning magnificently adorned with hoar frost stood revealed. Even the drainpipes, and the ground itself, were decked with hoar frost, and in the distance the tops of the lime trees in the exercise yard wore splendid silvery gray manes.

"How did you land in the sharashka, Spiridon?" Sologdin asked, looking closely at the yardman.

He was killing time. In all his years in the camps he had associated only with educated people, expecting to glean nothing worthwhile from less cultured prisoners.

Spiridon smacked his lips. "You may well ask. You're all learned folk, you and all the others they've lumped together in this place, and here am I bunged in with you. On my card it says I'm a glassblower. Well, I was a glassblower once, at our factory near Bryansk. But that's a long time ago, and now my eyesight's gone, and the work I did is no use in this place; what they want here is a really clever glassblower, like Ivan. There wasn't another like him in our whole factory, and never had been. But they just took a peep at my card and brought me here. Then they took a good look at me, and were going to send me packing, but the commandant, God bless him, set me on as a yardman."

Nerzhin came round the corner from the direction of the exercise yard and the one-story staff building. He was wearing unbuttoned overalls, a padded jacket draped round his shoulders, and a towel, prison issue, broad as it was long, round his neck.

He greeted them abruptly—"Morning, friends"—shedding garments, stripping off the upper part of his denims and removing his undervest as he came.

Sologdin looked askance at him. "Gleb, my boy, are you crazy? Where's the snow?"

"Right here," Nerzhin retorted, scrambling onto the roof of the woodshed, where there was a virgin layer of something fluffy which was partly snow and partly hoar frost. He scooped up handfuls of it and began vigorously rubbing chest, back, and sides. He rubbed himself with snow down to the waist all through the winter, although any warder who chanced to be near would try to stop him.

Spiridon shook his head: "Look what a sweat you're in now."

"Still no letter, Spiridon Danilovich?" Nerzhin called out.

"This time there was a letter for me."

"So why haven't you brought it for me to read? Is everything all right?"

"There was a letter, but I can't get it. The Snake's kept it."

"Myshin? Won't he hand it over?" Nerzhin stopped rubbing himself.

"He put my name up on the list, but the commandant had me cleaning the attic out, and before I knew it the Snake had shut up shop. It'll be Monday now."

"The rotters!" Nerzhin sighed, baring his teeth.

Spiridon waved it away.

"Don't damn the priests—leave it to the Devil," he said, with one eye on Sologdin, whom he didn't know well. "Right, I'm off."

In his big fur hat, with its flaps untied, Spiridon looked like a comically flop-eared mongrel as he set off for the guardroom, to which no other prisoner was admitted.

"Spiridon!"

Sologdin suddenly remembered and called after him. "What about the axe? Where's the axe?"

"The duty warder will bring it," Spiridon shouted back, and vanished.

"Well," said Nerzhin, vigorously rubbing his chest and back with his scrap of terry toweling. "I didn't come up to Anton's expectations. He says I treat Number Seven like 'a drunk's corpse under Marfino's fence.' Then yesterday evening he offered me a transfer to the cryptography group, but I refused."

A slight movement of Sologdin's head, and a grin perhaps expressed disapproval. Between his neatly clipped, graying ginger moustache, and matching beard, his smile revealed sparkling white teeth, sound teeth untouched by decay. The gaps had been made by outside forces.

"You're behaving more like a bard than a reckoner," he said.

Nerzhin was not surprised: "Mathematician" and "poet" had been replaced, in accordance with Sologdin's well-known whimsical habit of speaking the Language of Ultimate Clarity, and not using "bird language," that is, foreign words.

Still half-naked, unhurriedly toweling himself, Nerzhin gloomily agreed.

"Yes, it's not like me. But I suddenly felt so sick of it all that I didn't care any more. If I go to Siberia, I go to Siberia. . . . I'm sorry to find that Lyovka is right—I'm a failure as a skeptic. Obviously skepticism isn't just a system of ideas; it's mainly a matter of character. I want to intervene in what goes on. May even give somebody a smack in the chops."

Sologdin found a more comfortable position against the sawhorse.

"It gives me deep joy, my friend. Your hardened unbelief" (meaning what was called "skepticism" in the Language of Seeming Clarity) "was unavoidable on the road away from . . . the satanic drug" (he meant "Marxism," but he couldn't think of a Russian synonym for it) "to the world of truth. You are no longer a boy" (Sologdin was six years older) "you must find yourself spiritually, understand the relation between good and evil in human life. And you must choose."

Sologdin looked meaningfully at Nerzhin, who however showed no inclination to choose between good and evil there and then. He put on his shirt, which was too small, and answered back as he thrust his arms into his overall sleeves.

"That's a weighty statement. But shouldn't you also be reminding me that 'reason is feeble,' and that I myself am the 'source of error'?"

He rounded on his friend as though struck by a new thought.

"Look, you're supposed to have the 'light of truth' in you, yet you say that prostitution is morally beneficial, and that Dantes was in the right when he fought his duel with Pushkin."

Sologdin smiled complacently, baring a defective set of longish teeth with rounded edges.

"Well, didn't I successfully defend those propositions?"

"Yes, but the thought that in the same skull, the same breast. . . ."

"That's life. You must get used to it. I freely admit that I'm like one of those wooden eggs you can take apart. I am made up of nine spheres, one inside the other."

"Sphere is bird talk!"

"Sorry. You see how uninventive I am. I am made of nine roundnesses. It is not often that I let anyone see the inner ones. Don't forget that we live with our visors down. We have been forced to. And anyway, we are more complex than the people depicted in novels. Writers try to explain people completely—but in real life we never get to know anyone completely. That's why I love Dostoevsky. Stavrogin, Svidrigailov, Kirillov. What are they really like? The closer you get the less you understand them."

"Stavrogin? Which book is he in?"

"*The Possessed*. Haven't you read it?" Sologdin was astonished.

Nerzhin draped his damp, skimpy towel round his neck like a muffler, and pulled on his officer's service cap, which was so old that it was coming apart at the seams.

"*The Possessed*? Come off it. Where d'you think my generation could get hold of it? It's counterrevolutionary literature! Too dangerous!"

He put on his jacket.

"Anyway, I don't agree. When a new arrival crosses the threshold of your cell, you hang down from your bunk, and your eyes bore into him—is he friend or enemy? You size him up in a flash. And, surprisingly, you're never mistaken. Is it really as difficult as you say to understand a man? Remember how you and I first met. You arrived in the sharashka when the washbasin was still out on the main staircase, right?"

"Right."

"It was morning, and I was on my way downstairs, whistling some silly little tune. You were drying yourself, and you suddenly raised your face from the towel in the half-darkness. I was rooted to the spot. It was like looking at the face in an icon. Later on I looked more closely and you were by no means a saint—I don't mean to flatter you. . . ."

Sologdin laughed.

". . . Your face isn't at all gentle, but it is unusual. I felt at once that I could trust you, and after five minutes I was telling you. . . ."

"I was staggered by your rashness."

"But a man with eyes like yours can't be a stoolie!"

"It's too bad if I'm so easy to read. In a camp you need to look nondescript."

"Then that same day when I'd been listening to your evangelical revelations I tempted you with a question. . . ."

"Of the Karamazov variety."

"Ah, you remember! I asked you what should be done with professional criminals. Remember what you said? Shoot the lot! Right?"

Nerzhin, now as then, looked hard at Sologdin as though giving him a chance to retract.

But the bright blue of Dmitri Sologdin's eyes was untroubled. He folded his arms picturesquely over his chest, one of his most becoming poses, and loftily declared:

"My friend! They who want to destroy Christianity, and only they, would have it become the creed of eunuchs. But Christianity is the faith of the strong in spirit. We must have the courage to see the evil in the world and to root it out. Wait a while—you too will come to God. Your refusal to believe in anything is no position for a thinking man, it's just spiritual poverty."

Nerzhin sighed.

"You know, I don't even mind acknowledging a Creator, some sort of Higher Reason in the universe. I'll even say that I feel it to be so, if you want me to. But supposing I found out that there is no God—would I be any less moral?"

"Undoubtedly!"

"I don't think so. And why do you have to insist, why do all of you always insist, that we must recognize not just God in some general sense but a concrete Christian God, plus the Trinity, plus the Immaculate Conception?

Would my philosophical deism be the least bit shaken if I learn that not one of the Gospel miracles ever happened? Of course it wouldn't!"

Sologdin sternly raised a hand with an admonitory finger.

"There's no other way! If you begin to doubt a single dogma of the faith, a single word of the scriptures, all is lost! You are one of the godless!"

His hand slashed the air as though it held a saber.

"That's what repels people! All or nothing! No compromises, no allowances made. But suppose I can't accept it in toto? What can I be sure of? What can I rely on? I keep telling you—the one thing I know is that I know nothing."

Socrates' apprentice took hold of the saw and offered the other handle to Sologdin.

"Another time, then," Sologdin agreed. "Let's cut wood."

They had begun to feel the cold, and they sawed away briskly. Powdered brown bark sputtered from under the saw. The job had been done more skillfully with Spiridon at the other end of the saw, but after many mornings working together, the friends got along without recriminations. They sawed with the zeal, and the enjoyment, of men whose work is not performed under duress, or the lash of poverty.

Sologdin, flushed scarlet, growled once, when they were about to cut their fourth log: "Just try not to snag the saw."

And after the fourth log was cut, Nerzhin muttered: "It was a knotty one all right, that bastard."

Fragrant shavings, some white, some yellow, fell on the trousers and shoes of the sawyers at each swish of the saw. This rhythmical work soothed them and re-tuned their thoughts.

Nerzhin had woken up in a bad mood, but now he was thinking that camp life had left him stunned only for the first year. Now that he had his second wind, he would not fight tooth and nail for a trusty's job, he would not be afraid of general duties—now that he knew better what really mattered, he would join the morning work parade in his padded jacket, smirched with plaster or fuel oil, and slowly stick at it for the whole twelve-hour day—day in and day out for the five remaining years of his sentence: Five years wasn't ten years; five years you could survive. You just had to keep reminding yourself that prison was not just a curse—it was also a blessing.

These were his thoughts as he took alternate pulls at the saw. He could not possibly imagine that his partner, as he pulled the saw his way, thought of prison only as an unmitigated curse, from which he must sooner or later break free.

Sologdin was thinking now about his great secret achievement of the past few months, which held the promise of freedom. He would learn the definitive verdict on his work after breakfast, and he knew in advance that it would be favorable. Sologdin swelled with pride at the thought that his brain, exhausted by so many years of interrogation, and then of hunger in the camps, starved for so many years of phosphorus, had still succeeded in mastering a major engineering problem! How often we notice it in men approaching their forties—that sudden uprush of vital forces! Especially if the surplus energy of the flesh is not expended in procreation, but mysteriously transmuted into powerful thought.

The First Circle: Chapter 36

Phonoscopy

At noon Yakonov himself was missing from the velvety hush and glossy comfort of his office. He was in Number Seven, officiating at the "wedding" of the clipper and the scrambler. The idea of uniting those two devices, born that morning in the mercenary mind of Markushev, had been snapped up by many others who saw some advantage to themselves. Only Bobynin, Pryanchikov, and Roitman were against it, and nobody listened to them.

Present in the office were Selivanovsky, General Bulbanyuk (representing Ryumin), Smolosidov, a lieutenant on the strength at Marfino, and the prisoner Rubin.

Lieutenant Smolosidov was an unpleasant character. Perhaps you believe that there is some good in every living creature? Your search for it in Smolosidov would be rendered difficult by that unsmiling, iron-hard stare and the sour twist of those thick lips. He occupied one of the lowliest positions in his laboratory—he was little more than a radio fitter—and he was paid no more than that of the lowliest female employee, less than 2,000 a month. True, he stole another 1,000 from the Institute in the form of unobtainable radio parts which he sold on the black market—but everyone knew that there was more than this to be said about Smolosidov's position and income.

The free employees in the sharashka were afraid of him—even the friends who played volleyball with him. They were frightened by his face, in which it was impossible to awaken a spontaneous reaction. And by the special trust which the highest authorities showed him. Where did he live? Had he in fact a home? A family? He never accepted invitations from colleagues, never shared his leisure with them beyond the boundaries of the Institute. He had three war medals on his chest and in an unguarded moment had boasted that all through the war Marshal Rokossovsky had not spoken a single word which he, Smolosidov, had not heard. When asked how this could be, he replied that he had been the Marshal's personal wireless-operator. Nothing more was known about his past.

No sooner did the question arise as to which of the free workers could be trusted with the red hot secret tape, than the Minister's inner office gave the order: Smolosidov.

Smolosidov was now installing a tape recorder on a little varnished table, and General Bulbanyuk, whose head was like a grotesquely overgrown potato with three bulges for ears and nose, was saying:

"You, Rubin, are a prisoner. But you were a communist once, and you may be a communist again someday."

Rubin would have retorted, "I'm a communist right now!" but trying to convince Bulbanyuk of that was beneath his dignity.

"So the Soviet government, and our Organs, feel that they can trust you. The tape you are going to hear contains a state secret of world importance. We hope that you will help us to isolate this scoundrel, who wants to see his native land menaced by the atomic bomb. It goes without saying that if you make the slightest attempt to divulge the secret you will be annihilated. That clear?"

"Quite clear," snapped Rubin, whose greatest fear now was that he might not be allowed to hear the tape. Having lost all chance of private happiness long ago, Rubin had made mankind at large his family. The tape which he had yet to hear was already of personal concern to him.

Smolosidov pressed the "playback" button, and the quiet of the office was broken by the dialogue between a slow-witted American and a desperate Russian, with a faint rustling in the background. Rubin peered into the mottled diaphragm of the loudspeaker as though straining to discern the features of this enemy. Whenever he looked at anything so intently, his face became taut and harsh. It would be no good begging for mercy from a man with a face like that.

After the words (in bad Russian) "Who are you? Say your name," Rubin threw himself back in his chair. He was a different man. He had forgotten that others present were high-ranking officers, forgotten that it was a long time since major's stars had blazed on his shoulders. He relit his cigarette and rapped out: "Right. Just once more."

Smolosidov rewound the tape.

The others watched in awestruck silence.

Rubin chewed and mumbled the mouthpiece of his cigarette. He felt ready to burst. Suddenly he, of all people, the dishonorably discharged Rubin, was urgently needed! He too would have his chance to give Dame History a helping hand! He was back at his post! Once more defending the World Revolution!

Malignant Smolosidov hung over the tape recorder like a sullen dog. Jack-in-office Bulbanyuk, elbows on Anton's spacious desk, supported his impos-ing potato head in hands, half-hidden by his dewlap. From what stock had this impenetrably complacent breed proliferated? From the weed of commie-cockiness, maybe? How quick and clever his comrades had once been. Now the whole apparat had fallen into the hands of these people. And they were bulldozing the whole country along the road to perdition. How could it have happened?

Rubin could not look at them. They disgusted him so much that he would have liked to toss a hand grenade at them there and then, in that office, and blow them to bits!

But, as things were, at this crossroads in history, they represented the positive forces, embodying as they did the dictatorship, and the fatherland, of the proletariat.

He must rise above his feelings! Hateful as they were, he must help them!

Hogs of this sort, from an Army-Group Political Department, had slung Rubin in jail because his cleverness and his honesty were more than they could bear. Hogs of the same sort, in the Chief Military Prosecutor's De-partment, had in the space of four years binned a dozen anguished protesta-tions of innocence from Rubin.

Yes, he must rise above his own unhappy lot! To save the idea! To rescue the banner! To serve the world's most advanced society!

The tape came to an end.

Rubin crushed his dead cigarette in an ashtray.

"Right. We'll give it a try," he said. "But if you haven't got a suspect, what are we looking for? We can't tape the voices of everybody in Moscow. Whose voice do we compare this with?"

Bulbanyuk reassured him: "We picked up four people on the spot, near the telephone booth. But our man is most probably not one of them. There are five people in the Ministry of Foreign Affairs who could have known. Not counting Gromyko and one or two others, obviously. I've jotted down those five names, without initials, titles, or the posts they occupy, so you needn't be afraid to accuse any one of them."

He held out a page torn from a notebook. The names written on it were:

1. Petrov
2. Syagovity
3. Volodin
4. Shevronok
5. Zavarzin

Rubin read them, and made as if to copy the list, but Selivanovsky hastily prevented him.

"No, no! The list will be with Smolosidov."

Rubin handed it back. He was not offended but amused by all these precautions. As if the five names were not burnt into his memory already! Petrov! Syagovity! Volodin! Shevronok! Zavarzin! Linguistic speculation had become a matter of habit with Rubin, and he had automatically registered the derivation of the names "Syagovity" ("bouncy") and "Shevronok" (= "Zhavoronok," "skylark").

"Please record other phone calls made by each of the five," he said curtly.

"You'll get them tomorrow."

"Another thing. Put the age of each of them by his name." Rubin thought a bit. "And a list of the foreign languages he knows."

Selivanovsky assented. "I've been wondering myself why he didn't switch to a foreign language. What sort of diplomat is he? Maybe he's just very crafty?"

"Maybe our man got some uneducated simpleton to do it for him," Bulbanyuk said, slapping the table with his flabby hand.

"Who could you trust with a job like that?"

"What we need to find out as quickly as possible," Bulbanyuk explained, "is whether the culprit is in fact one of these five. If he isn't, we'll try another five, or another twenty-five for that matter!"

Rubin waited till he had finished, and nodded at the tape recorder.

"I shall need the tape the whole time, starting today."

"It will be with Lieutenant Smolosidov. You and he will be allocated a room to yourselves in the Top Secret zone."

"They're clearing it now," Smolosidov said.

Rubin's service experience had taught him to avoid the dangerous word "when," in case he was asked the same question. He knew that there was only work for a week or two in this, but that if you spun it out it could be good for months, whereas if you asked, "when do you want it?" the bosses would say "by tomorrow morning." He asked a different question:

"With whom can I discuss this work?"

Selivanovsky exchanged a glance with Bulbanyuk and answered.

"Only with Major Roitman. With Foma Guryanovich. And with the Minister himself."

"You remember my warning?" Bulbanyuk asked. "Want me to repeat it?"

Rubin rose without asking permission, looked at the general through half-closed eyes as though he was something very, very small, and said to no one in particular:

"I must go and think."

Nobody objected.

Rubin's face showed no emotion as he left the office. He walked unseeingly past the duty officer and down the strip of red stair-carpet.

He would have to draw Gleb into this new group. He would need to talk things over. The job would be a very difficult one. They had only just begun working on voices. Preliminary classification. Provisional terminology.

He looked forward to his research with a true scientist's excitement.

This was, in effect, a new science: identifying a criminal by a voiceprint.

Till then criminals had been identified by their fingerprints. That technique was called "dactyloscopy"—"finger-scanning"—and it had evolved over the centuries.

The new science could be called "voice-scanning" (that would be Sologdin's term), or "phonoscopy." And it had to be created in a matter of days.

Petrov. Syagovity. Volodin. Shevronok. Zavarzin.

The First Circle: Chapter 47

An Argument

All the really enlightened minds! All the greatest thinkers in the West! Sartre, for instance! They all support socialism! They're all against capitalism! That's almost a platitude by now! You're the only one who can't see it! Pithecanthropus erectus!"

Rubin loomed dangerously over Nerzhin and shook him with grappling fingers. Nerzhin planted his palms on Rubin's chest to push him away.

"Have it your way! Maybe I am an ape! But I refuse to use your terminology. I refuse to talk about what you call capitalism and socialism! I don't understand these words, and I won't use them!"

Rubin laughed and relaxed a little. "I suppose you prefer the Language of Utter Clarity?"

"Yes, if you like!"

"What do you understand?"

"I understand words like 'a family of one's own,' 'inviolability of the person.'"

"'Unlimited freedom,' perhaps?"

"No—moral self-limitation."

"Fetal philosopher! How far will you get with amorphous, protozoic concepts like that in the twentieth century? Those are all class-conditioned ideas! Dependent on. . . ."

"Are they, hell!" Nerzhin freed himself and stood up out of his niche. "Justice is never relative. . . ."

"It's a class concept! Of course it is," said Rubin, brandishing an open hand over Nerzhin's head.

"Justice is the cornerstone, the foundation of the universe!" Nerzhin too waved an arm. Anyone watching from a distance might have thought that they were about to start fighting. "We were born with a sense of justice in our souls; we can't and we don't want to live without it! Remember what

Fyodor Ioanich says: 'I am not strong, I am easily deceived, but I can distinguish white from black. Give me your keys, Godunov!'"

"You've got nowhere to hide!" Rubin said threateningly. "You'll have to declare some day which side of the barricade you're on."

Nerzhin answered just as angrily. "That's another word you blasted fanatics have done to death! You've put up barricades all over the world! That's the horror of it! A man may want to be a citizen of the world, a little lower than the angels—but they grab him by the legs and pull him down! 'Whoever is not with us is against us!' Just leave me room to move in! Room to move in, I tell you!" Nerzhin pushed him away.

"We would leave you room—it's those on the other side who won't."

"You would, you say? When did you ever let anybody move freely? It's tanks and fixed bayonets every inch of the way. . . ."

"My dear boy," said Rubin more gently, "look at it in historical perspective."

"To hell with your perspective! I want to live now, not 'in the long term'! I know what you're going to say! It's just a matter of bureaucratic distortions; this is a transitional period, a temporary state of affairs—but this transitional order of yours makes my life impossible; it tramples my soul underfoot, that's what your transitional system does, and I won't defend it, not being an imbecile!"

"I made a mistake disturbing you after your visit," Rubin said quite gently.

"Seeing my wife has nothing at all to do with it!" Nerzhin spoke as bitterly as ever. "I think just the same at any other time! We ridicule the Christians—silly so-and-sos, living in hopes of paradise and putting up with absolutely everything on this earth! But what have we got to look forward to? For whose sake do we suffer? For our mythical descendants? What difference does it make whether it's happiness for posterity or happiness in the next world? We can't see either."

"You never were a Marxist!"

"Alas, I was."

The First Circle: Chapter 60

But You Are Given Only One Conscience, Too

That afternoon Rubin had ordered additional recordings of calls made by each of the suspects. This was the first time Volodin had answered his telephone since then. As he raised the receiver a tape in the central exchange of the Ministry of State Security began rustling and recording: the voice of Innokentii Volodin.

As a precaution he had decided not to use the phone for the present. But his wife had gone out, leaving a note: He was to be at his father-in-law's that evening without fail.

He was calling now to cry off.

Throughout the last twenty-four hours his call to the Embassy had seemed to him suicidally rash. Nor could it possibly do any good. And anyway, to judge by that dithering idiot of an attaché, they were not worth defending.

There was nothing to show that he had been found out, but his heart ached with an inexplicable presentiment, and the anticipation of disaster grew stronger and stronger. The last thing he wanted was to go where people were enjoying themselves. He was trying to persuade his wife, speaking hesitantly as people do when they have something unpleasant to say. His wife persisted—and the peculiarities of his "individual speech pattern" were recorded on a narrow strip of magnetic tape, to be turned into the "sound pictures" on wet film which would be laid out before Rubin next morning.

His friends had long ago decided that Innokentii was an "Epicurean," and he readily accepted the label, without really knowing what it meant. Then one day, at home in Moscow with nothing to do, he had the amusing idea of reading up what his "master" had in fact taught. He started searching the cupboards left by his late mother for a book about Epicurus which he remembered seeing in his childhood.

Going through the old cupboards was a task which Innokentii began with an unpleasant sensation of stiffness, a reluctance to bend, to move heavy objects around, to breathe dust. Even this was unusually hard work for him, and he soon tired. But he forced himself to go on, and a refreshing breeze seemed to play on him from the depths of those old cupboards which had a ripe smell all their own. He found the book on Epicurus, among other things, and read it later, but more important was what he discovered, from her letters, about his late mother, whom he had never understood, and to whom he had felt close only as a child. Even her death had left him almost unmoved. In early childhood a vision of silvered bugles raised towards an ornate ceiling, and the song "Let leaping flames light up the blue night," had fused with Innokentii's idea of his father. A father whom he did not really remember at all: He had been killed in 1921, suppressing the peasant rebellion in Tambov province. But he was surrounded by people who never tired of telling him about the heroic naval officer's glorious role in the Civil War. Hearing his praises sung everywhere and by everybody, Innokentii began to feel very proud of his father and his fight for the common folk against rich people wallowing in luxury. Whereas he rather looked down on his anxious mother, nursing her unspoken grief in the midst of her books and hot-water bottles. Like most sons he did not stop to think that, beside himself and his upbringing, his mother had some sort of life of her own. That she could be ill and suffer. And now she had died at the age of forty-seven.

His parents had spent hardly any time together. But this too was something the boy had no occasion to think about, and it never occurred to him to question his mother.

Now the whole story unfolded in her letters and diaries. Their marriage was not a marriage but a whirlwind event, like everything in those years. Circumstances had flung them roughly and briefly together, circumstances allowed them to see very little of each other, and circumstances parted them. But in these diaries his mother was revealed as not just an appendage to his father, as their son had been accustomed to think, but as someone with a world of her own. Innokentii now learned that his mother had loved another man all her life, and had never been able to marry him. That it was perhaps only for the sake of her son's career that she had borne till the day she died a name that was alien to her.

Stored in the cupboards were bundles of letters tied with colored ribbons of fine fabric. Letters from girlhood friends, and from friends and acquaintances of later years, actors, artists, and poets long forgotten, or mentioned nowadays only disparagingly. Old-fashioned exercise books with blue morocco covers held his mother's diaries, written in Russian and French in her strange hand—it was as though a wounded bird had skimmed the page and scratched an erratic trail with its faltering claw. Recollections of literary soirées and theatrical events took up many pages. He was deeply moved by her description of herself, an enraptured girl, standing on the station in Petersburg one white June night among a crowd of admirers all weeping for joy as they welcomed the Moscow Arts Theater company. Pure love of art reigned triumphant in these pages. Innokentii could think of no such company nowadays, nor could he imagine anyone missing a night's sleep to welcome it, except those dragooned by the Department of Culture, carrying bouquets funded from the public purse. And obviously, no one would ever dream of shedding tears on such an occasion.

The diaries led him on and on. There were pages headed "Ethical Notes": "Goodness shows itself first in pity," said one of them.

Innokentii wrinkled his brow. Pity? A shameful feeling, degrading to the one who pities and the one who is pitied—so he had learnt at school, and in life.

"Never think yourself more right than other people. Respect other people's opinions even when they are inimical to yours."

That was pretty old-fashioned too. If I have a correct world view, can I really respect those who disagree with me?

He almost forgot that he was reading and seemed to hear clearly his mother's frail voice.

"What is the most precious thing in the world? I see now that it is the knowledge that you have no part in injustice. Injustice is stronger than you, it always was and always will be, but let it not be done through you."

If Innokentii had opened the diary six years earlier, he would not even have noticed those lines. But now he read them slowly, and with surprise. There was nothing esoteric in them, and much that was simply untrue, but still he was surprised. Even the words in which his mother and her women friends expressed themselves were outdated. In all seriousness, they began certain words with capital letters—Truth, Goodness, Beauty, Good and Evil, the Ethical Imperative. In the language used by Innokentii and those around him, words were more concrete and easier to understand: progressiveness, humanity, dedication, purposefulness.

But although Innokentii was progressive and humane and dedicated and purposeful (purposefulness was what all his contemporaries most prized and cultivated in themselves), sitting there on a low stool by the cupboards he felt that something he had lacked was stealing into his heart.

Shortly afterwards, Innokentii was posted to Paris. There he had access to all shades of world opinion, and to all Russian émigré literature (though, of course, he had to look over his shoulder at bookstalls). He could read and read and read! Though his duties, of course, got in the way.

Until then he had thought that his job was the best, and his lot the luckiest, that he could possibly have hoped for. But now he began to feel that there was something sordid about it. Being a Soviet diplomat meant not only delivering day in and day out statements at which people with their heads screwed on were bound to laugh. The other part of the job was more important—the secret part: meeting characters with code names, collecting information, passing on instructions and money.

In his carefree youth, before his crisis, Innokentii had seen nothing reprehensible about this backdoor business—he had thought it fun, and made light work of it. Now it was distasteful, repellent.

The great truth for Innokentii used to be that we only live once.

Now with the new feeling that had ripened in him, he became aware of another law: that we have only one conscience.

A life laid down cannot be reclaimed—nor can a ruined conscience.

But there was no one, no one at all in Innokentii's circle, not even his wife, to whom he could tell all these new thoughts. She had not understood or sympathized with the belated affection he had felt for his dead mother, nor did she understand why anyone should take an interest in events which were over and done with, never to return. If she had known that he had begun to despise his job, she would have been horrified: This job of his was the foundation of their glittering prosperity.

The gap between them had widened so far in the past year that he could no longer risk revealing himself.

This latest posting pleased him, but also frightened him. He liked the United Nations as an idea—not its Charter, but what it could be given: a general willingness to compromise and to avoid malicious point-scoring. He was very much in favor of world government. What else could save the planet? But that was the spirit in which Swedes or Burmese or Ethiopians could go to the UN. He was propelled by an iron fist at his back. Once again he was packed off with a secret mission, an undeclared purpose, a double memory, and a poisonous hidden brief.

During those months in Moscow he did at last find time to visit his uncle in Tver.

The First Circle: Chapter 61

The Uncle from Tver

The poverty-stricken look of the house made him surer than ever that he should not have come.

But still, this was his mother's brother, he knew about her life from childhood on, and was in fact Innokentii's only blood relation. Bolt now, and he would never learn all he needed to know, never even be able to think his own problem through.

And anyway, his uncle's directness, and his one-sided grin, pleased Innokentii. In those first few words he sensed that there was more to the man than had appeared in the two short letters.

In times of general mistrust and treachery, kinship gives at least an initial hope that the man you are dealing with has not been thrown in your way for some underhand purpose, that his route to you was a natural one. You can tell a kinsman, even a dim one, things that you could not discuss with the most luminous of sages.

Uncle Avenir was not just thin; he had withered away till there was only the indispensable minimum left on his bones. But such people are long-lived.

"How old are you, exactly, Uncle?"

(Innokentii hadn't even a rough idea.)

His uncle looked at him hard and answered enigmatically:

"I'm his contemporary."

"Whose?"

"The man himself."

His gaze was unwavering.

Innokentii smiled readily. This was familiar ground. Even in the years when he had enthused in unison with everybody else, The Man's vulgar manner, his crass speeches, his glaring stupidity had left a bad taste.

When his remark was met neither with polite incomprehension nor with lofty disapproval, Uncle Avenir brightened and risked a little joke.

"Ahem! You must admit that it would be presumptuous of me to die first. If I can squeeze into second place in the queue, I shall."

They both laughed. The first spark had leapt between them. After that it was easier. . . .

"Everything I do here I do with a clear conscience. When I empty the slops—it's with a clear conscience. I scrape the floor—with a clear conscience. If I rake out the ashes and light the stove—there's nothing bad in that. But if you've got a position to hold down, you can't live like that. You have to truckle . . . and you have to be dishonest. I beat a retreat every time. I couldn't even stand being a librarian, let alone a teacher."

"What's so hard about a librarian's job?"

"Just go and try it. You have to rubbish good books and praise bad ones. You have to mislead undeveloped minds. What job would you say can be done with a clear conscience?"

Innokentii knew too little about other jobs to say anything. The only job he had held was against his conscience.

Their conversation had got off to a good start. . . . They reminisced about Innokentii's mother. They looked at old snapshots, and Uncle made him a present of some of them. He had, however, been a lot older than his sister, and they had not been children together . . . .

They put the light out. But they didn't feel like sleeping. . . .

"It was all done by fraud," Uncle Avenir insisted. In the dark you would never have taken his firm voice for that of an old man. "Instead of a government true to its word—'Peace to the peoples! Bayonets into the ground!'—a year later Deserter Squads were hunting peasants in the woods and shooting them as a lesson to the rest! The Tsar never did that. 'Workers' Control of Production'? Nowhere did it last a single month. The central government got a stranglehold on everything. If they'd said in 1917 that production norms would be raised year in and year out—who would ever have followed them? An end of secret diplomacy, and secret appointments—and in no time they were stamping everything 'secret' or 'top secret.' Was there ever a country in which the people knew less about their government than we do?"

Skipping from decade to decade and subject to subject was somehow easier in the dark, and Uncle Avenir was soon telling Innokentii that throughout the war large contingents of NKVD troops were garrisoned in all big provincial towns and never moved up to the front. Whereas the Tsar had put all his "guards" regiments through the mincer and was left with no internal troops to put down revolution. As for the muddleheaded Provisional Government, it had no troops at all at its disposal. . . .

They had said good night twice, and Uncle Avenir had asked whether he should leave the door open because it was a bit stuffy—but then for some reason the atomic bomb surfaced, and he came back to whisper fiercely: "They'll never make it themselves!"

"They may do. In fact, I've heard that the first bomb will be tested very shortly."

"Poppycock!" Uncle Avenir said confidently. "They'll announce it—but who can check? They haven't got the industrial base for it. It would take them twenty years."

He turned to leave the room, and came back yet again.

"But if they do succeed in making it, we're done for, Inok. We shall lose all hope of freedom."

Innokentii lay on his back, his eyes drinking in the thick darkness.

"Yes, it will be dreadful. . . . They won't let it lie idle. . . . And without the bomb they'll never dare go to war."

"War is never the way out." (Uncle Avenir was back again.) "It isn't the advancing armies, the fires, and the bombing that make war terrible—it's terrible mainly because it gives stupidity legitimate power over intelligence. Still, that's the way it is with us even without war. . . . Now go to sleep."

Household chores will not stand neglect. All that Uncle Avenir had scamped that day awaited him next morning, in addition to his usual routine. Before he left for the market, he took down two wads of newspaper, and Innokentii, knowing by now that it would be impossible to read them in the evening, hastened to look at them by daylight. The dried-out and dust-laden pages were unpleasant to the touch and left nasty smudges on the tips of his fingers. At first he kept washing or wiping the dirt off, but after a while he stopped noticing it, as he had stopped noticing all the house's defects—the uneven floors, the poor light from the windows—and his uncle's shabbiness. The earlier the year, the stranger it was to read about. He knew now that he would not be leaving that day either . . .

They closed the shutters and bolted them. Then Uncle Avenir opened a chest in one of the box rooms and with the aid of an oil lamp (there was no wiring there) pulled out some warm clothes smelling of mothballs, some of them just rags. Then he held the lamp high and showed his nephew his treasure: The smooth, painted bottom of the chest was lined with a copy of *Pravda* from the second day of the October Revolution. The banner headline read,

"Comrades! With your blood you have ensured that the Constituent Assembly, the rightful master of our land, will be duly convened."

"That was before there had been any elections, of course. They didn't know yet how few would vote for them."

He repacked the chest slowly and neatly.

It was in the Constituent Assembly that the paths of Innokentii's father and uncle had crossed. Artem, his father, was one of the leaders of the land-based sailors who had dispersed the unspeakable Constituent Assembly, while Uncle Avenir had demonstrated in support of that long-promised and eagerly awaited body.

The demonstration with which Uncle Avenir had marched had gathered at the Troitsky Bridge. It was a mild, overcast winter day without wind or snow, and many of them wore open-necked shirts under their sheepskin coats. There were many students, high school pupils, and young ladies. Post office workers, telegraphists, civil servants. And miscellaneous individuals like Uncle Avenir. There were red flags carried by socialists and revolutionaries, and one or two green and white Kadet flags. A second demonstration, starting from the factories over the Neva, was entirely Social Democratic, also carrying red flags.

This story was told last thing at night, and in the dark again, so as not to annoy Raisa Timofeevna. The house was shut up tight and in uneasy darkness, as all houses in Russia used to be in the far-off and forgotten time of feuds and murders, when people listened anxiously to the menacing sound of footsteps in the street and peered out through cracks in the shutters if there was a moon. There was no moon that night, and the street lamp was some way from the house. There were no gaps in these shutters, but a faint light struggling through the unshuttered window in the corridor and the wide-open door of their room occasionally allowed Innokentii to distinguish the movements rather than the contours of his uncle's head against the surrounding blackness. Unsupported by the shine of his eyes and the tormented lines of his face, his voice asserted itself all the more youthfully and assuredly.

"We marched grimly, in silence, not singing. We understood the importance of the occasion—but perhaps we didn't fully understand. This was the one and only day of a free Russian parliament—something that had not existed in the preceding 500 years, and would not exist in the 100 years ahead. Who wanted this parliament anyway? How many of us had gathered, from all over Russia? Five thousand. . . . They opened fire on us from gateways, from rooftops, and then from the sidewalks—and they weren't shooting in the air but aiming point blank at the demonstrators, chest-high. Two or three fell out with each casualty, the rest marched on. . . . None of us returned their fire—we hadn't a single revolver between us. They wouldn't let us get as far as the Tauride Palace. It was densely surrounded by sailors and Latvian sharp-shooters. The Latvians decided our fate, little knowing what was in store for Latvia. On the Liteiny the Red Guards barred the way: "Break it up! Get on the pavement!" They opened fire in short bursts. Red Guards tore one of the red flags out of our hands—I could tell you a thing or two about those Red Guards.... They broke the pole and trampled the flag underfoot.... Some of the demonstrators scattered; some ran back the way they'd come. The Red Guards fired on them from behind and killed some. They found it so easy, those Red Guards, shooting peaceful demonstrators in the back. Just imagine it—and remember that the Civil War hadn't begun yet! But their code of behavior was already worked out."

Uncle Avenir took a deep breath. "Nowadays January 9th is a red-letter day in the calendar, but January 5th you can't even mention in a whisper."[1]

He heaved another sigh.

"And then there was the low trick they played, pretending that they opened fire on us because the demonstration was organized by supporters of Kaledin. What had we to do with Kaledin, I ask you? Some people can't understand the idea of opposition within their own ranks. Who are these people who walk among us, speak our language, and demand what they call freedom? We must at all costs disown them, connect them with the enemy outside, and then we can comfortably open fire on them."

The silence in the darkness was more tense and meaningful than ever.

The old wire mattress creaked as Innokentii pulled himself up against the headboard.

"What happened inside the Tauride?"

"On the eve of the Epiphany?" Uncle Avenir took a deep breath. "The mob, the *ochlos*,[2] was in full cry.... Deafening three-fingered whistles.... Filthy language drowned the speeches. They banged their rifle butts on the floor, with or without reason. They were on guard duty, you see. Guarding whom—against what? So-called soldiers and sailors, half of them drunk, spewing in the refreshment room, snoring on sofas, spitting out the husks of their sunflower seeds all over the foyer. Put yourself in the place of a deputy, an educated man, and tell me what you would do with that filthy rabble. A tap on the shoulder, or a quiet telling off would be blatant counterrevolution! An insult to sacred mob rule! Besides, they were wearing crossed

---

[1] January 9th refers to the massacre of workers marching in a large procession to try to present a petition to the Tsar in 1905; known as "Bloody Sunday," it was commemorated annually in the Soviet Union. January 5th refers to the date of the massacre of marchers in 1918 that Avenir has just described.

[2] *Ochlos*: Greek word for *mob*.

machine-gun belts over their tunics. They had grenades and Mausers at their belts. In the hall where the Constituent Assembly met, they sat with rifles even among the general public, stood in the gangways rifle in hand, leveled them at speakers as though they were targets on the range. Somebody would be talking about some sort of democratic peace and the nationalization of the land, and twenty muzzles would be trained on him, foresights and backsights in alignment. If they should kill him, it wouldn't even cost them an apology! Bring on the next one! Sitting there with their rifles aimed at the speaker's mouth! That's all you need to know about them. That's what they were like when they took over Russia, that's what they always had been, and that's what they'll be as long as they live. They may change in some respects, but not in essentials. Then there was Sverdlov, snatching the bell from the senior deputy's hand, shoving him aside, refusing to let him declare the Assembly open. Lewin sat in the government box laughing up his sleeve, reveling in it all. As for People's Commissar Karelin, one of the Left S.R.s, he was roaring his head off! He hadn't got the wit to realize what he was letting himself in for! In six months' time his own gang would be snuffed out! You know the rest . . . you've seen it at the cinema. The cloth-headed commissar with the cudgel, Drubber Dubenko, sent his lads to declare the superfluous assembly closed. The dry-land sailors with their cartridge belts and pistols rose to catch the chairman's eye. . . ."

"Including my father?"

"Yes, including your father. The great Civil War hero. Almost at the very time when your mother . . . gave in to him. They loved smacking their lips over delicately nurtured young ladies from good homes. That was the most mouth-watering prize the Revolution had to offer them."

Innokentii's brow, ears, cheeks, and neck were burning. He was on fire, as though he himself had taken part in some vile act.

His uncle pressed a hand on his knee, leaned closer and asked:

"Have you never felt the truth of the saying that the sins of the parents are visited on the children? And that you must cleanse yourself of them?"

The First Circle: Chapter 66

Going to the People

Rubin and Sologdin indulgently referred to Nerzhin's friendship with the yardman, Spiridon, as his "going to the people," in quest of that great homespun truth which Gogol, Nekrasov, Herzen, the Slavophiles, Lev Tolstoy, and finally the much-maligned Vasisuali Lokhankin had sought in vain before him.

Whereas Rubin and Sologdin themselves had never sought that homespun truth, because each of them possessed the ultimate truth, crystal clear and his very own.

Rubin knew for certain that "the people" is an artificial generalization, that every people is divided into classes, and that even they change as time goes by. Seeking a superior understanding of life in the peasant class was unimaginative and futile. The proletariat was the only consistently and thoroughly revolutionary class, the future belonged to the proletariat, and only the collectivism and selflessness of the proletariat gave life a higher meaning.

Sologdin was no less certain that "the people" is the formless raw material of history, from which the stout, crude, but indispensable legs of that Colossus—the Spirit of Man—are molded. "The people" was a collective term for the totality of crude and faceless creatures hopelessly straining in the harness to which they were born and from which death alone would release them. Only rare individuals scattered like brilliant stars about the dark sky of existence were endowed with superior insight.

They both knew that Nerzhin would get over it, grow up a bit, come to his senses.

Nerzhin had indeed already outgrown many of his wilder ideas.

Nineteenth-century Russian literature, so full of heartache for "our suffering brothers," had left him, as it leaves all who read it for the first time, with an image of "the People"—personified as a gray-haired saintly figure with a halo, in a silver frame, uniting in itself wisdom, moral purity, and spiritual greatness.

But the place for that image was the bookshelf—or that long-lost world, the fields and byways of the nineteenth century.

Russia in fact no longer existed—only the Soviet Union, and in it the big city in which Gleb had grown up. Success upon success had rained on young Gleb from the cornucopia of learning. He had discovered that he was a quick thinker, but there were others who thought even quicker and who overwhelmed him with their knowledge. "The People" stayed on his bookshelf, but in his mind the only people who mattered were those who carried in their heads the cultural treasures of the world—encyclopedic connoisseurs of antiquity and the fine arts, people of wide and varied erudition. He had to belong to this elite. Failure to win acceptance meant a life of misery.

Then the war came, and Nerzhin found himself serving in a horse-drawn transport unit. Choking with the indignity of it, he clumsily chased horses round the pasture, trying to throw a halter round their necks or jump on their backs. He had never learned to ride, he couldn't handle harness, he couldn't fork hay, and a nail would bend double under his hammer, as though deriding this unskillful workman! The worse things went for Nerzhin, the more raucously those around him—the unshaven, foulmouthed, pitiless, utterly unlikable people—guffawed.

In time Nerzhin made his way up from the ranks and became an artillery officer. Youthful and nimble again, he walked around smartly belted, elegantly flourishing a pliant twig broken off for the purpose—he carried nothing else.

He rode daringly on the footboards of trucks, swore roundly at river crossings, was ever ready to move out at midnight and in foul weather, and had behind him—obedient, devoted, eager to serve, and therefore decidedly likable—the People. And his own small sample of the people listened readily, or so it seemed, to his pep talks about the great People which had risen as one man to defend its country.

Then Nerzhin was arrested. In his first prisons, under investigation or awaiting transfer, and in the first camps, which had stunned and numbed him, he was horrified to discover that some of the elite had another side to them, in circumstances in which only firmness, willpower, and loyalty to friends showed the true worth of a prisoner and determined the fate of his comrades, these refined and sensitive and highly educated connoisseurs of the exquisite rather often turned out to be cowards, quick to surrender, and, thanks to their education, disgustingly ingenious in justifying their dirty tricks. Such people quickly degenerated into traitors and toadies. Nerzhin came to see himself as not so very different from them. He recoiled from those with whom he had once proudly identified himself. He began to loathe and to ridicule things he had revered. His aim now was to become ordinary, to shed the affectations—the exaggerated politeness, the preciosity—of the intellectuals. In the years of unrelieved disaster, in the worst moments of his shattered life, Nerzhin decided that the only valuable, the only important people were those who worked with their hands, planing timber, shaping metal, tilling the soil, smelting iron. He tried now to learn from simple laboring people the wisdom of their infinitely skillful hands and their philosophy of life. So Nerzhin had come full circle, and arrived at the idea so fashionable in the nineteenth century—that of "going to"—going down to—"the people."

But the circle was not quite a closed one: It ended in a spiraling tail unimaginable to our grandfathers. Unlike the educated gentlefolk of the nineteenth century, the zek Nerzhin could descend without dressing up in strange clothes and feeling with his foot for the ladder: He was simply slung bodily into the mass of the people, in ragged padded trousers, and a patched jerkin, and given a daily work quota. Nerzhin shared the lot of simple people not as a condescending gentleman—always conscious of the difference and so always alien—but as one of themselves, indistinguishable from them, an equal among equals.

It was not to ingratiate himself with the muzhik but to earn a soggy hunk of bread for the day that Nerzhin had to learn to knock nails in straight and plane planks so that they fitted perfectly. After his cruel training in the camps, another of Nerzhin's misconceptions fell away. He realized that he could lower himself no further. There was nothing, and no one, down there. He was cured, too, of his illusion that the People, with its age-old homespun wisdom, was superior to himself. Squatting with them in the snow at their escort's command, hiding with them from the foreman in the dark corners of a building site, heaving handbarrows over freezing ground, and drying his foot-rags in the huts with them, Nerzhin saw clearly that these people were in no way his betters. Their endurance of hunger and thirst was no greater than his. They were no more stouthearted than he was, faced with the stone wall of a ten-year sentence. No more farsighted and no more resourceful at critical moments—in transit from prison to camp or during body searches. They were, though, more gullible and more easily deceived by stool pigeons. They fell more readily for the crude deceptions of the authorities. They looked forward to an amnesty, though Stalin would sooner turn up his toes than grant it. If some thug of a warder happened to be in a good mood and smiled at them, they hastened to smile back. They were also much greedier for trivial favors: a "supplementary," 100 grams of rancid lardy-cake, a pair of hideous prison trousers, just as long as they were newish or a bit flashy.

Most of them lacked a "point of view" of the sort that a man treasures more than life itself.

All that was left to him, Nerzhin decided, was to be himself.

Once he had recovered—perhaps finally, perhaps not—from this last of many infatuations, Nerzhin saw the People differently. None of his books had prepared him for his new insight. "The People" did not mean all those who speak your language, nor yet the chosen few branded with the fiery mark of genius. Neither birth, nor the labor of your hands, nor the privileges of education admit you to membership of the People.

Only your soul can do that.

And each of us fashions his soul himself, year in and year out.

You must strive to temper and facet your soul so as to become a human being. And hence a humble component of your people.

A man with such a soul cannot as a rule expect to prosper, to go far in his career, to get rich. Which is why for the most part "the people" is not to be found at the higher levels of society.

The First Circle: Chapter 85

Prince Kurbsky

The capacity for heroic deeds—for actions which make extreme demands on a person's strength—depends to a greater or lesser extent on will-power. Some people are born heroes, others are not. The heroic acts that cost the greatest effort are those performed spontaneously by sheer will-power. Such actions are easier if they are the culmination of years of purposeful effort. And for the man born a hero great deeds are blessedly easy, as easy as breathing.

Ruska Doronin, for instance, had lived as an outlaw, a wanted man, sought all over the Soviet Union, with the carefree smile of an innocent child. The thrill of risk, the fever of adventure, must have been injected into his bloodstream at birth.

Respectable Innokentii, fortunate Innokentii, could never have brought himself to vanish and flit around the country under a false name. Arrest might be imminent, but it would never enter his head that he could do anything to prevent it.

He had made his telephone call to the Embassy on impulse, without stopping to think. His discovery had come as a surprise—and too late for him to wait those few days until he arrived in New York. He had called like a man possessed, although he knew that all telephones were bugged, and that he was one of the very few people in the Ministry who knew Georgii Koval's secret.

He had simply flung himself into the abyss because the thought that they could brazenly steal the bomb, and in a year's time start brandishing it, was intolerable. But he had not been prepared for the shattering impact of the stony bottom. He had cherished a wild hope that he could flutter out of it, escape responsibility, fly across the ocean, get his breath back, and tell his story to the press.

But even before he reached the bottom he had relapsed into impotent despair, spiritual exhaustion. His short-lived resolve had snapped, and terror was consuming him like a flame.

He had felt it most acutely that Monday morning, when he had to force himself to begin living again, to go to work, anxiously trying to detect menacing changes in the looks and voices of those around him.

Still outwardly self-possessed, Innokentii was internally a wreck, incapable of fighting back, of seeking a way out, of trying to escape.

It was not quite 11 a.m. when his boss's secretary, denying him access, informed Innokentii that his appointment—so she had heard—had been held up by the Vice-Minister.

This news, though not definite, came as such a shock that Innokentii did not insist on being seen and seeking confirmation. But nothing else could explain the delay, once his departure had been approved. The document accrediting him to the United Nations already bore Vyshinsky's stamp. He had obviously been found out.

The world seemed to have become a darker place. His shoulders felt as if he was carrying a yoke with two full pails. Back in his room it was as much as he could do to lock the door and remove the key so that they would think he had left. He could do this only because the usual occupant of the other desk had not returned from an official trip.

Innokentii's insides had turned into a nauseous jelly. He waited for the knock. He was terror-stricken. Any minute now they would come and arrest him. A fleeting thought—don't open the door. Make them break it down.

Or hang yourself before they come in.

Or jump out of the window. From the third floor. Right into the street. Two seconds in flight—and smash. Consciousness extinguished.

A thick sheaf of papers lay on the desk—the auditors' estimate of Innokentii's debts. He had to check the account and return it before leaving for abroad. But even the sight of it made him feel sick.

The heating was on but he felt cold, shivery.

His feebleness disgusted him! He was passively awaiting his doom.

Innokentii lay flat, face down, on the sofa. With the whole length of his body pressed against the sofa, he got from it some support, a kind of reassurance.

His thoughts grew confused.

Was it really him? Could he really have had the nerve to telephone the embassy? And if so—why? At the other end someone speaking Russian with an accent. "Ring from Canada. . . . Just who are you? How do I know you're telling the truth?" Those arrogant Americans! They'll live to see their farmers collectivized to a man. Serve them right.

Should never have called . . . sorry for myself . . . ending my life at thirty . . . perhaps under torture. . . .

But no, he didn't regret calling. It had to be done. It was as though someone had been leading him, and he had felt no fear.

No, it wasn't that he had no regrets—he no longer had the will to regret or not to regret. As his sense of imminent danger faded, he lay still; hardly breathing, hugging the sofa, wishing only that it would all end, that they would soon take him away . . . or something.

But luckily no one knocked, no one tried the door. And the telephone did not ring once.

He lost consciousness. Oppressive dreams, absurd dreams, pursued one another, until his head was bursting, and he awoke. Unrefreshed, indeed more jaded, feebler than before he had fallen asleep, exhausted by all the arrests or attempted arrests he had undergone in his dreams. He was too weak to rise from the sofa and shake off his nightmares, or indeed to stir at all. Too weak to resist the sickening drowsiness sucking him back into sleep.

He slept again at last, dead to the world. Slept with his mouth open, dribbling onto the sofa. The damp patch, and the midmorning bustle in the corridor woke him up.

He rose, unlocked the door, and went for a wash. They were bringing tea and sandwiches round.

No one was about to arrest him. The colleagues he met in the corridor and the main office behaved towards him as they always did.

This proved nothing. How could anyone else know?

But their unchanged looks and voices raised his spirits.

He asked the girl to bring him really hot, really strong tea, and drank two glasses of it with enjoyment. He felt his confidence growing.

But he still could not bring himself to insist on seeing the chief. To try and find out. . . .

The sensible solution was obviously to do away with himself. He would simply be obeying his instinct of self-preservation, sparing himself suffering.

But only if he knew for sure that they were going to arrest him.

Perhaps they weren't?

The telephone rang. Innokentii jumped. His heart stood still, then began beating quite audibly.

It was only Dotty. Dotty's marvelously musical telephone voice. Dotty talking like a wife reinstated in her conjugal rights. She asked how things were, and suggested going out somewhere that evening.

Once again Innokentii felt a glow of gratitude and affection. Bad wife or not, she was closer to him than anyone.

He did not tell her that his posting might have been canceled. Instead he imagined himself in a theater that evening, perfectly safe—people weren't arrested in the theater in full view of the audience!

"All right, get tickets for something cheerful," he said.

"The operetta, maybe? It's something called 'Akulina.' There's nothing much on otherwise. It's 'The Law of Lycurgus' at the little Red Army Theater and 'Voice of America' at the big one. The Arts is doing 'The Unforgettable.'"

"'Law of Lycurgus' sounds too good to be true. The worst plays always get great titles. Book for 'Akulina.' And we'll take in a restaurant after."

"Okay! Okay!" Dotty laughed happily into the telephone.

(And stay there all night so they won't find me at home! They always came in the night, of course.)

Innokentii was gradually recovering his self-possession. What if he was suspected? Shchevronok and Zavarzin were more familiar with the details than he was—they must surely be the prime suspects. And anyway suspicion was one thing, proof another.

Suppose I am in danger of arrest—there's nothing I can do about it. Should I be hiding things? There's nothing to hide. So why worry?

By now he felt strong enough to pace the floor as he thought it over. Suppose they are going to arrest me. It may not be today, or even this week. So should I stop living? Or should I spend my last few days enjoying myself like crazy?

Why had he panicked like that? Only last night, damn it, he had—oh, so wittily—defended Epicurus. Why not follow his advice? His ideas seemed sensible enough.

Thinking that he ought to look through his notebooks for entries best suppressed, he remembered that he had once jotted down excerpts from Epicurus. He found the place. "Our private feelings of satisfaction and dissatisfaction are the ultimate criteria of good and evil," he read.

That meant nothing to Innokentii in his present state of mind. He read on.

"Know that there is no such thing as immortality. Therefore death is not an evil, it is simply irrelevant to us: As long as we exist there is no death, and when death comes upon us we do not exist."

"Well said!" Innokentii leaned back in his chair. "Who was it I recently heard saying just that? Yes, of course—that young war veteran at the party last night."

Innokentii pictured to himself the Garden in Athens. Epicurus, a swarthy septuagenarian in a tunic, was holding forth from marble steps, while he, Innokentii, in modern dress, perched on a pedestal, in a casual sort of American pose, listening.

"Belief in immortality was born of the greed of insatiable people who squander the time that nature has allotted us. But the wise man will find that time sufficient to make the round of attainable delights and, when the time to die arrives, leave the table of life replete, making way for other guests. For the wise man one human span suffices, while the foolish man would not know what to do even with eternity."

Brilliant! But here's the rub: What if you are dragged from the table not by nature, in your seventies, but at thirty, by the Ministry of State Security?

"One should not fear physical suffering. He who knows the limits of suffering is proof against fear. Prolonged suffering is always insignificant, while acute suffering is never for long. The wise man will not lose his spiritual calm even under torture. His memory will bring back to him his former sensual and spiritual gratifications and, in spite of his present bodily suffering, will restore his spiritual equilibrium."

Innokentii began gloomily pacing the office floor.

That was what he dreaded—not actually dying, but being arrested and physically tortured.

Epicurus says you can rise above torture, does he? If only I had such strength of character.

Innokentii knew only too well that he did not.

He would die without regret if he knew that people would some day learn that there had been such a citizen of the world and that he had tried to save them from nuclear war.

If the communists got the atom bomb, the planet was doomed.

But they would shoot him like a dog in the dungeon, and hide his case file where it could never be found.

He threw back his head as a bird does to let water trickle down its taut throat.

But no—the idea that they might tell the world about him was more painful still. We are so befogged, he thought, that we cannot distinguish traitors from friends. What was Prince Kurbsky?[1] A traitor. And what was Ivan the Terrible? The beloved father of his people.

But *that* Kurbsky had escaped his terrible ruler. Innokentii had not been so lucky.

If he was exposed, his fellow-countrymen would enthusiastically stone him! How many would understand him? A thousand out of two hundred million if he was lucky. How many remembered the rejection of the sensible

---

[1] Andrey Mikhailovich Kurbsky (1528–83), a military leader and once a close friend of Tsar Ivan the Terrible, fearlessly and publicly criticized the tsar's acts of brutal cruelty.

Baruch plan: Deny yourselves the atom bomb, and the American bombs will be put under international lock and key? Above all: How did he have the audacity to decide what his country should do when that right belonged to the supreme power alone?

You prevented the Transformer of the World, the Forger of Happiness from stealing the bomb? That means you denied the bomb to your Motherland!

But what did the Motherland want with it? What did the village of Rozhdestvo want with it? That half-blind female dwarf? The old woman with the dead chicken? The one-legged peasant in rags and tatters?

Who, in all the village, would condemn him for that telephone call? Individually, they wouldn't begin to understand. But herd them into a village meeting and they would condemn him unanimously.

They were short of roads, textiles, planks, glass.... Give them back their milk, their bread, maybe even their church bells—but what good was the atom bomb to them?

What vexed Innokentii most was that his telephone call might not have prevented the theft after all.

The filigreed hands of the bronze clock pointed to 4:45.

It was getting dark.

Cancer Ward

After the sensational success of *One Day in the Life of Ivan Denisovich*, Solzhenitsyn tried to get *Cancer Ward* published. When this attempt failed, his standing as an author acceptable to the Soviet authorities ended. *Cancer Ward* and *The First Circle* appeared in the West in 1968 to critical acclaim.

Cancer Ward, like *The First Circle*, is autobiographical in inspiration, presents a cross section of society within a place of confinement, and uses a polyphonic structure to emphasize character rather than plot. One character, Oleg Kostoglotov, rises in significance above any other. He shares some qualities with Solzhenitsyn, though not as many as *The First Circle*'s Gleb Nerzhin. Like the author, Oleg had fought in World War II, served time in the gulag because of incautious comments about Stalin, experienced internal exile, developed cancer, and received treatment at the clinic in Tashkent. Unlike the author, Oleg comes from Leningrad, lacks formal education, and is unmarried.

Cancer forces the clinic's patients to ponder death, which is always the chief prompter of the human drama, and thus the novel focuses on the ultimate question of the meaning of life. Podduyev, a loud-mouthed liar, broaches the novel's thematic core when he reads in Tolstoy's story "What Men Live By" that the correct answer is "love." His quizzing of wardmates for answers to this same question elicits superficial answers: rations, air, water, one's pay, one's professional skills. Often the cancers correlate with their victims' defining traits: Podduyev dies of cancer of the tongue; throat cancer robs a philosopher of his speech. Since cancer, like the rain, falls on the just and the unjust alike, some cases underscore the mystery of suffering: An unpleasant Soviet bureaucrat leaves the clinic cured, but the good Doctor Dontsova develops cancer from the radiation dosages she selflessly administers.

The presence of many women in the hospital setting contributes to the distinctive flavor of *Cancer Ward* among Solzhenitsyn's works. Fittingly, then, the present selections focus on the role male-female relationships play in the search for meaning in life. In chapter 10, Dyomka dreads amputation of his cancerous leg. This thoughtful teenager has been instructed by Oleg and impressed by saintly old Aunt Styofa, though his Soviet schooling tells him not to accept her view that one's life depends on God. In contrast, Asya, a pretty girl preoccupied by sex, tells him that "life is for happiness." By chapter 28, Dyomka has undergone his amputation and accepted his loss. Asya, however, has learned that a mastectomy awaits her, and her outlook on life cannot accommodate this fateful news.

The most memorable male-female relationships among adults feature Oleg and two attractive women, both of whom see the virtuous qualities beneath his gruff exterior. The alluring and sexually experienced young nurse Zoya warns Oleg that the hormone therapy ordered by Dr. Dontsova will leave him impotent, to which news he roars, "I don't want to be saved *at any price!*" The "naturally kind" Dr. Vera Gangart (whom Oleg nicknames "Vega"), having turned inward after her fiancé's death in the war, responds to Oleg's candor, and these two contemporaries become friends.

Chapters 35 and 36 bring the novel to a bittersweet end. Their titles, "The First Day of Creation . . . and the Last Day," mirror Oleg's immediate exhilaration at leaving the clinic and his eventual resignation to the reality that his cancer is in retreat but not eradicated. These chapters comprise some of Solzhenitsyn's most lyrical passages, and their literary mix is enriched by his unusual incorporation of symbolism in the meanings Oleg attaches to the day's experiences. Oleg is astounded that both Zoya and Vega have offered him a night's lodging, but a sharp reminder of his sexual deficiency leads him to decide in favor of renunciation, and he heads for home. This decision is just one more stage of a morally mature man's spiritual liberation, hard-won through suffering and voluntary self-limitation.

Cancer Ward is Solzhenitsyn's least politically charged novel, though political overtones are not absent. Oleg, for example, sees the zoo's tiger as symbolic of Stalin. Nevertheless, precisely this novel caused Solzhenitsyn to identify the writer's task as attending to "the secrets of the human heart and conscience, the confrontation between life and death, the triumph over spiritual sorrow."

Cancer Ward: Chapter 10

The Children

All she did was run her fingers round Dyomka's tumor and hug his shoulders slightly. Then she moved on. But something fateful happened as she did it: Dyomka felt it. The twigs of his hope were snapped short.

He didn't feel it at once. First there was a lot of talk in the ward and everyone was saying goodbye to Proshka, then he started scheming about how he could move into Proshka's bed by the window, now a lucky one. The light was better there for reading; it was also nearer for talking to Kostoglotov. And then a "new boy" came in.

He was a young man, well tanned, with slightly wavy, tidy, pitch-black hair, probably over twenty years old. He was lugging three books under his left arm, and under his right three more.

"Hello, everyone!" he announced from the doorway. Dyomka took a liking to him, he looked so unassuming and sincere. "Where do I go?" he said, gazing around, for some reason not at the beds but at the walls.

"Will you be reading a lot?" asked Dyomka.

"All the time!"

Dyomka thought for a moment,

"Is it for your work or just reading?"

"For my work."

"Well, take that bed over there by the window, all right? They'll make it up for you in a minute. What are your books about?"

"Geology, pal," answered the newcomer.

Dyomka read one of the titles: *Geochemical Exploration of Mineral Deposits*. "Take the bed by the window, then. What's wrong with you?"

"My leg."

"With me it's my leg too."

Yes, the newcomer was moving one leg a bit cautiously. But his figure—it was neat as an ice skater's.

They made up the bed for him, and, as if this was the only reason he had come into hospital, he laid five of his books out on the window sill and stuck his nose into the sixth. He read for an hour or so without asking a question or telling anyone anything. Then he was summoned to see the doctors.

Dyomka too tried to read. First it was stereometry. He tried to build some models out of pencils, but the theorems wouldn't go into his head and the diagrams with their lopped-off straight lines and planes with jagged edges kept on reminding him, hinting at the same thing.

He changed to a book which was a bit easier, *The Water of Life* by someone called Kozhevnikov, which had already picked up a Stalin Prize. It was by A. Kozhevnikov, but there were also an S. Kozhevnikov and a V. Kozhevnikov. Dyomka was rather frightened at the thought of how many writers there were. In the last century there had been about ten, all of them great. In this century there were thousands; you only had to change a letter in one of their names and you had a new writer. There was Safronov and there was Safonov, more than one Safonov, apparently. And was there only one Safronov? No one could have time to read all their books, and when you did read one, it was as if you might just as well not have done. Completely unknown writers floated to the surface, won Stalin prizes, then sank back forever. Nearly every book of any size got a prize the year after it appeared. Forty or fifty prizes popped up every year.

Their titles too kept getting mixed up in Dyomka's head. A lot had been written about two films, *The Big Life* and *The Big Family,* one a very healthy influence, the other a very harmful one, but Dyomka simply couldn't remember which was which, especially as he hadn't seen either. It was the same with ideas; the more he read about them, the more confused they seemed. He had only just grasped that to analyze objectively meant to see things as they are in life. But then he read how Panova, a woman novelist, was being attacked for "treading the marshy ground of objectivism."

Nevertheless he had to cope with it all, understand and remember it.

When Dyomka read *The Water of Life* he couldn't make out whether the book was a drag, or whether it was the mood he was in.

Exhaustion and gloom pressed on him more and more heavily. Did he want someone to talk it over with? Or someone to complain to? Or just someone to have a heart-to-heart talk with, who might perhaps even show him a little pity?

Of course he had read and heard that pity is a humiliating feeling: whether you pity or are pitied.

Even so, he wanted someone to pity him.

Because throughout his life, no one had ever pitied Dyomka.

Here in the ward it was interesting listening and talking to people, but he couldn't talk to them in the way he now wanted. When you're with men you have to behave like a man.

There were women in the clinic, a lot of them, but Dyomka could not make up his mind to cross the threshold of their large, noisy ward. If they had all been healthy women there, it would have been fun to glance in on the way past on the chance of seeing something interesting, but confronted by that great nest of sick women he preferred to turn away from whatever he might see there. Their illness was like a screen of prohibition, much stronger than mere shame. Some of the women he met on the stairs or in the hallways were so depressed, so low-spirited, that they hardly bothered to pull their dressing gowns round them, and he could not avoid seeing their nightdresses round their breasts or below their waists. When this happened, though, he felt no joy, only pain.

This was why he always lowered his eyes when he saw them. It was no easy matter to make friends here.

Aunt Styofa noticed him. She began to ask questions, and they became friendly. She was a mother and a grandmother already, and had, like all grandmothers, wrinkles and an indulgent smile for human weakness. He and Aunt Styofa used to stand about near the top of the stairs and talk for hours. No one had ever listened to Dyomka so attentively and with such sympathy. It was as though she had no one nearer to her than he. And, for him, it was easy to tell her things about himself and even about his mother which he would never have revealed to anyone else.

Dyomka was two years old when his father was killed in the war. Then he had a stepfather, not affectionate but just, and quite possible to live with. His mother became—he had never spoken the word in front of Styofa although he himself had long been certain of it—a whore. His stepfather left her—quite rightly. After that his mother used to bring men to their one room. They always used to drink, and they tried to make Dyomka drink too, but he wouldn't take it. And then the men stayed with her: some till midnight, others till morning. There was no partition in the room, and no darkness because light came in from the street lamps. And it sickened Dyomka so much that the very thought of it, which his friends found so thrilling, seemed to him like so much pigswill.

And so it went on during the fifth and sixth classes. When he reached the seventh class, however, Dyomka went to live with the school watchman, an old man, and the school gave him two meals a day. His mother didn't even try to get him back. She was glad to wash her hands of him.

Dyomka spoke angrily about his mother, he couldn't speak calmly. Aunt Styofa listened to him, shook her head, and said strangely when she'd heard him out: "It takes all sorts to make a world. We're all in the world together!"

Last year Dyomka had moved into a factory housing estate. There was a night school there and they gave him a place in a hostel. He worked as a lathe-operator's apprentice, and later they made him a second-grade opera-tor. He wasn't very good at the job, but as he wanted to be different from his devil-may-care mother, he didn't drink or yell rowdy songs. Instead he stud-ied. He did well in the eighth class and finished the first half of the ninth.

Besides that there was only football. Sometimes he used to run about playing football with the boys. And fate punished him for this, the one little pleasure he enjoyed: in a scramble for the ball someone accidentally hacked him on the shin with his boot. Dyomka didn't even think about it at the time. He limped for a bit and then the pain was gone. But in the autumn his leg started to ache more and more. It was a long time before he went to the doctor with it. They gave him warm compresses for it but it got worse. They sent him along the usual medical obstacle course, first to the provincial cen-ter and now here.

"Why is it," Dyomka would ask Aunt Styofa, "that there's such rank injus-tice in fortune itself? There are people whose lives run smooth as silk from beginning to end, I know there are, while others' are a complete louse-up. And they say a man's life depends on himself. It doesn't depend on him a bit."

"It depends on God," said Aunt Styofa soothingly. "God sees everything. You should submit to him, Dyomusha."

"Well, if it's from God it's even worse. If he can see everything, why does he load it all on one person? I think he ought to try to spread it about a bit. . . ."

But there were no two ways about it—he had to submit. What else was there for him to do?

Aunt Styofa lived locally. Her daughters, sons, and daughters-in-law of-ten used to come and visit her and bring her things to eat. She didn't keep them for long. She shared them with her neighbors and the orderlies. She would call Dyomka out of his ward and slip an egg or a pastry into his hand.

Dyomka's appetite was never satisfied. All his life he had never had enough to eat. His constant, anxious thoughts of food had made his hunger seem greater than it really was. Still, he felt embarrassed at taking so much from Aunt Styofa. If he accepted the egg, he would try to refuse the pastry.

"Take it, take it!" she would say, waving it at him. "It's got meat in it. You can eat it now, while it's still Meat Week."

"Why, can't I eat it afterwards?"

"'Course you can't. Don't you know that?"

"So what comes after Meat Week?"

"Shrovetide, of course."

"That's even better, Aunt Styofa. Shrovetide's even better."

"Better in some ways, worse in others. But no meat!"

"Well, Shrovetide doesn't end then, does it?"

"What do you mean, doesn't end? It's gone in a week."

"So what do we do next?" asked Dyomka cheerfully, as he gobbled up the fragrant homemade meat pie, the like of which had never been baked in *his* home.

"Good heavens, doesn't anybody grow up Christian these days? No one knows anything. After that comes the Great Fast."

"But what's that for—the Great Fast? Why a fast—and why a Great Fast?"

"Because, Dyomusha, if you stuff your belly full it will pull you right down to the ground. You can't go on stuffing like that, you have to have a break sometimes."

"What's a break for?" Dyomka couldn't understand. He'd never known anything else but breaks.

"Breaks are to clear your head. You feel fresher on an empty stomach, haven't you noticed?"

"No, Aunt Styofa, I haven't."

Ever since he had been in the first class, before he could read or write, Dyomka had been taught, knew for certain, and fully understood that religion is a drug, a three-time reactionary dogma, of benefit only to swindlers. Because of it the working people in some places had been unable to free themselves from exploitation. But as soon as they got rid of religion, they would take up arms and free themselves. And Aunt Styofa with her funny calendar, with the word "God" always on her lips, with her carefree smile even in that gloomy clinic, and her pastry, was obviously a thoroughly reactionary figure.

Nevertheless on Saturday after lunch, when the doctors had gone and each patient was left alone with his thoughts, when the cloudy day still lent a little touch of light to the wards, while on the landings and in the corridors the lamps were already on, Dyomka would walk about, limping and searching everywhere for none other than the reactionary Aunt Styofa, who could give him no sensible advice except to submit.

He was afraid they'd take it away, amputate it. He'd have to give it up.

To give it up, not to give it up. To give it up, not to give it up. . . .

With the gnawing pain he felt, perhaps to give it up would be easier.

But Aunt Styofa was in none of her usual places. So he went down to the lower corridor, where it broadened out into the little lobby that was regarded as the clinic's "red corner"[1] (the main-floor duty nurse's table stood there with her medicine cupboard), and then he saw a girl, almost a child, wearing the same kind of faded gray dressing gown. But she was like a film star: yellow hair, the sort you never saw anywhere, with something light and rustling built up from it.

---

[1] Most Soviet institutions possessed a "red corner"—a room with magazines and Communist literature.

Dyomka had glimpsed her for the first time the day before and her hair, yellow like a bed of flowers, had made him blink. She seemed so beautiful that he had not dared to let his eyes rest on her. He had turned them away and walked past. Although there was no one closer to him in age in the whole clinic (except for Surhan, the boy whose leg had been amputated), he knew that girls like that were beyond his reach.

This morning he caught sight of her again, from behind. Even in her hospital dressing gown she had a waist like a wasp, you could recognize her at once. And her little sheaf of yellow hair quivered.

Dyomka had certainly not been looking for her. He knew he'd never be able to make up his mind to approach her. He knew that his mouth would stick like paste and he'd bellow something unintelligible and stupid. But he saw her and his heart missed a beat. Trying not to limp, trying to walk as evenly as possible, he made his way to the red corner, where he began to flip through the pile of the local *Pravda,* already thinned out by patients for packing and other uses.

Half the table, which was covered by a red cloth, was taken up by a bronze bust of Stalin with larger-than-lifesize head and shoulders. Opposite, at the corner of the table, stood an orderly, also heavily built and with a large mouth. She seemed to make a pair with Stalin. It was Saturday and she did not expect any rush, so she had spread a newspaper on the table in front of her and poured some sunflower seeds on to it. She was shelling them with relish, spitting out the husks onto the newspaper without any help from her hands. She'd probably only come in for a minute but been unable to tear herself away from the sunflower seeds.

A loudspeaker on the wall was hoarsely blaring dance music. At a small table two patients were sitting playing checkers.

The girl Dyomka was watching out of the corner of his eye was sitting on a chair by the wall, doing nothing, just sitting straight-backed holding together the neck of her dressing gown. They never had any hooks unless the women sewed them on themselves.

She sat there, a delicate yellow-haired angel, untouchable, who looked as though she might melt and vanish. But how good it would be to *talk* to her about something . . . even about his bad leg.

Dyomka was angry with himself. He kept turning the pages of the newspaper. He suddenly realized that when he had had his hair cut he had not asked them to leave the curl on his forehead. Not wanting to waste time, he'd let them clip his head all over with the clippers. Now she must think he looked like an idiot.

Then suddenly the angel spoke. "Why are you so shy? This is the second day you've been around. You haven't come up to me."

Dyomka jumped. He looked round. Well, who else could she be talking to? Yes, she must be, she was talking to *him*! The tuft or plume on her head trembled like the spikes of a flower.

"What's the matter? Are you the scared type? Go on, get a chair, pull it up, let's get to know each other."

"I'm . . . not scared." But something broke in his voice and stopped it ringing out in the normal way.

"Then get a chair. Park it next to me."

Dyomka took the chair. Making an extra effort not to limp, he carried it with one hand and put it next to her by the wall. He gave her his hand.

"Dyomka."

"Asya." She put her soft palm into his and then drew it away. He sat down, and it struck him as funny: There they were sitting next to each other like bride and groom. He couldn't even see her properly. He got up and moved the chair into an easier position.

"Why do you sit here not doing anything?" Dyomka asked.

"Why should I do anything? Anyway I am doing something."

"What are you doing?"

"I'm listening to music. I'm dancing in the mind. Can't you?"

"In the mind?"

"All right then, on the feet?"

Dyomka sucked his teeth, which meant "no."

"I saw you were rather green. We could have a turn round the floor now." Asya looked around. "Only there's nowhere to do it, and what kind of a dance is this anyway? So I just listen; silence always gets me down."

"Which is a good dance?" Dyomka was enjoying this conversation. "The tango?"

Asya sighed. "The tango! That's what our grandmothers used to dance. The thing today is rock-'n-roll. We don't dance it here yet, but in Moscow they do. Only professionals, of course."

Dyomka did not really take in all she was saying. It was nice just to talk to her and to be allowed to look straight at her. She had strange eyes with a touch of green. But you can't paint eyes, they stay the way they are. Even so they were pretty.

"That really is a dance!" Asya clicked her fingers. "Only I can't give you a demonstration. I've never seen it. How do you spend your time, then? Do you sing songs?"

"No-o, I can't sing."

"Why not? We always sing when silence gets us down. So what *do* you do? Do you play the accordion?"

"No-o," said Dyomka, covered with shame. He wasn't much compared to her, was he? He couldn't just blurt out to her that his passion was for social problems.

Asya was quite at a loss. What a funny type, she thought.

"Are you an athlete, then? I'm not bad at the pentathlon myself, by the way. I can do a hundred and forty centimeters and I can do thirteen point two seconds. . . ."

"No-o, I'm not." Dyomka realized bitterly how worthless he must seem to her. Some people could fix up their lives so easily. Dyomka would never be able to. He played a little football. . . .

And where had it got him?

"You do at least smoke? And drink?" Asya asked, still hoping. "Or is it only beer?"

"Beer . . ." sighed Dyomka. (He had never tasted beer in his life, but he couldn't let himself be completely disgraced.)

"Oh," groaned Asya, as though someone had knocked all the breath out of her. "What a lot of momma's boys you all are! No sporting spirit. The people at school are like you. Last September they moved us to a boys' school,[2] but the headmaster kept on just a few teachers' pets and bookworms and miserable types. All the best boys he stuck in the girls' school."

She did not mean to humiliate him, in fact she was sorry for him, but all the same he was hurt that she should think him a "miserable type."

"Which class are you in?" he asked.

"The tenth."

"So who lets you wear your hair like that?"

"Who lets us? They fight us! And we fight them!"

It was openhearted, the way she spoke. But let her tease him, let her even pummel him, the only thing that mattered was that they were talking.

The dance music stopped and the announcer began to speak of the people's struggle against the shameful Paris treaties, which were dangerous for France because they put her at the mercy of Germany, and intolerable for Germany because they put her at the mercy of France.

"So what do you do?" Asya was still trying to find out.

"I'm a turner," Dyomka said casually but with dignity.

Even the turner did not impress Asya. "How much do you earn?"

Dyomka was very proud of his pay, for it was his own and the first he had ever earned. But now he felt he couldn't let on how much.

"Oh, it's nothing. Nothing at all," he forced himself to say.

---

[2] In September 1954 coeducation was reintroduced in the Soviet Union.

"It's a complete waste of time," declared Asya quite categorically. "You'd do much better to become a sportsman. You've got what it takes."

"But you have to know how . . ."

"What do you have to know? Anyone can be a sportsman. You've only got to train a lot. And it pays! You travel for nothing. You get thirty rubles a day for food, *and* free hotels, and bonuses thrown in! And think of the places you see!"

"Where have you been?"

"I've been to Leningrad, Voronezh. . . ."

"Did you like Leningrad?"

"You bet! The shops in the Passage and the Gostiny Dvor! They've got separate stores for everything: stores for stockings, stores for handbags. . . ."

Dyomka could not imagine such things and he envied her. Perhaps it was true, perhaps the things this little girl was talking about so freely *were* the good things of life, and everything *he* depended on was musty and provincial.

The orderly was still standing by the table like a statue, spitting out husks without so much as bending her head.

"You're a sportswoman, but you're here?"

He would not have dared ask what part of her body actually hurt. The question might have been embarrassing.

"I'm only here for three days' examination." Asya waved her hand. The collar of her dressing gown kept falling open, and she had to keep holding it together or adjusting it with one hand. "This stupid dressing gown they make you wear here. I'm ashamed to put it on. A week here's enough to make you go crazy. And what have they picked you up for?"

"Me?" Dyomka sucked his teeth. He wanted to tell her about his leg, but he wanted to do it sensibly. Her lightning attack threw him off balance. "It's my leg."

Up to then the words "It's my leg" had been full of deep and bitter meaning for him, but faced with Asya's lightness of heart he was beginning to doubt whether it was really so grave. He spoke of his leg almost as he had of his pay, with embarrassment.

"What do they say about it?"

"Well, they don't really say anything, but they want to . . . to cut it off."

His face darkened as he said these words and he looked at Asya's bright face.

"Nonsense!" Asya slapped him on the back like an old friend. "Cut off your leg? They must be crazy. It's just that they don't want to treat it. Don't let them do it. It's better to die than live without a leg. What sort of life is it for a cripple, do you think? Life is for happiness."

Yes, of course. She was right again. What kind of life was it on crutches? He would be sitting next to her now, but where would he put the crutches? Where would he put the stump? He wouldn't even be able to bring up a chair by himself, she'd have to bring one for him. No, without legs it wouldn't be any sort of a life.

Life was for happiness.

"Have you been here long?"

"How long?" Dyomka thought to himself. "Three weeks."

"How awful!" Asya shook her shoulders. "How boring! No radio, no accordion! And I can imagine the sort of talk there is in the ward!"

Again Dyomka did not want to admit he'd spent whole days reading books and studying. All his values were tottering under the breeze of Asya's words; they seemed exaggerated, cardboard even.

He grinned, although inside he was not grinning at all, and went on, "Well, for instance, we were discussing what men live by."

"What do you mean?"

"Well, why they live, that sort of thing."

"Pah!" Asya had an answer for everything. "We had an essay about that at school: 'What does man live for?' They gave us study material full of cotton growers, milkmaids, Civil War heroes. 'What is your attitude to the brave deed of Pavel Korchagin?' 'What is your attitude to the heroism of Matrosov?'"[3]

"What *is* your attitude?"

"Well what? Should we do what they did? The teachers said we should. So we all wrote that we would. Why spoil things just before the exams? But Sashka Gromov said, 'Do I have to write all that? Can't I write what I really think?' Our teacher said, 'I'll give you what you really think. You'll get the worst mark you've ever known.' And one girl wrote—you should have been there, 'I don't know yet whether I love my country or not.' Our teacher quacked like a duck: 'What a lousy idea! How dare you *not* love your country?' 'Perhaps I do love it, but I don't know. I must find out for myself.' 'What is there to find out? You ought to drink in love for your country with your mother's milk. Write it all out again by the next lesson.' We call her 'Toad.' She comes to class and never smiles. Everyone knows why. She's an old maid. She hasn't made much of her private life, so she takes it out on us. Most of all she hates the pretty girls."

---

[3] Korchagin is a character from Nikolai Ostrovski's *How the Steel Was Tempered*. Matrosov was a hero of World War II who threw himself on a German machine gun, covering it with his body.

Asya was throwing the words out casually. She reckoned she knew all right what a pretty face was worth. It was obvious she hadn't been through the disease at all; the pain, the suffering, the loss of appetite and sleep. She hadn't yet lost her freshness or the color in her cheeks. She'd just popped in from one of her gyms or dance floors for a three-day examination.

"But there are *some* good teachers, aren't there?" Dyomka asked, only because he did not want her to fall silent, because he wanted her to keep talking while he sat and looked at her.

"No, not one. They're a lot of puffed-up turkeys. Anyway, school . . . who wants to talk about school?"

Her cheerful healthiness broke over Dyomka. He sat there grateful to her for her chattering, no longer inhibited, relaxed. He did not want to argue with her, he wanted to agree with everything she said in spite of his own beliefs. He'd have felt easier and more at peace with his leg too if it had stopped gnawing at him and reminding him he had done it an injury and that it was about to get its own back on him. Would it be halfway up the shin? Or up to the knee? Or half the thigh? Because of his leg the question, "What do men live by?" remained one of the most important things in his life. So he asked her, "No, but seriously, what do you think? What . . . what *do* people live for?"

Oh yes, this little girl understood a thing or two. She turned her greenish eyes toward Dyomka, as if not quite sure whether he was playing a joke on her or being serious.

"What for? What do you mean? For love, of course."

For love! Tolstoy had said "For love" too, but in what sense? And the girl's teacher had made them write "For love" too, but in what sense? After all, Dyomka was used to having things precise in his mind, to working them out for himself.

"But . . ." he began hoarsely. (It was simple enough, perhaps, but rather embarrassing to say.) "After all, love is . . . love isn't the whole of your life. It only happens . . . sometimes. From a certain age, and up to a certain age. . . ."

"What age? From what age?" Asya interrogated him angrily as though he had offended her. "It's best at our age. When else? What is there in life except love?"

Sitting there with her little raised eyebrows, she seemed so certain, it wasn't possible to object. Dyomka didn't object. He just wanted to listen to her, not to argue.

She turned toward him and leaned forward, and, without stretching out either of her arms, it was as if she were stretching them across the ruins of all the walls in the world.

"It is *ours* forever. And it is *today.* Don't listen to them wagging their tongues about whether this'll happen or that'll happen. It's love! That's all!"

She was so frank with him, it was as if they'd spent a hundred evenings talking, talking, and talking. And if it hadn't been for the orderly with her sunflower seeds, the nurse, the two checkers players, the patients shuffling along the corridors, she really might have been ready, there and then, in that little corner, at the finest age of their lives, to help him understand what men live by.

His leg had gnawed at him constantly, even in his sleep, even a second ago, but he had forgotten it now, it was as if it didn't exist. He looked at the open collar of Asya's dressing gown and his lips parted a little. What had repelled him so much when his mother did it, now for the first time struck him as innocent before the whole world, unstained, capable of outweighing all the evil on earth.

"What about you?" Asya half-whispered sympathetically, but ready to burst into laughter. "Haven't you ever . . . ? You silly, haven't you ever . . . ?"

A red-hot wave struck Dyomka, in the ears, the face and the forehead. It was as if he had been caught stealing. In twenty minutes this little girl had knocked him clean off all he had held fast to for years. His throat was dry as he asked her, like a man begging for mercy, "What about you . . . ?"

Just as behind her dressing gown there was nothing but her nightdress, her breasts, and her soul, so behind her words there was nothing hidden from him. She saw no reason to hide.

"Oh, me . . . since the ninth . . . There was one in our *eighth class* who got pregnant! And one got caught in an apartment; she was . . . for money, can you imagine? She had her own savings book. How did it come out? She left it in her exercise book and a teacher found it. The earlier you start, the more exciting it is. . . . Why wait? It's the atomic age!"

Cancer Ward: Chapter 28

Bad Luck All Around

Dyomka lay motionless, thinking pleasant thoughts: how he'd learn to walk on crutches, briskly and smartly; how one really summery day shortly before May Day he'd go out and explore the zoo from morning until the evening train; how he'd have plenty of time now to get quickly through his subjects at school and do well and read all the essential books he'd hitherto missed. There would be no more wasted evenings with the other boys, going off to a dance hall after tormenting himself about whether to go or not, even though he couldn't dance anyway. No more of that. He would just turn on his light and work at his books.

There was a knock at the door.

"Come in," said Dyomka.

(Saying "Come in" gave him a feeling of satisfaction. He had never known a situation where people had to knock at his door before entering.)

The door was flung open, letting in Asya.

Asya came in, or rather burst in. She rushed into the room as though someone was chasing her, pushed the door shut behind her and stood there by the door, one hand on the knob, the other holding the front of her dressing gown together.

She was no longer the Asya who had dropped in for a "three-day checkup," who was expected back in a few days' time by her track friends at the winter stadium. She had sagged and faded. Even her yellow hair, which couldn't change as quickly as the rest of her, hung down pitifully now.

She was wearing the same dressing gown, an unpleasant one without buttons that had covered many shoulders and been boiled in goodness knows what boilers. It looked more becoming on her now than before.

Asya looked at Dyomka and her eyelashes trembled a little. Had she come to the right place? Would she have to rush on somewhere else?

She was utterly crushed now. No longer Dyomka's senior by a full year in school, she had lost her advantage of extra experience, her knowledge of life and the three long journeys she had made. She seemed to Dyomka almost like part of him. He was very pleased to see her. "Asya, sit down! What's the matter?" he said.

They had had many talks together in hospital. They had discussed his leg (Asya had come out firmly against giving it up). After the operation she had come to see him twice, brought him apples and cookies. Natural though their friendship had been that first evening, it had since then become even more so. And she'd told him, although not all at once, exactly what was wrong with her. She had had a pain in her right breast, they had found some sort of hard lumps in it, they were giving her X-ray treatment for it and making her put pills under her tongue.

"Sit down, Asya. Sit down."

She let go of the doorknob and walked the few steps to the stool at the head of Dyomka's bed, dragging her hand behind her along the door, along the wall. It was as though she had to hold onto them and grope her way.

She sat down.

She sat down, and she didn't look Dyomka in the eye. She looked past him at the blanket. She wouldn't turn to face him, and he couldn't twist his body round to see her directly either.

"Come on now, what's the matter?" He had to play the "older man" again, that was his role. He threw his head back, craning his neck over the pile of pillows so that he could see her, still lying on his back.

Her lip trembled. Her eyelashes fluttered.

"As-asyenka!" Dyomka just had time to say the word. He was overcome with pity for her, he wouldn't have dared call her "Asyenka" otherwise. Suddenly she threw herself onto his pillow, her head against his, her little sheaf of hair tickling his ear.

"Please, Asyenka!" he begged her, fumbling over the blanket for her hand. But he couldn't see her hands and so he didn't find it. She sobbed into the pillow.

"What is it? Come on, tell me, what is it?"

But he'd almost guessed what it was.

"They're going to c-c-cut it off. . . !"

She cried and she cried. And then she started to groan, "O-o-oh!"

Dyomka couldn't remember ever hearing such a long-drawn-out moan of grief, such an extraordinary sound, as this "O-o-oh."

"Maybe they won't do it after all," he said, trying to soothe her. "Maybe they won't have to." But he knew somehow that his words wouldn't be enough to comfort her sorrow.

She cried and cried into his pillow. He could feel the place beside him; it was already quite wet.

Dyomka found her hand and began to stroke it. "Asyenka," he said, "maybe they won't have to."

"They will, they will! They're going to do it on Friday...."

And she let out such a groan that it transfixed Dyomka's soul.

He couldn't see her tear-stained face. A few locks of hair found their way through to his eyes. It was soft hair, soft and ticklish.

Dyomka searched for words, but they wouldn't come. All he could do was clasp her hand tighter and tighter to try to stop her. He had more pity for her than he had ever had for himself.

"What have I got to live for?" she sobbed.

Dyomka's experiences, vague as they were, provided him with an answer to this question, but he couldn't express it. Even if he could have done, Asya's groan was enough to tell him that neither he, nor anyone, nor anything at all would be able to convince her. Her own experience led to only one conclusion: There was nothing to live for now.

"Who in the world will w-w-want me n-n-now?" She stumbled the words out inconsolably. "Who in the world...?"

She buried her face in his pillow once again. Dyomka's cheek was by now quite wet.

"Well, you know." He was still trying to soothe her, still clasping her hand. "You know how people get married.... They have the same sort of opinions ... the same sort of characters...."

"What sort of fool loves a girl for her character?" She started up angrily, like a horse rearing. She pulled her hand away, and Dyomka saw her face for the first time—wet, flushed, blotched, miserable, and angry. "Who wants a girl with one breast? Who wants a girl like that? When she's seventeen!" She shouted the words at him. It was all his fault.

He didn't know how to console her.

"How will I be able to go to the beach?" she shrieked, as a new thought pierced her. "The beach! How can I go swimming?" Her body corkscrewed, then crumpled. Her head clutched between her hands, she slumped down from Dyomka toward the floor.

Unbearably, she began to imagine bathing suits in different styles —with or without shoulder straps, one-piece or two-piece, every contemporary and future fashion, bathing suits in orange and blue, crimson and the hue of the sea, in one color or striped with scalloped edges, bathing suits she hadn't yet tried on but had examined in front of a mirror—all the ones she would never buy and never wear.

She could never show herself on the beach again. It had suddenly struck her as the most excruciating, the most mortifying fact of her existence. Living had lost all meaning, and this was the reason why.

Dyomka mumbled something clumsy and inept from his pile of pillows. "Of course, you know, if no one will have you. . . . Well, of course, I realize what sort of a man I am now. . . . But I'll always be happy to marry you, you know that. . . ."

"Listen to me, Dyomka!" A new thought had stung Asya. She stood up, faced him, and looked straight at him. Her eyes were wide open and tearless. "Listen to me, you'll be the last one! You're the last one who can see it and kiss it. No one but you will ever kiss it! Dyomka, *you* at least must kiss it, if nobody else!"

She pulled her dressing gown apart (it wasn't holding together anyway). It seemed to him that she was weeping and groaning again as she pulled down the loose collar of her nightdress to reveal her doomed right breast.

It shone as though the sun had stepped straight into the room. The whole ward seemed on fire. The nipple glowed. It was larger than he had ever imagined. It stood before him. His eyes could not resist its sunny rosiness.

Asya brought it close to his face and held it for him.

"Kiss it! Kiss it!" she demanded. She stood there, waiting.

And breathing in the warmth her body was offering him, he nuzzled it with his lips like a suckling pig, gratefully, admiringly. Nothing more beautiful than this gentle curve could ever be painted or sculptured. Its beauty flooded him. Hurriedly his lips took in its even, shapely contour.

"You'll remember? . . . You'll remember, won't you? You'll remember it was there, and what it was like?" Asya's tears kept dropping onto his close-cropped head.

When she did not take it away, he returned to its rosy glow again and again, softly kissing the breast. He did what her future child would never be able to do. No one came in, and so he kissed and kissed the marvel hanging over him.

Today it was a marvel. Tomorrow it would be in the trash bin.

Cancer Ward: Chapter 35

The First Day of Creation . . .

Early in the morning while everyone was still asleep Oleg got up quietly, made his bed, folding the four corners of the blanket cover into the middle, as regulations required, and walked on tiptoe in his heavy boots out of the ward.

Turgun was asleep at the duty nurse's table, his head of thick black hair resting on folded arms over an open textbook.

The old orderly on the lower floor opened the bathroom for Oleg. The clothes he changed into there were his own, but they felt strange after two months in store, his old trousers, his army riding breeches, his cotton-and-wool blouse and his greatcoat. They had also been kept in store for him in the camps, so there was something left of them, they weren't completely worn. His winter hat was a civilian one he'd bought in Ush-Terek; it was too small for him and squeezed his head. The day promised to be a warm one, so Oleg decided not to put his hat on at all, it made him look too like a scarecrow. His belt he tied not round his greatcoat but round the blouse he wore under his greatcoat. To the ordinary passer-by he must have looked like a demobilized soldier, or one who had escaped from the guardroom. He tucked his hat into his old duffel bag, which was covered with grease stains and had a sewn-up shrapnel hole and a burn hole as well. He had had it in the front line and had asked his aunt to bring it to the prison in a parcel. He didn't want to take anything good with him to the camp.

After what he'd worn in hospital even clothes like these gave him a cheerful bearing. They made him feel healthy.

Kostoglotov was in a hurry to leave, afraid something might crop up to detain him. The old orderly removed the bar from across the handle of the outer door, and let him out.

He walked onto the porch and stood still. He breathed in. It was young air, still and undisturbed. He looked out at the world—it was new and turning green. He raised his head. The sky unfolded, pink from the sun rising somewhere unseen. He raised his head higher. Spindle-shaped, porous clouds, centuries of laborious workmanship, stretched across the whole sky, but only for a few moments before dispersing, seen only by the few who happened to throw back their heads that minute, perhaps by Oleg Kostoglotov alone among the town's inhabitants.

Through the lace, the cutout pattern, the froth and plumes of these clouds sailed the shining, intricate vessel of the old moon, still well visible.

It was the morning of creation. The world had been created anew for one reason only, to be given back to Oleg. "Go out and live!" it seemed to say.

But the pure, mirror-bright moon was not young. It was not the moon that shines on those in love.

His face radiated happiness. He smiled at no man, only at the sky and the trees, but it was with that early-morning springtime joy that touches even the old and the sick. He walked down the well-known pathways, meeting no one but an old street sweeper.

He turned round and looked at the cancer ward. Half hidden by the long brooms of the pyramidal poplars, the building was a towering mass of bright gray brick, brick upon brick and none the worse for seventy years of age.

Oleg walked on, bidding farewell as he went to the trees in the Medical Center. Already tassels hung in bunches from the maple trees, already the first flowers had appeared on the wild plum trees—white blossoms but given a greenish tinge by the leaves.

But there wasn't a single apricot tree, although he'd heard that they would be in flower by now. He might see one in the Old Town.

The first morning of creation—who can act rationally on such a day? Oleg discarded all his plans. Instead, he conceived the mad scheme of going to the Old Town immediately, while it was still early morning, to look at a flowering apricot tree.

He walked through the forbidden gates and came to the half-empty square where the trolley cars turned round, the same gates he had once entered as a hopeless, despondent man, soaked by the January rain, expecting only to die.

He walked out through the hospital gates thinking to himself, It's just like leaving prison.

Last January, when he had been struggling to make his way to the hospital, the screeching, jolting, overcrowded trolley cars had shaken him almost to death, but sitting there now with a window to himself he even began to enjoy the rattle of the machine. Going by trolley was a sort of life, a sort of freedom.

The trolley car dragged its way along a bridge across the river. Down below, weak-legged willow trees were bending over, their branches hanging into the tawny swift-moving water, already green, trusting in nature.

The trees along the sidewalk had also turned green, but not enough to hide the houses—one-story houses of solid stone, built unhurriedly by men who were in no hurry. Oleg looked at them enviously—lucky people who had actually lived in them! It was an amazing part of town flashing past the window now; very wide sidewalks and spacious boulevards. But what town does not look wonderful in the rosy early morning?

Gradually the style changed. The boulevards ended, the two sides of the street began to converge and hastily constructed buildings to flash by. They made no pretense to beauty or strength. Probably they had been built before the war. Oleg read the name of the street; it seemed familiar.

Then he knew why he recognized it—it was the street where Zoya lived!

He took out his rough-paper notebook and found the number. He looked out through the window again, and as the trolley car slowed down he spotted the house itself—two-story, with irregular-shaped windows and gates either permanently open or broken. There were a few outbuildings in the yard.

He could get out here, somewhere here.

He was by no means homeless in this town. He had an invitation, an invitation from a girl.

He didn't move from his seat. He sat there, almost enjoying the jolts and rumblings of the trolley car. It was not yet full. Opposite Oleg sat an old Uzbek in glasses—no ordinary Uzbek but a man with an air of ancient learning about him.

The lady conductor gave the man a ticket, which he rolled into a tube and stuck in his ear, and on they went, the twist of pink paper jutting out of his ear. It was an elementary touch that made Oleg feel gayer and more at ease as they entered the Old Town.

The streets grew even narrower. The tiny houses were crowded together, pushed shoulder to shoulder. Later on, even the windows disappeared. High clay walls rose blindly from the street. Some houses were built up higher than these walls; their backs were smooth, windowless, and smeared all over with clay. There were a few gates or little tunnels in the walls, so low that you'd have to stoop to enter. It was only a jump from the runningboard of the trolley car to the pavement, and only another step across the pavement before it ended. The whole street seemed to be falling under the trolley car.

So this must be the Old Town, where Oleg wanted to be. But there were no trees growing in the naked streets, let alone a flowering apricot.

Oleg couldn't let the streets go by any more. He got off.

What he saw now was the same scene as before, except that he was moving at walking pace. Without the rattle of the trolley car he could hear, he was sure he could hear, a sort of iron knocking noise. A moment later he spotted an Uzbek in a black and white skullcap and a long black quilted coat with a pink waist sash. He was squatting in the middle of the street hammering a hoe into a circle against one of the rails of the single trolley track.

Oleg stood there. He was touched—atomic age indeed! Even now in places like this, and in Ush-Terek, metal was such a rarity that there was nothing better than a trolley rail to use as an anvil. Oleg watched to see if the Uzbek would finish before the next trolley came. But he was in no hurry whatever. He hammered on carefully. When the oncoming trolley car sounded its horn he moved half a step to one side, waited for it to pass, and then squatted down again.

Oleg watched the Uzbek's patient back and the pink sash (which had drained the blue sky of its previous pinkness). He couldn't exchange two words with this Uzbek, but he still felt for him as a brother worker.

Hammering out a hoe on a spring morning—a real restoration of life that would be, wouldn't it?

Very good!

He walked slowly on, wondering where all the windows were. He wanted to peep behind the walls and look inside, but the doors, or rather the gates, were shut and it would be awkward just to walk in.

Suddenly Oleg saw light emerging from a small passageway in the wall. He bent down and walked along a dampish tunnel into a courtyard.

The courtyard hadn't yet woken up, but one could see that people lived here. Under a tree stood a bench dug into the ground and a table. Some toys were scattered about, quite modern ones, there was a water pump to provide the moisture of life, and a washtub too. There were many windows all around, all looking out in this direction, onto the courtyard. There wasn't one that faced the street.

He walked a bit further down the street and went into another courtyard through a similar sort of tunnel. Everything was the same, but there was also a young Uzbek woman looking after her little children. She wore a lilac shawl and her hair hung down to her waist in long, thin black braids. She saw Oleg and ignored him. He left.

It was completely un-Russian. In Russian villages and towns all the living-room windows looked straight onto the street, so that the housewives could peer through the curtains and the windowbox flowers, like soldiers waiting in a forest ambush, to see the stranger walking down the street, and who was visiting who and why. Yet Oleg immediately understood and accepted the Oriental way: I don't want to know how you live, and don't you peep in on me!

What better way of life could an ex-prisoner choose for himself after years in the camps, constantly exposed, searched, and examined, under perpetual observation?

He was getting to like the Old Town more and more.

Earlier on he'd noticed an empty teahouse in a space between two houses and the man who ran it just beginning to wake up. He now came across another one on a balcony above street level. He walked up into it. There were several men inside wearing skullcaps—purple or blue and some made of rug cloth—and an old man in a white turban with colored embroidery. There wasn't a single woman there. Oleg remembered he'd never seen a woman in a teahouse. There was no sign up to say woman were forbidden, it was just that they weren't invited.

Oleg thought it all over. It was the first day of his new life. Everything was new and had to be understood afresh. Did these men, by gathering together apart from women, mean to demonstrate that the most important part of life does not concern women?

He sat down by the balcony rail. It was a good point from which to observe the street. It was coming to life now, but no one seemed to be in the hurry habitual in towns. The passers-by moved along sedately, the men in the teahouse sat in endless calm.

One might imagine that Sergeant Kostoglotov, or Prisoner Kostoglotov, had served his time, had paid his debts to society, had sweated out the torment of his illness, and had died in January, and that some new Kostoglotov, tottering on two uncertain legs, had emerged from the clinic "so lovely and clean you can see through him," as they said in the camps, to live not an entire life but an extra portion, like the piece of bread they used to pin onto the main ration with a pine twig to make up the weight; it was part of the ration, but a separate bit.

As he embarked on this little additional piece of life, Oleg longed for it to be different from the main part he had lived through. He wished he could stop making mistakes now.

However, he'd already made one mistake, in choosing his tea. Instead of trying to be clever he should have chosen the ordinary black tea he knew well, but in his pursuit of the exotic he'd chosen *kok*—green tea. It turned out to have no strength, it didn't pep him up, it didn't really taste like tea at all, and when he poured some into the bowl it was full of tea leaves. He didn't want to swallow them, he'd rather pour it away.

Meanwhile the day was warming up and the sun was rising. Oleg wouldn't have minded a bite to eat, but this teahouse served nothing but two sorts of hot tea. They didn't even have sugar.

But he decided to adopt the changeless, unhurried manner of those about him. He didn't get up or set off in search of something to eat, but stayed sitting, adjusting his chair into a new position.

And then from the teahouse balcony he saw above the walled courtyard next door something pink and transparent. It looked like a puff dandelion, only it was six meters in diameter, a rosy, weightless balloon. He'd never seen anything so pink and so huge.

Could it be the apricot tree?

Oleg had learned a lesson. This was his reward for not hurrying. The lesson was—never rush on without looking around first.

He walked up to the railings and from on high gazed and gazed through this pink miracle.

It was his present to himself—his creation-day present.

It was like a fire tree decorated with candles in a room of a northern home. The flowering apricot was the only tree in this courtyard enclosed by clay walls and open only to the sky. People lived in the yard, it was like a room. There were children crawling under the tree, and a woman in a black headscarf with a green-flowered pattern was hoeing the earth at its base.

Oleg examined it—pinkness, that was the general impression. The tree had buds like candles. When on the point of opening, the petals were pink in color, but once open they were pure white, like apple or cherry blossoms. The result was an incredible, tender pink. Oleg was trying to absorb it all into his eyes. He wanted to remember it for a long time and to tell the Kadmins about it.

He'd planned on finding a miracle, and he'd found one.

There were many other joys in store for him today in this newly born world. . . .

The vessel of the moon had now disappeared.

Oleg walked down the steps into the street. His uncovered head was beginning to feel the sun. He ought to go and buy four hundred grams or so of black bread, stuff himself with it without any water, and then go downtown. Maybe it was his civilian clothes that put him in such good spirits. He felt no nausea and sauntered along quite easily.

Then he saw a stall set into a recess in the wall so that it didn't break the line of the street. It had an awning raised as a sun shield and propped up by two diagonal struts. Gray-blue smoke was blowing out from under the shield. Oleg had to bend low to get under. He stood stooping beneath, unable to straighten up.

A long iron grill ran across the whole length of the counter. In one place there was a fire of red-hot coals, the rest was full of white ashes. Across the grill and above the fire lay fifteen or so long, pointed aluminum skewers strung with pieces of meat.

Oleg guessed—it must be *shashlik!* Here was another discovery in his newly created world—the dish he'd heard so much about during those gastronomical discussions in prison. But in all his thirty-four years he had never had the chance to see it with his own eyes. He'd never been to the Caucasus or eaten in restaurants. In the pre-war canteens they had served nothing but stuffed cabbage and pearl-barley porridge.

Shashlik!

It was an enticing smell, the mixed odor of smoke and meat. The meat on the skewers wasn't charred, it wasn't even dark brown, it was the tender pinky-gray of meat nearly just right. The stallkeeper, round and fat of face, was unhurriedly turning the sticks round or moving them away from the fire and over the ashes.

"How much?" asked Kostoglotov.

"Three," the stallkeeper answered dreamily.

Oleg couldn't understand—three what? Three kopecks was too little, three rubles seemed too much. Perhaps he meant three sticks for a ruble? It was a difficulty he was always coming across since his release from the camp: He couldn't get the proper scale of prices into his head.

"How many for three rubles?" Oleg guessed, trying to find a way out.

The stallkeeper was too lazy to speak. He lifted one skewer up by the end, waved it at Oleg as one would to a child, and put it back on the fire.

One skewer, three rubles? Oleg shook his head. It was a scale beyond his experience. He only had five rubles a day to live on. But how he longed to try it! His eyes examined every piece of meat, selecting one for himself. Each skewer had its own special attraction.

There were three truck drivers waiting nearby, their trucks parked in the street. A woman came up to the stall, but the stallkeeper said something to her in Uzbek and she went away looking annoyed. Suddenly the stallkeeper began laying all the skewers out on a single plate. He sprinkled some chopped scallions on them with his fingers and splashed something out of a bottle. Oleg realized that the truck drivers were taking the whole stock of *shashlik,* five skewers each.

It was another example of the inexplicable, two-tiered price and wage structure that prevailed everywhere. Oleg couldn't even conceive of this second tier, let alone imagine himself climbing up to it. These truck drivers were just having a snack, fifteen rubles apiece, and very likely this wasn't their main breakfast either. No wage was enough to support such a life. Wage earners didn't buy *shashlik.*

"All gone," said the stallkeeper to Oleg.

"Gone? All gone?" asked Oleg miserably. Why on earth had he hesitated? It might be the first and last chance of a lifetime!

"They didn't bring any in today," said the stallkeeper, cleaning up his things. It looked as if he was getting ready to lower the awning.

"Hey, boys, give me one skewer!" Oleg begged the truck drivers. "One skewer, boys!"

One of them, a heavily tanned but flaxen-haired young man, nodded to him. "All right, take one," he said.

They hadn't paid yet. Oleg took a green note from his pocket, the flap of which was fastened with a safety pin. The stallkeeper didn't even pick it up. He just swept it off the counter into his drawer, as one sweeps crumbs or scraps off a table.

But the skewer was Oleg's! Abandoning his duffel bag on the dusty ground, he took the aluminum rod in both hands. He counted the pieces of meat—there were five of them, the sixth was a half—and his teeth began to gnaw them off the skewer, not whole chunks at a time but morsel by morsel. He ate thoughtfully as a dog eats after taking his food into a safe corner, and he thought how easy it was to whet human desires and how difficult it was to satisfy them once aroused. For years he had regarded a hunk of black bread as one of the most precious gifts on earth. A moment ago he had been ready to go and buy some for his breakfast, but then he had smelled the gray-blue smoke and the roast meat, the men had given him a skewer to gnaw and already he was beginning to feel contempt for bread.

The drivers finished their five skewers each, started up their engines and drove off, leaving Oleg still licking the last of his skewer. He was savoring each morsel with his lips and tongue—the way the tender meat ran with juice, the way it smelled, how perfectly it was cooked, not at all overdone. It was amazing the primeval pleasure, quite undulled, he derived from every mouthful. And the deeper he dug into his *shashlik* and the greater his enjoyment, the more he was struck by the cold fact that he wasn't going to see Zoya. The trolley car had been about to take him past her house, but he wouldn't get off. It was while lingering over the skewer of *shashlik* that he finally realized this.

The trolley car dragged him back along the same route into the town center, only this time it was jammed with passengers. Oleg recognized Zoya's stop and let two more go by. He didn't know which stop was best for him. Suddenly a woman appeared selling newspapers through the trolley-car window. Oleg decided to have a good look and see what was happening; he hadn't seen people selling newspapers in the street since he was a child. (The last time was when Mayakovsky[1] shot himself and little boys ran about selling a late-extra edition.) But on this occasion it was an aging Russian woman selling them, not at all briskly, taking her time over finding the right change. Still, her enterprise stood her in good stead and as each new trolley came along she managed to get rid of a few copies. Oleg stood there just to see how she was doing.

---

[1] Vladimir Mayakovsky, the great Futurist poet and supporter of the Russian Revolution, who shot himself in 1930.

"Don't the police chase you away?" he asked her.

"They haven't got round to it yet," the newspaper woman replied.

He hadn't been able to get a look at himself for a long time and he'd forgotten what he looked like. Any policeman who looked closely at them both would have demanded his documents before bothering about the woman's.

The electric clock in the street showed only nine, but the day was already so hot that Oleg began to unbutton the top loops of his greatcoat. Unhurriedly, letting himself be overtaken and pushed, he walked along the sunny side of the street near the square, screwing up his eyes and smiling into the sun.

There were many more joys in store for him today!

It was the sun of a spring he had not reckoned on living to see. And although there was no one around to rejoice after his return to life—in fact, no one knew about it—still, somehow the sun knew, and Oleg smiled at him. Even if there were never another spring, even if this were the last, nevertheless it was like a surprise gift, and he was grateful.

None of the passers-by was particularly pleased to see Oleg, but he was happy to see them all. He was delighted to have come back to them, to everything there was in the streets. He could find nothing in this newly made world of his that was uninteresting, unpleasant, or ugly. Whole months, years of life could not compare with today, this one supreme day.

They were selling ice cream in paper cups. Oleg could not remember the last time he'd seen those little cups. Goodbye to another one and a half rubles, off you go! His duffel bag, scorched and bullet-riddled, hung from his back leaving both hands free to skim the freezing layers off the top with the little wooden spoon.

Walking even more slowly, he came across a photographer's shopwindow in the shade. He leaned against the iron railings and stood there for a time stock still, gazing at the purified life and the idealized faces arranged in the window, especially the girls of course—they were in a majority. Originally, each girl had been dressed in her best clothes, then the photographer had twisted her head and adjusted the light ten times, then taken several shots and chosen the best one and retouched it, and then selected one shot each of ten such girls. That was how the window had been composed, and Oleg knew it, but still he found it pleasant to look in and believe that life actually was composed of girls like these. To make up for all the years he had lost, for all the years he would not live to see, and for all he was now deprived of, he gazed and gazed quite shamelessly.

The ice cream was finished and it was time to throw away the little cup. But it was so neat and clean and smooth that it occurred to Oleg it might be useful for drinking out of on the way. So he put it in his duffel bag. He put the little spoon in, too. That might come in handy as well.

Further on, he came across a pharmacist's. A pharmacist's is also a very interesting institution. Kostoglotov went inside immediately.

The counters were very clean—one right angle after another. He could have spent all day examining them. The goods on display looked bizarre to his camp-trained eye. He had never come across such things during the decades he had spent in the other world, while the objects he had seen as a free man he now found difficult to name. He could hardly remember what they were in. Overawed like a savage, he gazed at the nickel-plated glass and plastic shapes. There were herbs, too, in little packets with explanations of their properties. Oleg was a great believer in herbs—but where was the herb he wanted?

Next, there was a long display of pills. There were so many new names on them, names he had never heard before. All in all, the pharmacist's shop was opening up a complete new universe of observation and reflection. But all he did was walk from counter to counter, then ask for a thermometer, some soda, and some manganate, as the Kadmins had asked him to. There was no thermometer and no soda, but they sent him to the cashier, to pay three kopecks for the manganate. Afterward, Kostoglotov joined the line at the dispensary and stood there about twenty minutes. He had taken his bag off his back; he was still oppressed by a feeling of stuffiness. He was undecided—should he take the medicine? He pushed one of the three identical prescriptions Vega had given him the previous day through the little window. He hoped they would not have the medicine, in which case there would be no problem, but they did. They counted up on the other side of the window and wrote him out a bill for fifty-eight rubles and a few kopecks.

Oleg was so relieved he actually laughed as he left the window. The fact that at every stage in his life he was pursued by the figure 58 did not surprise him one jot.[2] But the idea of paying a hundred and seventy-five rubles for three prescriptions—that really was too much! He could feed himself for a month on money like that. He felt like tearing up the prescriptions and throwing them into the spittoon there and then, but it occurred to him that Vega might ask him about them, so he put them away.

He was sorry to leave the pharmacist's shop with its mirrored surfaces, but the day was already far advanced and calling him. It was his day of joy.

There were even more joys in store for him today!

---

[2] Oleg had originally been sentenced under Article 58 of the Soviet Penal Code.

He trudged on unhurriedly, moving from one shopwindow to the next, clinging like a burr to everything he saw. He knew he would meet something unexpected at every step.

Sure enough, there was a post office, and in the window an advertisement: "use our photo-telegraph!" Fantastic! It was something people had written about ten years ago in science-fiction stories, and here it was being offered to passers-by in the street. Oleg went in. There was a list hanging up of about thirty towns where photo-telegrams could be sent. Oleg started to work out where he could send one to and to whom, but among all those big towns scattered over one sixth of the world's land surface he could not think of a single person who would be glad to see his handwriting.

He wanted to find out more, so he walked up to the window and asked them to show him a form and tell him what length the letters had to be.

"It's broken," the woman answered; "it doesn't work."

Aha, it doesn't work! Well, to hell with them! That's more like what we're used to. That's reassuring somehow.

He walked on a bit further and read some billboard posters. There was a circus advertised and a few cinemas. There were matinees in all of them, but he couldn't waste the day he had been given to observe the universe on something like that. Of course, if he had plenty of time to spend in town, then it would do him no harm to go to the circus. After all, he was like a child, he had only just been born.

It was getting near the time when it would be all right to go and see Vega. If he was going at all. . . .

Well, why on earth shouldn't he go? She was his friend. Her invitation had been sincere. She'd even felt embarrassed about giving it. She was the only soul close to him in the town, so why shouldn't he go?

To go and see her was, secretly, the one thing in the world he most wanted to do. He wanted to go to her before he went on to inspect the universe of the town. But something held him back and kept producing counterarguments: Wasn't it a bit early? She might not be back yet, or she might not have had time to tidy the place up.

All right, a bit later. . . .

At every street corner he stopped and pondered. How could he avoid taking the wrong turning? Which was the best way to go? He did not ask anyone, but chose his streets by whim.

And so he ran across a wineshop, not a modern store with bottles but an old-fashioned vintner's with barrels. It was half dark, half damp, with a peculiar sourish atmosphere. They were pouring the wine out of the barrels straight into glasses. And a glass of the cheap stuff cost two rubles. After the *shashlik* this was cheap indeed! Kostoglotov pulled one more ten-ruble note out of the depths of his pocket and handed it over to be changed.

The taste turned out to be nothing special, but his head was so weak the wine made it turn even as he was finishing the glass. He left the shop and walked on. Life seemed even better, even though it had been good to him ever since morning. It was so easy and pleasant that he felt nothing could possibly upset him. For he had already experienced and left behind all the bad things of life, as many as there are, and he was left with the better part.

There were still more joys in store for him today.

For instance, he might run across another wineshop and be able to drink another glass.

But he did not see one.

Instead, there was a dense crowd occupying the whole sidewalk, making passers-by step into the road to go round. Oleg decided it must be a street incident. But no, they were all standing facing a broad flight of steps and some big doors, just waiting. Kostoglotov craned his neck and read: "Central Department Store."

He understood now. They must be giving out something important. But what exactly was it? He asked one man, then a woman, then another woman, but they were all very vague. No one would give him a straight answer. The only thing Oleg found out was that it was due to open very soon. Oh well, if that's the way it is. . . . Oleg pushed his way into the crowd.

A few minutes later two men opened the wide doors. With timid gestures they tried to restrain the first row of people, but then leaped aside as though avoiding a cavalry charge. The front rows of waiting men and women were all young; they galloped in through the doors and up the straight staircase to the second floor at the same speed as they would have left the building if it had been on fire. The rest of the crowd pushed their way in too, each running up the steps as fast as his age or strength allowed. One tributary flowed off across the ground floor, but the main stream was up on the second. As part of this attacking surge it was impossible to walk up the stairs quietly. Dark and ragged-looking, Oleg ran up with them, his duffel bag hanging from his back.

"Damn soldier!" the crowd kept swearing at him.

At the top of the stairs the flood separated at once. People were running in three different directions, but turning carefully on the slippery parquet floor. Oleg had a moment to choose in, but how could he decide? He ran blindly on, following the most confident of the racing streams.

He found himself in a growing line near the knitwear department. The assistants, however, in their light-blue uniforms were yawning and talking calmly, apparently quite unaware of the crush. To them it was just another boring, empty day.

As he regained his breath, Oleg discovered they were lining up for women's cardigans or sweaters. He whispered an obscenity and walked away.

Where the other two streams had run off to he could not discover. There was movement on all sides and people crowding at every counter. In one place the crowd was thicker and he decided it must be here. They were waiting for cheap blue soup plates. There they were unpacking boxes of them. Now that was something! There were no soup plates in Ush-Terek. The Kadmins ate off chipped ones. It would be quite something to bring a dozen plates like that to Ush-Terek. But he'd never manage to get them there, they'd all get broken on the way.

Oleg began to walk at random across the two floors of the department store. He looked at the photography department. Cameras, quite unobtainable before the war, were piled all over the shelves, together with all their accessories, teasing him and demanding money. It was another unfulfilled childhood dream of his, to take up photography.

He liked the men's raincoats very much. After the war he had dreamed about buying a civilian raincoat; he reckoned that was what a man looked his best in. But now he would have to lay out three hundred and fifty roubles, a month's wages. He walked on.

He did not buy anything anywhere, but in this mood he felt he had a wallet full of money and no needs. The wine inside him was evaporating, making him merry.

They were selling staple-fiber shirts. Oleg knew the words "staple-fiber." All the housewives in Ush-Terek would run off to the district store whenever they heard them. Oleg looked at the shirts, felt them, and fancied them. Mentally he decided to buy one of them, a green one with a white stripe. But it cost sixty roubles; he couldn't afford it.

While he was thinking about the shirts a man in a fine overcoat came up to the counter. He was not after these shirts, but the silk ones. He politely asked the assistant, "Excuse me, do you have size 40, collar size 16?"

Oleg winced. It was as if he were being scraped with iron files on both sides of his body. He started and turned round to look at this cleanshaven man, skin completely unscarred, wearing a fine felt hat with a tie hanging down his white shirt front. He looked at him as if the other had hit him across the ear, and one of them would soon be sent flying down the stairs.

What was this? There were men rotting in trenches, men being thrown into mass graves, into shallow pits in the permafrost, men being taken into the camps for the first, second and third times, men being jolted from station to station in prison trucks, wearing themselves out with picks, slaving away to be able to buy a patched-up quilt jacket—and here was this neat little man who could remember the size not only of his shirt but of his collar too!

It was the collar size that really stunned Oleg. He could not imagine a collar possibly having its own special number. Stifling a wounded groan, he walked right away from the shirts. Collar size too—really! What good was this refined sort of life? Why go back to it? If you remember your collar size, doesn't it mean you're bound to forget something else, something more important?

That collar size had made him feel quite weak. . . .

In the household goods department Oleg remembered how Elena Alexandrovna had dreamed of owning a lightweight steam iron, even though she had not actually asked him to bring her one. He hoped there would not be one, just as none of the other household necessities were available. Then both his conscience and his shoulders would be free of a great burden. But the assistant showed him just such an iron there on the counter.

"This iron, is it really a lightweight one, miss?" Kostoglotov was weighing it doubtfully in his hand.

"Why should I tell you a lie?" said the assistant, curling her lips. There was something metaphysical about her gaze. She was plunged deep in faraway thought, as if the customers hanging around the counter were not real people but shadows detached from this world.

"I don't mean you'd lie to me, but you might be making a mistake," suggested Oleg.

The assistant returned unwillingly to this mortal life. Undertaking the intolerable effort of shifting a material object, she put another iron down in front of him. After that she had no strength left to explain anything in words. Once again she floated off into the realm of the metaphysical.

Well, comparison reveals the truth. The lightweight one was in fact a full kilo lighter. Duty demanded that he buy it. She was quite exhausted after carrying the iron, yet her weary fingers still had to write him out a bill, her weakening lips to pronounce the word "Control." (What control was this? Who were they going to check? Oleg had completely forgotten. Goodness, it was difficult getting back into this world!)

But wasn't it she who was supposed to carry this lightweight iron all the way to the control point, her feet barely touching the floor? Oleg felt quite guilty at having distracted the assistant from her drowsy meditations.

He tucked the iron away in his duffel bag and immediately his shoulders felt the weight. Already he was beginning to feel hot and stuffy in his thick overcoat. He must get out of the store as soon as possible.

But then he saw himself in a huge mirror reaching from floor to ceiling. He knew it wasn't right for a man to stand gazing at himself, but the fact was there wasn't a mirror like that in the whole of Ush-Terek, he hadn't seen himself in a mirror that large for ten years. So, not caring what people thought, he just stood gazing at himself, first from a distance, then a little closer, then closer still.

There was no trace of the military man he considered himself to be. His greatcoat and boots only vaguely resembled a soldier's greatcoat and boots.

His shoulders had drooped long ago and his body was incapable of holding itself straight. Without a hat and without a belt, he looked less like a soldier than a convict on the run or a young lad from the country in town for the day to do a bit of buying and selling. But for that you needed a bit of bravado, and Kostoglotov looked exhausted, devastated, fearfully neglected.

It was a pity he had caught sight of himself. Until then he had been able to imagine himself a bold, soldierly figure who could look condescendingly down on the passers-by and ogle a woman as an equal. This terrible duffel bag on his back had stopped looking soldierly long ago, it now looked like a beggar's bundle. In fact, he could have sat there in the street and held out his hand and people would have thrown kopecks to him.

But he had to be going. . . .

Only how could he go to her looking like this?

He walked on a bit further and found himself in the haberdashery or gifts department. They were selling women's costume jewelry.

The women were twittering, trying things on, going through things and rejecting them, when this half-soldier, half-beggar, with the scar low down on his cheek stopped among them and stood dully on the spot, gazing around.

The assistant smiled. What did this chap want to buy for his country sweetheart? She kept an eye on him, too, in case he pinched anything.

But he did not ask to be shown anything or pick anything up. He just stood there looking dully round.

The whole department was glittering with glass. Precious stones, metals, and plastic. He stood before it, his head lowered like an ox before a road barrier smeared with phosphorus. Kostoglotov's head could not break through this barrier.

Then he understood. He understood how wonderful it is to buy something pretty for a woman, to pin it on her breast or hang it round her neck. So long as he had not known or remembered, he had been innocent. But he was conscious now, very acutely, that from this moment on he could not go to Vega without taking her a present.

He couldn't give her anything, he just didn't dare. He couldn't give her anything at all. There was no point in even looking at the expensive gifts. And as for the cheap stuff, what did he know about it? Those brooches, for instance—no, not brooches, those decorated pendants with pins, especially that hexagonal one with the sparkling glass crystals—wasn't that a good one?

But perhaps it was trashy and vulgar? . . . Perhaps a woman of taste would be ashamed even to take such a thing in her hand? . . . Perhaps they had given up wearing that type of thing long ago, it might be out of fashion? . . . How was he to know what they were not wearing?

How could he possibly manage it—arrive to spend the night and then offer her a brooch, tongue-tied and blushing?

Waves of confusion were battering him like a succession of balls in a bowling alley.

The dense complexity of this world was too much for him, a world where one had to know women's fashions, be able to choose woman's jewelry, look respectable in front of a mirror and remember one's collar size....

Yet Vega actually lived in this world, she knew everything about it and felt at home in it.

He felt embarrassed and depressed. If he was going to see her the time to go was now, now!

But ... he couldn't.

He ... he had lost the impulse. He ... he was afraid.

They were separated by this department store....

And so Oleg staggered out of the cursed temple into which, obedient to the idols of the marketplace, he had run so recently and with such coarse greed. He was weighed down by depression, as exhausted as if he had spent thousands of rubles, as if he had tried something on in every single department, had it all wrapped up for him, and was now carrying on his bent back a mountain of boxes and parcels.

But he only had the iron.

He was so tired, it was as if he had spent hours buying one vain object after another. And what had become of the pure, rosy morning promising him a completely new, beautiful life? Those feathery clouds which took centuries to design? And the diving vessel of the moon?

Where was it he had traded in his untouched soul of this morning? In the department store.... No, earlier on, he had drunk it away with that wine. Or even earlier, he had eaten it away with the *shashlik*.

What he should have done was to take one look at the flowering apricot and rush straight off to see Vega....

Oleg began to feel nauseous, not only from gaping at the shopwindows and signs, but also from jostling his way along the streets among that ever-thickening swarm of worried or cheerful people. He wanted to lie down somewhere in the shade by a stream, just lie there and purify himself. The only place in town he could go to was the zoo, the place Dyomka had asked him to visit.

Oleg felt that the animal world was more understandable anyway, more on his own level.

He was feeling weighed down too because he was appallingly hot in the heavy greatcoat. He didn't feel much like dragging it along with him separately, though. He started to ask people the way to the zoo, and was led there by a succession of well-laid-out streets, broad and quiet, with some paving slabs and spreading trees. No stores, no photographs, no theaters, no wineshops—nothing like that here. Even the trolley cars were rumbling somewhere far away. Here it was a nice, peaceful, sunny day, warming him through even under the trees. Little girls were jumping about playing hopscotch on the sidewalks. Householders were planting their front gardens or putting in sticks for climbing plants.

Near the zoo gates it was a veritable children's kingdom. It was a school holiday, and what a day!

The first thing Oleg saw as he walked into the zoo was the spiral-horned goat. There was a towering rock in its enclosure with a sharp slope and then a precipice. Right there, its front legs on the edge of the precipice, the proud goat stood motionless on its strong, slender legs, with its fantastic horns— long and curved, as though wound spiral after spiral out of a ribbon of bone. It wasn't a beard it had, but a luxuriant mane hanging low on each side to its knees, like a mermaid's hair. Yet the goat had such dignity that the hair did not make it look either effeminate or comic.

Anyone who waited by the spiral-horn goat's cage in the hope of seeing its self-assured little hoofs change position on the smooth rock would have despaired. It had stood there a long time just like a statue, like a continuation of the rock itself. And when there was no breeze to make its straggly hair flutter it was impossible to prove it was alive, that it wasn't just a trick.

Oleg stood there for five minutes and departed in admiration. The goat had not even stirred. That was the sort of character a man needed to get through life.

Walking across to the beginning of another path, Oleg saw a lively crowd, children mostly, gathered round one of the cages. There was something charging frantically about inside, rushing around, but always on the same spot. It turned out to be a squirrel in a wheel—exactly like the one in the proverb. But the proverb was by now a bit stale—and one had never really been able to picture it. Why a squirrel? And why in a wheel? But here was the squirrel, acting it out. It had a tree trunk inside its cage too and dry branches spreading out at the top. But someone had perfidiously hung a wheel next to the tree, a drum with one side open to the viewer. Along the inside rim were fixed cross pieces so that the whole rim was in fact a continuous, endless staircase. And there, quite oblivious of its tree and the slender branches up above, stood the squirrel in its wheel—even though no one had forced it there or enticed it with food—attracted only by the illusion of sham activity and movement. It had probably begun by running lightly up the steps out of curiosity, not knowing then what a cruel, obsessional thing it was. (It hadn't known the first time, but now at the thousandth time it knew well enough, yet it made no difference.)

The wheel was revolving at a furious pace. The squirrel's russet, spindly body and smoky-red tail unfurled in an arc of mad galloping. The cross pieces of the wheeled staircase rippled until they melted together with speed.

Every ounce of the animal's strength was being used. Its heart was nearly bursting, but still it couldn't raise its front paws higher than the first step.

The people who had been standing there before Oleg saw it running just as Oleg did during those few minutes. Nothing ever changed. There was no external force in the cage to stop the wheel or rescue the squirrel. There was no power of reason to make it understand. "Stop! It's all in vain!" No, there was clearly only one inevitable way out, the squirrel's death. Oleg didn't want to see that, so he walked on. Here were two meaningful examples, on the right and left of the entrance, two equally possible modes of existence with which the zoo greeted young and old alike.

Oleg walked past the silver pheasant, the golden pheasant, and the pheasant with red and blue feathers. He admired the indescribably turquoise neck of the peacock, the meter-wide spread of its tail and its pink and gold fringe. After his monochrome exile and life in hospital, his eye feasted on the colors.

It wasn't particularly hot here. The zoo was spaciously laid out and the trees were beginning to give shade. Oleg felt more and more rested as he walked past a whole poultry farm—Andalusian hens, Toulouse and Kholmogory geese—and climbed up the hill where they kept the cranes, hawks, and vultures. Finally, on a rock covered by a tentlike cage towering high over the whole zoo, he came to where the white-headed vultures lived. If it hadn't been for the sign, they might have been taken for eagles. They had been housed as high up as possible, but the roof of the cage was quite low over the rock, and these great, gloomy birds were in torment, spreading their wings and beating them although there was nowhere to fly.

When Oleg saw the tormented vultures he moved his shoulder blades as if about to spread his wings. (Or was it just the iron beginning to press into his back?)

Everything round him he explained in his own way. One of the cages had a notice on it: "White owls do not thrive in captivity." So they know that! And they still lock them up! What sort of degenerate owls, he wondered, did thrive in captivity?

Another notice read: "The porcupine leads a nocturnal life." We know what that means: They summon it at half-past nine in the evening and let it go at four in the morning.

Again: "The badger lives in deep, complicated burrows." Aha—just like us! Good for you, badger; how else can one live? He's got a snout of striped ticking, like an old bum's clothes.

Oleg had such a perverse view of everything that it was probably a bad idea for him to have come, just as he shouldn't have gone into the department store.

Much of the day had already gone by, but the promised joys had still not appeared.

Oleg emerged at the bears' den. A black one with a white "tie" was standing poking its nose into the wiring between the bars. Suddenly it jumped up and hung by its forepaws from the grill. It wasn't so much a white tie as a kind of priest's chain with a cross over the chest. It jumped up and hung there. What other way did it have of showing its despair?

In the next-door cell its mate was sitting with her cubs.

In the one after that a grizzly lived in misery. It kept stamping the ground restlessly, longing to walk up and down its cell, but there was only room for it to turn round and round, because the length from wall to wall was no more than three times its own.

So, according to a bear's measuring scale, it was a punishment cell.

The children were amused by the spectacle, saying to each other. "Hey, let's throw him some stones, he'll think they're candies."

Oleg did not notice the children looking at him. For them he was an animal too, an extra one free of charge. He couldn't see himself.

The path led down to the river where they kept the polar bear. At least they kept a couple there together. Several irrigation ditches flowed into their pit to form an icy basin into which they jumped every few minutes to refresh themselves, then climbed out again onto the cement terrace, squeezed the water out of their muzzles with their paws, and paced to and fro along the edge of the terrace above the water.

What must the summer down here be like for polar bears? It's forty degrees Centigrade. Oh well, the same as it was for us in the Arctic Circle.

The most confusing thing about the imprisoned animals was that even supposing Oleg took their side and had the power, he would still not want to break into the cages and liberate them. This was because, deprived of their home surroundings, they had lost the idea of rational freedom. It would only make things harder for them, suddenly to set them free.

This was the odd way Kostoglotov reasoned. His brain was so twisted that he could no longer see things simply and dispassionately. Whatever he experienced from now on, there would always be this shadow, this gray specter, this subterranean rumbling from the past.

Past the miserable elephant, the animal most deprived of space, past the sacred Indian zebu and the golden aguti hare, Oleg walked on up the hill, this time toward the monkeys.

Children and grownups were amusing themselves round the cages, feeding the monkeys. Kostoglotov walked past them without smiling. Quite hairless, as if clipped bare, sitting sadly on their plank beds, wrapped in their primitive sorrows and delights, they reminded him of many of his former acquaintances. In fact, he could even recognize individuals who must still be in prison somewhere.

One lonely, thoughtful chimpanzee with swollen eyes, hands dangling between his knees, reminded Oleg of Shulubin. It was exactly how he often used to sit.

On this bright, hot day Shulubin would be writhing in his bed between life and death.

Kostoglotov didn't think he would find anything interesting in the monkeyhouse. He moved quickly on and had begun to pass it when he noticed an announcement fixed to one of the further cages, and several people reading it.

He went there. The cage was empty but it had the usual notice reading "Macaque Rhesus." It had been hurriedly scrawled and nailed to the plywood. It said: "The little monkey that used to live here was blinded because of the senseless cruelty of one of the visitors. An evil man threw tobacco into the Macaque Rhesus's eyes."

Oleg was struck dumb. Up to then he had been strolling along, smiling with knowing condescension, but now he felt like yelling and roaring across the whole zoo, as though the tobacco had been thrown into his own eyes, "Why?" Thrown just like that! "Why? It's senseless! Why?"

What went straight to his heart was the childish simplicity with which it was written. This unknown man, who had already made a safe getaway, was not described as "anti-humanist," or "an agent of American imperialism"; all it said was that he was evil. This was what was so striking: How could this man be simply "evil"? Children, do not grow up to be evil! Children, do not destroy defenseless creatures!

The notice had been read and read again, but still the grownups and little children stood looking into the empty cage.

Oleg moved on, drawing his greasy, scorched, shrapnel-riddled duffel bag with the iron inside into the kingdom of reptiles, vipers, and beasts of prey.

Lizards were lying in the sand like scaly pebbles, leaning against each other. What had they lost in the way of freedom of movement?

A huge Chinese alligator with a flat snout, black as cast iron, was lying there. Its paws seemed twisted in the wrong direction. A notice announced that during hot weather it did not eat meat every day. It probably quite liked the well-organized zoo world with its ever-ready food.

There was a powerful python attached to a tree, like a thick dead branch. It was completely motionless except for its little sharp, flickering tongue. A poisonous ethis was coiled under a bell glass. There were ordinary vipers too, several of them.

But he had no wish to inspect all these. He was obsessed with picturing the face of that blinded macaque monkey.

He was already in the alley where they kept the beasts of prey. They were magnificent, vying with each other for the richest pelt: a lynx, a snow leopard, an ash-brown puma, and a tawny jaguar with black spots. They were prisoners, of course, they were suffering from lack of freedom, but Oleg felt toward them as he had toward the camp gangsters. After all, one can work out who are the guilty ones of this world. A notice said that the jaguar ate one hundred and forty kilograms of meat every twenty-four hours. Really, it was past all imagining! Their camp did not get as much meat in a week, and the jaguar had it every twenty-four hours. Oleg remembered the "trusties" in the camp who worked in the stables. They robbed their horses, ate their oats, and so survived.

A little further on he spotted "Mr. Tiger." His whiskers—yes, it was the whiskers that were most expressive of his rapacious nature. But his eyes were yellow. . . . Strange thoughts came to Oleg's mind. He stood there looking at the tiger with hatred.

In the camps, Oleg had met an old political prisoner who had once been in exile in Turukhansk.[3] He had told Oleg about those eyes—they were not velvet black, they were yellow.

Welded to the ground with hatred, Oleg stood in front of the tiger's cage.

Just like that, just like that . . . but why?

He felt sick. He didn't want to stay in the zoo any longer. He wanted to run away from it. He didn't go to see the lions. He began to look for the exit—where was it?

A zebra raced past. Oleg glanced at it and walked on. Then suddenly . . . he stopped dead in front of a miracle.

After all that carnivorous coarseness it was a miracle of spirituality: the Nilgai antelope, light brown, on fine, light legs, her head keen and alert but not in the least afraid. It stood close to the wire netting and looked at Oleg with its big, trustful and . . . gentle, yes, gentle eyes.

The likeness was so true it was unbearable. She kept her gentle, reproachful eyes fixed on him. She was asking him, "Why aren't you coming to see me? Half the day's gone. Why aren't you coming?"

It was witchcraft, it was a transmigration of souls, she was so obviously waiting for Oleg standing there. Scarcely had he walked up to her than she began asking him with those reproachful but forgiving eyes, "Aren't you coming? Aren't you coming? I've been waiting. . . ."

Yes, why wasn't he coming? Why wasn't he coming?

Oleg shook himself and made for the exit.

He might still find her at home.

---

[3] The place of Stalin's exile before the Revolution.

Cancer Ward: Chapter 36

. . . and the Last Day

He could not think of her either with greed or with the fury of passion. His one joy would be to go and lie at her feet like a dog, like a miserable beaten cur, to lie on the floor and breathe on her feet like a cur. That would be a happiness greater than anything he could imagine.

But such kind animal simplicity—arriving and prostrating himself at her feet—was of course something he could not allow himself. He would have to utter polite, apologetic words, then she'd have to do the same, and she would, because this was the complicated way things had been arranged for many thousands of years.

Even now he could see her as she was yesterday, with that glow, that flush on her cheeks as she said, "You know, you could quite easily come and stay with me—quite easily!" That blush would have to be redeemed. He couldn't let it touch her cheeks again, he would have to get round it with laughter. He couldn't let her make herself embarrassed again, and that was why he had to think up a few first sentences, sufficiently polite and humorous to soften the strangeness of the situation: his calling to see his doctor, a young woman living on her own, with the intention of staying the night—goodness knows why. But he'd rather not think up sentences, he'd rather open the door, stand there and look at her, and call her Vega from the start, that was essential— "Vega! I've come!"

But whatever happened it would be an uncontainable joy being with her, not in the ward or the doctor's consulting room but in an ordinary room, talking about something or other, he didn't know what. He would probably blunder, say the wrong things. After all he was no longer used to living among the human race. But his eyes would let him express what he wanted to say: "Have pity on me! Please, have pity on me, I am so unhappy without you!"

How could he have wasted so much time? Why ever hadn't he gone to Vega? He should have gone long ago. He was walking along briskly now, unhesitatingly, afraid only that he might miss her. After strolling round the town for half the day, he had grasped the layout of the streets and knew the way.

If they got on well together, if it was pleasant being with each other and talking, if there was a chance that at some point he might even take her by the hands, put his arms round her shoulders and look closely, tenderly into her eyes—wouldn't that be enough? And if there was to be even more, much more than that—wouldn't that be enough?

Of course with Zoya it wouldn't have been enough. But with Vega? The Nilgai antelope?

The very thought of taking her hands in his gave him a tense feeling inside his chest. He began to be quite excited about how it was going to happen.

Surely this would be enough?

He grew more and more excited the closer he came to her house. It was really fear, but a happy fear, a fainting delight. This fear was in itself enough to make him happy.

He kept walking, noticing only the street names, ignoring the shops, shopwindows, trolley cars, people, when suddenly he came to a street corner. There was an old woman standing there; he couldn't get past her at first because of the crush. He saw she was selling bunches of little blue flowers.

In no remote corner of his drained, plowed-over, adjusted memory was there a shadow of a notion that when calling on a woman one should bring her flowers. He had forgotten the convention as profoundly and finally as though it had never existed. He had been walking calmly along with his threadbare, patched, heavy duffel bag, not one doubt causing his step to hesitate, and now he had seen some flowers. For some reason these flowers were being sold to people. He frowned, and a vague recollection began to swim up in his mind like a drowned corpse out of a pool of murky water. That's right, that's right! In the long-past, almost nonexistent world of his youth, it had been the custom to give women flowers!

"These . . . What are they?" he asked the flowerseller shyly.

"They're violets, that's what," she said in an insulted tone. "One ruble a bunch."

Violets? Could they be those same violets, the ones in the poem? For some reason he remembered them differently. Their stems should be more graceful, taller, and the blooms more bell-shaped. But perhaps his memory was at fault. Or maybe it was some local variety. In any case there were no others to choose. Now he'd remembered, he realized it would be impossible to go without flowers, shameful too.

How could he possibly have walked along so calmly without flowers?

But how many should he buy? One? One didn't seem enough.

Two? Even two would be on the mean side. Three? Four? Appallingly expensive. A flash of labor camp cunning darted through his mind, like an adding machine ticking over. He could probably knock her down to one and a half rubles for two bunches or four for five bunches. But this sharp streak was apparently not the true Oleg. He held out two rubles and handed them over quietly.

He took the two bunches. They had a scent, but there again it wasn't the way the violets of his youth should have smelled, the violets of the poets. He could carry them along sniffing them like this, but it would look odd if he just carried them in his hands: a sick, demobilized, bareheaded soldier, carrying a duffel bag and some violets! There was no proper way of arranging them, so the best thing was to pull his hand up his sleeve and carry them inside, out of sight.

Vega's house—yes, this was the one!

Straight into the courtyard, she had said. He went into the courtyard, then turned left.

(Something in his chest seemed to be lurching from side to side.)

There was a long concrete veranda used by the whole house, open, but with an awning of slanting, interlaced ironwork under the railings. Things were thrown over the railings to air: blankets, mattresses, pillows, and some linen hanging on lines strung from pillar to pillar.

All in all, it was a very unsuitable place for Vega. The approaches were cluttered and untidy. Anyway, that wasn't her responsibility. A little further on, behind all that washing hanging out to dry, would be the door to her apartment, and behind that door the private world of Vega.

He ducked under some sheets and looked for the door. It was a door like any other, painted bright brown and peeling in places. It had a green box for mail.

Oleg produced the violets from the sleeve of his overcoat. He tried to tidy his hair. He was anxious and excited, and very glad to be so. He tried to imagine her without her doctor's white coat and in her home surroundings.

It wasn't just those few blocks from the zoo that his heavy boots had tramped. He had walked the far-flung roads of his country for twice seven years. And now here he was, demobilized at last, at the very door where for those past fourteen years a woman had been silently waiting for him.

He touched the door with the knuckle of his middle finger.

But he didn't have time to knock properly. The door was already beginning to open. (Could *she* have noticed him already through the window?) It opened and out came a great loutish, snout-faced young man with a flat, bashed-in nose, pushing a bright red motorcycle straight at Oleg. It looked enormous in that narrow doorway. He did not even ask what Oleg was doing or whom he had come to see. He wheeled it straight on as if Oleg wasn't there (he wasn't the sort to give way) and Oleg stepped to one side.

Oleg tried to figure it out but couldn't: What was the young man doing here if Vega lived on her own? Why should he be coming out of her apartment? Surely he couldn't have forgotten, even though it was years ago, that people didn't usually live by themselves, they lived in communal apartments? He couldn't have forgotten, and yet there was no reason why he should have remembered. In the labor camp barracks room one forms a picture of the outside world that is the barracks room's complete opposite, certainly not a communal apartment. Even in Ush-Terek people lived on their own, they didn't have communals there.

"Er, excuse me . . ." he said, addressing the young man. But he had pushed his motorcycle under the hanging sheet and was already taking it down the steps, the wheels bumping hollowly.

He had left the door open, though. Down the unlit depths of the corridor Kostoglotov could now see a door, and another, and a third. Which one? Then he made out a woman in the half-darkness. She didn't turn on the light.

"Who do you want?" she asked him aggressively.

"Vera Kornilyevna." Oleg spoke shyly, in a voice quite unlike his own.

"She's not here," the woman snapped back at him with sharp, confident hostility, without bothering to look or to try the door. She walked straight at Kostoglotov, forcing him to squeeze backward.

"Will you knock, please?" Kostoglotov recovered his old self. The expectation of seeing Vega had softened him, but he could still yap back at yapping neighbors. "She's not at work today," he said.

"I know. She's not here. She was, but she's gone out." The woman looked him over. She had a low forehead and slanting cheekbones.

She had already seen the violets, it was too late to hide them.

If it weren't for the violets in his hand he'd be able to stand up for himself. He'd be able to knock by himself, assert his independence, insist on asking how long she had gone out for, whether she would be back soon, and leave a message for her. Perhaps she had already left one for him?

But the violets had turned him into a suppliant, a bearer of gifts, a lovesick fool. . . .

The assault of the woman with the slanting cheekbones was so intense that he retreated onto the veranda.

She drove him from his bridgehead, pressing hard at his heels and observing him. There seemed to be a bulge in the old bum's bag. He might pinch something. (In here too!)

Out in the yard the motorcycle gave a number of impudent, explosive bursts. It had no silencer. The motor died, roared out, and died again.

Oleg hesitated.

The woman was looking at him with irritation.

How could Vega not be there? She had promised. But what if she had waited earlier on and then gone out somewhere? What a disaster! It wasn't a mere misfortune or a disappointment, it was a disaster.

Oleg drew his hand with the violets back into his overcoat sleeve, so that it looked as if his hand had been cut off.

"Excuse me, will she come back or has she gone to work?"

"She's gone," the woman cut him short.

It was no sort of an answer.

It would be equally absurd just to stand there opposite her, waiting.

The motorcycle twitched, spat, barked, and then died away. Lying on the railings were heavy pillows, mattresses, and blankets inside envelope-shaped covers, out to dry in the sun.

"What are you waiting for then, citizen?" Those enormous bastions of bedding had made Oleg's mind go blank.

The woman with the slanting cheekbones was staring at him. He couldn't think.

And that damn motorcycle was tearing him to shreds. It wouldn't start.

Oleg edged away from the bastions of pillows and retreated down the steps to where he'd come from. He was repulsed.

If it hadn't been for that pillow—one corner of it all crumpled, two corners hanging down like cows' udders, and the fourth sticking up like an obelisk—if it hadn't been for that pillow he could have collected himself and decided something. He couldn't leave suddenly like this. Vega might be coming back soon. And she'd be sorry he'd left. She'd be sorry.

But those pillows, mattresses, blankets, envelope-shaped blanket covers, and banner-like sheets implied such stable, tested experience that he hadn't the strength to reject it. He had no right.

Especially now. Especially him.

A man alone can sleep on planks or boards so long as his heart has faith or ambition. A prisoner sleeps on naked planks since he has no choice, and the woman prisoner, too, separated from him by force. But when a man and a woman have arranged to be together, the pillows' soft faces wait confidently for what is their due. They know they will not miss what is theirs.

So Oleg walked away from this unassailable fortress he could not enter, the lump of iron still weighing his shoulders down. He walked, one hand amputated, trudging toward the gate. The pillow bastions riddled him joyfully in the back with machine guns.

It wouldn't start, damn it.

Outside the gate the bursts sounded muffled. Oleg stopped to wait a little longer.

He still hadn't given up the idea of waiting for Vega. If she came back, she couldn't avoid passing this point. They'd smile and be so glad to see each other: "Hello. . . ." "Do you know that . . . ?" "Such a funny thing happened. . . ."

Was he to produce from his sleeve those crumpled, faded violets?

He could wait for her and then they'd go back into the courtyard, but they wouldn't be able to avoid those swollen, self-confident bastions again.

They would have to pass them whatever happened.

Someday, if not today, Vega, lightfooted and ethereal with those bright dark-brown eyes, her whole being a contrast to the dust of this earth, would carry her own airy, tender, delightful little bed out onto the same veranda. Yes, Vega too.

No bird lives without its nest, no woman lives without her bed.

However immortal, however rarefied she may be, she cannot avoid those eight inevitable hours of the night, going to sleep and waking up again.

It rolled out! The crimson motorcycle drove out through the gate, giving Kostoglotov the *coup de grâce.*

The lad with the bashed-in nose looked like a conqueror in the street.

Kostoglotov walked on his way, defeated.

He took the violets out of his sleeve. They were at their last gasp. In a few minutes they'd be unpresentable.

Two Uzbek schoolgirls with identical braids of black hair plaited tighter than electric wire were walking toward him. With both hands Oleg held out the two bunches.

"Here, girls, take these."

They were amazed. They looked from one to the other. They looked at him. They spoke to each other in Uzbek. They realized he wasn't drunk and wasn't trying to molest them. They may even have realized that some misfortune had made the old soldier give them flowers.

One of the girls took her bunch and nodded.

The second girl took hers and nodded.

Then they walked quickly, rubbing shoulders and chattering excitedly.

He was left with nothing but the dirty, sweat-soaked duffel bag on his shoulder.

Where could he spend the night? He'd have to think of something all over again.

He couldn't stay in a hotel.

He couldn't go to Zoya's.

He couldn't go to Vega's.

Or rather, he could, he could. And she'd be pleased. She'd never show how disappointed she'd been.

But it was a question of "mustn't" rather than "couldn't."

Without Vega the whole of this beautiful town with its wealth and its millions of inhabitants felt like a heavy bag on his back. Strange to think that this morning he had liked the place so much he'd wanted to stay longer.

And even stranger still, what had he been so happy about this morning? His cure no longer seemed like some special gift.

Oleg had walked less than a block when he felt how hungry be was, how sore his feet were, how utterly physically exhausted he was, and that still unbeaten tumor rolling around inside him. All he wanted was to get away as quickly as possible.

But even returning to Ush-Terek, to which the road was now open, no longer attracted him. Oleg realized he would sink even deeper into the gloom until he drowned.

At the moment he couldn't imagine any place or thing that could cheer him up.

Except—going back to Vega.

He would have to fall at her feet: "Don't turn me out, don't turn me out! It's not my fault!"

But it was a question of "mustn't" rather than "couldn't."

He asked a passer-by the time. After two o'clock. He ought to come to some decision.

He caught sight of a trolley car, the number that went toward the *komendatura*. He started to look around for a nearby stop.

With an iron screech, especially on the bends, as though gravely ill itself, the trolley car dragged him along the narrow stone streets. Oleg held onto the leather strap and bent his head to try and see something out of the window, but they were going through a part of town that had no greenery, no boulevards, only sidewalks and shabby houses. They flashed past a billboard poster advertising matinee shows at an outdoor moviehouse. It would have been interesting to see how it worked, but something had snuffed out his interest in the world's novelties.

She was proud to have withstood fourteen years of loneliness. But she didn't know what six months of the other thing could do to them: together, yet not together.

He recognized his stop and got off. He would now have to walk one and a half kilometers along a wide, depressing street in a factory neighborhood. A constant stream of trucks and tractors rumbled along both sides of the roadway. The footpath was lined by a long stone wall, then cut across a factory railway track and a coal-slack embankment, ran past a wasteland pitted with hollows, then across some more rails, then along another wall, and finally past some wooden, one-story barracks blocks—the sort described in official files as "temporary civilian accommodation" but which had remained standing for ten, twenty or even thirty years. At least there was none of the mud there had been in January during the rain, when Kostoglotov was looking for the *komendatura* for the first time. All the same, it was a depressing, long walk. One could hardly believe this street was in the same town as those ring boulevards, huge-girthed oak trees, buoyant poplars, and wondrous pink apricots.

However hard she tried to convince herself she ought to do it, that it was the right thing to do, it would merely mean that when it did break through the surface it would be all the more heartrending.

Whose idea could it have been to place the *komendatura*, the office that decided the fate of all the city's exiles, in such a tucked-away corner of town? But here it was, among the barracks blocks and the muddy pathways, the windows broken and boarded up with plywood, among the endless lines of washing. Here it was.

Oleg remembered the repulsive expression on the face of the *komendant*, who hadn't even been at work on a weekday, and how he had been received the last time. As he walked along the corridor of the *komendant's* barracks block, he slowed down and composed his features into a close, independent look. Kostoglotov would never permit himself to smile at his jailers even if they smiled at him. He considered it his duty to remind them that he re-membered everything.

He knocked and went in. The first room was bare and empty: only two long, wobbly, backless benches and, behind a board partition, a desk where presumably twice every month they performed the sacred rite of registering the local exiles.

There was no one there now, but further on was a door wide open with a notice on it: *Komendant.*

Oleg walked across so he could see through the door. "Can I come in?" he asked anxiously.

"Certainly, certainly!" A pleasant, welcoming voice invited him in.

Unbelievable! Oleg had never heard an NKVD man use such a tone. He went in. There was no one in the room but the *komendant*, sitting at his desk. But it wasn't the same one, not that enigmatic idiot with the wise-looking expression; it was an Armenian with the soft face of a well-educated man, not at all arrogant, wearing no uniform but a good suit that looked out of place in the barracks surroundings. The Armenian gave him a merry look, as if his job was selling theater tickets and he was glad to see that Oleg had come with a big order.

After his years in the camps Oleg couldn't be very well disposed toward Armenians. Few in number, they had looked after one another jealously and always taken the best jobs—in the storeroom or the bread room, or even where they could get at the butter. But to be fair, Oleg couldn't object to them because of that. It wasn't they who had invented the camps, they hadn't invented Siberia either. After all, what high ideal forbade them to help and save one another? Why should they give up commerce and peck away at the earth with pickaxes?

Seeing this merry-looking, friendly Armenian sitting behind his official desk, Oleg thought warmly that informality and enterprise must be the Armenians' special qualities.

Oleg gave him his name and that he was here on a temporary registration. The *komendant* got up eagerly and with ease, although he was a heavily built man, and began flipping through the cards in one of the files. At the same time, as though trying to provide Oleg with some diversion, he kept up a constant chatter: sometimes meaningless interjections, but occasionally naming people, which the most stringent instructions prohibited him from doing.

"Ye-es, now, let's have a look . . . Kalifotides . . . Konstantinides . . . Yes, do please sit down . . . Kulayev . . . Karamuriev. Oh dear, I've torn off the corner . . . Kazmagomayev . . . Kostoglotov!"

And again in blatant disregard of NKVD rules, he did not ask Oleg his first name and patronymic, but gave them himself. "Oleg Filimonovich?"

"Yes."

"I see. You've been under treatment in the cancer clinic since January 23. . . ." And he lifted his keen, kindly eyes from the paper. "Well, how did it go? Are you better?"

Oleg was genuinely moved; there was even a tightness in his throat. How little was needed. Put a few humane men behind these vile desks and life became completely different. He no longer felt constrained. He answered simply, "Well, how shall I put it . . . in one way better, in another way worse. . . ." (Worse? What an ungrateful creature man is! How could he be worse off than he had been lying on the clinic floor, longing to die?) "I mean, better on the whole."

"Well, that's good," said the *komendant* happily. "Why don't you sit down?"

Even filling out theater ticket orders takes a bit of time. You have to stamp them and write in the date in ink, then copy it into a thick book, and of course cross it out of another. All this the Armenian did happily and without fuss. He took Oleg's certificate with the travel permit from the file and held it out to him. His glance was expressive, his voice unofficial and a little quieter as he said, "Please . . . don't let it depress you. It'll all be over soon."

"What will?" asked Oleg in surprise.

"What do you mean? These registrations, of course. Your exile. *Komendant's* too!" he said with a carefree smile.

Obviously he had some more congenial job up his sleeve. "What? Is there already . . . an instruction?" Oleg hastened to extract the information.

"Not an instruction." The *komendant* sighed. "But there are certain signs. I'll tell you straight out, it's going to happen. Get better, and you will soon be going up in the world."

Oleg gave him a crooked smile. "I'm almost out of this world," he said.

"What's your profession?"

"I haven't one."

"Are you married?"

"No."

"That's good," said the *komendant* with conviction. "Those who marry in exile almost always get divorced afterwards and it's a terrible business. But you can get released, go back to where you came from and get married."

"Well, in that case, thank you very much." Oleg got up to go. The *komendant* nodded amiably but still didn't offer Oleg his hand.

As he walked out through the two rooms, Oleg wondered about the *komendant.* Had he always been like that or was it the changing times? Was he a permanent or a temporary? Or had they started specially appointing ones like him? It was very important to find out, but he couldn't go back now.

Back past the barracks again, past the railway lines, past the coal, Oleg set off along the long streetful of factories at a brisk pace, his step quicker and more even. He soon had to take off his overcoat because of the heat, and slowly the bucket of joy which the *komendant* had poured into him began to flood his whole being. Only gradually did he realize the full meaning of it all.

Only gradually because Oleg had lost the habit of believing the men who sat behind those desks. How could he forget the lies deliberately spread by officials, captains and majors in the years after the war, about how a sweeping amnesty for political prisoners was in preparation? Prisoners had believed them implicitly: "The captain told me so himself!" But the officials had simply been ordered to raise the prisoners' morale, to get them to carry on as before and fulfill their norms, to give them something to aim at and live for.

But as for this Armenian, if there was anything to suspect, it was that he knew too much, more than his post warranted. Still, hadn't Oleg himself expected something of the sort from the scraps of information he had read in the newspapers?

For heaven's sake, it was about time! It was long overdue. How could it be otherwise? A man dies from a tumor, so how can a country survive with growths like labor camps and exiles?

Oleg felt happy again. After all, he hadn't died. And here he was; soon he'd be able to buy himself a ticket to Leningrad. Leningrad! Would he really be able to go up and touch one of the columns of St. Isaac's? His heart would burst!

But what did St. Isaac's matter? Everything was changing now between him and Vega. It was enough to make his head spin. If he could really . . . if he could seriously. . . . No, it wasn't mere fantasy any longer. He'd be able to live here, with her.

To live with Vega! Together! Just imagining it was enough to burst his ribcase.

How glad she'd be if he went to her now and told her this. Why shouldn't he tell her? Why shouldn't he go? Who in the world was he to tell if not her? Who else was there interested in his freedom?

He had already reached the trolley-car stop. He'd have to choose which trolley to take—the one to the station, or the one to Vega's? And he'd have to hurry because she'd be going out. The sun was already quite low in the sky.

Again he began to feel agitated, and again he felt drawn toward Vega. Nothing remained of the convincing arguments he had amassed on his way to the *komendant's*.

He was not guilty, he was not covered in dirt, why should *he* avoid *her*? She'd known what she was doing, hadn't she, when she'd given him that treatment? Hadn't she become all silent, hadn't she left the stage when he was arguing with her and begging her to stop the treatment?

Why shouldn't he go? Why shouldn't they try to rise above the common level? Why shouldn't they aim higher? Weren't they human beings after all? At least, Vega was.

He was already pushing through the crowd to get to the trolley. There were a lot of people waiting at the stop, all surging forward to get to the one he wanted, all traveling his way. Oleg had his overcoat in one hand and his duffel bag in the other, so he couldn't grab hold of the handrail. He was squashed, spun round, and finally shoved onto the platform and into the car.

People were leaning on him savagely from all sides. He found himself behind two girls who looked like students. One fair, the other darkish, they were so close to him they must be able to feel him breathing. His arms were pulled apart and separately pinioned so that he could not pay the irate lady conductor, in fact he could not even move. His left arm, the one with the coat in it, seemed to be embracing the dark girl, while his whole body was pressed against the blonde. He could feel her all over, from knee to chin, and she couldn't possibly avoid feeling him in the same way. The greatest passion in the world could not have joined them as intimately as that crowd. Her neck, her ears, and her little curls were thrust closer to him than he would ever have thought possible. Through her worn old clothes he was absorbing her warmth, her softness, and her youth. The dark girl was still chatting to her friend about something going on at college. The blond girl had stopped answering her.

In Ush-Terek they had no trolley cars. Only in the shell holes had he ever been as close to people as this. But there hadn't always been women there. This sensation—he hadn't felt it, he hadn't had it confirmed for decades. It was all the more primeval for that, all the stronger.

It was a happiness, and it was a sorrow. There was in the sensation a threshold he could not cross whatever his powers of self-suggestion.

They had warned him, hadn't they? The libido remains, the libido but nothing else. . . .

They went past a couple of stops. After that it was still a crush, but there were not so many people pressing from behind. Oleg could have moved away from them a bit, but he didn't. He had no will left to put an end to this blissful torture. At this moment he wanted no more than to stay as he was for just a little longer, even if the trolley took him right back to the Old Town, even if it went out of its mind and took him clattering and circling nonstop until nightfall. Even if it ventured on a voyage round the world, Oleg had no will left to be the first to break away. As he prolonged this happiness, the greatest joy to which he could now aspire, he remembered gratefully the little curls of hair on the back of the blond girl's neck. Her face he hadn't even glimpsed.

She broke away from him and began to move forward.

And as he straightened his bent, weakened knees Oleg realized his journey to see Vega would end as a torture and a deceit.

It would mean his demanding more from her than he could ask from himself.

They had come to a high-minded agreement that spiritual communion was more valuable than anything else; yet, having built this tall bridge by hand together, he saw now that his own hands were weakening. He was on his way to her to persuade her boldly of one thing while thinking agonizingly of something else. And when she went away and he was left in her room alone, there he'd be, whimpering over her clothes, over every little thing of hers, over her perfumed handkerchief.

No, he should be more sensible than some teenage girl. He should go to the railway station.

He fought his way through to the rear platform—not forward, not past the student girls—and jumped off. Someone swore at him.

Not far from the trolley stop someone else was selling violets. . . .

The sun was already going down. Oleg put on his overcoat and took another trolley to the station. This time it wasn't so crowded.

He pushed his way all over the station, asking questions and getting the wrong answers. Finally he reached a sort of pavilion like a covered market, where they were selling tickets for the long-distance trains.

There were four booking-office windows, at each a line of a hundred and fifty to two hundred people. And there must be others in the line who were away for the moment.

The picture of railway station lines going on for days was one Oleg recognized at once, as though he'd always been familiar with it. Much had changed in the world: fashions, street lamps, the habits of young people, but this had remained constant for as long as he could remember. It had been like this in 1946, it had been the same in 1939, and in 1934 and in 1930. Shopwindows bursting with food he could even remember from the N.E.P.[1] period, but he couldn't imagine station booking offices that were easy to get to. The difficulties of travel were unknown only to those who had special cards or official vouchers.

As it happened, he had a voucher—not a very impressive one perhaps, but it would suit the occasion.

It was stuffy and he was sweating, but he pulled from his duffel bag a tight fur hat and squeezed it over his head as a hatmaker would over a stretching block. He slung his bag over one shoulder and assumed the expression of a man who less than two weeks earlier had lain on the operating table under Lev Leonidovich's knife. In this assumed condition of exhaustion, a dull stare in his eyes, he dragged himself between the lines right up to the booking-office window. There were no fights going on solely because a policeman was standing nearby.

In full view of everyone, Oleg made a feeble gesture to pull the voucher out of the slanting pocket under his greatcoat. Trustfully he handed it over to the "comrade militiaman."

The policeman was a fine upstanding Uzbek with a mustache, who looked like a young general. He ceremoniously read it through and announced to the people at the head of the line, "Let this man through. He's had an operation."

He made a sign to Oleg to take third place in the line.

Oleg glanced exhaustedly at his new neighbors in the line. He didn't even try to squeeze in, he just stood on one side, head bowed. A fat, elderly Uzbek, his face bronzed in the shadow of a brown velvet hat with a saucer-like brim, took him and pushed him into line.

---

[1] The New Economic Policy reintroduced limited private enterprise into the Soviet economy. It was begun by Lenin in 1921 as a temporary measure to revitalize the Soviet system after the excesses of "war communism."

He felt cheerful standing there near the window. He could see the girl's fingers as she pushed out the tickets. Clutched in the passengers' hands, he could see the sweat-drenched money, as much as was needed or more, that had been extracted from their sewn-up pockets or belts. He could hear the passengers making timid requests, all of which the girl refused mercilessly. It was clear that things were moving, and quickly.

Now it was Oleg's turn to bend down to the window.

"Please may I have one ordinary ticket to Khan-Tau," he said.

"Where?" the girl asked.

"Khan-Tau."

"Never heard of it." She shrugged her shoulders and started looking through a huge directory.

"Why do you want an ordinary ticket, dear?" a woman behind him asked sympathetically. "An ordinary ticket after you've had an operation? You'll split your stitches climbing up to your bunk. You should have got a reservation."

"I haven't any money," Oleg sighed.

It was the truth.

"There's no such station!" shouted the girl behind the window, slamming the directory shut. "Take a ticket to some other station."

"There must be." Oleg smiled weakly. "It's been working a whole year. I came from there myself. If I'd known, I'd have kept my ticket to show you."

"I don't know anything about that. If it's not in the directory it means there's no such station."

"The trains stop there. They do!" Oleg was beginning to argue more heatedly than someone who had just had an operation ought to. "It's even got a booking office."

"Move on, then, if you don't want a ticket, citizen. Next!"

"That's right, why should he hold us up?" came a disapproving murmur from behind. "Take a ticket to the station they give you. . . . He's just had an operation, all right, but why should he be so choosy?"

My God, Oleg could've given them an argument! How he longed to go the whole hog, demand to see the passenger-service director and the stationmaster. How he would have loved to get through to these thick skulls and see his bit of justice, a tiny, miserable bit but nevertheless justice. So long as he was fighting for it, he would feel like a human being.

But the law of supply and demand was an iron one, and so was the law of transport planning. The kind woman behind him, who had tried to persuade him to take a reservation, was already pushing her money over his shoulder. That policeman who had only just sent him to the front of the line was already lifting a hand to take him to one side.

"The one I want is thirty kilometers from where I live, the other's seventy." Oleg went on complaining into the window, but his words had become, in camp language, mere belly-aching. He was now eager to agree. "All right, give me one to Chu Station."

The girl recognized the station straightaway and knew what the price was. And there was a ticket left. All Oleg had to do was bless his good luck. He moved a little away from the window, checked the punchholes on the ticket against the light, checked the car number, checked the price, checked his change, and walked slowly away.

The further he got from the people who knew him as a post-operation case, the straighter he stood up. He took off his wretched little hat and put it back into his duffel bag. There were two hours before the train left and it was wonderful to be able to spend them with a ticket in his pocket. Now he could really celebrate: eat an ice cream (there was no ice cream in Ush-Terek), drink a glass of *kvas*[2] (there was no *kvas* either), and buy some black bread for the journey. Sugar too, he mustn't forget that. He'd also have to line up patiently and pour some boiled water into a bottle (it was a great thing, having your own water!). As for salt herrings, he knew he mustn't take any. How much more free and easy it was than traveling in those prison transports, in converted freight cars. They wouldn't search him before he got on, they wouldn't take him to the station in a paddy wagon, they wouldn't sit him on the ground surrounded by guards and make him spend forty-eight hours tormented by thirst. And if he managed to grab the luggage rack above the two bunks, he'd be able to stretch his whole length along it. This time there wouldn't be two or three people in the rack, there'd be just one! He'd lie down and feel no more pain from his tumor. This was happiness! He was a happy man. What was there to complain about?

That *komendant* had blabbed out something about an amnesty. . . . It was here, his long-awaited happiness, it was here! But for some reason Oleg hadn't recognized it.

After all, he'd heard Vega calling the surgeon "Lyova," speaking quite familiarly to him. And if not him, there might be someone else. There were so many opportunities. It's like an explosion when a man enters another person's life.

When he'd seen the moon this morning, he'd had faith! But that moon had been on the wane. . . .

He ought to go out onto the platform now, a good long time before they started letting passengers onto the train. When the train came in empty he'd have to watch out for his car, run to it, and get to the head of the line.

---

[2] A Russian national drink, a fermentation usually of bread.

Oleg went to look at the timetable. There was a train going in the opposite direction, Number 75. The passengers must already be getting in. Pretending to gasp for breath, he pushed his way quickly toward the door, asking everyone he met, including the ticket collector, half-hiding the ticket with his fingers, "Seventy-five, is this it? Is this it?"

He was terrified of being late for Number 75. The ticket collector didn't bother to check his ticket, he just pushed him on, slapping the heavy, bulging bag on his back.

Oleg began to walk quietly up and down the platform. Then he stopped and threw his duffel bag down on a stone ledge. He remembered another equally funny occasion in Stalingrad in 1939 during his last days of freedom. It was after the treaty with Ribbentrop had been signed, but before Molotov's speech and before the order to mobilize nineteen-year-olds.

He and a friend had spent the summer going down the Volga in a boat. In Stalingrad they sold the boat and had to get back by train to where they studied. But they had quite a lot of stuff left over from the boat trip, so much that they could hardly carry it in their four hands. And on top of that, Oleg's friend had bought a loudspeaker in some out-of-the-way village store. You couldn't buy them in Leningrad at that time.

The loudspeaker was a large, cone-shaped funnel without a case, and his friend was frightened it would get crushed as they got on the train. They went into the station at Stalingrad and immediately found themselves at the end of a long, bulky line that took up the whole station hall, cluttering it with wooden trunks, bags, and boxes. It was quite impossible to get through to the platform before their train came in, and it looked as if they would have to spend two nights without anywhere to lie down. Also a close watch was being kept to see they didn't get through onto the platform.

Suddenly Oleg had an idea: "Make an effort and get these things to the car door, even if you're the last man through." He took the loudspeaker and walked up to the staff door, which was locked. He waved the loudspeaker importantly through the glass at the girl on duty. She opened it. "Just this one to fix and I'm through," Oleg said. The woman nodded understandingly as if he'd spent the whole day carrying loudspeakers to and fro. The train pulled in and he got on first before all the others and grabbed two luggage racks.

That was sixteen years ago and nothing had changed.

Oleg wandered along the platform and saw there were others just as cunning as himself. They had also got through for a train that wasn't theirs and were waiting with their luggage. There were quite a few of them, but still there was much less of a crush on the platform than in the station and in the gardens in front of it. There were also some people from train Number 75 walking around carefree on the platform. These well-dressed types had no worries. They had numbered places which no one could grab from them. There were women with bunches of flowers they had been given, men with bottles of beer, and someone taking a photograph. It was a life quite inaccessible to Oleg. He could hardly understand it. The warm spring evening and the long platform under the awning reminded him of some place in the South he had known as a child, perhaps Mineralniye Vody.[3]

Then Oleg noticed a post office with an entrance onto the platform. There was even a little four-sided sloping desk on the platform for people to write letters at.

It suddenly dawned on him. He had to. And he'd better do it now before the day's impressions got blurred and faded.

He pushed his way in with his bag and bought an envelope—no, two envelopes and two sheets of paper—yes, and a postcard as well. Then he pushed his way back onto the platform, put his bag with the iron and the black bread between his feet, leaned against the sloping table and began with the easiest task, the postcard:

> Hello there, Dyomka! Well, I went to the zoo. It was quite something, I can tell you. I've never seen anything like it. You must go. There are white bears, can you imagine? Crocodiles, tigers, lions. Allow a whole day and go right round. They even sell pies in the place. Don't miss the spiral-horned goat. Don't be in a hurry, just stand and look at it—and think. And if you see the Nilgai antelope, do the same. There are lots of monkeys—they'll make you laugh. But there's one missing. An evil man threw tobacco into the Macaque Rhesus's eyes. Just like that, for no reason. And it went blind.
>
> The train's coming, I must dash.
>
> Get better and live up to your ideals. I'm relying on you.
>
> Give Aleksei Filippovich all the best from me. I hope he's getting better.
>
> > Best wishes,
> > OLEG.

He was writing quite easily, except that it was a very smudgy pen. The nibs were all crossed or broken, they tore the paper and dug into it like a spade, and the inkwell was a storehouse of scraps of paper. However hard he tried, the letter ended up looking terrible:

---

[3] A spa in the Northern Caucasus.

Zoyenka, my little Teddy bear, I'm so grateful for you for allowing my lips to get a taste of genuine life. Without those few evenings I should have felt absolutely, yes absolutely, robbed.

You were more sensible than I was, and I can go away now without any feelings of remorse. You asked me to come and see you but I didn't.

Thank you for that. You see, I thought—we'll stick with what we've had. We won't ruin it. I'll always remember everything about you with gratitude.

Honestly and sincerely I wish you the happiest of marriages!
OLEG.

It had been the same in the NKVD remand prison. On official complaint days they provided the same vile, rubbishy inkwell, the same sort of pen, and a piece of paper smaller than a postcard. The ink swam all over the place and went through the paper. Given that, you could write to anyone you liked about anything you liked.

Oleg read through the letter, folded it, and put it in the envelope. He wanted to seal the envelope—he remembered as a child reading a detective story where everything started with a mixup in some envelopes—but that wasn't so easy. There was only a dark line along the edges of the flap to mark the place where, according to State All-Union Regulations, there should have been glue—but of course there wasn't.

Oleg worked out which of the three pens had the best nib, wiped it clean and thought about what he was going to write in his last letter. Until then he had been standing there firmly enough, even smiling, but everything became unsteady now. He was sure he was going to write "Vera Kornilyevna" but instead he wrote:

Darling Vega (all the time I was dying to call you that, so I will now, just this once), I want to write to you frankly, more frankly than we've ever spoken to each other. But we have thought it, haven't we? After all, it's no ordinary patient, is it, to whom a doctor offers her room and her bed?

Several times today I set out to walk to your place. Once I actually got there. I walked along as excited as a sixteen-year-old—an indecency for a man with a life like mine behind him. I was excited, embarrassed, happy and terrified. It takes many years of tramping to realize the meaning of the words "God sent you to me."

You see, Vega, if I'd found you in, something false and forced might have started between us. I went for a walk afterwards and realized it was a good thing I hadn't found you in. Everything that you or I tormented ourselves with at least has a name and can be put into words. But what was about to begin between us was something we could never have confessed to anyone. You and I, and between us *this thing*: this sort of gray, decrepit, yet ever-growing snake.

I am older than you, I don't mean in years so much as in life. So believe me, you are right, right in everything, right in your past and in your present. Your future is the only thing you do not have the power to guess. You may disagree, but I have a prediction to make: Even before you drift into the indifference of old age you will come to bless this day, the day you did not commit yourself to share my life. (I'm not just talking about my exile. There are even rumors it's going to come to an end.) You slaughtered the first half of your life like a lamb. Please spare the second half!

Now that I'm going away anyway (if they end my exile I won't come back to you for checkups or treatment, which means we must say good-bye), I can tell you quite frankly: Even when we were having the most intellectual conversations and I honestly thought and believed everything I said, I still wanted all the time, *all the time,* to pick you up and kiss you on the lips.

So try to work that out.

And now, without your permission, I kiss them.

It was the same thing with the second envelope: a dark strip but no glue. Oleg had always suspected that for some reason this was done on purpose.

Meanwhile, behind his back—that was the result of all his scheming and cunning—the train had pulled into the platform and the passengers were running toward it.

He grabbed his bag, seized the envelopes, and squeezed his way into the post office. "Where's the glue? Have you got any glue, miss? Glue!"

"People are always taking it away," the girl shouted in explanation. She looked at him, then hesitatingly offered him the glue pot. "Here you are, glue it down now while I'm watching. Don't go away."

In the thick, black glue there were dried-up lumps like those a schoolchild would make. It was almost impossible to use and he had to employ the whole body of the brush to spread the glue—moving it across the envelope flap like a saw—wipe off the extra glue with his fingers, then stick it down, then use his fingers again to remove the extra glue pressed out by the flap.

All this time the people were running.

Now—glue back to the girl, pick up the duffel bag (he'd kept it between his legs to stop it being snatched), letters into the mailbox, and run!

He might be a prisoner on his last legs, completely worn out, but, goodness, how he ran!

He cut through some people who had dashed from the main exit gates and were dragging heavy luggage from the platform down onto the tracks and then up again onto the second platform. He reached his car and joined the line. He was about twentieth in the line, but then the ones in front were joined by friends and relations and he ended up about thirtieth. He'd never get a top bunk now, but his legs were so long he didn't really want one. He should be able to get hold of a luggage rack, though. They'd all have baskets thrown up on them—all right, he'd shove them out of the way.

They all carried the same sort of baskets, buckets as well. Maybe they were all full of spring vegetables? Were they on their way to Karaganda, as Chaly had described, to make up for mistakes in the supply system?

The old, gray-haired car attendant was shouting at them to stand in line along the car and not climb in because there'd be room for everyone. But the last remark did not sound too confident—the line behind Oleg was still growing. Then Oleg noticed the beginning of what he'd been afraid of, a movement to jump the line. The first one to make a move was some wild, raving creature. The ignorant eye might have taken him for a psychopath and let him go to the front of the line, but Oleg at once recognized him as a self-styled camp hoodlum. He was trying to frighten people, as his sort always does. The loudmouth was backed up by a number of ordinary quiet people: If he's allowed through, why aren't we? Of course it was a ruse Oleg could have tried, and he'd have had a proper bunk to himself. But the past years had made him tired of such tricks. He wanted things done honestly and in the proper way, just as the old car attendant did.

The attendant was still not letting through the maniac, who was pushing him in the chest and using foul language, quite naturally, as though they were the most ordinary words in the world. The people in the line were murmuring sympathetically, "Let him through! He's a sick man!"

Oleg lurched forward. In a few enormous strides he was beside the maniac. Then he yelled right in his ear, without sparing his ear-drums, "Hey! You! I'm from 'out there' too!"

The maniac jumped back, rubbing his ear. "Where's that?" he said.

Oleg knew he was too weak to fight, he was at his last gasp. But at least he had both hands free; the maniac had a basket in one. Towering over the maniac, he measured out his words quite softly: "The place where ninety-nine weep but one laughs."

The people in the line could not understand how the maniac was so suddenly cured. They saw him cool down, wink, and say to the tall chap in the overcoat, "I'm not saying anything. I don't mind. All right, get in first if you like."

But Oleg stayed there beside the maniac and the car attendant. If the worst came to the worst he could get on from here, but the ones who had been pushing were beginning to go back to their places in the line.

"That's all right by me," the maniac said with reproachful sarcasm. "I don't mind waiting."

On they came, carrying their baskets and their buckets. Under a sacking cover one caught the occasional glimpse of a long lilac-pink radish. Two out of three presented tickets to Karaganda. So these were the people Oleg had arranged the line for! The ordinary passengers were getting in too, including a respectable-looking woman in a blue jacket. Oleg got in and the maniac climbed confidently in behind him.

Oleg walked quickly along the car. He spotted a luggage rack—not one of the uncomfortable ones along the windows—which was still almost empty.

"Right," he announced. "We'll have to shift that basket."

"Where to? What's going on?" a man asked in alarm. He was lame but a sturdy fellow.

"Here's what's going on," Oleg replied. He was already up in the rack. "There's nowhere for people to lie down."

At once he made himself at home on the rack. He put his duffel bag under his head as a pillow, but only after removing the iron. He took off his overcoat and spread it out. He threw off his army jacket too. A man could do what he liked up here. Then he lay down to cool off. His feet and large-sized boots hung down over the corridor. They jutted out almost to calf length, but they were high enough not to get in anyone's way.

People were sorting themselves out down below as well, cooling off and getting to know each other.

The lame man seemed a sociable type. He told them he'd once been a vet's assistant. "Why did you give it up?" they asked him in surprise.

"What do you mean? Why should I get run in for every little sheep that dies? I'm better off on an invalid's pension carrying vegetables," he explained in a loud voice.

"Yes, what's wrong with that?" said the woman in the blue jacket. "It was in Beria's day they rounded people up for fruit and vegetables. They only do it for household goods now."

The sun's last rays would be shining on them if they hadn't been hidden by the station.

It was still quite light down below, but up where Oleg was it was twilight. The "soft"- and "hard"-class sleeper passengers were strolling along the platform, but in here they were sitting wherever they had managed to grab seats, arranging their things. Oleg stretched out full length. That was good! It was terrible traveling forty-eight hours with your legs tucked under you in those converted freight cars. Nineteen men in a car like this would be terrible. Twenty-three would be even worse.

The others hadn't survived. But he had. He hadn't even died of cancer. And now his exile was cracking like an eggshell.

He remembered the *komendant* advising him to get married. They'd all be giving him advice like that soon.

It was good to lie down. Good.

The train shuddered and moved forward. It was only then that in his heart, or his soul, somewhere in his chest, in the deepest seat of his emotion, he was seized with anguish. He twisted his body and lay face down on his greatcoat, shut his eyes and thrust his face into the duffel bag, spiky with leaves.

The train went on and Kostoglotov's boots dangled toes down over the corridor like a dead man's.

An evil man threw tobacco in the Macaque Rhesus's eyes.

Just like that. . . .

7

THE GULAG ARCHIPELAGO

The *Gulag Archipelago* is, by almost everyone's reckoning, one of the most important books of the twentieth century. Few books of any time can match its world-historical impact on concurrent events. By discrediting Soviet communism at home and abroad, this single book played an undeniable—perhaps a decisive—role in ending the Soviet Union and thus the Cold War. Thanks to one lone author, the word *gulag* is now fixed in the public mind as a one-word summary, along with *Holocaust*, of the era's totalitarian horrors. Solzhenitsyn was sure that his work "was destined to affect the course of history," and some critics, including observers frosty toward him, have called it *the* indispensable book about the distinctive character of the twentieth century.

The story of the composing of *The Gulag Archipelago* is almost as mind-boggling as the revelations in the work. Having successfully engineered the publication of *One Day in the Life of Ivan Denisovich* in 1962, Solzhenitsyn worked in public view to get other works into print but, meanwhile, was conducting virtually a second, "underground" life writing on forbidden subjects. He had begun writing *Gulag* in 1958 but wrote much of it during two intense spurts of creativity in the winters of 1965–66 and 1966–67 while hiding out in Estonia among ex-*zeks* and their friends. As an astonishing precaution, he never once had the whole manuscript before him while composing. When *Gulag* was completed in 1968, as the public campaign to vilify him was nearing white heat, he managed to have a microfilm copy of it spirited to the West for safekeeping. The KGB acquired its own copy by inflicting severe, nonstop interrogation upon a strong-willed woman who had worked hard for Solzhenitsyn but who overrode his instruction to destroy the copy in her keeping. That confiscation led Solzhenitsyn to initiate the publishing process in the West. The book's appearance was the immediate cause of his expulsion from the Soviet Union. *Gulag* was translated into some thirty-five languages and sold more than thirty million copies, at least three million in English alone.

The subject matter of *The Gulag Archipelago* is massive; it takes up eighteen hundred pages, which appear as three volumes but actually are divided into seven parts. The gulag comprises myriad prison installations spread all across the vast Soviet terrain, and Solzhenitsyn examines the history of this system from its inception in 1918 to his release from its grip in 1956. His overriding commitment was to find and tell the truth of history that Soviet propaganda falsified. Lacking access to archives and failing to recruit a coauthor, Solzhenitsyn read what he could and sought out eyewitness accounts—227 of these, he specifies. To his information base he added interpretive commentary. Indeed, he drew upon all his resources as a thinker and writer to marshal his multifarious materials into a "case" against the ideological state that eliminated millions of its own citizens. The unknowable number of terminated innocents, while almost surely lower than the 66 million calculated by an émigré demographer he cites, is estimated at 20 million in *The Black Book of Communism* and 35 million by Aleksandr Yakovlev, who led Russia's official investigation of the subject. A sense of obligation toward this "*zek* nation" motivated the writing of *Gulag*—as if, in his metaphor, he was rolling a boulder out of the path of his literary career.

Solzhenitsyn's challenge was to help readers imagine the unimaginable. Straightforward chronological narration would sanitize the gulag's nightmarish world and compress the magnitude of its torments. Conversely, lining up one horror story after another would risk imaginative overload and—oddly—make even unspeakable suffering seem monotonous. For the sake of maximum impact, Solzhenitsyn sacrificed predictability and inevitability, elevating kaleidoscopic shifts of subject and style to virtually a rhetorical method. Thus, some chapters offer generalized accounts of such common *zek* experiences as arrest, interrogation, trial, transportation, torture, death. Others feature chronologically ordered events. Yet others describe such groups as guards, thieves, women, children, religious believers. The heterogeneity extends to sections of legal transcripts, autobiography, and authorial analysis and speculation, among others. Throughout, vignettes of individuals' experiences vivify the generalizations. In sum, *The Gulag Archipelago* is *sui generis*, as befits its unique, complex purpose.

The subtitle, *An Experiment in Literary Investigation*, signals Solzhenitsyn's resort to literary techniques to intensify the narrative. The rhyming Russian title (*Arkhipelag Gulag*) combines history and literature; "Gulag" is an acronym for a real entity, the Chief Administration of Corrective Labor Camps," and "Archipelago" is an image likening the camps dotting the landmass to islands in a sea. Imagery abounds; one common strand likens prisoners to animals, such as scared rabbits or meek lambs. The novelist's powers of characterization enliven the anecdotes about individuals. The most effective feature of literary art in *Gulag* is simply the authorial voice. Its omnipresence holds together the sprawling text's many disparate elements and amalgamates information and interpretation. Its moods are many—lively, outraged, mordant, sarcastic, mournful, hopeful—and can change abruptly. Its shifting tone unsettles and challenges readers and, above all, leads them to feel involved.

Given the subject matter, readers might be tempted to approach *The Gulag Archipelago* in narrowly political terms. Solzhenitsyn meticulously cautions that he is not writing "a political exposé," though he never undercuts the importance of politics in its noblest sense, namely, the concern for the common good of a people or nation. In the supremely important passage that follows to his admonition (in the chapter "The Bluecaps"), he explains the moral vision that governs this book. The "line dividing good and evil" cuts through every human heart, shifting sometimes toward one side and then toward the other according to one's deeds. All persons, from the lowliest *zeks* to the loftiest officials, including Lenin and Stalin, are to be judged according to the same universal moral standards. All actions, for good or for ill, belong to "the history of *morals*." The political dimension of life is never far from Solzhenitsyn's mind, and the ultimate blame for the gulag's inhumanity lies in ideology, which for Solzhenitsyn is not a neutral synonym for "worldview" but refers to a sociopolitical theory beginning in utopianism and ending in social engineering. But he refuses to view the world primarily through the prism of politics, and thus he calls participants in the Soviet apparatus not ideologues but evildoers. Whereas villains in classic literature, such as Shakespeare's, knew they were doing evil, ideology builds in an excuse that allows its adherents to view their immediate evil deeds as ultimately good. Thus, ideology itself is measured in moral terms.

Solzhenitsyn's all-pervasive moral vision is grounded in his religious convictions. The autobiographical sections of *Gulag* add their portion to conveying these deeply held beliefs, none more so than the chapter "The Ascent." But at many points readers will observe his beliefs in operation, including the author's beliefs in a common human nature, the primacy of individuals, the need for human solidarity in developing one's full humanity, and the capacity of religious believers to turn physical deprivation into spiritual growth. Special notice should be paid to the importance of hope, for one organizing principle of *Gulag* is precisely the emotional movement from grief to hope. The early recital of unrelieved misery eventually gives way to celebrations of resistance to illegitimate authority and of instances of spiritual regeneration. Totalitarianism ultimately fails in its goal of achieving *total* control of everyone's outer and inner life. Readers who know only the early parts of *Gulag* cannot know that it concludes on the note of hope, as do virtually all of Solzhenitsyn's works. Improbably, *Gulag* turns out to be a book with a positive message. The author himself explained, in a letter guiding the abridgment, that "the main goal, the main sense of *Archipelago* [is] a moral uplifting and *catharsis*" [italics in the original].

Years after *The Gulag Archipelago* appeared, scholars with access to newly opened archives increased our stock of knowledge about the gulag, exactly as Solzhenitsyn hoped would happen. Yet none of these studies has had—or could fairly be asked to have—the impact on history that *Gulag* has had. Whatever verdict history eventually casts on Solzhenitsyn's *oeuvre*, this one book is a mighty guarantor that the name of Solzhenitsyn will endure.

The present selections come from the authorized abridgment, originally published in 1985. An untitled prefatory note brings in the literary device of imagery (salamander) while rebutting the doctrine of progress. Then come excerpts from the opening chapter, "Arrest," a generalized account that draws readers into a vicarious experience. Excerpts from this chapter highlight autobiographical references, which are prominent throughout the work. The next two chapters in the original illustrate the work's methodological shifts; one is a long, demanding historical overview of the origins and development of the gulag, with the compelling metaphorical title "The History of Our Sewage Disposal System," and then comes another generalized account, "The Interrogation." Then Solzhenitsyn tucks into "The Bluecaps," the chapter on the interrogators, one of his most important passages, the central exposition of his overarching moral vision.

Samplings from Part III starting with the powerful chapter "The Way of Life and Customs of the Natives." The devastation wreaked upon innocent human beings warrants the tone of outrage. The episodes in the chapter "The Kids" range from the appalling scene of boys at rape to the luminous Christian witness of Zoya Leshcheva, and the abhorrent brutalizing of children culminates in the chapter's unforgettable ironic closing lines. If "The Kids" is the most shocking chapter, the material of an absent chapter, "Women in Camps," is similarly dreadful.

With Part IV, the midpoint section, the suffocating darkness begins to yield to flickers of light. Its inspired title, "The Soul and Barbed Wire," intimates how incommensurable are the physical means of confinement (barbed wire) and the spiritual entities to be constrained (souls). The moral vision of *The Gulag Archipelago* reaches its acme in this section's first chapter, "The Ascent," which initiates the work's upward movement of spiritual triumph over the gulag's effort to dehumanize. This soaring chapter relates the dramatic events surrounding the key moment of Solzhenitsyn's own religious renewal. Yet an honest reckoning must balance stories of ascent with those of descent, so the next chapter is "Or Corruption?"

The next two selections come from Part V, which chronicles many episodes of the human spirit's resilience and its occasional victories. The brief chapter "Poetry Under a Tombstone, Truth Under a Stone" shows poetry persisting even under the greatest duress and Solzhenitsyn cleverly finding a way to compose and retain his own poems. "The Forty Days at Kengir" recounts the largest of all camp revolts. The tanks that crushed the mutiny show up again in the title of a never-filmed screenplay that Solzhenitsyn wrote, *Tanks Know the Truth*.

Two chapters from Part VI, plus an "Afterword," complete the present readings. "The Peasant Plague" scathingly describes Stalin's attempt to exterminate a whole social class, the *kulaks*. Killing these enterprising, successful farmers is a direct result of the class analysis of Marxist ideology. It is also exemplifies the process that Solzhenitsyn calls counterselection, which treats society's best human material as enemies of the state. In another instance of the same process, religious believers were the social grouping most overrepresented in the gulag's headcount. "Zeks at Liberty" reveals that even those *zeks* who were eventually released never returned to normal. Bearing the Gulag's scars for life, however, could have some positive effects, too. The gulag did more for Solzhenitsyn than provide literary materials; it gave definitive shape to his worldview as a whole.

Reading only a small sample of *The Gulag Archipelago*, while worthwhile, cannot convey the massiveness of the true story. And it can only hint at Solzhenitsyn's monumental achievement in writing it.

The Gulag Archipelago

Prefatory Note

In 1949 some friends and I came upon a noteworthy news item in *Nature*, a magazine of the Academy of Sciences. It reported in tiny type that in the course of excavations on the Kolyma River a subterranean ice lens had been discovered which was actually a frozen stream—and in it were found frozen specimens of prehistoric fauna some tens of thousands of years old. Whether fish or salamander, these were preserved in so fresh a state, the scientific correspondent reported, that those present immediately broke open the ice encasing the specimens and devoured them *with relish* on the spot.

The magazine no doubt astonished its small audience with the news of how successfully the flesh of fish could be kept fresh in a frozen state. But few, indeed, among its readers were able to decipher the genuine and heroic meaning of this incautious report.

As for us, however—we understood instantly. We could picture the entire scene right down to the smallest details: how those present broke up the ice in frenzied haste; how, flouting the higher claims of ichthyology and elbowing each other to be first, they tore off chunks of the prehistoric flesh and hauled them over to the bonfire to thaw them out and bolt them down.

We understood because we ourselves were the same kind of people as *those present* at that event. We, too, were from that powerful tribe of *zeks*, unique on the face of the earth, the only people who could devour prehistoric salamander *with relish*.

And the Kolyma was the greatest and most famous island, the pole of ferocity of that amazing country of *Gulag* which, though scattered in an Archipelago geographically, was, in the psychological sense, fused into a continent—an almost invisible, almost imperceptible country inhabited by the zek people.

And this Archipelago crisscrossed and patterned that other country within which it was located, like a gigantic patchwork, cutting into its cities, hovering over its streets. Yet there were many who did not even guess at its presence and many, many others who had heard something vague. And only those who had been there knew the whole truth.

But, as though stricken dumb on the islands of the Archipelago, they kept their silence.

By an unexpected turn of our history, a bit of the truth, an insignificant part of the whole, was allowed out in the open. But those same hands which once screwed tight our handcuffs now hold out their palms in reconciliation: "No, don't! Don't dig up the past! Dwell on the past and you'll lose an eye."

But the proverb goes on to say: "Forget the past and you'll lose both eyes."

Decades go by, and the scars and sores of the past are healing over for good. In the course of this period some of the islands of the Archipelago have shuddered and dissolved and the polar sea of oblivion rolls over them. And someday in the future, this Archipelago, its air, and the bones of its inhabitants, frozen in a lens of ice, will be discovered by our descendants like some improbable salamander.

I would not be so bold as to try to write the history of the Archipelago. I have never had the chance to read the documents. And, in fact, will anyone ever have the chance to read them? Those who do not wish to *recall* have already had enough time—and will have more—to destroy all the documents, down to the very last one.

I have absorbed into myself my own eleven years there not as something shameful nor as a nightmare to be cursed: I have come almost to love that monstrous world, and now, by a happy turn of events, I have also been entrusted with many recent reports and letters. So perhaps I shall be able to give some account of the bones and flesh of that salamander—which, incidentally, is still alive.

The Gulag Archipelago
Part I, Chapter I

Arrest

How do people get to this clandestine Archipelago? Hour by hour planes fly there, ships steer their course there, and trains thunder off to it— but all with nary a mark on them to tell of their destination. And at ticket windows or at travel bureaus for Soviet or foreign tourists the employees would be astounded if you were to ask for a ticket to go there. They know nothing and they've never heard of the Archipelago as a whole or of any one of its innumerable islands.

Those who go to the Archipelago to administer it get there via the training schools of the Ministry of Internal Affairs.

Those who go there to be guards are conscripted via the military conscription centers.

And those who, like you and me, dear reader, go there to die, must get there solely and compulsorily via arrest.

Arrest! Need it be said that it is a breaking point in your life, a bolt of lightning which has scored a direct hit on you? That it is an unassimilable spiritual earthquake not every person can cope with, as a result of which people often slip into insanity?

The Universe has as many different centers as there are living beings in it. Each of us is a center of the Universe, and that Universe is shattered when they hiss at you: "*You are under arrest.*"

If *you* are arrested, can anything else remain unshattered by this cataclysm?

But the darkened mind is incapable of embracing these displacements in our universe, and both the most sophisticated and the veriest simpleton among us, drawing on all life's experience, can gasp out only: "Me? What for?"

Mine was, probably, the easiest imaginable kind of arrest. It did not tear me from the embrace of kith and kin, nor wrench me from a deeply cherished home life. One pallid European February it took me from our narrow salient on the Baltic Sea, where, depending on one's point of view, either we had surrounded the Germans or they had surrounded us, and it deprived me only of my familiar artillery battery and the scenes of the last three months of the war.

The brigade commander called me to his headquarters and asked me for my pistol; I turned it over without suspecting any evil intent, when suddenly, from a tense, immobile suite of staff officers in the corner, two counterintelligence officers stepped forward hurriedly, crossed the room in a few quick bounds, their four hands grabbed simultaneously at the star on my cap, my shoulder boards, my officer's belt, my map case, and they shouted theatrically:

"You are under arrest!"

Burning and prickling from head to toe, all I could exclaim was:

"Me? What for?"

And even though there is usually no answer to this question, surprisingly I received one! This is worth recalling, because it is so contrary to our usual custom. Across the sheer gap separating me from those left behind, the gap created by the heavy-falling word "arrest," across that quarantine line not even a sound dared penetrate, came the unthinkable, magic words of the brigade commander:

"Solzhenitsyn. Come back here."

With a sharp turn I broke away from the hands of the SMERSH men and stepped back to the brigade commander. I had never known him very well. He had never condescended to run-of-the-mill conversations with me. To me his face had always conveyed an order, a command, wrath. But right now it was illuminated in a thoughtful way. Was it from shame for his own involuntary part in this dirty business? Was it from an impulse to rise above the pitiful subordination of a whole lifetime? Ten days before, I had led my own reconnaissance battery almost intact out of the *fire pocket* in which the twelve heavy guns of his artillery battalion had been left, and now he had to renounce me because of a piece of paper with a seal on it?

"You have . . ." he asked weightily, "a friend on the First Ukrainian Front?"

"It's forbidden! You have no right!" the captain and the major of counterintelligence shouted at the colonel. But I had already understood: I knew instantly I had been arrested because of my correspondence with a school friend, and understood from what direction to expect danger.

Zakhar Georgiyevich Travkin could have stopped right there! But no! Continuing his attempt to expunge his part in this and to stand erect before his own conscience, he rose from behind his desk—he had never stood up in my presence in my former life—and reached across the quarantine line that separated us and gave me his hand, although he would never have reached out his hand to me had I remained a free man. And pressing my hand, while his whole suite stood there in mute horror, showing that warmth that may appear in an habitually severe face, he said fearlessly and precisely:

"I wish you happiness, Captain!"

Not only was I no longer a captain, but I had been exposed as an enemy of the people (for among us every person is totally exposed from the moment of arrest). And he had wished happiness—to an enemy?

This is not going to be a volume of memoirs about my own life. Therefore I am not going to recount the truly amusing details of my arrest, which was like no other. That night the SMERSH officers gave up their last hope of being able to make out where we were on the map—they never had been able to read maps anyway. So they politely handed the map to me and asked me to tell the driver how to proceed to counterintelligence at army headquarters. I, therefore, led them and myself to that prison, and in gratitude they immediately put me not in an ordinary cell but in a punishment cell. And I really must describe that closet in a German peasant house which served as a temporary punishment cell.

It was the length of one human body and wide enough for three to lie packed tightly, four at a pinch. As it happened, I was the fourth, shoved in after midnight. The three lying there blinked sleepily at me in the light of the smoky kerosene lantern and moved over, giving me enough space to lie on my side, half between them, half on top of them, until gradually, by sheer weight, I could wedge my way in. And so four overcoats lay on the crushed-straw-covered floor, with eight boots pointing at the door. They slept and I burned. The more self-assured I had been as a captain half a day before, the more painful it was to crowd onto the floor of that closet. Once or twice the other fellows woke up numb on one side, and we all turned over at the same time.

Toward morning they awoke, yawned, grunted, pulled up their legs, moved into various corners, and our acquaintance began.

"What are you in for?"

But a troubled little breeze of caution had already breathed on me beneath the poisoned roof of SMERSH and I pretended to be surprised:

"No idea. Do the bastards tell you?"

However, my cellmates—tankmen in soft black helmets—hid nothing. They were three honest, openhearted soldiers—people of a kind I had become attached to during the war years because I myself was more complex and worse. All three had been officers. Their shoulder boards also had been viciously torn off, and in some places the cotton batting stuck out. On their stained field shirts light patches indicated where decorations had been removed, and there were dark and red scars on their faces and arms, the results of wounds and burns. Their tank unit had, unfortunately, arrived for repairs in the village where the SMERSH counterintelligence headquarters of the Forty-eighth Army was located. Still damp from the battle of the day before, yesterday they had gotten drunk, and on the outskirts of the village broke into a bath where they had noticed two raunchy broads going to bathe. The girls, half-dressed, managed to get away all right from the soldiers' staggering, drunken legs. But one of them, it turned out, was the property of the army Chief of Counterintelligence, no less.

Yes! For three weeks the war had been going on inside Germany, and all of us knew very well that if the girls were German they could be raped and then shot. This was almost a combat distinction. Had they been Polish girls or our own displaced Russian girls, they could have been chased naked around the garden and slapped on the behind—an amusement, no more. But just because this one was the "campaign wife" of the Chief of Counterintelligence, right off some deep-in-the-rear sergeant had viciously torn from three front-line officers the shoulder boards awarded them by the front headquarters and had taken off the decorations conferred upon them by the Presidium of the Supreme Soviet. And now these warriors, who had gone through the whole war and who had no doubt crushed more than one line of enemy trenches, were waiting for a court-martial, whose members, had it not been for their tank, could have come nowhere near the village.

We put out the kerosene lamp, which had already used up all the air there was to breathe. A *Judas hole* the size of a postage stamp had been cut in the door and through it came indirect light from the corridor. Then, as if afraid that with the coming of daylight we would have too much room in the punishment cell, they *tossed in* a fifth person. He stepped in wearing a newish Red Army tunic and a cap that was also new, and when he stopped opposite the peephole we could see a fresh face with a turned-up nose and red cheeks.

"Where are you from, brother? Who are you?"

"From the *other* side," he answered briskly. "A shhpy."

"You're kidding!" We were astounded. (To be a spy and to admit it—Sheinin and the brothers Tur had never written that kind of spy story!)

"What is there to kid about in wartime?" the young fellow sighed reasonably. "And just how else can you get back home from being a POW? Well, you tell me!"

He had barely begun to tell us how, some days back, the Germans had led him through the front lines so that he could play the spy and blow up bridges, whereupon he had gone immediately to the nearest battalion headquarters to turn himself in; but the weary, sleep-starved battalion commander hadn't believed his story about being a spy and had sent him off to the nurse to get a pill. And at that moment new impressions burst upon us:

"Out for toilet call! Hands behind your backs!" hollered a master sergeant *hardhead* as the door sprang open; he was just built for swinging the tail of a 122-millimeter cannon.

A circle of machine gunners had been strung around the peasant courtyard, guarding the path which was pointed out to us and which went behind the barn. I was bursting with indignation that some ignoramus of a master sergeant dared to give orders to us officers: "Hands behind your backs!" But the tank officers put their hands behind them and I followed suit.

Back of the barn was a small square area in which the snow had been all trampled down but had not yet melted. It was soiled all over with human feces, so densely scattered over the whole square that it was difficult to find a spot to place one's two feet and squat. However, we spread ourselves about and the five of us did squat down. Two machine gunners grimly pointed their machine pistols at us as we squatted, and before a minute had passed the master sergeant brusquely urged us on:

"Come on, hurry it up! With us they do it quickly!"

Not far from me squatted one of the tankmen, a native of Rostov, a tall, melancholy senior lieutenant. His face was blackened by a thin film of metallic dust or smoke, but the big red scar stretching across his cheek stood out nonetheless.

"What do you mean, *with us?*" he asked quietly, indicating no intention of hurrying back to the punishment cell that still stank of kerosene.

"In SMERSH counterintelligence!" the master sergeant shot back proudly and more resonantly than was called for. (The counterintelligence men used to love that tastelessly concocted word "SMERSH," manufactured from the initial syllables of the words for "death to spies." They felt it intimidated people.)

"And *with us* we do it slowly," replied the senior lieutenant thoughtfully. His helmet was pulled back, uncovering his still untrimmed hair. His oaken, battle-hardened rear end was lifted toward the pleasant coolish breeze.

"Where do you mean, *with us?*" the master sergeant barked at him more loudly than he needed to.

"In the Red Army," the senior lieutenant replied very quietly from his heels, measuring with his look the cannon-tailer that never was.

Such were my first gulps of prison air.

The Gulag Archipelago
Part I, Chapter 4

The Bluecaps[1]

Throughout the grinding of our souls in the gears of the great Nighttime Institution, when our souls are pulverized and our flesh hangs down in tatters like a beggar's rags, we suffer too much and are too immersed in our own pain to rivet with penetrating and far-seeing gaze those pale night executioners who torture us. A surfeit of inner grief floods our eyes. Otherwise what historians of our torturers we would be! For it is certain they will never describe themselves as they actually are. But alas! Every former prisoner remembers his own interrogation in detail, how they squeezed him, and what

---

[1] The term "Bluecaps" refers to interrogators, who were part of the state security system. The original shorthand term for this system as a whole was the Cheka (All-Russian Extraordinary Commission for Combating Counter-Revolution and Sabotage), which referred to a government department created by Lenin's decree on December 20, 1917. The new Soviet political police apparatus was headed by the fierce Polish revolutionary Felix Dzerzhinsky. It freely resorted to terror as a matter of state policy against real and imagined "enemies of the people." Subsequent incarnations of the Cheka include the GPU, the OGPU, the NKVD and GBU, the NKGB, MGB, MVD—with these abbreviations then generating neologisms, such as "gaybist" and "osobist"—and finally the KGB. This last would be the name of the Soviet secret police from 1954 until the collapse of the Soviet state in 1991. This apparatus was also called "the Organs," with the vulgar double entendre intended. Solzhenitsyn regularly refers to the "Cheka-KGB" and to Chekists in general to emphasize the fundamental continuity of the Soviet political police and intelligence services during the full length of the Soviet period. As George Leggett writes in his authoritative *The Cheka: Lenin's Secret Police* (Oxford, 1981), "It was under Lenin that the Soviet political police was conceived, served its grim apprenticeship, and came to maturity."

foulness they squeezed out of him—but often he does not even remember their names, let alone think about them as human beings. So it is with me. I can recall much more—and much more that's interesting—about any one of my cellmates than I can about Captain of State Security Yezepov, with whom I spent no little time face to face, the two of us alone in his office.

There is one thing, however, which remains with us all as an accurate, generalized recollection: foul rot—a space totally infected with putrefaction. And even when, decades later, we are long past fits of anger or outrage, in our own quieted hearts we retain this firm impression of low, malicious, impious, and, possibly, muddled people.

There is an interesting story about Alexander II, the Tsar surrounded by revolutionaries, who were to make seven attempts on his life. He once visited the House of Preliminary Detention on Shpalernaya—the uncle of the Big House—where he ordered them to lock him up in solitary-confinement cell No. 227. He stayed in it for more than an hour, attempting thereby to sense the state of mind of those he had imprisoned there.

One cannot but admit that for a monarch this was evidence of moral aspiration, to feel the need and make the effort to take a spiritual view of the matter.

But it is impossible to picture any of our interrogators, right up to Abakumov and Beria, wanting to slip into a prisoner's skin even for one hour, or feeling compelled to sit and meditate in solitary confinement.

Their branch of service does not require them to be educated people of broad culture and broad views—and they are not. Their branch of service does not require them to think logically—and they do not. Their branch of service requires only that they carry out orders exactly and be impervious to suffering—and that is what they do and what they are. We who have passed through their hands feel suffocated when we think of that legion, which is stripped bare of universal human ideals.

Although others might not be aware of it, it was clear to the interrogators at least that the *cases* were fabricated. Except at staff conferences, they could not seriously say to one another or to themselves that they were exposing criminals. Nonetheless they kept right on producing depositions page after page to make sure that we rotted. So the essence of it all turns out to be the credo of the blatnye—the underworld of Russian thieves: "You today; me tomorrow."

They understood that the cases were fabricated, yet they kept on working year after year. How could they? Either they forced themselves *not to think* (and this in itself means the ruin of a human being), and simply accepted that this was the way it had to be and that the person who gave them their orders was always right. . . .

But didn't the Nazis, too, it comes to mind, argue that same way?

Or else it was a matter of the Progressive Doctrine, the granite ideology. An interrogator in awful Orotukan—sent there to the Kolyma in 1938 as a penalty assignment—was so touched when M. Lurye, former director of the Krivoi Rog Industrial Complex, readily agreed to sign an indictment which meant a second camp term that he used the time they had thus saved to say: "You think we get any satisfaction from using *persuasion?* We have to do what the Party demands of us. You are an old Party member. Tell me what would you do in my place?" Apparently Lurye nearly agreed with him, and it may have been the fact that he had already been thinking in some such terms that led him to sign so readily. It is after all a convincing argument.

But most often it was merely a matter of cynicism. The bluecaps understood the workings of the meat grinder and loved it. In the Dzhida camps in 1944, interrogator Mironenko said to the condemned Babich with pride in his faultless logic: "Interrogation and trial are merely judicial corroboration. They cannot alter your fate, which was *previously* decided. If it is necessary to shoot you, then you will be shot even if you are altogether innocent. If it is necessary to acquit you, then no matter how guilty you are you will be cleared and acquitted."

"Just give us a person—and we'll create the *case!*" That was what many of them said jokingly, and it was their slogan. What we think of as torture they think of as good work. The wife of the interrogator Nikolai Grabishchenko (the Volga Canal Project) said touchingly to her neighbors: "Kolya is a very good worker. One of them didn't confess for a long time—and they gave him to Kolya. Kolya talked with him for one night and he confessed."

What prompted them all to slip into harness and pursue so zealously not truth but *totals* of the processed and condemned? Because it was *most comfortable* for them not to be different from the others. And because these totals meant an easy life, supplementary pay, awards and decorations, promotions in rank, and the expansion and prosperity of the *Organs* themselves. If they ran up high totals, they could loaf when they felt like it, or do poor work or go out and enjoy themselves at night. And that is just what they did. Low totals led to their being kicked out, to the loss of their feedbag. For Stalin could never be convinced that in any district, or city, or military unit, he might suddenly cease to have enemies.

That was why they felt no mercy, but, instead, an explosion of resentment and rage toward those maliciously stubborn prisoners who opposed being fitted into the totals, who would not capitulate to sleeplessness or the punishment cell or hunger. By refusing to confess they menaced the interrogator's personal standing. It was as though they wanted to bring *him* down. In such circumstances all measures were justified! If it's to be war, then war it will be! We'll ram the tube down your throat—swallow that salt water!

225

Excluded by the nature of their work and by deliberate choice from the *higher* sphere of human existence, the servitors of the Blue Institution lived in their lower sphere with all the greater intensity and avidity. And there they were possessed and directed by the two strongest instincts of the lower sphere, other than hunger and sex: greed for *power* and greed for *gain*. (Particularly for power. In recent decades it has turned out to be more important than money.)

Power is a poison well known for thousands of years. If only no one were ever to acquire material power over others! But to the human being who has faith in some force that holds dominion over all of us, and who is therefore conscious of his own limitations, power is not necessarily fatal. For those, however, who are unaware of any higher sphere, it is a deadly poison. For them there is no antidote.

Here attraction is not the right word—it is *intoxication!* After all, it *is* intoxicating. You are still young—still, shall we say parenthetically, a sniveling youth. Only a little while ago your parents were deeply concerned about you and didn't know where to turn to launch you in life. You were such a fool you didn't even want to study, but you got through three years of *that* school—and then how you took off and flew! How your situation changed! How your gestures changed, your glance, the turn of your head! The learned council of the scientific institute is in session. You enter and everyone notices you and trembles. You don't take the chairman's chair. Those headaches are for the rector to take on. You sit off to one side, but everyone understands that you are head man there. You are the Special Department. And you can sit there for just five minutes and then leave. You have that advantage over the professors. You can be called away by more important business—but later on, when you're considering their decision, you will raise your eyebrows or, better still, purse your lips and say to the rector: "You can't do that. There are *special considerations* involved." That's all! And it won't be done. Or else you are an osobist—a State Security representative in the army—a SMERSH man, and a mere lieutenant; but the portly old colonel, the commander of the unit, stands up when you enter the room and tries to flatter you, to play up to you. He doesn't even have a drink with his chief of staff without inviting you to join them. You have a power over all the people in that military unit, or factory, or district, incomparably greater than that of the military commander, or factory director, or secretary of the district Communist Party. These men control people's military or official duties, wages, reputations, but you control people's freedom. And no one dares speak about you at meetings, and no one will ever dare write about you in the newspaper—not only something bad but anything *good!* They don't dare. Your name, like that of a jealously guarded deity, cannot even be mentioned. You are there; everyone feels your presence; but it's as though you didn't exist. From the moment you don that heavenly blue service cap, you stand higher than the publicly acknowledged power. No one dares check up on what *you* do. But no one is exempt from your checking up on him. And therefore, in dealing with ordinary so-called citizens, who for you are mere blocks of wood, it is altogether appropriate for you to wear an ambiguous and deeply thoughtful expression. For, of course, you are the one—and no one else—who knows about the *special considerations*. And therefore you are always right.

There is just one thing you must never forget. You, too, would have been just such a poor block of wood if you had not had the luck to become one of the little links in the *Organs*—that flexible, unitary organism inhabiting a nation as a tapeworm inhabits a human body. Everything is yours now! Everything is for you! Just be true to the *Organs!* They will always stand up for you! They will help you swallow up anyone who bothers you! They will help move every obstacle from your path! But—be true to the Organs! Do everything they order you to! They will do the thinking for you in respect to your functions too.

The duties of an interrogator require work, of course: you have to come in during the day, at night, sit for hours and hours—but not split your skull over "proof." (Let the prisoner's head ache over that.) And you don't have to worry whether the prisoner is guilty or not but simply do what the *Organs* require. And everything will be all right. It will be up to you to make the interrogation periods pass as pleasurably as possible and not to get overly fatigued. And it would be nice to get some good out of it—at least to amuse yourself. You have been sitting a long time, and all of a sudden a new method of *persuasion* occurs to you! Eureka! So you call up your friends on the phone, and you go around to other offices and tell them about it—what a laugh! Who shall we try it on, boys? It's really pretty monotonous to keep doing the same thing all the time. Those trembling hands, those imploring eyes, that cowardly submissiveness—they are really a bore. If you could just get one of them to resist! "I love strong opponents! *It's such fun to break their backs!*"

And if your opponent is so strong that he refuses to give in, all your methods have failed, and you are in a rage? Then don't control your fury! It's tremendously satisfying, that outburst! Let your anger have its way; don't set any bounds to it! Don't hold yourself back! That's when interrogators spit in the open mouth of the accused! And shove his face into a full cuspidor! That's the state of mind in which they drag priests around by their long hair! Or urinate in a kneeling prisoner's face! After such a storm of fury you feel yourself a real honest-to-God man!

Or else you are interrogating a "foreigner's girl friend." So you curse her out and then you say: "Come on now, does an American have a special kind of ——! Is that it? Weren't there enough Russian ones for you?" And all of a sudden you get an idea: Maybe she learned something from those foreigners. Here's a chance not to be missed, like an assignment abroad! And so you begin to interrogate her energetically: *How?* What positions? More! In detail! Every scrap of information! (You can use the information yourself, and you can tell the other boys too!) The girl is blushing all over and in tears. "It doesn't have anything to do with the case," she protests. "Yes, it does, speak up!" That's power for you! She gives you the full details. If you want, she'll draw a picture for you. If you want, she'll demonstrate with her body. She has no way out. In your hands you hold the punishment cell and her *prison term.*

And if you have asked for a stenographer to take down the questions and answers, and they send in a pretty one, you can shove your paw down into her bosom right in front of the boy being interrogated. He's not a human being after all, and there is no reason to feel shy in his presence.

In fact, there's no reason for you to feel shy with anyone. And if you like the broads—and who doesn't?—you'd be a fool not to make use of your position. Some will be drawn to you because of your power, and others will give in out of fear. So you've met a girl somewhere and she's caught your eye? She'll belong to you, never fear; she can't get away! Someone else's wife has caught your eye? She'll be yours too! Because, after all, there's no problem about removing the husband. No, indeed! To know what it meant to be a bluecap one had to experience it! Anything you saw was yours! Any apartment you looked at was yours! Any woman was yours! Any enemy was struck from your path! The earth beneath your feet was yours! The heaven above you was yours—it was, after all, like your cap, sky blue!

The passion for gain was their universal passion. After all, in the absence of any checking up, such power was inevitably used for personal enrichment. One would have had to be *holy* to refrain!

If we were able to discover the hidden motivation behind individual arrests, we would be astounded to find that, granted the rules governing *arrests* in general, 75 percent of the time the particular choice of *whom* to arrest, the personal cast of the die, was determined by human greed and vengefulness; and of that 75 percent, half were the result of material self-interest on the part of the local NKVD (and, of course, the prosecutor too, for on this point I do not distinguish between them).

The motivations and actions of the bluecaps are sometimes so petty that one can only be astounded. Security officer Senchenko took a map case and dispatch case from an officer he'd arrested and started to use them right in his presence, and, by manipulating the documentation, he took a pair of foreign gloves from another prisoner. (When the armies were advancing, the bluecaps were especially irritated because they got only second pick of the booty.) The counterintelligence officer of the Forty-ninth Army who arrested me had a yen for my cigarette case—and it wasn't even a cigarette case but a small German Army box, of a tempting scarlet, however. And because of that piece of shit he carried out a whole maneuver: As his first step, he omitted it from the list of belongings that were confiscated from me. ("You can keep it.") He thereupon ordered me to be searched again, knowing all the time that it was all I had in my pockets. "Aha! what's that? Take it away!" And to prevent my protests: "Put him in the punishment cell!" (What Tsarist gendarme would have dared behave that way toward a defender of the Fatherland?)

Every interrogator was given an allowance of a certain number of cigarettes to encourage those willing to confess and to reward stool pigeons. Some of them kept all the cigarettes for themselves.

Even in accounting for hours spent in interrogating, they used to cheat. They got higher pay for night work. And we used to note the way they wrote down more hours on the night interrogations than they really spent.

Interrogator Fyodorov (Reshety Station, P. O. Box No. 235) stole a wristwatch while searching the apartment of the free person Korzukhin. During the Leningrad blockade Interrogator Nikolai Fyodorovich Kruzhkov told Yelizaveta Viktorovna Strakhovich, wife of the prisoner he was interrogating, K. I. Strakhovich: "I want a quilt. Bring it to me!" When she replied: "All our warm things are in the room they've sealed," he went to her apartment and, without breaking the State Security seal on the lock, unscrewed the entire doorknob. "That's how the MGB works," he explained gaily. And he went in and began to collect the warm things, shoving some crystal in his pocket at the same time. She herself tried to get whatever she could out of the room, but he stopped her. "That's enough for you!"—and he kept on raking in the booty.

There's no end to such cases. One could issue a thousand "White Papers" (and beginning in 1918 too). One would need only to question systematically former prisoners and their wives. Maybe there are and were bluecaps who never stole anything or appropriated anything for themselves—but I find it impossible to imagine one. I simply do not understand: Given the bluecaps' philosophy of life, what was there to restrain them if they liked some particular thing? Way back at the beginning of the thirties, when all of us were marching around in the German uniforms of the Red Youth Front and were building the First Five-Year Plan, they were spending their evenings in salons like the one in the apartment of Konkordiya Iosse, behaving like members of the nobility or Westerners, and their lady friends were showing off their foreign clothes. Where were they getting those clothes?

As the folk saying goes: *If you speak for the wolf, speak against him as well.*

Where did this wolf-tribe appear from among our people? Does it really stem from our own roots? Our own blood?

It is our own.

And just so we don't go around flaunting too proudly the white mantle of the just, let everyone ask himself: "If my life had turned out differently, might I myself not have become just such an executioner?"

It is a dreadful question if one really answers it honestly.

I remember my third year at the university, in the fall of 1938. We young men of the Komsomol[2] were summoned before the District Komsomol Committee not once but twice. Scarcely bothering to ask our consent, they shoved an application form at us: You've had enough physics, mathematics, and chemistry; it's more important to your country for you to enter the NKVD school. (That's the way it always is. It isn't just some person who needs you; it is always your Motherland. And it is always some official or other who speaks on behalf of your Motherland and who knows what she needs.)

One year before, the District Committee had conducted a drive among us to recruit candidates for the air force schools. We avoided getting involved that time too, because we didn't want to leave the university—but we didn't sidestep recruitment then as stubbornly as we did this time.

Twenty-five years later we could think: Well, yes, we understood the sort of arrests that were being made at the time, and the fact that they were torturing people in prisons, and the slime they were trying to drag us into. But it isn't true! After all, the Black Marias were going through the streets at night, and we were the same young people who were parading with banners during the day. How could we know anything about those arrests and why should we think about them? All the provincial leaders had been removed, but as far as we were concerned it didn't matter. Two or three professors had been arrested, but after all they hadn't been our dancing partners, and it might even be easier to pass our exams as a result. Twenty-year-olds, we marched in the ranks of those born the year the Revolution took place, and because we were the same age as the Revolution, the brightest of futures lay ahead.

It would be hard to identify the exact source of that inner intuition, not founded on rational argument, which prompted our refusal to enter the NKVD schools. It certainly didn't derive from the lectures on historical

---

[2] Komsomol: The League of Young Communists, the youth arm of the Communist Party.

materialism we listened to: It was clear from them that the struggle against the internal enemy was a crucial battlefront, and to share in it was an honorable task. Our decision even ran counter to our material interests: At that time the provincial university we attended could not promise us anything more than the chance to teach in a rural school in a remote area for miserly wages. The NKVD school dangled before us special rations and double or triple pay. Our feelings could not be put into words—and even if we had found the words, fear would have prevented our speaking them aloud to one another. It was not our minds that resisted but something inside our breasts. People can shout at you from all sides: "You must!" And your own head can be saying also: "You must!" But inside your breast there is a sense of revulsion, repudiation. I don't want to. *It makes me feel sick.* Do what you want without me; I want no part of it.

Still, some of us were recruited at that time, and I think that if they had really put the pressure on, they could have broken everybody's resistance. So I would like to imagine: If, by the time war broke out, I had already been wearing an NKVD officer's insignia on my blue tabs, what would I have become? What do shoulder boards do to a human being? And where have all the exhortations of grandmother, standing before an icon, gone? And where the young Pioneer's daydreams of future sacred Equality?

And at the moment when my life was turned upside down and the SMERSH officers at the brigade command point tore off those cursed shoulder boards, and took my belt away and shoved me along to their automobile, I was pierced to the quick by worrying how, in my stripped and sorry state, I was going to make my way through the telephone operator's room. The rank and file must not see me in that condition!

So let the reader who expects this book to be a political exposé slam its covers shut right now.

If only it were all so simple! If only there were evil people somewhere insidiously committing evil deeds, and it were necessary only to separate them from the rest of us and destroy them. But the line dividing good and evil cuts through the heart of every human being. And who is willing to destroy a piece of his own heart?

During the life of any heart this line keeps changing place; sometimes it is squeezed one way by exuberant evil and sometimes it shifts to allow enough space for good to flourish. One and the same human being is, at various ages, under various circumstances, a totally different human being. At times he is close to being a devil, at times to sainthood. But his name doesn't change, and to that name we ascribe the whole lot, good and evil.

Socrates taught us: *Know thyself!*

Confronted by the pit into which we are about to toss those who have done us harm, we halt, stricken dumb: It is after all only because of the way things worked out that they were the executioners and we weren't.

From good to evil is one quaver, says the proverb.

And correspondingly, from evil to good.

Whoever got in by mistake either adjusted to the milieu or else was thrown out, or eased out, or even fell across the rails himself. Still . . . were there no good people left there?

In Kishinev, a young lieutenant gaybist went to Father Viktor Shipovalnikov a full month before he was arrested: "Get away from here, go away, they plan to arrest you!" (Did he do this on his own, or did his mother send him to warn the priest?) After the arrest, this young man was assigned to Father Viktor as an escort guard. And he grieved for him: "Why didn't you go away?"

When the interrogator Goldman gave Vera Korneyeva the "206" form on nondisclosure to sign, she began to catch on to her rights, and then she began to go into the *case* in detail, involving as it did all seventeen members of their "religious group." Goldman raged, but he had to let her study the file. In order not to be bored waiting for her, he led her to a large office, where half a dozen employees were sitting, and left her there. At first she read quietly, but then a conversation began—perhaps because the others were bored—and Vera launched aloud into a real religious sermon. (One would have had to know her to appreciate this to the full. She was a luminous person, with a lively mind and a gift of eloquence, even though in freedom she had been no more than a lathe operator, a stable girl, and a housewife.) They listened to her impressively, now and then asking questions in order to clarify something or other. It was catching them from an unexpected side of things. People came in from other offices, and the room filled up. Even though they were only typists, stenographers, file clerks, and not interrogators, in 1946 this was still their milieu, the *Organs*. It is impossible to reconstruct her monologue. She managed to work in all sorts of things, including the question of "traitors of the Motherland." Why were there no traitors in the 1812 War of the Fatherland, when there was still serfdom? It would have been natural to have traitors then! But mostly she spoke about religious faith and religious believers. *Formerly,* she declared, unbridled passions were the basis for everything—"Steal the stolen goods"— and, in that state of affairs, religious believers were naturally a hindrance to you. But now, when you want to *build* and prosper in this world, why do you persecute your best citizens? They represent your most precious material: After all, believers don't need to be watched, they do not steal, and they do not shirk. Do you think you can build a just society on a foundation of self-serving and envious people? Everything in the country is falling apart. Why do you spit in the hearts of your best people? Separate church and state properly and do not touch the church; you will not lose a thing thereby. Are you materialists? In that case, put your faith in education—in the possibility that it will, as they say, disperse religious faith. But why arrest people? At this point Goldman came in and started to interrupt rudely. But everyone shouted at him: "Oh, shut up! Keep quiet! Go ahead, woman, talk." (And how should they have addressed her? Citizeness? Comrade? Those forms of address were forbidden, and these people were bound by the conventions of Soviet life. But "woman"—that was how Christ had spoken, and you couldn't go wrong there.) And Vera continued in the presence of her interrogator.

So there in the MGB office those people listened to Korneyeva—and why did the words of an insignificant prisoner touch them so near the quick?

And why is it that for nearly two hundred years the Security forces have hung onto the color of the heavens? That was what they wore in Lermontov's lifetime—"and you, blue uniforms!" Then came blue service caps, blue shoulder boards, blue tabs, and then they were ordered to make themselves less conspicuous, and the blue brims were hidden from the gratitude of the people and everything blue on heads and shoulders was made narrower—until what was left was piping, narrow rims . . . but still blue.

Is this only a masquerade?

Or is it that even blackness must, every so often, however rarely, partake of the heavens?

It would be beautiful to think so. But when one learns, for example, the nature of Yagoda's striving toward the sacred. . . . An eyewitness from the group around Gorky, who was close to Yagoda at the time, reports that in the vestibule of the bathhouse on Yagoda's estate near Moscow, icons were placed so that Yagoda and his comrades, after undressing, could use them as targets for revolver practice before going in to take their baths.

Just how are we to understand that? As the act of an *evildoer?* What sort of behavior is it? Do such people really exist?

We would prefer to say that such people cannot exist, that there aren't any. It is permissible to portray evildoers in a story for children, so as to keep the picture simple. But when the great world literature of the past—Shakespeare, Schiller, Dickens—inflates and inflates images of evildoers of the blackest shades, it seems somewhat farcical and clumsy to our contemporary perception. The trouble lies in the way these classic evildoers are pictured. They recognize themselves as evildoers, and they know their souls are black. And they reason: "I cannot live unless I do evil. So I'll set my father against my brother! I'll drink the victim's sufferings until I'm drunk with them!" Iago very precisely identifies his purposes and his motives as being black and born of hate.

But no; that's not the way it is! To do evil a human being must first of all believe that what he's doing is good, or else that it's a well-considered act in conformity with natural law. Fortunately, it is in the nature of the human being to seek a *justification* for his actions.

Macbeth's self-justifications were feeble—and his conscience devoured him. Yes, even Iago was a little lamb too. The imagination and the spiritual strength of Shakespeare's evildoers stopped short at a dozen corpses. Because they had no *ideology*.

Ideology—that is what gives evildoing its long-sought justification and gives the evildoer the necessary steadfastness and determination. That is the social theory which helps to make his acts seem good instead of bad in his own and others' eyes, so that he won't hear reproaches and curses but will receive praise and honors. That was how the agents of the Inquisition fortified their wills: by invoking Christianity; the conquerors of foreign lands, by extolling the grandeur of their Motherland; the colonizers, by civilization; the Nazis, by race; and the Jacobins (early and late), by equality, brotherhood, and the happiness of future generations.

Thanks to *ideology*, the twentieth century was fated to experience evildoing on a scale calculated in the millions. This cannot be denied, nor passed over, nor suppressed. How, then, do we dare insist that evildoers do not exist? And who was it that destroyed these millions? Without evildoers there would have been no Archipelago.

There was a rumor going the rounds between 1918 and 1920 that the Petrograd Cheka, headed by Uritsky, and the Odessa Cheka, headed by Deich, did not shoot all those condemned to death but fed some of them alive to the animals in the city zoos. I do not know whether this is truth or calumny, or, if there were any such cases, how many there were. But I wouldn't set out to look for proof, either. Following the practice of the bluecaps, I would propose that they prove to us that this was impossible. How else could they get food for the zoos in those famine years? Take it away from the working class? Those enemies were going to die anyway, so why couldn't their deaths support the zoo economy of the Republic and thereby assist our march into the future? Wasn't it *expedient?*

That is the precise line the Shakespearean evildoer could not cross. But the evildoer with ideology does cross it, and his eyes remain dry and clear.

Physics is aware of phenomena which occur only at *threshold* magnitudes, which do not exist at all until a certain *threshold* encoded by and known to nature has been crossed. No matter how intense a yellow light you shine on a lithium sample, it will not emit electrons. But as soon as a weak bluish light begins to glow, it does emit them. (The threshold of the photoelectric effect has been crossed.) You can cool oxygen to 100 degrees below zero Centigrade and exert as much pressure as you want; it does not yield, but remains a gas. But as soon as minus 183 degrees is reached, it liquefies and begins to flow.

Evidently evildoing also has a threshold magnitude. Yes, a human being hesitates and bobs back and forth between good and evil all his life. He slips, falls back, clambers up, repents, things begin to darken again. But just so long as the threshold of evildoing is not crossed, the possibility of returning remains, and he himself is still within reach of our hope. But when, through the density of evil actions, the result either of their own extreme degree or of the absoluteness of his power, he suddenly crosses that threshold, he has left humanity behind, and without, perhaps, the possibility of return.

From the most ancient times justice has been a two-part concept: Virtue triumphs, and vice is punished.

We have been fortunate enough to live to a time when virtue, though it does not triumph, is nonetheless not always tormented by attack dogs. Beaten down, sickly, virtue has now been allowed to enter in all its tatters and sit in the corner, as long as it doesn't raise its voice.

However, no one dares say a word about vice. Yes, they did mock virtue, but there was no vice in that. Yes, so-and-so many millions did get mowed down—but no one was to blame for it. And if someone pipes up: "What about *those who . . .*" the answer comes from all sides, reproachfully and amicably at first: "What are you talking about, comrade! Why *open* old *wounds?*" Then they go after you with an oaken club: "Shut up! Haven't you had enough yet? You think you've been rehabilitated!"

In that same period, by 1966, *eighty-six thousand* Nazi criminals had been convicted in West Germany. And still we choke with anger here. We do not hesitate to devote to the subject page after newspaper page and hour after hour of radio time. We even stay after work to attend protest meetings and vote: *"Too few!* Eighty-six thousand are too few. And twenty years is too little! It must go on and on."

And during the same period, in our own country (according to the reports of the Military Collegium of the Supreme Court) about *ten men* have been convicted.

What takes place beyond the Oder and the Rhine gets us all worked up. What goes on in the environs of Moscow and behind the green fences near Sochi, or the fact that the murderers of our husbands and fathers ride through our streets and we make way for them as they pass, doesn't get us worked up at all, doesn't touch us. That would be "digging up the past."

Meanwhile, if we translate 86,000 West Germans into our own terms, on the basis of comparative population figures, it would become *one-quarter of a million.*

But in a quarter-century we have not tracked down anyone. We have not brought anyone to trial. It is their wounds we are afraid to reopen. And as a symbol of them all, the smug and stupid Molotov lives on at Granovsky No. 3, a man who has learned nothing at all, even now, though he is saturated with our blood and nobly crosses the sidewalk to seat himself in his long, wide automobile.

Here is a riddle not for us contemporaries to figure out: *Why* is Germany allowed to punish its evildoers and Russia is not? What kind of disastrous path lies ahead of us if we do not have the chance to purge ourselves of that putrefaction rotting inside our body? What, then, can Russia teach the world?

In the German trials an astonishing phenomenon takes place from time to time. The defendant clasps his head in his hands, refuses to make any defense, and from then on asks no concessions from the court. He says that the presentation of his crimes, revived and once again confronting him, has filled him with revulsion and he no longer wants to live.

That is the ultimate height a trial can attain: when evil is so utterly condemned that even the criminal is revolted by it.

A country which has condemned evil 86,000 times from the rostrum of a court and irrevocably condemned it in literature and among its young people, year by year, step by step, is purged of it.

What are we to do? Someday our descendants will describe our several generations as generations of driveling do-nothings. First we submissively allowed them to massacre us by the millions, and then with devoted concern we tended the murderers in their prosperous old age.

What are we to do if the great Russian tradition of penitence is incomprehensible and absurd to them? What are we to do if the animal terror of hearing even one-hundredth part of all they subjected others to outweighs in their hearts any inclination to justice? If they cling greedily to the harvest of benefits they have watered with the blood of those who perished?

It is clear enough that those men who turned the handle of the meat grinder even as late as 1937 are no longer young. They are fifty to eighty years old. They have lived the best years of their lives prosperously, well nourished and comfortable, so that it is too late for any kind of *equal* retribution as far as they are concerned.

But let us be generous. We will not shoot them. We will not pour salt water into them, nor bury them in bedbugs, nor bridle them into a "swan dive," nor keep them on sleepless "stand-up" for a week, nor kick them with jackboots, nor beat them with rubber truncheons, nor squeeze their skulls in iron rings, nor push them into a cell so that they lie atop one another like pieces of baggage—we will not do any of the things they did! But for the sake of our country and our children we have the duty to *seek them all out and bring them all to trial!* Not to put them on trial so much as their crimes. And to compel each one of them to announce loudly:

"Yes, I was an executioner and a murderer."

And if these words were spoken in our country *only* one-quarter of a million times (a just proportion, if we are not to fall behind West Germany), would it, perhaps, be enough?

It is unthinkable in the twentieth century to fail to distinguish between what constitutes an abominable atrocity that must be prosecuted and what constitutes that "past" which "ought not to be stirred up."

We have to condemn publicly the very *idea* that some people have the right to repress others. In keeping silent about evil, in burying it so deep within us that no sign of it appears on the surface, we are *implanting* it, and it will rise up a thousandfold in the future. When we neither punish nor reproach evildoers, we are not simply protecting their trivial old age, we are thereby ripping the foundations of justice from beneath new generations. It is for this reason, and not because of the "weakness of indoctrinational work," that they are growing up "indifferent." Young people are acquiring the conviction that foul deeds are never punished on earth, that they always bring prosperity.

It is going to be uncomfortable, horrible, to live in such a country!

The Gulag Archipelago
Part III, Chapter 7

The Way of Life and Customs of the Natives

To describe the native life in all its outward monotony would seem to be both very easy and very readily attainable. Yet it is very difficult at the same time. As with every different way of life, one has to describe the round of living from one morning until the next, from one winter to the next, from birth (arrival in one's first camp) until death (death). And simultaneously describe everything about all the many islands and islets that exist.

No one is capable of encompassing all this, of course, and it would merely be a bore to read whole volumes.

Philosophers, psychologists, medical men, and writers could have observed in our camps, as nowhere else, in detail and on a large scale the special process of the narrowing of the intellectual and spiritual horizons of a human being, the reduction of the human being to an animal and the process of dying alive. But the psychologists who got into our camps were for the most part not up to observing; they themselves had fallen into that very same stream that was dissolving the personality into feces and ash.

Just as nothing that contains life can exist without getting rid of its wastes, so the Archipelago could not keep swirling about without precipitating to the bottom its principal form of waste—the *last-leggers*. And everything built by the Archipelago had been squeezed out of the muscles of the last-leggers (before they became last-leggers). And those who survived, who reproach *the last-leggers with being themselves to blame*, must take upon themselves the disgrace of their own preserved lives.

And among the surviving, the orthodox Communists now write me lofty protests: How base are the thoughts and feelings of the heroes of your story *One Day in the Life of Ivan Denisovich!* Where are their anguished cogitations about the course of history? Everything is about bread rations and gruel, and yet there are sufferings much more unbearable than hunger.

Oh—so there are! Oh—so there are indeed much more unbearable sufferings (the sufferings of orthodox thought)? You in your medical sections and your storerooms, you never knew hunger there, orthodox loyalist gentlemen!

It has been known for centuries that Hunger . . . rules the world! (And all your Progressive Doctrine is, incidentally, built on Hunger, on the thesis that hungry people will inevitably revolt against the well-fed.) Hunger rules every hungry human being, unless he has himself consciously decided to die. Hunger, which forces an honest person to reach out and steal ("When the belly rumbles, conscience flees"). Hunger, which compels the most unselfish person to look with envy into someone else's bowl, and to try painfully to estimate what weight of ration his neighbor is receiving. Hunger, which darkens the brain and refuses to allow it to be distracted by anything else at all, or to think about anything else at all, or to speak about anything else at all except food, food, and food. Hunger, from which it is impossible to escape even in dreams—dreams are about food, and insomnia is over food. And soon—just insomnia. Hunger, after which one cannot even eat up; the man has by then turned into a one-way pipe and everything emerges from him in exactly the same state in which it was swallowed.

And this, too, the Russian cinema screen must see: how the last-leggers, jealously watching their competitors out of the corners of their eyes, stand duty at the kitchen porch waiting for them to bring out the slops in the dishwater. How they throw themselves on it, and fight with one another, seeking a fish head, a bone, vegetable parings. And how one last-legger dies, killed in that scrimmage. And how immediately afterward they wash off this waste and boil it and eat it. (And inquisitive cameramen can continue with their shooting and show us how, in 1947 in Dolinka, Bessarabian peasant women who had been brought in from *freedom* hurled themselves with that very same intent on slops which the last-leggers had *already checked over*.) The screen will show bags of bones which are still joined together lying under blankets at the hospital, dying almost without movement—and then being carried out. And on the whole . . . how simply a human being dies: He was speaking—and he fell silent; he was walking along the road—and he fell down. "Shudder and it's over." How the fat-faced, socially friendly work assigner jerks a zek by the legs to get him out to line-up—and he turns out to be dead, and the corpse falls on its head on the floor. "Croaked, the scum!" And he gaily gives him a kick for good measure. (At those camps during the war there was no doctor's aide, not even an orderly, and as a result there were no sick, and anyone who pretended to be sick was taken out to the woods in his comrades' arms, and they also took a board and rope along so they could drag the corpse back the more easily. At work they laid the sick person down next to the bonfire, and it was to the interest of both the zeks and the convoy to have him die the sooner.)

What the screen cannot catch will be described to us in slow, meticulous prose, which will distinguish between the nuances of the various paths to death, which are sometimes called scurvy, sometimes pellagra, sometimes alimentary dystrophy. For instance, if there is blood on your bread after you have taken a bite—that is scurvy. From then on your teeth begin to fall out, your gums rot, ulcers appear on your legs, your flesh will begin to fall off in whole chunks, and you will begin to smell like a corpse. Your bloated legs collapse. They refuse to take such cases into the hospital, and they crawl on all fours around the camp compound. But if your face grows dark and your skin begins to peel and your entire organism is racked by diarrhea, this is pellagra. It is necessary to halt the diarrhea somehow—so they take three spoons of chalk a day, and they say that in this case if you can get and eat a lot of herring the food will begin to hold. But where are you going to get herring? The man grows weaker, weaker, and the bigger he is, the faster it goes. He has already become so weak that he cannot climb to the top bunks, he cannot step across a log in his path; he has to lift his leg with his two hands or else crawl on all fours. The diarrhea takes out of a man both strength and all interest—in other people, in life, in himself. He grows deaf and stupid, and he loses all capacity to weep, even when he is being dragged along the ground behind a sledge. He is no longer afraid of death; he is wrapped in a submissive, rosy glow. He has crossed all boundaries and has forgotten the name of his wife, of his children, and finally his own name too. Sometimes the entire body of a man dying of starvation is covered with blue-black pimples like peas, with pus-filled heads smaller than a pinhead—his face, arms, legs, his trunk, even his scrotum. It is so painful he cannot be touched. The tiny boils come to a head and burst and a thick wormlike string of pus is forced out of them. The man is rotting alive.

If black astonished head lice are crawling on the face of your neighbor on the bunks, it is a sure sign of death.

Fie! What naturalism. Why keep talking about all that?

And that is what they usually say today, those who did not themselves suffer, who were themselves the executioners, or who have washed their hands of it, or who put on an innocent expression: Why remember all that? Why rake over old wounds? (*Their* wounds!!)

The Gulag Archipelago
Part III, Chapter 17

The Kids

The Archipelago had many ugly mugs and many bared fangs. No matter what side you approached it from, there wasn't one you could admire. But perhaps the most abominable of all was that maw that swallowed up *the kids.*

The kids were not at all those besprizorniki or waifs in drab tatters who scurried hither and thither thieving and warming themselves at asphalt caldrons on the streets, without whom one could not picture the urban life of the twenties. The waifs were taken from the streets—not from their families—into the colonies for juvenile delinquents (there was one attached to the People's Commissariat of Education as early as 1920), into workhouses for juveniles (which existed from 1921 to 1930 and had bars, bolts, and jailers, so that in the outworn bourgeois terminology they could have been called prisons), and also into the "Labor Communes of the OGPU" from 1924 on. They had been orphaned by the Civil War, by its famine, by social disorganization, the execution of their parents, or the death of the latter at the front, and at that time justice really did try to return these children to the mainstream of life, removing them from their street apprenticeship as thieves.

But where did the young offenders come from? They came from Article 12 of the Criminal Code of 1926, which permitted children *from the age of twelve* to be sentenced for theft, assault, mutilation, and murder (Article 58 offenses were also included under this heading), but they had to be given moderate sentences, not "the whole works" like adults. Here was the first crawl hole into the Archipelago for the future "kids"—but it was not yet a wide gate.

We are not going to omit one interesting statistic: In 1927 prisoners aged sixteen (they didn't count the younger ones) to twenty-four represented 48 percent of all prisoners.

What this amounts to is that nearly *half* the entire Archipelago in 1927 consisted of youths whom the October Revolution had caught between the ages of *six and fourteen*. Ten years after the victorious Revolution these same girls and boys turned up in prison and constituted half the prison population! This jibes poorly with the struggle against the vestiges of bourgeois consciousness which we inherited from the old society, but figures are figures. They demonstrate that the Archipelago never was short of young people.

But the question of *how* young was decided in 1935. In that year the Great Evildoer once more left his thumbprint on History's submissive clay. Among such deeds as the destruction of Leningrad and the destruction of his own Party, he did not overlook the children—the children whom he loved so well, whose Best Friend he was, and with whom he therefore had his photograph taken. Seeing no other way to bridle those insidious mischiefmakers, those washer-women's brats, who were overrunning the country in thicker and thicker swarms and growing more and more brazen in their violations of socialist legality, he invented a gift for them: These children, from twelve years of age (by this time his beloved daughter was approaching that borderline, and he could see that age tangibly before his eyes), should be sentenced *to the whole works* in the Code. (Including capital punishment as well.)

Illiterates that we were, we scrutinized decrees very little at the time. More and more we gazed at the portraits of Stalin with a black-haired little girl in his arms.... Even less did the twelve-year-olds read the decrees. And the decrees kept coming out, one after another. On December 10, 1940, the sentencing of juveniles from the age of twelve for "putting various objects on railroad tracks." (This was training young diversionists.) On May 31, 1941, it was decreed that for all other varieties of crime not included in Article 12 juveniles were to be given full sentences from the age of fourteen on!

But here a small obstacle arose: The War of the Fatherland began. But the law is the law! And on July 7, 1941—four days after Stalin's panicky speech in the days when German tanks were driving toward Leningrad, Smolensk, and Kiev—one more decree of the Presidium of the Supreme Soviet was issued, and it is difficult now to say in what respect it is more interesting for us today—in its unwavering academic character, showing what important questions were being decided by the government in those flaming days, or in its actual contents. The situation was that the Prosecutor of the USSR (Vyshinsky?) had complained to the Supreme Soviet about the Supreme Court (which means His Graciousness had heard about the matter), because the courts were applying the Decree of 1935 incorrectly and these brats were being sentenced only when they had *intentionally* committed crimes. But this was impermissible softness! And so right in the heat of war, the Presidium of the Supreme Soviet elucidated: This interpretation does not correspond to the text of the law. It introduces limitations not provided for by the law! And in agreement with the prosecutor, the Presidium issued a clari-fication to the Supreme Court: Children must be sentenced and the full measure of punishment applied (in other words, "the whole works"), even in cases where crimes were committed not intentionally but as a result of *care-lessness.*

Now that is something! Perhaps in all world history no one has yet ap-proached such a radical solution of the problem of children! From twelve years on for carelessness . . . up to and including execution! And that is when all the escape holes were shut off to the greedy mice! That is when, finally, all the collective-farm ears of grain were saved! And now the granaries were going to be filled to overflowing and life would flourish, and children who had been bad from birth would be set on the long path of correction.

And none of the Party prosecutors with children the same age shud-dered! They found no problem in stamping the arrest warrants. And none of the Party judges shuddered either! With bright eyes they sentenced little children to three, five, eight, and ten years in general camps!

And for "shearing sheaves" these tykes got not less than eight years!

And for a pocketful of potatoes—one pocketful of potatoes in a child's trousers!—they also got eight years!

Cucumbers did not have so high a value put on them. For a dozen cu-cumbers Sasha Blokhin got five years.

And the hungry fourteen-year-old girl Lida, in the Chingirlau District Center of Kustanai Province, walked down the street picking up, mixed with the dust, a narrow trail of grain spilled from a truck (doomed to go to waste in any case). For this she was sentenced to only *three* years because of the alleviating circumstances that she had not taken socialist property directly from the field or from the barn. And perhaps what also inclined the judges to be less harsh was that in that same year of 1948 there had been a clarification of the Supreme Court to the effect that children need not be tried for theft which had the character of childish mischief (such as the petty theft of apples in an orchard). By analogy the court drew the conclusion here that it was possible to be just a wee bit less harsh. (But the conclusion we draw is that from 1935 to 1948 children *were* sentenced for taking apples.)

And a great many were sentenced for running away from Factory Appren-ticeship Training. True, they got only six months for that. (In camp they were jokingly called *death-row prisoners.* But joke or no joke, here is a scene with some such "death-row prisoners" in a Far Eastern camp: They were assigned to dump the shit from latrines. There was a cart with two enormous wheels and an enormous barrel on it, full of stinking sludge. The "death-row prison-ers" were hitched up, with many of them in the shafts and others pushing from the sides and from behind [the barrel kept swaying and splashing them]. And the crimson-cheeked *bitches* in their twill suits roared with laughter as they urged the children on with clubs. And on the prisoner transport ship from Vladivostok to Sakhalin in 1949, the *bitches used* these children at knifepoint for carnal enjoyment. So even six months was sometimes enough too.)

And it was then that the twelve-year-olds crossed the thresholds of the adult prison cells, were equated with adults as citizens possessing full rights, equated by virtue of the most savage prison terms, equated, in their whole unconscious life, by bread rations, bowls of gruel, their places on the sleeping shelves—that is when that old term of Communist re-education, "minors," somehow lost its significance, when the outlines of its meaning faded, became unclear—and Gulag itself gave birth to the ringing and impudent word "kids." And with a proud and bitter intonation these bitter citizens began to use this term to describe themselves—not yet citizens of the country but already citizens of the Archipelago.

So early and so strangely did their adulthood begin—with this step across the prison threshold!

And upon the twelve- and fourteen-year-old heads burst a life style that was too much for brave men who were experienced and mature. But the young people, by the laws of their young life, were not about to be flattened by this life style but, instead, grew into it and adapted to it. Just as new languages and new customs are learned without difficulty in childhood, so the juveniles adopted *on the run* both the language of the Archipelago—which was that of the thieves—and the philosophy of the Archipelago—and whose philosophy was that?

From this life they took for themselves all its most inhuman essence, all its poisonous rotten juice—and as readily as if it had been this liquid, and not milk, that they had sucked from their mothers' breasts in infancy.

They grew into camp life so swiftly—not in weeks even, but in days!—as if they were not in the least surprised by it, as if that life were not completely new to them, but a natural continuation of their free life of yesterday.

Even out in freedom they hadn't grown up in linens and velvets; it had not been the children of secure and powerful parents who had gone out to clip stalks of grain, filled their pockets with potatoes, been late at the factory gate, or run away from Factory Apprenticeship Training. The kids were the children of workers. Out in freedom they had understood very well that life was built upon injustice. But out there things had not been laid out stark and bare to the last extremity; some of it was dressed up in decent clothing, some of it softened by a mother's kind word. In the Archipelago the kids saw the world as it is seen by quadrupeds: Only might makes right! Only the beast of prey has the right to live! That is how we, too, in our adult years saw the Archipelago, but we were capable of counterposing to it all our experience, our thoughts, our ideals, and everything that we had read to that very day.

Children accepted the Archipelago with the divine impressionability of child-hood. And in a few *days* children became beasts there! And the worst kind of beasts, with no ethical concepts whatever. The kid masters the truth: If other teeth are weaker than your own, then tear the piece away from them. It be-longs to you!

There were two basic methods of maintaining kids in the Archipelago: in separate children's colonies (principally the younger kids, not yet fifteen) and in mixed-category camps, most often with invalids and women (the se-nior kids).

Both were equally successful in developing animal viciousness. And nei-ther rescued the kids from being educated in the spirit of the thieves' ideals.

Take Yura Yermolov. He reports that when he was only twelve years old (in 1942) he saw a great deal of fraud, thievery, and speculation going on around him, and arrived at the following judgment about life: "*The only people who do not steal and deceive are those who are afraid to.* As for me—I don't want to be afraid of anything! Which means that I, too, will steal and deceive and live well." And yet for a time his life somehow developed differently. He became fascinated by the shining examples whose spirit he was taught in school. However, having got a taste of the Beloved Father, at the age of four-teen he wrote a leaflet: "Down with Stalin! Hail Lenin!" They caught him on that one, beat him up, gave him 58-10, and imprisoned him with the kids and thieves. And Yura Yermolov quickly mastered the thieves' law. The spirit of his existence spiraled upward steeply—and at the age of fourteen he had executed his "negation of a negation": He had returned to the concept of thievery as the highest and the best of all existence.

And what did he see in the children's colony? "There was even more injustice than in freedom. The chiefs and the jailers lived off the state, shielded by the correctional system. Part of the kids' ration went from the kitchen into the bellies of the instructors. The kids were beaten with boots, kept in fear so that they would be silent and obedient."

The simplest reply to the overpowering injustices was to create injustices oneself! This was the easiest conclusion, and it would now become the rule of life of the kids for a long time to come (or even forever).

But here is what's interesting! In giving the cruel world battle, the kids didn't battle against one another! They didn't look on each other as enemies! They entered this struggle as *a collective*, a united group! Was this a budding socialism? The indoctrination of the instructors? Oh, come on, cut the cackle, big-mouths! This is a descent into the law of the thieves! After all, the thieves are united; after all, the thieves have their own discipline and their own ring-leaders. And the juveniles were the apprentices of the thieves, they were mastering the precepts of their elders.

No one could avoid being cooked up in that mash! No boy could remain a separate individual—he would be trampled, torn apart, ostracized, if he did not immediately declare himself a thieves' apprentice. And *all of them* took that inevitable oath.... (Reader! Put *your own* children in their place....)

Who was the enemy of the kids in the children's colonies? The jailers and the instructors. The struggle was against them!

Say they were marching a column of kids under armed guard through a city, and it seems even shameful to guard children so strictly. Far from it! They had worked out a plan. A whistle—and all who wanted to scattered in different directions! And what were the guards to do? Shoot? At whom? At children? ... And so their prison terms came to an end. In one fell swoop 150 years ran away from the state. You don't enjoy looking silly? Then don't arrest children!

Here is one of their boastful stories about themselves, which, knowing the typical pattern of the kids' actions, I fully believe. Some excited and frightened children ran to the nurse of a children's colony and summoned her to help one of their comrades who was seriously ill. Forgetting caution, she quickly accompanied them to their big cell for forty. And as soon as she was inside, the whole anthill went into action! Some of them barricaded the door and kept watch. Dozens of hands tore everything off her, all the clothes she had on, and toppled her over; and then some sat on her hands and on her legs; and then, everyone doing what he could and where, they raped her, kissed her, bit her. It was against orders to shoot them, and no one could rescue her until they themselves let her go, profaned and weeping.

In general, of course, interest in the female body begins early among boys, and in the kids' cells it was intensely heated up by colorful stories and boasting. And they never let a chance go by to let off steam. Here is an episode. In broad daylight in full view of everyone, four kids were sitting in the compound of Krivoshchekovo Camp No. 1, talking with a girl called Lyuba from the bookbinding shop. She retorted sharply to something they had said. The boys leaped up, grabbed her legs, and lifted them in the air. She was in a defenseless position; while she supported herself on the ground with her hands, her skirt fell over her head. The boys held her that way and caressed her with their free hands. And then they let her down—and not roughly either. Did she slap them? Did she run away from them? Not at all. She sat down just as before and continued the argument.

These were sixteen-year-old kids, and it was an adult camp, with mixed categories. (It was the same one that had the women's barracks for five hundred where all the copulation took place without curtains and which the kids used to enter importantly like men.)

In the children's colonies the kids worked for four hours and then were supposed to be in school for four. (But all that schooling was a fake.) When transferred to an adult camp, they had a ten-hour working day, except that their work norms were reduced, while their ration norms were the same as adults'. They were transferred at the age of sixteen, but their undernourishment and improper development in camp and before camp endowed them at that age with the appearance of small frail children. Their height was stunted, as were their minds and their interests.

After the children's colony their situation changed drastically. No longer did they get the children's ration which so tempted the jailers—and therefore the latter ceased to be their principal enemy. Some old men appeared in their lives on whom they could try their strength. Women appeared on whom they could try their maturity. Some real live thieves appeared, fat-faced camp storm troopers, who willingly undertook their guidance both in world outlook and in training in thievery. To learn from them was tempting—and not to learn from them was impossible.

For a *free* reader does the word "thief" perhaps sound like a reproach? In that case he has understood nothing. This word is pronounced in the underworld in the same way that the word "knight" was pronounced among the nobility—and with even greater esteem, and not loudly but softly, like a sacred word. To become a worthy thief someday . . . was the kid's dream.

On one occasion, at the Ivanovo Transit Prison, I spent the night in a cell for kids. In the next bunk to me was a thin boy just over fifteen—called Slava, I think. It appeared to me that he was going through the whole kid ritual somehow unwillingly, as if he were growing out of it or was weary of it. I thought to myself: This boy has not perished, and is more intelligent, and he will soon move away from the others. And we had a chat. The boy came from Kiev. One of his parents had died, and the other had abandoned him. Before the war, at the age of nine, Slava began to steal. He also stole "when our army came," and after the war, and, with a sad, thoughtful smile which was so old for fifteen, he explained to me that in the future, too, he intended to live only by thievery. "You know," he explained to me very reasonably, "that as a worker you can earn only bread and water. And my *childhood* was bad so I want to live well." "What did you do during the German occupation?" I asked, trying to fill in the two years he had bypassed without describing them—the two years of the occupation of Kiev. He shook his head. "Under the Germans I worked. What do you think—that I could have gone on stealing under the Germans? They shot you on the spot for that."

Here, as recounted by A. Y. Susi, are several pictures from Krivoshchekovo (Penalty) Camp No. 2 of Novosiblag. Life was lived in enormous half-dark dugouts (for five hundred each) which had been dug into the earth to a depth of five feet. The chiefs did not interfere with the life inside the compound—no slogans and no lectures. The thieves and kids held sway. Almost no one was taken out to work. Rations were correspondingly meager. On the other hand, there was a surplus of time.

One day they were bringing a breadbox from the bread-cutting room under the guard of brigade members. The kids started a fake fight in front of the box itself, started shoving one another, and tipped the box over. The brigade members hurled themselves on the bread ration to pick it up from the ground. Out of twenty rations they managed to save only fourteen. The "fighting" kids were nowhere to be seen.

The mess hall at this camp was a plank lean-to not adequate for the Siberian winter. The gruel and the bread ration had to be carried about 150 yards in the cold from the kitchen to the dugout. For the elderly invalids this was a dangerous and difficult operation. They pushed their bread ration far down inside their shirt and gripped their mess tin with freezing hands. But suddenly, with diabolical speed, two or three kids would attack from the side. They knocked one old man to the ground, six hands frisked him all over, and they made off like a whirlwind. His bread ration had been pilfered, his gruel spilled, his empty mess tin lay there on the ground, and the old man struggled to get to his knees. (And other zeks saw this—and hastily bypassed the dangerous spot, hurrying to carry their own bread rations to the dug-out.) And the weaker their victim, the more merciless were the kids. They openly tore the bread ration from the hands of a very weak old man. The old man wept and implored them to give it back to him: "I am dying of starvation." "So you're going to kick the bucket soon anyway—what's the difference?" And the kids once decided to attack the invalids in the cold, empty building in front of the kitchen where there was always a mob of people. The gang would hurl their victim to the ground, sit on his hands, his legs, and his head, search his pockets, take his makhorka and his money, and then disappear.

It was enough for a careless free worker to go into the camp compound with a dog and turn his head for one second. And he could buy his dog's pelt that very same evening outside the camp compound: The dog would have been coaxed away, knifed, skinned, and cooked, all in a trice.

Their ears simply didn't admit anything that they themselves didn't need. If irritated old men started to grab them and pull them up short, the kids would hurl heavy objects at them. The kids found amusement in just about anything. They would grab the field shirt off an elderly invalid and play "Keep away"—forcing him to run back and forth just as if he were their own age. Does he become angry and leave? Then he will never see it again! They will have sold it outside the compound for a smoke! (And they will even come up to him afterward innocently: "Papasha! Give us a light! Oh, come on now, don't be angry. Why did you leave? Why didn't you stay and catch it?")

For adults, fathers and grandfathers, these boisterous games of the kids in the crowded conditions of camp could cause more anguish and be more hurtful than their robbing and their rapacious greed. It proved to be one of the most sensitive forms of humiliation for an elderly person to be made equal with a young whippersnapper—if only it were equal! But not to be turned over to the tyranny of the whippersnappers.

That is how small stubborn Fascists were trained by the joint action of Stalinist legislation, a Gulag education, and the leaven of the thieves. It was impossible to invent a better method of brutalizing children! It was quite impossible to find a quicker, stronger way of implanting all the vices of camp in tiny, immature hearts.

Even when it would have cost nothing to soften the heart of a child, the camp bosses didn't permit it. This was not the goal of *their* training. At Krivoshchekovo Camp No. 1 a boy asked to be transferred so that he could be with his father in Camp No. 2. This was not permitted. (After all, the rules required families to be broken up.) And the boy had to hide in a barrel to get from one camp to the other and lived there with his father in secret. And in their confusion they assumed he had escaped and used a stick with spikes made of nails to poke about in the latrine pits, to see whether or not he had drowned there.

Stalin's immortal laws on kids existed for twenty years—until the Decree of April 24, 1954, which relaxed them slightly: releasing those kids who had served more than one-third . . . of their *first* term! And what if there were fourteen? Twenty years, twenty harvests. And twenty different age groups had been maimed with crime and depravity.

So *who* dares cast a shadow on the memory of our Great Coryphaeus?

There were nimble children who managed to *catch* Article 58 very early in life. For example, Geli Pavlov got it at twelve (from 1943 to 1949 he was imprisoned in the colony in Zakovsk). For Article 58, in fact, *no minimum age* existed! That is what they said even in public lectures on jurisprudence—as, for example, in Tallinn in 1945. Dr. Usma knew a six-year-old boy imprisoned in a colony under 58. But that, evidently, is the record!

And where, if not in this chapter, are we going to mention the children orphaned by the arrest of their parents?

The children of the women of the religious commune near Khosta were fortunate. When their mothers were sent off to Solovki in 1929, the children were softheartedly left in their own homes and on their own farms. The children looked after the orchards and vegetable gardens themselves, milked their goats, assiduously studied at school, and sent their school grades to their parents on Solovki, together with assurances that they were prepared to suffer for God as their mothers had. (And, of course, the Party soon gave them this opportunity.)

Considering the instructions to "disunite" exiled children and their parents, how many of these kids must there have been even back in the twenties? And who will ever tell us of their fate? . . .

Even a superficial glance reveals one characteristic: The children, too, were destined for imprisonment; they, too, in their turn would be sent off to the promised land of the Archipelago, sometimes even at the same time as their parents. Take the eighth-grader Nina Peregud. In November, 1941, they came to arrest her father. There was a search. Suddenly Nina remembered that inside the stove lay a crumpled but not yet burned humorous rhyme. And it might have just stayed there, but out of nervousness Nina decided to tear it up at once. She reached into the firebox, and the dozing policeman grabbed her. And this horrible sacrilege, in a schoolgirl's handwriting, was revealed to the eyes of the Chekists:

> The stars in heaven are shining down
> And their light falls on the dew;
> Smolensk is already lost and gone
> And we're going to lose Moscow too.

And she expressed the desire:

> We only wish they'd bomb the school,
> We're awfully tired of studies.

Naturally these full-grown men engaged in saving their Motherland deep in the rear in Tambov, these knights with hot hearts and clean hands had to scotch such a mortal danger. Nina was arrested. Confiscated for her interrogation were her diaries from the sixth grade and a counterrevolutionary photograph: a snapshot of the destroyed Vavarinskaya Church. "What did your father talk about?" pried the knights with the hot hearts. Nina only sobbed. They sentenced her to five years of imprisonment and three years' deprivation of civil rights (even though she couldn't lose them since she didn't yet have them).

In camp, of course, she was separated from her father. . . .

Oh, you corrupters of young souls! How prosperously you are living out your lives! You are never going to have to stand up somewhere, blushing and tongue-tied, and confess what slops you poured over souls!

But Zoya Leshcheva managed to outdo her whole family. And here is how. Her father, her mother, her grandfather, her grandmother, and her elder adolescent brothers had all been scattered to distant camps because of their faith in God. But Zoya was a mere ten years old. They took her to an orphanage in Ivanovo Province. And there she declared she would never remove the cross from around her neck, the cross which her mother had hung there when she said farewell. And she tied the knot of the cord tighter so they would not be able to remove it when she was asleep. The struggle went on and on for a long time. Zoya became enraged: "You can strangle me and then take it off a corpse!" Then she was sent to an orphanage *for retarded children*—because she would not submit to their training. And in that orphanage were the dregs, a category of kids worse than anything described in this chapter. The struggle for the cross went on and on. Zoya stood her ground. Even here she refused to learn to steal or to curse. "A mother as sacred as mine must never have a daughter who is a criminal. I would rather be a political, like my whole family."

And she became a political! And the more her instructors and the radio praised Stalin, the more clearly she saw in him the culprit responsible for all their misfortunes. And, refusing to give in to the criminals, she now began to win them over to her views! In the courtyard stood one of those mass-produced plaster statues of Stalin. And mocking and indecent graffiti began to appear on it. (Kids love sport! The important thing is to point them in the right direction.) The administration kept repainting the statue, kept watch over it, and reported the situation to the MGB. And the graffiti kept on appearing, and the kids kept on laughing. Finally one morning they found that the statue's head had been knocked off and turned upside down, and inside it were feces.

This was a terrorist act! The MGB came. And began, in accordance with all their rules, their interrogations and threats: "Turn over the gang of terrorists to us, otherwise *we are going to shoot the lot of you* for terrorism!" (And there would have been nothing remarkable if they had: so what, 150 children shot! If He Himself had known about it, he would himself have given the order.)

It's not known whether the kids would have stood up to them or given in, but Zoya Leshcheva declared: "I did it all myself! What else is the head of that papa good for?"

And she was tried. And she was sentenced *to the supreme measure*, no joke. But because of the intolerable humanitarianism of the 1950 law on the restoration of capital punishment the execution of a fourteen-year-old was forbidden. And therefore they gave her a "tenner" (it's surprising it wasn't twenty-five). Up to the age of eighteen she was in ordinary camps, and from the age of eighteen on she was in Special Camps. For her directness and her language she got a second camp sentence and, it seems, a third one as well.

Zoya's parents had already been freed and her brothers too, but Zoya languished on in camp.

Long live our tolerance of religion!

Long live our children, the masters of Communism!

And let any country speak up that can say it has loved its as we have ours!

The Gulag Archipelago
Part IV, Chapter I

The Ascent

A nd the years go by. . . .
Not in swift staccato, as they joke in camp—"winter-summer, winter-summer"—but a long-drawn-out autumn, an endless winter, an unwilling spring, and only a summer that is short.

Even one mere year, whew, how long it lasts! Even in one year how much time is left for you to think! For 365 days you stomp out to line-up in a drizzling, slushy rain, and in a piercing blizzard, and in a biting and still subzero cold. For 365 days you work away at hateful, alien work with your mind unoccupied. For 365 evenings you squinch up, wet, chilled, in the end-of-work line-up, waiting for the convoy to assemble from the distant watch-towers. And then there is the march out. And the march back. And bending down over 730 bowls of gruel, over 730 portions of grits. Yes, and waking up and going to sleep on your multiple bunk. And neither radio nor books to distract you. There are none, and thank God.

And that is only one year. And there are ten. There are twenty-five. . . .

And then, too, when you are lying in the hospital with dystrophy—that, too, is a good time—*to think.*

Think! Draw some conclusions from misfortune.

And all that endless time, after all, the prisoners' brains and souls are not inactive?! In the mass and from a distance they seem like swarming lice, but they are the crown of creation, right? After all, once upon a time a weak little spark of God was breathed into them too—is it not true? So what has become of it now?

For centuries it was considered that a criminal was given a *sentence* for precisely this purpose, to think about his crime for the whole period of his sentence, be conscience-stricken, repent, and gradually reform.

But the Gulag Archipelago knows no pangs of conscience! Out of one hundred natives—five are thieves, and their transgressions are no reproach in their own eyes, but a mark of valor. They dream of carrying out such feats in the future even more brazenly and cleverly. They have nothing to repent. Another five . . . *stole* on a big scale, but not from people; in our times, the only place where one can steal on a big scale is from the state, which itself squanders the people's money without pity or sense—so what was there for such types to repent of? Maybe that they had not stolen more and divvied up— and thus remained free? And, so far as another 85 percent of the natives were concerned—they had never committed any crimes whatever. What were they supposed to repent of? That they had thought what they thought?

No, not only do you not repent, but your clean conscience, like a clear mountain lake, shines in your eyes. (And your eyes, purified by suffering, infallibly perceive the least haze in other eyes; for example, they infallibly pick out stool pigeons. And the Cheka-GB is not aware of this capacity of ours to see with the eyes of truth—it is our "secret weapon" against that institution.)

It was in this nearly unanimous consciousness of our innocence that the main distinction arose between us and the hard-labor prisoners of Dostoyevsky. There they were conscious of being doomed renegades, whereas we were confidently aware that they could haul in any free person at all in just the same way they had hauled us in; that barbed wire was only a nominal dividing line between us. In earlier times there had been among the majority . . . the unconditional consciousness of personal guilt, and among us. . . the consciousness of disaster on a mammoth scale.

Just not to perish from the disaster! It had to be survived.

Wasn't this the root cause of the astounding rarity of camp suicides? Yes, rarity, although every ex-prisoner could in all probability recall a case of suicide. But he could recall even more escapes. There were certainly more escapes than suicides! (Admirers of socialist realism can praise me: I am pursuing an optimistic line.) And there were far more self-inflicted injuries, too, than there were suicides! But this, too, is an act indicating love of life—a straightforward calculation of sacrificing a portion to save the whole. I even imagine that, statistically speaking, there were fewer suicides per thousand of the population in camp than in freedom. I have no way of verifying this, of course.

It is a very spectacular idea to imagine all the innocently outraged millions beginning to commit suicide en masse, causing double vexation to the government—both by demonstrating their innocence and by depriving the government of free manpower. And maybe the government would have had to soften up and begin to take pity on its subjects?—well, hardly! Stalin wouldn't have been stopped by that. He would have merely picked up another twenty million people from freedom.

But it did not happen! People died by the hundreds of thousands and millions, driven, it would seem, to the extremity of extremities—but for some reason there were no suicides! Condemned to a misshapen existence, to waste away from starvation, to exhaustion from labor—they did not put an end to themselves!

And thinking the whole thing over, I found that proof to be the stronger. A suicide is always a bankrupt, always a human being in a blind alley, a human being who has gambled his life and lost and is without the will to continue the struggle. If these millions of helpless and pitiful vermin still did not put an end to themselves—this meant some kind of invincible feeling was alive inside them. Some very powerful idea.

This was their feeling of universal innocence. It was the sense of an ordeal of the entire people—like the Tatar yoke.

But what if one has nothing to repent of—what then, what then does the prisoner think about all the time? "Poverty and prison . . . give wisdom." They do. But—where is it to be directed?

Here is how it was with many others, not just with me. Our initial, first prison sky consisted of black swirling storm clouds and black pillars of volcanic eruptions—this was the heaven of Pompeii, the heaven of the Day of Judgment, because it was not just anyone who had been arrested, but I—the center of this world.

Our last prison sky was infinitely high, infinitely clear, even paler than sky-blue.

We all (except religious believers) began from one point: We tried to tear our hair from our head, but our hair had been clipped close! . . . How could we? How could we not have seen those who informed against us?! How could we not have seen our enemies? (And how we hated them! How could we avenge ourselves on them?) And what recklessness! What blindness! How many errors! How can they be corrected? They must be corrected all the more swiftly! We must write. . . . We must speak out. . . . We must communicate. . . .

But—there is nothing that we can do. And nothing is going to save us!

Then there begins the period of transit prisons. Interspersed with our thoughts about our future camp, we now love to recall our past: How well we used to live! (Even if we lived badly.) But how many unused opportunities there were! When will we now make up for it? If I only manage to survive—oh, how differently, how wisely, I am going to live! The day of our future *release?* It shines like a rising sun!

And the conclusion is: Survive to reach it! Survive! At any price! This is simply a turn of phrase, a sort of habit of speech: "at any price."

But then the words swell up with their full meaning, and an awesome vow takes shape: to survive *at any price.*

And whoever takes that vow, whoever does not blink before its crimson burst—allows his own misfortune to overshadow both the entire common misfortune and the whole world.

This is the great fork of camp life. From this point the roads go to the right and to the left. One of them will rise and the other will descend. If you go to the right—you lose your life, and if you go to the left—you lose your conscience.

One's own order to oneself, *"Survive!,"* is the natural splash of a living person. Who does not wish to survive? Who does not have the right to survive? Straining all the strength of our body! An order to all our cells: Survive! A powerful charge is introduced into the chest cavity, and the heart is surrounded by an electrical cloud so as not to stop beating. They lead thirty emaciated but wiry zeks three miles across the Arctic ice to a bathhouse. The bath is not worth even a warm word. Six men at a time wash themselves in five shifts, and the door opens straight into the subzero temperature, and four shifts are obliged to stand there before or after bathing—because they cannot be left without convoy. And not only does none of them get pneumonia. They don't even catch cold. (And for ten years one old man had his bath just like that, serving out his term from age fifty to sixty. But then he was released, he was at home. Warm and cared for, he burned up in one month's time. That order—"Survive!"—was not there. . . .)

But simply "to survive" does not yet mean "at any price." "At any price" means: at the price of someone else.

Let us admit the truth: At that great fork in the camp road, at that great divider of souls, it was not the majority of the prisoners that turned to the right. Alas, not the majority. But fortunately neither was it just a few. There are many of them—human beings—who made this choice. But they did not shout about themselves. You had to look closely to see them. Dozens of times this same choice had arisen before them too, but they always knew, and knew their own stand.

Take Arnold Susi, who was sent to camp at the age of about fifty. He had never been a believer, but he had always been fundamentally decent, he had never led any other kind of life—and he was not about to begin any other. He was a "Westerner." And what that meant was that he was doubly unprepared, and kept putting his foot into it all the time, and getting into serious difficulties. He worked at general work. And he was imprisoned in a penalty camp—and he still managed to survive; he survived as exactly the same kind of person he had been when he came to camp. I knew him at the very beginning, and I knew him . . . afterward, and I can testify personally. True, there were three seriously mitigating circumstances which accompanied him throughout his camp life: He was classified as an invalid. For several years he received parcels. And thanks to his musical abilities, he got some additional nourishment out of amateur theatricals. But these three circumstances only explain why he survived. If they had not existed, he would have died. But he would not have changed. (And perhaps those who died did die because they did not change?)

And Tarashkevich, a perfectly ordinary, straightforward person, recalls: "There were many prisoners prepared to grovel for a bread ration or a puff of makhorka smoke. I was dying, but I kept my soul pure: I always called a spade a spade."

It has been known for many centuries that prison causes the profound rebirth of a human being. The examples are innumerable—such as that of Silvio Pellico: Through serving eight years he was transformed from a furious Carbonaro to a meek Roman Catholic. In our country they always mention Dostoyevsky in this respect. These transformations always proceed in the direction of deepening the soul. Ibsen wrote: "From lack of oxygen even the conscience will wither."

By no means! It is not by any means so simple! In fact, it is the opposite! Take General Gorbatov: He had fought from his very youth, advanced through the ranks of the army, and had no time at all in which to think about things. But he was imprisoned, and how good it was—various events awakened within his recollection, such as his having suspected an innocent man of espionage; or his having ordered by mistake the execution of a quite innocent Pole. (Well, when else would he have remembered this? After rehabilitation he did not remember such things very much?) Enough has been written about prisoners' changes of heart to raise it to the level of penological theory. For example, in the pre-revolutionary *Prison Herald* Luchenetsky wrote: "Darkness renders a person more sensitive to light; involuntary inactivity in imprisonment arouses in him a thirst for life, movement, work; the quiet compels profound pondering over his own 'I,' over surrounding conditions, over his own past and present, and forces him to think about his future."

Our teachers, who had never served time themselves, felt for prisoners only the natural sympathy of the outsider; Dostoyevsky, however, who served time himself, was a proponent of punishment! And this is something worth thinking about.

The proverb says: "Freedom spoils, and lack of freedom teaches." But Pellico and Luchenetsky wrote about *prison*. But Dostoyevsky demanded punishment—in prison. But *what kind of* lack of freedom is it that educates?

Camp?

That is something to think about.

Of course, in comparison with prison our camps are poisonous and harmful.

Of course, they were not concerned with our souls when they pumped up the Archipelago. But nonetheless: Is it really hopeless to stand fast in camp?

And more than that: Was it really impossible for one's soul to rise in camp?

Here is E. K., who was born around 1940, one of those boys who, under Khrushchev, gathered to read poems on Mayakovsky Square, but were hauled off instead in Black Marias. From camp, from a Potma camp, he writes to his girl: "Here all the trivia and fuss have decreased. . . . I have experienced a turning point. . . . Here you harken to that voice deep inside you, which amid the surfeit and vanity used to be stifled by the roar from outside."

At the Samarka Camp in 1946 a group of intellectuals had reached the very brink of death: They were worn down by hunger, cold, and work beyond their powers. And they were even deprived of sleep. They had nowhere to lie down. Dugout barracks had not yet been built. Did they go and steal? Or squeal? Or whimper about their ruined lives? No! Foreseeing the approach of death in days rather than weeks, here is how they spent their last sleepless leisure, sitting up against the wall: Timofeyev-Ressovsky gathered them into a "seminar," and they hastened to share with one another what one of them knew and the others did not—they delivered their last lectures to each other. Father Savely—spoke of "unshameful death," a priest academician—about patristics, one of the Uniate fathers—about something in the area of dogmatics and canonical writings, an electrical engineer—on the principles of the energetics of the future, and a Leningrad economist—on how the effort to create principles of Soviet economics had failed for lack of new ideas. Timofeyev-Ressovsky himself talked about the principles of microphysics. From one session to the next, participants were missing—they were already in the morgue.

That is the sort of person who can be interested in all this while already growing numb with approaching death—now that is an intellectual!

Pardon me, you . . . love life? You, you! You who exclaim and sing over and over and dance it too: "I love you, life! Oh, I love you, life!" Do you? Well, go on, love it! Camp life—love that too! It, too, is life!

> There where there is no struggle with fate,
> There you will resurrect your soul. . . .

You haven't understood a thing. When you get there, you'll collapse.

Along our chosen road are twists and turns and twists and turns. Uphill? Or up into the heavens? Let's go, let's stumble and stagger.

The day of liberation! What can it give us after so many years? We will change unrecognizably and so will our near and dear ones—and places which once were dear to us will seem stranger than strange.

And the thought of freedom after a time even becomes a forced thought. Farfetched. Strange.

The day of "liberation"! As if there were any liberty in this country! Or as if it were possible to liberate anyone who has not first become liberated in his own soul.

The stones roll down from under our feet. Downward, into the past! They are the ashes of the past!

And we ascend!

It is a good thing *to think* in prison, but it is not bad in camp either. Because, and this is the main thing, there are no *meetings*. For ten years you are free from all kinds of meetings! Is that not mountain air? While they openly claim your labor and your body, to the point of exhaustion and even death, the camp keepers do not encroach at all on your thoughts. They do not try to screw down your brains and to fasten them in place. And this results in a sensation of freedom of much greater magnitude than the freedom of one's feet to run along on the level.

No one tries to persuade you *to apply* for Party membership. No one comes around to squeeze membership dues out of you in *voluntary* societies. There is no trade union—the same kind of protector of your interests as an official lawyer before a tribunal. And there are no "production meetings." You cannot be elected to any position. You cannot be appointed some kind of delegate. And the really important thing is . . . that they cannot compel you to be a propagandist. Nor—to listen to propaganda. Nor—will they ever drag you off to the electoral precinct to vote freely and secretly for a single candidate. No one requires any "socialist undertakings" of you. Nor—self-criticism of your mistakes. Nor—articles in the wall newspaper. Nor—an interview with a provincial correspondent.

A free head—now is that not an advantage of life in the Archipelago?

And there is one more freedom: No one can deprive you of your family and property—you have already been deprived of them. What does not exist—not even God can take away. And this is a basic freedom.

It is good to think in imprisonment. And the most insignificant cause gives you a push in the direction of extended and important thoughts. Once in a long, long while, once in three years maybe, they brought a movie to camp. The film turned out to be—the cheapest kind of "sports" comedy. It was a bore. But from the screen they kept drumming into the audience the moral of the film:

The result is what counts, and the result is not in your favor.

On the screen they kept laughing. In the hall the audience kept laughing too. But blinking as you came out into the sunlit camp yard, you kept thinking about this phrase. And during the evening you kept thinking about it on your bunk. And Monday morning out in line-up. And you could keep thinking about it as long as you wanted. And where else could you have concentrated on it like that? And slow clarity descended into your brain.

This was no joke. This was an infectious thought. It has long since been inculcated in our Fatherland—and they keep on inculcating it over and over. The concept that only the material result counts has become so much a part of us that when, for example, some Tukhachevsky, Yagoda, or Zinoviev was proclaimed . . . a traitor who had sidled up to the enemy, people only exclaimed in a chorus of astonishment: "*What more could he want?*"

Now that is a high moral plane for you! Now that is a real unit of measure for you! "What more could he want?" Since he had a belly full of chow, and twenty suits, and two country homes, and an automobile, and an airplane, and fame—what more could he want?!! Millions of our compatriots find it unthinkable to imagine that a human being (and I am not speaking here of this particular trio) might have been motivated by something other than material gain!

To such an extent has everyone been indoctrinated with and absorbed the slogan: "The result is what counts."

Whence did this come to us?

If we look back at our history, maybe about three hundred years—could anything of the kind have taken place in the Russia of Old Believers?

All this came to us from Peter I, from the glory of our banners and the so-called "honor of our Fatherland." We were crushing our neighbors; we were expanding. And in our Fatherland it became well established that: The result is what counts.

And then from our Demidovs, Kabans, and Tsybukins. They clambered up, without looking behind them to see whose ears they were smashing with their jackboots. And ever more firmly it became established among a once pious and openhearted people: The result is what counts.

And then—from all kinds of socialists, and most of all from the most modern, infallible, and intolerant Teaching, which consists of this one thing only: The result is what counts! It is important to forge a fighting Party! And to seize power! And to hold on to power! And to remove all enemies! And to conquer in pig iron and steel! And to launch rockets!

And though for this industry and for these rockets it was necessary to sacrifice the way of life, and the integrity of the family, and the spiritual health of the people, and the very soul of our fields and forests and rivers—to hell with them! The result is what counts!!!

But that is a lie! Here we have been breaking our backs for years at All-Union hard labor. Here in slow annual spirals we have been climbing up to an understanding of life—and from this height it can all be seen so clearly: It is not the result that counts! It is not the result—but *the spirit!* Not *what*—but *how*. Not what has been attained—but at what price.

And so it is with us the prisoners—if it is the result which counts, then it is also true that one must survive at any price. And what that means is: One must become a stool pigeon, betray one's comrades. And thereby get oneself set up comfortably. And perhaps even get time off sentence. In the light of the Infallible Teaching there is, evidently, nothing reprehensible in this. After all, if one does that, then the result will be in our favor, and the result is what counts.

No one is going to argue. It is pleasant to win. But not at the price of losing one's human countenance.

If it is the result which counts—you must strain every nerve and sinew to avoid *general work*. You must bend down, be servile, act meanly—yet hang on to your position as a trusty. And by this means . . . survive.

If it is the essence that counts, then the time has come to reconcile yourself to *general work*. To tatters. To torn skin on the hands. To a piece of bread which is smaller and worse. And perhaps . . . to death. But while you're alive, you drag your way along proudly with an aching back. And that is when—when you have ceased to be afraid of threats and are not chasing after rewards—you become the most dangerous character in the owl-like view of the bosses. Because . . . what hold do they have on you?

And as soon as you have renounced that aim of "surviving at any price," and gone where the calm and simple people go—then imprisonment begins to transform your former character in an astonishing way. To transform it in a direction most unexpected to you.

And it would seem that in this situation feelings of malice, the disturbance of being oppressed, aimless hate, irritability, and nervousness ought to multiply. But you yourself do not notice how, with the impalpable flow of time, slavery nurtures in you the shoots of contradictory feelings.

Once upon a time you were sharply intolerant. You were constantly in a rush. And you were constantly short of time. And now you have time with interest. You are surfeited with it, with its months and its years, behind you and ahead of you—and a beneficial calming fluid pours through your blood vessels—patience.

You are ascending....

Formerly you never forgave anyone. You judged people without mercy. And you praised people with equal lack of moderation. And now an understanding mildness has become the basis of your un-categorical judgments. You have come to realize your own weakness—and you can therefore understand the weakness of others. And be astonished at another's strength. And wish to possess it yourself.

The stones rustle beneath our feet. We are ascending....

With the years, armor-plated restraint covers your heart and all your skin. You do not hasten to question and you do not hasten to answer. Your tongue has lost its flexible capacity for easy oscillation. Your eyes do not flash with gladness over good tidings nor do they darken with grief.

For you still have to verify whether that's how it is going to be. And you also have to work out—what is gladness and what is grief.

And now the rule of your life is this: Do not rejoice when you have found, do not weep when you have lost.

Your soul, which formerly was dry, now ripens from suffering.

And even if you haven't come to love your neighbors in the Christian sense, you are at least learning to love those close to you.

Those close to you in spirit who surround you in slavery. And how many of us come to realize: It is particularly in slavery that for the first time we have learned to recognize genuine friendship!

And also those close to you in blood, who surrounded you in your former life, who loved you—while you played the tyrant over them...

Here is a rewarding and inexhaustible direction for your thoughts: Reconsider all your previous life. Remember everything you did that was bad and shameful and take thought—can't you possibly correct it now?

Yes, you have been imprisoned for nothing. You have nothing to repent of before the state and its laws.

But... before your own conscience? But... in relation to other individuals?

... Following an operation, I am lying in the surgical ward of a camp hospital. I cannot move. I am hot and feverish, but nonetheless my thoughts do not dissolve into delirium—and I am grateful to Dr. Boris Nikolayevich Kornfeld, who is sitting beside my cot and talking to me all evening. The light has been turned out—so it will not hurt my eyes. He and I—and there is no one else in the ward.

Fervently he tells me the long story of his conversion from Judaism to Christianity. This conversion was accomplished by an educated, cultivated person, one of his cellmates, some good-natured old fellow like Platon Karatayev.[1] I am astonished at the conviction of the new convert, at the ardor of his words.

We know each other very slightly, and he was not the one responsible for my treatment, but there was simply no one here with whom he could share his feelings. He was a gentle and well-mannered person.

It is already late. All the hospital is asleep. Kornfeld is ending up his story thus:

"And on the whole, do you know, I have become convinced that there is no punishment that comes to us in this life on earth which is undeserved. Superficially it can have nothing to do with what we are guilty of in actual fact, but if you go over your life with a fine-tooth comb and ponder it deeply, you will always be able to hunt down that transgression of yours for which you have now received this blow."

I cannot see his face. Through the window come only the scattered reflections of the lights of the perimeter outside. And the door from the corridor gleams in a yellow electrical glow. But there is such mystical knowledge in his voice that I shudder.

These were the last words of Boris Kornfeld. Noiselessly he went out into the nighttime corridor and into one of the nearby wards and there lay down to sleep. Everyone slept. And there was no one with whom he could speak even one word. And I went off to sleep myself.

And I was wakened in the morning by running about and tramping in the corridor; the orderlies were carrying Kornfeld's body to the operating room. He had been dealt eight blows on the skull with a plasterer's mallet while he still slept. (In our camp it was the custom to kill immediately after rising time, when the barracks were all unlocked and open and when no one yet had got up, when no one was stirring.) And he died on the operating table, without regaining consciousness.

And so it happened that Kornfeld's prophetic words were his last words on earth. And, directed to me, they lay upon me as an inheritance. You cannot brush off that kind of inheritance by shrugging your shoulders.

But by that time I myself had matured to similar thoughts.

I would have been inclined to endow his words with the significance of a universal law of life. However, one can get all tangled up that way. One would have to admit that on that basis those who had been punished even more cruelly than with prison—those shot, burned at the stake—were some sort of super-evildoers. (And yet . . . the innocent are those who get punished most zealously of all.) And what would one then have to say about

---

[1] Platon Karatayev: An admirable character and prisoner of war in Tolstoy's *War and Peace*, whose simple presence influences others toward spiritual growth.

our so evident torturers: Why does not fate punish *them?* Why do they prosper?

(And the only solution to this would be that the meaning of earthly existence lies not, as we have grown used to thinking, in prospering, but . . . in the development of the soul. From *that* point of view our torturers have been punished most horribly of all: They are turning into swine, they are departing downward from humanity. From that point of view punishment is inflicted on those whose development . . . *holds out hope.*)

But there was something in Kornfeld's last words that touched a sensitive chord, and that I accept quite completely *for myself.* And many will accept the same for themselves.

In the seventh year of my imprisonment I had gone over and reexamined my life quite enough and had come to understand why everything had happened to me: both prison and, as an additional piece of ballast, my malignant tumor. And I would not have murmured even if all that punishment had been considered inadequate.

Punishment? But . . . whose?

Well, just think about that—*whose?*

I lay there a long time in that recovery room from which Kornfeld had gone forth to his death, and all alone during sleepless nights I pondered with astonishment my own life and the turns it had taken. In accordance with my established camp custom I set down my thoughts in rhymed verses—so as to remember them. And the most accurate thing is to cite them here—just as they came from the pillow of a hospital patient, when the hard-labor camp was still shuddering outside the windows in the wake of a revolt.

> When was it that I completely
> Scattered the good seeds, one and all?
> For after all I spent my boyhood
> In the bright singing of Thy temples.
>
> Bookish subtleties sparkled brightly,
> Piercing my arrogant brain,
> The secrets of the world were . . . in my grasp,
> Life's destiny . . . as pliable as wax.
>
> Blood seethed—and every swirl
> Gleamed iridescently before me,
> Without a rumble the building of my faith
> Quietly crumbled within my heart.

But passing here between being and nothingness,
Stumbling and clutching at the edge,
I look behind me with a grateful tremor
Upon the life that I have lived.

Not with good judgment nor with desire
Are its twists and turns illumined.
But with the even glow of the Higher Meaning
Which became apparent to me only later on.

And now with measuring cup returned to me,
Scooping up the living water,
God of the Universe! I believe again!
Though I renounced You, You were with me![2]

Looking back, I saw that for my whole conscious life I had not understood either myself or my strivings. What had seemed for so long to be beneficial now turned out in actuality to be fatal, and I had been striving to go in the opposite direction to that which was truly necessary to me. But just as the waves of the sea knock the inexperienced swimmer off his feet and keep tossing him back onto the shore, so also was I painfully tossed back on dry land by the blows of misfortune. And it was only because of this that I was able to travel the path which I had always really wanted to travel.

It was granted me to carry away from my prison years on my bent back, which nearly broke beneath its load, this essential experience: *how* a human being becomes evil and *how* good. In the intoxication of youthful successes I had felt myself to be infallible, and I was therefore cruel. In the surfeit of power I was a murderer, and an oppressor. In my most evil moments I was convinced that I was doing good, and I was well supplied with systematic arguments. And it was only when I lay there on rotting prison straw that I sensed within myself the first stirrings of good. Gradually it was disclosed to me that the line separating good and evil passes not through states, nor between classes, nor between political parties either—but right through every human heart—and through all human hearts. This line shifts. Inside us, it oscillates with the years. And even within hearts overwhelmed by evil, one

---

[2] A new translation of this poem, made by Ignat Solzhenitsyn specifically for this volume, appears with the title "Acathistus" on page 21.

small bridgehead of good is retained. And even in the best of all hearts, there remains . . . an unuprooted small corner of evil.

Since then I have come to understand the truth of all the religions of the world: They struggle with the *evil inside a human being* (inside every human being). It is impossible to expel evil from the world in its entirety, but it is possible to constrict it within each person.

And since that time I have come to understand the falsehood of all the revolutions in history: They destroy only *those carriers* of evil contemporary with them (and also fail, out of haste, to discriminate the carriers of good as well). And they then take to themselves as their heritage the actual evil itself, magnified still more.

The Nuremberg Trials have to be regarded as one of the special achievements of the twentieth century: They killed the very idea of evil, though they killed very few of the people who had been infected with it. (Of course, Stalin deserves no credit here. He would have preferred to explain less and shoot more.) And if by the twenty-first century humanity has not yet blown itself up and has not suffocated itself—perhaps it is this direction that will triumph?

Yes, and if it does not triumph—then all humanity's history will have turned out to be an empty exercise in marking time, without the tiniest mite of meaning! Whither and to what end will we otherwise be moving? To beat the enemy over the head with a club—even cavemen knew that.

"Know thyself!" There is nothing that so aids and assists the awakening of omniscience within us as insistent thoughts about one's own transgressions, errors, mistakes. After the difficult cycles of such ponderings over many years, whenever I mentioned the heartlessness of our highest-ranking bureaucrats, the cruelty of our executioners, I remember myself in my captain's shoulder boards and the forward march of my battery through East Prussia, enshrouded in fire, and I say: "So were *we* any better?"

When people express vexation, in my presence, over the West's tendency to crumble, its political shortsightedness, its divisiveness, its confusion—I recall too: "Were we, before passing through the Archipelago, more steadfast? Firmer in our thoughts?"

And that is why I turn back to the years of my imprisonment and say, sometimes to the astonishment of those about me: "*Bless you, prison!*"

Lev Tolstoi was right when he *dreamed* of being put in prison. At a certain moment that giant began to dry up. He actually needed prison as a drought needs a shower of rain!

All the writers who wrote about prison but who did not themselves serve time there considered it their duty to express sympathy for prisoners and to curse prison. I . . . have served enough time there. I nourished my soul there, and I say without hesitation:

"*Bless you, prison,* for having been in my life!"

(But from the burial mounds I hear a response; "It's very well for you to say that—you who've come through alive!")

The Gulag Archipelago
Part IV, Chapter 2

Or Corruption?

But I have been brought up short: You are *not talking about the subject* at all! You have got off the track again—onto prison! And what you are supposed to be talking about is *camp.*

But I was also, I thought, talking about camp. Well, all right, I'll shut up. I shall give some space to contrary opinions. Many camp inmates will object to what I have said and will say that they did not observe any "ascent" of the soul, that this is nonsense, and that corruption took place at every step.

More insistent and more significant than others (because he had already written about all this) was Shalamov's[1] objection:

> In the camp situation human beings never remain human beings—
> the camps were created to this end.
>
> All human emotions—love, friendship, envy, love of one's fellows, mercy, thirst for fame, honesty—fell away from us along with the meat of our muscles. . . . We had no pride, no vanity, and even jealousy and passion seemed to be Martian concepts. . . . The only thing left was anger—the most enduring of human emotions.
>
> We came to understand that truth and falsehood were kin sisters.

There is only one distinction here to which Shalamov agrees: Ascent, growth in profundity, the development of human beings, is possible in *prison*. But

> . . . camp—is wholly and consistently a negative school of life. There is nothing either necessary or useful that anyone derives

---

[1] Varlam Shalamov: Author of *Kolyma Tales*, short stories about life in the gulag.

from it. The prisoner learns flattery, falsehood, and petty and large-scale meanness. . . . When he returns home, he sees not only that he has not grown during his time in camp, but that his interests have become meager and crude.

Y. Ginzburg[2] also agrees with this distinction: "Prison ennobled people, while camp corrupted them."

And how can one object to that?

In prison, both in solitary confinement and outside solitary too, a human being confronts his grief face to face. This grief is a mountain, but he has to find space inside himself for it, to familiarize himself with it, to digest it, and it him. This is the highest form of moral effort, which has always ennobled every human being. A duel with years and with walls constitutes moral work and a path upward (if you can climb it). If you share those years with a comrade, it is never in a situation in which you are called on to die in order to save his life, nor is it necessary for him to die in order for you to survive. You have the possibility of entering not into conflict but into mutual support and enrichment.

But in camp, it would appear, you do not have that path. Bread is not issued in equal pieces, but thrown onto a pile—go grab! Knock down your neighbors, and tear it out of their hands! The quantity of bread issued is such that one or two people have to die for each who survives. The bread is hung high up on a pine tree—go fell it. The bread is deposited in a coal mine—go down and mine it. Can you think about your own grief, about the past and the future, about humanity and God? Your mind is absorbed in vain calculations which for the present moment cut you off from the heavens—and tomorrow are worth nothing. You *hate* labor—it is your principal enemy. You hate your companions—rivals in life and death. You are reduced to a frazzle by intense *envy* and alarm lest somewhere behind your back others are right now dividing up that bread which could be yours, that somewhere on the other side of the wall a tiny potato is being ladled out of the pot which could have ended up in your own bowl.

Camp life was organized in such a way that envy pecked at your soul from all sides, even the best-defended soul.

And in addition you are constantly gripped by *fear* of slipping off even that pitifully low level to which you are clinging, of losing your work which is still not the hardest, of coming a cropper on a prisoner transport, of ending up in a Strict Regimen Camp. And on top of that, you got beaten if you were weaker than all the rest, or else you yourself beat up those weaker than

---

[2] Yevgenia Ginzburg: Author of *Journey into the Whirlwind,* a gulag memoir.

you. And wasn't this corruption? *Soul mange* is what A. Rubailo, an old camp veteran, called this swift decay under external pressure.

Amid these vicious feelings and tense petty calculations, when and on what foundation could you ascend?

So isn't it the right time not to object, and not to rise to the defense of some sort of alleged camp "ascent," but to describe hundreds, thousands of cases of genuine soul corruption? To cite examples of how no one could resist the camp philosophy of Yashka, the Dzhezkazgan work assigner: "The more you spit on people, the more they'll esteem you." To tell how newly arrived front-line soldiers (in Kraslag in 1942) had no sooner scented the thieves' atmosphere than they themselves undertook *to play the thief—to plunder* the Lithuanians and to fatten up off their foodstuffs and possessions: You greenhorns can go die! Or how certain Vlasov men began *to pass for thieves* out of the conviction that that was the only way to survive in camp. Or about that assistant professor of literature who became a thief Ringleader.

And how much corruption was introduced by that democratic and progressive system of "trusty watchmen"—which in our zek terminology became converted to *self-guarding*—introduced back in 1918? After all, this was one of the main streams of camp corruption: the enlistment of prisoners in the trusty guards!

And ... he grows proud. And ... he tightens his grip on his gun stock. And ... he shoots. And ... he is even more severe than the free guards. (How is one to understand this: Was it really a purblind faith in social initiative? Or was it just an icy, contemptuous calculation based on the lowest human feelings?)

After all, it was not just a matter of "self-guarding" either. There were also "self-supervision," and "self-oppression"—right up to the situation in the thirties when all of them, all the way up to the camp chief, were zeks. Including the transport chief. The production chief. Yes, and even *security chiefs* were zeks too. One could not have carried "self-supervision" any further than that: The zeks were conducting interrogations of themselves. They were recruiting stool pigeons to denounce themselves.

Yes, yes. But I am not going to examine those countless cases of corruption here. They are well known to everyone. They have already been described, and they will be described again. It is quite enough to admit they took place. This is the general trend, this is as it should be.

Why repeat about each and every house that in subzero weather it loses its warmth? It is much more surprising to note that there are houses which retain their warmth even in subzero weather.

And how is it that genuine religious believers survived in camp (as we mentioned more than once)? In the course of this book we have already mentioned their self-confident procession through the Archipelago—a sort of silent religious procession with invisible candles. How some among them were mowed down by machine guns and those next in line continued their march. A steadfastness unheard of in the twentieth century! And it was not in the least for show, and there weren't any declamations. Take some Aunt Dusya Chmil, a round-faced, calm, and quite illiterate old woman. The convoy guards called out to her: "Chmil! What is your article?"

And she gently, good-naturedly replied: "Why are you asking, my boy? It's all written down there. I can't remember them all." (She had a bouquet of sections under Article 58.)

"Your term!"

Auntie Dusya sighed. She wasn't giving such contradictory answers in order to annoy the convoy. In her own simplehearted way she pondered this question: Her term? Did they really think it was given to human beings to know their terms?

"What term! . . . Till God forgives my sins—till then I'll be serving time."

"You are a silly, you! A silly!" The convoy guards laughed. "Fifteen years you've got, and you'll serve them all, and maybe some more besides."

But after two and a half years of her term had passed, even though she had sent no petitions—all of a sudden a piece of paper came: release!

How could one not envy those people? Were circumstances more favorable for them? By no means! It is a well-known fact that the "nuns" were kept only with prostitutes and thieves at penalty camps. And yet who was there among the religious believers whose soul was corrupted? They died—most certainly, but . . . they were not corrupted.

And how can one explain that certain unstable people found faith right there in camp, that they were strengthened by it, and that they survived uncorrupted?

And many more, scattered about and unnoticed, came to their allotted turning point and made no mistake in their choice. Those who managed to see that things were not only bad for them, but even worse, even harder, for their neighbors.

And all those who, under the threat of a penalty zone and a new term of imprisonment, refused to become stoolies?

How, in general, can one explain Grigory Ivanovich Grigoryev, a soil scientist? A scientist who volunteered for the People's Volunteer Corps in 1941—and the rest of the story is a familiar one. Taken prisoner near Vyazma, he spent his whole captivity in a German camp. And the subsequent story is also familiar. When he returned, he was arrested by us and given a tenner. I came to know him in winter, engaged in general work in Ekibastuz. His forthrightness gleamed from his big quiet eyes, some sort of unwavering forthrightness. This man was never able to bow in spirit. And he didn't bow in camp either, even though he worked only two of his ten years in his own field of specialization, and didn't receive food parcels from home for nearly the whole term. He was subjected on all sides to the camp philosophy, to the camp corruption of soul, but he was incapable of adopting it. In the Kemerovo camps (Antibess) the security chief kept trying to recruit him as a stoolie. Grigoryev replied to him quite honestly and candidly: "I find it quite *repulsive* to talk to you. You will find many willing without me." "You bastard, you'll crawl on all fours." "I would be better off hanging myself on the first branch." And so he was sent off to a penalty situation. He stood it for half a year. And he made *mistakes* which were even more unforgivable: When he was sent on an agricultural work party, he refused (as a soil scientist) to accept the post of brigadier offered him. He hoed and scythed with enthusiasm. And even more stupidly: In Ekibastuz at the stone quarry he refused to be a work checker—only because he would have had to pad the work sheets for the sloggers, for which, later on, when they caught up with it, the eternally drunk free foreman would have to pay the penalty. (But would he?) And so he went to break rocks! His honesty was so monstrously unnatural that when he went out to process potatoes with the vegetable storeroom brigade, he did not steal any, though everyone else did. When he was in a good post, in the privileged repair-shop brigade at the pumping-station equipment, he left simply because he refused to wash the socks of the free bachelor construction supervisor, Treivish. (His fellow brigade members tried to persuade him: Come on now, isn't it all the same, the kind of work you do? But no, it turned out it was not at all the same to him!) How many times did he select the worst and hardest lot, just so as not to have to offend against conscience—and he didn't, not in the least, and I am a witness. And even more: Because of the astounding influence on his body of his bright and spotless human spirit (though no one today believes in any such influence, no one understands it) the organism of Grigory Ivanovich, who was no longer young (close to fifty), grew stronger in camp; his earlier rheumatism of the joints disappeared completely, and he became particularly healthy after the typhus from which he recovered: in winter he went out in cotton sacks, making holes in them for his head and his arms—and he did not catch cold!

So wouldn't it be more correct to say that no camp can corrupt those who have a stable nucleus, who do not accept that pitiful ideology which holds that "human beings are created for happiness," an ideology which is done in by the first blow of the work assigner's cudgel?

Those people became corrupted in camp who before camp had not been enriched by any morality at all or by any spiritual upbringing. (This is not at all a theoretical matter—since during our glorious half-century millions of them grew up.)

Those people became corrupted in camp who had already been corrupted out in freedom or who were ready for it. Because people are corrupted in freedom too, sometimes even more effectively than in camp.

If a person went swiftly bad in camp, what it might mean was that he had not just gone bad, but that that inner foulness which had not previously been needed had disclosed itself.

M. A. Voichenko has his opinion: "In camp, existence did not determine consciousness, but just the opposite: Consciousness and steadfast faith in the human essence decided whether you became an animal or remained a human being."

Yes, camp corruption was a mass phenomenon. But not only because the camps were awful, but because in addition we Soviet people stepped upon the soil of the Archipelago spiritually disarmed—long since prepared to be corrupted, already tinged by it out in freedom, and we strained our ears to hear from the old camp veterans "how to live in camp."

But we ought to have known how to live (and how to die) without any camp.

Yes, the camps were calculated and intended to corrupt. But this didn't mean that they succeeded in crushing *everyone*.

Just as in nature the process of oxidation never occurs without an accompanying reduction (one substance oxidizes while at the same time another reduces), so in camp, too (and everywhere in life), there is no corruption without ascent. They exist alongside one another.

In the next part I hope still to show how in other camps, in the Special Camps, a different *environment* was created after a certain time: The process of corruption was greatly hampered and the process of ascent became attractive even to the camp careerists.

The Gulag Archipelago
Part V, Chapter 5

Poetry Under a Tombstone,
Truth Under a Stone

At the beginning of my camp career I was very anxious to avoid general duties, but did not know how. When I arrived at Ekibastuz[1] in the sixth year of my imprisonment I had changed completely, and set out at once to cleanse my mind of the camp prejudices, intrigues, and schemes, which leave it no time for deeper matters. So that instead of resigning myself to the grueling existence of a general laborer until I was lucky enough to become a trusty, as educated people usually have to, I resolved to acquire a skill, there and then, in *katorga*.[2] When we joined Boronyuk's team (Oleg Ivanov and I), a suitable trade (that of bricklayer) came our way. Later my fortunes took a different turn and I was for some time a smelter.

I was anxious and unsure of myself to begin with. Could I keep it up? We were unhandy cerebral creatures, and the same amount of work was harder for us than for our teammates. But the day when I deliberately let myself sink to the bottom and felt it firm under my feet—the hard, rocky bottom which is the same for all—was the beginning of the most important years in my life, the years which put the finishing touches to my character. From then onward there seem to have been no upheavals in my life, and I have been faithful to the views and habits acquired at that time.

I needed an unmuddled mind because I had been trying to write a poem for two years past. This was very rewarding, in that it helped me not to no-

---

[1] Ekibastuz: A huge prison camp for political prisoners located in central Kazakhstan, it served as the setting for *One Day in the Life of Ivan Denisovich*.

[2] *katorga*: In tsarist times this term meant "hard labor" or "penal servitude." In Stalin's reintroduction of the term, it meant, in essence, "murder camps." *Katorga* is the title for the whole of Part V of *The Gulag Archipelago*.

tice what was being done with my body. Sometimes in a sullen work party with Tommy-gunners barking about me, lines and images crowded in so urgently that I felt myself borne through the air, overleaping the column in my hurry to reach the work site and find a corner to write. At such moments I was both free and happy.

But how could I *write* in a Special Camp?

Memory was the only hidey-hole in which you could keep what you had written and carry it through all the searches and journeys under escort. In the early days I had little confidence in the powers of memory and decided therefore to write in verse. It was of course an abuse of the genre. I discovered later that prose, too, can be quite satisfactorily tamped down into the deep hidden layers of what we carry in our head. No longer burdened with frivolous and superfluous knowledge, a prisoner's memory is astonishingly capacious, and can expand indefinitely. We have too little faith in memory!

I started breaking matches into little pieces and arranging them on my cigarette case in two rows (of ten each, one representing units and the other tens). As I recited the verses to myself, I displaced one bit of broken match from the units row for every line. When I had shifted ten units I displaced one of the "tens." Every fiftieth and every hundredth line I memorized with special care, to help me keep count. Once a month I recited all that I had written. If the wrong line came out in place of one of the hundreds or fifties, I went over it all again and again until I caught the slippery fugitives.

In the Kuibyshev Transit Prison I saw Catholics (Lithuanians) busy making themselves rosaries for prison use. They made them by soaking bread, kneading beads from it, coloring them (black ones with burnt rubber, white ones with tooth powder, red ones with red germicide), stringing them while still moist on several strands of thread twisted together and thoroughly soaped, and letting them dry on the window ledge. I joined them and said that I, too, wanted to say my prayers with a rosary but that in my particular religion I needed one hundred beads in a ring (later, when I realized that twenty would suffice, and indeed be more convenient, I made them myself from cork), that every tenth bead must be cubic, not spherical, and that the fiftieth and the hundredth beads must be distinguishable at a touch. The Lithuanians were amazed by my religious zeal, but with true brotherly love helped me to put together a rosary such as I had described, making the hundredth bead in the form of a dark red heart. I never afterward parted with this marvelous present of theirs; I fingered and counted my beads inside my wide mittens—at work line-up, on the march to and from work, at all waiting times; I could do it standing up, and freezing cold was no hindrance. I carried it safely through the search points, in the padding of my mittens, where it could not be felt. The warders found it on various occasions, but supposed that it was for praying and let me keep it. Until the end of my sentence (by which time I had accumulated 12,000 lines) and after that in my place of banishment, this necklace helped me to write and remember.

I realized that I was not the only one, that I was party to a great secret, a secret maturing in other lonely breasts like mine on the scattered islands of the Archipelago, to reveal itself in years to come, perhaps when we were dead, and to merge into the Russian literature of the future.

How many of us were there? Many more, I think, than have come to the surface in the intervening years. Not all of them were to survive. Some buried manuscripts in bottles, without telling anyone where. Some put their work in careless or, on the contrary, in excessively cautious hands for safekeeping. Some could not write their work down in time.

Even on the isle of Ekibastuz, could we really get to know each other? encourage each other? support each other? Like wolves, we hid from everyone, and that meant from each other, too. Yet even so I was to discover a few others in Ekibastuz.

Meeting the religious poet Anatoly Vasilyevich Silin was a surprise which I owed to the Baptists. Day in and day out he was meek and gentle with everyone, but reserved. Only when we began talking to each other freely, and strolling about the camp for hours at a stretch on our Sundays off, while he recited his very long religious poems to me (like me, he had written them right there in the camp), I was startled not for the first time or the last to realize what far from ordinary souls are concealed within deceptively ordinary exteriors.

A homeless child, brought up an atheist in a children's home, he had come across some religious books in a German prisoner-of-war camp, and had been carried away by them. From then on he was not only a believer, but a philosopher and theologian! "From then on" he had also been in prison or in camps without a break, and so had spent his whole theological career in isolation, rediscovering for himself things already discovered by others, perhaps going astray, since he had never had either books or advisers. Now he was working as a manual laborer and ditchdigger, struggling to fulfill an impossible norm, returning from work with bent knees and trembling hands—but night and day the poems, which he composed from end to end without writing a word down, in iambic tetrameters with an irregular rhyme scheme, went round and round in his head. He must have known some twenty thousand lines by that time. He, too, had a utilitarian attitude to them: They were a way of remembering and of transmitting thoughts.

His sensitive response to the riches of nature lent warmth and beauty to his view of the world. Bending over one of the rare blades of grass which grew illegally in our barren camp, he exclaimed:

"How beautiful are the grasses of the earth! But even these the Creator has given to man for a carpet under his feet. How much more beautiful, then, must we be than they!"

"But what about 'Love not this world and the things that are of this world'?" (A saying which the sectarians often repeated.)

He smiled apologetically. He could disarm anyone with that smile. "Why, even earthly, carnal love is a manifestation of a lofty aspiration to Union!"

His theodicy, that is to say his justification of the existence of evil in the world, he formulated like this:

> Does God, who is Perfect Love, allow
> This imperfection in our lives?
> The soul must suffer first, to know
> The perfect bliss of paradise. . . .
> Harsh is the law, but to obey
> Is for weak men the only way
> To win eternal peace.

Christ's sufferings in the flesh he daringly explained not only by the need to atone for human sins, but also by God's desire to *feel* earthly suffering to the full.

"God always *knew* these sufferings, but never before had he *felt* them," Silin boldly asserted. Even of the Antichrist, who had

> Corrupted man's Free Will—perverted
> His yearning toward the One True Light

Silin found something fresh and humane to say:

> The bliss that God had given him
> That angel haughtily rejected:
> He nothing knew of human pain;
> He loved not with the love of men—
> By grief alone is love perfected.

Thinking so freely himself, Silin found a warm place in his generous heart for all shades of Christian belief.

> This is the crux:
> That though Christ's teaching is its theme
> Genius must ever speak with its own voice.

The atheist's impatient refusal to believe that spirit could beget matter only made Silin smile.

"Why don't they ask themselves how crude matter could beget spirit? That way round, it would surely be a miracle. Yes, a still greater miracle!"

My brain was full of my own verses, and these fragments are all that I have succeeded in preserving of the poems I heard from Silin—fearing perhaps that he himself would preserve nothing. A doomed and exhausted slave, with four number patches on his clothes, this poet had more in his heart to say to living human beings than the whole tribe of hacks firmly established in journals, in publishing houses, in radio—and of no use to anyone except themselves.

Silin ate from the same pot as the Baptists, shared his bread and warm victuals with them. Of course, he needed appreciative listeners, people with whom he could join in reading and interpreting the Gospel, and in concealing the little book itself. But Orthodox Christians he either did not seek out (suspecting that they would reject him as a heretic), or did not find. The Baptists, however, seemed to respect Silin, listened to him; they even considered him one of their own: but they, too, disliked all that was heretical in him, and hoped in time to bend him to their ways. Silin was subdued when he talked to me in their presence, and blossomed out when they were not there—it was difficult for him to force himself into their mold, though their faith was firm, pure, and ardent, helping them to endure *katorga* without wavering, and without spiritual collapse. They were all honest, free from anger, hard-working, quick to help others, devoted to Christ.

That is why they are being rooted out with such determination. In the years 1948–1950 several hundred of them were sentenced to twenty-five years' imprisonment and dispatched to Special Camps *for no other reason* than that they belonged to Baptist communes (a commune is of course an *organization*).

The camp is different from the Great Outside. Outside, everyone uninhibitedly tries to express and emphasize his personality in his outward behavior. In prison, on the contrary, all are depersonalized—identical haircuts, identical fuzz on their cheeks, identical caps, identical padded jackets. The face presents an image of the soul distorted by wind and sun and dirt and heavy toil. Discerning the light of the soul beneath this depersonalized and degraded exterior is an acquired skill.

But the sparks of the spirit cannot be kept from spreading, breaking through to each other. Like recognizes and is gathered to like in a manner none can explain.

The Gulag Archipelago
Part V, Chapter 12

The Forty Days of Kengir

For the Special Camps there was another side to Beria's fall: By raising their hopes it confused, distracted, and disarmed the *katorzhane*. Hopes of speedy change burgeoned. Their anger cooled.

In that fateful year, 1953, the fall of Beria made it urgent for the security ministry to prove its devotion and its usefulness in some signal way. But how?

The mutinies which the security men had hitherto considered a menace now shone like a beacon of salvation. Let's have more disturbances and disorders, so that *measures will have to be taken*. Then staffs, and salaries, will not be reduced.

In less than a year the guards at Kengir opened fire several times on innocent men; and it cannot have been unintentional.

They shot Lida, the young girl from the mortar-mixing gang who hung her stockings out to dry near the boundary fence.

They winged the old Chinaman—nobody in Kengir remembered his name, and he spoke hardly any Russian, but everybody knew the waddling figure with a pipe between his teeth and the face of an elderly goblin. A guard called him to a watchtower, tossed a packet of makhorka near the boundary fence, and when the Chinaman reached for it, shot and wounded him.

Then there was the famous case of the column returning to camp from the ore-dressing plant and being fired on with dumdum bullets, which wounded sixteen men.

This the zeks did not take quietly—it was the Ekibastuz story over again. Kengir Camp Division No. 3 did not turn out for work three days running (but did take food), demanding punishment of the culprits.

A commission arrived and persuaded them that the culprits would be prosecuted. They went back to work.

But in February, 1954, another prisoner was shot at the woodworking plant—"the Evangelist," as all Kengir remembered him (Aleksandr Sisoyev, I think his name was). This man had served nine years and nine months of his *tenner*. His job was fluxing arc-welding rods and he did this work in a little shed which stood near the boundary fence. He went out to relieve himself near the shed—and while he was at it was shot from a watchtower. Guards quickly ran over from the guardhouse and started dragging the dead man into the boundary zone, to make it look as though he had trespassed on it. This was too much for the zeks, who grabbed picks and shovels and drove the murderers away from the murdered man.

The woodworking plant was in an uproar. The prisoners said that they would carry the dead man into camp on their shoulders. The camp officers would not permit it. "Why did you kill him?" shouted the prisoners. The bosses had their explanation ready: the dead man himself was to blame—he had started it by throwing stones at the tower. (Can they have had time to read his identity card; did they know that he had three months more to go and was an Evangelical Christian? . . .)

In the evening after supper, what they did was this. The light would suddenly go out in a section, and someone invisible said from the doorway: "Brothers! How long shall we go on building and taking our wages in bullets? Nobody goes to work tomorrow!" The same thing happened in section after section, hut after hut.

A note was thrown over the wall to the Second Camp Division. In this division, which was multinational, the majority had *tenners* and many were coming to the end of their time—but they joined in just the same.

In the morning the men's Camp Divisions, 2 and 3, did not report for work.

This bad habit—striking without refusing the state's bread and slops—was becoming more and more popular with prisoners.

They held out like this for two days. But the strike was mastered. . . .

For the second time in Kengir, a ripening abscess was lanced before it could burst.

But then the bosses went too far. They reached for the biggest stick they could use on the 58's—for the thieves!

The bosses now renounced the whole principle of the Special Camps, acknowledged that if they segregated political prisoners they had no means of making themselves *understood*, and brought into the mutinous No. 3 Camp Division 650 men, most of them thieves, some of them petty offenders (including many minors). "A *healthy batch* is joining us!" the bosses spitefully warned the 58's. "Now you won't dare breathe."

The bosses understood well enough how the restorers of order would begin: by stealing, by preying on others, and so setting every man against his fellows.

But here again we see how unpredictable is the course of human emotions and of social movements! Injecting in Kengir No. 3 a mammoth dose of tested ptomaine, the bosses obtained not a pacified camp but the biggest mutiny in the history of the Gulag Archipelago.

Events followed their inevitable course. It was *impossible* for the politicals not to offer the thieves a choice between war and alliance. It was *impossible* for the thieves to refuse an alliance. And it was *impossible* for the alliance, once concluded, to remain inactive.

The obvious first objective was to capture the service yard, in which all the camp's food stores were also situated. They began the operation in the afternoon of a nonworking day (Sunday, May 16, 1954). . . .

All these quite undisguised operations took a certain time, during which the warders managed to get themselves organized and obtain instructions. . . .

The service yard was now firmly held by the punitive forces, and machine-gunners were posted there. But the Second Camp Division erected a barricade facing the service yard gate. The Second and Third Camp Divisions had been joined together by a hole in the wall, and there were no longer any warders, any MVD authority, in them.

How can we say what feelings wrung the hearts of those eight thousand men, who for so long and until yesterday had been slaves with no sense of fellowship, and now had united and freed themselves, not fully perhaps, but at least within the rectangle of those walls, and under the gaze of those quadrupled guards? So long suppressed, the brotherhood of man had broken through at last!

Proclamations appeared in the mess hall: "Arm yourselves as best you can, and attack the soldiers first!" The most passionate among them hastily scrawled their slogans on scraps of newspaper: "Bash the Chekists, boys!" "Death to the stoolies, the Cheka's stooges!" Here, there, everywhere you turned there were meetings and orators. Everybody had suggestions of his own. What demands shall we put forward? What is it we want? Put the murderers on trial!—goes without saying. What else? . . . No locking huts; take the numbers off! But beyond that? . . . Beyond that came the most frightening thing—the real reason why they had *started it all*, what they really wanted. We want freedom, of course, just freedom—but who can give it to us? The judges who condemned us in Moscow. As long as our complaints are against Steplag or Karaganda, they will go on talking to us. But if we start complaining against Moscow . . . we'll all be buried in this steppe.

Well, then—what do we want? To break holes in the walls? To run off into the wilderness? . . .

Those hours of freedom! Immense chains had fallen from our arms and shoulders! No; whatever happened, there could be no regrets! That one day made it all worthwhile!

Late on Monday, a delegation from command HQ arrived in the seething camp. The delegation was quite well disposed. Our side learned that generals had flown in from Moscow. They found the prisoners' demands *fully justified!* (We simply gasped: justified? We aren't rebels, then? No, no, they're *quite* justified!) "Those responsible for the shooting will be made to answer for it!" "But why did they beat up women?" "Beat up women?" The delegation was shocked. "That can't be true." Anya Mikhalevich brought in a succession of battered women for them to see. The commission was deeply moved: "We'll look into it, never fear!" "Beasts!" Lyuba Bershadskaya shouts at the general. There were other shouts: "No locks on huts!" "We won't lock them any more." "Take the numbers off!" "Certainly we'll take them off." "The holes in the wall between camp areas must remain!" They were getting bolder. "We must be allowed to mix with each other." "All right, mix as much as you like." "Let the holes remain." Right, brothers, what else do we want? We've won, we've won! We raised hell for just one day, enjoyed ourselves, let off steam—and we won! Although some among us shake their heads and say, "It's a trick, it's all a trick," we believe it!

We believe because that's our easiest way out of the situation. . . .

All that the downtrodden can do is go on hoping. After every disappointment they must find fresh reason for hope.

So on Tuesday, May 18, all the Kengir Camp Divisions went out to work, reconciling themselves to thoughts of their dead.

That morning the whole affair could still have ended quietly. But the exalted generals assembled in Kengir would have considered such an outcome a defeat for themselves. They could not seriously admit that prisoners were in the right!

When the columns of prisoners returned to camp in the evening after giving a day's work to the state, they were hurried in to supper before they knew what was happening, so that they could be locked up quickly. On orders from the general, the jailers had to play for time that first evening—that evening of blatant dishonesty after yesterday's promises.

But before nightfall the long-drawn whistles heard on Sunday shrilled through the camp again—the Second and Third Camp Divisions were calling to each other like hooligans on a spree. The warders took fright, and fled from the camp grounds without finishing their duties.

The camp was in the hands of the zeks, but they were divided. The towers opened fire with machine guns on anyone who approached the inside walls. They killed several and wounded several. Once again zeks broke all the lamps with slingshots, but the towers lit up the camp with flares. . . .

They battered at the barbed wire, and the new fence posts, with long tables, but it was impossible, under fire, either to break through the barrier or to climb over it—so they had to burrow under. As always, there were no shovels, except those for use in case of fire, inside the camp. Kitchen knives and mess tins were put into service.

That night—May 18–19—they burrowed under all the walls and again united all the divisions and the service yard. The towers had stopped shooting now, and there were plenty of tools in the service yard. Under cover of night they broke down the boundary fences, knocked holes in the walls, and widened the passages, so that they would not become traps.

That same night they broke through the wall around the Fourth Camp Division—the prison area—too. The warders guarding the jails fled. The prisoners wrecked the interrogation offices. Among those released from the jail were those who on the morrow would take command of the rising: former Red Army Colonel Kapiton Kuznetsov and former First Lieutenant Gleb Sluchenkov.

Mutinous zeks! These eight thousand men had not so much raised a rebellion as *escaped to freedom*, though not for long! Eight thousand men, from being slaves, had suddenly become free, and now was their chance to . . . live! Faces usually grim softened into kind smiles. Women looked at men, and men took them by the hand. Some who had corresponded by ingenious secret ways, without even seeing each other, met at last! Lithuanian girls whose weddings had been solemnized by priests on the other side of the wall now saw their lawful wedded husbands for the first time—the Lord had sent down to earth the marriages made in heaven! For the first time in their lives, no one tried to prevent the sectarians and believers from meeting for prayer. Foreigners, scattered about the Camp Divisions, now found each other and talked about this strange Asiatic revolution in their own languages. The camp's food supply was in the hands of the prisoners. No one drove them out to work line-up and an eleven-hour working day.

The morning of May 19 dawned over a feverishly sleepless camp which had torn off its number patches. Many took their street clothes from the storerooms and put them on. Some of the lads crammed fur hats on their heads; shortly there would be embroidered shirts, and on the Central Asians bright-colored robes and turbans. The gray-black camp would be a blaze of color.

Orderlies went around the huts summoning us to the big mess hall to elect a commission for negotiations with the authorities and for self-government.

For all they knew, they were electing it just for a few hours, but it was destined to become the government of Kengir camp for forty days.

The days ran on. And the generals were regretfully forced to conclude that the camp was not disintegrating of its own accord, and that there was no excuse to send troops in to the rescue.

The camp *stood fast* and the negotiations changed their character. Golden-epauleted personages, in various combinations, continued coming into the camp to argue and persuade. They were all allowed in, but they had to pick up white flags, and they had to undergo a body search. In return, the rebel staff *guaranteed* their personal safety! . . .

They showed the generals around, wherever it was allowed (not, of course, around the *secret* sector of the service yard), let them talk to prisoners, and called big meetings in the Camp Divisions for their benefit. Their epaulets flashing, the bosses took their seats in the presidium as of old, as though nothing were amiss.

The discussions sometimes took the form of direct negotiations on the loftiest diplomatic model. Sometime in June a long mess table was placed in the women's camp, and the golden epaulets seated themselves on a bench to one side of it, while the Tommy-gunners allowed in with them as a bodyguard stood at their backs. Across the table sat the members of the Commission, and they, too, had a bodyguard—which stood there, looking very serious, armed with sabers, pikes, and sling-shots. In the background crowds of prisoners gathered to listen to the powwow and shout comments. (Refreshments for the guests were not forgotten!)

The rebels had agreed on their demands (or requests) in the first two days, and now repeated them over and over again:

- Punish the Evangelist's murderer.
- Punish all those responsible for the murders on Sunday night in the service yard.
- Punish those who beat up the women.
- Bring back those comrades who had been illegally sent to closed prisons for striking.
- No more number patches, window bars, or locks on hut doors.
- Inner walls between Camp Divisions not to be rebuilt.
- An eight-hour day, as for free workers.

- An increase in payment for work (here there was no
question of equality with free workers).
- Unrestricted correspondence with relatives, periodic visits.
- Review of cases.

Although there was nothing unconstitutional in any of these demands, nothing that threatened the foundations of the state (indeed, many of them were requests for a return to the old position), it was impossible for the bosses to accept even the least of them, because these bald skulls under service caps and supported by close-clipped fat necks had forgotten how to admit a mistake or a fault. Truth was unrecognizable and repulsive to them if it manifested itself not in secret instructions from higher authority but on the lips of common people.

Still, the obduracy of the eight thousand under siege was a blot on the reputation of the generals, it might ruin their careers, and so they made promises. They promised that nearly all the demands would be satisfied— only, they said, they could hardly leave the women's camp open, that was against the rules (forgetting that in the Corrective Labor Camps it had been that way for twenty years), but they could consider arranging, should they say, *meeting days*. To the demand that the Commission of Inquiry should start its work inside the camp, the generals unexpectedly agreed. (But Sluchenkov guessed their purpose, and refused to hear of it: While making their statements, the stoolies would expose everything that was happening in the camp.) Review of cases? Well, of course, cases would be re-examined, but prisoners would *have to be patient*. There was one thing that couldn't wait at all—the prisoners must get back to work! to work! to work!

But the zeks knew that trick by now: dividing them up into columns, forcing them to the ground at gunpoint, arresting the ringleaders.

No, they answered across the table, and from the platform. No! shouted voices from the crowd. The administration of Steplag have behaved like provocateurs! We do not trust the Steplag authorities! We don't trust the MVD!

"Don't trust *even* the MVD?" The vice-minister was thrown into a sweat by this treasonable talk. "And who can have inspired in you such hatred for the MVD?"

A riddle, if ever there was one.

There were weeks when the whole war became a war of propaganda. The outside radio was never silent: Through several loudspeakers set up at intervals around the camp it interlarded appeals to the prisoners with information and misinformation, and with a couple of trite and boring records that frayed everybody's nerves.

Through the meadow goes a maiden,
She whose braided hair I love.

(Still, to be thought worthy even of that not very high honor—having records played to them—they had to rebel. Even rubbish like that wasn't played for men on their knees.) These records also served, in the spirit of the times, as a *jamming device*—drowning the broadcasts from the camps intended for the escort troops.

On the outside radio they sometimes tried to blacken the whole movement, asserting that it had been started with the sole aim of rape and plunder. At other times they tried telling filthy stories about members of the Commission. Then the appeals would begin again. Work! Work! Why should the Motherland keep you for nothing? By not going to work you are doing enormous damage to the state! (This was supposed to pierce the hearts of men doomed to eternal *katorga!*) Whole trainloads of coal are standing in the siding, there's nobody to unload it! (Let them stand there—the zeks laughed—you'll give way all the sooner!)

The Technical Department, however, gave as good as it got. Two portable film projectors were found in the service yard. Their amplifiers were used for loudspeakers, less powerful, of course, than those of the other side. (The fact that the camp had electricity and radio greatly surprised and troubled the bosses. They were afraid that the rebels might rig up a transmitter and start broadcasting news about their rising to foreign countries.)

The camp soon had its own announcers. Programs included the latest news, and news features (there was also a daily wall newspaper, with cartoons). "Crocodile Tears" was the name of a program ridiculing the anxiety of the MVD men about the fate of women whom they themselves had previously beaten up.

But there was not enough power to put on programs for the only potential sympathizers to be found in Kengir—the free inhabitants of the settlement, many of them exiles. It was they whom the settlement authorities were trying to fool, not by radio but with rumors that bloodthirsty gangsters and insatiable prostitutes were ruling the roost inside the camp; that over there innocent people were being tortured and burned alive in furnaces.

How could the prisoners call out through the walls, to the workers one, or two, or three kilometers away: "Brothers! We want only justice! They were murdering us for no crime of ours, they were treating us worse than dogs! Here are our demands"?

The thoughts of the Technical Department, since they had no chance to outstrip modern science, moved backward instead to the science of past ages. using cigarette paper, they pasted together an enormous air balloon. A bundle of leaflets was attached to the balloon, and slung underneath it was a brazier containing glowing coals, which sent a current of warm air into the dome of the balloon through an opening in its base. To the huge delight of the assembled crowd (if prisoners ever do feel happy they are like children), the marvelous aeronautical structure rose and was airborne. But alas! The speed of the wind was greater than the speed of its ascent, and as it was flying over the boundary fence the brazier caught on the barbed wire. The balloon, denied its current of warm air, fell and burned to ashes, together with the leaflets.

After this failure they started inflating balloons with smoke. With a following wind they flew quite well, exhibiting inscriptions in large letters to the settlement:

"Save the women and old men from being beaten!"

"We demand to see a member of the Presidium."

The guards started shooting at these balloons.

Then some Chechen prisoners came to the Technical Department and offered to make kites. (They are experts.) They succeeded in sticking some kites together and paying out the string until they were over the settlement. There was a percussive device on the frame of each kite. When the kite was in a convenient position, the device scattered a bundle of leaflets, also attached to the kite. The kite fliers sat on the roof of a hut waiting to see what would happen next. If the leaflets fell close to the camp, warders ran to collect them; if they fell farther away, motorcyclists and horsemen dashed after them. Whatever happened, they tried to prevent the free citizens from reading an independent version of the truth. (The leaflets ended by requesting any citizen of Kengir who found one to deliver it to the Central Committee.)

The kites were also shot at, but holing was less damaging to them than to the balloons. The enemy soon discovered that sending up counter-kites to tangle strings with them was cheaper than keeping a crowd of warders on the run.

A war of kites in the second half of the twentieth century! And all to silence a word of truth.

In the meantime the Technical Department was getting its notorious "secret" weapon ready. Let me describe it. Aluminum corner brackets for cattle troughs, produced in the workshops and awaiting dispatch, were packed with a mixture of sulfur scraped from matches and a little calcium carbide. When the sulfur was lit and the brackets thrown, they hissed and burst into little pieces.

But neither these star-crossed geniuses nor the field staff in the bathhouse were to choose the hour, place, and form of the decisive battle. Some two weeks after the beginning of the revolt, on one of those dark nights without a glimmer of light anywhere, thuds were heard at several places around the camp wall. This time it was not escaping prisoners or rebels battering it down; the wall was being demolished by the convoy troops themselves!

In the morning it turned out that the enemy without had made about a dozen breaches in the wall in addition to those already there and the barricaded gateway. (Machine-gun posts had been set up on the other side of the gaps, to prevent the zeks from pouring through them.) This was of course the preliminary for an assault through the breaches, and the camp was a seething anthill as it prepared to defend itself. The rebel staff decided to pull down the inner walls and the mud-brick outhouses and to erect a second circular wall of their own, specially reinforced with stacks of brick where it faced the gaps, to give protection against machine-gun bullets.

How things had changed! The troops were demolishing the boundary wall, the prisoners were rebuilding it, and the thieves were helping with a clear conscience, not feeling that they were contravening their *code*.

Additional defense posts now had to be established opposite the gaps, and every platoon assigned to a gap, which it must run to defend should the alarm be raised at night.

The zeks quite seriously prepared to advance against machine guns with pikes.

There was one attack in the daytime. Tommy-gunners were moved up to one of the gaps, opposite the balcony of the Steplag Administration Building, which was packed with important personages holding cameras or even movie cameras. The soldiers were in no hurry. They merely advanced just far enough into the breach for the alarm to be given, whereupon the rebel platoons responsible for the defense of the breach rushed out to man the barricade—brandishing their pikes and holding stones and mud bricks—and then, from the balcony, movie cameras whirred and pocket cameras clicked (taking care to keep the Tommy-gunners out of the picture). Disciplinary officers, prosecutors, Party officials, and all the rest of them—Party members to a man, of course—laughed at the bizarre spectacle of the impassioned savages with pikes. Well-fed and shameless, these grand personages mocked their starved and cheated fellow citizens from the balcony, and found it *all very funny.*

Then warders, too, stole up to the gaps and tried to slip nooses with hooks over the prisoners, as though they were hunting wild animals or the abominable snowman, hoping to drag out a *talker.*

But what they mainly counted on now were deserters, rebels with cold feet. The radio blared away. Come to your senses! Those who come over will not be tried for mutiny!

The Commission's response, over the camp radio, was this: Anybody who wants to run away can go right ahead, through the main gate if he likes; we are holding no one back!

In all those weeks only about a dozen men fled from the camp.

Why? Surely the rest did not believe in victory. Were they not appalled by the thought of the punishment ahead? They were. Did they not want to save themselves for their families' sake? They did! They were torn, and thousands of them perhaps had secretly considered this possibility. But the social temperature on this plot of land had risen so high that if souls were not transmuted, they were purged of dross, and the sordid laws saying that "we only live once," that being determines consciousness, and that every man's a coward when his neck is at stake, ceased to apply for that short time in that circumscribed place. The laws of survival and of reason told people that they must all surrender together or flee individually, but they did not surrender and they did not flee! They rose to that spiritual plane from which executioners are told: "The devil take you for his own! Torture us! Savage us!"

And the operation, so beautifully planned, to make the prisoners scatter like rats through the gaps in the wall till only the most stubborn were left, who would then be crushed—this operation collapsed because its inventors had the mentality of rats themselves.

No one supported the island of Kengir. It was impossible by now to take off into the wilderness: The garrison was being steadily reinforced. The whole camp had been encircled with a double barbed-wire fence outside the walls. There was only one rosy spot on the horizon: The lord and master (they were expecting Malenkov) was coming to dispense justice. But it was too tiny a spot, and too rosy.

They could not hope for pardon. All they could do was live out their last few days of freedom, and submit to Steplag's vengeance.

There are always hearts which cannot stand the strain. Some were already morally crushed, and were in an agony of suspense for the crushing proper to begin. Some quietly calculated that they were not really involved, and need not be if they went on being careful. Some were newly married (what is more, with a proper religious ceremony—a Western Ukrainian girl, for instance, will not marry without one, and thanks to Gulag's thoughtfulness, there were priests of all religions there). For these newlyweds the bitter and the sweet succeeded each other with a rapidity which ordinary people never experience in their slow lives. They observed each day as their last, and retribution delayed was a gift from heaven each morning.

The believers . . . prayed, and leaving the outcome of the Kengir revolt in God's hands, were as always the calmest of people. Services for all religions were held in the mess hall according to a fixed timetable. The Jehovah's Witnesses felt free to observe their rules strictly and refused to build fortifications or stand guard. They sat for hours on end with their heads together, saying nothing. (They were made to wash the dishes.) A prophet, genuine or sham, went around the camp putting crosses on bunks and foretelling the end of the world.

Some knew that they were fatally compromised and that the few days before the troops arrived were all that was left of life. The theme of all their thoughts and actions must be how to hold out longer. These people were not the unhappiest. (The unhappiest were those who were not involved and who prayed for the end.)

But when all these people gathered at meetings to decide whether to surrender or to hold on, they found themselves again in that heated climate where their personal opinions dissolved, and ceased to exist even for themselves. Or else they feared ridicule even more than the death that awaited them.

And when they voted for or against holding out, the majority were *for.*

Why did it drag on so long? What can the bosses have been waiting for? For the food to run out? They knew it would last a long time. Were they considering opinion in the settlement? They had no need to. Were they carefully working out their plan of repression? They could have been quicker about it. Were they having to seek approval for the operation *up top?* How high up? There is no knowing on what date and at what level the decision was taken.

On several occasions the main gate of the service yard suddenly opened—perhaps to test the readiness of the defenders? The duty picket sounded the alarm, and the platoons poured out to meet the enemy. But no one entered the camp grounds.

In the middle of June several tractors appeared in the settlement. They were working, shifting something perhaps, around the boundary fence. They began working even at night. The unfriendly roar made the night seem blacker.

Then suddenly the skeptics were put to shame! And the defeatists! And all who had said that there would be no mercy, and that there was no point in begging. The orthodox alone could feel triumphant. On June 22 the outside radio announced that the prisoners' demands had been accepted! A member of the Presidium of the Central Committee was on his way!

The rosy spot turned into a rosy sun, a rosy sky! It is, then, possible to get through to them! There *is,* then, justice in our country! They will give a little, and we will give a little. If it comes to it, we can walk about with number patches, and the bars on the windows needn't bother us, we aren't thinking of climbing out. You say they're tricking us again? Well, they aren't asking us to report for work *beforehand!*

Just as the touch of a stick will draw off the charge from an electroscope so that the agitated gold leaf sinks gratefully to rest, so did the radio announcement reduce the brooding tension of that last week.

Even the loathsome tractors, after working for a while on the evening of June 24, stopped their noise.

Prisoners could sleep peacefully on the fortieth night of the revolt. *He* would probably arrive tomorrow; perhaps he had come already. . . .

In the early dawn of Friday, June 25, parachutes carrying flares opened out in the sky, more flares soared from the watchtowers, and the observers on the rooftops were picked off by snipers' bullets before they could let out a squeak! Then cannon fire was heard! Airplanes skimmed the camp, spreading panic. Tanks, the famous T-34's, had taken up position under cover of the tractor noise and now moved on the gaps from all sides. (One of them, however, fell into a ditch.) Some of the tanks dragged concatenations of barbed wire on trestles so that they could divide up the camp grounds immediately. Behind others ran helmeted assault troops with Tommy guns. (Both Tommy-gunners and tank crews had been given vodka first. However *special* the troops may be, it is easier to destroy unarmed and sleeping people with drink inside you.) Operators with walkie-talkies came in with the advancing troops. The generals went up into the towers with the snipers, and from there, in the daylight shed by the flares (and the light from a tower set on fire by the zeks with their incendiary bombs), gave their orders: "Take hut number so-and-so! . . ."

The camp woke up—frightened out of its wits. Some stayed where they were in their huts, lying on the floor as their one chance of survival, and because resistance seemed senseless. Others tried to make them get up and join in the resistance. Yet others ran right into the line of fire, either to fight or to seek a quicker death.

The Third Camp Division fought—the division which had started it all. They hurled stones at the Tommy-gunners and warders, and probably sulfur bombs at the tanks. . . . Nobody thought of the powdered glass. One hut counterattacked twice, with shouts of "Hurrah."

The tanks crushed everyone in their way. (Alla Presman, from Kiev, was run over—the tracks passed over her abdomen.) Tanks rode up onto the porches of huts and crushed people there. The tanks grazed the sides of huts and crushed those who were clinging to them to escape the caterpillar tracks. Semyon Rak and his girl threw themselves under a tank clasped in each other's arms and ended it that way. Tanks nosed into the thin board walls of the huts and even fired blank shells into them. Faina Epstein remembers the corner of a hut collapsing, as if in a nightmare, and a tank passing obliquely over the wreckage and over living bodies; women tried to jump and fling themselves out of the way: Behind the tank came a truck, and the half-naked women were tossed onto it.

The cannon shots were blank, but the Tommy guns were shooting live rounds, and the bayonets were cold steel. Women tried to shield men with their own bodies—and they, too, were bayoneted! Security Officer Belyaev shot two dozen people with his own hand that morning; when the battle was over he was seen putting knives into the hands of corpses for the photographer to take pictures of dead *gangsters*. Suprun, a member of the Commission, and a grandmother, died from a wound in her lung. Some prisoners hid in the latrines, and were riddled with bullets there.

As groups of prisoners were taken, they were marched through the gaps onto the steppe and between files of Kengir convoy troops outside. They were searched and made to lie flat on their faces with their arms stretched straight out. As they lay there thus crucified, MVD fliers and warders walked among them to identify and pull out those whom they had spotted earlier from the air or from the watchtowers. (So busy were they with all this that no one had leisure to open *Pravda* that day. It had a special theme—a day in the life of our Motherland: the successes of steelworkers; more and more crops harvested by machine. The historian surveying our country as it was *that day* will have an easy task.)

The victorious generals descended from the towers and went off to breakfast. Without knowing any of them, I feel confident that their appetite that June morning left nothing to be desired and that they drank deeply. An alcoholic hum would not in the least disturb the ideological harmony in their heads. And what they had for hearts was something installed with a screwdriver.

The number of those killed or wounded was about six hundred, according to the stories, but according to figures given by the Kengir Division's Production Planning Section, which became known some months later, it was more than *seven hundred*.

All day on June 25, the prisoners lay face down on the steppe in the sun (for days on end the heat had been unmerciful), while in the camp there was endless searching and breaking open and shaking out.

The members of the Commission and other suspects were locked up in the camp jail. More than a thousand people were selected for dispatch either to closed prisons or to Kolyma (as always, these lists were drawn up partly by guesswork, so that many who had not been involved at all found their way into them).

May this picture of the pacification bring peace to the souls of those on whom the last chapters have grated.

On June 26, the prisoners were made to spend the whole day taking down the barricades and bricking in the gaps.

On June 27, they were marched out to work. Those trains in the sidings would wait no longer for working hands!

The tanks[1] which had crushed Kengir traveled under their own power to Rudnik and crawled around for the zeks to see. And draw their conclusions. . . .

---

[1] This episode is reflected in Solzhenitsyn's screenplay, *Tanks Know the Truth*, written in 1959 and published in Russian in his *Complete Works* (1981).

The Gulag Archipelago
Part VI, Chapter 2

The Peasant Plague

This chapter will deal with a small matter. Fifteen million souls. Fifteen million lives.

They weren't educated people, of course. They couldn't play the violin.

In the First World War we lost in all three million killed. In the Second we lost twenty million (so Khrushchev said; according to Stalin it was only seven million. Was Nikita being too generous? Or couldn't Iosif keep track of his capital?). All those odes! All those obelisks and eternal flames! Those novels and poems! For a quarter of a century all Soviet literature has been drunk on that blood!

But about the silent, treacherous Plague which starved fifteen million of our peasants to death, choosing its victims carefully and destroying the backbone and mainstay of the Russian people—about that Plague there are no books.

Our country as well as our European neighbors keep silent about the six million people who were subsequently starved to death during the famine artificially brought about by the Bolsheviks. In the prosperous Poltava region, corpses were left lying around in the villages, on the roads and in the fields. It was impossible to walk through the groves near the stations: The stench of rotting corpses, among them those of babies, would make one faint. The situation was perhaps most horrible in the Kuban region. In many places in Byelorussia special crews had to be brought in from other regions to collect the corpses; those on the spot who were still alive were too few to bury the dead.

No bugles bid our hearts beat faster for them. Not even the traditional three stones mark the crossroads where they went in creaking carts to their doom. Our finest humanists, so sensitive to today's injustices, in those years only nodded approvingly: Quite right, too! Just what they deserve!

It was all kept very dark, every stain carefully scratched out, every whisper swiftly choked.

Where did it all start? With the dogma that the peasantry is *petit bourgeois?* (And who in the eyes of these people is not petit bourgeois? In their wonderfully clear-cut scheme, apart from factory workers [not the skilled workers, though] and big-shot businessmen, all the rest, the whole people—peasants, office workers, actors, airmen, professors, students, doctors—are nothing but the "petite bourgeoisie.") Or did it start with a criminal scheme in high places to rob some and terrorize the rest?

From the last letters which Korolenko wrote to Gorky in 1921, just before the former died and the latter emigrated, we learn that this villainous assault on the peasantry had begun even then, and was taking almost the same form as in 1930.

But as yet their strength did not equal their impudence, and they backed down.

The devastating peasant Plague began, as far as we can judge, in 1929—the compilation of murder lists, the confiscations, the deportations. But only at the beginning of 1930 (after rehearsals were complete, and necessary adjustments made) was the public allowed to learn what was happening—in the decision of the Central Committee of the Party dated January 5. (The Party is "justified in shifting from a policy of restricting the exploiting tendencies of the kulaks to a policy of liquidating the kulaks as a class.")

The savage law of the Civil War (Ten for every one! A hundred for every one!) was reinforced—to my mind an un-Russian law: Where will you find anything like it in Russian history? For every activist (which usually meant big-mouthed loafer: A. Y. Olenyev is not the only one to recall that thieves and drunkards were in charge of "dekulakization")—for every *activist* killed in self-defense, hundreds of the most industrious, enterprising, and level-headed peasants, those who should keep the Russian nation on an even keel, were eliminated.

Yells of indignation! What's that? What do you say? What about the *bloodsuckers?* Those who squeezed their neighbors dry? "Take your loan—and pay me back with your hide"?

I suppose that bloodsuckers were a small part of the whole number (but were all the bloodsuckers there among them?). And were they bloodsuckers born? we may ask. Bloodsuckers through and through? Or was it just that all wealth—and all power—corrupts human beings? If only the "cleansing" of mankind, or of a social estate, were so simple! But if they had "cleansed" the peasantry of heartless bloodsuckers with their fine-toothed iron comb, cheerfully sacrificing fifteen millions for the purpose—whence all those vicious, fat-bellied rednecks who preside over collectivized villages (and District Party Committees) today? Those pitiless oppressors of lonely old women and all defenseless people? How was the root of this predatory weed missed during dekulakization? Surely, heaven help us, they can't have sprung from the *activists*? . . .

The principle underlying dekulakization can also be clearly seen in the fate of the children. Take Shurka Dmitriyev, from the village of Masleno (Selishchenskie Kazarmy, near the Volkhov). He was thirteen when his father, Fyodor, died in 1925, and the only son in a family of girls. Who was to manage his father's holding? Shurka took it on. The girls and his mother accepted him as head of the family. A working peasant and an adult now, he exchanged bows with other adults in the street. He was a worthy successor to his hard-working father, and when 1929 came his bins were full of grain. Obviously a kulak! The whole family was driven out!

Adamova-Sliozberg has a moving story about meeting a girl called Motya, who was jailed in 1936 for leaving her place of banishment without permission to go to her native village, Svetlovidovo near Tarussa, *two thousand kilometers on foot*! Sportsmen are given medals for that sort of thing. She had been exiled with her parents in 1929 when she was a little schoolgirl, and deprived of schooling forever. Her teacher's pet name for her was "Motya, our little Edison": The child was not only an excellent pupil, but had an inventive turn of mind, had rigged up a sort of turbine worked by a stream, and invented other things for the school. After seven years she felt an urge to look just once more at the log walls of her unattainable school—and for that "little Edison" went to prison and then to a camp.

Did any child suffer such a fate in the nineteenth century?

Every *miller* was automatically a candidate for dekulakization—and what were millers and blacksmiths but the Russian village's best technicians?

Let us look at one village blacksmith. In fact, we'll start with his father, as Personnel Departments like to do. His father, Gordei Vasilyevich, served for twenty-five years in the Warsaw garrison, and earned enough silver to make a tin button: This soldier with twenty-five years' service was denied a plot of land. He had married a soldier's daughter while he was in the garrison, and after his discharge he went to his wife's native place, the village of Barsuki in the Krasnensky district. The village got him tipsy, and he paid off its tax arrears with half of his savings. With the other half he leased a mill from a landowner, but quickly lost the rest of his money in this venture. He spent his long old age as a herdsman and watchman. He had six daughters, all of whom he gave in marriage to poor men, and an only son, Trifon (their family name was Tvardovsky). The boy was sent away to serve in a haberdasher's shop, but fled back to Barsuki and found employment with the Molchanovs, who had the forge. After a year as an unpaid laborer, and four years as an apprentice, he became a smith himself, built a wooden house in the village of Zagorye, and married. Seven children were born (among them Aleksandr, the poet), and no one is likely to get rich from a forge. The oldest son, Konstantin, helped his father. If they smelted and hammered from one dawn to the next they could make five excellent steel axes, but the smiths of Roslavl, with their presses and their hired workmen, undercut their price. In 1929 their forge was still wood-built, they had only one horse, sometimes they had a cow and a calf, sometimes neither cow nor calf, and besides all this they had eight apple trees—you can see what bloodsuckers they were. . . . The Peasant Land Bank used to sell mortgaged estates on deferred payments. Trifon Tvardovsky had taken eleven desyatins[1] of wasteland, all overgrown with bushes, and the year of the Plague found them still sweating and straining to clear it: They had brought five desyatins into cultivation, and the rest they abandoned to the bushes. The collectivizers marked them down for dekulakization—there were only fifteen households in the village and somebody had to be found. They assessed the income from the forge at a fantastic figure, imposed a tax beyond the family's means, and when it was not paid on time: Get ready to move, you damned kulaks, you!

If a man had a brick house in a row of log cabins, or two stories in a row of one-story houses—there was your kulak: Get ready, you bastard, you've got sixty minutes! There aren't supposed to be any brick houses in the Russian village, there aren't supposed to be two-story houses! Back to the cave! You don't need a chimney for your fire! This is our great plan for transforming the country: History has never seen the like of it.

But we still have not reached the innermost secret. The better off were sometimes left where they were, provided they joined the kolkhoz[2] quickly, while the obstinate poor peasant who failed to apply was deported.

This is very important, the most important thing. The point of it all was not to dekulakize, but to force the peasants into the kolkhoz. Without frightening them to death there was no way of taking back the land which the Revolution had given them, and planting them on that same land as serfs.

It was a second Civil War—this time against the peasants. It was indeed the Great Turning Point, or as the phrase had it, the Great Break. Only we are never told what it was that broke.

It was the backbone of Russia.

---

[1] desyatin: 2.7 acres.
[2] kolkhoz: A Soviet collective farm.

We can find described in books, or even see in films, barns and pits in the ground, full of grain hoarded by bloodsuckers. What they won't show us is the handful of belongings earned in a lifetime of toil: the livestock, the utensils—things as close to the owner as her own skin—which a weeping peasant woman is ordered to leave forever.

What they will not show us are the little bundles with which the family are allowed onto the state's cart. We shall not learn that in the Tvardovsky house, when the evil moment came there was neither suet nor bread; their neighbor Kuzma saved them: He had several children and was far from rich himself, but brought them food for the journey.

The journey itself, the peasant's *Via Crucis*, is something which our socialist realists do not describe at all. Get them aboard, pack them off—and that's the end of the story. Episode concluded. Three asterisks, please.

They were loaded onto carts . . . if they were lucky enough to be taken in the warm months, but it might be onto sledges in a cruel frost, with children of all ages, babes in arms as well. In February, 1931, when hard frosts were interrupted only by blizzards, the strings of carts rolled endlessly through the village of Kochenevo (Novosibirsk oblast), flanked by convoy troops, emerging from the snowbound steppe and vanishing into the snowbound steppe again. Even going into a peasant hut for a warm-up required special permission from the convoy, which was given only for a few minutes, so as not to hold up the cart train. They all shuffled into the Narym marshes—and in those insatiable quagmires they all remained. Many of the children had already died a wretched death on the cruel journey.

This was the nub of the plan: The peasant's seed must perish together with the adults. Since Herod was no more, only the Vanguard Doctrine has shown us how to destroy utterly—down to the very babes. Hitler was a mere disciple, but he had all the luck: His murder camps have made him famous, whereas no one has any interest in ours at all.

It is hard to believe in such cruelty: On a winter evening out in the taiga they were told: You've arrived! Can human beings really behave like this? Well, they're moved by day so they arrive at nightfall—that's all there is to it. Hundreds and hundreds of thousands were carried into the wilds and dumped down like this, old men, women, children, and all.

As the Plague approached in 1929, all the churches in Archangel were closed: They were due to be closed anyway, but the very real need for somewhere to put the dekulakized hurried things along. Great streams of deported peasants poured through Archangel, and for a time the whole town became one big transit prison. Many-tiered sleeping platforms were put up in the churches, but there was no heat. Consignment after consignment of human cattle was unloaded at the station, and with dogs barking around them, the bast-shod went sullenly to church and a bed of planks. (S., then a boy, would never forget one peasant walking along with a shaft bow around his neck: He had been hurried away before he could decide what would be most useful. Another man carried a gramophone with a horn. Cameramen—there's work for you in this! . . .) In the Church of the Presentation, an eight-tiered bed platform which was not fastened to the wall collapsed in the night and several families were crushed. Their cries brought troops rushing to the church.

This was how they lived in that plague-stricken winter. They could not wash. Their bodies were covered with festering sores. Spotted fever developed. People were dying. Strict orders were given to the people of Archangel not to help the *special resettlers* (as the deported peasants were now called)! Dying peasants roamed the town, but no one could take a single one of them into his home, feed him, or carry tea out to him: The militia seized local inhabitants who tried to do so and took away their passports. A starving man would stagger along the street, stumble, fall—and die. But even the dead could not be picked up (besides the militia, plainclothesmen went around on the lookout for acts of kindness). At the same time market gardeners and livestock breeders from areas near big towns were also being expelled, whole villages at a time (once again—what about the theory that they were supposed to arrest exploiters only?), and the residents of Archangel themselves dreaded deportation. They were afraid even to stop and look down at a dead body.

The plight of these peasants differed from that of all previous and subsequent Soviet exiles in that they were banished not to a center of population, a place made habitable, but to the haunt of wild beasts, into the wilderness, to man's primitive condition. No, worse: Even in their primeval state our forebears at least chose places near water for their settlements. For as long as mankind has existed no one has ever made his home elsewhere. But for the *special settlements* the Cheka (not the peasants themselves—they had no right of choice) chose places on stony hillsides. Three or four kilometers off there might be convenient water meadows—but no, according to instructions no one was supposed to settle there. So the hayfields were dozens of kilometers away from the settlement, and the hay had to be brought in by boat. Sometimes settlers were bluntly *forbidden to sow grain crops.* (What they should grow was also determined by the Cheka!) Yet another thing we town folk do not understand—what it means to have lived from time immemorial with animals. A peasant's life is nothing without animals—and here he was condemned for many years never to hear neighing or lowing or bleating; never to saddle, never to milk, never to fill a trough.

On the river Chulym in Siberia, the special settlement of Kuban Cossacks was encircled with barbed wire and towers were put up, as though it were a prison camp.

Everything necessary seemed to have been done to ensure that these odious work fiends should die off quickly and rid our country of themselves and of bread. Indeed, many such special settlements died off to a man. Where they once stood, chance wayfarers are gradually burning what is left of the huts, and kicking the skulls out of sight.

No Genghis Khan ever destroyed so many peasants as our glorious *Organs,* under the leadership of the Party.

Take, for instance, the Vasyugan tragedy. In 1930, 10,000 families (60,000–70,000 people, as families then went) passed through Tomsk and from there were driven farther, at first on foot, down the Tom although it was winter, then along the Ob, then upstream along the Vasyugan—still over the ice. (The inhabitants of villages on the route were ordered out afterward to pick up the bodies of adults and children.) In the upper reaches of the Vasyugan and the Tara they were marooned on patches of firm ground in the marshes. *No food or tools were left for them.* The roads were impassable, and there was no way through to the world outside, except for two brushwood paths, one toward Tobolsk and one toward the Ob. Machine-gunners manned barriers on both paths and let no one through from the death camp. They started dying like flies. Desperate people came out to the barriers begging to be let through, and were shot on the spot.

They died off—every one of them.

And yet—exiles survived! Under their conditions it seems incredible—but live they did.

True, when during the war there was a shortage of reckless Russian fighting power at the front, they turned among others to the "kulaks": They must surely be Russians first and kulaks second! They were invited to leave the special settlements and the camps for the front to defend their sacred fatherland.

And—they went. . . .

Not all of them, however. N. Kh—v, a "kulak's" son—whose early years I used for Tyurin,[3] but whose subsequent biography I could not bring myself to recount—was given the chance, denied to Trotskyite and Communist prisoners, however much they yearned to go, of defending his fatherland. Without a moment's hesitation, Kh—v snapped back at the head of the Pris-

---

[3] Tyurin: Zek leader of the work "gang" to which Ivan Denisovich belonged in *One Day in the Life of Ivan Denisovich.*

oner Registration and Distribution Section: "It's your fatherland—you defend it, you dung-eaters! *The proletariat has no fatherland!*"

Marx's exact words, I believe.

The things that could have been done with such people if they had been allowed to live and develop freely!!!

The Old Believers—eternally persecuted, eternal exiles—they are the ones who three centuries earlier divined the ruthlessness at the heart of Authority! In 1950 a plane was flying over the vast basin of the Podkamennaya Tunguska. The training of airmen had improved greatly since the war, and the zealous aviator spotted something that no one before him had seen in twenty years: an unknown dwelling place in the taiga. He worked out its position. He reported it. It was far out in the wilds, but to the MVD all things are possible, and half a year later they had struggled through to it. What they had found were the Yaruyevo Old Believers. When the great and longed-for Plague began—I mean collectivization—they had fled from this blessing into the depths of the taiga, a whole village of them. And they lived there without ever poking their noses out, allowing only their headman to go to Yaruyevo for salt, metal fishing and hunting gear, and bits of iron for tools. Everything else they made themselves, and in lieu of money the headman no doubt came provided with pelts. When he had completed his business he would slink away from the marketplace like a hunted criminal. In this way the Yaruyevo Old Believers had won themselves twenty years of life! Twenty years of life as free human beings among the wild beasts, instead of twenty years of kolkhoz misery. They were all wearing homespun garments and homemade knee boots, and they were all exceptionally sturdy.

Well, these despicable deserters from the kolkhoz front were now all arrested, and the charge pinned on them was . . . guess what? Links with the international bourgeoisie? Sabotage? No, Articles 58-10, on Anti-Soviet Agitation (!?!?), and 58-11, on hostile organizations. (Many of them landed later on in the Dzhezkazgan group of Steplag, which is how I know about them.)

In 1946 some other Old Believers were stormed in a forgotten monastery somewhere in the backwoods by our valiant troops, dislodged (with the help of mortars, and the skills acquired in the Fatherland War), and floated on rafts down the Yenisei. Prisoners still, and still indomitable—the same under Stalin as they had been under Peter!—they jumped from the rafts into the waters of the Yenisei, where our Tommy-gunners finished them off.

Warriors of the Soviet Army! Tirelessly consolidate your combat training!

The Gulag Archipelago
Part VI, Chapter 7

Zeks at Liberty

We have had a chapter in this book on "Arrest." Do we need one now called "Release"?

Of those on whom the thunderbolt of arrest at one time or another fell (I shall speak only of 58's), I doubt whether a fifth, I should like to think that an eighth, lived to experience this "release."

And anyway, release is surely something everybody understands.

It has been described so often in world literature, shown in so many films: Unlock my dungeon—out into the sunshine—the crowd goes wild—open-armed relatives.

But there is a curse on those "released" under the joyless sky of the Archipelago, and as they move into freedom the clouds will grow darker.

Only in its long-windedness, its leisureliness, its otiose flourishes (what need has the law to hurry now?), does release differ from the lightning stroke of arrest. In all other respects, release is arrest all over again, the same sort of punishing transition from state to state, shattering your breast, the structure of your life and your ideas, and promising nothing in return.

Because in this country, whenever someone is released, somewhere an arrest must follow.

The space between two arrests—that is what release meant throughout the forty pre-Khrushchev years.

A life belt thrown between two islands—splash your way from camp to camp! . . . The walk from one camp boundary to the next—that's what is meant by release.

You will not be given a residence permit in a town, even a small one, nor will you ever get a decent job. In the camp at least you received your rations, but here you do not.

Moreover, your freedom of movement is illusory. . . .

Not "released," but "deprived of exile" would be the best description of these unfortunates. Denied the blessings of an exile decreed by fate, they cannot force themselves to go into the Krasnoyarsk taiga or the Kazakh desert, where there are so many of their own kind, so many *exes,* all around. No, they plunge deep into the tormented world of *freedom,* where everyone recoils from them, and where they are marked men, candidates for a new spell inside.

It's a vicious circle: no job without a residence permit, no residence permit unless you have a job. And without a job you have no bread card either. Former zeks did not know the rule that the MVD is required to find them work. And those who did know were afraid to apply in case they were *put back inside. . . .*

You may be free, but your troubles are only beginning.

But on the Kolyma there was really not much choice: They *hung on to* people. The discharged zek immediately signed a *voluntary* undertaking to go on working for Dalstroi. (Permission to leave for the mainland was even harder to obtain than your discharge.)

Just as a common illness develops differently in different people, the effects of freedom upon us varied greatly.

Its physical effects, to begin with . . . Some had overstrained themselves in the fight to end their time in the camps alive. They had endured it all like men of steel, consuming for ten whole years a fraction of what the body requires; working and slaving; breaking stones half-naked in freezing weather—and never catching cold. But once their sentence was served, once the inhuman pressure from outside was lifted, the tension inside them also slackened. Such people are destroyed by a sudden drop in pressure. The giant Chulpenyov, who had never caught cold in seven years as a lumberjack, contracted a variety of illnesses once he was freed.

There used to be a saying: The hard times brace you, and the soft times drive you to drink. Sometimes a man's teeth would all fall out in a year. Sometimes he would grow old overnight. Another man's strength would give out as soon as he got home, and he would die burned out.

Yet there were others who took heart when they were released. For them, it was time to grow younger and spread their wings. It comes as a sudden revelation: Life after all is so *easy* when you're free! There, on the Archipelago, the force of gravity is quite different, your legs are as heavy as an elephant's, but here they move as nimbly as a sparrow's. All the problems which tease and torment men who have always been free we solve with a single click of the tongue. We have our own cheerful standards: "Things have been worse!" Things used to be worse—so now everything is quite easy. We never get tired of repeating it: Things have been worse! Things have been worse!

But the pattern of a man's future may be even more firmly drawn by the emotional crisis which he undergoes at the moment of release. This crisis can take very different forms. Only on the threshold of the guardhouse do you begin to feel that what you are leaving behind you is both your prison and your homeland. This was your spiritual birthplace, and a secret part of your soul will remain here forever—while your feet trudge on into the dumb and unwelcoming expanse of *freedom*.

The camps bring out a man's character—but so does release! This is how Vera Alekseyevna Korneyeva, whom we have met before in our story, took leave of a Special Camp in 1951. "The five-meter gates closed behind me, and although I could hardly believe it myself, I was weeping as I walked out to freedom. Weeping for what? . . . I felt as though I had torn my heart away from what was dearest and most precious to it, from my comrades in misfortune. The gates closed—and it was all finished. I should never see those people again, never receive any news from them. *It was as though I had passed on to the next world. . . .*"

To the next world! . . . Release as a form of death. Perhaps we had not been released? Perhaps we had died, to begin a completely new life beyond the grave? A somewhat ghostly existence, in which we cautiously felt the objects about us, trying to identify them.

It was as though our freedom was stolen, not authentic. Those who felt like this seized their scrap of stolen freedom and ran with it to some lonely place. "While in the camp almost all my closest comrades thought, as I did, that if ever God allowed us to leave the camp alive, we would not live in towns, or even in villages, but somewhere in the depths of the forest. We would find work as foresters, rangers, or failing that, as herdsmen, and stay as far away as we could from people, politics, and all the snares and delusions of the world." (V. V. Pospelov) For some time after he was discharged Avenir Borisov shunned other people and took refuge in the countryside. "I felt like hugging and kissing every birch tree, every poplar. The rustle of fallen leaves (I was released in autumn) was like music to me, and tears came to my eyes. I didn't give a damn that I only got 500 grams of bread—I could listen to the silence for hours on end, and read books, too. Any sort of work seemed easy and simple now that I was free, the days flew by like hours, my thirst for life was unquenchable. If there is any happiness in the world at all, it is certainly that which comes to any zek in the first year of his life as a free man!"

It is a long time before people like this want to *own* anything: They remember that property is easily lost, vanishes into thin air. They have an almost superstitious aversion to new things, go on wearing the same old clothes, sitting on the same old broken chairs. One friend of mine had furniture so rickety that there was nothing you could safely sit or lean on. They made a joke of it. "This is the way to live—between camps." (His wife had also been inside.)

But people vary. And many crossed the line to freedom with quite different feelings (especially in the days when the Cheka-KGB seemed to be closing its eyes a little). Hurrah! I'm free! One thing I solemnly swear: Never to land inside again! Now I'm going all out to make up for what I've missed.

For two centuries Europe has been prating about equality—but how very different we all are! How unlike are the furrows life leaves on our souls. We can forget nothing in eleven years—or forget everything the day after. . . .

Each year on the anniversary of my arrest I organize myself a "zek's day": In the morning I cut off 650 grams of bread, put two lumps of sugar in a cup, and pour hot water on them. For lunch I ask them to make me some broth and a ladleful of thin mush. And how quickly I get back to my old form: By the end of the day I am already picking up crumbs to put in my mouth, and licking the bowl. The old sensations start up vividly.

I had also brought out with me, and still keep, my number patches. Am I the only one? In some homes they will be shown to you like holy relics.

Associations of former zeks gather once a year, varying the place from time to time, to drink and reminisce. "And strangely enough," says V. P. Golitsyn, "the pictures of the past conjured up are by no means all dark and harrowing; we have many warm and pleasant memories."

Another normal human characteristic. And not the worst.

"My identification number in camp began with *yery*," V. L. Ginzburg rapturously informs me. "And the passport they issued to me was in the 'Zk' series!"

You read it—and feel a warm glow. No, honestly—however many letters you receive, those from zeks stand out unmistakably. Such extraordinary toughness they show! Such clarity of purpose combined with such vigor and determination! In our day, if you get a letter completely free from self-pity, genuinely optimistic—it can only be from a former zek. They are used to the worst the world can do, and nothing can depress them.

I am proud to belong to this mighty race! We were not a race, but they made us one! They forged bonds between us, which we, in our timid and uncertain twilight, where every man is afraid of every other, could never have forged for ourselves. The orthodox and the stoolies automatically removed themselves from our midst when we were freed. We need no explicit agreement to support each other. We no longer need to test each other. We meet, look into each other's eyes, exchange a couple of words—and what need for further explanation? We are ready to help each other out. Our kind has friends everywhere. And there are millions of us!

Freedom has something else in store for former convicts—reunion with family and friends. Reunion of fathers with sons. Of husbands with wives. And it is not often that good comes out of these reunions. In the ten or fifteen years lived apart from us, how could our sons grow in harmony with us: Sometimes they are simply strangers, sometimes they are enemies. Nor are women who wait faithfully for their husbands often rewarded: They have lived so long apart, long enough for a person to change completely, so that only his name is the same. His experience and hers are too different—and it is no longer possible for them to come together again.

This is a subject which others can make into films and novels, but there is no room for it in this book.

The Gulag Archipelago

From the Afterword

Instead of my writing this book alone, the chapters should have been shared among people with special knowledge, and we should then have met in editorial conference and helped each other to put the whole in true perspective.

But the time for this was not yet. . . .

I had to conceal the project itself, my letters, my materials, to disperse them, to do everything in deepest secrecy. . . . I must explain that *never once* did this whole book, in all its parts, lie on the same desk at the same time. . . . The jerkiness of the book, its imperfections, are the true mark of our persecuted literature. Take the book for what it is.

I have stopped work on the book not because I regard it as finished, but because I cannot spend any more of my life on it.

Besides begging for indulgence, I want to cry aloud: When the time and the opportunity come, gather together, all you friends who have survived and know the story well, write your own commentaries to go with this book, correct and add to it where necessary (but do not make it too unwieldy, do not duplicate what is there already). Only then will the book be definitive. God bless your work!

8

THE RED WHEEL

Weighing in at a daunting six thousand pages, *The Red Wheel* (*Krasnoe koleso*) is Solzhenitsyn's multivolume epic on the 1917 revolutionary cataclysm that ushered in the Soviet regime, as well as the events leading up to the revolution. It is arguably the author's *chef d'oeuvre* and has been described by Solzhenitsyn himself as "the chief artistic design of my life." This authorial claim has been met with perplexity, and sometimes even with derision, by critics for whom the events that Solzhenitsyn describes are far removed from the concerns of contemporary Western readers, too alien or "Russian," their comprehension too demanding to be of real interest to the harried contemporary reader. But Solzhenitsyn counters that the Russian revolutions of 1917 were the central event of the twentieth century—the decisive turning point from which so many of its other evils flowed. The destinies of not only Russia but also Europe and the wider world were irreversibly shaped by the events described in this work. They are well worth the supreme effort of historical recovery to which Solzhenitsyn has devoted the central decades of his life.

In *The Red Wheel*, Solzhenitsyn aims to bring to light the underlying complex meaning of "1917," to uncover the multiple sources of the Soviet tragedy. To begin with, he writes in explicit opposition to both Tolstoyan fatalism and Marxist historical determinism. Solzhenitsyn emphatically denies that there was anything "inevitable" or "fated" about the victory of Bolshevism in October 1917. If the principal noncommunist actors in the drama had made more responsible or brave decisions, if Russia's most capable statesman in two centuries, Pyotr Stolypin, had not been assassinated in September 1911, things might have turned out quite differently in the Russian twentieth century. Solzhenitsyn's work is a vindication of human freedom and responsibility against any view of history that makes human beings mere playthings of impersonal historical forces. *The Red Wheel* is thus philosophical historiography as well as literary art. Solzhenitsyn combines the two in order to display the role of choice and accident in the great and terrible events that shaped the destiny of the twentieth century.

But the repudiation of revolutionary historicism was not central to Solzhenitsyn's purposes when he first embarked on this ambitious project in the late 1930s. Long before he made his definitive spiritual and intellectual break with communism, the October Revolution and the events leading up to it fascinated the young Solzhenitsyn. In 1936 and 1937, as an aspiring writer who was very much a committed Marxist-Leninist, Solzhenitsyn set out to write an epic centered on the events of the First World War and the Russian Revolution. Remarkably, he was able to incorporate a good deal of the material that he wrote at that time into the first chapters of *August 1914*, published in Russian (in the West) in 1971 and a year later in English. In the late 1930s, Solzhenitsyn was also able to collect information on the "Samsonov catastrophe" that plays such a central role in the same volume.

When Solzhenitsyn returned to the work in the 1960s and '70s, the design of *The Red Wheel* had grown to breathtaking proportions. He now envisioned his narrative in no less than twenty "knots"—"discrete periods of time"—covering the period from 1914 to 1922, from the outbreak of the First World War until the consolidation of Bolshevik control in Russia at the end of the Civil War. (He also foresaw a series of five additional epilogues that would carry the narrative forward to 1945). When it became apparent to Solzhenitsyn that it would be beyond his—or anyone's—powers to complete this project in a single lifetime, he chose to limit himself to four still very sizable "knots": the volumes that would be published as *August 1914*, *November 1916* (because of a thirteen-day gap between Russian and Western calendars at the time, the title of the Russian original is *October 1916*), *March 1917*, and *April 1917*. Only the first two of these knots have appeared in English (in the remarkably faithful translations rendered by the late Harry Willetts). The nine chapters from *March 1917* and the two chapters from *April 1917* that are included in this reader are the first excerpts from these books to appear in English.

Like *The Gulag Archipelago*, *The Red Wheel* merits being called "an experiment in literary investigation" (although the comparison is inexact, since *The Red Wheel* has fictional characters and thus fictional episodes and *The Gulag Archipelago* does not). Not only does it combine history and literature in truly novel ways, but it freely experiments with literary forms and devices that stretch the limits of the conventional novel, even that of so-called historical fiction. It makes ready use of historical documents, excerpts from newspapers, cinematic or screen sequences (two of which—chapter 58 of *August 1914* and chapter 418 of *March 1917*—are reproduced below), and aptly placed Russian proverbs (see, for example, the conclusion of chapter 69 of *August 1914*). Just as Solzhenitsyn's politics attempts to bring together respect for tradition with an ungrudging recognition of the need for reform and a place for innovation, so too does his conception and practice of literary art combine apparently heterogeneous elements.

The Red Wheel is a unique work that (to cite the entry on Solzhenitsyn in the *Dictionary of Literary Biography*) "eludes ready classification in terms of genre." It is a "novel" that contains many chapters of "dramatized history" as well as carefully researched and detail-filled chapters on Tsar Nicholas II, Prime Minister Pyotr Stolypin, Lenin in Zurich and in Petrograd, and the Duma and the principal political groupings (Octobrists, Kadets, and assorted revolutionaries) in Russia on the eve of the revolutions of 1917. It is a work of faithful historical reconstruction that includes a central role for fictional characters such as Colonel Georgi Vorotyntsev, a keen and capable strategist who is burning with love of country. Vorotyntsev has no tolerance for ineffectual and timeserving Tsarist courtiers and generals, even as he repudiates the self-destructive nihilism of Russia's homegrown revolutionaries. If the tough-minded reformist Prime Minister Pyotr Stolypin is the "historical" protagonist of *The Red Wheel*, Vorotyntsev is undoubtedly its "fictional" protagonist. His patriotism and commitment to the revitalization of Russia are equally at odds with the irresponsible histrionics of Russia's *soi-disant* liberals ("false liberals" Solzhenitsyn calls them, as they never manage to see enemies on their left) and the blindness and ineptitude of the Tsarist old guard. He embodies the patriotic single-mindedness of those intelligent, forward-looking officers who represented Russia's best hopes for renewal amidst the devastation of war and revolution (see *April 1917*, chapter 186).

The various "knots" of *The Red Wheel* capture certain crucial moments that reveal the nature of the unfolding revolutionary juggernaut, the "red wheel" of the book's title. These huge, sprawling books are "novelistic" in a real but qualified sense. Above all, they are *polyphonic* works that allow dozens of characters (including those for whom Solzhenitsyn has no sympathy, such as Lenin) to speak from their own points of view. This does not preclude the author from speaking in his own voice, particularly in the more historical chapters. The movement back and forth from historical-political analyses to fictional representations of its heroes such as Sanya Lazhenitsyn (a fictional representation of Solzhenitsyn's father—see chapter six of *November 1916* below) as well as Vorotyntsev, no doubt taxes those who have little interest in the political and spiritual fate of Russia or even in the Russian revolution. In the first instance, this is a book directed especially at Russians and students of Russia. But for all those who truly share—or come to share—Solzhenitsyn's desire to comprehend the underlying meaning of 1917, for those who have the discipline to encounter and engage with an artful mixture of history, philosophy, and literature in the pursuit of a truth that goes beyond narrowly nationalistic limits and concerns, Solzhenitsyn's masterwork will delight and instruct.

August 1914 is the first and best known of the four knots that constitute *The Red Wheel*. By concentrating on a couple of crucial weeks at the beginning of the First World War, Solzhenitsyn highlights the underlying sclerosis and vulnerability of a Russian old regime whose stability was erroneously taken for granted by revolutionaries and reactionaries alike. In fact, the regime's ignorance and incompetence reared its head at the Battle of Tannenberg in East Prussia, a great military confrontation between the Russian 1st and 2nd armies and the German 8th Army that took place between August 17 and September 1, 1914. Tannenberg was not only a catastrophic defeat—with ninety thousand Russian troops killed or captured—but also a portent of disasters to come. Much of *August 1914* is dedicated to describing the mistakes, misjudgments, and false assumptions that culminated in the Russian defeat at Tannenberg. These mistakes even included the failure to encrypt messages that were sent to commanders on the front!

The commander of the Russian 2nd Army, General Aleksandr Samsonov, is in important respects an admirable figure: He is decent, pious, and imbued with a deep and abiding love of "Mother Russia." He embodies the best of old Russia but not a few of its vices as well. Influenced by the "spiritualism" of Tolstoy and by an excessively "fatalistic" confidence in Providence that borders on superstition, he was finally incapable of providing clear and effective leadership. He lacked the imagination to act decisively, to transform situations through his own initiative. The suicide in the forests of East Prussia of this faithful and tragic figure is movingly described in chapter 48 of *August 1914.* Samsonov's suicide provides an opportunity for shameless self-exculpation on the part of a military and political class that refuses to take responsibility for the mistakes that led to the disaster at Tannenberg.

This collective abdication of responsibility leads to one of the most dramatic confrontations in the entire work. In chapter 82 of *August 1914,* Colonel Vorotyntsev, in the presence of the supreme commander of Russia's Imperial forces, Grand Duke Nikolai Nikolaevich, takes the leaders of Russia's armed forces to task for their vicious scapegoating of General Samsonov and for their criminal refusal to come to terms with the generalized corruption and incompetence of the regime. For this act of courage, Vorotynstev is posted to an isolated front, where he does his duty for the duration of a war the wisdom of which he does not hesitate to question.

With the publication of *August 1914,* Solzhenitsyn lost many admirers and supporters in liberal circles in both Russia and the West. It ought to have been apparent to all fair-minded critics that Solzhenitsyn was no uncritical defender of the Russian old regime. His was a devastating indictment of a regime that had seemingly lost the ability to renew itself. But Solzhenitsyn clearly had no sympathy for Russia's revolutionaries or for those false liberals who had no other aim than to contribute to the subversion of the existing social and political order (this theme is developed to great effect in chapter 7 of *November 1916*). Solzhenitsyn wrote as a patriot and Christian who supported an exiguous "middle line" of development between reactionaries and revolutionaries. This became particularly clear in the augmented edition of *August 1914* published in Russian in 1983 and in English in 1989.

In eight remarkable chapters of that work (the so-called Stolypin cycle), Solzhenitsyn painted a portrait of the statesman Pyotr Stolypin, scourge of both the revolutionary left and the reactionary right and the last, best hope for Russia's salvation. Prime minister of Russia from 1906 until 1911, Stolypin was abidingly concerned with promoting far-reaching agrarian reforms that would lead to the creation of a "solid class of peasant proprietors" in Russia. He believed that a property-owning peasantry would provide the social basis for a revitalized monarchy in Russia. He was a "liberal conservative" who rejected pan-Slavist delusions and who advocated a monarchy that respected the rule of law, and governed in cooperation with a "society" that had an increasing stake in the existing social order. But Stolypin was shot (in the presence of the Tsar) at the Kiev opera house in September 1911. His assassin was, quite strikingly, a double agent of the secret police and revolutionary terrorists.

In chapter 69 of *August 1914*, Solzhenitsyn provides a powerful description of Stolypin's last days. It gradually dawns on the dying prime minister that he will not survive the assassination attempt that has been made against him. Stolypin is anxious to discuss the future of Russia with an emperor who does not sufficiently appreciate how fragile was the prime minister's achievement in "defeating revolution and restoring his country to him in good health." The dying Stolypin mentally reviews his five-year tenure as prime minister—the violence and terror that had torn the country apart, to be sure, but also the triumphant trip to Siberia in 1910 to survey the first dramatic effects of the agrarian reforms that were beginning to lay the foundations for a new class of citizen proprietors in a free and lawful Russia. Stolypin leaves the world with firm confidence in God's purposes but with an aching sense that his work has only begun. He knows that Russia lacks a sufficiently intelligent and vigorous political class, and he fears the "corruptors" who have been at their work for half a century now. He laments the fact that civil society is imbued with a rabid and malignant hostility to imperial power, and he realizes that his reform program will need time to take firm root.

In exploring a relatively quiescent period, *November 1916* allows Solzhenitsyn to survey painstakingly the full range of left-liberal and revolutionary opposition to the existing regime, the very sects and sectarians who would come to the forefront during the revolutionary year of 1917. Solzhenitsyn draws a particularly insightful portrait of Lenin during his Zurich exile. The future leader of the Soviet state is disheartened about the prospects for revolution in Russia (so much for the alleged "science" of historical inevitability). He is shown in all his conspiratorial glory, manipulating the socialist community abroad and expressing his limitless contempt for peaceful, prosperous, and "bourgeois" Switzerland (where he laughably suggests that the worldwide "socialist" revolution might begin). Yet only five months later, Lenin (in the final chapters of *March 1917*) is plotting with the Germans to return in a sealed train car to a Russia that has been transformed beyond recognition by revolutionary agitation and chaos. The road has been prepared for a seizure of power by the most committed and fanatical of revolutionary sectarians and sects.

November 1916 is arguably the most explicitly Christian of Solzhenitsyn's novels. Its Christian sensibility and symbolism are especially apparent in chapters 5, 6, and 75 (the latter two chapters are reproduced here). In the first two chapters, readers are privy to a moving and instructive discussion between Sanya Lazhenitsyn and his army chaplain, Father Severyan. The half-pacifist Lazhenitsyn (who had initially volunteered for the army because he felt "sorry for Russia") is overwhelmed with feelings of guilt for having to kill his fellow human beings with seeming impunity. In response, the sympathetically drawn cleric gives voice to a Christian wisdom that affirms that war, especially in defense of state and nation, is "not the vilest form of evil." The state, for all its limitations, is an indispensable precondition of the common good, a necessary instrument for avoiding the evils that flow from imperfect human nature. These chapters powerfully emphasize the distinction, even chasm, between properly Christian wisdom and the secular humanitarianism that too often goes by that name. The views expressed by Father Severyan (on the disgraceful treatment of Russia's Old Believers, the limits of Voltairean and Tolstoyan humanitarianism, the fact that war is not the greatest of evils and that no religion has a monopoly on the truth) converge with Solzhenitsyn's most deeply held convictions on all of these subjects.

The final chapter of *November 1916* (chapter 75, "An Arduous Confession") is among the most luminous in *The Red Wheel*. In that chapter a second-level fictional character named Zina, who had a disastrous affair and a child out of wedlock, and whose self-preoccupation has led to the death of her child, finds herself drawn ineluctably into a church in the city of Tambov. Through the act of confession, she begins to experience unconditional forgiveness, the forgiveness of a God who is Love. In this most "novelistic" of chapters, Solzhenitsyn conveys his deep conviction that the crisis afflicting Russia and the world is in no small part a spiritual crisis, a crisis of men who have forgotten their humanizing dependence upon God and their common need for repentance and spiritual healing.

The third and fourth "knots" of *The Red Wheel, March 1917* and *April 1917,* chronicle the massive chaos unleashed by the "February revolution" of 1917. It is Solzhenitsyn's judgment that the "February revolution" is *the* formative event in modern Russian history. Far from being a positive phenomenon that brought liberty to the long-oppressed Russian people, it was marked by chaotic violence from the start, a disintegration of order, and the *diktat* of radicals wielding ever more revolutionary slogans and demands, while the supposedly triumphant liberal forces cowered in impotence or displayed limitless indulgence toward the Bolsheviks, thus allowing them to seize power almost effortlessly in October 1917. As demonstrated in chapter 27 of *April 1917*, the disintegration of society was so rapid that no power could be marshaled even for so small a task as properly treating and honoring the disabled veterans who had fought and given their limbs in World War I. No one, it turns out, can protect and defend them from thuggery.

And there are universal lessons to be drawn from these very Russian developments: Liberty can never arise from the willful destruction of a social order that is open to change or amelioration, and lawful government cannot coexist with the delirium and nihilism of revolutionary mobs. There is another. As Solzhenitsyn put it in a 1979 interview with the BBC Russian service, the refusal of liberals and socialists in the Duma and the Provisional Government to stand up to the hard left reflects a "process of weakening and self-capitulation" that has been "repeated on a worldwide scale since those days."

In a series of short, dramatic chapters, Solzhenitsyn conveys the anarchy that took hold of the streets of Petersburg during the February revolution. In scene after scene, the reader witnesses the inebriation of crowds who are caught up in a playful but deadly revolutionary carnival. The engineer Obodovsky, who is broadly sympathetic to the revolution but who is no friend of Bolshevism or of mob violence, reflects on the peculiarity of the revolutionary mob in chapter 17 of *March 1917*: "A crowd was such a peculiar kind of creature! At once human and inhuman. It ran on legs and had heads aplenty, but once a part of it, each individual was absolved of his normal responsibilities, and his strength swelled in proportion to the number in the crowd, even as they drained him of his willpower." Yet the unhistorical legend persists that the February revolution created a working democracy rather than revolutionary chaos and delirium. Moreover, that "democracy" is said to be the only moment of authentic liberty in a millennium of unremitting Russian autocracy and oppression. Solzhenitsyn demonstrates the opposite of both propositions.

Even amidst these frightful events, some noble souls continued to do their duty. In chapters 101, 122, and 185 of *March 1917*, the reader is introduced to Colonel Balkashin, the commander of a "Wheeled Battalion" in Petrograd's Lesnoi district. This decent and honorable military officer, cut off from instructions from his superiors, attempts to maintain order in his own compound amidst an increasingly threatening crowd. He and his men are brutally gunned down, a display that reveals the true nature of a revolutionary mob severed from law and morality. And the fictional Vorotyntsev does his best to organize midlevel Russian officers to save what can possibly be saved amidst the vacuum of power—and the moral and political disorder—that defined the "democratic" dispensation inaugurated in February 1917. Solzhenitsyn clearly suggests that people can act even amidst wreckage, that in history no one is doomed by impersonal forces.

In choosing excerpts from *March 1917* and *April 1917*, the editors have been careful to select chapters that convey both the spirit of the work (and that time) as well as Solzhenitsyn's impressive artistry. The sundry "street scenes," the dramatic account of the abdication of the Tsar, and the portrayal of the assassination of Admiral Nepenin contain some of the most vivid and captivating writing in Solzhenitsyn's entire corpus. It should also be noted that the selections from *March 1917* are drawn from two volumes of extracts from that work *(The Revolution at Last)* that were published in Russia in 2001. Along with two other volumes of extracts (*Stolypin and the Tsar* and *Lenin in Zurich and Petrograd*) published that same year, these "frigates" were sent sailing into the new Russian book market to suit modern times, rather than staying in port and forcing every reader to buy and process the full work. Solzhenitsyn's decision to publish these extracts reflects his keen desire to have his readers recover the truth about the events leading up to the revolution and especially to correct the erroneous and pernicious identification of the anarchy and unrest of February 1917 with "true democracy." The relevance of these concerns for postcommunist Russia is readily apparent.

The Red Wheel, a quintessentially "Russian" book, reminds us that the searching exploration of certain pregnant particulars provides the best access to universal truth. It conveys quite palpably that the destinies of Russia and the West have intertwined and will inexorably continue to intertwine.

The Red Wheel
August 1914 – Chapter 48

The Final Hours of Commander Samsonov

They led him, carried him. His body was moved by others. He himself could only meditate. The shifting strata had finally collapsed. The dust had settled. The veil was rent. The air was cleared. All vague and uncertain movements were over. The world as it was now, and the world as it had been in times past, stood out clearly.

The tight blindfold was removed from his reason, and his heart had shed a great burden. From the time when he had inspected the troops at Orlau, thanked them, and taken his leave of them, the weight had disappeared of itself and his mind had been easier. Although the handful of soldiers on the hill at Orlau could not speak for the whole army or all Russia, it was their forgiveness his soul had thirsted for. He gave little thought to a possible trial for dereliction of duty: Those who are highly placed are not put on trial, they are reprimanded, kept on the reserve for a while, given a fresh command. "Shame doesn't eat your eyes out." They might, of course, appoint a commission of inquiry, but it would search in vain—no one would ever be able to disentangle the facts, it was too late already. What had happened was part of God's plan and men were not meant to understand it, or not yet.

No longer a proud horseman, but a rider in a cart, jolting over roots and tussocks, bumping shoulders with Postovsky, but exchanging never a word with him, in fact forgetting him altogether, Samsonov thought his long thoughts.

He did not think about Army Group HQ and Zhilinsky, did not dwell on the insults and humiliation which had tried him so sorely in the past few days. He made no effort to think up proofs that Zhilinsky was more to blame for all that had happened than he was himself. His resentment had cooled to a hard bright realization that Zhilinsky would wriggle out of it, get off scot-

318

free. It no longer galled him. It was strange that an accusation of treachery from that contemptible person had been so hurtful just a little while ago, and had affected his handling of whole corps.

He was thinking rather of something else: how hard it was for the Emperor to choose himself worthy helpers. Self-seeking mediocrities are more pushy than the good and loyal, they acquire great ingenuity in flaunting their specious loyalty and their specious talents. Nobody ever sees as many liars and deceivers as the Tsar does—and how could he, a mere human, acquire the godlike perspicacity to penetrate the darkness of other men's souls? So he became the victim of wrong choices, and these self-seekers were sapping the Russian state like worms gnawing at a mighty tree.

These were thoughts for a man on horseback, not one jolting and rocking in a cart.

Samsonov's reflections, calm and detached, had no relevance to the object of the staff group's journey, which was to find a chink in the encircling forces and slip through it. When his musings were interrupted he did not immediately understand what people were telling him: that the road to Janow, by which they were traveling, had been cut, that there were Germans on the road ahead of them, and that the way out of the forest was under fire. His staff officers suggested changing direction from south to east, making a detour all the way around to Willenberg. Willenberg at least ought to be in Russian hands (Blagoveshchensky's). Samsonov nodded—Samsonov had no objection.

They had to go back the way they had come, losing versts and time, then turn into a convenient path to the east. Samsonov took no interest in any of it—the choice of path, or the loss of time and distance. A protective shutter in his mind barred the way to all possible unpleasantnesses and annoyances from the outside world. The faster and more irremediably external events flowed, the slower the motions in Samsonov's own body, the more deliberate his thoughts.

He had meant well and the results were extremely bad, as bad as they possibly could be. But if he with the best intentions could be left without a stitch to cover his nakedness, what would the actions of the selfish lead to in this war? And if Russia's defeats were repeated, would there not be another upheaval like the one that followed the Japanese war?

It was painful and terrifying to think that he, General Samsonov, had served his Emperor and Russia so ill.

It was getting on toward evening. The sun was quite low. The majority opinion among the staff officers favored an attempt to turn south again and look for a way through there. The commander nodded agreement to everything they said, without really trying to understand.

The terrain had become forbidding: They had left the dry elevation with its reddened pines and were riding over low-lying ground overgrown with bushes, along paths where the wheels were slowed by tacky sand, fording too many unexpected streams and drainage channels.

On a number of occasions the Cossack scouts rode forward, but the chatter of machine guns was shortly heard and they returned—occupied territory ahead.

What sort of Cossacks were they anyway, this squadron escorting HQ staff? Second- or third-rate, flimsy fellows, timidly diving into the bushes as soon as the firing started. It almost seemed that Russia's supply of Cossacks had dried up too. The ataman of the Semirechye and Don Cossacks hadn't a single good squadron to his name!

He needed to think, to do a lot more thinking before the day was out. Postovsky or Filimonov ought to be able to deputize for him to the extent of leading the little staff group, but they had both gone soft. The greedy, predatory look had been wiped from Filimonov's face and he was puffing and sniffling as though he had influenza. Near the village of Saddek, no more than four versts from the highway, the younger staff officers asked permission from the commander himself to attack with the Cossack squadron and try to break through. As they emerged from the forest there was more than a verst between them and the higher ground along the road, and the treeless terrain gave little prospect of success, but the officers were so insistent on making one try at least that Samsonov consented, as though in a dream, without really thinking about it.

Colonel Vyalov tried to talk the Cossacks into attacking. They jibbed, didn't want to leave the forest, objected that their horses were exhausted, whereupon Staff Captain Ducimetière cried, "Hurrah!" and galloped off alone with drawn sword in the direction of the machine gun. Vyalov and two other officers followed, and only then did the Cossacks stir. They charged in disorder, firing randomly into the air, whooping and yelping, not so much to scare the enemy as to give themselves courage. However, three of them were unhorsed, and fifty paces from the machine gun the others turned off into the trees. Seeing this disgraceful conduct restored Samsonov's powers of action and decision. He called them all off, forbade the officers to try a second attack, on foot this time, and ordered them all to retrace their steps northward and then turn east again toward Willenberg.

Once more they rode into the pine wood, darker now, scrambled onto the stony track, and moved quickly and unhindered in the direction of Willenberg. But as they emerged into the twilight three versts from the town they met a Polish peasant and asked him whether there were many Russian soldiers there.

He scratched his head. *"Nie, panowie, tam wcale niema Rosjan, tylko Niemcy, duo Niemeow dzis przyszlo."*[1]

The staff officers drooped. They sat and despaired. Where could Blagoveshchensky and his corps be?

Samsonov seated himself on a tree stump, and his head sank onto his chest. If even the army staff was too late to break out, what must await the army as a whole the next day?

The staff officers discussed the situation: They would have to steal through somewhere during the night, that very night. It was their last chance.

Samsonov saw the hand of God in it. Who had darkened his mind and made him leave his army? Yes, the hand of God was in it! He steeled himself and announced: "You all have my permission to leave, gentlemen. General Postovsky, take charge of the breakthrough of HQ staff. I am returning to the 15th Corps."

(The 15th Corps or the 13th, it made no difference—in those twilight minutes twenty-five versts to Samsonov's rear the two corps were inextricably entangled at the fatal forest crossroads, and were rapidly ceasing to exist as separate units.)

However, the staff officers, irrespective of rank, rushed as one man to surround the commander and urge on him, speaking all at once but each with arguments of his own, the impossibility, the error, the absurdity, the impermissibility, the wrongheadedness of his decision. He was in command of the whole army . . . his duty to the flanking corps . . . his duty to the Northwestern Army Group . . . were just as important . . . he and only he could reunite the forces remaining to them in a matter of hours and so save Russia from invasion by the enemy. . . .

Yesterday, when they objected to leaving Neidenburg for Nadrau, they had not dared to protest so emphatically. But a great deal had happened in the hours between.

Samsonov sat on the low throne which the forest had grown for him, listened to them, and closed his eyes. He was thinking how uncongenial to him his staff officers all were: They had been brought together by chance, yet all of them, in heart and mind, were alien. He felt some kinship only with Krymov, whom he had sent away.

The staff officers' arguments were solidly built, but to Samsonov they had a hollow ring. He did not reproach them with it, but he could tell from their voices that their concern was not for him or for the army but for themselves. None of them wanted to go back with him, but army discipline made it impossible for them to escape without him.

---

[1] No, there are no Russians there at all, only Germans. A lot of Germans arrived today.

Yet Samsonov no longer had the strength to argue with a dozen importunate subordinates; worse still, he no longer had the strength to set off into the dark distance with only his orderly, Kupchik, for company.

There was a third possibility—to summon all the fighting units to this place and try to fight their way out—that no one suggested. It occurred to no one. The question was: how to escape? "We won't get out of it with that gang"—looking at the Cossack squadron, every man of them had the same thought. The Cossacks were dismissed, to make their way out as best they could while the staff officers continued on foot. It seemed sensible to suppose that, in the night and on bad roads, they would have a better chance without horses. The local inhabitants were Poles, and sympathetic.

Samsonov sat on his stump, beard on chest, oblivious. The defeated general was calmer than any of his staff.

He was waiting for the fuss, which distracted him from his thoughts, to end, waiting for the smooth motion to begin again so that he could think calmly.

But even when they were rid of the Cossacks, even after unbridling and releasing the horses, the staff officers were still not ready for the night march, still found things to fuss about. In the fading gray light, with a glimmer of moonlight showing, Samsonov could dimly see that a hole was being dug and the officers laying in it something from their pockets. He saw it, but attached no importance to it. He was commander no longer, he had ceased ordering them to do this and not to do that. He was waiting, endlessly it seemed, to be led away.

Postovsky, polite but insistent, approached and loomed over him. "Your Excellency! Permit me to remark. We don't know what may happen to us.... If we should fall into the hands of the enemy ... there may be documents or badges they shouldn't get.... Why present them with a prize like that?"

Prize? Badges? Samsonov did not understand.

"Aleksandr Vasilievich, we're burying everything we don't need ... marking the spot ... We shall come back later, or send somebody.... If you've got any documents ... anything that gives away names....

From the eminence that Samsonov had reached in that long day these worries seemed piffling. But here came the younger officers, strutting up to tell him earnestly that he must not let the enemy know who their prisoner was—let them think that he had slipped through their fingers: After all, if a regimental flag couldn't be carried away safely, it was cut up or burned or buried, but never surrendered....

How quickly things had changed. A quarter of an hour ago he could have consented or refused to go with them. They had implored him to go, it was all-important to them. Now, they didn't much care what he thought they should do. He was like a golden idol, the god of a savage tribe—if they brought him back safely the curse would not fall on their heads.

Not on theirs. But on his.

Now they were moving, in single file, with Samsonov somewhere in the middle and Kupchik behind him carrying the saddlecloth from his abandoned horse. The faint light of the moon filtering into the less dense parts of the forest made it possible to distinguish tree trunks, thickets, piles of brushwood, and clearings, but only very close up. And they could see each other only at a very short distance. Then there was no moon, and those in the lead almost groped their way along, stopping to consult a luminous compass. When they did so all the others stopped too. It was quite impossible to go straight ahead: They had to get around holes in the ground, boggy patches, thickets, and every time they had to make sure of their direction again.

General Samsonov was at liberty to resume his meditations. There was no more talk, nothing at all to prevent him from thinking his thoughts through.

Only he found that there was nothing more for him to think about. Nothing at all. All the thinking had been done, all the decisions made. The room was swept and garnished. All that was left was remembrance.

The memories that came to him were not of his rural childhood in Yekaterinoslav, not of his cadet school, not of the cavalry training establishment, not of the many, many places in which he had served, his eventful career, those who had served with him. Shutting out all else, the Cossack cathedral on the hill loomed in his mind again; huge, menacing, with its intricately patterned brickwork. He was born in the Ukraine, had been in Moscow, lived in St. Petersburg, in Warsaw, in Turkestan, and beyond the Amur River, yet—though he was no son of the Don by birth—he was carried irresistibly to the broad-browed hill at Novocherkassk. Not to the upper part, where Yermak's monument rears up, but downhill toward the Kreshchensky descent, where, on a granite plinth raised only slightly above the cobblestones, lie a Caucasian cloak and a tall Caucasian cap in bronze, as though their owner, Baklanov, had carelessly flung them down and just left.

Left for his grave, in the vaults of the church.

For a soldier's burial.

With victories to be carved in granite.

Walking was difficult. His legs had lost the habit, and worse still was his shortness of breath: Just walking, with nothing to carry, made him wheeze and pant as though he had asthma.

When a man loses his position of superiority, his means of locomotion, and his means of protection, his body is put to the test, and he finds that the truth about him is expressed, not by his general's tabs, but by a flagging heart, lungs that refuse to expand fully, as though they were two-thirds blocked, weak legs, and unreliable feet that tread awkwardly, stub the ground, stumble over tussocks, moss beds, and fallen branches. If anything can give him pleasure it is not that he is making progress, not the thought that he may yet scrape through, but the holdups ahead, when everybody has to stop and he can lean against a trunk and try to get his breath.

Samsonov was ashamed to ask for a rest, but out of consideration for him they stopped every hour and sat down. Kupchik always spread the horse blanket with alacrity for the commander, whose aching legs were grateful for a chance to stretch out and rest.

But they could not sit for long. The short night and their last chance were hurrying away. Around midnight the stars were obscured and it was too dark to see anything at all. The little group plodded on, single file, informed of each other's whereabouts only by the snapping of twigs, heavy breathing, or the occasional touch of a hand. The path got worse—at one moment boggy ground squelched underfoot, at the next unthinned bushes or dense clusters of young trees barred the way. They assumed that it would be dangerous to stray in the direction of Willenberg. But there were other dangers—they might bump into a German patrol, or get lost altogether. They clung together, called to each other in whispers. There were no more stops for rest. When they came to a ditch Kupchik and the Cossack captain helped Samsonov across, almost dragging him.

Samsonov was oppressed by the burden of his body. Only his body was pulling him on to more pain and suffering, more shame and disgrace. To escape from the disgrace, the pain, the heaviness he had only to release himself from his body. It would he a blissful liberation, it would be like taking the first deep breath after the lungs have been congested.

Only yesterday he had been an idol to whom his staff officers looked for redemption. Since midnight he had been a fallen idol, a millstone around their necks.

Slipping away from Kupchik was the one difficulty. The Cossack orderly kept close behind his general, touching his back or his hand from time to time. But Samsonov tricked him: As they went around a thicket of bushes he stepped aside and stood hidden.

The heavy steps, the crackling, the snapping, passed him by, grew distant, then he could no longer hear them.

There was silence. The perfect silence of peacetime, with no reminders of battle. The only sound was that of the fresh night breeze sighing in the treetops. This was not an enemy forest, it was neither German nor Russian. It was God's forest, giving shelter to any of His creatures.

Samsonov rested his weight against a tree trunk and listened to the forest—close to his ear, the rustle of peeling pine bark; closer to the sky, the cleansing wind.

He felt more and more at peace with himself. He had served long years in the army, had accepted danger and sudden death as his fate, had faced death and been ready for it, yet had never known that it could be as easy as shedding a burden.

But suicide was accounted a sin.

A faint sound—his revolver cocked itself. Samsonov laid his upturned cap on the ground with the revolver in it. He took off his sword and kissed it. He fumbled for the locket with his wife's picture and kissed it.

He took a few steps to an open space. The sky had clouded over. Only one star was visible—obscured for a while, it peered out again. He sank to his knees on the warm pine needles. Not knowing where the east was, he looked up at the star as he prayed.

At first he prayed in remembered words, then without words, kneeling, gazing at the sky, breathing. Then he groaned aloud, shamelessly, like a dying forest creature.

"O Lord, forgive me if Thou canst, and take me into Thy rest. Thou seest that I could do no other, and can do no other."

The Red Wheel
August 1914 — Chapter 58

Through the Eyes of a Horse

Screen[1]

  =   A horse's head.

Not a thoroughbred. A bay horse. A Russian peasant's
horse. A defenseless, unresentful face.

As well able as any human face to express despair: What
is happening to me? What have I come to? So many
deaths I have seen! And now I am going to die myself.

Its collar has not been removed. Or even eased.

It is exhausted, its legs can scarcely support it. It has not
been fed, not been unharnessed, only flogged unmer-
cifully—Pull harder! Save us—until it snapped the
traces and broke loose itself.

Twitching one ear, then the other, it wanders away,
hopelessly, to some place

where its foot sticks fast in

the squelching

quagmire.

It bucks, frees itself with an effort from the treacherous
spot,

---

[1] The "Publisher's Note" to *August 1914* provides instructions for approaching the
"screen" sequences in *The Red Wheel*: The four different margins are used to
represent four sets of technical instructions for the shooting of a film. These, from
left to right on the page, are sound effects, camera direction, action, dialogue. The
symbol = indicates "cut to."

wanders off again, catching its feet in the traces, which
  trail along the ground,
its head is bent low, but it is not looking for grass, there is
  none.
Fearfully, it steps around
the corpses of horses with distended bellies and all four
  legs in the air like posts.
How swollen they are! Extraordinary how much bigger a
  horse becomes when it dies.
Whereas a man becomes smaller. As he lies face down,
  crumpled, small, you would never believe that he was
  the cause of all that thunder, all that gunfire, all the
  marching and countermarching of masses of men
now abandoned, laid low. A cart on its side in a ditch,
its upper wheel looks like a steering wheel . . .
A wagon, on its back, holds up its shafts in horror . . .
a frenzied cart rears up on its hind wheels . . .
a harness, tangled and torn, litters the field . . .
a whip . . .
rifles, bayonets, broken off from guns, and gunstocks
  knocked off . . .
first-aid kits . . .
officers' chests . . .
forage caps . . . belts . . . boots . . . swords . . . officers' field
  pouches . . .
soldiers' kit bags—sometimes on dead men . . .
barrels—undamaged or holed or empty . . .
sacks, full or half full, tied up or untied . . .
a German bicycle intercepted on its journey to Russia . . .
abandoned newspapers . . . *Russian Word* . . .
documents from regimental offices flutter in the breeze.
The corpses of those two-legged creatures who harness
  us, drive us, flog us . . .
and more of our own kind, more dead horses.
If a horse is disemboweled—

Close-up
  —flies, gadflies, gnats hum greedily over the protruding
  and rotting entrails.
While higher and higher still
  birds circle, swoop toward the carrion,
and screech in dozens of different voices.

= Our horse will never forget this. Nor is it
= alone here! There are so many of them wandering over
 the battlefield,
 on the low-lying, marshy ground, the accursed place
 where all these things have been abandoned, dropped,
 overturned,
 among corpses, corpses, corpses.
= Horses roam the field in dozens and hundreds,
 bunch together in herds,
 or in two or threes,
 lost, exhausted, mere skin and bones, still just about alive,
 some of them have succeeded in struggling free of a
 dead team,
 others are still in harness, like our horse,
 or trail broken shafts around
 or—here are two, with a snapped-off center pole dragging between them . . .
 there are wounded horses too . . .
 the heroes, undecorated, unmentioned in dispatches of
 this battle, who have lugged over a distance of one
 hundred or two hundred versts
 all this artillery, dead now and drowned in the bog . . .
 all this gun fodder, these shell boxes slung from chains—
 try hauling them!
= Those who did not free themselves—this is their fate: two
 teams, every horse dead, sprawl across each other . . .
 seem to trample and crush each other, though they are
 dead.
 Or perhaps they are not all dead, but there is no one to
 unharness and save them.
= Look again—dead teams, caught in a bombardment as
 they were approaching to move a battery to a new
 position. The battery fought to the last man; shattered
 guns,
 dead gunners all around.
 The colonel, a crooked bean pole of a man, had obviously
 taken over from the sergeant bombardier . . .
 But there are dead Germans too, killed in the attack,
 lying in heaps on the field in front of the battery.
= Back to the horses. People chase us., grab at us, try to
 catch us. . .

We horses shy away from them . . .
they try again, they tie us up . . .
They are German soldiers,
their unenviable orders are to chase the horses,
mustn't let the spoils of war, all those thousands of horses,
    go to waste.
=   But it is not only horses they chase. Look there—on the
    edge of the forest they are lining up
a column of Russian prisoners,
some of them with undressed wounds.
Deeper in the forest, deeper,
there are still many men lying on the ground, in a state of
    collapse, or sleeping,
or wounded,
and the Germans are combing the forest,
and when they find them, when they track them down
like wild beasts,
they make them stand up—
and if a man is badly wounded . . .

A shot.

    . . . they finish him off.
=   Now see the column of prisoners, shuffling along, almost
    unguarded.
Prisoners' faces. It is a cruel fate—those who have
    experienced it know.
Prisoners' faces. Captivity is not escape from death, it is
    the point at which suffering begins.
They are bent already, they stumble.
It is especially hard on those with leg wounds.
The only hope is that a loyal comrade will help you along
    if you put your arm around his neck, half carrying
    you.
=   Other prisoners are still worse off; not traveling light, but
    harnessed like horses to haul and maul
their own Russian cannon, German booty now,
to the highroad for the victors, where armored cars are
    driving around,
and there are armed bicyclists,
and machine gunners sit at their guns, ready to shoot.
=   Rows and rows of Russian cannon, howitzers, and ma-
    chine guns are already drawn up there.

= And here is something else, hefty cart horses are drawing
    a huge farm wagon with a hayrack along the road. It is
    carrying someone else, though—

Close-up
    Russian generals!
    Generals to a man! Nine all told.
    Sitting quietly on the straw with their legs tucked under
        them.
    Their heads all turned in the same direction, looking
        humbly homeward, humbly submitting to their fate.
    Some look black, but others are very calm: Their war is
        over, and most of their troubles.
= The wagon is stopped by a German general standing by
    his car, a shortish, sharp-eyed man, rather jumpy,
    overexcited perhaps by his triumph.
    General von François, wearing a victor's frown,
    feels no pity for these generals, but is disgusted by their
        wretched circumstances. He gestures:
    Get out! Why on earth are you on that cart? We have
        plenty of cars for generals—get into those four over
        there.
= Stretching their numbed legs, the Russian generals get
    down from the hay wagon
    and take their seats in the German cars
    looking sheepish, yet quite pleased to be treated with
        such respect.
= The column of footsloggers is marched into
    a compound with a temporary, almost a token
    fence of barbed wire
    stretched between temporary poles in the open field.
    The prisoners scatter to lie or sit on the bare ground,
        holding their heads,
    or stand or walk around,
    exhausted, bedraggled, bandaged, with bruises or open
        wounds.
    Some, for whatever reason, in their underwear,
    others without shoes,
    and all, of course, unfed.
    They stare at us through the barbed wire, forlorn and sad.
= A novel idea! To keep so many people
    in an open field, and make sure they don't run away!

Where else could you put them?
=   A novel solution! The con-cen-tra-tion camp!
The fate of future decades!
The harbinger of the twentieth century!

                                                        Document No. 7
1 September 1914

FROM THE HEADQUARTERS OF THE SUPREME COMMANDER

Following a buildup of reinforcements drawn from the whole front thanks to the highly developed rail network, superior German forces fell upon Russian forces of about two corps, which were subjected to extremely heavy bombardment by heavy artillery as a result of which we suffered great losses. Information received shows that our troops fought heroically; Generals Samsonov, Martos, Pestich, and several staff officers fell in battle. All measures necessary to counter this lamentable event are being taken with the utmost vigor and determination. The Supreme Commander still firmly believes that God will help us to carry them out successfully.

The Red Wheel
August 1914 — Chapter 69

Stolypin's Last Days

His eyes were fixed on one point on the ceiling—his body would permit no more. He could not turn onto his right side at all, and turning onto his left was painful. He had to lie supine, his weight crushing his backbone just as when he had been pinned to the barrier, aware the whole time of the bullet still there under his shoulder blade.

The first night had been a dangerous one. Death had stared him in the face. His heart had kept slowing down.

In the morning there was a remission. The wound stopped throbbing.

He was fully conscious, his mind was clear and moving freely, as our higher faculties always should be. He no longer believed that he was going to die.

When he looked in the mirror his color was good, his face was not that of a dying man. He had no temperature. The racking pains of the first few hours had subsided (or was that just the effect of the morphine?) and the feeling of nausea had diminished. He so wanted to forget his body's troubles and withdraw into his mind—how easily he could live there!

Where had the most damaging bullet struck? The doctors explained that it had struck his Order of St. Vladimir, which had reduced its impact and deflected it.

For the better, or for the worse?

They said that there was no blood in his sputum, no peritonitis—that was good.

A sick man or a wounded man immediately ceases to count as a grown-up independent person. He loses not only control over his situation but his right to know what is happening to him. If Stolypin had not remembered some Latin from student days he would not have understood from the doctors' cryptic utterances that the bullet had pierced the diaphragm and made a lesion in the liver.

At least it wasn't his heart or his throat, or he would have died immediately. It could have been worse.

But we have only one liver.

Enemies know the thing to peck out is the liver.

Was he really going to die?

They had got through to him after all.

His helpless right hand was maimed forever. He must have tried to shield himself with it.

He asked about the wounded musician. The man wasn't seriously hurt.

Though it no longer mattered, it would be "interesting" to know how the assassin had managed to get into the theater. The things of this world meant less and less to him, but this riddle still teased him.

Why the theater anyway, when it would have been so easy to kill him any day during the Kiev celebrations?

All those policemen were the same! Too busy chasing promotion. Remember Gerasimov in St. Petersburg, in the worst revolutionary years—how many times he had self-effacingly saved the Tsar and Stolypin and others. The terrorists had avenged themselves by slandering him, and Kurlov had gobbled him up.

Kurlov! That ignorant, muddled, conceited mediocrity, foisted on him as chief of all police forces! He had not dismissed the man when he should have done so, had not interfered with his crackpot security exercises because he didn't want to hurt the Emperor's feelings. But how he would like to look the man in the eye now!

He sent for Kurlov, but Kurlov was too crafty to come. He had gone off junketing with the Emperor.

What made Stolypin think that he still had the authority to summon people?

Did Stolypin really think that he had ever had complete authority even when he was head of the government?

How simple it all was: Someone had killed the head of the Russian government—and no one even came along to tell him how and why.

Still, on the first day he felt reasonably well, so well that he expected to pull through and to look into the whole thing when he was up and about again. The doctors did not keep from their patient what they had read in the newspapers—that the shots had been fired by an Okhrana agent, Bogrov.[1]

---

[1] Solzhenitsyn discusses Bogrov's motives for shooting Stolypin in chapter 63 of *August 1914.*

Bogrov? The man they had been talking about yesterday? The secret agent who had informed on the terrorists? It defied belief.

These questions would have intrigued him, would have set him fidgeting, if any of it had mattered any longer. What difference did it make who had done it and why? They had got through to him.

In fact, his spirit floated freely, unresentfully. His mind was clearer than ever.

Pyotr Arkadievich was waiting for the most important conversation in his life.

Waiting.

For the Emperor.

As soon as they had brought him to the hospital the night before and bandaged his wounds, and even before taking Communion, Stolypin had asked those around to let the Emperor know that he was ready to die for him.

Throughout that first dreadful night, with death hanging over him, he had expected the Emperor from hour to hour.

He had expected him all the more confidently that morning when he began to feel better.

There was so much to tell him, so much to warn him against. After what had happened Stolypin could talk to him as never before, frankly and without reservations.

But the day was running out and the Emperor did not come.

Stolypin knew his Emperor—how he knew him! He may have remembered that even on the day of the Khodynka catastrophe the French ambassador's ball had not been canceled. He may have remembered that the Emperor loved and enjoyed nothing more than military parades, that according to plan the main parade was to take place on 15 September, at some distance from the city, and that tens of thousands of men had been brought in for it. How could the schedule possibly be changed?

He knew all this. And he waited.

He waited even more confidently toward the evening of 15 September, when the Emperor was due to return to Kiev.

But still the Emperor did not come.

Stolypin's most lucid day went by and was lost.

Could the Emperor not have altered the program of the celebrations just a little bit?

Was it really of no importance to him to be told about matters of state? About what remained to be done? About future dangers? To hear a dying man's thoughts? Pyotr Arkadievich's wish was to explain his whole reform plan to the Emperor that very day—to bequeath it to him and commit him to carrying it out. Not in memory of Stolypin's past services, not as a reward to Stolypin for defeating revolution and restoring his country to him in good health, but for the sake of his own future! For his own sake! He obviously did not see what a tight corner Russia was in, even now, and what she must do to break out of it.

There was one visitor—an investigating officer, not a very high-ranking one. He questioned Stolypin and drew up a statement: what exactly had happened in the theater, where exactly and next to whom the Prime Minister had been standing, how the assassin had approached him and in which hand he was holding. . . .

Another visitor allowed in by the doctors was Kokovtsov, already acting Prime Minister.

It might have happened twice before, if Stolypin had been dismissed. Now it had. Kokovtsov was taking over his post.

He was not an enemy. But he was narrow, intellectually and emotionally. Was there any way of deepening his understanding, of enlarging his sympathies? He needed to be braver at heart if he was to pull this load.

Why not Krivoshein? . . .

The Emperor had so willed.

Stolypin shared some of his thoughts with Kokovtsov. Among the most important: Kokovtsov must get the Emperor to replace Sukhomlinov—it was becoming obvious that the War Ministry was in a state of chaos.

Into the vacuum created by the Emperor's absence a secretary brought bundles of telegrams—good wishes for his recovery from all corners of Russia.

In the hour of anguish we hear these encouraging cries from friends—always too late. How much more valuable it would have been to have one sixteenth of their number beside us while we were still capable of action.

Besides the telegrams there were newspaper reports of church services—in the capitals especially they went on uninterruptedly. Local people brought along icons, and more icons. The Bishop of Chernigov brought oil from the relics of St. Barbara the Martyr.

How Russia loved such excesses! But they were no substitute for the work of every day. It was easier to pray for someone than to give him support. Easier than doing what needed to be done.

Stolypin had always been conscious of a God above him, urging him on, inspiring him, guiding him.

His first endeavor had been to fill the peasant's barn.

Must he now take his leave? Before the most important of his reforms?

He longed to hear a clear, firm voice promising to continue his work with the same strength of purpose. But nowhere in Russia was such a voice raised. Perhaps there was no such voice?

To depart—at forty-nine, and still at the height of his powers. Leaving behind a Russia still rent by the rabid hostility of civil society toward the imperial power. By malicious lies. By ignorant prejudice.

It is as Thou hast ordered it, O Lord, Thou whose designs are beyond our understanding. However much it is Thy will for each of us to do, however many times we exceed the limit of all we had thought possible, at each new horizon, even at the final horizon of death, there is still more left undone to trouble us.. . . . There is so much for which I feel myself needed, but Thou hast bidden me be still and struggle no more. And what of Olga? What of the six children, some grown up, some still infants?

Whether it was a punishment from God or a mercy, there was no relief, except just occasionally in a short sleep, from his uninterrupted awareness that he was wounded and might die.

I shall surely die.

There was nothing new in the telegrams and rumors. It was no good trying to make sense of the pains and the murmurings inside him, to try to guess what was going on, whether *this* was breaking down or *that* was healing, whether the blood was clotting or whether the tired heart was pumping it away.

The doctors didn't seem to be giving him any treatment. Morphia and caffeine, that was all. They said he would be up in three weeks. They wouldn't disturb him to change his dressings. They thought of extracting the bullet, but left it there. They were waiting for an eminent colleague from St. Petersburg.

He who had been perpetually active found himself peremptorily cut off from everything. He had no one to talk to. Nor any way of sending messages. The mind destined never to have any part in the future reviewed his past.

1906. Mutinies and rebellions everywhere.

1907. "You can't frighten me."

How apt such unstudied phrases can be. The joy of standing fast! And the misery of stumbling about among quarreling factions instead of maneuvering flexibly with the serried ranks of state power behind you.

But how could he complain? He might have died on Aptekarsky Island without achieving anything. Instead, he had been granted five years to do his work.

Though the whole burden of Russia rested on his shoulders he had not hesitated for a moment to challenge that loudmouth to a duel.

This too had been a duel of sorts. Except that the enemy had crept up on him stealthily, and an active man's breast is always exposed.

He had been struck by the expression on the assassin's face, his triumphant certainty that he was right. Yet even as he exulted in victory there was a wry smile on his intellectual face: Would the world realize how clever he had been?

They had all been perverted in this way. The corruptors had been at it for half a century.

What did Russia matter to them? What did they care about the tasks facing it?

No, no, this was no Okhrana agent.

In the course of our lives we receive prophetic warnings, adumbrations of what is to come. They seem irrelevant at the time yet affect us more than we think. We usually fail to recognize them. When he had made his speech on Azef he had refused to entertain the obscene notion that an Okhrana agent had directed terrorists. But his enemies in the Duma had prophesied that the government itself would perish at the hands of such informers! Perhaps there was a freakish resemblance between the Azef affair and what had happened to him.[2]

They had been disappointed that time. Their triumph now would be complete.... For so many people Bogrov could not have timed his shot better. It put the finishing touch to the April sessions of the Duma.

He ought to have made time to deal with the police. He shouldn't have shrunk from it.

1909. Russia's development steadily gaining speed.

1910. A year of great achievements. Individual homesteads already spreading over the face of Russia, changing the face of nature. His own happy trip to Siberia, truly the supreme moment of his life, since he could tell himself, "All this is your creation."

Perhaps, then, he had done all that he was meant to do. It is not given to any single individual to do so very much. One man cannot change the whole course of history.

Yet even in that finest hour, indeed especially then, he was beset on all sides, tied hand and foot....

No, that was wrong. No, Lord, I thank Thee, giver of all good things, that it was granted to me to accomplish so much.

The high point of the journey had been in mid-September: The very days so boringly taken up this year by the Kiev ceremonies had last year been so spacious, so rich in incident, out on the Siberian steppe with the grain elevators rising around him, amid hills of grain.

If only he could go there again, just once!

---

[2] Y. F. Azef was a prominent social revolutionary terrorist who also worked for the Okhrana, the tsarist secret police. He famously arranged the assassination of the tsar's minister of the interior to protect his cover.

The night of 15–16 September went by, with less cause for alarm than the night before. His temperature remained at thirty-seven, his pulse was not over ninety, and he tried hard to believe that his chances were as good as the doctors said. He was neither feverish nor delirious. It was just that his immobilized body seemed swollen and heavy, and he was so weak. His right side, around the wound, was as heavy as iron. What mysterious process was going on in the depths there? The bleeding had stopped, and they weren't changing the dressing. They weren't giving him any treatment at all. Perhaps there was nothing they could do?

Olga arrived from their Kovno estate.

"Well, you can see how it is, my dear... Well... There we are...."

But the Emperor did not appear late that evening after the parade, nor yet early next morning.

Would he come that afternoon?

What was on his program? Oh, yes, he would be going out of Kiev again—to Korosten and Ovruch.

So he wouldn't come?

He didn't come.

Yes, Pyotr Arkadievich knew his Emperor. But all the same he awaited his arrival. He made ready to speak, not like a subject but like a man on his deathbed, to say things he could say to no one else.

Your Majesty, do not delude yourself that all is now well. One violent storm will bring it all tumbling down again! The same two forces seek to disrupt us—the irresponsible and the insane. And one of the two is entirely at your mercy—clear away this rank growth, Your Majesty!

Pinned down as he was, right and left, with an excruciating, tearing pain in his shoulders, whom should he suggest to the Emperor as his own replacement? There was no one.

Did he regret not having raised his voice to shake the Emperor before this? Or did he, on the contrary, regret that he had not done more to retain the Emperor's goodwill?

He had always behaved as his feelings told him to. He could not dissemble, he could not falsify the facts.

Well, he had perhaps become too heated that spring over the western zemstvos.

Let the man who has governed a state condemn him.

Nobody could judge every little detail perfectly.

Why is it that if you get on successfully with the main task, all around become your enemies?

He had said once in a speech that the enemy furiously hacks away at the scaffolding as we try to build, and someday it will surely collapse—yes, he had said "surely"—and crush us beneath the wreckage (you too, vengeful Rodichev, will never get your scaffolding built, you will tumble first!), but let it be when the framework of the renewed Russia is already in being.

But was it yet in being? Had the main work been done? Oh God—only now did Pyotr Arkadievich see what was most important, only now, when he no longer had the strength to raise himself on one elbow.

There was nothing terrible about dying. He had not known the fear of death for a long time past, he was surprised himself how little he feared it, although he was still under fifty. His fears had always been for Russia.

Alas, he could no longer help her!

It was frightening to think that he would have no heirs and that his work would never be completed. Why are we never allowed to take a hand in the real work? Why instead of us are Germans planted everywhere, or decrepit Russian freaks, and if someone with a firm guiding hand sets out to build a road they fly at him from every side to knock compass, yardstick, pick, or shovel from his hold.

. . . Your Majesty, if the two sides are not made to see sense we may yet come to grief. It is unthinkable that the country should go on living so dangerously divided. I have dark forebodings, Sire—and not only because this bullet was my lot. The year 1905 may repeat itself, Your Majesty—God forbid there should be another war. You must tenderly nurture the new healthy growth. And put no trust in self-seeking people, of whom there are so many around you!

The day dragged on endlessly, and his mind was less clear than on the day before. At times everything went dark, or he felt sick, or broke into a sweat which left him weaker, and he was more conscious all the time of the heavy lump of iron where his liver should be, and even when Zeidler arrived from St. Petersburg the surgeons were still reluctant to do anything.

Meanwhile the Emperor was opening a church at Ovruch.

Stolypin longed for Guchkov[3] to appear: He remembered the years when they had got on so well—perhaps now they could renew their understanding.

He was somewhere on the way or was just setting out, but he too was in no hurry. He sent an Old Believers' icon on ahead.

Stolypin was feeling worse all the time.

"Bury me in Kiev, Olga. I shall sleep peacefully in this city."

---

[3] A. I. Guchkov (1862–1936) was the leader of the center-right Octobrist Party in the third Duma, a party that often cooperated with Stolypin's government. He served in the "Provisional Government" between March and May 1917 and emigrated to the West in 1918.

He had long ago expressed a solemn wish to be buried "where he was killed"—his intimates all knew of it. As it turned out, he had been killed in the cradle of Russia, the city in which Russia had its earliest roots. This, and not bureaucratic Petersburg, not Kadet-dominated Moscow, was where Russian national feeling had flourished most vigorously in recent years. It was for Kiev's sake that he had fought his battle over the western zemstvos last spring.

It had almost broken his heart at the time, but now it might even have helped stem the hemorrhage.

By evening his mind had begun to wander—just when it occurred to him that he could write down all that he wanted to say to the Emperor. Why hadn't he thought of it before! Sentences formed themselves more eloquently than when he was fully conscious. At last he knew how to convince the Emperor, who could not fail to do his bidding. What happiness!

He asked for paper, something to use as a pad, a pen—and suddenly he remembered that his right hand had always written with the support of his left, and now it was wounded. How could he write? His courage failed him.

Delirious dreams crowded in. His wife and Dr. Afanasiev, who had sat through both nights, were at his bedside.

In the morning consciousness returned. The doctors were alarmed, they found that his peritoneum was inflamed and that he had a pulse of 120. Three days late, they made up their minds to change his dressings, and operated to remove the murderous bullet from his back.

Pyotr Arkadievich asked to see it.

He was too weak by now to speak at any length and with any force, even if the Emperor did come.

The Emperor, it seemed, had been in the clinic late the previous evening, while the patient was unconscious. He had left Kiev yet again that morning, loyal to his timetable.

17 September was a day of interruptions, intermittent dozing, injections.

Broken thoughts passed through his mind.

He had thrown wide the gates to the Russian future. He could not be sure that they would not be shut again.

Oh God, how should I picture the future? Will it be sunlit and sublime or wreathed once more in dark mists? If only I could see the continuation of the changes I have set in motion, see which way it will go.

He yearned to fling himself into it, to become part of it. I belong there! I belong there, all of me!

But another feeling—of resigned detachment—was growing within him. It has nothing to do with me. It's over—and I am glad.

On the morning of the 18th Pyotr Arkadievich regained consciousness completely and asked the professors a question: "How can you lie to me on the last day of my life?"

The professors avoided answering. His right hand was bandaged, and with his left he could not feel his own pulse—if there was any pulse to feel. They gave him oxygen, and caffeine.

Stolypin lay there, conscious, thinking hard.

He knew very well that he was dying.

And that day the Emperor had simply not come.

He was a weak man, unhappy in the knowledge of his weakness, unable to face unpleasant realities—and he had just not come.

It was God's will to send us such an Emperor at such a time.

It is not for us, O Lord, to weigh Thy purposes.

O God, our Creator! Illuminate his mind and his heart! Grant him the strength to face great hardships!

All day on 18 September the sick man suffered dreadfully as his mind grew darker, groaning and tossing and turning. They were surprised that his heart was still holding out—at tines it seemed to have stopped altogether and only caffeine started it beating again.

They should probably have operated the day before, when they discovered the hemorrhage under the diaphragm, to drain the blood and plug the liver. They had hesitated too long.

No more outsiders were allowed into the room,

In the evening as he was lapsing into oblivion, he asked for the electric light to be switched on. "Give me paper. . . . Give me a pen! . . . What's the good of a penholder without a nib?"

Then there was something about the way to rule Russia.

Several times he repeated the word "Finland" quite distinctly, and his left hand traced pictures on the bedsheet.

They brought him pencil and paper but he could not use them.

By 8 p.m. his extremities were getting cold. He was having great difficulty with his breathing.

At nine he spoke his last: "Turn me on my side." Dr. Afanasiev did so.

Then he lost consciousness altogether.

They began letting people in to make their farewells.

The archpriest read the prayer for the dying.

His face retained its fresh color to the very last.

His wife stood like a woman turned to stone.

At 10 p.m., at about the hour when the assassin had struck, after four days of struggle, Stolypin died.

Dr. Afanasiev, who had kept watch over him four nights on end, confided that he had seen many people of outstanding intelligence and talent when they were doomed to die, and most of them had clung desperately to life, betrayed their sense of helplessness, their lack of spirit, pleading with the doctors to save them, searching their faces for any sign of hope. But from this patient he had heard no entreaties. Knowing that he was doomed, he had shown a rare equanimity and self-possession.

Stolypin went to meet death as an equal. He passed like a sovereign from one kind of life to another.

WHO MAKES US SEE THE LIGHT

THAT'S THE ONE WE HURT ALL RIGHT

Convocation at Headquarters

There were no large rooms in the building. The biggest of them would hold twenty in a pinch. There were in fact just twenty officers in the Quartermaster General's department, but more than half as many again had gathered that morning.

Two short tables had been placed at right angles to each other. At the head of one sat the Supreme Commander, even when seated the tallest man present. Next to him—they were inseparable—was his brother, Grand Duke Pyotr Nikolaevich, dutifully taking it all in (although everybody knew that for years past he had been preoccupied with church architecture and uninterested in military matters). Next to him was their cousin, the choleric Prince Pyotr of Oldenburg ("Poppycock Pasha"). Then came the Adjutant General, Illustrious Prince Dmitri Golitsyn (master of the royal hunt in recent years). Then General Petrovo-Solovovo, the debonair marshal of the Ryazan nobility, now a "general-in-waiting." Then Lieutenant General Yanushkevich, the Supreme Commander's Chief of Staff, deftly sorting his papers with an ingratiating little smile on his sly face. Then the Quartermaster General, Lieutenant General Danilov ("Black" Danilov), with his rectangular forehead, his spreading jowls, and his fixed glare. Then the "duty general" who dealt with awards and appointments. Immediately facing the Grand Duke, by the opposite wall, where the two tables met, sat the Commander-in-Chief Northwestern Army Group, General of Cavalry Zhilinsky, a man of sixty or so with a hard, sallow face and a coldly contemptuous manner. Also present were the head of the Diplomatic Section, the head of the Naval Section, and the Chief of Army Communications.

Those for whom there was no room at the tables—members of the Operations Section, the Supreme Commander's adjutant, the Kalmyk prince who was Yanushkevich's adjutant, and Zhilinsky's adjutant—had chairs by the window or the stove and held their notebooks on their knees.

The stove had been lit earlier that morning, and the room was not over-heated. Bursts of cold rain pattered against the windowpane more and more frequently. It was so dull and cheerless outside that they wondered whether to switch the lights on.

They were wedged in so tightly that they agreed to speak sitting down. It looked more businesslike anyway. They were there to compare views, not to make speeches.

At the Grand Duke's invitation Zhilinsky spoke first. He did not once raise his gray eyelids fully. He could afford not to look at most of those present. For the most part he kept his eyes on his papers or on the Grand Duke. The head with the gray topknot moved only occasionally as he widened his field of vision. He spoke as he always did, without emotional emphasis. He evidently did not expect any of those present to treat him as though he was on trial. He lectured them in his harsh, crackling voice as though he was the Grand Duke's equal called in to discuss on equal terms an unpleasant but not very significant occurrence.

The deplorable failure of the 2nd Army, he said, was entirely the fault of the late General Samsonov. To begin with, he had failed to carry out Army Group HQ's basic directive about the line of advance. (Details followed.) By deviating without authorization from the specified direction General Samsonov had inadmissibly overextended his frontage, made his corps march unnecessarily long distances, and so lengthened his lines of communication. Worse still, he had opened up a gap between the 1st and 2nd armies, disrupting cooperation between them. Unlike the punctilious General Rennenkampf, Samsonov had interpreted several other orders to suit himself. (Details followed.) His order to the central corps on the night of 27–28 August to continue their advance, although he knew that the flanking forces had withdrawn, was incomprehensible to any normal, sensible person. This gross error was aggravated by his ill-considered order to cut off telegraph communication from Neidenburg, which made it impossible for Army Group HQ to prevent the shattering defeat of his army. When Army Group HQ had, after some delay, realized what the position was, he, Zhilinsky, had immediately telegraphed orders to all corps to withdraw to their starting lines, and it was entirely the fault of General Samsonov that the central corps were unable to receive this message.

The Commander-in-Chief Northwestern Army Group did not raise his croaking voice to denounce Samsonov, and this made what had happened seem still more simple and obvious: The deceased Army Commander was directly and grossly at fault. There was no real reason, then, for anyone there present to feel guilty or ill at ease.

Not a murmur of protest, not a skeptical cough was heard. The only sound was that of flies, brought to life by the heat of the stove, buzzing about the room and settling in black clusters on the whitewashed stovepipe and the ceiling.

Vorotyntsev writhed and fumed. No one in Russia, no one in the whole of warring Europe was more hateful to him at that moment than this Living Corpse. He hated the clipped voice, the clayey face adorned with an elaborate mustache that hid much of his cheeks and curled upward at the tips to make him look imposing, and his so far unchallenged haughtiness. But it was not only for today's work that Vorotyntsev hated this gravedigger. All the stupidities, the blunders, and the oversights of which he had been guilty during his tenure as Chief of Staff were so many links in a chain around the neck of the Russian army, dragging it down to destruction. And there he was, giving his meticulously weighed account with not the slightest fear of rebuttal or even demur, let alone of punishment. Even if he was dismissed another very agreeable post would be found for him. He had, after all, carried out his most important duty—his duty to his French allies and to General Joffre. If worst came to worst he could go to France to collect bouquets from French ladies and lunch with the President.

Still, General Zhilinsky would not leave his listeners altogether without hope. He would make up for the timorous Samsonov with his own boldness: He planned nothing less than a repetition of the combined operation of the 1st and 2nd armies around the Masurian Lakes! Rennenkampf, now deep inside Prussia, was excellently placed for it. It remained only to reinforce the 2nd Army, re-form certain corps, and dispatch Sheideman by the route chosen before hostilities began.

The Grand Duke sat, upright and majestic, as though he expected the national anthem to be played at any moment.

Zhilinsky seemed to have covered everything, but naturally General Danilov now felt called upon to speak, since everyone there regarded him as the best strategic thinker in the Russian army. In his position it was no good saying just anything. He had to exhibit the results of profound thought, let them see that a constant stream of ideas flowed through that head (the head was thick, the stream sluggish, the ideas stillborn!), and so the Quartermaster General, with the supreme self-assurance common in dimwits, began speaking in a voice that brooked no contradiction.

He agreed completely with the general picture drawn by the Army Group Commander. (And went over it again.) But some important additions were necessary. If Samsonov had crossed the Russian frontier earlier, as he had been ordered to, and if he had struck at the enemy's flank in the area of the Masurian Lakes, as instructed, instead of waiting until the Germans turned to face him, we would undoubtedly have thrown them into confusion and would now be celebrating a major victory. The fatigue of the 2nd Army had also played no small part, and General Samsonov must bear the blame for disregard of the normal rest days provided for in infantry regulations. Many errors of lesser importance could be laid at his door.

More eloquent than what he said was the stupefying silence into which he now lapsed, his features rectangular and lifeless, expressing nothing, his eyes staring fixedly, his shapeless ears flat against his head. Even the handle-bar mustache did nothing to improve his appearance. The pomposity of the man! He behaved as though he had narrowly avoided disclosing a secret too deep to be mentioned in such a large gathering. Military secrets and the complexities of strategy were burdens which this martyr to duty shouldered alone. He was the expert, and he would unravel these matters when the time came. No one else had the key to this lock: Officers lower in rank inevitably lacked both his knowledge and his talents, while above him there was only the sensible but ineffectual Yanushkevich and the impetuous and impractical Grand Duke.

In the natural order of things it was now the turn of the Supreme Commander's Chief of Staff to speak. How gladly dark-eyed Yanushkevich, with his puffy face and his fluffy mustache, his ingratiating manner, his affectionate handling of files and papers (and probably of women), would have forgone his turn! A kindhearted monarch had offered him this post in a generous moment. Suave Yanushkevich felt as much at home with strategy and operational planning as Little Red Riding Hood in the dark forest. His heart had missed a beat, but then at the thought of how delightful it would be to occupy such a high post his heart had jumped for joy. And anyway he could not possibly upset his blue-eyed Emperor, who was just as easily embarrassed as himself, by confessing that he understood nothing of such matters.

Whether he was riding in a carriage or walking over spacious parquet floors in the palaces of St. Petersburg, Yanushkevich was always conscious of the impression he was making, and would tell himself over and over again, and with dread and delight, that he was Lieutenant General Yanushkevich, Chief of the General Staff! He had held that position only four months, and the main effort so far required of him had been to prevent the war from failing to break out. That done, he had intended to remain aloof from subsequent menacing developments, but War Minister Sukhomlinov, that incorrigible optimist, had promoted him to be Chief of Staff to the Supreme Commander.

How could he bring himself to refuse what was undoubtedly a great advance in his career? From his first day at Supreme HQ, however, Yanushkevich had been in thrall to Danilov, the only one there who knew anything or could do anything. Danilov's tone was a constant reproach—why was Yanushkevich Chief of Staff, and not he himself? One thing Yanushkevich quickly grasped was that though there were better strategists than Danilov in the Russian army, he too was Sukhomlinov's choice, and it might be more advantageous to leave him where he was, deferring to him in private and promising to obtain for him awards and promotions equal to his own. They were like two boats tied together, and only together could they navigate this war, Yanushkevich dealing with organizational matters and Danilov with strategy.

But what torments he suffered every morning, when he was forced to endure strategic discussions and look sagacious. What an effort it cost him right now to rise and look important, taking care that no one noticed how frightened he was of slipping up and how tiresome and incomprehensible he found it all. In any case, he could say nothing against Zhilinsky, who though formally his subordinate was a full general and had been his predecessor as Chief of the General Staff, while he himself was an upstart, promoted over the heads of his seniors.

Yanushkevich simply repeated, and went on repeating, in rounded phrases and courteous tones all that had been said before, adding nothing and omitting nothing, merely rearranging it a little, so that it became clearer all the time to the conference how gravely at fault he had been, that deceased commander who had destroyed his own army. It was a relief that he had removed himself! Other generals, it seemed, could never make such mistakes, and the conference began to lose all sense of urgency. Every point had been covered, and the subject was exhausted.

Vorotyntsev's agitated pencil had noted all their evasions on a piece of paper resting on his map case—together with ways of hitting back at them. At the top of the page, more evenly and precisely written in black ink, were the main points he had jotted down with his Japanese fountain pen the night before. He made no notes on Yanushkevich's contribution, and scarcely listened to it. Sitting with his eyelids lowered so as not to see them all, he saw instead Samsonov's honest, vulnerable face, not as he was now, lying in some untraceable thicket, not even as he was when he took leave of his troops at Orlau, but back at Ostrolenka, when he was still free to act as he chose, when it was still possible for him not to lose the battle. Even then his helpless vulnerability was written on his face. Vorotyntsev had a vision of Kachkin's savage grin as he crashed through the thickets like a wild boar, carrying Ofrosimov over his shoulder. And of Blagodarev flopping down, plunging his knife into the ground as though it was the plowshare with which he had just turned up a hundred desyatins.[1]

He was about to leap up from his chair and speak without permission, but Svechin, sitting beside him, gave his elbow a cautionary squeeze. The Supreme Commander did not even look at him. He was sitting with one lean

---

[1] desyatin: 2.7 acres.

cavalry officer's leg over the other, remote and unbending as always, expressionless, except that his pursed lips raised the ends of his mustache. He had eyes only for Zhilinsky's sallow face and stupidly raised eyebrows. It was not so long ago that he himself had authorized Zhilinsky to replace Samsonov if necessary. But since yesterday it had gradually become clear to him that Zhilinsky might well be the main culprit in the catastrophe, and that removing *him* at once would be the most effective way of asserting his own authority and teaching all the generals a lesson. It might, however, be a rash move. Zhilinsky considered his present post beneath him and would gladly relinquish it. He would dash off to St. Petersburg to whisper his complaint in the highest circles and tell tales to Sukhomlinov. In the viper's nest at court whatever happened next would be used against Nikolai Nikolaevich. If the war went badly he would be incompetent, ill equipped to hold the Supreme Command. If the war went well he would be called ambitious, and a threat to the Tsar and his family. God saw how he grieved for the flower of the officer corps and for the stout soldiers who had suffered so dreadfully in encirclement. But ninety thousand men surrounded and twenty thousand dead was not the whole of Russia. Russia had a hundred and seventy million people. To save all Russia he needed not just a victory or two in the field, but, more important still, to win the biggest battle of all, that at court for the heart of the Emperor: He had to get rid of the unscrupulous Sukhomlinov, exclude the vile Rasputin, and undermine the influence of the Empress. With all this in front of him he could not afford just now to reinforce the other side with a resentful Zhilinsky. Loyalty to the greater Russia made it the Grand Duke's immediate duty to suppress his compassion for the lesser Russia, for Samsonov's army, which was in any case beyond salvation.

But he would see to it that Zhilinsky had a rough time, he would scare him by setting Vorotyntsev on him. That much he must do! The Grand Duke had been aware of Vorotyntsev the whole time, and had noticed from the corner of his eye how restive he was.

Outside the gloom was thickening. Raindrops spattered the windows. It was getting dark in the room, and they turned the electric lights on. The whitewashed walls made the room very bright, and every man there could see the minutest detail in the appearance of his neighbors. The head of the Diplomatic Section, Supreme HQ, was the next to speak. He requested the generals not to lose sight of foreign policy implications and the country's international commitments. The French public was convinced that Russia could be making a greater contribution. The French government took the view that Russia had not fielded all available forces, that the East Prussian offensive was not an adequate effort, that the Germans had transferred two corps from the eastern to the western front, and not the other way around (on this point French and Russian intelligence reports conflicted), and that

France had the right to remind her ally of the promise to launch an all-out attack on Berlin.

That last word the Grand Duke and the generals ignored as though it was one of those embarrassing noises which good manners require us not to notice in company, keeping their eyes on the window or the wall or the papers before them.

But if that one word had no resonance for them, the force of the Diplomatic Section's statement and the will of the Emperor were unmistakable: They must at all costs and with all speed save their French ally! Their hearts, of course, ached for Russia's losses, but it was important not to let her allies down.

The Chief of Army Communications then reported that the reinforcement of the East Prussian front was being treated as a matter of the greatest urgency. Troops were being continually transferred from the Asian borderlands for this purpose. Two corps from the Caucasus, one from Turkestan, and one from Siberia would arrive shortly. So that the immediate second offensive, which was morally imperative, was already materially provided for.

Zhilinsky said that this had been his reason for asking the gentlemen there present to sanction a repetition of the operation around the Masurian Lakes.

If this meant losing all he had, his career, the army, his epaulets—no, if they scalped him for it, tore the skin from his burning head, Vorotyntsev had to jump in. Lies! Lies! All lies! The man could not be allowed to go on lying indefinitely! He wrenched his elbow from Svechin's grip and, forgetting that on this occasion speakers were expected to keep their seats, rose to his feet in a rage with no idea what his first furious words would be—and heard the Grand Duke's commanding voice: "Now I shall ask Colonel Vorotyntsev to give us his personal impressions. He has been with the 2nd Army."

There was no explosion. The hissing steam of his fury escaped invisibly. He cautiously restrained his leaping heart, remembering the proverb that "the man who masters his wrath can master everything."

"Our review of the situation is all the more essential, Your Imperial Highness, in that Rennenkampf's army is under threat at this very minute, and may come to an even worse end than Samsonov's."

(Too loud. Must be quieter. Lower the steam pressure.)

It was as though someone had broken the window and a cold, wet wind had burst in on them. They shrank and shifted uneasily in their seats, the Grand Duke as well as the others.

But Vorotyntsev became more fluent with every sentence, and delivered what sounded like a carefully prepared and judiciously weighed speech:

"Gentlemen! No one from the 2nd Army has been invited to our conference—there is hardly anyone left to invite. But I was with them at the time, and perhaps I may be permitted to say what I think those now dead or in captivity might have said. Dead men may be forgiven for speaking plainly, as we were all trained to do. . . ."

(Just as long as his voice did not fail him! Just as long as he didn't choke on his words!)

". . . I am not going to talk about the valor of our soldiers and officers—no one here has called it into question. Among those whose names should be inscribed in the rolls of honor are regimental commanders Alekseev, Kabanov, Pervushin, and Kakhovskoy. If more than fifteen thousand men escape from encirclement they owe it to a handful of colonels and staff captains, not to Army Group HQ! Except where the German artillery had a two-to-one advantage (and sometimes even where they did) our units came out on top in tactical engagements. They held their defensive positions under the heaviest fire—the Vyborg Regiment at Usdau, for instance. The 15th Corps, led by the brilliant General Martos, attacked, and attacked successfully, from first to last. Yet in spite of all this the battle ended not, as people here have put it, in failure but in a crushing defeat."

He hurled the word into the room like a bomb. The blast lashed their faces.

It was a challenge to the Grand Duke too. He could not acknowledge to the emperor that "defeat" was the right word, although he was ready to "put his head on the block" if the Emperor thought he should. But though he could not admit the truth of what Vorotyntsev had said he did not interrupt. He sat there as tall and imposing and aristocratically haughty as ever (so close to the throne—and yet so far away).

"I am bound to say that we should have been on guard. The Russian General Staff knew from intelligence the assumptions on which the German High Command was acting: In German war games the Russians always took the offensive, just as the 2nd Army now did, and it was always against the left flank on the Narew that the Germans launched their successful counterattack. They even had General Samsonov moving as in fact he did. I have been told that the blame rests entirely on him. The dead cannot answer back—and if it were true it would be very convenient for us, there would be no need for us to mend our ways. But if we act on that assumption you must forgive me for predicting that the same thing will happen over and over again, and we are very likely to lose the war altogether!"

There was a rustle of protest. Zhilinsky's lusterless eyes rested on the Supreme Commander: It was time he interrupted this brash colonel and put him in his place.

But the Supreme Commander, who could be so peremptory, sat motionless with his head thrown back. His expression said only that he was in control of the situation.

"I must, though, object on behalf of the late Aleksandr Vasilievich to some of the things said here. He arrived at Bialystok straight from Turkestan and was presented with a ready-made plan, according to which the army would march deep into the Masurian wilderness, where there was nothing but fortresses and corridors between lakes. He saw that this was ludicrous and sent alternative suggestions of his own, intended for the Supreme Commander and submitted to Lieutenant General Oranovsky, Chief of Staff, Northwestern Army Group, on 11 August."

(Vorotyntsev's voice was rising steadily. He did his best to control it.)

"When several days went by with no response to his memorandum he did not know what to think. He asked me to be sure to inquire about it at Supreme HQ, and I learned yesterday that Samsonov's message had never reached the Grand Duke!"

The Living Corpse turned a death's-head grin on Vorotyntsev. Since the Supreme Commander was silent the time had come for him to intervene himself.

"I know nothing of this memorandum."

"That makes it even worse, Your Excellency!" Vorotyntsev seemed glad of the interruption and addressed Zhilinsky directly. "Obviously, we shall never know the truth of the matter without an inquiry. If there is one, I shall ask for that piece of paper to be produced!"

Generals' faces quivered indignantly. Everything had been sufficiently explained; what did the insolent fellow mean by his talk of an inquiry? They all looked at the Supreme Commander, mutely begging him to stop this crazy colonel.

But the Supreme Commander sat inscrutably, with his beautifully molded head in the air, looking somewhere above Zhilinsky.

Zhilinsky, usually so terse and phlegmatic, retorted with uncharacteristic heat: "General Samsonov probably retracted the memorandum."

"No, he didn't. I'm quite sure of that," Vorotyntsev insisted, looking only at Zhilinsky—a supraterrestrial being when seen, or rather not seen, from Ostrolenka or Neidenburg or Orlau, but now, within touching distance, just a bony old man with a bad back. "The plan which General Samsonov put forward, and as far as possible followed, was sound. It enabled him to outflank a large proportion of the enemy's forces, though still not enough of them. The inexplicable obstinacy of the Army Group HQ in hanging on to that corner of the Masurian Lakes is at least equally to blame for the overextension of Samsonov's front."

Zhilinsky, more irritated still, interrupted. "Our main concern was to coordinate the operations of the two armies."

Vorotyntsev had sensed by now the Supreme Commander's tacit agreement not to interrupt him. No one else there would be able to talk him down. He had reached his goal! His journey hadn't been in vain! He became colder and more rational. His lips twisted in a mocking smile. He cast sentence after sentence at Zhilinsky, like so many nooses around his neck.

"How can you speak of coordination when one army was made to attack prematurely and the other practically stood down? When General Rennenkampf's five cavalry divisions were not thrown in to pursue the enemy after Gumbinnen, or sent to save the 2nd Army from disaster? Army Group HQ seems to have deliberately prevented the two armies from coordinating their movements, by making the 1st Army attack a week too early. Why? Do you call it coordination when Sheideman's corps is taken away from Samsonov and given to Rennenkampf on 23 August, then assigned to the Warsaw area on the 27th—as though apparently its presence had become unnecessary just when the 2nd Army was facing its decisive battle?"

How did Vorotyntsev know all this? These sins lay at the door of Supreme HQ. Danilov turned a suspicious eye on Svechin and said nervously: "There were good strategic grounds for that. We were getting the 9th Army ready to move on Berlin. . . ."

"So the 2nd Army could be thrown to the wolves?" Vorotyntsev retorted. "Anyway, Sheideman's corps was sent to help the 2nd Army on the 28th—only Army Group HQ misdirected it! On the 29th the corps was assigned to Warsaw yet again, but on the 30th General Rennenkampf carried it off northward. Do you call that coordination between armies? Northwestern Army Group HQ was created solely for the purpose of coordinating them. General Samsonov has been accused of irresolution but the Army Group command was guilty of the worst kind of indecision when it kept back half of the army to protect the rear and maintain communications!"

"What do you mean, half of it? Where do you get that from?" Danilov clamored indignantly, with an obtuse colonel known as "Treacherous Vanka," a favorite of his, seconding him.

"Just think, gentlemen: two army corps, the right and the left, and three cavalry divisions—exactly half of the army. And Samsonov is ordered to attack and win with the other half. Since Army Group HQ had held back the flanks, it should have sent them to help the center out. General Samsonov made mistakes, certainly, but they were tactical mistakes. The strategic mistakes have to be laid at the door of Army Group HQ. Samsonov did not have forces larger than those of the enemy at his disposal, but Army Group HQ did—and still the battle was lost. We have to draw the inescapable conclusions, gentlemen; otherwise, what is the point of this conference? What are staff officers for? The conclusion I draw is that we are incapable of leading any unit bigger than a regiment!"

"Your Imperial Highness, I must ask you to put a stop to this colonel's nonsensical statement!" Zhilinsky proved that he was not quite a corpse by thumping the table.

The Grand Duke's big, eloquent, oval eyes surveyed him coldly. He spoke quietly but firmly.

"What Colonel Vorotyntsev says is very much to the point. I am learning a lot from him. As I see it, Supreme HQ" (he looked at Danilov, who lowered his bovine brow, while a shiver seemed to run down Yanushkevich's sensitive spine) "took practically no part in supervising the operation, but left it entirely to the Northwestern Army Group." He knew his Danilov. The Grand Duke often grasped the essentials long before Danilov had finished chewing the cud of reports he had written himself. "And if the colonel gets something wrong you can correct him immediately."

Zhilinsky grunted, rose, and went out to relieve himself.

The Supreme Commander was greatly tempted. He had the evidence before him. Why not set up a commission of inquiry to examine it further? Zhilinsky could be banished in disgrace, and Supreme HQ would be safe from all accusations.

But only the day before the Emperor's gracious telegram had shown the Grand Duke a different way: the way of forgiveness, with all recriminations laid aside. Besides, he had received an imperial decree (not yet made public) promoting Oranovsky to the rank of full general. Promotion procedures take their own course, independently of military operations, and there is no way of arresting them.

Once its charge has carried it beyond the enemy's defenses a cavalry unit's losses are behind it, and it has time in hand and an unimpeded gallop. So it was with Vorotyntsev. The real discussion was about to begin!

"However, I should like to deal with broader issues. What was the 2nd Army's strength squandered on? On subduing a deserted and pathless tract of our own territory! Before they could even reach the frontier or make contact with the enemy our corps had to flounder in the sands for five or six days. Ammunition, food, supplies would have to be lugged across the same expanse. How? Why didn't someone think of planting supply dumps along the frontier before the war?"

Yanushkevich frowned. Listening to this impertinent Young Turk from Golovin's class at the Academy caused him pain. The snake's tongue flickered under the fluffy mustache.

"If we had done that the enemy might have seized the supplies."

Vorotyntsev reared up, his jaw purple with anger. "So you would sooner lose twenty thousand dead and seventy thousand prisoners than a dozen quarter-master's stores?"

He could not look at the man without feeling sick. Every effeminate movement gave him away: "General" Yanushkevich was an impostor. How could such a man be Chief of Staff to the Supreme Commander?! And what was to prevent him from sending all of Russia's fighting forces to their destruction?

"The reason no stores were put near the frontier," Danilov said heavily, "was because we expected to be on the defensive in this region, not attacking."

That was true. But the supposition was part of a plan for the whole war which had been hastily changed, then further modified by Zhilinsky, when he was Chief of Staff, *and* by the War Minister, *and* by the Emperor! For that matter, the Grand Duke himself had favored the change. Vorotyntsev could not afford to let himself be sidetracked. He had more pointed and more provocative things to say now that Zhilinsky had reentered the room and was stumping back to his seat.

"But the main reason for the destruction of Samsonov's force is that neither it nor the Russian army as a whole was ready to take the offensive so soon. Everybody here knows that according to our original estimate the army was to have been ready to go into action two months from the day of mobilization. One month was the minimum."

Zhilinsky had reached his chair, but did not sit down. The contest had become too hot for that. He confronted Vorotyntsev, resting his clenched fists on the table. The colonel, crimson with tension, chest thrown out as though he too was ready for fisticuffs, flung his next words in Zhilinsky's face.

"We made a fatal decision just to please the French, thoughtlessly promising to begin operations a fortnight after mobilization, when we were only one-third ready. Only an ignoramus could have promised to lead our units into battle piecemeal and in a state of unreadiness!"

"Your Imperial Highness, this is an insult to the Russian state and to the Emperor, who approved of the decision! According to our convention with our French allies. . . ."

Vorotyntsev, hurriedly taking advantage of the last second before the Grand Duke lost patience, retorted in a voice full of hatred: "Under the convention Russia promised to give 'resolute aid,' not to commit suicide! It was you who signed Russia's suicide note, Your Excellency!"

(Yanushkevich, forgotten by everyone, sat with his head lowered. It was he, though, who had demanded that the Northwestern Army Group should act four days earlier still.)

"It is also an insult to the Minister of War!" Zhilinsky yelled, but his voice was cracked and unfrightening. "And the decision had His Majesty's approval! There is no room for officers like you at GHQ! Nor indeed in the Russian army!"

The Grand Duke sat like a handsome statue, his legs crossed and turned away from the table. He spoke stonily, through stern lips: "Yes, Colonel. You have exceeded the limits of the permissible. It was not for this that I allowed you to speak."

He would not be allowed to say his last word, the last, perhaps, of his army career. He could not bear to forgo a single syllable, could not bear to know and not tell what he knew. He had nothing more to lose or to fear, he was free of all constraints. He saw only the men of the Dorogobuzh Regiment carrying a dead colonel and a wounded lieutenant on their shoulders; Staff Captain Semechkin, that merry, mettlesome bantam of a man, breaking through the enemy lines with two companies of the Zvenigorod Regiment . . . and he answered the Supreme Commander in ringing tones: "Your Imperial Highness! I too am an officer of the Russian army, like you and like General Zhilinsky. And we, all of us, every officer in that army, share responsibility for our country's history. We cannot and must not lose one campaign after another. Those same Frenchmen will look on us with contempt tomorrow!"

The Grand Duke rarely lost his temper but now he flared up: "*Colonel!* Leave the conference room at once!"

Vorotyntsev felt only relief. The white-hot arrow tip had been plucked from his breast. Bringing flesh with it, but no matter. Not another sound. Thumbs along the seams of his trousers. About-face, with a stamp of the heel. March to the door.

As he reached it a beaming adjutant entered.

"Your Imperial Highness! A telegram from the Southwestern Army Group!"

This was it, what they had all been waiting for! The Grand Duke unfolded his limbs and rose. The others got to their feet.

"Gentlemen! The Mother of God has not deserted our Russia! The city of Lvov has been taken. A colossal victory! We must issue a communiqué to the press."

Document No. 10
Telegram, 2 September

I am happy to give Your Majesty the glad news of the victory won by General Ruzsky's army at Lvov after seven days of uninterrupted fighting. The Austrians are returning in total disorder, in some places abandoning light and heavy weapons, artillery, and supply wagons as they flee. The enemy has sustained enormous losses, and many prisoners have been taken. . . .

Supreme Commander
Adjutant General NIKOLAI

UNTRUTH DID NOT START WITH US AND WILL NOT END WITH US.

1937	Rostov-on-Don
1969–70	Rozhdestvo on the Istya; Ilinskoye
1976; 1980	Vermont

The Red Wheel
November 1916 – Chapter 6

Not the Vilest Form of Evil

A t confession? When was that?"

"In Lent. You'd only just joined us."

"Ah, that's probably the reason. I've got a poor memory for faces and I see new ones all the time."

The second lieutenant wasn't finding it any easier now. It was like making his confession all over again.

"I complained to you . . . that I found fighting difficult. I told you I'd joined up without waiting to be drafted. I could have finished my university course. But I volunteered. Which means that I voluntarily took all the sins and murders committed here upon myself."

"Yes, yes, yes!" Father Severyan had remembered. "Of course! It was the only confession of that sort I heard from an officer, and I wouldn't have missed it for anything. We'd have gone on from there if it hadn't been in my first few days. Absolutely everybody was coming to confess—it was Passion week. But why didn't you come again?"

"I had no way of knowing that it had made any impression. I thought maybe others talk like that and you were a bit bored with it all. Or maybe there was no answer. The main thing was that you gave me absolution for my sin and my doubts—but I hadn't absolved myself. It all came back to plague me again. Should I have gone back to you? A second and a third time? To repeat what I'd already said, in the very same words—as if I was rejecting the absolution you'd given me? And even if you didn't reproach me, what could you do? Only repeat: 'I, an unworthy priest, by the authority given to me by God. . . .' And I would be answering back, as you covered my head with your robe: 'No, don't forgive me, it won't help!' In confession there's no avoiding it: you have to pardon me in the end." He looked at the priest quizzically. "Couldn't you not forgive me? If I'm to bear the very same burden tomorrow, because you can't relieve me of it, don't forgive me! Send me away unrelieved. That would be more honest. How can I ever relieve myself of it while the war goes on? I can't. The fact that I can't see the people I'm killing doesn't change matters. I wonder what the final score will be. And how I shall justify myself? The only way out is for me to get killed. I don't see any other."

Father Severyan followed closely the movements of Sanya's mind and his eager interest showed in his mobile young features.

"Well, you know, in the ancient Church warriors returning from a campaign were not immediately absolved. They were made to do penance first. But there is another way out: change your ideas."

"I've tried. Tried to see things simply. Like all the others, like Chernega, for instance. He fights—and is cheerful about it. I tried to do the same. For several months. It didn't work. You bombard the enemy and get no answer. It's Cheverdin who gets the answer."

The priest wasn't at all put out by the second lieutenant. His keen gaze searched the features of his slow-spoken companion.

How unusual it was to meet such a person among the officers of this brigade (most of them regulars, following their vocation formally, shamefacedly or laughingly)—and a student at that. Such people were even more unusual among students. Back home in Ryazan, Father Severyan's activities were conducted in a murky atmosphere of ridicule and contempt created by the whole educated stratum of society—contempt not just for him but for the whole Orthodox Church. Repulsed by their contempt, he, who came from the same sort of family and the same cultured milieu, was driven back toward the ignorant and uneducated petty bourgeois who still thickheadedly saw some sense in lighting candles and going to church instead of reading newspapers and attending theaters and lectures. Father Severyan did not blush for his calling and his costume, and would have been content to remain with the educated stratum to which he belonged, but he was forced out of it. He had had to come all the way from the Ryazan diocese to the front line to hear a student talk like this.

But Sanya went on bitterly. "Besides, the way I look at it, Father Severyan, since we're in the same brigade and your job is to contribute to the success of Russian arms, there's little comfort you can give to me. You are too involved in it all, and—forgive me for saying so—may be sinning yourself. You distribute amulets, and make sure every last man has one around his neck. You carry the cross along the trenches before an attack, and sprinkle the men with holy water. Or you take an icon around the dugouts for tomorrow's corpses to kiss. Priests have been known, when there are no officers left, to jump at the chance of relaying their regimental commander's battle orders. But the most dreadful thing of all is when a service is held in the field, and the candles are placed on pyramids of four rifles leaning together."

Father Severyan did not lower his head. Father Severyan did not avert his eyes. He listened attentively to the second lieutenant's reproaches, even urging him on with expressive movements of his eyebrows, asking for and welcoming more of the same.

"I realize that you did not come here of your own free will, that you were sent."

"You're mistaken. It was my idea."

"Yours?"

"Well, what about you? Priests aren't drafted. Either they volunteer or their diocese sends them to fill an official quota. But a diocese will keep back those it thinks best, and send the dross to the army in the field: the weak ones, those who have been convicted of offenses, political undesirables. Though I myself might well have been included in the last category because of my reformist ideas. But I didn't wait for that, I volunteered. I actually thought that this was the more natural place for me to be in time of war."

"For most men, yes." The second lieutenant still wasn't convinced.

"For a priest too," the priest insisted with the stubbornness he had shown in learning to ride. "Life as it is must be our field of action."

It was strange to hear a priest speak like that. Something along the lines of "Love those who hate you" is what you would have expected. The second lieutenant smiled and murmured, "The overturned cart."

"What?"

"I think the same, just the same. But you. . . . Your position is a special one, a delicate one. Can a priest voluntarily go to war?"

Father Severyan propped himself up higher, on his elbow. His eyes blazed.

"Isaaki . . ."

"Filippovich."

"Isaaki Filippovich!" All that he had not managed to say at confession came tumbling out in one breath. "At no time has the world been without war. Not in seven or ten or twenty thousand years. Neither the wisest of leaders, nor the noblest of kings, nor yet the Church—none of them has been able to stop it. And don't succumb to the facile belief that wars will be stopped by hotheaded socialists. Or that rational and just wars can be sorted out from the rest. There will always be thousands of thousands to whom even such a war will be senseless and unjustified. Quite simply, no state can live without war, that is one of the state's essential functions." Father Severyan's enunciation was very precise. "War is the price we pay for living in a state. Before you can abolish war you will have to abolish all states. But that is unthinkable until the propensity to violence and evil is rooted out of human beings. The state was created to protect us from violence."

The second lieutenant seemed to have risen slightly from his seat without leaving it and his face shone brighter although the stove was no longer red-hot and the lamp was burning with an even flame. Father Severyan kept his mind fixed on the same thought, resisting any temptation to digress.

"In ordinary life thousands of bad impulses, from a thousand foci of evil, move chaotically, randomly, against the vulnerable. The state is called upon to check these impulses—but it generates others of its own, still more powerful, and this time one-directional. At times it throws them all in a single direction—and that is war. So then, the dilemma of peace versus war is a superficial dilemma for superficial minds. 'We only have to stop making war and we shall have peace.' No! The Christian prayer says 'peace on earth and goodwill among men.' That is when true peace will arrive: when there is goodwill among men. Otherwise even without war men will go on strangling, poisoning, starving, stabbing, and burning each other, trampling each other underfoot and spitting in each other's faces."

Meanwhile, carefree Chernega, who knew nothing of such problems, was snoring up above—the only sound to be heard anywhere on the Russo-German front.

The stove was no longer crackling. The coals were glowing noiselessly.

Father Severyan's ready answer flowed effortlessly.

"War is not the vilest form of evil, not the most evil of evils. An unjust trial, for instance, that scalds the outraged heart, is viler. Or murder for gain, when the solitary murderer fully understands the implications of what he means to do and all that the victim will suffer at the moment of the crime. Or the ordeal at the hands of a torturer. When you can neither cry out nor fight back nor attempt to defend yourself. Or treachery on the part of someone you trusted. Or mistreatment of widows or orphans. All these things are spiritually dirtier and more terrible than war."

Lazhenitsyn rubbed his brow. One of his ears, that nearer to the stove, was burning. He rubbed his brow, feeling somewhat easier, but still examining the priest's words fastidiously. He could never answer quickly, or in monosyllables.

"Not the vilest form of evil? But the most wholesale form. The victims of individual murders, or individual miscarriages of justice, are individuals...."

"Multiplied by thousands! There are just as many of them. Only they are not assembled in one place in one short period of time, like those killed in war. Think of the great tyrants—Ivan the Terrible, Biron, Peter. Or—yes—the reprisals against the Old Believers. No need for war there—they were effectively suppressed without it. Over the years, and counting all countries, the sum of suffering is no less without war than with it. It may even be greater."

Lazhenitsyn was livening up. Brightening. And the priest spoke with even greater ease, beginning to look his own age, thirty-five or thirty-six, again.

"The real dilemma is the choice between peace and evil. War is only a special case of evil, concentrated in time and space. Whoever rejects war without first rejecting the state is a hypocrite. And whoever fails to see that there is something more primitive and more dangerous than war—and that is the universal evil instilled into men's hearts—sees only the surface. Mankind's true dilemma is the choice between peace in the heart and evil in the heart. The evil of worldliness. And the way to overcome this worldliness is not by antiwar demonstrations, processions along the streets with signs bearing slogans. We have been granted not just one generation, not just an age, not just an epoch, to overcome it, but the whole of history from Adam to the Second Coming. And throughout history our combined forces have failed to overcome it. You could rightly reproach neither the student nor the priest who voluntarily joined the fighting army—they naturally went where so many others were suffering—but those who do not struggle against evil. "

But did Sanya mean to reproach anyone? Himself, yes—but no one else. He was thinking it over, easier in his mind but still uncertain, afraid to step too hastily on this new and crucial terrain.

An idea so wide-ranging would need lengthy consideration. But he would risk one obvious objection: "Does any of this make murder in battle more forgivable than murder with malice aforethought? Or murder by a torturer, or a tyrant. It's just that here we have a ritual, it's made to look like a matter of routine—'everybody else is doing it, I can't be the odd man out'—and this ritual deludes us. Gives us a false reassurance."

"Yes, but if you think about it, a ritual has to have some sort of basis in reality. Nobody has yet made a ritual of killing the defenseless. In fact, torturers sometimes go mad. There is no folklore about torture chambers, about unjust courts, about the general disharmony. But about war—there's no end of it! War divides, yes—but it also creates comradely union, it calls on us to sacrifice ourselves—and how readily men answer the call! When you go to war, you risk being killed yourself. Say what you like, war is not the greatest of evils."

Sanya was thinking.

Father Severyan gave him time to reply. He expected objections, but heard none.

If you knew Sanya you would know that it was difficult to change his mind, that he would never hastily adopt new beliefs and was slow to part with old ones. But when he did yield to an argument he seemed pleased rather than resentful. He was thinking it through carefully, so as not to make a mistake. There was a pause for reflection in every sentence.

"What you say . . . comes as a surprise to me. I hadn't thought enough about it. It's a great relief. But everybody should be told about these things. Nobody knows about them."

He opened the stove and stirred the fire. In the warm light of the glowing coals he was silent. The priest's arguments had hit home with him.

Chance, the quiet time of night, and like-mindedness had united them. There was probably no one else in the whole brigade for either of them to talk to.

"Yes, they need to be told."

Sanya again: "As it is, malicious people say that the Church sanctifies war. Anyway . . . forcing religion on young soldiers in barracks simply kills it." He stirred the fire and stared into the embers. "Anyway . . . Mankind has lapsed from Christianity as water trickles through the fingers. There was a time when Christians, by their sacrifices, their martyrdoms, their incomparable faith, did indeed command the spirit of humanity. But, with their quarrels, their wars, and their complacency, they lost it all. And it is doubtful whether any power could restore it to them."

"If you believe in Christ," the priest said, remote in the darkening depths, "you don't need to count his present-day followers. Maybe there are only two of us Christians left in the whole world. 'Fear not, my little flock, for I have conquered the world!' He has given us the freedom to go astray—and left us with the freedom to find our way home."

Sanya poked the fire.

"Ah, Father Severyan," he answered quietly, "there's no shortage of reassuring quotations, but things are pretty bad all the same." Sanya raked the coals into one last little heap. There was still a faint glow.

"And why, in this situation, when all the world is the loser, does every denomination insist on its unique and exclusive rightness? The Orthodox, the Catholics, and all the other Christians. They all say they're the only ones, they're superior. This can only accelerate the general decline."

Should one rage against the apostates, the doubters, the seekers who refused to find? Should one not rather marvel at the way in which the idea of God is awakened even in those whom the Good News has not reached? For thousands of years the earth teems with mean and trivial creatures—then suddenly, like a blinding light, comes the realization. Hearken, fellow men! All this did not come into being of itself! It was not created by our own miserable efforts! There must be someone up there above us! . . .

Sanya stared fixedly into the dying embers.

How could anyone suppose that the Lord would withhold the true faith from all the remote races? That throughout the whole history of the planet Earth only one small people in one small place would be allowed to see the light, then the neighbors apprised of it—and no one else? So that the yellow and black continents and all the islands would be left to perish? They had prophets of their own—were they not from the same, the one God? Were those peoples doomed to eternal darkness simply because they did not acquire from us our superior faith? Can a Christian really believe that?

"The one way for a religion to prove itself superior is to approach other religions without arrogance."

"Yes, but no creed can command belief without the assurance that it is absolute truth." There was a hint of steel in Father Severyan's voice. "The exclusiveness of my creed does not demean the beliefs of others."

"I . . . er . . . I don't know. . . ."

In fact, any sect, once it has broken away, starts insisting that it has a monopoly of truth. Exclusiveness and intolerance have marked all the movements in world history. The one way in which Christianity could have surpassed them was to forswear exclusiveness and grow into a tolerant and receptive creed. To accept that we have not cornered all the truth in the world. Let us curse no one for his imperfection.

It was getting dark in the dugout.

God's truth was like "Mother Truth" in the folktale. Seven brothers rode out to look at her, viewed her from seven sides and seven angles, and when they returned each of them had a different tale to tell: One said that she was a mountain, one that she was a forest, one that she was a populous town. . . . And, for telling untruths, they slashed each other with swords of tempered steel, and with their dying breaths bade their sons slash away at each other, to the death. They had all seen one and the same Truth, but had not looked carefully.

It was getting darker.

The Red Wheel
November 1916 — Chapter 37

The Skittle Club

Their meetings in the Stüssihof restaurant were known as the Skittle Club, although there was no skittle alley.

"... The Swiss government is the executive committee of the bourgeoisie...."

"Skittle Club" was somebody's idea of a joke: Their politics made no sense, but plenty of noise.

"... The Swiss government is a pawn in the hands of the military clique...."

But they had cheerfully adopted the name. We'll knock the capitalists down like ninepins!

(He had educated them. He had cured them of religion. He had implanted in them an appreciation of the historical role of violence.)

"... The Swiss government is shamelessly selling out the masses to the financial magnates."

It was some years now since Nobs had started the discussion table in the restaurant on Stüssihof Square. He had brought together the younger people, the activists. Then Lenin had gradually started coming.

(How many humiliations he had had to endure in this conceited country! The Social Democrats in Bern had always looked down on him. When he had moved to Zurich last spring he had tried to get a few Russian émigrés together for lectures—but the few who came at all had soon drifted away. Then he had transferred his attentions to the young Swiss. Some men of forty-seven might think it beneath their dignity—fishing for baby-faced supporters and working them over one by one—but if you could wrest a single one of them from the opportunist Grimm[1] it was time well spent.)

---

[1] Robert Grimm was a Swiss Social Democratic leader who presided over the "internationalist" Zimmerwald and Kienthal conferences that are referred to in this chapter.

". . . The Swiss government is toadying to European reaction and encroaching on the democratic rights of the people."

Across the table sits simpleminded, broad-faced Platten, the fitter (since he had broken his arm he had been a draftsman, but fitter sounded more proletarian). His big face is busy absorbing what is said—it is all so difficult. His brow is knotted and his soft ripe lips pursed with effort, helping his eyes and ears not to miss a word.

". . . Swiss Social Democrats must show complete lack of confidence in their government. . . ."

The table has been made longer for a jolly Swiss gathering. No cloth covers, its planed surface pitted with knotholes, polished by a century of elbows and plates. All nine of them have arranged themselves on two benches, giving themselves plenty of room, and one place is blocked by a pillar. Some have ordered snacks, some beer, just to keep up appearances, and because the Swiss always do. (Everyone pays for himself.) A lantern hangs from the pillar.

That elongated, triangular face under the unruly lick of hair, the keenest face there, belongs to Willi Münzenberg, the German from Erfurt.[2] He is very quick on the uptake, and in fact it's all much too slow for him. His long restless hands reach out for more. These are the clichés he rings out himself at public meetings.

(He'd had luck with the younger people in Zurich. There were half a dozen of them here—all youth leaders. Not like in 1914, when he had sent Inessa to see the Swiss leftists—Naine was fishing, Graber helping his wife to hang the washing out—and nobody wanted to know.)

". . . We must learn not to trust our governments. . . ."

Lenin is at the corner of the table by the pillar, which conceals him from one side. Nobs is at the far end, diagonally opposite, as far out of range as possible, watchful, ingratiating, catlike. He started it all—does he now regret it? In years he is one of them—they are all around thirty—but in party status, in self-importance, and even in girth he has ceased or is ceasing to belong.

Over every table hangs a lamp of a different color. The one over the Skittle Club is red. A reddish light plays on every face—Platten's broad open features, the black forelock and starched collar of the self-assured and foppish Mimiola, Radek's unkempt and tousled curls, his irremovable pipe, his permanently parted wet lips.

". . . In every country stir up hatred of your own government! This is the only work worthy of a socialist. . . ."

---

[2] Willi Münzenberg (1889–1949) was a prominent German Social Democrat turned Communist who later became a master propagandist for Soviet causes.

(Work with the young was the only thing worth doing. There was nothing humiliating about it. It was simply taking the long view. Grimm wasn't so very old—he was eleven years Lenin's junior—but he already had a handhold on power. He wasn't stupid, but theory was over his head. He didn't want an armed rising, yet he had leftish hankerings. When Lenin had entered Switzerland in 1914, mentioning Greulich's name, and established himself there with Grimm as his sponsor, they had met and talked far into the night. Grimm had asked, "What do you think the Swiss Social Democrats should do in the present situation?" To see what he was made of, Lenin had answered in a flash, "I would immediately declare civil war!" For a moment Grimm was scared. But then he had decided that it was just a joke.)

". . . The neutrality of Switzerland is a bourgeois fraud and means submission to the imperialist war. . . ."

Platten's brow is convulsed, his eyes strained and bewildered. How difficult, how terribly difficult it is to master the lofty science of socialism! These grandiose formulas somehow refuse to fit in with your own poor limited experience. War is a fraud and neutrality is a fraud—so neutrality is just as bad as war? . . . But a sideways glance at your comrades shows you that they understand it all, and you are ashamed to admit that you don't, so you pretend.

(It was not just facile phrasemongering. He had brought forth these ideas in a fit of inspiration on his journey across Austria, written a definitive summary of them when he reached Bern, introduced them in a Central Committee manifesto, then defended them in his tussle with Plekhanov at Lausanne. You could know your Marxism inside out and still not find the answer when a real crisis burst upon you: The man who finds it makes an original discovery. In the autumn of 1914, when four-fifths of Europe's Socialists had taken a stand in defense of the fatherland, while one-fifth timidly bleated "for peace," Lenin alone in the ranks of world socialism had pointed the way for the others: *for war!*—but a *different* war!—and immediately!!)

Lenin too has a mug of beer in front of him. The Swiss politician at the tavern table is a species he can't endure, but this is the ritual. Bronski looks sleepy and imperturbable as always. But Radek, with the black whiskers that run from ear to ear under his chin, with his horn-rimmed glasses, his quick glance, and his buckteeth, restlessly switching his eternally smoking black pipe from corner to corner of his mouth—Radek has heard it all before, and now finds it too elementary, too tame, and too slow.

". . . The petty ambition of petty states to stand aloof from the great battles of world history. . . ."

Platten is quietly floundering, trying not to give himself away. The idea of world revolution is easy to understand but it is so difficult to apply to his

Switzerland. His mind consents. Since they have avoided the universal blood-bath, they mustn't sit calmly by but summon the people to class battles. But his heart is unreasonable: It is good that in those houses clinging to the mountain ledges peasants can live in peace, that the men are all at home, that grass is mown in the meadows four times in a summer, however steep the slopes may be, that the tall barns will be filled to the roof with the store of hay, that the tinkling of hundreds of little bells, sheep bells and cow bells, sounds from spur to spur, as though the mountains themselves were ringing.

"... The narrow-minded egoism of privileged small nations...."

The plodding walk of herdsmen. Now and then, the deafening crack of a bullwhip on the stony road, echoing through the folds in the hills. Water troughs at mountain springs, long enough for twenty cows to drink. Shifting winds over swaying grass, shifting mists steaming over wooded gorges, and when sunlight breaks through the rain, there may be no room for the rainbow's arc, and it will stand upright like a pillar on the mountain. The quiet inscription on a hostel in the wilderness: "The motherland shelters her children with her forest cloak."

"... Industry bound up with tourism ... Your bourgeoisie trades in the beauties of the Alps, and your opportunists help them at it...."

Platten gives up his attempt at concealment, and innocently, trustingly, his face reflects his doubts.

Lenin has noticed! From where he sits at the corner of the table—the only older man among all those youngsters, looking well over fifty—he strikes home with a swift, shrewd, sideways thrust.

"... *A republic of lackeys!* That's what Switzerland is!"

The keynote of his harangue.

Radek guffaws happily, deftly switches his pipe—the fingering is different every time—and sucks in imposing quantities of damp smoke. Willi mischievously tries to catch Teacher's eye, his long hands writhing impatiently: encore! encore!

Platten isn't arguing. Platten is merely puzzled. Perhaps his country is like an ornate hotel, but lackeys are obsequious, fussing, and fawning, while the Swiss are staid and dignified. Even ministers' wives don't keep lackeys, but beat their own carpets.

(But it had never been known for a letter to go astray in Switzerland, and the libraries were magnificently run: Books were sent without charge and immediately to remote pensions in the mountains.)

"... Sops for docile workers in the form of social reforms—to persuade them not to overthrow the bourgeoisie...."

It has taken three weeks of effort to arrange this meeting and they have finally got them all together on the evening of Friday, the third—the eve of the Party Congress. Radek has been a great help, made himself very useful.

(When Radek was nice, he was really nice, a super pal. At present there was no living without him. And how well he spoke and wrote German! He took the sharpest bends in the road with ease—there was no need to waste time explaining. A scoundrel, but a brilliant one—such people were invaluable. But at times he was loathsome. In Bern they had avoided meeting, communicated through the mail, and in February broken off relations forever. At the Kienthal Conference he had spoken like an out-and-out provocateur.)

". . . The Swiss people are more cruelly hungry every day, and risk being drawn into the war and killed in the interests of capitalism. . . ."

Nobs's skeptical amber cigarette holder balances unaided on his nether lip.

(What a business it had been, starting, without a single supporter in Europe, the struggle for the renewal of the International, or rather its demolition and the construction of a new, Third International. At one minute scraping together any of the Bolshevik émigrés who would agree to come; the next, rallying with Grimm's help three dozen women—the International Conference of Socialist Women—and, since he could hardly attend in person to give them the guidance they needed, sitting for three days in the café of the Volkshaus while Inessa, Nadya, and Zinka Lilina ran to report and ask for instructions.)

". . . Will you go to the slaughter for interests which are foreign to your own? Or will you instead make great sacrifices for socialism, for the interests of nine-tenths of mankind?"

(Then there was the International Socialist Youth Conference. They had mustered fewer than a score, mostly people who had evaded the call-up and were sure to be against the war, and again he had sat in the same café for three days, while Inessa and Safarov trotted to him for instructions. This was when Willi had appeared on the scene.)

If you're twenty-seven, with ten turbulent years of the youth movement behind you—meetings, organizations, conferences, demonstrations. . . . And if, among your peers, you discover that you have a voice, courage, luck—people listen to you, you rise step by step as though to a platform where you can be seen better, and suddenly find yourself in demand as a public speaker, delegate, secretary. . . . And the party leaders immediately try to draw you into their orbit, and urge you not to listen to that Asiatic with his wild ideas, yet it is from him and from the incendiary Trotsky that you always learn what is right and what matters!

". . . 'Defense of the fatherland' is a fraud on the people, and can never be 'war for democracy.' And Switzerland is no different. . . ."

Twenty-seven! The things he'd been through! His mother's early death, beatings from his stepmother, beatings from his father, serving in his father's tavern, playing cards and talking politics with the customers, at the washtub under his stepmother's eye, always suffering because his clothes were ragged and his boots the wrong size, drawn into propaganda work while he was apprenticed to a shoemaker, emigration to Zurich when he was only twenty to work as a pharmacist's dispenser and join in all the class battles. . . .

In the reddish light from the lamp Münzenberg's devoted and determined face is trustful and expectant. The tempered strength of his will shows in the sharp jut of his narrow chin. His brows are knit in an eager frown of welcome for revolutionary ideas. He has already often done as Lenin said and the results have been good. He rallied more than two thousand people for a Youth Day on the Zürichberg and led them through the city singing the "Internationale," waving red flags and shouting, "Down with the war!" He had earned an invitation to Kienthal and joined Lenin in signing the resolution of the left.

". . . In Switzerland too, 'defense of the fatherland' is a humbugging phrase. It paves the way for the massacre of workers and small peasants. . . ."

Schmidt from Winterthur, an ungainly figure at the far end of the bench, is puzzled and peers past his neighbors to say, "The war can't affect our country, we're neutral. . . ."

"Ah, but Switzerland may enter the war at any moment!"

Nobs chews his amber holder under his fluffy blond mustache. He smiles like an amiable cat, but his eyes are mistrustful and a tuft of hair stands up like a question mark.

"Of course, refusal to defend the fatherland makes exceptionally high demands on revolutionary consciousness!"

(All his life he had been the leader of a minority, pitting himself with a handful of followers against all the rest, and aggressive tactics had been essential. His tactics were to whittle down the majority resolution as far as he could—and then still not accept it! Either you record our opinion in the minutes or we leave! . . . But you're in the minority, why are you dictating to us? . . . All right—we're leaving! A breakdown! A public brawl! A disgrace! . . . That was how it had been at all those conferences, and there had never been a majority that hadn't weakened. *The wind always blows from the far left!* No Socialist in the world could afford to ignore that fact. That was why Grimm was so unsure of himself, and why he had hurriedly called the Zimmerwald Conference.)

" . . . Not a single penny for a regular army, not even in Switzerland! . . ."

"Not even in peacetime?"

"Even in peacetime Socialists must vote against military credits for the bourgeois state!"

(Lenin had had to wait a long time for his invitation to Zimmerwald, and had been very depressed. Grimm might not summon him, and it would be quite unseemly to force himself on them. What sort of conference would it be anyway? A bunch of silly shits would get together and declare themselves "for peace and against annexations." *For peace*—he couldn't bear to hear those words! . . . Meanwhile, he had discreetly used his influence to insinuate as many of his supporters as he could into the list of delegates. Those who were against their own governments—they would be the nucleus of a left International! . . . But they could muster only eight: himself, Grishka, and Radek, that was three, Platten, one Latvian, and three Scandinavians. Still the *whole* of the "old" International, fifty years after its foundation, had barely filled the four wagons that carried the participants into the mountains so as not to attract the attention of the authorities, who in fact noticed neither the arrival of the delegates in Switzerland nor their dispersal. They had learned of it only from the foreign press.)

"But the special character of Switzerland . . ."

"Special character nothing! Switzerland is just another imperialist country!"

Platten recoils. His brow is an open book. He struggles to bring the creases of astonishment under control. His unregenerate heart rebels: Our Switzerland may be a tiny country, but surely it is a very special one. Since the first three cantons were united, have we ever annexed anybody? With intense mental effort he strives to accept these advanced ideas. His big, strong, helpless hands lie palm upward on the table.

(Platten was good material to work on. Through Platten alone he could bring the whole Zurich organization into line. If only he would work harder at educating himself.)

"And so we, the Zimmerwald left, are now completely unanimous: We *reject* defense of the fatherland!"

Some of the awkward squad didn't understand.

"But if we reject defense of the fatherland, are we to leave the country defenseless?"

"A radically incorrect formulation! The right way to put it is this: Either we let ourselves be killed in the interests of the world imperialist bourgeoisie or, at the cost of fewer casualties, we carry out a socialist revolution in Switzerland—the only way to deliver the Swiss masses from rising prices and hunger!"

(In Zimmerwald he had hardly spoken at all, but had directed his left-wing supporters from the shadows. That was the most effective way to deploy his forces. The speech making could be safely left to Radek—he'd be witty, resourceful, relaxed, self-confident. His own duty as leader was to weld his small group more firmly together. An ordinary enemy is only half an enemy. But the man who used to be with us and suddenly wobbles off the line is doubly our enemy! We must hit him first and hardest! But it is better to anticipate trouble and prime your followers in caucus between sessions.)

"... The disgusting thing about pacifists is that they dream of peace without a socialist revolution."

Radek is always ready for marching orders. His pockets bulge with newspapers, books, all he needs for a day: If he has to hurry off to a revolution he can go as he is. How interesting he finds it all!!!

(But the rogue needed watching. He might change sides, might betray, at any minute. And he sometimes got things wrong—trying to reconcile Grimm and Platten, for instance, when it was important to keep them quarreling.)

"... Revolution is absolutely essential for the elimination of war. ..."

Just look at Bronski, dozing again. He might as well not be here at all. He is only needed so that we have enough people. When his vote is wanted, it will be there. And when required he will say what is required. (Yes, he is stupid. But there are so few of us that everyone counts.)

"... Only a socialist system can deliver mankind from war. ..."

Difficult to say whether Nobs really approves. His eyes and lips sympathize, but his ears are still and his brow is unruffled. Yet he is editor in chief of the main left-wing paper and is effortlessly advancing to the commanding heights of the Party. They all have great need of him.

He needs them too, though. Nobs knows perfectly well that the wind always blows from the left. Small as their group is, it may change the course of the whole Swiss Party. Only he doesn't want them to be a millstone around his neck.

"... It is illogical for anyone who aims at ending the war to reject socialist revolution. ..."

(When Liebknecht's letter was read to the Zimmerwald Conference, Lenin had sprung to his feet shouting: "CIVIL WAR IS A SPLENDID THING!" Caution is all very well nine times out of ten, but the tenth time you must overstep the mark. Take the proletarian slogan—"fraternization"—to the trenches! Preach class struggle to the troops. Tell them to turn their bayonets against their fellow countrymen! THE AGE OF THE BAYONET IS AT HAND! It was risky, of course, for an émigré in a neutral country to carry on like this, but he had always gotten away with it. At Zimmerwald, though, that foul German crook Ledebour had said, "You can put your name to it here, because you're safe. Why don't you go to Russia and *send* your signature?" That was the level of debate with such people!)

"... The Swiss Party is stubbornly stuck in the rut of strict legality and is making no preparations for revolutionary mass struggle. ..."

From the counter with its two potbellied old barrels and its dozens of colorful bottles a waiter with blunt Swiss features is slowly carrying golden tankards and dark red glasses and tumblers to the table. From the serving hatch another waiter brings yellow trays with thin brown slices of smoked sausage and plates of roast meat or fish. Swiss bellies are unhurriedly packing away inordinately lavish Swiss helpings, each enough for four. And at every glutton's elbow a second helping is keeping warm over a little flame.

"... The socialist reorganization of Switzerland is perfectly feasible and urgently necessary. Capitalism is completely ripe for transformation into socialism—here and now...."

(At the last session of the Zimmerwald Conference, from midday on all through the night, the left had raised a storm over each amendment, demanded at every turn that its dissenting opinion be recorded, and by these means shifted the resolution considerably to the left. They hadn't, of course, succeeded in putting through either the "Civil War" or "A New International" resolution. Still, the Zimmerwald left had emerged as a new wing of the international movement, and Lenin was no longer a mere Russian sectarian, but its chief. The official leadership, however, had remained with the centrists and the hero of the conference in newspapers throughout the world was Grimm. Though not much more than thirty, he was already on the Executive Committee of the International, because he was hand in glove with the opportunists. Lenin had been visiting or living in Switzerland for twenty years on and off, long before Grimm was ever heard of.)

Willi's thin, eager face. He agrees, agrees completely; but it is essential for him to understand exactly what must be done, and where to start.

"In Switzerland it will be necessary to expropriate ... a maximum of ... thirty thousand bourgeois at the very most. And of course to seize all the banks right away. And Switzerland will then be a proletarian country."

From his place by the pillar, Lenin observes them obliquely, his domed brow inclined, bringing the full pressure of his mind and his hard gaze to bear on them, skillfully checking how much each of them has taken in. His thinner hair is a richer red in the light from the lantern.

"Strike at the roots of the present social order *by concrete action*. And *now!*"

That is the step which Socialists everywhere find so difficult. Nobs screws up his eyes as though in pain. Even the proletarian from Winterthur looks a bit down in the mouth. And Mimiola's high starched collar is choking him.

A fine fellow, our Ulyanov, but much too extreme. Nowhere on earth, let alone in Switzerland or Italy, would you find anyone so extreme.

It is hard, so hard on them.

Lenin's gaze slides rapidly, restlessly over all those heads, so different, yet all so nearly his for the taking.

They all dread his lethal sarcasm.

(When you can't force something through a narrow opening it often helps to pile on extra weight.)

He addresses the table at large, simultaneously pursuing each of the six Swiss in his thoughts. His voice is tense, but lacking in resonance—it seems always to get lost in his chest, his larynx, or his mouth, and it slurs the *r*'s.

"The only way to do it is to *split the Party!* It's a bourgeois affectation to pretend that 'civil peace' can reign in Swiss social democracy!"

They shudder. They freeze.

But he goes on: "The bourgeoisie has reared the social chauvinists to serve it as watchdogs! How can you speak of *unity* with them?" (Keep hitting the same spot, over and over again, varying the words just slightly—that's the first rule of propagandists and preachers.)

"It's a disease that affects Social Democrats not only in Switzerland, not only in Russia, but all over the world—this maudlin hankering after 'reconciliation'! They're all ready to renounce their principles for the sake of a bogus 'unity'! Yet short of a complete organizational break with the social patriots, it's impossible to advance a single step toward socialism!!"

However unresponsive they are, whatever they may be thinking, he has the assurance of a teacher confronting his class: The whole class may disagree, but Teacher is right just the same. His voice becomes still more guttural, more impatient, more excited.

"The question of a split is of fundamental importance! Any concession here is a *crime!* All those who vacillate on this are *enemies of the proletariat!* True revolutionaries are never afraid of a split!"

(Split, split, and split again! Split at all stages of the movement! Go on splitting until you find yourself a tiny clique—but nonetheless the Central Committee! Those left in it may be the most mediocre, the most insignificant people, but if they are united in a single obedience you can achieve anything!!!)

"It is high time for a split at the international level! We have excellent reports on the split in the German Socialist Party. The time has come to break with the Kautskyites in your own and all other countries! *Break* with the Second International—and start building a Third!"

(A method tried and proven at the very dawn of the century. He had pierced and slain the Economists with the death ray of *What Is to Be Done?*, his scheme for a band of professional conspirators. He had shaken off the clammy clinging incubus of Menshevism with his *One Step Forward, Two Steps Back.* He did not want power for its own sake, but how could he help taking the helm when all the rest steered so incompetently? He could not let his incomparable qualities of leadership atrophy and go to waste.)

Yet the idea might have been born there and then, at the table, might have been an instantaneous and irresistible revelation: *Split* your party—and thereby ensure the victory of the revolution!

Nobs, stiff with delicious fear, doesn't even murmur. If you refuse, who knows, you may be the loser. Perhaps the best place to be is right here, at this table?

Platten's paw has frozen on the handle of his tankard.

Mimiola has triumphed over his constricting collar, risen clear of it. But he looks gloomy.

Willi wears a little smile of startled enlightenment. He is ready. And he will carry the young with him. He will repeat every word of it from the platform.

The heavy brow batters away at the breached wall.

"My book on imperialism proves conclusively that revolution is imminent and inevitable in all the industrialized countries of Europe."

There are still a couple of them who want to believe, but can't quite see it.

There you are, living in a room you've grown used to, and one morning you go out into the street, with familiar buildings all around you, and you start a revolution. But how? . . . Who is going to show you how? There has never been anything quite like it.

"Yes, but this is Switzerland. . . ."

"What of it? That was a glorious strike in Zurich in 1912! And what about this summer? Willi's marvelous demonstration on the Bahnhofstrasse! A baptism of blood!"

Yes, this was Willi's proudest boast.

"All those casualties!"

Even the first of August hadn't been as good as the third, in honor of the fallen.

They hem and haw. . . . In Switzerland? . . .

How can they disbelieve him? He treats every youngster as his equal with perfect seriousness. Not like those leaders who snub their juniors once they get one foot on the ladder. He never begrudges the effort spent on conversation with the young, wearing them down with questions, questions, questions, until he can slip a noose on them.

"Yes, but in Switzerland. . . ."

While they are clearing up this little matter, Radek has found time to read two of the newspapers from his bulging pockets and leaf through a book. And still they don't understand!

Radek pokes the stem of his pipe at them. "Your own Party Congress last year . . . adopted a resolution on revolutionary action by the masses! What about that?"

Well, what about it? . . . All sorts of resolutions are passed. Passing resolutions is easy enough.

'Then there's Kienthal!"

Five of those present had been at Kienthal, including Nobs and Münzenberg. Among the forty-five delegates they had been part of the minority of twelve. They had threatened once again to wreck the meeting by walking out, had in fact left the hall and returned. So the majority had given way to the minority, and they had pushed the resolution further and further to the left: *"Only the acquisition of political power by the proletariat can ensure peace!"*

True enough, but you can say anything in resolutions. . . .

"No, but here in Switzerland. . . ."

The most patient of men couldn't listen to these numskulls without exploding! Then—he amazes himself with a fresh revelation, which comes out in a hoarse cracked whisper.

"Don't you realize that Switzerland is the most revolutionary country in the world??!"

They are all rocked back in their seats, clutching tankards, plates, forks. . . . The lantern on the pillar sways in the wind of his voice. Nobs grabs at his cigarette holder as it falls from his mouth.

??????????????? . . .

(He saw it all! Saw the barricades that would soon rise in Zurich, not, perhaps, on the Bahnhofstrasse, where all the banks were, but over toward the working-class district by the Volkshaus on the Helvetiaplatz!)

And with a caustic flash of the Mongol eyes, in a voice without depth or resonance, but with the cutting edge of a Kalmyk saber, catching only on the *r*'s: "Because Switzerland is the only country in the world where soldiers are given weapons and ammunition to take home!"

So. . . ?

"Do you know what revolution means? It means seizing the banks! The railway station! The post office and telegraph! The big enterprises! And that's all! Once you've done that the revolution is victorious! And what do you need to do it? *Only weapons!* And the weapons are there!"

The things Fritz Platten hears from this man, who is his fate and his doom! Sometimes his blood freezes. . . .

Lenin has abandoned persuasion and is rapping out orders to these recalcitrants, these incompetent muddlers.

"So what are you waiting for? What more do you need? Universal military training? Well then, the time has come to demand it!"

He is improvising, thinking between sentences, picking his way among his thoughts, but his voice never falters.

"Officers must be elected by the people. Any group of . . . a hundred can demand military training! With instructors paid from the public purse. It is *precisely* the civic freedom of Switzerland, its effective democracy, that makes revolution immensely easier!"

Bracing himself against the table, he looks as though he were about to spread his wings, fly up from the dining room of the Stüssihof restaurant, and soar above the five-cornered, enclosed medieval square, itself no bigger than a good-sized public hall, glide over the comic warrior with a flag on the fountain, spiral past the jutting balconies, past the fresco of the two cobblers hammering away on their stools three floors up, past the coats of arms on the pediments five floors up, and over the tiled roofs of old Zurich, over the mountain pensions and the overdecorated chalets of the lackeys' republic.

"Begin propaganda in the army *immediately!* Make the troops and young men of call-up age see that it is right and inevitable for them to use their arms to liberate themselves from hireling slavery! . . . Put out leaflets calling for an *immediate* socialist revolution in Switzerland!"

(Rather rash words for a foreigner without a passport, but this was the one time in ten that made the difference between victory and defeat.)

"Take executive control of all working-class associations immediately! Insist that the Party's parliamentary representatives publicly preach socialist revolution! The compulsory takeover of factories, mills, and agricultural holdings!"

What? Go and take people's property away from them, just like that? Without passing a law? The Swiss blockheads couldn't blink fast enough.

"To reinforce the revolutionary elements in the country, all foreigners should be naturalized without charge. If the government makes the slightest move toward war, create underground workers' organizations! And in the event of war . . ."

Greatly daring, Münzenberg and Mimiola, leaders of youth, finished it for him: ". . . refuse to perform military service!"

(Luckily Münzenberg and Radek, deserters from the German and Austro-Hungarian armies, respectively, cannot be deported under Swiss law.)

Not one little thing have they understood! A mocking smile but not an unfriendly one, passes over Lenin's face. He has no other choice—down, down he comes, past the cobblers hammering away at their work with slavish diligence, over the blue column of the fountain, to alight with a rush in his old place in the restaurant.

"Under no circumstances must they refuse; what can you be thinking of? In Switzerland especially! When they give you arms, take them! Demand demobilization—yes, but without giving up your arms! Keep your arms and get out into the streets! Not a single hour of civil peace! Strikes! Demonstrations! Form squads of armed workers!!! And then *an armed uprising!!!*"

Broad-browed Platten is bowled over as though by a blow on the head: "But with all Europe at war . . . will the neighboring powers . . . tolerate a revolution in Switzerland? They'll intervene. . . ."

This is the nub of Lenin's scheme—the utter, unreproducible uniqueness of Switzerland.

"That's what is so splendid! While all Europe is at war—barricades in Switzerland! A revolution in Switzerland! Switzerland speaks three major European languages. And through those three languages the revolution will overflow in three directions and flood all Europe! The alliance of revolutionary elements will expand to include the proletariat of all Europe! A sense of class solidarity will be aroused in the three neighboring countries! If there is any intervention, revolution will flare up *through Europe!!* That is why SWITZERLAND IS THE CENTER OF WORLD REVOLUTION TODAY!!!"

Singed by the red light, the members of the Skittle Club sit fixed as the words chance to find them. The narrow triangle of Münzenberg's intrepid face is thrust forward into the glow. Nobs's fluffy mustache is also touched with the flame. Mimiola looks as if he was about to pull his tie off and lead his hot-blooded Italians over the ruins of Europe. Bronski in his sad, sly way is trying to look eager for battle. Radek wriggles, licks his lips, and excitement flashes behind his glasses: If that's how it's going to be, what fun he will have!

(The Skittle Club is the Third International in embryo!)

"You are the best part of the Swiss proletariat!"

Radek has a resolution ready and waiting for tomorrow's Congress of the Swiss Party. If only Nobs will print it. . . .

Hmmmmm . . .

But who will put it to the Congress?

Hmmmmm . . .

Since the restaurant would soon be closing, the party broke up.

There were three streetlamps on Stüssihof Square, and lights shone from the windows of houses all around. You could easily read the plaque telling how in 1443 Burgomaster Stüssi had fallen in battle not far from here. His family home had stood for sixty years before that. That must be Stüssi too, the comic Swiss warrior in armor and blue hose standing in the middle of the fountain. You could hear the thin jets of water splashing into the bluish basin. The air was dry and cold for this part of the world.

They were still talking as they took leave of each other and walked away over the smooth cobbles. The square seemed completely shut in, and unless you knew where to look for the crevices which were streets, you might wonder whether you would ever get out. Some of the company went off down a bumpy cobbled slope, and took the side street which led to the embankment. Others turned off at the tavern called the Franciscan. Willi, however, accompanied his teacher along the same street in the opposite direction, past the Voltaire cabaret on the next corner, where the arty set raved the night away, and on the narrow pavements they encountered prostitutes who were still waiting for customers. Past the Voltaire they turned steeply uphill under an antiquated lamp on an iron post, along a street like a stairway, so narrow that with arms outstretched you could almost touch both walls at once, and there was hardly room to walk two abreast; up and up they went.

The heels of Lenin's stout mountain boots clattered on the cobbles.

Willi wanted his teacher to reassure him over and over again. He had not forgotten the fight on the Bahnhofstrasse that summer, but every trace had been hosed and swept away, the shopwindows were as dazzling as ever, the bourgeoisie strolled around as comfortably as before, and the workers placidly obeyed their accommodating leaders.

"Yes, but the people aren't ready for it...."

At a sharp turning in the alley, in the dim light of someone's sleepless upper windows, the voice from under the dark cap was quiet but as sharp-edged as ever.

"Of course the people aren't ready. But that doesn't give us the right to postpone the *beginning*."

In spite of the platform victories behind him, the yells of assembled youth in his ears, Willi persisted.

"But we are such a small minority!"

Lenin stopped, and out of the darkness came something not revealed even to the select gathering at the Skittle Club.

"The majority is always stupid, and we cannot wait for it. A resolute minority must act—and then it becomes the majority."

The Congress opened the following morning, across the river in the Merchants' Hall. Lenin, as leader of a foreign party, was invited to deliver greetings. Radek was also there, ostensibly representing the Polish Party. Two from "our" side, speaking in succession.

On the first morning not all the delegates had arrived, and the audience was no larger than at a good lecture. (Lenin, in fact, was not used to large audiences; he had never known what it was like to address a thousand people at a time—except just once, at a mass meeting in Petersburg when he had lost his tongue.)

As soon as he looked out over the hall caution overcame him. Just as at Zimmerwald, just as at Kienthal, he had no overpowering urge to speak his mind fully—no, the full fervor of his conviction was naturally reserved for a closed meeting of his supporters. Here, of course, he did not call for action either against the government or against the banks. Standing before this nominally Social Democratic but in reality bourgeois mass of self-satisfied, fat-faced Swiss, lounging at their little tables, Lenin sensed immediately that they did not and would not understand him, and that he had practically nothing to say to them. He somehow couldn't even bring himself to remind them of the highly revolutionary resolution which they themselves had adopted last year—and anyway it might spoil everything.

So his salutations would have been quite short, if he had not gotten painfully entangled with the Adler affair. (Two weeks earlier, Fritz Adler, Secretary of the Austrian Social Democratic Party, had shot and killed the Prime Minister of Austria-Hungary—killed the head of the imperial government in time of war!) This assassination had captured everyone's imagination, there was a lot of talk about it, and before making up his own mind Lenin had inquired carefully into the circumstances. Who had influenced Adler? (His Russian Socialist Revolutionary wife, perhaps?) Because he was secretly preoccupied with this problem, a perpetual source of disagreement with the Russian SRs here at the Congress, he had devoted half of his speech to an irrelevant discussion of terrorism. . . . He had said that the greetings sent to the terrorist by the Central Committee of the Italian Party *deserved full sympathy*, if the assassination were understood as a signal to the Social Democrats to abandon opportunist tactics. And he had defended at length the Russian Bolsheviks' opposition to individual terror: It was *only* because terror ought to be a *mass* activity.

Meanwhile the Swiss munched and swigged and mooed and tippled—there was no way to understand them.

Still, the Saturday session had gone well and raised his hopes. Platten was applauded by the majority, and Papa Greulich, a seventy-five-year-old with a luxuriant gray mop of hair, started joking about the Party's "adoption of new pets." (Nothing to the round Schweizerdeutsch rudenesses we'll heap on you when the time comes! When we come to power, we'll hang you!) It had worked, it had gone off beautifully! Lenin had cheered up and felt like an old warhorse in the swirl of battle. Moreover, the circumspect Nobs had not refused to put forward the Skittle Club's (i.e., Radek's) resolution: that the Congress should adhere to the Kienthal decisions. (The stupid Swiss might vote for it just to be in fashion, without really knowing what the Kienthal decisions were—and then they'd be caught! After that, you could bait your hook with their own resolution and catch the whole bunch of them! Grimm as well!)

Trivialities? No! That is how history is made—from one hard-won resolution to the next, through the pressure of the minority, you push and push every resolution—leftward, ever leftward!

Then the next step. That Saturday evening, on the Skittle Club's initiative, by individual invitation, a separate, secret, private meeting of all young delegates was held away from the Congress building; they gambled on the normal sympathy of the young for the left. The plan was simple: to work out with their help a resolution (or rather submit a ready-made one brought along by Radek) for them to put forward and force through the Congress on the following day, Sunday.

At this private conference of young delegates, Willi, of course, was in the chair—making lavish use of his commanding gestures, his bold, cheerful voice, and his tumbling hair—and Radek was at his side, smothered in curls, wearing his merrily militant spectacles, reading his resolution, explaining it, answering questions. (He was a good speaker too—but his pen was beyond price.) Lenin, as he always preferred to, had sat inconspicuously among the rest, and contented himself with listening attentively.

All might have gone well. The young delegates listened closely to their Russo-Polish comrade and seemed in agreement.

All might have gone well if something extremely unpleasant hadn't happened. They had not had the sense to lock the door. And through the unlocked door, unnoticed at first, came two malicious tale-bearers, two horrid old bags: Madame Blok, who was Grimm's friend no less, and Martov's lady friend, Dimka Smidovich. Once these wretched females were in, there was no getting them out: They'd scream and make a scene! And the whole meeting could hardly move elsewhere! Anyway, they'd already seen and heard Radek speaking, and realized, of course, that a resolution for the Swiss Congress was being drafted by Russians.

What an infernal nuisance! What a colossal fiasco! Loathsome creatures with their filthy little intrigues! Of course, they'd rushed off to Grimm and whispered in his ear. And he, the brute, the blackguard, the utter swine, had believed the stupid wenches. He'd tried to start a vulgar brawl by printing vile innuendos in his *Berner Tagwacht*, which were absolutely incomprehensible to ninety-nine percent of its readers: "A *certain small group of foreigners,* who look at our workers' movement through spectacles of their own, and are utterly indifferent to Swiss affairs, are trying in a fit of impatience to provoke an artificial revolution in our country! . . ."

Poppycock! Unmitigated hogwash! And that is what they call a working-class leader?

Then at the Congress they'd laughed down Nobs's resolution. When he proposed making it a rule for the future that only those opposed to national self-defense should be nominated for parliament, Greulich had been greatly amused. If we elect such deputies, he said, their hotheadedness may land them in the *skittle alley.*

The Congress roared with laughter.

Moreover, consideration of the Kienthal resolution had been postponed—until February 1917.

What a tragedy it all was! So much effort, so many evenings, so much conviction, lucid thought, and revolutionary dynamite had gone into it! And the result was—a heap of vulgar, stupid opportunist debris, like dingy cotton wool, like the dust of junk rooms.

In musty Switzerland the bacillus of petty bourgeois cretinism reigned triumphant.

And the bourgeois world still stood, unexploded.

FOR FOLK LIKE YOU WITH NIMBLE TONGUE

THE ROAD AHEAD IS NEVER LONG.

FOR FOLK LIKE ME WITH NO BOOK LEARNING

IT'S THE LONG, LONG LANE THAT HAS NO TURNING.

The Red Wheel
November 1916 — Chapter 75

An Arduous Confession

Darkness.
Silence.

But this is not the grave. You are still alive. For one brief moment you lie there forgetful of your grief. Then you are wide awake.

Half a second at most. Then a stab of pain. Remembering what happened last, what happened yesterday. But not just that—the whole series of events, each one a knife wound. And all the time your head is aching, your breast is aching, leaving you helpless. If only you could lie there, remembering nothing. Just resting, listening to the hush, the profound silence all along Arapovskaya Street, all over Tambov. But no—it all comes back, like a tattoo of hammerblows. Yesterday's letter. A child's grave. Zhenya's grave, the Little Guy's grave. His last days. You got back too late. From here, from Tambov. The desolate bitterness left by that lovers' meeting, those two blissful days with no thought of disaster. In this very room?

A little grave in a country graveyard. On a damp autumn day.

And now—*he* had another woman!

The searing current ran through her brain, along the same grooves again and again, cauterizing. . . . Switch it off! Let go of me!

Why does he write to me like this now?

She fought against it, broke the circuit. Lay there as if in a swoon, a healing sleep, disconnected from the chain of stinging shocks.

But the burning sensation returned. By a roundabout route. As if what she now remembered belonged to another life. Her mother had lain dying, and she had gone into hiding because she was pregnant, and it would be better for mother not to see daughter at all than to see her like that. She had not arrived in time to close her mother's eyes.

Then, from a third life, something now easily borne, so remote that it no longer rankled—Zhenya's father.

At the time it had seemed impossibly complicated, an insoluble problem. How could she persuade him to tell his wife? Left to himself he would never have the courage. But why had it seemed so important? She no longer remembered. She had no thought of stealing him, weak and irresolute as he was. But the indignity of it choked her—the idea of being an invisible appendage, a thief in the night, not a person in her own right. No, there must be clarity.

Such a weak man. But where were the strong ones? Under nervous strain not one of them was strong. Wasn't Fyodor just as weak?

Weak! Blind! Hopelessly muddled! Floating like a bit of wood wherever the current carried him. When you were with him you forgave him, because of his naïveté, his emerald eyes, you found yourself wanting to believe in him, to draw him upward, but when you parted—what was there left? A void. And to cap it all, he writes to say. . . !

Let me go! Switch it off.

She could think of Zhenya's father calmly now. It was a relief, even. Try to concentrate on *him*.

She had once seen him as one of those characters whom Chekhov portrayed so faithfully. They were at large everywhere, nice, amiable people who wouldn't hurt a fly and would never make anything of themselves. Was it angst, or just dreaminess? Eternally seeking—but not striving to find. Satisfied with whatever comes along: Life's like that—make the best of it. (Fyodor was just the same!) It was easy to foresee, right from the beginning, how it would end: He would remain in his shell forever, seeking (but not too eagerly), and only Zinaida herself would be shattered. When he was seeing her off to the country to have her child he had promised to come quickly, to come at once, promised faithfully. And afterward to reorganize his life, for his son's sake! And he had not been lying, he had meant every word.

But he had not even come to look at his son.

Men's lives are roomier, easier, they do not even have to try to understand themselves, they feel no need to examine themselves in depth. But a woman's life is narrow, and she must live in depth.

The other woman too? Was it the same for her? Did she live in depth? If she were only half a woman, wouldn't she feel the same hurt?

But the Little Guy was dead!!! Her little boy! Little Zhenya! Before he had time to learn the first thing about the world, before he could distinguish places, or faces, or even the parts of his own body. He had recognized only his mother, and only vaguely. He had struggled out of nonexistence, slept away three-quarters of his time, and promptly returned there. That old-mannish look with which newborn infants survey this inhospitable world had only just left him. His soft hair had only just begun to grow, his head was just assuming a more human shape, the fold in his neck had disappeared . . . when suddenly his lips turned blue. And he was no more.

"They'll say"—damn them! For herself Zina had never been in the least afraid of what "they'll say." Still, she wasn't going to risk killing her mother. But hadn't she given the sick woman a push in that direction by not going to see her? Shouldn't she at least have gone to the funeral? More "they'll say." She shuddered.

Perhaps it was the same for that other woman. Perhaps she was not so much concerned to hold on to her husband as afraid of what "they'll say." It could be too much for her to take.

Yet for Fyodor's sake she had rushed here, braving the disapproval of her sister and brother-in-law, fearlessly inviting him into their home. And here, in the drawing room of their childhood, the drawing room in which he had once been introduced to her family, and she, a high school girl, had gazed in rapturous awe on this former member of the Duma, who had suffered for his principles (!), and was a writer (!), and had twinkling emerald eyes (!) . . . in that very same drawing room, she had walked around naked at his request while he lay on the sofa lazily looking her over with those same emerald eyes.

It was only three weeks ago, only three weeks, since they had dallied around here shamelessly, while her son was falling sick in Korovainovo!

For six years she had been tantalized, allured, even when she was an unripe girl and far away, by the presentiment that with Fyodor some revelation awaited her. In those two days together with him she had been lost to the world—yet all the time a feeling of emptiness, of disillusionment was growing within her, and as soon as they parted, as soon as she was aboard the train to Kirsanov, it suffused her whole being, all her raptures seemed degrading, all illusion, all dross, and in her revulsion she could not understand why she had ever gone there. She must hurry back to her son! Her anxiety for her abandoned child was excruciating. What if something had happened to him? What if he were ill?

A peasant woman, beside her in the Korovainovo cemetery, had called her own tiny dead child "a piece torn from my womb."

Torn . . .

From my . . .

Womb . . .

Gone . . .

I wish I had gone too.

So—now?

So no one had ever seen her secret infant. Neither his father. Nor his . . . stepfather? There had not been time. It was as though he had never lived, except in his mother's memory. There wasn't even a photograph. Nothing to show anyone, ever.

Was that what she had wanted? To keep him hidden? "Stepfather"! He had scattered and abandoned children of his own, lovelessly—he himself probably didn't know where. He had made only one of them an exception and adopted him. What inferior creatures men were, if they could not even love their own children.

But supposing they had had a child of their own? Surely she would have won him over, endeared it to him?

On the train to Kirsanov she had been desperate: It had only just begun—and it was all over. It could not go on! Over as soon as begun—and nothing left to remember! He was hopelessly coarse-grained, primitive, incapable of understanding higher things. Over the years his letters had been so many cruel lessons to her, he wrote gratuitously about other women, tried to put her off, rapped her fingers to break her hold on him, and she had thought it was all just a rough game, could not believe that he cared nothing for her, that he might write her off at any moment, that he meant every word when he said that as far as women were concerned he did not pick and choose, he was content with those who cost least to woo, he wasted no effort on conquest, but let no opportunity slip. . . . And still she remembered his radiant smile, his endearing shyness in literature classes, she had always believed that he had a soul, dormant it was true, but needing only to be cleansed, needing only the help of a woman's hand, and his front-row pupil was perfectly capable of providing that! For six years she had been true as a compass needle amidst his sordid revelations, believed that it was all a pose, that beneath the surface there was some hidden treasure, as yet unmined, known to no one. He was cynically frank because he had never known what it was to be loved.

How her hopes had soared, how she had exulted, when she found that he could rise above jealousy of another man's child!

And then they were alone together, in each other's arms. And . . . and it was as if none of it had ever happened.

In fact, she had always been afraid of getting to know him more closely. Eager to—and afraid to. . . .

Before she got back to her son, before she was told about his illness, she was already in despair, already full of revulsion—determined never to meet Fyodor again, perhaps not even to write to him.

EMPTINESS!

Emptiness! Zhenya could have lived, filled her life with his own, but now there was nothing but emptiness! A vacuum never to be filled by any other human being, any other child! *That* being would never exist again on this earth. A life that never was, that would remain a mirage, a life linked with, intersected by, no other.

She had not wanted to write to him anyway. But when Little Guy vanished everything had gone dark, and she was dumbstruck. What could she write to him? There would be no miracle.

Such treachery: abandoning a helpless little boy, so that by herself she could. . . .

But there was a second and worse betrayal: under that very roof, in that same empty house, listening to that very clock striking, to be thinking of him now, burning for him again, when she should be thinking only of Zhenya.

Unexpectedly, and unthinkingly, she had found herself drawn by her son's death to the church. It was a path she had never once taken in her young days. Now, it was as if she had been going there all her life. The peasant women who were her neighbors had stood so unobtrusively around the little coffin. They had carried it to the cemetery.

But to stay on in Korovainovo after the funeral and until the ninth-day service would have been too much for her. She abandoned his lonely grave, lonely forever now, since it was his destiny to remain forever in the Korovainovo cemetery, and rushed off to see her aunt in the Convent of the Ascension at Tambov.

Her aunt had told her to come at any time: If anything goes wrong, come and see me. But all she ever had to offer was the promise of solace in the world to come, none of it had anything to do with the turmoil of life here and now. Zinaida would answer her rudely. Forget it, Auntie, God the Comforter is an absurdity. Why go to such trouble to create a world which was going to need consoling?

Now, though, she had found that it was all very simple, and that this solace was very much needed, like fragrant pitch cooling to fill deep ruts and smooth over sharp stones. It was with her aunt that Zinaida began to recover her balance.

Instead of brooding over the future she could no longer look forward to with her son, she asked herself: Where was he now? That he was nowhere was unthinkable: To have lived only a little while could not be the same as never having been conceived.

My . . . womb . . . torn from. . . .

Then she had come across Father Aloni in the church at nearby Utkino—a kindly priest, serious-minded as simple Russian people generally are, broad-shouldered and benevolent. After conducting the ninth-day service he had talked to Zinaida at length, and with serene ease. After which her equilibrium was even more secure.

Zina had of old defended the Church against the "progressives," even when she was an unbeliever. Just to be contrary.

Now that she had recovered her equilibrium and was thinking more calmly Zina had found the strength and the equanimity to write to Fyodor about the death of her son. Perhaps this was how her recovery could begin. But she was not to reach the twice-ninth day without shocks. Yesterday, like a bolt out of the blue, she had received his letter. It had passed hers in the mail—otherwise he would not have written it. You should know, he wrote, that I have someone else, and that it is serious.

Someone else—a third someone, a twentieth.... Why, then, had he come to her? Why had he not admitted it? Why this blissful reunion (or meaningless farce)? That was what really hurt, that was her hell. Was it for him, was it for this that she had destroyed her little boy?

Was this the man she had wanted to save? To purify?

To think that she had believed in him! Danced to his tune!

Who are you? Tell me.

She was sitting up in bed.

She lit the lamp.

Replaced the glass chimney with a firm hand.

Her childhood home, untidy and deserted now, seemed still gloomier. Dark doorways opened into other dark rooms.

This was where she had displayed herself to him.

She must tear herself away! From this bed, before all her ribs were crushed! From these rooms. This house. Go anywhere. So long as she was not alone!

Alone—she would hang herself, there would be nothing else to do. She would not be able to go on! Life would be impossible! Especially here. She must get away from this vault, this blackness, this silence, in which her mother had lain dying, and in which they had indulged their passion—while in that other place her baby was dying.

Why did you ask me to come? If you hadn't I wouldn't have rushed to join you—and *he* would not have taken sick!

Now she was dressed.

I must go somewhere, anywhere! To somebody, anybody! Fall on someone's breast—I ... can't go on alone!

The simplest thing would be to go to her aunt. The convent gates would be open by now—the nuns rose before daylight.

But for some reason she could not go to her aunt. It would have been so natural, and so salutary, to run to her immediately after Zhenya's death. But *now* it was impossible.

How have all these troubles piled up? At twenty-two, for other people, life is just beginning. But your path is blocked by a landslide of troubles. Life has no place for you, hang yourself, why don't you!

Yes, hang yourself! This yellow scarf will do. A long, strong scarf.

To have been so pure, to know yourself to be upright, noble even, and then in a single year to wreak such havoc, ruin so many lives, become so hopelessly entangled. That other family—shattered! Mama betrayed! Little Zhenya—betrayed.

He was the only one she hadn't betrayed.

So he had betrayed her.

It wasn't so very early. People were up and around. It was dark because this was November. Anyway, I must get out of here.

She covered her head with her scarf. Can't stay here. Can't be by myself—it'll end badly.

But somehow it seemed absolutely impossible to go to her aunt in the convent.

My hands are trembling. Now I've dropped the key. I won't be able to find it. . . . Perhaps it's slipped into that crack on the doorstep. . . . Why don't I leave it and just go. . . . No, I mustn't, it's my sister's home.

She burst into tears. She had held out as long as she could, but now she was weeping. Where could it be, that piece of iron?

Not a soul to be seen on Arapovskaya Street. If lamps had been lit it was behind shuttered windows. People took their time getting up. Took their time living. Spent an hour over their prayers.

There were streetlamps on the corner of High Street. And one on the corner of Dolevaya Street, but its light did not reach her.

She went back inside for matches. What was her aunt really like? She had been in the convent for a long, long time. Being a saint was easy enough. But understanding a sinful woman was impossible for her. A woman who had not suffered this ordeal could not possibly understand one who had.

She struck match after match, but the wind blew them all out. In the end she found where the key had hidden itself.

She locked the door, and set off.

The way to her aunt would have taken her along Bolshaya Street, past Studenets, as far as Voznesensky Street. For no particular reason she walked toward Dolevaya instead.

It was damp. And dark. Breezy too, along Dolevaya, and she felt the wind through her flimsy head scarf. It was bracing.

She walked on, alone, no one on the street, no one standing at a front gate. She might have spoken to the first person she met, but there was no one. On warm evenings, all Tambov sat on benches, or stood at garden gates. Now the city was deserted.

To whom could she turn? Everything was closed. Everyone was indoors.

She used to think that the worse things were, the more interesting life became; when things got better they settled down into a too peaceful pattern, a humdrum routine. But no. That was all very well until the ice gave way under you. When it did, you would be crying out, "Give me a hand! Give me a hand! Pull me out of here!"

She had loved Fyodor for six years, and little Zhenya for only six months. But to him she had been his whole world. He had known nothing and no one else.

And that was all she had needed. So what was the point of those letters? Why, when she was fulfilled, had she called to *him*? She had held out for so many years, determined not to be importunate, hedging words of affection with irony, rewriting anything that sounded too affectionate. And after all that she had thrown herself at him.

It was not as if he would find happiness with "the other one." Of course not. But then he had no need of love or happiness, or of anyone to share his life. He was mean-spirited and probably beyond salvation.

Her little one would never toddle on his own little feet. Never even say "mama." He had been given time for nothing.

How could she face her aunt after getting that letter yesterday? How could such a trollop ever hold her head up again? It had been bad enough having a child by a married man.

Now she was crossing Dvoryanskaya. The cold wind blew still stronger there, rounding the curved façade of the Gentry Assembly. Two cabs dashed by, one after the other, returning empty from the station, their drivers leaning into the wind.

Zinaida came to a stop, out in the wind, in the middle of the square.

The Utkino church stood there before her. A faint light shone through the elongated windows. A few shadowy figures were making their way there from different directions.

She had not consciously intended to come there. Her legs had brought her unbidden.

But where *could* she go? Not back where she had come from. Not home, to be by herself—anything but that.

The windows were suffused with light, as on a feast day. But a subdued light, soothing to a sick soul.

Since those obligatory services at school she had hardly ever entered a church except for the blessing of the Easter cakes. Though she had sometimes wanted to, by way of protest against the prevailing fashion. True, she had attended a communion service with organ music in a Lutheran church in Moscow, but she had thought of that as a concert.

There too, her thoughts had been of him. Conscious of her own nothingness, in the presence of sublime music she had remembered him, and become so sorry for him: His one thought was to get on, to rise in the world, to achieve something, but he was already in his forties, he had done nothing, he had no niche of his own, he was a failure. And she had yearned to save him.

All by herself?

She passed by two or three beggars in the doorway—she had come out without her purse—and entered the church. There were lamps before all the icons, and a few candles, but just one electric light, over the choir. Not a single chandelier was lit. That explained the subdued half-light.

Zina loved icon lamps. Her mother used to have one at home. In the intimacy of the attic bedroom, the woman and the icon, with a lamp between them. It gave only a little light, but it knew a great deal. What bottomless depths there were in that dialogue. All the things said there, all the blessings asked!

The service was just beginning in the side chapel on the right, the Chapel of Our Lady, where there was an icon, modest in size but renowned throughout the country, of the Tambov Virgin. Almost all the parishioners had congregated. A cantor recited some incomprehensible and interminably dreary rigmarole, while a priest, invisible in the sanctuary, interpolated occasional brief responses.

Zina, almost oblivious of her surroundings, went down the broad, empty middle aisle. She stood near a pillar and looked upward.

The pillar ended in an arch which carried her eyes along its smooth curve until it merged with the vaulted dome.

The dome itself, up above the nave, was like a miniature round heaven. Enough diffused light from icons and lamps reached the heights for her to see that this celestial hemisphere was wholly occupied by a head-and-shoulders representation of God the Father looking down from the clouds. When morning came the dawn light would reach that spot through narrow windows in the dome. The sun's first and last rays would find it. At present it was in semi-darkness but, lit from below, the countenance of the Lord of Hosts, majestic in conception, was half visible and half recognizable. There was no trace of consolatory tenderness in the Creator's tense expression, but nor could vengefulness or menace have any place there. He Himself was the heaven above us all, and we were sustained by Him. This attempt to show the face of God in human lineaments, humanized, had been arrogant presumption on the part of the artist. But from beyond and through what was painted there the unimaginable looked down—a portrayal of the Power that sustains the world. And whoever encountered the gaze of those celestial Eyes, and whoever was privileged to glimpse even momentarily that Brow, understood with a shock not his own nullity but the place which he was designed and privileged to occupy in the general harmony. And that he was called upon not to disrupt that harmony.

There Zinaida stood, and went on standing, with her head thrown back, staring into that immensity, deaf to what was happening in the church, with no thought of praying, no thought of anything. What floated above her could not be conveyed in words, was indeed out of reach of thought. It was a wave of life-giving will, surging also into the human breast. Her vocal cords tightened, heat flooded her swollen neck, her legs were unsteady but she had not the strength to tear herself away. Chilled by what she had seen, she stood shivering like a sacrificial victim awaiting the stroke, stood for as long as her neck could endure the strain, scarcely feeling the floor beneath her, unable to pray, to beseech, to question. . . .

A passive receptacle of the Divine Will, she began to feel easier and stronger. Gone was the burning desire she had felt at home to break out, run away, see someone, anyone, talk. Standing there, she felt no urge to run. She stood staring upward, her neck growing numb, but the iron bands that had immobilized her for so many days relaxed, gradually fell away, released her.

She was beginning to feel giddy. She put her hands to her head and with an effort restored it to its normal position. She walked on a little way over the flagstones.

In the side chapel to the right a priest emerged from the sanctuary and bowed to the closed gates, but it was not Father Aloni.

Zinaida found herself, with no one else near her, facing a large icon of Christ, with a big pink lamp burning before it. The icon and its lamp filled her field of vision, shutting out the rest of the church. Somewhere a service was in progress, but she did not catch a single word. She stood gazing on the Savior's brown-tinted face.

It was a completely human face, though its complexion was not of this world. It had other peculiarities: The hair descended in two straggling locks, the nose was impossibly long and thin, the raised fingers were frozen in a gesture of benediction. The eyes held an enigmatic omniscience . . . knowing all, from the beginning to the end of time, things of which we never dream. A mind at ease might not have responded to these depths. But Zinaida, with her heightened perception, saw that Christ was suffering acutely, suffering yet not complaining. His compassion was for all those who approached him— and so at that moment for her. His eyes could absorb whatever pain there might yet be—all her pain, as they had absorbed many times as much before, and would absorb whatever pain was still to come. He had learned to live with pain as something inevitable. And he could grant release from all pain.

A weight was lifted from her.

The pink glass of the icon lamp, and the light it gave, were also unusual. This was not the pinkness of a dawn sky, or of a blush. It was a pinkness with an otherworldly mauve tint, remote from all earthly colors. And that strange light made the dark brown, all-knowing countenance seem all the more perceptive.

In that ghostly pink light it seemed more impossible than ever to believe that her son was . . . nowhere. She could see now that *somewhere* there was *something*.

The icon and the lamp swam before her eyes.

How fortunate that she had strayed unthinkingly to this place. She had no wish to go elsewhere. No wish to pour her heart out to anyone else, as she had longed to a little while ago. That was now the last thing she needed.

Now she could hear the chant from nearby: "For my iniquities have risen above my head, they have weighed me down like a heavy burden. . . . I cry out in the torment of my heart: O Lord, all my desires are open to Thee, and my lamentations are not hidden from Thee."

She shuddered. Her whole story had been known here before her coming. They were proclaiming it aloud.

She made no attempt to pray. She scarcely knew how to. But some kind of block, some inhibition had been removed from her mind and her breast, and she found herself thinking again. Thinking not in jerks and jolts, which hurt and burned, but contemplating herself as though she were someone else.

She thought that as the Church defined sin she was a sinner three times over.

No, four.

Five, even. (Her reckoning came easily—it might as well have concerned someone else.)

She had seduced a married man, and the damage she had done was not merely superficial. By insisting that he should "tell" she had split that family irreparably. She had abandoned her dying mother. She had abandoned her son for her lover. She . . . that made four. What was the fifth? There was a fifth sin somewhere.

"For my soul is overwhelmed with calamities, and my life is close to the bottomless pit."

Her eyes too became clear, and now, at an angle and in front of her, she saw—and her heart leapt to see him—Father Aloni standing sideways to her by the central pulpit, hearing confessions. Matins was still in progress in the side chapel, but he was hearing confessions, soundlessly, it seemed. Standing beside the lectern, head bowed, he listened closely to another bowed head, then covered it with his stole, made the sign of the cross, and dismissed the penitent. There were several of them waiting, and the line was moving slowly.

Zinaida observed this as something which did not concern her. She had no need to confess. She could see into herself clearly enough without that.

When she reviewed her past feelings she knew that she had never been two-faced, never set out to deceive or to damage anyone. She had wanted only to follow her natural, womanly path. Surely she, like any other woman, had a right to do that? She had not succeeded, she had made only false starts, and—oh, God!—how difficult it was to start at all. You emerge from adolescence feeling so free, so light—why did things immediately become so difficult and confused, why were other people, all of them, and their destinies, always in your way, so that at every move you had to step over or else collide with someone else? How could you start again from the beginning?

She had never meant to harm anyone! Why, then, at every turn in her life did she have to tread on someone?

No, she was being unfair to herself. There was one person toward whom she felt no guilt. For him she had always wanted the best—little though he realized it. She had wanted to open his eyes to the talent of which he was unaware, and likely to remain so all his life. Reading his complacent confidences with bated breath she had seen more and more certainly that she and she alone was the one he needed! She alone could enlarge his life and help him to fulfill himself—but largeness and diversity were not in his character. He was base and trivial. And he bore all the blame—because he had weakly let her go her own way, because he had been ready to surrender her to the first taker. It was he who had driven her to it. And then—to behave as he had yesterday, as much as to say be off and take your devotion and your sacrifices somewhere else! Yet even in rejecting her he had been false! If he loved another (if only he could, if only he were mercifully granted the grace to love, but he was incapable of it), if he loved another why had he gone out of his way to Tambov?

Ah, that was it, the fourth sin, or was it the fifth, wrenched from her like something that had become part of her. It was as if her dress had caught fire, and tearing it off and not tearing it off were alike impossible—her fifth sin had stuck to her, merged with her! She had stayed away from her aunt because she knew the answer she would get, and that it was not the one she needed, not the one she would have thought up for herself.

Father Aloni dismissed his last penitent and looked around for others. His eyes swept over the central aisle, he saw her and nodded an invitation, assuming that she had come to see him.

She had not, of course. But he stood waiting. Upright, solid, simple, broadfaced, his thick, wavy hair brushed back from a large, smooth brow, the eyes beneath it bright.

He beckoned, waited.

She had not come there for him!

But still he waited, and called out to her, thinking, of course, that she was still struggling with her fresh grief.

Well, since she was there ... And he was still waiting. And if not him, who was it she had come to see? Why had she come there?

One step, another, a third—she was walking toward him, unintentionally, surprising herself.

Careful—don't trip on the steps up to the choir stalls. She had eyes only for that broad-browed face, framed by an auburn beard, and for his encouraging gaze.

She bowed her head toward the lectern. Her forehead rested on the tooled cover of the Gospel, and there was a crucifix to her right.

Gospel and crucifix watched over her confession. The lectern—she saw it now—was a steep slope, a rough steep slope—and up that slope she had to drag her whole life, struggling under the burden, and against the friction.

Confession at school had been a joke, a giggle. One wave of the stole over your head and you were absolved. The priest's questions were condescending, meant for infants. You almost expected him to get you a bonbon from the sideboard. "I have sinned, Father, I have sinned"—and off you flitted. She had never been to confession since. Now she waited impatiently for him to question her.

The priest, hovering unseen above her, also waited. She could not raise her head, look into his eyes and speak to him simply, one human being to another, as she had after the requiem. She felt that she must answer to a superior being.

It was good that she was not looking into his eyes.

In fact, she could not see him at all. Nor anyone else. Only the crucifix, as she knelt with her brow pressed to the Gospel.

No questions were asked, no answers demanded. She must struggle through the darkness unaided.

She had not wanted to hear what her aunt or her sister nuns might say, they were all too holy to understand. But could she speak now?

Speak, yes, but not say what hurt most! Let her thoughts come tumbling out—tell everything (but not quite everything)! You know all the things you've done, you've gone over them a hundred and twenty times. Can't you, just this once, wrest them out of their protective covering of complicitous silence, say it all out loud? Impossible. (Everything else—yes—but not that one thing!)

Hopeless. But no more hopeless than sitting at home alone in an empty house. And wherever she might go it would be just as hopeless. How could she haul herself up this steep incline beside the crucifix? Tell another person, a stranger, all that had happened? Without mincing her words, without dissembling? (Easier to do such things than to talk about them! Would she have voice enough, breath enough?) She plunged in without preliminary explanation, throat dry, voice cracked.

"I have seduced a married man."

She was over the first threshold. No—that was all in the past. Why had she done it? That was the question.

"I seduced him without really loving him. In fact . . . when I really loved someone else. . . . It was just that . . . I'd reached the age. . . . I had to have an outlet for my emotions."

If only some question were asked above her bowed head! An opinion expressed, a condemnation delivered! Or perhaps some murmur of sympathy? But was she even being listened to?

"I made him confess to his wife. And by doing so . . . I suppose . . . I ruined their lives . . . forever."

The second threshold. A life as heavy as lead. How to haul it up the slope? But every time she put something into words a weight seemed to fall away.

She had not yet finished, though. She must punish herself to the full.

"It was all for no purpose . . . all for nothing. . . . I am profoundly penitent."

Not true. It had a purpose. Not altogether clear or precise, but . . . I knew beforehand that we should part. . . . No, I didn't. . . .

"It was for a contemptible purpose. . . . To snatch him for myself. . . . No, it was simply out of vanity. Because the other man didn't love me."

It had suddenly become so much easier to speak.

"You see, I've loved him . . . the other one . . . all my life."

When you speak of love you should feel that you have wings. But she was struggling up that slope, every sin a stone over which she stumbled and slithered backward, nose to the ground.

"And then I . . . concealed my pregnancy from my mother. I decided to hide myself in the country. My mother fell ill, she was dying, and I didn't get there. . . . I let her down . . . for the child's sake."

Untrue. Another equivocation.

"No, it was because I was ashamed. Because of my vanity."

It was like using the grapnel at a wellhead, with three hooks facing different ways—and what you have to do is find down there, in the dark depths of your soul, a hot stone, fish for it, grip it, only the hooks won't take hold, it breaks loose, seventy times over it breaks loose until at last, with delicate movements, as cautiously as if it was your dearest treasure, you latch on to it, draw it upward, raise it carefully, carefully, then seize it. You burn your fingers but you have rid your soul of it.

"I abandoned my child . . . for a lovers' meeting . . . Like a mad thing . . . And while I was away he got sick . . . And because I wasn't there he died. . . ."

Another great stone dragged painfully, breathlessly, upward, and tipped onto the surface. Her brow was bathed in cold sweat.

What could the priest think of her now? He had been so full of pity for the grief-stricken young mother.

But it was as if every stone thrown out had ceased to be part of her—forever? or just for the moment?—so that she could look at it objectively instead of dragging it around inside her.

She had not once raised her head to glance at the priest, she wouldn't dare to, and none of the other penitents had done so. But, without hearing a single sound from him, she realized that it was not the priest hovering invisibly over her who was hearing her confession! He was only the necessary witness.

That was what made it so hard—that she was left to herself. But it was also a relief. A relief for how long? Could a word she said aloud outweigh guilt, sin, evil?

Yet strangely, incomprehensibly, as soon as the words were out a weight was lifted from her. If only for the moment.

As for forgiveness—who could forgive such things? How could any other person grant you forgiveness? You must bear the burden alone, labor on alone.

But that means movement. All that is piled up in a living breast cannot lie there inert forever. If it did, we would ourselves be stones.

But what does he mean by it, hovering over me without saying a word? He might help with a question, a sound of some sort, a murmur of encouragement.

But once you have learned how to drag these stones out with your grappling hook—your throat is less dry, speech becomes less hesitant, confession flows faster, until your words tumble over themselves as you hurry to snatch at and identify all your betrayals (your own betrayals! You were blaming *him* a little while ago, but that was a lie!), mention them for the second time (all futile! all rejected!), or perhaps it wasn't the second time? Perhaps this was another betrayal? Yes, I have betrayed you again, sinned not against your life this time, but against the still fresh, still warm memory of you, before your little grave has been smoothed over, that will have to wait till next spring—and who is it I am thinking of again? Of *him,* of *him,* that is why I fled, among flying sparks, like a mad thing swerving so as not to burn myself, at times even leaping through the flames, unable to find the straight path, which anyway did not exist, over the baking-hot earth, the soles of my feet burning, returning to the same place—he rapped my fingers, said keep away, get your claws out of me—for six years I had thought of him, and now I am thinking of him again, I have sacrificed my little son, and before I am out of mourning here it comes again, for the fifth time like a tornado, and now . . . there is no pulling this stone out, it is ablaze! Scorched as I am, desire writhes in me like a fiery serpent—the desire to conceive again! Conceive a child of his! He has never known this joy—with me!

And however much the priest might object, and try to forbid it, whether he forgave her or not, she realized, horrified, that she was fatally tied. Tied to *him.*

Was she doomed, then, yet again, to deprive someone else? To snatch, to steal what was not hers? Was it impossible to walk this earth without trampling others? Simply to walk on the grass-grown earth?

How treacherous the earth's crust was! At every step there was molten lava underfoot! If you tried to run it would cave in under you!

Flinching from the flames, she dropped her hook, staggered back from the well, and—oh, God!—had all the stones crashed back down there? Help me, O God! You see that I want to tear myself away! I want to change! But this is one disaster too many. . . .

She had struggled as far as she could up the slope, and now lay prostrate, one temple against the crucifix, her meager strength, that of a single human being, exhausted.

She was silent.

She felt the weight of something woven rest on her head, shutting out the little she could still see. And through the fabric she felt the touch of a hand making the sign of the cross.

And a voice—no ordinary voice, one capable of soaring above a thousand others, of supplication, of suffering, of repentance, now hushed and meant for her alone, but with the same significance as when it reverberated in the dome.

"May the Lord Our God Jesus Christ through His grace and the munificence of His love for mankind . . ."

She had blurted out all she had to say, however horrible it was she had done all she had to do, and now she crouched with her head pressed to the crucifix, breathless.

But another Breath, the Spirit, hovered over her and stole tremulously into her.

". . . forgive you, my child, all your transgressions. And I, an unworthy priest, with the authority vested by Him in me . . ."

He stressed not his authority, but his unworthiness. Grief-stricken witness of her struggle against grief, he testified to her forgiveness.

"I pardon you and absolve you of all your sins. . . ."

He pronounced these words as weightily and as meaningfully as if he knew of many details which she had not mentioned and, having weighed them, nonetheless unhesitatingly forgave her.

But Zinaida herself did not feel that all was forgiven, forgotten, and over. And that her labor had not been in vain.

She still had a question to ask. Perhaps she had already formulated it when she was jumping about to avoid being burned.

He withdrew his stole, and she quietly raised her uncovered head to look at Father Aloni.

She saw his frank gaze, his honest, firm, guileless, big-browed face. Yes, he had understood her question, and let it be seen that he had.

But, with splayed fingers, he gently but firmly pressed her head down.

She was at a loss until she saw the Gospel there beneath her.

She kissed the ancient dark red cover with its half-effaced embossed pattern.

Still gripping her head with his fingers, he guided it toward the crucifix.

She pressed her lips to its silvery surface.

And again threw back her head with that mute question still in her gaze.

Father Aloni's eyes were moist with unshed tears.

He had said what was required of him, and need say no more. But she waited, head thrown back, for words meant only for her.

His thick lips moved among the dark auburn undergrowth.

"In each of us there is a mystery greater than we realize. And it is in communion with God that we are able to catch a glimpse of it. Learn to pray. Truly, you are capable of it."

But as yet she did not feel herself to be capable of it. For her this was no answer.

His gray eyes gazed on her sorrowfully, compassionately. He saw that she wanted him to continue.

"The world holds no sufferings worse than those caused by family problems. They leave festering sores on the heart itself. For as long as we live this is our earthly lot. You can rarely decide for another that he or she should do or not do this or that. How can anyone forbid you to love when Christ said that there is nothing higher than love? And He made no exceptions, for love of any kind whatsoever."

The Red Wheel
March 1917 — Chapter 17

The Toppled Tram

It was a motor-driven tram, and it lay overturned and alone at the beginning of Syezhin Street, not far from Kronverk Avenue. There must have been plenty of people around while it was being tipped over, but now even the street-kids, tired of sitting and jumping around on it, had run off to find other places to play. People passing by barely checked their stride, and none lingered long, as if the sight of an upturned tram in the middle of the street was nothing out of the ordinary. Perhaps the sights they had just seen—or those they were hurrying off to see—were even more extraordinary.

But one tall passer-by had stopped—clad in a dark cloth jacket and an engineer's peaked cap, with a leather satchel slung military-fashion over one shoulder, he stood, hands thrust into his pockets and collar turned up at the neck—bare cloth with no fur trimming. He stood, and stood, poised beside the toppled giant.

The tram's paintwork was a dirty green natural color, like the hide of certain large animals—and it lay on the dirty snow, a hulking working buffalo, wheezing its last, if not already dead. Its glass forehead was a web of cracks where they had stunned it repeatedly before the coup de grâce had sent it crashing to the ground. The flank onto which it had rolled was battered and crumpled, slashed with shards of glass. Far behind the creature's back, contorted at an unnatural angle, stretched its trunk with the rope still attached. Its four lifeless paws of rounded cast-iron jutted out parallel to the ground, exposing the damage done to the track as they were wrenched free. And here, too, was the miserable creature's underbelly, once hidden from prying eyes, but now exposed to general ridicule, its pendulous secrets bespattered with the filth of the streets.

And its masters had not come to retrieve their maimed beast. It lay abandoned by all.

How, indeed, would they go about getting it back on its feet now?

Leaning over the body, Obodovsky looked in through the upper windows to check the condition of its lower side; walking all round it, he peered in to the driver's cabin and tested the bow collector with his hand. Dusk was already falling when he trudged on his way.

He did not have far to go, for it was right here on Syezhin Street that they lived, just before it curved round onto Bolshoi Avenue.

And here, with that familiar soft, warm embrace and a kiss on the lips, was Nusya to meet him.

Nusya had not walked far today, but there had been plenty to see close at hand. In particular, she knew just how the tram had come to be stopped: It had been traveling under escort, with a police officer on the front platform urging the driver to keep his nerve and press on. But two lumps of ice hurled from the crowd had struck the officer on the side of the head, injuring him, the driver had leapt from the other side of the tram, and the passengers had been forced off.

As ever, Obodovsky paid no attention to the food he was eating. As he chewed, the skin on the whole of his skull moved and his ears twitched nervously.

A crowd was such a peculiar kind of creature! At once human and inhuman. It ran on legs and had heads aplenty, but once a part of it, each individual was absolved of his normal responsibilities, and his strength swelled in proportion to the number in the crowd, even as they drained him of his willpower.

In this part of town the main activity of the day had been breaking windows—at the baker's, the haberdasher's, the greengrocer's—smashing them out of sheer spite. But in every crowd there would always be people, adolescents or adults, who were also after the takings.

It had been the same along the River Okhta—so Obodovsky had been told—they'd smashed the windows and made off with the cash.

It was this looting—going on all over Petrograd, it would seem—that was nudging events beyond the point of no return, just like the shootings. There would have to be more destruction, more looting tomorrow to cover the tracks of the perpetrators.

And as for events in the center—well, those he had witnessed for himself. Never had he dreamt he would live to see the day—to stand there in front of the Kazan Cathedral, beloved assembly point for student revolutionaries these thirty years or more, and watch them openly singing "Arise, Working People, Rise up from Your Thrall!" with no one lifting a finger to stop them, then unfurling the red banner—and your heart's skipping along to the old familiar beat—you just can't help it.

A tiny, fragile human skiff—two pairs of eyes, a man's, a woman's—always together, ever at one, a delicate interlacing of gaze and feeling, fine-tuning each other's every move as they grope their way through pounding, shifting seas. The twin poles of a magnetic needle finding its bearings in the teeth of these tempestuous forces.

And a key was turning. The key to the whole story, the key that made sense of all the sights and scenes of the day.

The Cossacks had not been intervening! It was happening all over town. They had let a whole crowd of youths and women cross over the Nikolai Bridge. That the Cossacks should remain neutral was the most stunning part of it all; never had there been such a thing!

An exhilarating sense of anticipation was creeping over him.

Of course, looting shops is disgusting, but you always get that during mass upheavals.

He was torn in two directions.

That toppled tram, so senselessly vandalized, such a marvelous work of human hands.

After the arrests of the Workers' Group, Obodovsky had been so outraged that he could have smashed the Internal Affairs Ministry with his bare fists, hammered down its callous façade. How could they be so asinine! They never learn, they haven't the wit to grasp what Gvozdev meant for them and what he might have become! Such insensitivity to nuances is the mark of a braying ass!

But now it's apparently *our own* people that have risen up?

Does that mean they'll come slithering out of the woodwork again now—all these "social democrats" (hideous sort of name), the brazen, pushy ones and the ones spouting abstruse nonsense and wriggling their way through the chinks in a dozen amendments and provisos?

And along with it all comes the fear that everything we've managed to put right since 1915 will go to ruin—all the work on military supplies, all the specialist training for the artillery—and what will become of our spring offensive?

There's even something suspicious about the disturbances in some of the munitions factories and at the Putilovsky works, almost as if someone were secretly pulling the strings.

No, what's suspicious is the government's failure to intervene for the second day running: not a shot fired, not a single arrest. You'd think it was some well-drilled piece of street theater: Could the whole thing be an elaborate provocation? to be followed by reprisals on an unimaginable scale? What if the authorities were deliberately standing by, hoping to provoke even worse disturbances—then drown them in blood?

For a hundred years? Another hundred years of reaction!! Oh, our poor, miserable country!

But perhaps it's not that at all, perhaps they're wavering? ready to compromise even? Maybe they'll get rid of that idiot Protopopov? or agree to make ministries accountable?

Or could it actually be that this entire monstrous edifice might be sapped of strength? might even collapse?

Collapse, just like that? this ponderous, indestructible Leviathan? . . .

And will the radiant, egalitarian society dawn at last? Where no obtuse officials with inflated salaries and chests bespangled with stars can block the paths to progress? Where no one will be indifferent to the common good?

One's heart beats fit to burst: O please let the Revolution triumph!

Then slumps again: No, not in the middle of a war like this! The timing couldn't be worse! It's madness. . . .

"You won't believe it, Nusya, but when I was standing by the Kazan Cathedral with everyone singing and the red flags flying, it wasn't just that I wasn't happy; I was ready to stand up like one of those priests spouting appeasement and beseech the crowd with arms outstretched: No, brothers, this isn't the way! You must endure a little longer! Think what evil times we live in! Think how this will gladden the Germans' hearts. Wait till our Spring offensive. It will all be over soon—and *then*, then's the time. . . ."

The Red Wheel
March 1917 — Chapter 29

On the Streets

What was special about today was the absence of that festive, almost playful mood of the previous two days. There were no more chants of "Bread! Give us bread!" and even the looting had abated. The masses were entirely convinced that the troops, and especially the Cossacks, were on their side. (Women had been walking right up to their horses and adjusting the bridles.) For the third day the street demonstrations passed off without casualties—for people had lost their fear of the police, too. In fact, it was the crowds who were setting about the police, and ever more ferociously.

As for the police, their confidence had plummeted. No one stood up for them, not even the authorities themselves, and dotted among the teeming thousands in forlorn little groups they were supposed to keep things in check.

The power of the streets was beginning to make itself felt.

*   *   *

By now all the cordons set up in the suburbs were being penetrated by increasingly large crowds heading for the center of town, and that was where the main events were unfurling. Here, and especially along the Nevsky Prospekt, the ranks of their fellow-demonstrators were swelling. From the sidewalks burghers and office workers stared out at the marchers, their faces betraying neither sympathy nor censure. While those in the road shouted at them:

"What are you standing around for? Get off the sidewalk, you bourgeois trash! Clear off!"

The number of young people in the crowd had grown—intellectuals, or semi-intellectuals at least. Red flags began to appear, dotted here and there, but at many different points in the crowd. And when speakers rose to address the throng, it was no longer grain shortages they thundered about, but beating up the police and overthrowing this criminal regime that had sold out to the Germans!

*   *   *

On Znamenie Square there was now a non-stop political meeting in progress: The crowds and speakers might change, but the meeting went on uninterrupted. And the whole throng was gathered round the monument to Tsar Alexander III!

It is hard to imagine anything more incongruous than this steadfast, unyielding, dispassionate figure of the Emperor, astride his mighty steed standing poised with glowering, lowered head! Tall metal lampposts ring him about, and close behind stands a little church with five cupolas.

The speakers were inaudible above the din and the cheering. The whole square was packed. Cossacks and mounted police had been deployed near the railway station and on either side of Liga Avenue. One of the police officers with drawn saber would shout, "Leave the Square! Or be driven out!" The crowd does not take him seriously, does not budge. He gesticulates to the Cossacks with his sword, yelling: "Clear the Square!" The crowd ebbs away before their sullen, half-hearted advance only to return the moment they have gone. Or the mounted police would charge with sabers bared; the crowd stirs in agitation, tenses itself—but no blow falls.

No one has any idea what to do with the crowd.

And the Nevsky is filled to overflowing with people, a sea of heads and red flags.

*   *   *

A large crowd has assembled by the Kazan Cathedral and the Ekaterina Canal. The respectable portion of the public includes some extremely excitable ladies, who, like the men, gather in knots to argue the issues and hold their emergency meetings.

Some in the crowd start pelting the police with empty bottles. Then half a dozen revolver shots are fired at them, wounding one in the stomach, another in the head; others still are hurt by flying bottles.

A police officer fires two shots in reply. The wounded policemen are carried away.

*   *   *

From about four in the afternoon at various points along the Nevsky—at Pushkin Street, Vladimir Avenue, the Anichkov Bridge—the crowds were disarming policemen and beating them savagely.

*   *   *

A young man in a student's cap draws an object from under his coat, taps it against his boot, and throws it along the ground into the thick of the mounted police. A deafening crash and horses are hurled in the air by the blast, their riders falling flat on their backs.

* * *

And in Znamenie Square—beneath the heavy-footed mount of Alexander III—the meeting was still going on, with speakers holding forth from the red-granite pedestal of the monument. Beside it a large red banner was held aloft.

Into the Square from the direction of Gonchar Street rode a police officer, Captain Krylov, with five mounted policemen and a unit of Don Cossacks. He sat on his horse like a skilled cavalryman. Unsheathing his saber and raising it high, he rode into the crowd.

And his men followed—the policemen with drawn swords, the Cossacks apathetically, their swords still sheathed.

The crowd parted, swayed uncertainly. People began breaking away, fleeing past the monument: "Look out! They're using their swords!"

But not a blow had been struck. Krylov rode out in front alone.

And no one hindered him as he rode right up to the flag.

Seizing it, he drove the flag-bearer before him, back towards the station. Past the policemen. Past the Cossacks.

And all at once—struck from behind by a saber blow to the head—he slumped from his horse, dropping the flag as he fell to the ground.

The mounted police rushed to protect him, only to be driven back—by the Cossacks!

And the crowd erupted into an exultant roar, waving their caps and headscarves.

"Hooraaay for the Cossacks! One of the Cossacks has killed a policeman!"

They finished off the police captain with anything that was to hand—a janitor's shovel, the heels of their shoes.

And his sword was handed up to one of the speakers, who raised it repeatedly aloft: "Look! The sword of the tyrant!"

The Cossack detachment sat on their mounts, regaled with a chorus of grateful shouts. Afterwards, over by the gates to the station one of the Cossacks was being tossed in the air by the jubilant crowd. Was it the one who struck the blow? Or someone else?

* * *

As a young man, Krylov had served in a regiment of the Guards. He had fallen in love with a girl from an impoverished family, but his mother—who was rich and well-connected—refused to consent to the marriage. Krylov introduced his fiancée to his commanding officer and obtained his permission to wed. He introduced her to his fellow-officers: She was charming, well-bred, and the officers approved his choice. And so Krylov was married. It was then that his mother arrived to speak to the Colonel: Force Krylov to resign his commission, or I shall take my complaint to the Minister of War, and higher still. The Colonel summoned Krylov, who saw that there was nothing for it but to leave the regiment. He began casting about for a post in some other service, but everywhere his mother had forestalled him and all avenues were closed.

He did manage to find a post—but only with the police. . . .

*   *   *

And there he lay, eyes closed in death. Blood ran from his temples and nose, trickling down his neck.

People gathered round and gazed.

The Red Wheel
March 1917 — Chapter III

_____

About Town

No one will ever tell who set fire to the Circuit Court building or when—there are no witnesses.

At the height of the blaze the crowd refused to let the fire brigade near, so the firemen drove off again. People stood and stared, approvingly. Boys from the nearby school were pilfering files just for the fun of it. They carried off case histories bearing the photographs of convicted criminals. One young man, an official of the court, stood reproaching the crowd, his voice growing louder as his courage grew—it was shameful that the public notary's archive was burning, a real calamity, and he explained why. A sullen-faced artisan spat on the ground and swore:

—*** you and your archive! We can divide up the land and houses without any archive.

*   *   *

But on Sadovaya Street—everything looks normal: The shops and stores are open; Apraksin and Shchukin Markets are thronged with customers, salesmen touting for trade, peddlers with their trays try to outshout one another, laughing and joking.

*   *   *

When the raid on the Arsenal started, they got away with 40,000 rifles in a single day as well as smashing open lots of cases of revolvers.

*   *   *

A truck full of soldiers is bowling along Suvorov Avenue. Its deep-throated horn bellows incessantly. Crowds come running at the sound. Rifles and sabers are flung from the back of the truck as it moves along. Young people gather them up, trying to sort out how the straps and slings work. But it's the adolescents who go wild with joy; they're the first to grab the weapons.

*　　*　　*

By the entrances to yards and buildings the inquisitive gather—tenants, officials, upper-class girls, sometimes even officers with their ladies. It's dangerous to watch, but interesting too. Knots of onlookers push forward into the crowd for a better look. Then dart back again; officers arm in arm with their ladies do the same.

Townsfolk roam the streets in mingled curiosity and dread, asking people they meet what's going on there and whether it's safe to pass.

*　　*　　*

Seven prisons were stormed that day. In the streets prisoners and convicts from the chain gang stroll merrily about in dressing gowns and prison uniforms, embracing one and another and hugging the soldiers too.

Every last one has been released, no questions asked. The common criminals were all set free along with the political prisoners (and far outnumber them). Within hours a wave of robberies, arson attacks, and murders breaks out all over the city.

*　　*　　*

Workers disarmed the guards at the Finland Station and took control. They cut off the signals, and the trains ground to a halt. The gunsmiths from the Sestroretsk Small Arms Factory occupied the Beloostrov stop as well.

Men from the Putilovo Works took over firearms shops and used the weapons to disperse the last detachments of police in the area of the factory.

*　　*　　*

Everywhere in the streets people are disarming officers—peacefully: Let's have your sword and your revolver—now be on your way, your Honor.

*　　*　　*

So many rifles are firing, everywhere and all the time—you'd think they were going off of their own accord.

In the streets trucks are becoming more and more common. But where do they all come from? The war's been going on for three years, and no one's ever seen so many. They move along in the midst of the crowds like great bristling animals. The soldiers are festooned with belts of machine-gun bullets crisscrossing their chests, draped over their shoulders, girding their waists, wrapped round the barrels of their rifles. Their faces exude joy, and impatience, and a flicker of hatred.

—"Hoora-a-a-ay!" they keep shouting to the crowd. And the crowd surges forward to meet them, waving rags and scraps of red cloth:

—"Hoora-a-ay!"

*   *   *

On Suvorov Avenue a group of soldiers walk up to an officer and tear off his epaulets. He turns aside, walks a few steps—and shoots himself.

*   *   *

At the gates to the barracks of the Izmailov Battalion, mutinous soldiers approach the duty officer, who responds by refusing them entry. He is bayoneted on the spot, impaled by two of them simultaneously; the body is shaken loose onto the ground. (Later it is stripped and thrown naked into a storeroom.)

The Red Wheel
March 1917 — Chapters 101, 122, 185

The Wheeled Battalion

The wheeled reserve battalion stationed at the very edge of St. Sampson Avenue, almost in the Lesnoi district, stood out from the other reserve battalions in Petrograd: It was not just a sump for underage conscripts, prematurely drafted and then left to languish untrained and unskilled, but was made up of soldiers of above-average ability, old enough for combat and led by officers who were likewise fit and combat-ready. The battalion was perhaps the only military unit in the capital that could boast a frontline fighting spirit. Its function was to train specialized companies, equipped with machine guns mounted on motorcycle sidecars supported by motor-driven transport columns, and ship them to the front. Such companies were still a novelty and were intended for combined operations with the cavalry in the major offensive planned for this spring. Training was vigorous and intensive, often taking up ten or twelve hours a day, Sundays included, for there was so much to get through and the soldiers were keen and well-motivated. Utterly focused on the tasks in hand, the battalion scarcely noticed what was going on in the capital, or even in the country at large.

Although the officers had been apprised as early as mid-February of the District Commander's orders assigning them to protect a particular area of town in the event of major disturbances in Petrograd, they had for the most part seen a good deal of active service before being recalled from the front, and so treated the instruction with skepticism and some distaste: They felt neither the desire nor the obligation to carry out what were surely police duties.

Nor had events in the city in the closing days of February made any impression on the battalion: They had not posted pickets in the city, everything was peaceful enough here in Lesnoi district, their training routine had not been interrupted by so much as a day, and if crowds of factory workers headed off into town from here to kick up a din—well, that left it all the quieter here at the base.

*   *   *

The Battalion comprised ten companies: Two were already at full strength and ready to be shipped off to the front, four more were combat units but still in the process of formation, while the remaining four were reserve companies. They were quartered in barrack blocks (the whole base, including barracks and perimeter fence, was made of wood, offering no protection from bullets), and here too they kept their six machine guns, with a further eight in the battalion arsenal.

Colonel Ivan Nikolaevich Balkashin, commanding officer of the Wheeled Battalion, began his rounds of the companies under training. The troops all knew about the attacks on the Vyborg Side by now, and they were seething: He did not have to waste time convincing them that the crowd was playing right into the Germans' hands. Balkashin asked each company to uphold law and order, and as one man they roared back: "We will, sir! We will!"

The troops felt affection for him personally, as he was aware.

Without further ado he assigned two companies to picket duty and ordered them to march out and station themselves across St. Sampson Avenue, facing outwards in both directions—but they were to maintain order by peaceful means and do their best to avoid opening fire.

Every two hours he had these companies relieved.

For a long while the crowd kept its distance. Balkashin had time to arm all the men and especially the machine-gun section.

For the first few hours yesterday, Balkashin was still in telephone contact with District Headquarters, but they could give him no orders or advice whatsoever. It was up to him to work out his own tactics in the light of local conditions.

Balkashin had already worked out that his small unit, stranded deep in a sprawling working-class district and housed in wooden barracks to boot, would need more than its excellent fighting spirit to take on the tens of thousands of local insurgents, many of them already armed. The best he could do was try to hold out till help arrived, and deterrence would be more use than actual firing.

By the end of yesterday, District HQ was not responding at all, even when other phone connections were operating.

Then the telephone link with the city went completely dead—perhaps they had cut the wires? Only that morning the mechanized battalion had been stationed in the capital of its own country; now suddenly it was pinned down on an encircled landing strip deep in hostile territory.

Before darkness fell, vast crowds advanced on the battalion positions from both directions along St. Sampson Avenue. They surged up to the companies he had posted there, yelling, haranguing the soldiers to join the uprising, but not shooting—which made it all the more unthinkable that the mechanized troops should fire into the crowd. There was nothing for it but to fall back.

Then, to stop the crowd from breaking into the barracks yard, Balkashin stationed a further company outside on what little of the Avenue remained unoccupied and began to fire volleys into the air.

The crowd came to a halt.

But with night falling, even to keep these companies in their present position made less and less sense. So Balkashin pulled his men back inside the gates in stages, leaving only one platoon on guard outside, and setting up his machine guns inside the yard facing the gateway.

Now the crowds coming from both directions could freely merge, flooding the whole roadway and moving up and down the avenue, but they were wary of touching the troops from the Wheeled Battalion. That didn't stop them from jeering, yelling, and urging them to kill their officers.

After a while the crowd would surely disperse, and that was how Balkashin and his battalion hoped to get through the night.

*　*　*

During the night he had had an idea: They should march out in full combat formation before the crowds had time to reassemble, and proceed to the center of town. There would have been no impediment, for the insurgents were all asleep. But he had no authority to abandon the battalion's substantial logistical support and technical gear—it would all be plundered.

There had been nothing to indicate that there was fighting going on in the city, loyal troops putting up resistance. But the idea that a garrison 150,000 strong could lapse into insensibility and impotence at a stroke was even harder to conceive.

And so Balkashin held his troops in position.

He gave orders to dig an inner perimeter of foxholes in the frozen earth. But there were not enough crowbars and pickaxes to go round.

In the meantime, out on St. Sampson Avenue crowds of armed workers and soldiers had started to build up once again—and they were in an ugly mood.

Then two armored cars drove up to join them—a fearful weapon in street fighting! They brought their machine guns to bear on the troops' barracks—and there they stood.

Charge at them now and it was bound to cost lives.

Anyway, we cannot be the ones who fire first.

And that was when the third armored car arrived.

Oh, why didn't we pull out during the night!

Shouts were heard, telling them to surrender.

The troops made no reply.

And then—the machine guns opened up.

And there was nowhere to take cover! Whatever position they held, they were sitting ducks—just wait there till the bullet gets you. Every barrack had its dead and wounded.

Their own six machine guns could at least shoot back, through windows and cracks in the walls, but that drew the enemy fire, and they couldn't take cover either.

There was nothing to bandage the wounded with—there had never been any preparations for combat here—nor was there anywhere they could be evacuated to. They just lay in agony and endured as best they could.

Yet the battalion held its position, even under such withering fire. The rebels fell silent. The din abated.

One of the company commanders started urging Colonel Balkashin to surrender. Balkashin shamed him into silence.

The crowd advanced right up to the perimeter and set about breaking down the fence. They were partly successful, and at two points the demolished fencing was set on fire.

Balkashin's heart bled for his poor troops. But it would have violated every article in the military code to surrender to a wild mob. He went from barrack to barrack persuading each company to hold firm.

By now the barracks at the far end of the base had been set alight as well. They had to be abandoned and the troops concentrated in the central ones.

It was already afternoon when two three-inch field guns were rolled up to join the besieging forces. They took up their firing position—and from point-blank range began to blast the barracks apart, leaving gaping holes and walls ablaze!—it was worse than being at the front; at least they had dugouts. The ceilings caved in, the floors collapsed, bunks and lockers were shattered—the barracks ceased to offer any refuge, and the survivors leapt out into the yard, diving behind mounds of snow, some flinging away their rifles.

And then, as a last resort, Colonel Balkashin assembled his corps of instructors, placing the battalion band in front, in a bid to take the insurgents by surprise and spearhead a breakthrough for the remaining troops to follow.

But they were raked with grapeshot and machine-gun fire even before they could form up for the charge; and with that the troops from the Wheeled Battalion broke and ran.

Fighting their way out was a forlorn hope anyway. The whole of St. Sampson Avenue was inundated with people stretching far, far into the distance.

At this point Balkashin raised his hand as a sign to his men in the yard that he was going to put everything right. And without exchanging a further word with his officers, he walked out of the yard alone.

His appearance was so unexpected that the firing came to a halt. Balkashin, who held the St. George Cross for valor, had already been wounded more than once, but here, too, he held up his hand, calling the crowd to order, and in a deep, authoritative voice he pronounced:

—Listen, all of you! The soldiers of this battalion are not to blame, so stop shooting at them. The order to fight back was given by me in accordance with my oath as a military officer. But now I am giv . . .

They suddenly recollected themselves. A ragged volley rang out—some reacted more quickly than others—the Colonel fell dead.

But that didn't stop them from rushing to finish him off with bayonets and knives.

Meanwhile the crowd dashed past—and in through the gates, bent on killing any officers they came across. And beating up the soldiers.

A few managed to escape, fleeing across the snow-covered vegetable patches.

All over the barracks fires were burning, curls of smoke rising.

The men of the wheeled battalion came out with their hands up to surrender.

The beating began.

The Red Wheel
March 1917 — Chapter 204

The Streets Rejoice

*   *   *

High on the main spire of the Peter and Paul Fortress, the red flag has been raised aloft. People stare in delight, passing the word to those who have not seen. A sense of general elation. Here—in the last stronghold of tsarism!

This sprawling, multifaceted stone fortress above the Neva has tormented the best minds of the country: How many doomed political prisoners must be languishing within? At the gates the crowd was working itself up, demanding the release of the prisoners. Finally, a delegation of witnesses was admitted to inspect the cells. And convinced itself that the place was empty—from the first bastion to the last ravelin. The nineteen mutineers from the Pavlovsk Battalion, arrested a day ago, had already been released. The delegates emerged, rejoined the crowd, desultorily cheering, and everyone began to disperse.

*   *   *

After the withdrawal of government troops from the Admiralty building, it was gradually overrun by a rabble that then set about plundering the Naval General Staff and the workshops. Yet another headache for Grigorovich, Minister for Naval Affairs: He started pressing Duma President Rodzyanko to assign guards to protect the buildings.

*   *   *

Here and there on the gates and railings of the Winter Palace, the eagles and imperial monograms are draped with scraps of red cloth.

And a new fashion sweeps the town—tearing down the Russian tricolor flag.

*   *   *

Across Theater Square two ugly-looking brutes were dragging a little sledge with the body of a policeman tied to it, lying flat on his back. Some of those they met stopped and jovially inquired how the "flatfoot" was killed. And two boys, about fourteen years old, were running along behind the sled trying to stick a cigarette between the dead man's lips.

Sometimes the bodies of murdered policemen were dumped in garbage pits.

*   *   *

At Nikolai Station soldiers mobbed the snack bar, demanding something to eat. Then they broke in, drove away the cooks, ate all they could, smashed every last plate in the place, and made off with the silverware and linen. They claimed they were taking it to the State Duma.

*   *   *

And on the streets you keep hearing the sound of the Marseillaise! Bands play it, people sing it in chorus—always ineptly, cacophonously—but still it rings out again and again, spreading still further, never-ending.

*   *   *

A detachment marching in step to the beat of the drum. Suddenly from somewhere behind—a single stray shot. The whole formation scatters.

Soldiers. But with no officers! . . .

*   *   *

Soldiers who have gone over to the revolution—many with greatcoats unbelted and unbuttoned. Faces joyful, but bewildered. Many bedecked with belts of machine-gun cartridges, across their shoulder, round their waist, or just carrying them in their hands, without a machine gun.

*   *   *

A group of armed men bursts into the administrative offices of the Putilovo Works: "Hand over the cashbox!" Flat refusal. They seize the military director of the factory, Major-General Dubnitsky: "You're coming to the Duma!" His assistant, also a general: "We've served together and I'm not leaving you. . . ." Once past the Narva Gate, they made the generals get out: "Waste of time driving bloodsuckers like you around!" They forced them at bayonet point to the Baltic Station, beating them all the way—then drowned them under the ice of the Flood Diversion Canal.

* * *

On many streets they'll warn you: "Don't go any further. There's shooting down there!"

* * *

They call it *picking off the cops.* The building under suspicion is raked with fire from pistols, rifles, machine guns; they pepper the walls, too, shattering the windows. It's all done in festive mood, a hundred guns blasting away with gusto. (And afterwards they're keen to pose for photographs: soldiers in tall fur hats, others in caps, a chauffeur with his goggles pushed up onto the peak of his cap, and a man in civvies wearing a fedora.)

And whom are they exchanging fire with? They search the staircases, checking every apartment—maybe there are officers hiding there? or a cache of weapons? (or maybe a watch or cigar case?). They get up on the roofs and wander about, waving their arms up there, too. The only thing they don't do—not anywhere, not ever—is "pick off" a single cop, or even find one. They're *so* elusive.

They warn people: Any building where we find a machine gun—gets burned down.

* * *

Finance Minister Bark was arrested by his own footman, who then mocked him.

* * *

A woman gallops past on horseback, hatless, face wild with delight, hair streaming out behind her.

* * *

The crowd is no less remarkable for who *isn't* there. Today, just like yesterday, there has been no sign of priests in the streets. As soon as they've finished a service, they go back home.

Except that a member of the Duma, Father Popov the First, appeared on the steps of the Tauride Palace in the middle of the day. He had emerged to bless the armed forces: "Let this day remain in our memory for now and ever shall be!" But the forces of the revolution didn't have much use for his blessing. They didn't flock to kiss the cross he was holding out.

* * *

Have a drink, then a hair of the dog!—just a question of finding where. The number of drunks in the crowd is growing fast.

In the Kolomna part of town drunken sailors from the naval depot are bursting into private apartments to steal. Any military personnel they find are arrested and driven off in trucks.

* * *

A janitor in a yellow sheepskin and a clean apron is using a wooden spade to scrape up lumps of blood-soaked snow. A faint haze of steam rises from the snow.

The Abdication of Nicholas II

With red ribbons strung across its iron breast and sporting little red flags, the locomotive brought its two carriages to rest at the Pskov Station shortly before ten in the evening and not far from the platform where the Imperial train, "Priority Clearance A," was standing. A pair of sentries, posted outside the royal train, and various officials of the bodyguard and the imperial suite were stunned to see, by the light of the station lamps, a number of soldiers jump down from the guard's van of the newly arrived train wearing red ribbons in their buttonholes and clumsily dragging their rifles along any way they pleased—a vivid image of revolutionary Petrograd. The railway carriages had come to a halt at the adjacent platform, obliquely opposite the royal lounge car.

The two Duma deputies, Shulgin and Guchkov, had first wanted to see General Ruzsky, so as to have a precise picture of the situation and avoid any false moves. But scarcely had they set foot from their carriage when an aide-de-camp who had been on the lookout bore down on them and invited them to appear before His Majesty. A refusal was out of the question—not just for time-honored notions of propriety, but also because it would have suggested indecisiveness and ruined the very mission that had brought them here.

And so the stocky, corpulent Guchkov with his slight limp, wrapped in an opulent fur coat, and the tall, lean, lightly dressed figure of Shulgin in a cat-skin cap set off for the imperial carriage as if that had always been their first port of call, stepping down onto the rails and climbing up again onto the opposite platform.

On the way the aide-de-camp Mordvinov asked Shulgin what was afoot in Petrograd, and Shulgin, still relatively young and impressionable, answered him frankly without thinking about how it affected their mission:

—It's simply unimaginable! We are completely in the hands of the Council of Workers' Deputies. We slipped away in secret, and they may well arrest us on our return.

Mordvinov was astounded: —Then what hope can there possibly be?

—What we're hoping—said Shulgin in all sincerity—is that His Majesty will help us.

They went into the dining section of the carriage. A footman helped the deputies off with their coats. Passing through the doors, they entered the lounge car. The blinds were lowered, and the room was bathed in light and dazzlingly clean—something the Deputies had grown unused to in Petrograd of late. The walls were upholstered in light green leather. There was a piano. A small, elegant clock hung on one wall.

The Sovereign had been in the adjacent carriage, but now he came in: not with his customary light and youthful tread, but with a figure as trim as ever, set off by a long, gray Cossack coat with stitched-on cartridge belts and colonel's epaulets. Recent events had cast a shadow over his features and left a tracery of deep wrinkles. He did not pause for the deputies to approach him with due ceremony, but walked over to them himself and shook hands quite informally; his grip was firm.

That he should live to see the day! Throughout these seven terrible hours from his agreement to abdicate that afternoon up to the arrival of the deputies, he had been awaiting this personal foe and enemy of his family as a savior and in his heart had impatiently anticipated their meeting. Seven hours during which he had endured tea and dinner with his retinue. And read the heartening telegram from Sakharov. And the cheerless one from Admiral Nepenin, saying that unless his abdication was submitted within the next few hours, Russia would be overtaken by catastrophe. And the telegram from General Alekseev, containing Duma President Rodzyanko's confident announcement of the formation of a self-proclaimed government, and telling how they had chosen General Kornilov as their own head of the Petrograd Military District. Several times he had reread the abdication manifesto, so adroitly drafted by the diplomatic section of General Headquarters, but in no way dishonorable.

On this occasion he was not confident that his eyes could conceal his hopes and anxieties— might the deputies have brought something to soften the blow? Impatiently, he tried to guess just what had brought them here. He was ready to accept an accountable ministry, and to make his bête noire Guchkov President of the Council of Ministers (and then work with him and endure his endless reports)—anything to put an end to this agonizing feud with Petrograd and let him continue his journey to Tsarskoe Selo without hindrance.

The Tsar sat down at a small square table against the wall, large enough for two to sit at each side, and leaned lightly against the greenish leather upholstery of the wall. Guchkov and Shulgin sat facing him and Count Frederiks on a separate chair in the middle of the room. In the corner at another small table, General Naryshkin of the Imperial Suite, who was Head of the Field Chancellery, held his pencil poised over a sheet of paper, ready to take notes.

Realizing that Guchkov was the senior of the two, the Tsar nodded to him to begin.

Oh, there was so much that Guchkov could say to this man. How many of his reports had passed between the two of them by now?—reports that in 1905 and 1906 had been accepted with every sign of confidence, leaving him full of hope that action might follow, only to be rejected by the uncomprehending President of the Third Duma. And that was in addition to all those other reports to the Tsar that he had prepared in his head at various times, all those monologues addressed to him, letters exposing this or that injustice. Not one single scar from the last decade had been smoothed away or forgotten. But the slippery monarch had contrived to dodge every one of his set speeches. Time had since moved on, and it was too late for reproaches and raking over past wrongs—except, at best, for the satisfaction of getting his own back. And now in the Tsar's eyes Guchkov could glimpse no enmity—only uncertainty.

So he must press on by the shortest route and finish the job of breaking his august interlocutor down—a man who had never let himself be pinned down.

And Guchkov began—simply, point by point, telling it as it was:

—Your Majesty. We have come to report on the events of the past days in Petrograd. And, furthermore ... to seek advice (that was nicely put) on what steps might be taken to save the situation.

What he was *not* striving for was—brevity. He could see with the utmost clarity the route he must take, and the desirable outcome, but even he could not bring himself to enunciate it without due preparation—while the Emperor's need for preparation was all the greater. For Guchkov a lengthy, circumstantial, convincing delivery offered the best prospect of propelling the Tsar through the mire of doubts and equivocation that lay ahead. And so he related in detail how it had all begun and how it had gone on from there.

—You can see, your Majesty, that this was not the result of some conspiracy or premeditated coup ... —he hadn't intended to put it quite in those words, but that was how it came out; it was as if his tongue were a criminal, drawn back to the scene of the crime. —No, it was to stop the revolt from degenerating into total anarchy that we formed the Provisional

Committee of the State Duma. And we have already been taking measures to put officers back in command of the other ranks. However, apart from us there is another committee sitting in the same Duma building—the Council of Workers' Deputies, and, regrettably, we found ourselves under its authority, and even subject to its censorship. Their slogans are—"A Socialist Republic" and "All Land to the Peasants," and the soldiers find this immensely appealing. There is a real danger that we moderates will be swept aside. We're already being swamped by this movement of theirs. And, if we go, then they will have Petrograd entirely in their hands.

Such a forthright exposition of the true state of affairs perhaps bore unforeseen risks. For the Provisional Committee was regarded here as an all-powerful government, and if that turned out not to be so, then who were Guchkov and the rest, and what was the point of negotiating with them at all?

But sometimes when his gaze met the unguarded, candid eyes of the Tsar, Guchkov could sense how those few feeble sparks of hope that at first seemed to animate them were dying away as he watched. Telling the whole truth like this was clearly more efficacious: They had come here as moderates, not bitter foes of the crown, as once the Tsar had imagined, and this predisposed him—not to submit to them as a source of real power—but to help them as at least partial allies.

And now a change of tack that was surely both persuasive and expedient, something they must be particularly responsive to here: What if the mutiny were to spread to the front? It was like tinder waiting for a spark, and any unit that breathed the air of insurrection would be infected. That was why it was hopeless to send forces against the Petrograd garrison; as soon as the troops made contact with the rebels, they would inevitably go over to their side.

There hadn't been any cases of this yet, but was there anything to stop the rot from spreading?

—Your Majesty, there is nothing to be gained by conflict. It is beyond your powers to crush this rising!

Whether this was actually so, or whether Guchkov was laying it on thick to dispel the Tsar's lingering hopes and conceal what was exercising the Duma deputies themselves—the Monarch raised no objections or counterarguments. His bowed head was motionless, his expression impenetrable. Sitting there, he seemed the calmest of those present.

Indeed, this was always the way: However worked up he might be before a decisive moment, he would calm down as soon as it arrived. And, realizing that his visitors had brought no relief, he had now entirely regained his composure. As his last hope fled, it took his remaining agitation with it. He listened indifferently—was he hearing something new, or merely confirming what he had already made up his mind to do?

Though he concealed it, he was still surprised at how decently Guchkov was behaving, not a hint of impertinence. He had expected him to be downright offensive.

Outside the door a caustic voice was haranguing someone for failing to send the deputation to see him first. When he had finished, Ruzsky came in. He did not ask permission to be present—not by so much as a nod of his head—or to join the three of them at the table; instead he simply sat down at the third side of the table, nearest to Shulgin, fiddling irritably with his aiguillettes.

Through Guchkov's even tones the hammer blows were beginning to resound. He seemed bent on making absolutely sure he had got through to the Tsar. Inexorably he enumerated all those units who had come to welcome the Duma and acknowledge its authority—deputations from the Royal Escort, the Royal Railway Regiment, the Free Regiment of Guards, and even the Court Police of Tsarskoe Selo. Everyone who was in any way entrusted with the Monarch's personal protection.

And it was evident that this was having its effect on the Tsar—the eyebrows began to twitch; the shoulder gave a slight jerk.

And elaborating further on the same theme: All of these units have been ordered to continue to provide the protection they were assigned to. However, other units in Tsarskoe Selo have joined the mutiny, and the common crowd is armed, so there is, of course, a danger (Guchkov did not spell out "for your family").

He was trying to jolt the Emperor out of his composure.

But again the Monarch was giving nothing away.

For all his simplicity, he was nevertheless the Tsar, and something within him would not let that be forgotten.

Now, for the first time, the Tsar interrupted, albeit fairly diffidently:

—But have you given due thought to the impression this will make on Russia. . . ? How can one be confident that my departure will not lead to even greater bloodshed?

Guchkov, ponderous in his inertia, and Shulgin, inspired, dynamic—two voices responding with but a single thought: That is precisely what the Committee of the Duma wants to avoid; after the abdication there will no longer be anything to prevent a fully unified Russia from pursuing the war to a victorious conclusion.

—Even judging by Kiev—Shulgin emerged from his silence, speaking with conviction—public opinion has now left its monarchist sympathies far behind.

What? Kiev, too? Kiev, the ancient capital? Monarchist Kiev? . . .

The Sovereign looked at this man—a known monarchist, indeed once a staunch, even prominent supporter of the crown. He looked at the pointed tips of his foppish little mustache, seeming to see him for the first time since the conversation began—and there was sadness in his gaze. And he asked—not him, but Guchkov once again:

—But won't there be disturbances in the Cossack regions?

Guchkov smiled:

—Oh no, your Majesty, no! The Cossacks are all on the side of the new order! The conduct of the Don regiments in Petrograd left no doubt about that.

Ruzsky was starting to get restless: They were going over the same ground again, while the Tsar was quite capable of sitting in silence like that for a whole hour. Meanwhile you'd think the abdication didn't already exist. Guchkov was wasting his efforts. The telegram, signed that day by the royal hand, was lying in Ruzsky's pocket!

But since it was impossible in the Tsar's presence to break into the conversation and make a statement on his own behalf (high time they put an end to these insufferable formalities), Ruzsky began to fidget, leaned over to Shulgin, and, losing all sense of propriety, whispered ostensibly to him, but in reality intending that Guchkov should overhear:

—It's already been resolved, signed even. I. . . .

He was the one who had broken the Tsar's will, and people ought to know it!

But Guchkov neither heard nor understood! Before the audience with the Tsar, a quick word in his ear would have kept him from saying any of this and tempting the former Emperor into thinking he might yet cling to a corner of the throne! But Guchkov didn't understand, and with his disheveled tie and his eyes inflamed behind his pince-nez, he was talking again in his assertive way:

—Events are moving so fast that the extremists regard Rodzyanko and me and other moderates as traitors. They, of course, are opposed to this way out, since they see it as preserving the principle of monarchism.

He did not add "which both of us hold dear," but the implication was clear enough. Whether spontaneously or by design, the deputies' position had now taken shape: They had not come as adversaries or negotiators; they could even be seen as allies of his Majesty in his efforts to save all that was most sacred.

It was then that it suddenly dawned on the Tsar, quite inappropriately and out of the blue, what the animal was that Ruzsky had always reminded him of—a ferret! A ferret in spectacles, its face flattened out as it rose from his pronounced cheekbones up towards his temples. A young ferret, more precisely, but with a prematurely aged expression.

Now Guchkov could see for himself that there would be no conflict: The Tsar was on the point of capitulation.

After a pause Guchkov added condescendingly:

—Perhaps your Majesty would wish to be alone now? For further deliberation? Or for prayer?

The Tsar cast a look of amazement and alarm at Guchkov.

Guchkov laid before him the crumpled draft of the abdication statement he and Shulgin had composed on the way here.

Yes! Shulgin's instincts hadn't let him down: He had known it was right for him to come. His presence here would rule out any hint of coercion or humiliation. Two monarchists—for Guchkov, too, was a monarchist—two men of good breeding, unarmed, duty-bound to come before the Sovereign with slow and muted tread and recount in hoarse, weary voices all that had passed. In such circumstances abdication was not degrading for a monarch who loved his country.

But the Tsar still kept his silence, occasionally smoothing his mustache with his thumb and index finger. His shoulders were slumped, not at all regally but like the simplest of mortals. He looked out through his large, blue, sickly eyes. And after listening for so long, at last he said:—I've been thinking about this. . . . I have been thinking. . . .

Ruzsky was in torments of frustration, unable to spread before the deputies the abdication that was already signed and sealed. Although in a sense the Tsar was no longer tsar—all the power he once enjoyed lay folded in four here in the inside pocket of Ruzsky's tunic—yet the power of etiquette, instilled in Ruzsky since his youth, did not relax its grip. To announce the abdication himself was more than he dared. Yet the Emperor's acquiescent tone, the way he drew out the word "thinking"—surely this amounted to a statement of assent? and gave Ruzsky the right (this was how he envisaged it)—the right to draw the paper from his pocket and, even as he was handing it back to the Tsar across the table, to announce:

—His Majesty has already resolved the matter.

It was a genial move! Cutting off the Tsar's retreat!

But having once let the manifesto slip from his grasp, then having failed all day to retrieve it from Ruzsky, Nicholas II did not now unfold the document or make any statement to the Duma deputies, but merely concealed it in his pocket.

He had stolen his abdication back?! What a blunder the General had made! How could he have been so stupid, so gullible!

And Ruzsky was on the point of announcing it himself, saying out loud just what the document contained: After all, it hadn't been destroyed; it was right here in the Tsar's pocket.

But no, to Ruzsky's relief, the Tsar had not been playing the fox. Surely, he was just searching for his words? That was it. Although—he didn't seem agitated. But then, did he even know what it meant to be agitated? It was a normal human quality, but you had to wonder whether he possessed it at all. He was more composed than anyone else present, as if he were affected least of all by what was happening.

But of his sadness he made no disguise. And he sat looking at Guchkov, not seeking any answering gaze.

Though he did not address his words to anyone in particular, it was clear nevertheless that he was speaking to Guchkov alone, and his voice sounded simple and natural:

—I have been thinking. All morning. The whole day. But do you think— he digressed in the timid tones of a supplicant—do you think that once the heir has accepted the crown, he will be able to stay with me and his mother until he comes of age?

And he looked on, defenseless, with hope.

Guchkov shook his head categorically:

—Certainly not. No one will bring themselves to entrust the education of the future monarch to those who . . . —His voice took on a hard edge, this wasn't regarding the present company—who have brought the country to its present state.

—But what does that leave for me?—the Tsar inquired, his voice dwindling to the faintest of murmurs.

—You, your Majesty, will be obliged to travel abroad.

The Tsar nodded his head sadly.

—Well then, gentlemen. At first, I was ready to take the step of abdicating in favor of my son. I signed a statement to precisely that effect at three o'clock this afternoon. But now, after thinking it over once more, I realize. . . . That I cannot bring myself to be parted from him.

Guchkov's head came up with a jerk, and he looked at the Tsar.

The Sovereign's voice was not at all statesmanlike. But neither was it indifferent; it trembled with pain:

—I realized that . . . I hope you will understand this. . . . His health is delicate and I cannot. . . . Therefore, I have decided I will give up the throne—not to my son, but to Grand Duke Michael.[1]

And he lowered his eyes. It had been an effort for him to speak.

The Deputies exchanged startled glances, for the first time since the conversation began. And now Shulgin broke in, hastily, as if afraid that others might forestall him

—Your Majesty! This proposal takes us completely by surprise. We had not anticipated an abdication other than in favor of Tsarevich Aleksei.

---

[1] Grand Duke Michael (1878–1918) was the younger brother of Nicholas II. He refused the crown after the tsar's abdication. He was later assassinated by the Bolsheviks.

We came here to propose what we have communicated to you, and nothing else.

Such a simple change, such a simple transposition of one object for another, and those who sent them were unprepared: No one had considered it beforehand. . . .

Guchkov, too, was searching for an objection he could raise:

—One of the factors we considered was that the image of the little heir would very much soften the transfer of power in the eyes of . . . the masses. . . .

Everyone back there in the new government, everyone at the Duma's center of power, was reckoning on having an heir, Aleksei, who is not yet of age, and a regent, Michael, whose hands are tied. . . . But where does this leave us now?

The Tsar's position was fraught with boundless difficulties of his own. But he could not go out and take advice; there was no one to consult; all he could do was ask these men, who had come in enmity, the same question as before:

—But I have to be sure of . . . how the rest of Russia will react to this. — And his bewildered blue-eyed gaze sought a response in theirs, avoiding Ruzsky: —Won't it reflect badly upon . . . —he was at a loss for a way of putting it modestly.

—No, no, your Majesty, not at all!—Guchkov was adamant. —That isn't where the danger lies at all. The danger is that others may declare a republic before us, and if they do. . . . Then civil strife will break out. We must act swiftly to strengthen the monarchy before that can happen.

But there seemed to be no convincing the Tsar; he couldn't take it all in:

—But, gentlemen, I would like some guarantee that my departure will not cause new bloodshed. . . .

Oh no, Shulgin urged, quite the contrary! It's entirely the other way about! Abdication is the only way of saving Russia from the prospect of civil war!

That was right: We'd get a return to peaceful relations, after all.

But as for the Tsar's amendments to the draft abdication—of course, that would need. . . . Let's say, a quarter of an hour for consultations.

Guchkov, however, needed less effort and less time to accept them. After all, he had come here knowing the unparalleled obstinacy of this man, steeling himself for an utterly grueling, perhaps fruitless, duel, that would send him back empty-handed, save for the promise of an accountable government and a scrap of a constitution. And instead—they had broken down the defenses, the abdication had been served up on a plate, all that society had long struggled and striven for had now been prized loose—they must seize it while it was still being proffered.

And the hatred he felt for this man now failed him. He spoke magnanimously:

—Your Majesty! I do not, of course, consider that I have any right to interfere where paternal feelings are concerned. In that area there is no place for politics, and exerting pressure is out of the question. Against your proposal we shall raise no. . .

A faint flicker of gratification appeared in the long-suffering face of the Tsar.

They had found the point at which he would dig in his heels—his right to his only son.

The Deputies were at a loss what to say, and the Tsar did not press them further. He rose quietly and left to return to his own carriage. The Deputies' draft statement—remained where it lay.

Was he giving them time for thought, or had he already decided for himself? That he did not say.

Those left in the lounge car wandered about, lit cigarettes. They were joined, uninvited, by the thickset General Danilov, who till now had been left standing enviously outside on the platform, shuffling from one foot to the other.

Now as the conversation began, it occurred to them that there must surely be some laws governing the succession to the throne, and it would be no bad thing to consult them. Count Naryshkin, who up to now had been making a transcript of the discussion, went out and returned bearing the relevant volume of the legislation of the Russian Empire. They leafed though the pages, trying to find out whether a father who was his son's guardian could abdicate on behalf of that son. But they came up with nothing.

They could not find the different categories of abdication either, nor even could they find the section that dealt with abdication in general.

For twenty years people had been struggling to limit the Tsar's powers or get rid of him altogether, but—here was an odd thing!—no one had given any real thought to the law.

Now Guchkov and Shulgin conferred, or rather, each of them pursued his own disorderly chain of thoughts.

If Grand Duke Michael were to take on a central role, then he would also be able to pursue unpredictable and independent policies of his own. Or again, the Tsar might not actually accept the suitably decorous image they had in mind—with the Monarch acting the part, but not actually ruling. That was an outcome that flew in the face of the Provisional Government's resolution and their express desires.

It took time to reach a considered view, and there simply wasn't long enough to reach agreement. Shulgin would have liked to say, waxing romantic: Your Majesty! Aleksei is the natural heir, an incarnation of the idea of monarchy that is comprehensible to all. He is untainted by blemish or reproach. There will be no small number of Russians ready to give their lives for this little tsar. . . .

But perhaps there were also advantages to the situation? If the Tsarevich is left on the throne, then it will be very difficult to isolate him from his father's influence and, above all, from that of his hated mother. If these influences persist as before, then his parents' withdrawal from power will seem a sham. But if the boy remains on the throne and is actually separated from his parents, that is, if they go abroad—then this will adversely affect his frail health, and he will be forever thinking of his parents—which might nurture far-from-benevolent feelings towards those who came between them.

There is another important argument: If a boy ascends to the throne, will his oath of allegiance to the constitution be valid in law? The Duma Committee sets great store by such an oath to prevent the new Tsar from restoring the independence of the throne. In the case of Grand Duke Michael, they can insist on such an oath without further ado. As regent Michael will have to uphold all the rights and entitlements of the Heir. As tsar, however, his powers can be limited from the moment of his accession, and this will be a telling consideration. . . .

Guchkov did not want to accept the Tsar's variant. But his enervated brain could not come up with a cogent counterargument.

More than that, he was so stunned at how little resistance the Tsar had shown to the idea of abdication! For those who had spent decades living in the shadow of this imperial colossus, it was impossible to anticipate such a thing, or even to conceive of it! When such a happy outcome as this fell into your hands unbidden, could there be any question of not taking it? With one step Guchkov was achieving something unprecedented in Russian history: With luck he was reining in this revolutionary turmoil, while at the same time rescuing the principle of monarchy!

However, no one seemed to be waiting on their decision. The Tsar had not returned. Did that mean he thought the matter already settled? Or perhaps he himself had gone off to give it more thought?

But what if one looked at it the other way round? If no agreement were reached now, then, presumably, there would be no abdication at all, and they would leave empty-handed? And given their situation as virtual captives in the Tauride Palace, that would presumably mean that the abdication issue would just be turned over to the increasingly bold and brazen Petrograd riffraff, the Council of Workers' Deputies? That would be the worst calamity of all, something to be avoided come what may. That was the way of the guillotine and the republic. . . .

In other words, they had to take whatever abdication was on offer. There was simply no choice.

The main thing was to get it soon, then set off within the hour and announce it in Petrograd—*soon*!

The Tsar returned at a quarter past eleven—no more shaken than when he left, armored in self-possession as before—and he held out two typewritten sheets of paper:

—Here is the document. Read it.

They were all on their feet already, having risen at the Tsar's entrance. And Guchkov, with Shulgin to one side, leaned over the table, reading in rapid bursts, sotto voce.

—In these days of our mighty struggle against the foreign foe.... The mass disturbances now underway are threatening to undermine the conduct of this long and stubborn war.... At this decisive moment We have deemed Ourselves conscience-bound to afford Our people unity and solidarity . . . and in one accord with the State Duma, We have seen fit to abdicate the throne of the Russian State.... Not wishing to be parted from Our beloved son . . . we pass the succession to Our brother.... We call upon all true sons of the Fatherland . . . to set them on the path to victory, prosperity, and glory....

And more about Germany lusting to enslave Russia. And how the Tsar was standing down for the sake of Russia's victory.

Ruzsky could see that this was a far cry from the abdication manifesto that had been sent from GHQ. Could the Tsar really have reworked it so quickly and so smoothly on his own?

Guchkov raised no objections.

Shulgin suggested that the statement should be marked "3 p.m.," the time when the Tsar had reached his decision to abdicate—before their arrival.

This was in anticipation of any later reproaches that the deputies had wrung the abdication from the Tsar.

And with a bold hand his Majesty signed the abdication—using a simple pencil.

Guchkov expressed his reluctance to risk carrying the original of the Manifesto during such turbulent times and asked whether a second original might not be prepared and left with Ruzsky.

They took it away to type out another copy.

And now the three of them—the former Sovereign and the two representatives of the new government—faced the prospect of staring at each other in silence for a further twenty minutes.

However, one couldn't just abandon everything as if it were someone else's problem. Order had to be maintained. The throne went to his brother, all right. But who was the Cabinet to go to?

The Tsar did not want it to be Rodzyanko. Krivoshein was the one who should be appointed.

The deputies advised giving it to Prince Lvov.

—Agreed.

And as Supreme Commander?—Grand Duke Nikolai Nikolaevich,[2] of course. Who else could it be?

Decrees to the Senate were written. That would bolster both parties' position.

They were sent for retyping.

After that—silence.

And then, then. . . . Talking about oneself was the hardest thing of all. This was something quite unprecedented—being without the crown. And where was he to go?

Finding the right tone proved difficult. You couldn't even be sure who was subordinate to whom now. It wouldn't do to act willfully, but it was humiliating having to ask. . . .

The Tsar gave a shrug of his shoulder.

—There would be no obstacle to my leaving for Tsarskoe Selo now?

Guchkov's brow went up like a barrier. Earlier in the day he had supposed it possible, but. . . . Behind the Tsar's back he glimpsed his supreme foe with her imperious, malevolent bearing.

(For the Tsar to be reunited with his willpower—no, that was out of the question. He might even revoke his abdication.)

Guchkov did not explicitly forbid it. But the tension of his whole manner, the forehead flushed red, the very silence. . . .

Which dragged on.

Until he said that insurrection had broken out in Luga. There was no way of guaranteeing him safe passage.

The Tsar swayed almost imperceptibly—then went limp as if struck by a blow.

(He couldn't go to Tsarskoe? But that was all he had ever wanted. That was why he had been in a hurry to absolve all these formalities. And now he couldn't go? . . .)

It would only be for a while, after all, just till the children got better. Then they'd all leave together—to Livadia, say. . . .

So where to now? To GHQ? . . .

There were matters there that needed to be handed over.

"To GHQ"—the words rang out, then hung in the air. Was this a question? A statement? Was he asking permission, or was he not? The situation was all so impenetrable.

---

[2] Grand Duke Nikolai Nikolaevich was supreme commander of Russian imperial forces from August 1914 until August 1915 (see chapter 82 of *August 1914*).

Guchkov looked at the Tsar once again, staring him full in the face, through his pince-nez, scarcely concealing the fact that he was seeing a broken man.

(GHQ, the center of the armed forces? With General Alekseev there, and without the Empress, he will never dare something serious. He isn't capable of it.)

All right, then.

General Ruzsky positively squirmed at this, bewildered and indignant—but how can you let a Supreme Commander who's just abdicated go back to GHQ?

Yet he could not get the words out to object out loud to Guchkov.

The second original of the abdication document was brought in.

Now the Imperial train could leave for Mogilev. After three days and nights spent driving round in a senseless, frenetic circle, losing a crown on the way, it could return to the place it should never have left.

The Red Wheel
March 1917 — Chapter 418

The Killing of Nepenin

SCREEN[1]

This is the way they are led: in front—no escort guards
    (prison ways are alien to sailors).
In front walks Admiral Nepenin. Alone.
His face somewhat rotund, with astute, lively features,
    and only the mouth slightly covered by his beard and
    mustache.
But he is tense; he did not expect to be treated like this.
And behind him, marching in step, is his adjutant, a
    lieutenant.
And at their side, also in step—two sailors.
Cap ribbons fluttering above their pea jackets, they must
    be moving quickly.
Yes, you can tell from the swing of their shoulders, too.
While further back—more sailors, forming a kind of
    horseshoe behind them.
And within the span of the horseshoe's sides there are
    more officers of various ranks, all the way up to full
    captain.

---

[1] The "Publisher's Note" to *August 1914* provides instructions for approaching the
"screen" sequences in *The Red Wheel*. The four different margins are used to
represent four sets of technical instructions for the shooting of a film. These, from
left to right on the page, are sound effects, camera direction, action, dialogue. The
symbol = indicates "cut to."

Some are impassive, others obviously frightened. No one
was expecting this. No one's ready for it. But is any of
us ever ready for his life to be turned upside down?
Behind the front line of the horseshoe are more and more
sailors, merging into a single dense crowd.
Like this: in a throng of sixty or more, not marching in
formation, not like an escort, but in a tightly packed
malevolent crowd, their carbine barrels pointing
forward and upward,
they are leading
a cluster of officers in their midst,
unarmed, the short swords have gone from their sides.
The sailors walk along confidently, brutally aware of their
destination.
Irregular steps merging into a continuous tramp of feet.
Is it the sailors' uniform, is it the life a sailor leads, or
were these men specially selected, that they look so
fierce and pitiless?
On some faces the expression has almost ceased to be
human at all. Where can so much malice come from?
And the officers' faces—are their bones different? a
different lifestyle? The black uniform they share is
similar, but here there is culture and refinement.
And now there is confusion, too; they glance about as if
lost.
No, they can never coexist! How can they live together,
these two breeds of men?
these men we see now walking along, caught in a single
frame?
But walking where to?
The officers have their suspicions. For they know what
happened during the night on other ships.
The sailors know it, too.
And do not so much as waver.
If the sailors were marching in ranks, then it would not be
so terrible. But in a crowd, shoulder to shoulder,
almost jaw to jaw, barrel to barrel, they come, forging
confidently ahead!
Tramping feet on the snowy road.
From a low angle
nothing but legs, close to the ground.

Here among these legs and black trousers there is more
    similarity between the leaders and
the led.
Higher
    = And the admiral with responsive, mobile features, feels
        this pressure and momentum at his back, senses them
        without turning round,
    and walks along just as confidently and briskly himself.
    As if he is leading them!
    That's right! As if it is he who is leading them, in accor-
        dance with his plans as admiral.
    Leading this bunch of men just as he led the entire fleet.
    His downy mustaches trembling from time to time, his
        acute gaze.
    How well he explained it to them, with candor and
        sympathy! How he trusted in the stirrings of their
        hearts! How he depended upon them!
    Our sacred nation!
    The sailors. Jaw to jaw.
    = There at the back of the line of officers—a flurry of
        movement.
    Like someone falling.
The whole time we see from in front—
    see in full close-up the Admiral's face,
    not yet disillusioned even now,
    how he trusted and hoped.
    But there at the rear—sailors' hands are shoving the
        officers back,
    dragging them back,
    pulling them aside, now to the right,
    now to the left.
    they fling them back, through the encompassing line of
        black, beribboned sailors—
    what happens next—whether they are marched away or
        just thrown aside we cannot see,
     all we see is officers disappearing one after the other
        from the grip of the horseshoe.
    but it draws ever closer, towards the admiral, jaws upon
        jaws.
    On the cap bands, if you are quick, you can pick out
        "Glory," "Andrew." . . .

And what is this terrible uniform the sailors wear? What
    are these ribbons, with their delicate fluttering, so
    unnatural on the heads of men,
on the heads of beasts
such cruel little ribbons?
= View of the Sveaborg Fortress.
= Snow-covered banks.
= Trampled snow in the street along which they are
    leading
= the Admiral with that lively, open face, who so believed
    in these heroes in black,
just as he is leading them now, without ever glancing
    round.
But at the rear the last of the officers are hurled aside,
and not one of them cries out, this terrible silence, nothing but the
    tramp of sailors' feet,
    and the Admiral striding along, confident that he is
        leading the entire complement of officers of the
        "Gyrfalcon," the staff officers of the fleet,
while further back all that remains of them is this one
    little adjutant.
= But behind the Admiral's back we see the foremost
    sailor in the encircling horseshoe line,
a sailor-revolutionary straight from the posters and the
    film clips that we shall see again and again and again.
= Two figures: the Admiral, rather short, solidly built—
    and behind him the looming, lanky figure of the
    sailor.
Now! It's going to happen now!
= Legs. Someone kicks from behind, kicks another man in
    the back of the knee, it's a thin leg—the adjutant's!
Losing his balance, the adjutant stumbles, topples forward.
From in front
= The Admiral! unchanged, still convinced that right is
    on his side. And the sailor from the posters
has suddenly raised his carbine!
= Filling the whole screen—the Admiral's back and the
    muzzle of a carbine—spurting flame!
A shot!
= Once more—the Admiral's face!
still with that newfound simplicity and innocence—

understanding only now,
fully grasping only now the truth that he was seeking!
= But already he is sliding down out of the picture.
And falls.
The enveloping line of sailors has come to a halt.
They look down. In curiosity.
And—shoot again to finish him, firing down at where he
    fell.
A shot. Another shot.

The Red Wheel
March 1917 — Chapter 531

Produced for Inspection

On the Tsar's return to Tsarksoe Selo,[1] his first hours were spent with his children—first with the heir Alexei whose room was brightly lit, since he had already recovered. Next he saw his daughters: The elder princesses were on the mend; little Anastasia, his youngest, was still unwell, while Maria, who was seriously ill, lay in a fever in a completely darkened room. She could not fully take in the fact of her father's arrival and drifted between wanting to make sure he really had come and rambling on about some mob of terrible men who were coming to kill Mama.

After spending only a while in their rooms, Nicholas could feel what a burden his dear wife had borne in tending all these sick children at the same time, especially in times like these.

But Olya and Tanya were simply elated at father's homecoming. Though they were still lying down, they assured him that they were really quite better now. To them his arrival put an end to all their woes.

That was all they could talk about, as they squirmed around on their pillows—now we're all together again, Papa and Mama, we're not afraid of a thing!

Alexei had cheered up too, and Nicholas took him in his arms and hugged him, not speaking and trying not to betray how lost he felt. Talking had become such an effort for him.

---

[1] On March 3, 1917, the Provisional Government gave the former tsar permission to travel to Tsarskoe Selo to be with his family. On the same day, the executive committee of the Petrograd Soviet voted to arrest the royal family in an effort to prevent them from accepting asylum in Great Britain. On the 9th of March, Nicholas returned to Tsarskoe, where, along with his family, he was held under house arrest.

438

While Benkendorf was present, he tried to speak of trivial matters, but habit and all the self-possession he could muster were unequal to the task. There was such an aching hollow feeling within him that all he could do was shut himself away, close his eyes, and lie in silence, stiff and numb. Powerless now to evince any sign of life, Nicholas could not bear to be alone with anyone other than Alix.

And they went down to their private rooms.

Locked the doors behind them.

Walking in the park was forbidden, but Nicholas could replenish his strength by spending a few hours with Alix—slumped in silence. He had to go through this interval of wordless immobility in order to emerge revivified.

Alexandra made him lie down on a couch. She sat beside him, applying cold damp cloths to his brow.

The Empress's chambermaid did not so much knock as gently stroke the door:

—Your Majesty . . . Count Benkendorf begs to speak with you.

Alix rose quietly and left the room.

Agitated and embarrassed, his narrow side-whiskers atremble, Count Benkendorf told a garbled tale of how some commissar or other from the Council of Workers' Deputies had arrived, and His Majesty must appear before him.

—"Appear?"—the Empress snapped angrily. She could still feel her own reserves of strength, and her sense of responsibility grew even as those of her royal consort waned. The Tsar has not scheduled any audiences.

The Count wrung his hands; how could an old courtier like him not understand it! But the military commander of the palace said there was no other way out. Would it please Her Majesty to hear his explanation in person?

As always, the man's duties, the man's decisions fell to her lot. In his present condition Nicki was incapable of deciding for himself.

The Empress walked through into the green drawing room just as she was—the dress she wore for tending the children had become her habitual attire—and there received Staff-Captain Kotzebue.

Kotzebue explained that he had no choice; he was powerless to argue with the Petrograd Council. And the Council wished to assure itself that His Majesty was indeed here.

It was enough to make you choke!

—But where do they think he's got to? Where else could he possibly be?

However, Kotzebue held his ground. If it came to a clash with the Council's forces, that would spell trouble for all concerned. But with a great deal of difficulty they found a way of arranging things peaceably. And really it would be quite a trivial formality, not too burdensome for His Majesty. He did not have to receive this commissar, nor talk to him, nor even greet him. The plan was that upstairs, at that place by the picture gallery where the corridors intersect, the Tsar would walk along one corridor without stopping, and this commissar would watch from the other corridor, and that was all there was to it. The commissar would be surrounded by armed officers from the Escort Regiment—he wouldn't be able to move or give any offense.

There was nothing for it but to agree. Being virtual prisoners, they hardly had much choice in the matter.

Yet the Empress knew the state she had left the Emperor in. Would he be able to appear at all, mute and enfeebled as he was?

But surely this business can be put off for a couple hours? Even just for one hour?

Alas, would that it could—the Staff Captain was deeply worried. In an hour any chance of a peaceful outcome might be lost. Her Majesty cannot begin to imagine what dangers have already been averted.

Obviously, she had to give in.

Alexandra went to prepare Nicki. He was lying on his back sunk in a drowsy torpor, his mouth half open, groaning. Her heart bled to see him like this. What had he done to deserve this new suffering and humiliation?

She cradled his head in both hands and caressed him as she woke him.

He had trouble comprehending what was going on. But why? Where do I have to go? What for? But he believed her.

Onerously, laboriously he raised himself a little, then sat up.

He changed out of his dressing-gown in the bedroom, putting on his Household Cavalry uniform. He always changed swiftly and easily, a habit acquired in the army.

His eyes and his many deep wrinkles showed up like pits in his somber face.

Alix made the sign of the cross over him, and he went out to join Benkendorf and Dolgorukov, though it was hard to say whether he had understood or was still in a daze.

Thank Heaven, he did not have to speak to anyone!

It was just like taking a little stroll along the corridor, since, after all, the park was out of bounds now.

But how shameful even a stroll could be for a deposed monarch! . . .

They went up to the second floor. Benkendorf respectfully explained to the Tsar where and how he was to walk—as far as the room of his valet Vokov. Oh, and it had to be done without headgear.

Had he understood or had he not?

He took off his Hussar's cap and placed it on a windowsill in the corridor.

Benkendorf himself hurried on ahead with Dolgorukov to take up their positions, while the Tsar was supposed to linger here for two or three minutes.

Then he set off—as if oblivious or sleepwalking, as if he were not involved, not even present at all.

He opened the broad paneled doors himself. Beyond them, down where the corridors crossed beneath glass roofs that now scarcely let through the light of the dying day, every single lamp was brightly lit.

The pain made Nicholas screw up his eyes a little.

He walked along slowly, aimlessly.

Three paces from the intersection stood the commissar, dressed in the uniform of an official in the Military Commission but wearing a large, shaggy Caucasian fur hat on his head. One of his short legs was thrust forward.

Behind him two tense officers stood guard, and it was impossible to miss their unnatural position, right hands resting inside their pockets.

There, too, stood the Staff Captain of the Uhlans.

Neither he nor the other officers saluted, but they came to attention. Benkendorf followed suit.

But the commissar did not stir and did not remove his hat. He stood there with that same wild appearance, one foot forward, as if he had taken a step towards the Tsar. And nobody told him—too late, perhaps?—to get his hat off.

And no one could bring himself to reach out and whip it off for him.

In the silence that fell, you could hear people breathing.

There was something tentative about the Tsar's steps, not at all his usual way of walking, with a faint, resonant tinkling of his spurs. As he walked, his very gait conveyed his bewilderment—what was he supposed to do now?

And having no hat on was odd. It made it hard to hold one's head up firmly like a military man.

His haggard appearance, the inflamed eyelids and drooping bags under the eyes, his limp mustache—how he had aged!

All he had to do was cross the junction of the corridors as quickly as possible, without looking round, not so much as a sidelong glance, and walk away, make his escape—that was all.

But the Tsar could not pass by without noticing the tense group of men standing off to one side. He naturally turned his head towards them—then slowed his step—then changed direction—took half a step this way, then another, searching their faces in confusion, baffled at first as to why they were standing there. And why in this odd configuration? And who is that in the snakelike fur hat?

But more serpentine still were the eyes. The hatred in them stung and burned. The commissar's face was contorted; he quivered as if in a fever.

Confronted with this stark manifestation of pure malice, the Tsar stopped, came to himself, and sensed what was before him. His ravaged, swollen face revealed lucid understanding—and with it, utter enervation.

He swayed slightly from one foot to the other. One shoulder twitched. And he was already turning to go—but could not refrain, out of politeness, from nodding farewell to the group.

He nodded.

And set off, unsteadily, not walking off in the same direction, straight ahead, but—back the way he had come.

Lenin's Pirouettes

No one could talk of anything but the journey. Several émigré committees and all the party directorates had asked Grimm to negotiate with the German ambassador, Romberg. (Since Martov's proposal to release one German prisoner of war for every émigré repatriated.) Excellent, excellent. The *Martov plan* was working.

And Grimm had taken it on. (Better still.) But he was not just the Zimmerwald leader, he was also a member of the Swiss Parliament, and it would have been unwise for him to take such a step without the sympathy of the government, of Foreign Minister Hoffmann, for instance. (This meant that there must have been consultations. Why should Switzerland be against it, anyway? The Swiss themselves wouldn't mind sending that rowdy bunch packing. Switzerland itself was in an uncomfortable position, with the war on every side.) Grimm went to see Romberg again and again, negotiating *in absolute secrecy*, not a word must filter through to the press, there must be no stain on Swiss neutrality—but he didn't mind reporting to the main representatives of each party (Natanson, Martov, Zinoviev). We're all in the know.

It was going at a snail's pace. But never mind, never mind.

Romberg said yes to everybody, and Grimm considered that he had made light work of it. If he says yes, it's yes. All that remains is for you, comrades, to request permission from your Provisional Government.

Oh, thank you! Excuse us for not taking off our caps to you! And after that we spend our lives kowtowing to Louis Blanc–Kerensky?[1]

---

[1] Aleksandr Kerensky (1881–1970) was a lawyer and SocialRevolutionary who served as the second prime minister of the Russian Provisional Government in 1917. Radical revolutionaries compared him to the French politician, historian, and moderate socialist Louis Blanc, who played a major role at the beginning of the French revolution of 1848.

Through all these anxious days the rogue Radek was missed terribly: They summoned him by telephone from the Davos sanatorium where he was recuperating, but even for the Russian revolution he wouldn't come immediately. Before he arrived, though, he had understood the situation, and thought up yet another diversionary maneuver—through a German correspondent in Bern.

Romberg had given him the same answer as all the others: Yes, yes, of course we will let through all those who wish to go.

Still the German frontier would not open, and all those *desirous* of traveling got no further than making inquiries, comparing notes, asking the Provisional Government's permission in telegrams to Kerensky, and mostly just dithering.

Everyone agreed—and nothing had begun to happen. These old-fashioned diplomatic methods were so clumsy.

Nothing could begin to happen until the great dark fish in the depths had finished their run.

Until Sklarz had reported Lenin's counterproposals in Berlin.

Until the German General Staff said its final yes.

Until the German Ministry of Foreign Affairs took fright: By now there had been much public discussion of their return and Prince Lvov[2] had told the Swiss minister frankly that the speedy departure of the émigrés from Switzerland was undesirable. They must hurry (who could be causing the delay?). Germany would never have another chance like this.

On Saturday, March 31, Ambassador Romberg in Bern at last received instructions to inform Lenin as quickly as possible that his proposals concerning extraterritoriality had been accepted, and that there would be no individual checks or discriminatory conditions.

On Saturday—and "immediately"! So that there was no question of lazily putting it off over Sunday. Breaking all the laws of discretion, and using the emergency line, the German ambassador started calling around, and finally found the German socialist Paul Levi in the Volkshaus: "Please inform Lenin as quickly as possible that...."

Another ring called Ulyanov[3] to the neighbors' telephone at home in the Spiegelgasse, and he went along in some agitation, thinking it might be Inessa.[4]

But no—it was his answer!!

---

[2] Prince Georgi Lvov (1861–1927) was the first prime minister of the Russian Provisional Government. He held office from March 23 until July 21, 1917. He escaped to the West after the Bolsheviks came to power.

[3] Ulyanov: Lenin's family name.

[4] Inessa Armand (1874–1920) was a leading Bolshevik and a close friend and companion of Lenin's after 1909.

At long last the way was open! At last they could fix the departure of a group of forty for the day after tomorrow, giving the comrades just time enough to pack, return their library books, put their financial affairs in order, assemble from Geneva, Clarens, Bern, Lucerne, and buy provisions for the journey. They could be away by Tuesday, and the following Saturday— a week later than if he had accepted Sklarz's first proposal—take a hand in the Russian revolution.

While he was still in the gloom of the musty staircase, and then in the dim daylight of his cell-like room (heavy snow with intervals of sleet had been falling all day long), gripping the lapels of his vest to prevent his hands from flinging themselves prematurely into action, soothed by the greatcoat-like weight of his greasy old jacket—Lenin forced himself not to rush off and announce the news to someone but to think. Think. Think, rapidly pacing.

A strong man never loses his head in defeat and despondency. But losing your head in moments of success is easy, and for a politician this is the greatest of dangers.

The way was wide open—and still it was impossible to make use of it: There would be no explaining afterward by whom and how it had been arranged that the leading Bolsheviks alone should suddenly be provided with a carriage, and why they had taken it.

A few more baffling and misleading moves must be made first.

There was no room here to stretch his legs, he couldn't go out in such weather (and reading rooms were long since forgotten). His restless pacing made him dizzy, and fiery spirals bored into his brain.

The way was open—but *where to?* To a forced wait on the Finnish frontier? Or to one of the Provisional Government's prisons? It was easy to imagine how the gales of chauvinism were howling in Russia by now! In the petit-bourgeois way of thinking, what he was doing was "treason." Even here in Switzerland the Mensheviks, the S.R.'s, and the rest of the spineless émigré riffraff would cry treason.

No!

No.

N-n-no. . . .

(One thing I can do for now is contact Hanecki. He's been refused a travel permit by the British! It's high time he shouted it from the rooftops!)

It was one thing to be restrained by circumstances—but how difficult it was to restrain yourself when you were set free and longing to go.

The next thing to do was to . . . was to . . .

The events which had glided like heavy dark fish near the seabed must now be seen passing over the surface like little white sailing boats.

The negotiations are *concluded*? So now's the time to *begin* them! Let's make it appear that we're only beginning today!

What more suitable personage for this task than guileless, trusttful Platten?

Obviously, a group must be got ready. And a list already exists.

(Inessa! Won't you go even now? It's monstrous! You won't go with us? To Russia! To the great day we have waited for for so long? You want to stay in this putrid place? . . .)

Forty people can hardly be accused of treason. If there are forty the blame will be spread too thin to matter. We could, of course, pick up a few Maximalists and a mixed bunch of desperate characters, and it would all look a little more innocent. But . . . it is better not to take outsiders along, not to have unnecessary witnesses to every move we make—and who knows what may happen? Anyway, what profit is there in transporting our competitors by our own efforts, in our own carriage, to Petersburg, just to fight them there? No! Every detail, including the date and time of departure, must be kept secret until the last moment.

Only the fact that negotiations are going on must be public.

Without an agreement already in your pocket, you couldn't possibly begin such negotiations. What a humiliation it would be if they failed! But now that we have an agreement, we can go ahead.

Like all proletarian business, like every step in the proletarian cause, this journey needs to be highly organized. Bind them with hoops of iron. Can't have some turd slithering out of it afterward. We must all be in the same boat. No one must be able to evade responsibility, no one must be able to say, "I had no part in it! I never suspected what was going on!"

Every one of them, then, must sign his name to it. As though he is taking a solemn oath. Like bandits kissing the knife. So that no one can break ranks later on and rush to expose us. . . . It's a very serious responsibility and all forty of us must share it.

(Surely Inessa will come? . . .)

He sat down at once to draw up such a pledge. On his chair by the window, in the half darkness, with a snowstorm outside, he balanced the paper on his knees and wrote—his slanting handwriting, bigger than usual in these days of agitation, tumbling over itself as it pursued his thoughts obliquely across the page—sketching out points which might be included. "I confirm that I have been informed of the conditions proposed by the German Embassy to Comrade Platten . . . and that in agreeing to conform to them I accept full political responsibility for the possible consequences. . . ."

Suddenly out in the corridor he heard Radek's pleasantly sharp, mocking voice. He had come, then! No guest or assistant could be more welcome just then. Karl, Karl, how are you, take your coat off, oh, the snow's got under your collar. You'll never guess what news we have for you!

The little yelps, the flashing teeth which his upper lip could not cover, the crop of curls, the halo of whiskers—Radek the mischievous chuckling schoolboy.

Come on, then, let's draft it together. And draw up equally firm conditions for Romberg.

"*You* make conditions for *them*?"

"Yes. What of it?"

"That's delightful!"

Radek was just the man for this sort of prank. His advice was as good as his jokes; he was inspired and yet circumspect.

Only, smoking wasn't allowed in this room, he had to suck an empty pipe. And . . . oh, no. . . .

"Vladimir Ilyich! What do we do about *me*! Surely you wouldn't think of not taking me?"

"Why shouldn't we take you?"

"Well, if we say here 'Russian émigrés'—I'm an Austrian subject."

So he was, damn it! Damn it all! They'd got used to thinking of him as one of themselves—he was a "Polish comrade" only for form's sake. But how could they not take him? A Radek couldn't be left behind.

Radek had already seen a way out. If Platten made a written agreement with Romberg (and if there was only an oral understanding, it would be still easier to confuse the issue), he must leave out the word "Russian" and put in "political émigrés." Since only they were under discussion, the Germans would put their fist to it without a second thought.

Normally, tricks would be impermissible at such an enormously important juncture, in such an extremely serious matter, and the German General Staff was not a partner to joke with. But for Radek—that irreplaceable, that incomparable fount of ingenuity—for sharp, caustic, impudent Radek, perhaps he should risk it?

"But will Platten agree to handle the negotiations? Will he then want to go with us?"

"There's nobody else. So he will agree."

"What if Münzenberg were to go? He's a bit firmer."

"Willi? No, he counts as a German deserter. How can he deal with the ambassador? Or travel through Germany?"

"Even so"—Radek rattled his pipe stem against his teeth—"even so, Platten is party secretary here, how can he travel with émigrés? Besides, he will be worried to death that it may somehow harm his Switzerland."

"How can it? Switzerland can only benefit."

No, Lenin had no doubts on this score. Platten as a rule sheepishly deferred to Grimm, but in the most important things he would go along, once he saw the point. He was a workingman, a proletarian to the marrow. Of the discussions with Parvus[5] he knew and would know nothing.

Whereas Radek knew it all, whether you told him about Parvus or not. Radek had an almost indecent admiration for Parvus: In the taverns of Bern he might revile Parvus, as his international duty obliged him to, for his rash step toward the chauvinists, his wealth, his shady deals, his dishonesty, his love life—but he gaped and drooled so that you could see he thought Parvus a fine fellow and longed to be like him! . . .

"As for Sklarz, I've told Platten that he's a two-bit errand boy of the German government, and that I threw him out! I shall say about Grimm that there's something suspicious in his behavior, he's holding up our departure, seeing what's in it for himself. But we can wait no longer, the revolution calls! Let's act like proletarians, openly, without secrets—and apply directly to the German Embassy! And he'll do it!" Lenin spoke with assurance.

What should they instruct him to say to Romberg? A completely new text was required. "In Russia things are taking a turn which endangers the cause of *peace*. Russia must be wrested from the British and French warmongers. We shall of course endeavor in return to liberate the German prisoners of war." (Hold us to it if you can! . . .) "But we must be insured against embarrassment, and have guarantees that we shall not be pestered on the journey. . . . We are prepared to travel in locked compartments, with the blinds down if necessary. But we must be sure that the carriage will not be stopped. . . ."

Lenin dominated the room, pacing rapidly along its diagonal, three paces this way, three paces that, with one hand behind his back, and flourishing the other, while Radek wrote, steadying the page with his empty pipe.

Radek always stirred in new ideas: If we're taking a step like this, it might help to collect supporting signatures from Western socialists. . . . Socialists, of course, but why not some eminently respectable people, too? . . .

"Where can we find them? . . .

"Romain Rolland, for instance?"

What a brainy fellow! Just the thing!

They must cast the hook at once. Who would dangle it in front of Rolland for them?

Since Radek's arrival, Lenin had ceased to feel as though his head were bursting with a searing eddy of thoughts. He had an outlet for his ideas, he

---

[5] Parvus (nom de guerre of Israel Lazarevich Galfand [1867–1924]) played a major role in the revolution of 1905. He was a successful businessman who funded revolutionaries, especially Bolsheviks.

could express them and receive an answer. Here was another: If they demonstratively started fresh negotiations through Platten, shouldn't they just as demonstratively break with Grimm?

Break with a loud snap!

"Taking care to shift all the blame onto him."

"And giving the blackguard a bit extra for what we owe him. Make him regret postponing the Swiss congress."

The way to do it was first of all to publish all the confidential information on his secret negotiations.

That hurts every time—the sudden publication of confidential matters. Leaves the enemy simply stunned.

So why not immediately, without further ado, prepare such a publication?

"Dotting all the *i*'s. . . ."

"And publish it tomorrow!"

Yes, with Radek the most strenuous work turned into a merry game. That was what Lenin particularly liked about Radek—the way he entered into the spirit of things.

They were both sitting now—Radek writing, worrying his empty pipe with his teeth—no time for a smoke in the corridor—occasionally laughing and bobbing up and down on his chair as he thought of a neat phrase, while Lenin sat beside him and gave advice.

Radek was the only person to whom Lenin could completely surrender his pen, and sit by with nothing to do but laugh. There had never been a cleverer pen in the whole Bolshevik Party. Lunacharsky, Bogdanov, Bukharin were all weaker writers.

"Another important thing is that it will look as though it's the Swiss who are negotiating, because they want to get rid of us. It's none of our doing."

He was so clever, so quick, simply priceless.

"We'll get it published right away, tomorrow, by Nobs or. . . ."

"Tomorrow's Sunday. But I tell you what!" Sparks danced behind Radek's glasses. "As it's Sunday tomorrow, we'll send Grimm a telegram *immediately*. Right now, on Saturday evening." Radek grinned and bobbed up and down as though there were splinters in his chair.

Lenin, too, bounced happily in his seat.

They talked and talked, interrupting each other, correcting each other, and Radek wrote it all down:

"Our party has decided . . . to accept unconditionally . . . the proposal to travel through Germany . . . and to organize this journey at once. . . . We are *absolutely* unable to take responsibility . . . for further delay . . . emphatically protest . . . and are leaving *on our own!*"

"Beautiful," said Radek, scratching behind his ear. "We'll coat it with chocolate for him. 'We *earnestly* request you to reach an immediate agreement. . . .' Reach agreement tomorrow, on a Swiss Sunday! What's more, tomorrow is also April 1!"

"April 1!!" Lenin hadn't laughed so much in a long time. All the tension of the last few weeks burst from his breast in loud, harsh, liberating spasms of laughter. "This will be a nice box of chocolates for the centrist swine!"

"'Reach immediate agreement . . . and if possible *tomorrow.*'"

"While all Switzerland is snoozing!"

"'Inform us of the decision! . . . Gratefully yours. . . .'"

It was like in a game of chess when you make a well-thought-out move and then see that it is even more effective and promising than you had calculated. But this bit of fun—Grimm's Sunday chore on April Fool's Day—was thought up by Radek the jester.

"And if he doesn't do it on Sunday—on Monday we shall be free to act ourselves!"

"On Tuesday, anyway. . . ."

Ah, but Radek had an even better idea. "Vladimir Ilyich! What about Martov?[6] We must write to Martov, particularly as he's the *initiator of the plan!?*" Radek was choking with laughter.

"Write what to Martov?" Even Lenin's mind couldn't work quite so quickly.

"To tell him that we accept immediately *Grimm's proposal for us to travel via Germany!* That way we can make a fool of Grimm by making it look like his proposal!! Tell the whole world it comes from him. That the Swiss socialists are shoving us out. A member of the Swiss Parliament!"

Now, this really was a stroke of genius! Bravo, Radek! Grimm would set up a howl! Make frantic excuses! But it's always easier to spit than to wipe it off—you have to learn to spit first and at the right moment.

"The scoundrel will wish he'd printed my pamphlet after all."

"It's getting late, though. We'll have to mail it at the Fraumünster."

"I can run down, Vladimir Ilyich."

"Let's go together since we're in the mood."

In that case they must look around and think what else needed to be done. Of course, a letter to Hanecki in Stockholm—"Urgent that you wire three thousand crowns for travel expenses!"

(May as well write to Inessa, then: "Don't worry about money . . . we have more than we thought. . . . The comrades in Stockholm are giving us a lot of help. . . . I hope that we will have you traveling with us?")

---

[6] Yuri Martov (1873–1923) headed the Menshevik faction of the Russian Social Democratic Party after its split with Lenin and the Bolsheviks in 1903.

Another thing—he must draw out the hundred francs he had deposited in the cantonal bank as a condition of residence in Switzerland. No point in pampering the lackeys' republic.

Lenin put on his iron-heavy quilted greatcoat, and Radek the thin summer coat in which he ran around all through the winter, his pockets crammed with books.

He filled his pipe and had his matches ready.

Lenin said aloud: "That's fine. What can Platten's negotiations with Romberg amount to? Romberg will just take the documents out of his desk drawer. But we had to fling those few days in the chauvinists' ugly faces."

Radek, light-footed and pleased with himself, danced about like an adolescent.

"My hands itch, my tongue itches! I can't wait for the wide-open Russian spaces, can't wait to start agitating!"

And, letting Lenin go first, holding a match ready to strike in the corridor, he said: "It comes to this, Vladimir Ilyich: Six months from now either we will be ministers or we will be hanged."

DOCUMENTS[7]

March 31. *Berlin*
(Memo by an official of the Foreign Ministry with the General Staff)

> ... Above all, we must avoid compromising the travelers by excessive attentiveness on our part. It would be very desirable to have some sort of declaration from the Swiss government. If we suddenly send these restless elements to Sweden without such a declaration, it may be used against us.

March 31
(Assistant Secretary of State to Ambassador Romberg in Bern. In cipher)

> Urgent! The journey of the Russian émigrés through Germany should take place very quickly, since the Entente has already started countermeasures in Switzerland. Speed up the negotiations as much as possible.

---

[7] Documents no. 30, 31, from Werner Hahlweg's *Lenin's Rükkehr nach Russland,* 1917.

April 2

(Count Brockdorff-Rantzau, German ambassador in Copenhagen, to the Ministry of Foreign Affairs. Top secret)

... We must now definitely try to create the utmost chaos in Russia. To this end we must avoid any discernible interference in the course of the Russian revolution. But we must secretly do all we can to aggravate the contradictions between the moderate and the extreme parties, since we are extremely interested in the victory of the latter, for another upheaval will then be inevitable, and will take forms which will shake the Russian state to its foundations. ...

Support by us of the extreme elements is preferable, because in this way the work is done more thoroughly and achieves its results more quickly. According to all forecasts, we may count on the disintegration being so far advanced in three months or so that military intervention by us will guarantee the collapse of Russian power.

The Red Wheel
April 1917 — Chapter 27

Disabled Veterans Demonstrate

Some folk come through the war with nothing worse than the memory of it. *No hill so steep it can't be skirted, no woe too deep to overcome*—and in five or ten years the whole damned business has withered away without trace. But for you who left your arm or leg back there, you with your innards ravaged for life by poison gas, with your own dear eyes put out for good—*you* will never shake this war off, not till you quit this life for good. And that little garden by the farm will stay imprinted in your memory, the one where you sat with your elbow pouring blood, nursing your wounded arm for the last time. Or those big, bushy trees way over in the village of Brusno-Novo— you were thinking about which of the poplars was taller and which was shorter and more rounded—and that's the last thing you'll see for the rest of your days; the image will hover before you as you fumble and stumble your way through the world.

And after that you're bounced around in carts and railway wagons, you squirm and groan the hours away in hospital cots—here in this dank, gray Petersburg too (you never thought you'd end up here!), shunted from one hospital to another month after month. And then, just when it's nearly time to be signed off and sent home—not much of a worker any more with your missing limbs or sightless eyes (and not much use as a husband for that matter)—just when you're wondering how you can eke out what's left of your life, you start hearing rumors that some fellow called Lenin's been shipped in through Germany and left here; he speaks our language, and it seems there are others here who are with him, too. They're for ending the war and making peace with the Germans, without defeating them first—stopping the war just like that. And these Petersburg people, mooching around the streets with fags in their mouths, they don't know any better—you won't get one of them near the frontline, oh no!

So that's the way it is! We've all been taken for a ride. It really chokes me up to think of it: They've been crippling us, leading us to the slaughter, and who's it all been for? We're supposed to crawl round on our stumps now, while you whoop it up—is that it?

Throughout the second week after Easter, they chewed it over among themselves; many of the nurses helped them get organized, some of the doctors too. And that Sunday they gathered—every disabled serviceman in Petersburg—and held meetings of their own.

Some headed for the Kazan Cathedral: There was a gathering of invalids there too, a great crowd of them. People gave speeches: We're already in this war now, so we've got to end it in a right and proper way, and that means finishing off the Germans—for the sake of all those who've been killed or gassed, and for the sake of our own wounds as well. Let's make sure they never try to come at us again. And there were more speeches—even one from a thirteen-year-old lad, not crippled, thank God, who'd already won the St. George Cross.

Afterwards, those who were fit enough to walk formed up in ragged ranks and set off on foot, while others were supported by their nurses, and others still—amputees from all the different military hospitals, some in bandages, some who had already been discharged—were driven along by units of the Household Cavalry in long, open carriages, or in trucks, even in ordinary motor cars. And they all headed for the Tauride Palace. At the head of the maimed and bandaged ranks, the scorched and blinded faces, marched three military bands, playing to keep up the spirits of soldiers and spectators alike. And those in the marching ranks and up on the carriages who had anything left to grip with held up placards saying: "Glory to the Fallen. Their sacrifice must not be in vain."—"We fight for freedom, till our dying breath!"—"Lenin & Co., get back to Germany!"—"Able-bodied men, relieve your sick brothers in the trenches!"—"See our wounds! They cry out for victory."—"Review the pension laws." And, once again: "Send Lenin back to Kaiser Bill!"—"Down with Lenin, a disgrace to Russia."

They even managed to pick up the mutilated Russian POWs who had just arrived at the Finland Station and bring them along too. These were men who had dragged their sick and mangled bodies through all the privations and brutality of the German camps.

Along the way, people doffed their hats before the advancing procession. One woman in mourning fell weeping to her knees. At the corner of Liteiny Avenue, a crowd of workers applauded the crippled veterans as they passed.

They reach the Palace, and as is the way of these things, out onto the porch comes someone keen to meet them. Young-looking, tow-haired, but fat-faced and well-fed. It's Skobelev, a member of the Executive Committee:

—The people has succeeded in uprooting the rotten stump of Russian Tsarism, and now it will take the destiny of the country into its hands. The Proletariat will not permit. . . . But we are with you in supporting the Provisional Government, because so far it has kept to the promises it gave in the well-known program. . . .

From down below, right beneath the porch, a disabled officer tells him outright:

—We've come to find out what Lenin's up to and what you think of him.

Skobelev:

—I don't have any problem discussing this with you, because I'm no supporter of Lenin or his tactics. In fact, I've been opposed to him for fourteen years. But let me tell you how we see it: Every citizen of our new, free Russia has a right to express his opinions freely. Your banners read: "Send Lenin back to Germany!" "Down with Lenin!" Comrades, that's not the right way to do things. We have to be tolerant towards his views, as well; everyone must be at liberty to say whatever he wants to say. We'll still keep our own heads screwed on the right way!

A swirling clamor of voices breaks out above the crowd of invalids:

—Down with him! . . . Down with him! . . . We don't want to hear people defending Lenin.

And the officer who spoke before now mounts the steps to stand next to Skobelev:

—So does that mean we've been fighting for the well-being of those people who are now shouting "Down with the war"? But we've put our lives on the line, and we can't stand by while a bunch of scoundrels and provocateurs seize power in Russia for their German paymasters. We've sacrificed our arms and legs, and now we're supposed to watch while these cowards yell "Down with the war!"—is that it? No chance! We may be only half the men we were, but let them finish us off first; then you can make your alliance with Germany over our dead bodies.

—Hear, hear! You tell him!—came the shouts of the crippled men, and you could hear the sickly voices among them. The officer went on:

—Yes, we're ready to sacrifice what's left of our strength for the triumph of liberty. But for us the only way to assert our freedom is by victory over Germany.

Skobelev has another try, kneading the dough. . . .

—We're saying the same thing as you—press on with the war until all sides renounce their conquests; we're ready to back up that slogan with the bayonet. And you are profoundly wrong, comrade officer, to say we'll stand aside or retreat from our positions. No, dear comrades, we'll stick with you till the bitter end or die with you in the attempt. But, comrades, we mustn't forget freedom of speech either. Let the Leninists say what they like, but we won't let them put their plans into action.

But again there is heckling from the crowd, and he beats a swift retreat.

So who do we talk to now? And with that the invalids begin to drift and barge their way into the Palace itself—anyway, it's chilly outside.

There was so much room inside—like standing in a town square! They halted in the long entrance hall with column after column stretching away, and began to congregate there, while some older fellow, short and ginger-haired (no one caught his name), came out onto the landing above them and went on about the Council and the proletariat, but not so much as a whisper about Lenin. No one could make out what he was getting at. He was followed by Gvozdev, who kept it a bit simpler:

—Comrades, I'm just back from Minsk, where we've been holding the Congress of Front-line Troops, and I'll give you a report of the results.

They listened for a while. There were all kinds of matters raised. But the lads up at the front can see what's what, and they can be left to sort it out for themselves. What they can't see is what's happening back here in Petersburg, and they don't know a thing about Lenin.

—And what's happening about Lenin?—the invalids yell.

—As far as Lenin's concerned, I have to inform you, comrades, that the way you propose to fight against him is utterly inadmissible. His movement is not to be put down, and he himself is not to be arrested. He isn't a reactionary or counterrevolutionary. And yes, of course, we must put an end to the war, but the way to do it is by reaching agreement with the German proletariat. Your slogan "Fight on till victory!" may have the effect of further embittering the working class over there.

At that point utter pandemonium broke out—such roaring, yelling, shouts of "Down with him!" that Gvozdev could not finish, and he was driven from the podium altogether.

Now it was the invalids who got themselves up onto the landing, some of them helped up by the nurses. And every speech was the same: Down with Lenin! Pack him off to Germany! All these bigwigs snug in their palace—they've grown spoiled and persnickety, they've never seen combat, and they'll never understand us.

—We're not saying Lenin should be killed, but if he's a provocateur or a German spy, then why shouldn't he be arrested? And why can *he* arrest people who come near the house he's in?

—All right then, we'll arrest him ourselves, just us invalids! We can still muster enough strength for that, even if he's surrounded himself with machine guns and armored cars. So come on, lads—up and at him!

But while this is going on, some of the disabled servicemen have wandered out of the entrance hall and pressed on into the building to see what they can find. Coming across a large, white hall with armchairs surrounding a circular dais, they start to settle down in the chairs, some on the dais itself, others in the body of the hall. And now news photographers turn up to get shots of them for their papers. Soon this room, too, is full to overflowing. A tall man with black curly hair mounts the rostrum, all set to deliver a long, prepared speech, but the invalids immediately start yelling about Lenin. The speaker replies:

—Comrades, I hear indignant shouts of "Down with Lenin" from some among you, and there are even those calling for repressive measures to be taken against him. I declare, in the name of the Executive Committee of the Council of Workers' and Soldiers' Deputies, that we take an entirely different view from Lenin. He has parted company with us.

—And with the rest of Russia!—comes a voice from the floor.

—But it's our considered opinion that to ban Lenin and his supporters from saying what they think is not the right way to oppose them, for a free country has to have freedom of speech.—What freedom does he deserve—they shout—when he's a German provocateur and spy?

From up on the dais the black-haired speaker responds:

—You can't fight ideas with violence, but only with reasoned arguments.

No way! They yell and shout. No one is listening to him. Unable to finish, the speaker comes down from the dais and leaves the hall.

And who's that getting up in his place? Ah, it's our Rodzyanko, the old warhorse. The invalids are already clapping before he can even mount the podium, and the nurses join in.

—... I have come to greet you—you who have not spared your blood in our struggle against the foe. I bow down before you and in reverence for the sacred wounds you have borne. A free Russia will show its appreciation of your exploits.... It is you who must now be the first priority of our government. Everything will be given to you; the government will recompense you for all the sacrifices you have made.... But our enemy is on the watch, eager to snatch away the freedom that is so dear to us and reinstate the old order. This we will never allow! I am certain that the great Russian people will triumph and that their victory will usher in an era of brotherhood and equality. ... Above all we must ensure the survival of our dear Mother Russia!...

The hall clapped and yelled its approval. Breathless but happy, Rodzyanko towered above them. The Russian people had not forgotten him! The Russian people loved him still!

One of the wounded officers called for three cheers in honor of the first citizen of Russia. The cheers re-echoed again and again.

Ever since this morning Rodzyanko had been hearing the same kind of thing. From the window of his house on Furshtadt Street, he had seen a throng of Sunday strollers gathering not far away to welcome an American delegation and had gone out and mingled with them just like one of the crowd. But with his face and figure, how could he hope to remain incognito? Ambassador Francis had recognized him from the balcony and invited him up to join him. And the crowd roared out its delight when Rodzyanko took up his place next to the Ambassador and heard the transatlantic guest declare: "There is no corner of the earth that does not know the President of the State Duma to be a hero of freedom and human rights! . . ."

The disabled veterans lingered long in the Tauride Palace, filling the entire building, while in the Duma chamber a resolution was debated and ushered through. It was then that the professional chatterboxes came out—not invalids themselves, but uttering the words the disabled men had been waiting to hear.

The Provisional Government has our full confidence! (But the Council keeps the right to exercise control over it.) We are categorically opposed to the line that Lenin is pushing: It sows dissent in the revolutionary army and pits one section of our democracy against another. It was tactless of Lenin to return via Germany and harmful to the interests of the Russian people. The Council of Workers' Deputies must seek to neutralize his activities by all the means at its disposal. We must replace our fighting men from earlier waves of conscription with draft dodgers from the revolutionary classes. And we send greetings to all who have remained in the trenches. Land must be allocated to all who can work it by their own labor. And finally for the maimed veterans: Their children should receive a free education up to the age of fifteen, while they themselves should have their artificial limbs renewed at state expense for the rest of their lives and be allowed free travel back to their homes and to places of medical treatment.

That was all they were going to get out of the welter of benefits promised by Rodzyanko.

. . . What the crippled servicemen did not know was that, after they had left the Kazan Cathedral, that same morning a group of demonstrators bearing black banners had been defending Lenin when the crowd ripped up their black flags and dragged them off to the Commissariat. There the officials duly refused to arrest them.

And now when it was already after three in the afternoon and the invalids were coming out of the Tauride Palace to board their carriages and trucks, out of nowhere came running various soldiers and workers, who blithely tore the furled banners and placards from their feeble grasp, yelling:

—To hell with this army of bourgeois hirelings!

They leaped up onto the trucks, and in place of "Fight on till victory is ours!" they stuck their own placards—"Down with the war!"—prepared specially and brought along for the purpose. First one, then another of the invalids was dragged off the truck and sent sprawling on the ground.

And there was no one to stand up for them.

One of the soldiers who had climbed onto a truck even delivered a harangue, telling the invalids they were no better than a herd of sheep.

—What about you? Have you been at the front?—the crippled men retorted.

—Yes, I have. (Who can say if it was true?) But I'm not stupid enough to want to lose my arms or legs.

The maimed veteran who responded was close to tears:

—Not just our arms and legs—we're ready to lay down our lives for a Russian victory! . . .

But the Leninists weren't going to let him have his say. They talked the band into striking up the funeral march and drowned the veterans out.

They kept it up for quite some time.

And though this was all happening right next to the Palace where both Council and Duma convened, there was no one to intervene on the invalids' behalf—no strong, able-bodied men to stand up to the troublemakers, no one from the palace commandant's detachment or the militia, not one of those who that same morning had applauded from the sidewalk as the veterans passed by.

The nurses went round trying to persuade the thugs not to prevent the patients from boarding their transports—they had not eaten since seven in the morning.

The Leninists desisted, but stayed on to shower the invalids with obscenities.

The Red Wheel
April 1917 – Chapter 186

Vorotyntsev on the Mogilev Rampart

Vorotyntsev had been in Mogilev for more than a month now, and the Rampart was right next to GHQ. Yet not once had he walked over and climbed up onto it—never since that warm, yet wild and stormy October night.[1]

But today he set off for the Rampart after lunch, mulling over the speech he was to give in two days' time. He had been promised an opportunity to speak on the second day of the Officers' Congress.

The speech was already composed in his head, scorching his brain.

Like an electric charge, the message could be passed to hundreds of men in a trice.

And they could then relay it to hundreds more.

At the same time, though, he would have to weigh every syllable. You couldn't openly say who you were rousing them *against*. And nothing too specific about the Government and what he thought of it. As for the Council, there was scarcely anything you *could* say.

But who were they against? Did he even understand, himself? It was all such a hellish, vertiginous state of affairs. Just who were they up against? Certainly, the Leninists had declared themselves clearly enough, but they weren't the only ones. What about these councils and soviets of every shape and hue? And all those little army committees with their yes-men and hangers-on? Thanks to them, even the soldiers are getting more and more carried away with it all. They don't understand any better, they're easily duped, and soon there will be millions of them. So what does that make them? Are they on their way to becoming enemies too? Surely not our own lads—not you! . . .

---

[1] A reference to Vorotyntsev's stormy affair with the historian Olda Andozerskaya (see *November 1916*).

460

It's like some terrible landslide! Everything is slipping away.

What we have is a vicious circle, with everyone deceiving everyone else—that's the enemy we face.

But how do we break through it? This isn't something we've had to deal with before. We don't know how to go about it.

What's needed is a speech that will pierce like a sword.

It was truly an event, to gather three hundred officers—fighting men straight from the front, representing thousands of serving officers—and to do so amidst the seething unrest of these desperate, anarchic times. Nor was the congress intended to be the end of the matter. An All-Russian Union of Officers would be established—everyone else is setting up councils, so why shouldn't we? It will lift the morale of the officer corps and help close ranks.

And the Union's Central Committee will be based here at GHQ. (He must try to get on it.) It will be like a second GHQ attached to the real one, but free from that direct military line of command that staff officers must observe. It would have greater freedom of movement. While working to assist the Supreme Commander.

Or the Leader? But where might this Leader be? If only someone would come right out and issue a rallying call! But not one of the powerful generals will venture that far; they're all tangled up in events.

That's the curse of the present situation—no one can avoid being embroiled.

General Alekseev got back from Petrograd today. He's not giving the slightest thing away. He will be the one who opens the congress. And directs its proceedings.

But what kind of lead will he give? It's clear by now what a feeble role he played in the first few days of March.

He had been following the paths along the crest of the Rampart and now emerged at its easternmost end, near where it dropped sharply away. The steep slope was already covered in a growth of new grass, and a gravel footpath slanted across it, leading down to the quayside. A green slope, chopped off right before it reached the embankment.

There were few people up on the Rampart during the day. Here at the edge of the drop stood a solitary bench. It was empty, for the worst of the floods had passed and the locals were tired of admiring the view.

He sat down.

It can't be helped, but a soldier's eye is trained to see all the wrong things—instead of the height and the beauty, the views on all sides, his first involuntary glance homes in on every natural feature, every twist in the contours of the land: How do we mount an attack here? And hard on its heels comes the second look: And how do we defend it?

It was no different with this steep drop. Forcing a crossing over the Dnieper, then taking the hill—now that *would* be tough! Perhaps in winter?

There were two barges moored at the landing stages. And another being towed upstream by a little steamboat.

The floodwater was receding, but still had a long way to go before it regained its banks. For now the grayish blue waters flowed in a broad expanse.

And on the far side of the Dnieper, the floodplains stretched back a good three miles. Now that *is* wide!

And beyond the flat stretch of floodlands lies a small tannery. And another one. Then a village. A second village. And after that the forests start.

What a delight—this broad view from on high, out over the river below, over the water meadows, and away into the distance. It's like being borne aloft while your life stretches out below you.

This is the way to be buried: on the steep bank of a Russian river facing a broad floodplain. It must be the left bank and with your feet towards the river and your grave dipping slightly so that even as you lie there, you can always see the wide expanse of water and farther off you can watch the sun rise each day.

The color of the sky is no longer blue, but tending to white and tinged with gold. Here and there a fringe of light clouds like strands of hair. Hanging motionless.

It's a rare event to see so much of Russia all at one time.

If you traverse the forest, bearing slightly to the left in an east-northeasterly direction, then fly up and onwards, the first province that opens before you is Smolensk, followed by that of Moscow, then Vladmir. Till finally you reach our own Kostroma lands. It's scarcely more than four hundred miles, a good bit shorter than the front. Not far at all.

Oh, my dear, sad, cheated Kostroma homeland. What has kept me away from you for so very, very long?

Even on flying visits to the estate at Zastruzhie as a grown man, there was still that aching, mournful yearning that always gripped him there—was it the meager look of the fields that caused it? or the way the road twisted?—it ran along here, then wound and twisted before turning off altogether. Perhaps it was the distant windmill? And that same yearning reached him here too, catching and tugging at his heart even here.

Or did he sense that he would never return there again?

O, my Mother Russia! We fail in our duty and serve you ill.

And look what our service has brought us to.

It's right here, close behind us, just beyond those trees—Nechvolodov used to insist—the revolution is *already here!* How many years now has it been blowing us this way and that while we don't so much as raise a finger.

In the past they would have called him a gentle, valorous knight.

But at the time we didn't want to believe him.

And now our much-vaunted Russian troika has taken a drunken lurch into the ravine, leaving us stuck shaft-deep in the mire.

We could never stop boasting.

Where did we pick up this habit of putting on airs? All this devil-may-care strutting and posturing?

Today the first of the delegates will start to gather—officers from fourteen different armies! It's vital to meet as many as ever possible, to spend time with them, talk to them.

To form a nucleus.

No, there is still strength to be found in the officer corps. If not there, then nowhere.

However crushed, divided, and dispersed they may be, who else is ready to face death with head held high? (A head that has already seen its share of battles on all the different fronts.)

However few men we can muster, neither the government nor the Council can deprive us of our ultimate right—the right to fight again.

It has been growing and swelling, and now conflict is inevitable. The fight will surely come.[2]

And if victory cannot be ours, we must seek a worthy death.

The chill of the impending crisis and its very irrevocability bring a new sense of relief all their own.

On the face of it, how can anything get worse? We've slipped over the edge, and we're stuck in the mire. Every sacrifice is in vain. And we cannot tell where we should be or where to take our stand.

Yet his shoulders straightened up once more. No, there is still light ahead. Not everything has been frittered away.

But to which fork should we hurry? And under which stone shall we lay our bones to rest?

---

[2] Vorotyntsev is clearly anticipating the coming Russian Civil War.

9

RUSSIA IN COLLAPSE

At the beginning of his 1990 essay *Rebuilding Russia*, Solzhenitsyn warned that, while "time [had] finally run out for communism," great care had to be given to the means by which Russia exited from totalitarianism. Without thoughtful consideration of the national future, Russia risked being crushed "beneath the rubble" of communism's crumbling edifice. In that work, Solzhenitsyn himself laid out a reasoned program for dissolving the Soviet Union, as well as for resuscitating a mutilated civil society and introducing a balanced political order that would combine adequate presidential authority with a true "democracy of small areas." Local self-government was particularly important for Solzhenitsyn, since without it "there can be no stable or prosperous life, and the very concept of civic freedom loses all meaning."

Unfortunately, Solzhenitsyn's counsel was all but ignored during the chaotic transition to post-Soviet rule. While the Soviet Union was dissolved, little thought was given to the fate of 25 million Russians who consequently found themselves adrift in the so-called "near abroad." The necessary effort to establish democracy and a market economy was treated as an exclusively "technical" problem that could be handled through "shock therapy" and the rapid transfer of public property to the "private sector." Next to no attention was paid to the moral foundations of a free society, to strengthening family life, the church, or education as Solzhenitsyn recommended. "Reformers" such as Yegor Gaidar even appealed to the example of the nineteenth-century "robber barons" in the United States to excuse the depredations of the new "oligarchs" who came to wield nearly unlimited authority at the commanding heights of the Russian state and society.

After Solzhenitsyn's return to his native Russia in 1994, he traveled widely in every part of the country and listened attentively to the concerns of an increasingly disheartened and desperate people. To protest the willful confusion of the market economy with a ravenous "market ideology" and of authentic democracy with the rule of unscrupulous oligarchs and unrepentant apparatchiks, Solzhenitsyn penned *Russia in Collapse*, published in 1998. In this vigorously written work, Solzhenitsyn repudiated the Red-Brown coalition that had emerged as well as any conception of Russian patriotism that accommodated itself to the blood-soaked ideology of communism. But he equally refused to endorse "reforms" that justified the pilfering of Russia's national resources and the domination of the nation by a corrupt and unaccountable elite.

Solzhenitsyn's book chronicles Russia's "Third Time of Troubles" and points the way toward a decent, democratic future. Although the book brims with righteous indignation, it is informed throughout by a moderate and humane vision of Russia's future.

The following selections from *Russia in Collapse* highlight the enduring relevance of Solzhenitsyn's analysis. Here the Russian writer defends a measured and self-critical patriotism against liberal intellectuals who confuse patriotism with fascism and extreme nationalists who confuse love of country with xenophobia and imperialism. Solzhenitsyn also provides a fascinating description of the Russian national character. He shows that, whereas Russian generosity and magnanimity are rooted in the best Orthodox traditions, they have been severely undermined by a Bolshevik tyranny that privileged mendacity, betrayal, and self-preservation over elementary human decency. Even without the brutal Bolshevik assault on national mores, Solzhenitsyn suggests that Russians have always been haunted by "an age-old vice ... —a sluggishness, laziness in civic life." To overcome such debilitating passivity, Solzhenitsyn recommends vigorous local self-government as well as civic and social initiatives that do not depend upon the approval of a distant, centralized state. Despite everything, Solzhenitsyn refuses to lose hope in the capacity of decent Russians to revitalize the national spirit. He calls for his compatriots to put themselves at the service of their homeland, to which they owe an enduring debt, rather than bowing before "ephemeral constitutions" that do not always represent the noblest traditions of the nation. *Russia in Collapse* admirably shows how a true patriot can serve intelligently and courageously during a period of great dislocation and trial.

Place names referred to in *Russia in Collapse*, as excerpted

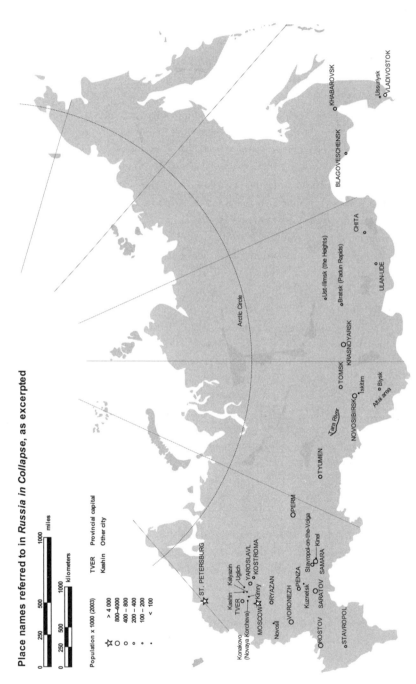

Notes: With the exception of Moscow and St. Petersburg, this map shows only the place names in *Russia in Collapse*, as excerpted. Parentheses are used for small places that do not appear on most maps. Names outside parentheses indicate the nearest city. Stavropol-on-the-Volga was renamed Togliatti under the Soviet regime. Its original name has not been restored.

Russia in Collapse

Foreword

"Time has finally run out for communism. But its concrete edifice has not yet crumbled. May we not be crushed beneath its rubble instead of gaining liberty." That alarm begins my 1990 work, *Rebuilding Russia.*

That year, however, people were gripped by the television screen, following heatedly the sessions of the Supreme Soviet, expecting that the path to a new life was about to open up there. Then, 1991 swirled with even greater excitement—as did 1992, for some.

Now, all admit that Russia has been flattened.

Those who justify this insist that it could not have gone otherwise; that there was no other way; that these are just the "difficulties of transition." Those of clearer mind are certain that good paths existed, for good paths are always available in the life of a nation.

Convinced though I am that the latter group is correct, the argument has become moot: We must now think only about how to crawl out from under the rubble.

— I. On Russia's disjointed expanses —

Over the past four years, I have been able to visit twenty-six provinces of Russia. Sometimes, this meant only their capitals, but more often it included trips to smaller cities and farther, into the rural countryside. I took part in nearly a hundred public meetings (attendance ranged from 100–200 to 1500–1700, with open and unfettered discussion on any theme). After each meeting people would gather around, and the exchange of ideas and words would continue. Thus—with thousands of people. In addition, there were separate meetings one-on-one, as well as discussions in small groups (often with provincial leaders). All this together formed in me a vibrant and unfading impression of the life of our people in various layers of society, and their frame of mind. It is an impression reinforced time and again by thousands of letters from across the country.

As I write this small book, I continue to be embraced by that multitude of people, scattered and isolated over the expanses of Russia, but suffering in such similar ways. Their questions, worries, concerns were repeated, and repeated, and repeated. No matter how much Russia is being ripped into hunks, she is still a single entity! As I write, their words blow like a breeze upon me: their guidance, their instructions, their requests, and their farewells. I shall never again set my eyes on so voluminous a swath of our homeland, but the breath I drew in shall last me to the end of my days. (Or else, I would still be racing back and forth across the Russian land, never getting enough; for I had left my heart in every such place.) And so I write this book sensing those gazes upon me: demanding and inquiring, disconsolate, angry, imploring.

I will not struggle to relate even a minor portion of what I heard, for that would require a large volume. I will present just a few highlights.

"Everything is ripped out of our hands." "No one cares for anything. The government has no plan." "We yearned for democracy, but now we don't believe anyone." (Words spoken at the Krasnoyarsk combine works.)

"Whoever works honestly has no future in life anymore." "We work only out of habit; no one sees any way forward." "Nothing depends on us." (Biysk chemical plant. It is heartrending to see the denigrated sadness in the eyes of young men who now perform menial work because their specialist jobs are gone.)

"The law on land gets put together by people who never lived out in the country" (a village elder from Ussuriysk district). The scientists of the Oceanographic Institute do not just complain about their own poverty, but that we are polluting the water, killing the lower organisms in the food chain, and thus consigning whole species to future extinction. (The Institute is so poor that the scientists bring their own instruments and even their own pencils.) At a street fair in Krasnoyarsk, amidst the bright colors of imported Chinese fabrics, an old woman "shuttle-trader" says: "I am a teacher; I am ashamed of what I am doing, but this is how I am forced to earn my bread." I told her, "It is Russia that should be ashamed."

Students: "Will we live to see the day when science is valued more than making a buck?" "Kids in school go faint from hunger." We have a new term now: *refused* children (their parents refused to keep them). An old man says: "I set money aside, saved it all my life, and now they've turned it into nothing. What did they rob me for?" And from everywhere: "Where do we get money for funerals?" "There is no money for burials." "A veteran died recently, we collected money as a community." "What are we to do?" "How do we go on?" "How do we go on??" That refrain I heard everywhere, even at the smallest stations during two-minute stops.

One sight I shall never forget is "the Heights," next to Ust-Ilimsk. This was the place of the first "descent" of construction workers sent to build the next great hydroelectric dam. The builders' first housing was little more than temporary boxes, yet thirty years later, alongside a "socialist city," those flimsy shacks continue to stand, bunched together. Those who weren't fast and clever enough are stuck living there still, along with some furloughed prisoners. At the main intersection in the village is a metal-and-glass mountain of trash ("for eleven years they won't give us a truck to move it out"). The only water here is brought in, for pay, and only to drink, being too precious to use for washing or watering the garden. Laundry is done far away, "down by the hydrant," but then the hydrant has no pressure in summer. There is no telephone in this place, and the nearest store is two kilometers away. How many such "heights" do we have in today's Russia?

By summer 1994, one could hear the desperation all across Siberia: "How do we survive? *Why* are we still alive?" (a meeting in Ulan-Ude). "Tragedy has struck, from which Russia may never recover" (a Tomsk meeting). "How many times have we been deceived already?" "What is all this being done *for*?" (Iskitim, a place full of gloom). "I don't want to say it, but we're coming to an end, we're dying" (a worker in Tyumen). "I don't want my son to be a slave in this country, better he leave!" (Chita, at the train station). A year later, in Kuznetsk, Penza province: "A little more time will pass, and it will be too late to save anything."

Throughout 1994, so many voices in so many places repeated the same thing: "The common man is being robbed." "I don't believe anything these authorities say." "Our citizens trust neither the leadership, nor the deputies, nor the President." "Legalized bandits[1] occupy our highest levels of power."

Wherever you look, "a black pall covers the soul when you see what is happening" both to people and to the environment.

People drink rotten river water (from the Tara river). "Yellow babies" was the term for a strange illness among infants in Altai. The number of birth defects grows; babies are born deaf, and develop thyroid cancer (Voronezh—the radioactive terminology of Chernobyl reached there, too). Parents themselves fix the schools, for not a penny comes from the budget. A bathroom has been reconstructed into a classroom. Even with three school sessions a day, the breaks between them—to clear in and out, turn around and start all over—are just five minutes. A beginning schoolteacher makes the equivalent of twelve dollars per month (what a fairly low-skilled American worker makes in an hour). But even an experienced teacher, with senior status and a

---

[1] Literally, "thieves-in-law."

thirty-hour weekly workload, worries: "If I should fall ill, I have no money for getting better." (Novaya Korcheva, Tver province). "I cannot afford decent clothes, I am ashamed in front of my students" (Novosil district). Textbooks in school libraries fall apart when you pick them up, and the distribution centers don't send any new ones. "We cannot go on without textbooks."

I was pained to look at a group of conscripts on their way to boot camp (Padun Rapids along the Baikal-Amur Railway): scrawny adolescents in poor health with sad eyes, a look of despondency. Others (in the Stravropol area) weren't able to wiggle out, and now got stuck in the army, never even finished technical school.

Nowadays "people worship the green piece of paper" (Rostov). Nowadays "whatever makes you money makes you right" (Ryazan). "We now are ruled by an ideology of seizing and envy" (Kinel). "Kids watch, and whoever steals they see living well, while my dad is a bumpkin because he wants to live honestly." "Girls from twelve years of age go off into love."

Sometimes the words grew to anger. "The government has taken up pillaging." "Not a single official comes before a court." "The democrats turned out to be the biggest bribe-takers of all." "How did they become millionaires overnight, out of nothing?" (Yaroslavl). An old pensioner in Tver: "As long as I can remember, we were always *building* something—now it's 'a rights-based government'; yet there is no setting anyone to rights." "How do you wreck in two years something that took centuries to build?" (Kostroma). "The authorities commit unbelievable stupidities." "For how long will the country be ruled by unworthy men?" (Penza, to the loud applause of the auditorium). A high-school graduate in Novosibirsk: "Television has turned to trash." Samara: "The guys at my plant are calling us to take up arms, like in 1917." Perm: "If a firm hand doesn't put an end to this, there is going to be a crash."

Yet many other voices reflect self-examination. "We ourselves are at fault: We all have a welfare mentality; each of us needs to have the impulse to act." "Look at us: We know how to talk, but not how to do." (Indeed, almost no one talked of *self-government*, and how to set it up; it was not on their minds; usually I was the one raising that point.) "We keep waiting for someone to unite us." They do seek it; they ask: "How can we band together?"

Alas, that very action, that quality is quite absent among us Russians.

Very many are simply thoughtful, without irritation, but in a constant search: "Could there really not have been a third way?" "But what is the way out of the aimless policies of today?" "Is there a way out of this looting and downfall?" "The young generation is dying spiritually." "You can restore a destroyed factory, but once a person has tasted of an effortless ruble, you can never restore him."

"We are in for difficult times ahead." That much everyone recognizes very well, despite the government's sprightly assertions to the contrary. What the people have to say is incomparably more sober than what Ministers and Dumies[2] babble in front of the television cameras. "Give the people an opportunity to express themselves!" "As if anyone would listen to us....." Suddenly, though, comes a question like this (at Tver University): "How does one not live by lies *today*?" Or even more directly: "How can we save Russia?" (Ulan-Ude). Try finding an answer....

And so the lamplights flicker, warmly, all across the land. "No, Russia has not died! But how do we ease the path to a rebirth?" (Stavropol). In a privileged Vladivostok private school a student gets up to ask, "Shouldn't we be worried about the needy kids? Where are they going to go to school?" I meet a biologist in Krasnoyarsk, who has four children, and his mother is paralyzed by a stroke. He is tackling this concern: that the bureaucracy forces out all the talented and honest people from its ranks; and so he is putting together a proposal for a system that lets talented people rise to the top. (As if our authorities have any interest in talented people....) People like this—whether individuals (some have also written me letters) or little groups, and despite their being burdened by want, put down by poverty—labor on, so that the lamplights might not be extinguished. In Stavropol-on-the-Volga there is a "school of culture" for children from fifth grade and up. In the part of Saratov province that lies east of the Volga, teachers ask, "How do we teach adolescents about the good and the eternal, when television and everything else around us is against it?" In Novaya Korcheva (Tver province), four hundred children attend an extracurricular "center of culture." In Kalyazin there is a "school of the arts," with more than sixty attending. In Kimry—a "home of crafts and folklore," which over five years has turned two hundred children into craftsmen. "The people long to find a common effort. We need to save the soul of the people!" (V. I. Beliakova). In Kashin, people on their last legs put together a "festival of the rebirth of Russia," for the young ones. The library in Kashin—it is a hundred years old, and it has seen better days—radiates knowledge and culture as best it can, for it cannot afford editions of the classics. "We will stand here to the last!" says director G. B. Volkova. (What a charming city Kashin is, but how dilapidated. A local engraver calls it "a gem turned to a trash pile.") There is so much history in each of our "small cities," and much fertile ground for a future.

Across the landscape of Russia, much strength is still not sapped. Take just the librarians, who hold things together amidst hunger and ruin.... No, the people are not finished, the people are alive.

---

[2] Solzhenitsyn's satirical reference to members of the Duma, the legislature.

And here, it seems, another message hints at itself. It repeats itself constantly. All the way from Vladivostok: "We Russians do not value our own culture. But if we do not save our culture, we cannot save the Russian people." At a meeting of the Khabarovsk intelligentsia: "Will the Russian people retain its spiritual consciousness?" In Blagoveschensk an elderly Orthodox woman: "None of us need a Russia without God. And none of us need freedom without Russia." "If we do not come forward in repentance, Russia is not worth a dime." And all through my travels westward, at almost every public meeting, such words could be heard, always pushed off to the side but never squelched entirely. "No, Orthodoxy today is not a sufficient buttress for the state; it is weak." A loader in Samara: "Russians are being squeezed all around. And the moment Russians stand up for themselves, right away cries of 'fascism!' follow." In Saratov University: "It cannot be that the Russian people are hopeless!" A young man in Uglich asks, ahead of the meeting, "Tell us, what does it mean to be a Russian today?"

And so, my friends, in this work I will try to give what answers I can. As best I can.

Russia in Collapse

Will We Russians Continue to Be?

—26. Patriotism —

There are probably many definitions of patriotism. Nevertheless, I will present here the definition that I repeated on many occasions at public meetings in different parts of the country, and which was always received with understanding: "Patriotism is an integral and persistent feeling of love for one's homeland, with a willingness to make sacrifices for her, to share her troubles, but not to serve her unquestioningly, not to support her unjust claims, rather, to frankly assess her faults, her transgressions, and to repent for these."

Patriotism is an organic, natural feeling. It requires no justification or theoretical basis, while all types of prefixes that have been attached to patriotism display either an ignorance of it or an intentional desire to mock it. P. Vyazemsky once appended the epithet "kvas" patriotism,[3] a term that came into much favor among Russia's liberal circles. Yet it reveals his own aristocratic condescension toward the straightforward, thoroughly grounded love that simple people feel for their country.

It may be fashionable here, this branding of patriotism almost as a cousin of "fascism." In the United States, however, patriotism occupies a high place indeed. Not only is there no shame in it; America breathes its patriotism, is proud of it, and various subgroups of society become as one through it. In every American classroom hangs the national flag, and in many schools an oath of allegiance to the flag is recited.

---

[3] *Kvas*: a lightly fermented grain-based drink highly popular in Russia for centuries; a modern American analogy to Vyazemsky's dismissive phrase might be "six-pack" patriotism.

Patriotism is to be found in many countries, including all the countries of Europe. Patriotism is a foundation that does not separate but rather unifies a nation with mankind. Of course, like any human feeling, patriotism can also be skewed and distorted.

Is it not similar to what has happened to the concept of freedom in today's world, and especially in shock-stressed Russia? Freedom has been elevated to a total eclipse of a person's *obligations*, to a freedom *from* any obligation. Yet we only remain human beings insofar as we constantly sense our duty—within ourselves, above ourselves.

Just as a society cannot survive if it fails to grasp the lessons of civic responsibility, the same goes for a country—especially a multinational country—that loses a sense of responsibility for the polity itself.

A multinational country must rely in difficult moments of its history upon the support of *all* of its citizens. *Every one* of its peoples must live with the conviction that it, too, desperately needs a singular defense of the interests of the state as a whole.

That type of feeling, a patriotism for the country, is utterly lacking in Russia today. It has come to this for many reasons, beyond just the active encouragement of ethnic patriotisms in the special-status autonomous provinces. Here we see the general influence of our chaos, and the absolutely unworthy behavior of the government authorities, who have dropped so low in the esteem of the people nationwide. One officer at a meeting in Yaroslavl put it this way: "The new Russia has not stood itself up as a motherland."

— 27. A people comatose —

Love for one's people is as natural as love for one's family. No one can be faulted for this love, only respected. After all, no matter how much the modern world whirls and jerks about, we still aim to keep intact our *family*, and we hold it in special regard, suffused with sympathy. A nation is a family, too, except an order of magnitude higher in numbers. It is bound by unique internal ties: a common language, a common cultural tradition, a shared historical memory, and a shared set of problems to resolve in the future. Why, then, should the self-preservation of a people be held a sin?

On this count, in terms of their own patriotisms, many smaller peoples of our country clearly outpace the ethnic Russians. Theirs is a firm national sense.

And ours? Our national sense is trampled upon and ripped to shreds. For the brief period of the war with Germany, Russian patriotism was permitted, indeed elevated, glorified—and then, having served its purpose, shoved backed in the drawer and turned into a straw man.

I speak here about a clean, loving, constructive Russian patriotism and not of a radical nationalist bent ("only our type!" or "only our faith!"); not of the elevation of one's nationality above our higher spiritual plank, above our humble stance before Heaven. Needless to say, let us not call "Russian patriotism" the school that prefers a small-minded alliance with our communist destroyers.

Russian patriotism is not forbidden directly, as if by some decree—but almost. No small efforts are expended, both within the country and from without, to erase Russians' national identity.

And we? We have given in to it. Under the avalanche of our defeats in the twentieth century, we have surrendered our will to defend our face, our uniqueness, our organic spirit. We are in so many ways responsible for our own fall.

Let us remember the words of Gogol: "There is much ignorance of Russia in Russia." And Ivan Aksakov (in a speech about Pushkin): "Is not the cause of the full measure of our troubles and travails, that we all—aristocrats, democrats—have such a weak Russian historical consciousness, such a dead sense of our history?"

Most distressing of all is the absence among Russians today of any feeling of unity, a weak feeling to begin with. Today, when the majority of the peoples of Russia are living through great troubles, many of them find strength by pulling together and working for their local good. In this regard, the Russian people are in the worst shape, because among our chain of losses we have let go of our mutual cohesion, which could salvage us—and with it we have lost the sense of our own *place* within the country.

Our national consciousness has fallen into lethargy. We barely live, wandering from a past bereft of memory toward the menacing specter of our very disappearance.

We are a people comatose.

While insistent nationalisms grow more abundant in the world, the coma of our national consciousness drains even our lifeblood, our instinct of self-preservation.

I fear that, after all the bitter things we have lived through and are living through now, a weakening, a decline, a fall is the fortune that awaits the Russian people.

— 30. The evolution of our character —

Of course, the character of a people is not fixed eternally. It shifts over centuries, sometimes over just decades, depending on the environment and landscape that fills the soul, on the events that occur with a people, on the spirit of the age—especially during a time of sharp changes. The Russian character changed too.

Our seventeenth-century Time of Troubles gave free rein for a dynamic segment of our population, the Cossacks in particular, to turn to pillaging and cruelty. Yet it did not shake the people's moral foundations, which remained intact.

Far deeper and more damaging was the religious seventeenth-century Schism. It created that fateful fissure at which Peter would then wield his club, indiscriminately battering our customs and mores. Since that time, the original Russian character held firmly within the isolated environment of the Old Believers—and *them* you cannot accuse of being spoiled; or corrupt; or lazy; or unable to run an industrial, agricultural or merchant business; nor of being illiterate; nor, most certainly, of being indifferent to spiritual questions. That which we have been labeling for the third century in a row as the "Russian character" is already the result of its distortion by the cruelly mindless Schism, by the age of Nikon and Aleksei Mikhailovich,[4] then once again by the cruelly enterprising Peter and the fossils who succeeded him.

How these heirs, the Petersburg dynasty, wasted the people's energy—mostly for no reason—I have already described in another essay (*"The Russian Question" at the End of the Twentieth Century*, 1994). The bitter truth is commonly known: that for more than a hundred years the dynasty and the nobility selfishly protracted the serfdom of a large portion of the Russian peasantry, taking advantage of the humble nature of the latter.

After that hundred-year delay, the liberating reform was enacted—but it was weak, not granting the peasants enough land, and even what little it granted the peasants were required to pay for, albeit in gradual installments. The reform was not farsighted and did not take care to help the peasantry through this massive transitional shock, whether economically or socially or morally. The consequences did not take long to manifest themselves in the spasms of the national character, which could not adapt to the new system of interactions, to that devastating "blow of the ruble" (Gleb Uspensky). Some segments of the population—but far, far from all—descended amid broken households, moral degradation, flashes of criminal behavior, and a cresting wave of drunkenness. This wreckage is noted by many of our authors besides Uspensky. K. Leontiev wrote in 1891: "Our people are drunk. They lie. They are dishonest. And they have already, in just thirty years, gotten accustomed to an unnecessary stubbornness and harmful pretensions." And he predicted: If this continues apace, the Russian people "in just a half-century

---

[4] Nikon was the Russian Orthodox patriarch whose governance of the church led to the schism of 1667; Aleksei Mikhailovich was the tsar during that period, and the father of Peter the Great.

or so . . . gradually, without even noticing it, will be transformed from a 'God-bearing people' into a 'God-destroying people.'" His prediction came true ahead of time. . . .

General Denikin, whose experience with Russian soldiers spanned many years, observed: "Religious feeling was shaken by the turn of the twentieth century. The people were losing their Christian countenance and falling into basic material interests, in which they began to see the meaning of life." (Many others note the same thing.)

In 1905 the newfound embitterment manifested itself in arsons and looting of the properties of landed gentry, but the actual attempt at revolution in 1905, followed by the 1906 revolutionary-criminal aftershock that Stolypin firmly cut short, did not reach the masses at their core and did not add to the destruction of the national character.

As late as 1917, based on testimony before the United States Senate's "Overman Committee" by George Simons, a Protestant minister who had lived for several recent years among the Russians: "I want to tell you that I have not found a better type of a man or woman than in the Russian villages, and even among the workmen, of whom I knew thousands, and I always felt pretty safe among them until these Bolsheviki came in power."[5]

The Bolsheviks, for their part, quickly put the Russian character in irons and redirected it to their own ends. With their *reverse selection*, their deliberate destruction of all that was bright, remarkable, of a higher level—the Bolsheviks set about changing the Russian character root and branch, ripping, pulling, and twisting it. I have already written enough of the meltdown of the people's morals under the yoke of Bolshevism (*Gulag Archipelago*, part IV; and in many essays). I will recapitulate briefly. A paralyzing fear spread over the country, a fear not only of arrest but of any action of the leadership (given the total and utter worthlessness of anyone's rights, and the inability to escape from arbitrary rule by relocating). A network of informants saturated the population. Secrecy and distrust permeated the people, so much so that any overt activity was perceived as a provocation. How many denunciations there were against one's own close relatives! or against friends who had fallen under the sword! A total, deafening indifference toward those who perished all around. An overpowering plume of betrayal. It was unavoidable: If you want to survive, lie. Lie and pretend. In place of all the good that was dying away, ingratitude, cruelty, and a thoroughly rude self-centered ambition now rose and established themselves. As Boris Lavrenyov put it in the 1920s, after the Civil War: "The Bolsheviks reboiled Russian blood upon a

---

[5] *Oktiabrskaia revolutsiia pered sudom amerikanskikh senatorov.* Moscow, Leningrad: GIZ, 1927, 18; quoting 66th Congress, 1st session, Document no. 62, Reports and Hearings of the Subcommittee on the Judiciary, vol. 4, p. 159. [Author's note.]

fire." True, true enough; and does not this constitute a change, a complete rebranding of the national character?

The Soviet regime abetted the rise and success of the worst personalities. We should rather be amazed that a core of goodness yet remained among so many. And we should be amazed that our people had not been imploded completely, for otherwise how could they have gathered the titanic strength necessary to fight the Soviet-German war?

The Soviet-German war, and our recklessly incurred, uncounted losses in that war, coming on the heels of internal self-destruction, collapsed the heroic strength of the Russian people for a long time to come, perhaps a hundred years. Perish the thought that it might be forever.

The stupor of the people under Khrushchev and Brezhnev is not marked by any giant breakpoints that would have altered the national character. As Leontiev had once predicted, there came a drowsy and seemingly cozy subservience. The juices of the fading Russian giant fed the rapid nourishment of the peripheral peoples, as they strengthened toward the leap to independence—while we were simply happy that no longer was anyone leading us, by the multitude, to execution.

Then, we were yanked into two thoughtless, totally uncalculated Great Leaps, one under Gorbachev and the other under Yeltsin. With no time to look around, to adjust ourselves to the changes, to prepare ourselves and our children, to preserve the remnants of our meager property, we leapt—we were thrown—not into the "Market," but into a "Market Ideology" (without the market): "Let dog eat dog"; "I might die tomorrow, but why don't you die today." This ruble-dollar shock turned out to be much more far-reaching than the "blow of the ruble" from the times of Alexander II. (And despite all our blood "reboiled upon a fire," we set yet another world record for patience: to humbly go on working without receiving our salaries. Instead, we could be found ripping out an underground military cable in order to sell a piece of scrap metal.)

More frightening than any mass poverty, there also came out of the gaichubaian[6] "reform" a new spiritual decomposition of the people. The humblest, hardest-working, and most trusting among us turned out to be the least prepared to weather the mighty gusts of the Breakdown. How can we shelter from this Breakdown the last untrampled remnants of the national character? What remnants of magnanimity do we still have? What feelings of empathy for the plight of another (even as you are in a plight yourself)? What willingness to help others (when things have gone from bad to worse for you, too)? And then, the most important, the main question: How in the

---

[6] Solzhenitsyn's satirical reference to Yegor Gaidar and Anatoly Chubais, Yeltsin's key ministers who pushed through the early 1990s economic "shock therapy."

face of this corrosive, rude, triumphant corruption do we protect our children?

Of the old traits of the national character, we lost those that made us good, while developing those that made us weaker. That is what rendered us defenseless against the trials of the twentieth century.

Is it not our erstwhile total openness that turned into a propensity to surrender to the influence of others, a spiritual spinelessness? Did it not also show itself in the lack of unity and solidarity amongst us? Or, most bitterly, in our recent rejection of Russian refugees from the neighboring republics? One can only be amazed by this lack of caring by Russians for other Russians. Rarely among any people are mutual sympathy and assistance so completely lacking as with us. Could it be just a matter of the current decline? Or maybe it is a trait carved into us by the Soviet decades? After all, we once had cooperative artels; we had vibrant communities. Perhaps a togetherness can be restored?

Then again, it will no longer suffice simply to restore the health of the people. The high demands of the coming electronic-information age mean that, if we want to amount to something among other people, we must reorient our character toward a twenty-first century that promises to be highly intensive. Throughout our history, we have ever so lacked intensity.

The Russian character today is swaying on shaky ground. And there is no telling where it will end up.

— 31. Will we continue to be Russian? —

In late 1919, as the Volunteer Army was making its final, fatal retreat, General Peter Wrangel rallied it thus: "With us are all who in heart are Russian." No better way to say it. Nationality need not be planted in our blood, but in the attachments of our heart and in the spiritual vector of the person. This was especially important in the formation of the Russian people. By virtue of being the group that for centuries *encompassed* the rest, Russians also became a *regenerating people*. Many of those foreigners who took up government service, or who vibrantly and comprehensively immersed themselves in Russian culture and daily life, became truly Russian in their soul.

This part began with the question, "Will we Russians continue to be?" This question has been stifled for well-nigh eighty years: first, because it "conflicts with internationalist values"; then, because it "interferes with the program of democratic reforms." Yet the question looms menacingly: Are the Russians to exist in the future upon the Earth? The upcoming census in 1999 is certain to show a sharp decline in our population, due mainly to an explosion of deaths and fewer births.

The merciless dial of this question turns also to its corollary: *Will we continue to be Russian?* Even if we survive physically, will we keep our Russianness, the whole of our faith, our soul, our character—our place in the worldwide firmament of cultures? Can we persevere with our spirit intact, speaking our language, conscious of our historical traditions?

— 33. Local self-government —

People's real everyday life, four-fifths of it or more, depends not on the events taking place on the national level, but on local events, and therefore on *local self-government* that directs the course of life in a small district. This is exactly how life is regulated in the nations of the West: through effective local self-government, where each has the opportunity to participate in the decisions that most directly affect his existence. Only this type of arrangement can be called a *democracy.*

But what were our own local *soviets?*[7] From their very beginning, in 1917, these councils—a distorted copy of prerevolutionary *zemstvo*, or land, councils—were set up not as bodies representing the entire population, but for a political goal, as organs of the dictatorship of one segment (workers, soldiers) over other segments. As the revolution progressed, the councils lost even this role, becoming mere ornaments in the power structure of the Communist Party.

After the events of August 1991 there arose the best possible opportunity in Russia to create democratic popular self-rule—a "democracy of small spaces." This opportunity was still not lost in October 1993, with the dissolution of the soviets. But the central authorities made nary a step in that direction; their heads were full of other designs.

Our State Duma, in both its sessions, one as indifferent as the other, put the brakes on any substantive legislation enabling local self-government, refusing to vest it with real authority and an independent financial base.

But even if no one will open the gates to local self-government, it is still in the vital interest of the people to act! Let all who have not yet lost their resolve act on their own, without waiting for the blessing of an enabling statute out of the calcified Center, which may yet take a long time before it awakens. Much already is not functioning in today's Russia, and we must not let the rest of it stall.

---

[7] A soviet (pl. *soviety*) was a council made up of "workers' deputies" operating at various levels of government. Such councils originally gave the Soviet Union its name and survived through the Communist period as nominally elected representative bodies in the formally democratic structure of the USSR. Not only the Supreme Soviet but all soviets were disbanded after the standoff of October 1993, which Yeltsin won by force of arms.

We should begin with patient decision-making about specific local problems, coming together to address each and every issue that arises affecting the community: physical, professional, cultural, social. We should come together in active civic, professional, and cultural groups. In whatever place, and in however small a number, we must work on every short-term and every long-term task. Every such association, in form and substance, bridges the void of our ill, indifferent times.

To become the driving and working force of local self-government is the most urgently needed vocation for the intelligentsia in our heartland. Not only are these talents underused today, but they have been consigned to poverty and swept into irrelevance by the broom of all those "shock" reforms. Yet this intelligentsia is honest, highly literate, hard-working, selflessly idealistic, caring for the plight of others, a direct heir of its prerevolutionary forerunners, a prized heritage of Russia.

Every time that there forms a little center, a link in a chain, an initiative—whether around culture, education, child-rearing, a particular profession, local history, the environment, community planning, even just gardening—such groups are the seedlings of local self-government, and may even become component parts in its future structure. It is for them to form in a common endeavor, and to begin to guide local life—with wisdom, toward its preservation, and not into a dead end, where many a boss and many a Decree has led us. At the outset, it may be necessary to come together even before the law permits real and meaningful elections of local government.

Some will complain: But we *do not know how*. Our people have weak awareness of their rights. However, the calamities that have befallen the people are actively sharpening such awareness. It will gain strength through the very *process* of fighting for popular self-government. Besides, one cannot create the finished product all at once, but only by stepwise approximations, through constant attempts.

And finally, let us remember that not all among the new wealthy class carry a crazed and cruel heart. Some of them are open to charity, as had always been the tradition in Russia. Among the newly grown entrepreneurs, now financially secure, there are decent people, and through donations they are already helping to do good. Yet others will help tomorrow. Those of them who share a sense of responsibility for Russia's future will have great ability to influence the quality of our education, our culture, and more. An *entire* people never acts as one; and we needn't expect the entire people all at once to begin contemplation and to act. A river begins with rills. Various individual concerns will intersect, will combine—and so will gather themselves into a broader stream.

If we are not ready to organize ourselves, we have no one else to blame.

481

— 36. Let us build —

The great majority of the Russian people, having been robbed clean, is bowed down in helplessness, in poverty. But we must recognize an even scarier truth: Over the course of the twentieth century, the Russian people as a whole have suffered an historic defeat, both spiritual and material. For decades we paid for the national catastrophe of 1917, and we pay now for our exit from it, also a catastrophic one. We did not just rupture the communist system, but are demolishing what remains of our own vital foundation.

To recognize—does not mean to accept or to succumb. It means, rather, to reawaken before all our time is up; to find our way out and to apply our strength toward that end.

And above all else—toward our internal healing.

For our spiritual crisis is more painful and perilous than the chaos of our mismanagement. If we let the soul of the nation be undermined, that already is its destruction. "There is no sense trying to restore a Russia without conscience and without faith" (Ivan Ilyin).

If we are truly to free ourselves from the notion that circumstance and setting determine our consciousness—a primitive, materialistic worldview in which we were raised for decades—we must first understand and accept that our, our children's, our people's future depends first and foremost on our consciousness, our spirit, and not on the economy.

More dreadful than the fact of the looting and sale of Russia is this question: How could there grow from within us this cruel, monstrous set, these covetous, greedy thieves, who have grabbed even the mantle of "new Russians"; who with such relish and chic have grown fat off the people's calamity? More destructive than our want, after all, is this wholesale disgrace, this triumphant degenerative vulgarity that has permeated the new elite and is belched out at us from every TV set.

And then—what of these easily bought "*killery*"?[8] (The good Lord took pity, and no Russian word could be found for them.)

Where ends this steady slide?

Whom can our youth take as an example? Of whom can they be proud?

Are we any longer *ourselves*? Are we even recognizable from the past string of centuries? Is the motto "the richer the better!" in our country's tradition? This intense chase that powerfully grips so many hearts: "my personal success!" "I must succeed at any cost!"—is that some timeless trait of ours? Indeed not: For centuries we were a laughingstock precisely because we lacked such a trait.

---

[8] Russian neologism from the 1990s, taken directly from the English word *killers* and used to describe paid hitmen.

And could it possibly be that we would yield the hearts of our children to be skewed by this new corrosion? They are being led away from us; they will leave! We are already losing them, another age group each and every year.

What we lost in *land*—that is not yet a loss for Russia. Even after all that has been cut away from us, Russia is populated at a density too low for the twenty-first century to permit. The "great" communist resettlement projects destroyed what demographers call the *living fabric* of the population. Before entire republics left, taking with them millions of Russians, we inside the country cast aside our heartland, our own cradle, as "having no future."

No, our greatest damage does not come from lost expanses of land. The spiritual life of a nation is more important than its territory and more important, even, than its level of economic prosperity. The greatness of a people is in its level of internal development, not external.

And thus, the very Spirit of the people—the last thing that we have to lose—is being grabbed, and stolen, and shattered day by day, the casualty of this thieving, polluting atmosphere that envelops us from all sides.

Having traveled far and wide across Russia these past four years, having watched, having listened, I am willing to state, under oath if need be: No, our Spirit yet lives! In its core it is uncorrupted! There, in the meeting halls—I didn't say it, people would tell me, would try to convince me: "Just save the soul of the people! The rest will save itself."

Yes, the *Spirit* is capable of reversing the direction of even the most fatal process. It can pull us back even from the brink. Some will find this difficult to believe. But those who in their lives have come to see the justness and might of a higher power above us—those will believe that, despite a crushing century for Russians, there is hope for us yet. It has not been taken away.

If only each of us could sense it: I am not some lone fragment; I *can* influence what goes on—sometimes through fearless acts, sometimes through endurance. Who else will do it if not we?—our children, our grandchildren? Why should it be any easier for them?

We will never receive anything from powerful benefactors until we ourselves come to believe that we are the makers of our fate. *Each and every* one of us, if we have the willpower not to disappear off the face of the planet entirely (for that threat is real), must lift ourselves out of our aimless, perilous state. We must change our very behavior, our tired indifference to our own fate.

How can we overcome that age-old vice of ours—a sluggishness, a laziness in civic life?

Of course, every vice is the flip side of a virtue. No less a harsh critic of Russian fortunes than Chaadayev wrote in a letter to Tyutchev: "Why have we still not come upon our purpose in the world? Might not the reason be in that same spirit of self-abnegation, which you correctly point out as a distinguishing trait of our national character?" Perhaps, our self-abnegation, or maybe some other moral shoots might come in handy to someone else in the world?

My *spirit*, my *family*, and my *labor*—it must be honest, tireless, utterly indifferent to the all-engrossing greed of thieves—for how else can we pull ourselves out? For even if the sword falls upon the thieves (which will not happen), nothing will ever be created without labor. The saying goes, "No good can be made without labor." Nor can a free and independent person.

The way is tortuous indeed. Yet if our decline took almost an entire century, then what to expect of our ascent? Just to recognize all our losses and our illnesses will take us years and years.

Whether or not we preserve ourselves physically and as a nation-state, the Russian *culture* is still a unique phenomenon, with an inimitable image and soul, and part of a system of a dozen or so major world cultures. And it would ill behoove us to give up and lose our face, to let fall the spirit of our long history. We would lose more of our own goodly heritage than we would stand to gain in return.

We must not serve our government, but our Homeland. Our Homeland is what produced us all. It stands higher than any ephemeral constitution. No matter how shattered right now is Russia's multifaceted life—we still have time to hold fast, to become worthy of our inexpungible eleven-hundred-year past. That is the inheritance of dozens of generations, both before us and after us.

Then let us not become the generation that betrays them all.

10

Two Hundred Years Together

After meeting with Solzhenitsyn in the spring of 2001, the Israeli statesman Shimon Peres announced the stunning news that the Nobel laureate had completed a major historical work on Russia's "Jewish question." As Solzhenitsyn himself declared, this was a subject he would have preferred to avoid. It had given rise to "mutual reproaches" and fierce polemics on both the Russian and Jewish sides. Many Jewish commentators reduced the essence of Russian history to a particularly virulent form of anti-Semitism, while extreme Russian nationalists blamed Jews for all the calamities that afflicted their homeland in the twentieth century. And some of Solzhenitsyn's fevered critics were all too eager to confuse his patriotism and Orthodox faith with a badly concealed anti-Semitism.

But Solzhenitsyn's work on *The Red Wheel* had convinced him that the "Jewish question," however difficult to navigate, was a topic that could not remain taboo and should not be left to the distortions of irresponsible extremists. He had only touched upon this question in *The Red Wheel* because he wanted to avoid giving any encouragement to fringe elements who blamed the Russian revolutions of 1905 and 1917 on the conspiratorial machinations of Jews. But since no fair-minded historian had jumped into the breach, Solzhenitsyn felt obliged to embark on this monumental project. Instead of "ever-increasing reproaches and accusations," there needed to be a "quest for all points of understanding, and all possible paths into the future, cleansed from the acrimony of the past." *Two Hundred Years Together* aims to understand the past accurately, equitably, while paving the way toward mutual understanding and full reconciliation between Russians and Jews.

The first volume of *Two Hundred Years Together* (published in Russian in the summer of 2001) treats the encounter between Russians and Jews from 1772, when 100,000 Jews first entered the Russian empire, to the eve of the revolutionary conflagrations of 1917. The second volume (published at the very end of 2002) covers the period from the revolutions of 1917 until the exodus of hundreds of thousands of Jews for Israel and the West in the early 1970s. The first volume aimed primarily "to report" events and was generally marked by a restrained tone; the second, more passionately written, volume describes events that Solzhenitsyn either knew firsthand or had spent decades investigating and writing about in *The Gulag Archipelago* and *The Red Wheel.*

Critics of *Two Hundred Years Together* have often failed to come to terms with the larger intellectual and moral concerns that inform Solzhenitsyn's analysis. Some commentators have perversely gone out of their way to read the book selectively, keeping scorecards of "good" and "bad" Jews in its pages and prying quotations egregiously out of context. These critics treat Solzhenitsyn's expressed goal of encouraging mutual understanding between Russians and Jews as a subterfuge. They accuse him of minimizing the Russian state's responsibilities for pogroms in 1882, 1903, and 1905–7. And some have mendaciously claimed that Solzhenitsyn holds Jews uniquely responsible for the criminal totalitarianism of the twentieth century. Nothing could be further from the truth.

Solzhenitsyn in no way minimizes the damage the pogroms did to the lives and liberties of ordinary Jews, to the "reasonable evolution" of the Russian state, or to Russian-Jewish relations. He establishes that, with one notable exception, the pogroms were not government-sponsored but instead were instigated spontaneously from below. But a "scandalously" weak Russian state did little to protect Russia's Jews or to bring the culprits to justice. However, Solzhenitsyn refuses to distinguish between good and bad forms of lawlessness: Peasants burning the homes and estates of landowners after the revolution of 1905 unleashed "pogroms" as unjustifiable as the mass violence against Jews in Moldavia, Ukraine, and southwest Russia. A strong, self-respecting, law-based state was the most sensible response to both forms of "incendiary" violence. The powerful excerpt from chapter 18 provides a particularly grim tally of the murderous anti-Semitism that gripped the Ukraine during the Civil War. Much of this violence was instigated by Whites, and some by Ukrainian nationalists and by marauding elements of the Red Army. These pogroms took the lives of up to 200,000 Jews and inflicted untold spiritual and psychological damage on survivors.

In particularly emphatic passages, Solzhenitsyn declares that none of the Russian revolutions can be blamed on a "malicious Jewish plot." The Russian writer freely mocks those fanatics who think they have discovered "the root cause that explained it all: the Jews!" They mistakenly maintained "Russia would long ago have ascended to the pinnacles of power and glory were it not for the Jews!" It was in truth the full panoply of "Russian failings," which Solzhenitsyn so powerfully explicates in the concluding paragraphs of chapter 9, that "determined [Russia's] sad historical decline."

While "it would be quite wrong to say that the Jews 'organized' the revolutions of 1905 and 1917," Solzhenitsyn believes that all parties must take responsibility for their "renegades," those who collaborated with an essentially totalitarian and terroristic regime after 1917. For Solzhenitsyn, though, it is always a question of collective *responsibility* and never of collective guilt. It is not a matter of answering before other peoples, "but to oneself, to one's conscience, and before God." In decisive respects, *Two Hundred Years Together* renews Solzhenitsyn's high-minded defense of "repentance and self-limitation" in the life of nations.

In chapter 21, Solzhenitsyn does justice to the singularity of the Holocaust on Soviet territory. He clearly acknowledges the monstrousness of the war against the Jewish people, without ever minimizing the comparable evils that were the gulag and collectivization. Solzhenitsyn refuses to "privilege" one form of murderous totalitarianism over another or to set the sufferings of Russians and Jews against each other. The "totality of suffering" experienced by both Russians and Jews at the hands of the National Socialist and Communist regimes is "so great, the weight of the lessons inflicted by History so unsupportable" that it is imperative that it produce good and not only bitter fruit. It must give rise to mutual empathy, understanding, and reflection on the part of both Russians and Jews. In making these appeals, Solzhenitsyn never loses sight of our common humanity or the rigorous demands of the moral law. And transcending all polemics, he affirms that a "mysterious Design" continues to connect Russians and Jews in their third century of cohabitation. Fidelity to it requires a strenuous effort to do justice to their *common past*.

Two Hundred Years Together
Introduction

Approaching the Theme

Through a half-century of work on the history of the Russian Revolution, I repeatedly came face to face with the question of Russian-Jewish interrelations. Time and again it would enter as a sharp wedge into events, into people's psychology, and arouse blistering passions.

I never lost hope that there would come, before me, a writer who might illumine for us all this searing wedge, generously and equitably. More often, alas, we meet one-sided rebukes, either pertaining to Russians' culpability toward Jews, and even the primordial depravity of the Russian people (there is quite a profusion of such views)—or, from those Russians who did write about this mutual dilemma, mostly agitated tendentious accounts that refuse to see any merit on the other side.

It's not that there is a paucity of public commentators—in Russia the Jewish side, especially, abounds in them, more so than the Russian side. But, despite this dazzling array of minds and ideas, there still has not appeared such an exposition or elucidation of our common history as might meet with understanding from both sides.

Yet we must learn not to tauten these tense, interwoven strings to their breaking point.

I would be glad not to test my strength in such a thorny thicket, but I believe that this history, and attempts to study it, must not remain "forbidden."

The history of the "Jewish question" in Russia (and not only in Russia) is, first and foremost, a *rich* one. To write about it means to hear new voices and to convey them to the reader. (In this book Jewish voices will sound far more frequently than Russian ones.)

But because of the atmosphere surrounding this theme, writing about it turns out, in fact, to be like walking a razor's edge. One feels from *two* sides all manner of possible, impossible, and ever-increasing reproaches and accusations.

Yet what leads me through this narrative of the two-hundred-year-long cohabitation of the Russian and Jewish peoples is a quest for all points of common understanding and all possible paths into the future, cleansed from the acrimony of the past.

The Jewish people—like all other peoples and like all persons—is both an active subject of history and its anguished object. Furthermore, Jews often carried out, perhaps unconsciously, major tasks allotted them by History. The "Jewish question" has been treated from numerous angles, always with passion but also, oftentimes, with self-delusion. And yet the events that befall any people in the course of History are sometimes determined not by that people alone, but also by the other peoples who surround it.

An exaggerated hotheadedness on either side is humiliating to both. There cannot be a question upon earth that is unsuited for contemplative discourse among people. To converse broadly and openly is more honest—and in our case it is also indispensable. Alas, mutual grievances have accumulated in both our people's memories, but if we repress the past, how can we heal them? Until the collective psyche of a people finds its clear outlet in the written word, it can rumble indistinctly or, worse, menacingly.

We cannot shut the door on the last two hundred years; and in any case, our planet has shrunk, and, no matter how one parses it, we become neighbors again.

For many years I postponed this work and would still now be pleased to avert the burden of writing it. But my years are nearing their end, and I feel I must take up this task.

I have never conceded to anyone the right to conceal that which *was*. Equally, I cannot call for an understanding based on an unjust portrayal of the past. Instead, I call both sides—the Russian and the Jewish—to patient mutual comprehension, to the avowal of their own share of the blame. Yet isn't it so easy to turn away from it, saying, "That wasn't really *us*. . ."? I earnestly have tried to understand both sides of a historic conflict. To do this, I delve into events, not polemics. I try to *show*, taking up an argument only in those unavoidable cases where the truth has been enveloped in layer upon layer of falsehood. I dare anticipate that this book will not be met with the anger of implacable extremists, but instead will serve the cause of harmony. I hope to find benevolent collocutors among both Jews and Russians.

I conceive of my ultimate aim as discerning, to the best of my ability, mutually agreeable and fruitful pathways for the future development of Russian-Jewish relations.

1995

I wrote this book guided only by the demands of the historical material itself, as well as seeking beneficent solutions for the future. But let us not lose sight of the fact that, in recent years, Russia's condition has so precipitously been transformed that the question we are examining has been significantly marginalized, and has grown dimmer, when compared with Russia's other problems.

2000

Two Hundred Years Together
Volume I, Chapter 8

At the Turn of the Twentieth Century

By the beginning of the twentieth century, then,[1] the Pale of Settlement had outlived the purpose for which it had been created. It did not bar Jews from acquiring solid positions in the most vital areas of national life, whether economy and finance or the intellectual sphere. No longer of practical significance, it failed, too, in its political and economic goals. But what it did accomplish was to aggravate Jewish feelings of bitterness toward the regime, to fan smoldering social tensions, and, importantly, to stigmatize the Russian government in the eyes of the West.

But then again, was there any area or any undertaking whatever in which the Russian Empire did *not* lag behind throughout the nineteenth century and the pre-Revolutionary decades—given its general sluggishness, its unresponsive bureaucracy, and the inflexible thinking at the top? The Empire was unable to cope with a dozen issues absolutely crucial to the country's existence, such as those bearing on local self-government, on rural *zemstvos*, on land reform, on the Church and its ruinously humiliating status, on ways of making the government's thinking comprehensible to society, on the need to shift mass education into high gear, and on support for the development of Ukrainian culture. In just the same way, it was fatally late in reexamining the actual state of affairs relating to the Pale and the effect it was having on the situation in the entire state.

Over the course of more than a century, the regime proved incapable of solving the problem of its Jewish population, neither offering an acceptable form of assimilation nor allowing the Jews to remain in the kind of voluntary isolation that had prevailed a century earlier when they were first incorporated into the empire.

---

[1] In the preceding chapters, the author has enumerated a multitude of prominent Jewish entrepreneurs in the Russia of the late nineteenth century.

Meanwhile, the three decades between the 1870s and the early twentieth century had become a time of rapid development in Russia's Jewish community, with an undisputed flowering of intellectual energy among its elite, who now felt hemmed in not only by the Pale of Settlement but by the confines of the Russian Empire as well.

This general picture should certainly be kept in mind when focusing on the specific ways in which Russian Jews were denied equal rights, on the Pale of Settlement, and on the restrictive quotas in various fields of endeavor. Despite the growing significance of the Jewish presence in the US, at the beginning of the twentieth century Jews in Russia constituted roughly one half of the world's Jewish population[2]—a crucial circumstance for subsequent Jewish history. Looking back across the historical divide of the Revolution, I. M. Bikerman wrote the following in 1924: "Tsarist Russia was the home of more than half the world's Jews. . . . It is therefore only natural that the Jewish history of the generations closest to us in time has primarily been the history of Russian Jews."

And although in the nineteenth century

> Western Jews were wealthier, more influential, and more advanced in cultural terms, the life force of the Jews was in Russia. It was a force that grew in strength together with the flourishing of the Russian Empire. . . . The renaissance [of the Jews] began only with the incorporation into Russia of the lands populated by them. The Jewish population increased rapidly in number, to the point that it could even expatriate a huge contingent to the New World; Jews began accumulating wealth; a significant middle class came into existence; the material level of the lower classes was constantly improving; by dint of effort, Russian Jews were overcoming the physical and moral taint brought out of Poland; European-style education was spreading among Jews, and we were able to accumulate so much inner strength that we could afford the luxury of having a literature in three languages. . . .

This education and wealth had all been acquired by Jews in Russia. And "in terms of sheer numbers and the vitality of the forces it contained," Russian Jewry revealed itself to be "the backbone of the entire Jewish people."[3]

---

[2] *Kratkaia evreiskaia entsiklopediia* (Jerusalem, 1976–[ongoing]), II, 313–14. [Author's note.]

[3] I. M. Bikerman, "Rossiia i russkoe evreistvo," in *Rossiia i evrei*, Sbornik I (Berlin, 1924; reprinted Paris, 1978), 84–85, 87. [Author's note.]

This portrayal by a witness of the events described is echoed in 1989 by one of our contemporaries: "At the turn of the twentieth century, the public aspects of life had for Russian Jews attained a scope and a level of development that could have been a source of envy for many other national minorities in Europe."[4]

It must be said that the one thing that the alleged "prison-house of nations"[5] cannot be accused of is the denationalization of Jews or of any other national group.

True, some Jewish commentators complain that in the 1880s the St. Petersburg-based Jewish intelligentsia "took virtually no part in representing Jewish interests," and that these concerns were being upheld through the efforts of Baron Ginzburg and other wealthy and well-connected Jews.[6]

"Jews in Petersburg [where they numbered some thirty or forty thousand by the end of the century] were scattered throughout the city, and the overwhelming majority of the Jewish intelligentsia of the day had little concern for Jewish needs and interests."[7]

But in the very same years, "the holy spirit of renewal . . . hovered over the Jewish Pale, awakening forces in the rising generation that had been slumbering for centuries. . . . It was a veritable spiritual revolution."

Among young Jewish women, "the striving for education . . . was literally religious in its fervor," and soon in Petersburg, too, "many Jewish students of both genders . . . enrolled in institutions of higher education." By the beginning of the twentieth century "a significant part of the Jewish intelligentsia began to feel . . . that it was duty-bound to return to its own people."[8]

This spiritual awakening among Russian Jews gave rise to very divergent tendencies that had little in common with one another. Some of them would later play a role in determining the fate of the entire world in the twentieth century.

The Russian Jews of the period envisioned at least six different kinds of futures, many of which were mutually exclusive:

> —retaining their religious identity by self-isolation, as had been the case for centuries (but this option was rapidly losing appeal);

---

[4] E. Finkel'shtein, "Evrei v SSSR. Put' v XXI vek," *Strana i mir* [Munich], 1989.1: 70. [Author's note.]

[5] A hostile moniker for Russia in use in the nineteenth century.

[6] G. B. Sliozberg, *Dela minuvshikh dnei. Zapiski russkogo evreia*, 3 vols. (Paris, 1933–34), I, 145. [Author's note.]

[7] M.A. Krol', *Stranitsy moei zhizni*, vol. 1 (New York, 1944), 267. [Author's note.]

[8] Krol', pp. 260–61, 267, 299. [Author's note.]

—assimilation;

—struggling for cultural and national autonomy of the Jews in Russia, with the goal of an active but separate existence in the country;

—emigration;

—enlisting in the Zionist movement;

—joining the revolutionary cause.

Two Hundred Years Together
Volume I, Chapter 9

In the Revolution of 1905

How can we sum up the effect of the 1905 Revolution on Russian Jews as a whole? On the one hand, "The revolution of 1905 had an overall positive outcome. Though Jews still did not have equal civil rights, it granted them political equality. ... The Jewish question had never been so positively viewed in public opinion as after the so-called 'Libertarian Movement.'"[1]

But on the other hand, as a result of the significant participation of Jews in the events of 1905, all Jews as a group now more than ever came to be identified with the revolution.

An official plan of government reforms published August 25, 1906, promised to look into restrictions aimed at Jews in order to see which ones could be immediately revoked because they "generated nothing but irritation, and were clearly obsolete."

But at the same time the Russian government was profoundly dismayed by the revolution itself (which dragged on for two more years in the form of widespread and at times simply criminal terrorism, barely contained by Stolypin)—as well as by the prominent participation of Jews in it.

Angered by the persistent nature of revolutionary violence, as well as by the humiliating defeat in the war with Japan, the ruling circles in Petersburg were not above yielding to the temptingly simple view that there was nothing organically wrong with Russia and that the entire revolution, from beginning to end, was a malicious Jewish plot, part and parcel of a worldwide Jewish-Masonic conspiracy. Here was the root cause that explained it all: the Jews! Russia would long ago have ascended to the pinnacles of power and glory were it not for the Jews!

---

[1] G. A. Landau, "Revoliutsionnye idei v evreiskoi obshchestvennosti," in *Rossiia i evrei*, Sbornik I, 116. [Author's note.]

It was a myopic and facile explanation, which made the impending fall of these high officials all the more irrevocable.

The superstitious faith in the historical potency of conspiracies (even if such may occur, formed by groups small or large) utterly overlooks the principal reason why individuals and entire state structures fail, namely, human weaknesses.

It was our Russian failings that determined our sad historical decline, from the senseless Nikon-inspired schism, the cruel inanities and perversities launched by Peter, and, throughout, the national shock occasioned by the zigs and zags of the post-Petrine period, a century-long squandering of Russian strength on campaigns foreign and irrelevant to the country, together with a hundred years of arrogant smugness by the nobility and a bureaucratic sclerosis for the duration of the nineteenth century. It was not some alien conspiracy that allowed us to abandon our peasants to centuries of mere existence. No outside conspiracy caused the stately and cruel Petersburg to repress the warm culture of Ukraine. No outside plot was involved when four ministries at a time could squabble for years over jurisdiction over a particular matter, endlessly bouncing the issue off four bureaucratic walls, and through each and every section office. And no foreign plot is to blame for the fact that none of our successive emperors was attuned to the tempo of the world's development and to the genuine needs of the day. If we had preserved the spiritual strength and purity that earlier in our history had flowed from St. Sergius of Radonezh, we would have had no need to fear any plot or conspiracy.

No, it would be quite wrong to say that the Jews "organized" the revolutions of 1905 and 1917, just as it was not organized by any other nation as such. In the same way, neither the Russians nor the Ukrainians, considered as nations, had organized Jewish pogroms.

It would be easiest for all of us to look back at the revolution and to renounce our "renegades." They were, it is claimed, "non-Jewish Jews,"[2] or else "internationalists, not Russians." No nation, however, can shirk its responsibility for its members. As nations, we contribute to their formation.

In the case of young Jewish revolutionaries (and, alas, their mentors), as well as those Jews to whom the encyclopedia refers as "the important driving force of the revolution,"[3] what was forgotten was the wise counsel of the prophet Jeremiah to the Jews taken to Babylon: "Seek the welfare of the city where I [the Lord] have sent you into exile, and pray to the Lord on its behalf: For in its welfare you will find your welfare" (Jer. 29:7).

---

[2] See, for example, Paul Johnson, *A History of the Jews* (New York, 1987), 448. [Author's note.]

[3] *Kratkaia evreiskaia entsiklopediia*, VII, 349. [Author's note.]

In contrast, the Russian Jews who had joined the revolutionary movement were burning with eagerness to tear that city down. They were blind to the consequences.

The role of the small but energetic Jewish people in the long and complex history of the world is undisputed, powerful, persistent, and even striking. Their impact on the history of Russia is a case in point. Yet this role has remained a riddle for all of us.

And for Jews as well.

Indeed, this strange mission brings them no happiness.

Two Hundred Years Together
Volume II, Chapter 15

Among the Bolsheviks

The topic is only too familiar: Jews amid the Bolsheviks. It has been written about innumerable times. Those who wish to prove that the Revolution was un-Russian and "of alien stock" point to Jewish names and pseudonyms in an effort to clear Russians of blame for the revolution of 1917. Jewish authors, on the other hand (both those who used to deny the marked participation of Jews in the Bolshevik regime and those who never disputed this point), are unanimously of the opinion that these were not Jews *in spirit*. They were *renegades*.

We are in full agreement with this view. Individuals should indeed be judged in the light of their *spirit*. Yes, these people were renegades.

But neither were the leading Russian Bolsheviks Russian in spirit. Many were distinctly anti-Russian, and all were certainly anti-Orthodox. In them, Russian culture manifested itself only through the distorting lens of political doctrine and calculation of partisan advantage.

Let us pose the question differently: How many random renegades does it take to create a tendency that is no longer accidental? What proportion of one's people needs to be involved? About Russian renegades we know that there was a depressingly, unforgivably large number among the Bolsheviks. But what about Jews? How actively did Jewish renegades take part in setting up the Bolshevik regime?

A further question arises: What is the attitude of a people to its renegades? For this can vary widely, ranging from curses to acclaim, and from avoidance to participation. It manifests itself in the actions of the population, be it Russian, Jewish, or Latvian, in other words in life itself, and only in a minor and secondary sense in the accounts of historians.

And so, can nations disavow their renegades? Would such a disavowal have meaning? Should a people remember its renegades or not; should it preserve a memory of the fiends and demons that it engendered? The answer to that last question should surely not be in doubt: *We must remember.* Every people must remember them as *its own*; there is simply no other way.

There is probably no more striking example of a renegade than Lenin, but it is impossible not to acknowledge him as a Russian. True, old Russia evoked disgust and loathing in him, as did the whole of Russian history, to say nothing of Russian Orthodoxy. And it seems that of Russian literature he assimilated only Chernyshevsky and Saltykov-Shchedrin, while also amusing himself with Turgenev's liberalism and Tolstoy's denunciations. There was not even any sign of attachment to the Volga Region, where he grew up (he sued the peasants on his estate for damaging his crops)—on the contrary, he pitilessly delivered the whole area to the horrifying famine of 1921. All that is undeniable. But it was we Russians who brought into being the social environment in which Lenin grew and filled with hate. It was *in us* that the weakening of the Orthodox faith took place, that faith in which he could have matured instead of trying to destroy it. A more characteristic exemplar of a renegade is difficult to imagine, and yet Lenin is Russian, and we Russians must answer for him.

If one chooses to raise the issue of Lenin's ethnic roots, it will change nothing to say that he was of very mixed heritage: His grandfather on his father's side, Nikolai Vasilyevich, was of Kalmyk and Chuvash background; his grandmother, Anna Alekseyevna Smirnova, was a Kalmyk. On his mother's side, the grandfather was a converted Jew, Israel, then Alexander, Davidovich Blank; his grandmother, Anna Johannovna (Ivanovna) Grosschopf, had a German father and a Swedish mother, Anna Beata Östedt. But none of this gives us the right to claim that Lenin does not belong to Russia. We must acknowledge him not only as a genuine offspring of Russia as a country, for all the ethnic groups to which he owes his existence were part of the fabric of the Russian Empire, but also as an offspring specifically of the Russian people, being the product of a country and a social atmosphere shaped by us Russians; even though *in spirit*, ever alienated from Russia and at times fiercely anti-Russian, Lenin was for us indeed an alien formation. And yet for all that we simply cannot disavow him.

And what about Jewish renegades? As we have seen,[1] there was no specifically Jewish gravitation toward the Bolsheviks over the course of 1917. But energetic Jewish activism did manifest itself in the revolutionary maneuvers of the period. At the last congress of the Russian Social Democratic Party prior to 1917 (London, 1907) where, it is true, Mensheviks were included, out of the 302 (or 305) delegates more than half—160—were Jewish. And at the April conference in 1917 (where Lenin's explosive "April

---

[1] Chapters 13 and 14.

Theses" were announced), among the nine members of the newly chosen central committee we see Grigori Zinoviev, Lev Kamenev, and Yakov Sverdlov. At the summer VI Congress of the newly named Russian Communist Party of Bolsheviks, eleven members were elected to the central committee, including Zinoviev, Sverdlov, Sokolnikov, Trotsky, and Uritsky.[2] Next came the so-called "historic meeting" of October 10, 1917, on Karpovka Street, in Himmer and Flakserman's flat, where the decision to undertake the coup was taken. Among the twelve participants were Trotsky, Zinoviev, Kamenev, Sverdlov, Uritsky, and Sokolnikov. At the same occasion the first "Politburo" (an appellation with a brilliant future) was organized, and of the seven members we see the same Trotsky, Zinoviev, Kamenev, Sokolnikov. Not a small number by any count. D. S. Pasmanik puts it succinctly: "There can be no doubt that the number of Jewish renegades greatly exceed the restrictive quotas of old . . . and that they occupy far too much space among the Bolshevik commissars."[3]

Of course all this relates to the upper echelons of Bolshevism and is in no sense indicative of any mass Jewish movement. Moreover, the Jews in the Politburo did not act in any coordinated manner. At the October meeting, for example, Zinoviev and Kamenev were opposed to launching the coup at that particular time. It was Trotsky who was the leader and guiding genius of the October seizure of power, and he has in no sense exaggerated his role in his *Uroki Oktiabria* (The Lessons of October). Lenin, with his cowardly retreats into hiding, was not a significant contributor to the coup proper.

In accordance with his internationalist view, and particularly after his 1903 polemics with the Bund (the Jewish Social Democratic Labor Party), Lenin did not believe that there should be any such thing as a "Jewish nationality"; in his view, in fact, it did not exist but was a reactionary fiction invented in order to sow dissension in the revolutionary camp. (Stalin concurred, deeming Jews "a paper nation" and prophesying their inevitable assimilation.) Lenin accordingly considered anti-Semitism a capitalist stratagem, a device useful to the counterrevolution, but not something that had organic reality. At the same time, he had an excellent understanding of the mobilizing potential of the Jewish question on the ideological battlefield. And, needless to say, he was ever ready to make the most of any special bitterness felt by Jews to further the revolutionary cause.

And it so happened that from the first days of the revolution Lenin found himself forced to seize on this very circumstance. Just as he had not foreseen crucial developments on the state level, Lenin did not anticipate the degree

---

[2] *Kratkaia evreiskaia entsiklopediia*, VII, 399. [Author's note.]

[3] D. S. Pasmanik, *Russkaia revoliutsiia i evreistvo: Bol'shevizm i iudaizm* (Paris, 1923), 155. [Author's note.]

to which educated and semi-educated Jews (who were scattered throughout Russia because of the war) would come to the rescue of his government in critical months and years, beginning with the episode when they replaced the Russian civil servants who were on a mass strike against the Bolsheviks. These were the Jewish inhabitants of Russia's western borderlands who had been evicted from their homes[4] and had not returned to their previous areas of residence after the war. (For example, of the Jews evicted during the war from Lithuania, those returning after 1918 were mostly inhabitants of small towns and villages, whereas the urbanized Lithuanian Jews as well as the younger generation remained in the large towns of Russia.)[5]

Right "after the annulment of the Pale of Settlement in 1917, there followed a great exodus of Jews from the lands bordered by the Pale to the interior of Russia."[6] This was not a movement of refugees or formerly evicted persons but a migration of individuals seeking to resettle for good. Here is a sample of a Soviet report from 1920. "Several tens of thousands of Jewish refugees and evictees have settled in Samara alone"; in Irkutsk "the Jewish population has grown to fifteen thousand ... [and] large Jewish communities have arisen in Central Russia, along the Volga, and in the Urals." However, "the majority is still being supported by social welfare agencies and various philanthropic organizations." And the paper ends with an exhortation: "Party organizations, Jewish sections of the Party and of the Peoples' Commissariat of Nationalities must mount the most vigorous and broad-based campaign against any return to the areas holding the 'graves of forefathers' and on behalf of a reorientation toward productive labor in Soviet Russia."[7]

Try putting yourself in the shoes of the small body of Bolsheviks who had seized power and were barely holding on to it. Whom could they trust? To whom should they turn for help? Semyon (Shimon) Dimanshtein, a Bolshevik from way back, and since January 1918 head of the Jewish Commissariat (a specially created subsection of the Commissariat for Nationalities), gives this account of the remarks Lenin had made to him:

> Of great benefit to the revolution was the fact that due to the war, a significant portion of the Jewish middle intelligentsia happened to be in Russian cities. They foiled the widespread sabotage which we encountered immediately after the October Revolution and

---

[4] See ch. 12. [Author's note.]

[5] S. Gringauz, "Evreiskaia natsional'naia avtonomiia v Litve i drugikh stranakh Pribaltiki," in *Kniga o russkom evreistve*, 1917–1967 (New York, 1968), 46. [Author's note.]

[6] *Kratkaia evreiskaia entsiklopediia*, II, 312. [Author's note.]

[7] *Izvestiia*, October 12, 1920, 1. [Author's note.]

which was extremely dangerous for us. Jews, though far from all of them, sabotaged this sabotage, thereby rescuing the Revolution in a difficult moment.

Lenin considered it

inexpedient to emphasize this point in the press, but made it clear that taking control of the governmental apparatus and altering it significantly was achieved exclusively due to this reserve of literate, reasonably competent and sober-minded new civil servants.[8]

As we see, the Bolsheviks invited Jews starting with the very first days after assuming power, offering both leadership positions and administrative work within Soviet governmental structures. The result? Many, very many, responded positively, doing so without delay. What the Bolshevik regime needed above all were functionaries who would be absolutely loyal, and it found many such individuals among young secularized Jews along with their Slavic and international confrères. These people were not at all necessarily "renegades," since some were not members of the party, had no particular revolutionary sympathies, and seemed apolitical prior to this point. And for many this might have been a simple household decision rather than one based on ideology. The fact remains, though, that it was a mass phenomenon. And Jews were not dispersing to the previously closed rural areas they had cherished, preferring Moscow and Petersburg.

Thousands of Jews thronged to the bolsheviks, seeing in them the most determined champions of the revolution, and the most reliable internationalists. . . . Jews abounded at the lower levels of the party machinery.[9]

A Jew, as an individual who was clearly not a member of the nobility, of the clergy, or of the old civil service, automatically became part of a promising subset in the new clan.[10]

---

[8] S. Dimanshtein, "Vvedenie," in N. Lenin, *O evreiskom voprose v Rossii* (Moscow, 1924), 17–18. [Author's note.]

[9] Leonard Schapiro, "The Rôle of Jews in the Russian Revolutionary Movement," *The Slavonic and East European Review*, 40 (1961–62): 164. [Author's note.]

[10] M. Kheifets, "Nashi obshchie uroki," *22* [Tel Aviv], No. 14 (1980): 162. [Author's note.]

And in order to encourage Jewish participation in the Bolshevik enterprise, "at the end of 1917, when the Bolsheviks were only just setting up their institutions, the Jewish section in the Commissariat of Nationalities was already functioning."[11] Soon thereafter, starting in 1918, this body was transformed into a separate "Jewish Commissariat," and in March 1919, in preparation for the VIII Congress of the Party, it was planned to announce the formation of a "Jewish Communist Union of Soviet Russia" which would be an organic but separate part of the Russian Communist Party. (The idea was to bring this new formation into the Comintern as well, so as to undermine the Bund.) A special Jewish section of the Russian telegraph agency (ROSTA) was also established.

D. Shub's justifying comment to the effect that "significant numbers of young Jews were attracted to the Communist Party" as a result of the pogroms that had taken place on the territories held by the Whites during the Civil War[12] (that is, starting in 1919) is quite mistaken. The mass influx of Jews into Soviet structures occurred in late 1917 and 1918. There is no doubt that the events of 1919 (discussed in chapter 16) could only have served to strengthen the Jewish connection to the Bolsheviks, but this certainly did not originate the phenomenon.

Another author, a Communist, explains "the particularly important role of the Jewish revolutionary in our labor movement" by the fact that Jewish workers demonstrate a "special development of certain psychological qualities necessary for leadership"—attributes that are only beginning to grow in Russian workers, namely, outstanding levels of energy, cultural development, and orderliness.[13]

Few commentators deny the *organizing* role of Jews in Bolshevism. D. S. Pasmanik puts it this way: "The appearance of Bolshevism [in Russia] resulted from the peculiarities of Russian history ... but the methodical organization of Bolshevism was in part achieved by the activity of Jewish commissars."[14] The dynamic role of Jews in Bolshevism at the time was also noted with approval by American observers: "The rapid emergence of the Russian Revolution from the destructive phase and its entrance into the constructive phase is a conspicuous expression of the constructive genius of Jewish dis-

---

[11] *Evreiskaia tribuna* [Paris], September 7, 1923, 1. [Author's note.]

[12] D. Shub, "Evrei v russkoi revoliutsii," in *Evreiskii mir*, Sbornik II (New York, 1944), 142. [Author's note.]

[13] Iu. Larin, *Evrei i antisemitizm v SSSR* (Moscow & Leningrad, 1929), 260–62. [Author's note.]

[14] D. S. Pasmanik, "Chego zhe my dobivaemsia?" in *Rossiia i evrei*, Sbornik I, 212. [Author's note.]

content."[15] While the October Revolution was riding high, there were any number of Jews who spoke about their energetic input into Bolshevism with head held high.

Let us recall that in the period before 1917, revolutionaries and radical liberals readily and actively capitalized on the restrictions placed on Jews, not at all because of any love for them but as a way to further their own political agendas. In much the same way, in the months, then years, following the October coup, the Bolsheviks were only too happy to make use of the services of Jews in their administrative and Party structures, motivated once again not by feelings of solidarity with Jews but by the benefits received from their talents, their intelligence, and their alienation from the Russian populace. Latvians, Hungarians, and Chinese were utilized in similar ways— no sentimental hang-ups could be expected from them.

The attitude of the Jewish population at large toward the Bolsheviks was guarded, if not hostile. But having finally attained full freedom thanks to the revolution,[16] and together with it, as we have seen, a true flowering of Jewish activity in the social, political, and cultural realms, all superbly organized, Jews did not stand in the way of the rapid advancement of other Jews who were Bolsheviks and who then exercised their newly acquired power to cruel excess.

Starting with the late 1940s, when the Communist regime had a serious falling out with the world's Jews, the vigorous Jewish participation in the Communist revolution began to be soft-pedaled or entirely concealed by Communists and Jews alike. It was an annoying and troubling reminder, and attempts to recall this phenomenon or to refer to it were classified as egregious anti-Semitism by the Jewish side.

In the 1970s and 1980s, as information about the past began to pile up, the early revolutionary years came into sharper focus. And more than a few Jewish voices began to speak out about this phenomenon in the public forum.

Indeed, there are many explanations as to why Jews joined the Bolsheviks (and the Civil War produced yet more weighty reasons). Nevertheless, if Russian Jews' memory of this period continues seeking primarily to *justify* this involvement, then the level of Jewish self-awareness will be lowered, even lost.

---

[15] S. Tonjoroff, "Jews in World Reconstruction," *The American Hebrew & Jewish Messenger*, September 10, 1920, 507. [Author's note.]

[16] The complete removal of all legal restrictions on Jews in Russia was accomplished by the Provisional Government in March 1917. This is described in ch. 13.

Using this line of reasoning, Germans could just as easily find excuses for the Hitler period: "Those were not real Germans, but scum"; "they never asked us." Yet every people must answer morally for all of its past—including that past which is shameful. Answer by what means? By attempting to *comprehend*: How could such a thing have been allowed? Where in all this is *our* error? And could it happen again?

It is in that spirit, specifically, that it would behoove the Jewish people to answer, both for the revolutionary cutthroats and the ranks willing to serve them. Not to answer before other peoples, but to oneself, to one's consciousness, and before God. Just as we Russians must answer—for the pogroms, for those merciless arsonist peasants, for those crazed revolutionary soldiers, for those savage sailors. (I think I rendered them descriptively enough in *The Red Wheel*. I will add another example, of that Red Army man Basov. He is the one who kept under guard Andrei Shingaryov, a defender of the people and lover of truth. First, Basov took spending money from the arrested Shingaryov's sister for transporting the latter under guard from the Peter and Paul Fortress to the Mariinsky hospital—in other words, for not giving Shingaryov a minute of freedom. In just a few hours, that same night, he brought sailors to the hospital to shoot Shingaryov and Fyodor Kokoshkin.[17] In that disgusting type, how much is ours!!)

To answer, just as we would answer for members of our own family.

For if we release ourselves from any responsibility for the actions of our national kin, the very concept of *a people* loses any real meaning.

---

[17] *Dnevnik A. I. Shingaryova. Kak eto bylo: Petropavlovskaia krepost'*, 27.XI.1917–5.I.1918, 2nd ed., Moscow, 1918, 66–68. [*Diary of A. I. Shingaryov. How it happened: Peter and Paul Fortress*, 27 Nov. 1917–5 Jan. 1918.] [Author's note.]

Two Hundred Years Together
Volume II, Chapter 16

During the Civil War

The dark eruption of pogroms against Jews in Ukraine continued through 1919 and into the beginning of 1920. In their breadth, scope, and cruelty, these pogroms outstripped beyond measure all that we have read, previously, of 1881–1882, 1903, and 1905.[1] The high-ranking Soviet official Yuri Larin wrote in the 1920s that what occurred in Ukraine in the Civil War was "a most lengthy series of massive pogroms against the Jewish population, far outnumbering previous occurrences both in terms of the number of victims and the *number of participants*." Vinnichenko[2] is supposed to have said: "The pogroms will end when the Jews stop being communists."[3]

All the victims of those pogroms were never tallied up with certainty. Naturally, given the circumstances, reliable statistics could not be kept either during or following the course of events. A book on Jewish pogroms in 1918–1921 states that "the number of those killed in Ukraine and Belorussia during the period from 1917 through 1921, inclusively, ranges from 180 to 200 thousand. . . . Just the number of those orphaned stands in excess of 300 thousand, a testimony to the colossal scale of the catastrophe."[4] The first edition of the Soviet Encyclopedia gives the same data.[5] The modern Jewish Encyclopedia reports that "by various estimates, the number of dead ranges from 70 to 180–200 thousand Jews."[6]

---

[1] Chapters 5, 8, and 9, respectively.

[2] Volodymyr Vinnichenko, writer and social-democrat revolutionary who was prime minister during the Ukrainian Directorate (December 1918 through February 1919). [Editor's note.]

[3] Iu. Larin, *Evrei i antisemitizm v SSSR* (Moscow & Leningrad, 1929), 38. [Author's note.]

[4] *Evreiskiie pogromy, 1918–1921*, 74. [Author's note.]

[5] *Bolshaya Sovetskaya Entsiklopedia*, 1st ed., Moscow, 1932, Vol. 24, 148. [Author's note.]

[6] *Kratkaya evreiskaia entsiklopedia*, VI, 569. [Author's note.]

Summarizing data from various Jewish sources, a contemporary historian counts up to 900 massive pogroms, of which 40% were conducted by Petliura's forces, and the defenders of the Ukrainian Directorate; 25% by the forces of Ukrainian warlords; 17% by Denikin's army; and 8.5% by Budyonny's First Cavalry and other Red army forces.[7]

How many torn-apart lives underlie those numbers!

---

[7] G. V. Kostyrchenko, *Tainaia politika Stalina*, 56. [Author's note.]

II

ESSAYS AND SPEECHES

Solzhenitsyn's many essays, speeches, and interviews, while less important intrinsically than his literary works, valuably distill his ideas in expository form. During his years in prison and as an underground writer, he could hardly have imagined being begged from all directions to speak his mind freely. But as soon as he landed in exile in 1974, invitations flooded in. So, while not welcoming distractions from his literary writing, he addressed numerous European and American audiences over the next few years and later visited Japan and Taiwan. Everywhere, he shared his analysis of the twentieth century, with special attention to the effects of communism and the experience of Russia.

Solzhenitsyn's discourses met with a mixed response. Starting with his programmatic *Letter to the Soviet Leaders* (1974) and extending through his kindly intended criticisms of the West, his nonliterary views often clashed with those of Western opinion shapers. Naïvely taking the West's trumpeted freedom of speech at face value, Solzhenitsyn sometimes painted in broad brushstrokes and incautiously employed a peremptory tone. The elites' negative reactions gradually hardened into a consensus. Feeling rebuffed, he sharply reduced his public speaking. He did wrap around his return home in 1994 another flurry of speeches saying goodbye to the West and hello to postcommunist Russia.

Solzhenitsyn's Nobel and Harvard addresses are well known; others, such as the Templeton and Liechtenstein addresses, are also meritorious, as are many of the essays composed strictly at his own initiative. The fog of incomprehension that enshrouded his pronouncements in the 1970s has lifted considerably now that Soviet communism has collapsed. The titles used for essays and speeches in this volume are those that Solzhenitsyn prefers.

Open Letter to the Secretariat
of the RSFSR Writers' Union

Solzhenitsyn's 1969 letter definitively ended his seven years as an officially approved Soviet writer. Shortly after the 1962 appearance of *One Day in the Life of Ivan Denisovich* made Solzhenitsyn famous, he was inducted into the Soviet Writers' Union. A few other small works appeared. But soon, in well-documented episodes, further publication was blocked, press vilifications grew fierce, and overt harassment commenced. At crucial meetings of writers during 1967, some encouraged Solzhenitsyn, but general opinion congealed into antagonism. In 1969 the Writers' Union of the Russian Federation (RSFSR), a component of the Soviet Writers' Union, handed its Ryazan branch the grubby chore of purging the obstreperous author. His letter to officials of the RSFSR organization advocates freedom of thought and speech with the same word, *glasnost* ("openness"), that Mikhail Gorbachev later popularized. The theme that "we belong first and foremost to humanity" was to resurface in a speech in New York charging communism with being "anti-humanity" and asserting that "that which is against communism is for humanity."[1] Solzhenitsyn's anticommunism derives from his foundational pro-humanity position.

Shamelessly trampling upon your own regulations, you have expelled me *in absentia*, in emergency fashion, failing even to send me a summoning telegram, failing even to give me the four hours needed to travel from Ryazan and be present. You have brazenly shown that the *decision* preceded the "dis-

---

[1] *Warning to the West* (New York: Farrar, Straus and Giroux, 1976), 58–59.

cussion." Perhaps you feared allocating ten minutes to me also? I am now compelled to substitute for them with this letter.

Wipe your clock dials!—your watches have fallen behind the times. Throw open your lavish heavy curtains!—you do not even suspect that, outside, day is breaking. Ours is no longer that stifling, grim, hopeless time when you expelled Akhmatova with this same obsequiousness. Nor yet is it that timid and chilly time when you expelled Pasternak, howling your derision. Did that shame not suffice for you? Do you yearn to deepen it? But the hour draws near when each of you will seek to scratch out your signature from under today's resolution.

Blind leaders of the blind! You do not even perceive that you are wandering in a direction opposite to the one you have proclaimed. In this hour of crisis you are able to offer our profoundly ill society nothing constructive, nothing good, but only your hatred and your vigilance, your "hold them tight and don't let go."

Your flabby articles crumble apart, your mindlessness flails about listlessly, but arguments you have none—only your voting and administration. That is why neither Sholokhov, nor all the rest of you put together, dared answer the famous letter of Lydia Chukovskaya, the pride of Russian literati. Meanwhile, the administrative pincers are being made ready: How could she have allowed her unpublished book to be read? If the *authorities* have decided not to publish you—crush yourself, smother yourself, stop existing! don't let anyone read you!

They're setting up for expulsion also Lev Kopelev—a war veteran who has already served a ten-year sentence for nothing—now guilty of standing up for the persecuted, and of making public a sacred covert conversation with an influential personage—of violating secrets of the halls of power. Well, why do you carry on conversations that need to be concealed from the people? Were we not promised, fifty years ago, that there would never again be secret diplomacy, secret negotiations, secret baffling appointments and transfers, and that the masses would know about everything, and judge openly?

"Enemies will hear us": That is your excuse; your eternal, omnipresent "enemies" form a convenient basis for your positions in society and for your very existence. As if there were no enemies when immediate openness was promised us. Goodness, what would you do without "enemies"? Your very survival would not be possible without them, since you have chosen for your barren atmosphere—hate, a genuine hate that yields nothing to racism. But through this we lose any sense of a single common humanity—and so its doom draws nearer. Why, if tomorrow the ice of just Antarctica were to melt, and we all to turn into a drowning race, into whose face would you then rub your "class warfare"? Not to mention—when the remnants of bipeds roam the radioactive Earth, and die.

It's high time to remember that our first allegiance is to the human race. And the human race broke away from the animal world through thought and speech. It is natural that these should be free. And if they are shackled—we return to our animal state.

Glasnost, forthright and total glasnost—this is the first prerequisite for the health of any society, including our own. Whoever does not desire glasnost for our country is indifferent to his fatherland and thinks of nothing but his personal gain. Whoever does not desire glasnost for his fatherland—does not wish to cleanse it from diseases, but, rather, to drive them inside, there to fester.

A. Solzhenitsyn
November 12, 1969

Nobel Lecture

In 1970 Solzhenitsyn received the Nobel Prize in Literature "for the ethical force with which he has pursued the indispensable traditions of Russian literature." His worldwide reputation rocketed further upward, but Soviet authorities viewed the award as a Cold War provocation. Newspaper headlines trumpeted yet another dramatic episode in Solzhenitsyn's life. "Nobeliana," a riveting chapter in *The Oak and the Calf*, describes this feverish stage of the continuing battle between author and regime, and it explains Solzhenitsyn's decision to accept the prize in absentia. The text of his Nobel speech appeared in 1972, and once in exile he went to Sweden to receive the Nobel insignia in person in 1974.

The *Nobel Lecture* encapsulates Solzhenitsyn's literary theory. He opens with a spiritual justification of art and proceeds to the social uses that art, especially literature, can serve. Some writers, beholden to the concept of the autonomous self, look only inward to get their artistic bearings. Solzhenitsyn prefers those writers who move beyond subjectivity, take as their premise the universality of the human condition, and reckon with God and the created order. These writers relate literature to life in the real world. Literature can transmit the truth of human experience from one age to another and from one nation to another. In so doing, literature can provide a world riven by different cultures and clashing moral standards a common scale for judging good and evil. Solzhenitsyn articulates a high, hopeful, and ultimately practical view of the purpose and function of literature.

ONE

Just as the savage in bewilderment picks up . . . a strange object cast up by the sea? . . . something long buried in the sand? . . . a baffling object fallen from the sky?—intricately shaped, now glistening dully, now reflecting a brilliant flash of light—just as he turns it this way and that, twirls it, searches for a way to utilize it, seeks to find for it a suitable lowly application, all the while not guessing its higher function . . .

So we also, holding Art in our hands, confidently deem ourselves its masters; we boldly give it direction, bring it up to date, reform it, proclaim it, sell it for money, use it to please the powerful, divert it for amusement—all the way down to vaudeville songs and nightclub acts—or else adapt it (with a muzzle or stick, whatever is handy) toward transient political or limited social needs. But art remains undefiled by our endeavors and the stamp of its origin remains unaffected: Each time and in every usage it bestows upon us a portion of its mysterious inner light.

But can we encompass the *totality* of this light? Who would dare to say that he has *defined* art? Or has enumerated all its aspects? Moreover, perhaps someone already did understand and did name them for us in the preceding centuries, but that could not long detain us; we listened briefly but took no heed; we discarded the words at once, hurrying—as always—to replace even the very best with something else, just so that it might be new. And when we are told the old once again, we won't even remember that we used to have it earlier.

One artist imagines himself the creator of an autonomous spiritual world; he hoists upon his shoulders the act of creating this world and of populating it, together with the total responsibility for it. But he collapses under the load, for no mortal genius can bear up under it, just as, in general, the man who declares himself the center of existence is unable to create a balanced spiritual system. And if a failure befalls such a man, the blame is promptly laid to the chronic disharmony of the world, to the complexity of modern man's divided soul, or to the public's lack of understanding.

Another artist recognizes above himself a higher power and joyfully works as a humble apprentice under God's heaven, though graver and more demanding still is his responsibility for all he writes or paints—and for the souls which apprehend it. However, it was not he who created this world, nor does he control it; there can be no doubts about its foundations. It is merely given to the artist to sense more keenly than others the harmony of the world, the beauty and ugliness of man's role in it—and to vividly communicate this to mankind. Even amid failure and at the lower depths of existence—in poverty, in prison, and in illness—a sense of enduring harmony cannot abandon him.

But the very irrationality of art, its dazzling convolutions, its unforeseeable discoveries, its powerful impact on men—all this is too magical to be wholly accounted for by the artist's view of the world, by his intention, or by the work of his unworthy fingers.

Archaeologists have yet to discover an early stage of human existence when we possessed no art. In the twilight preceding the dawn of mankind we received it from hands which we did not have a chance to see clearly. Neither had we time to ask: *Why* this gift for us? How should we treat it?

All those prognosticators of the decay, degeneration, and death of art were wrong and will always be wrong. It shall be we who die; art will remain. And shall we even comprehend before our passing all of its aspects and the entirety of its purposes?

Not everything can be named. Some things draw us beyond words. Art can warm even a chilled and sunless soul to an exalted spiritual experience. Through art we occasionally receive— indistinctly, briefly—revelations the likes of which cannot be achieved by rational thought

It is like that small mirror of legend: you look into it but instead of yourself you glimpse for a moment the Inaccessible, a realm forever beyond reach. And your soul begins to ache. . . .

Two

Dostoyevsky once let drop an enigmatic remark: "Beauty will save the world." What is this? For a long time it seemed to me simply a phrase. How could this be possible? When in the bloodthirsty process of history did beauty ever save anyone, and from what? Granted, it ennobled, it elevated—but whom did it ever save?

There is, however, a particular feature in the very essence of beauty— a characteristic trait of art itself: The persuasiveness of a true work of art is completely irrefutable; it prevails even over a resisting heart. A political speech, an aggressive piece of journalism, a program for the organization of society, a philosophical system, can all be constructed—with apparent smoothness and harmony—on an error or on a lie. What is hidden and what is distorted will not be discerned right away. But then a contrary speech, journalistic piece, or program, or a differently structured philosophy, comes forth to join the argument, and everything is again just as smooth and harmonious, and again everything fits. And so they inspire trust—and distrust.

In vain does one repeat what the heart does not find sweet.

But a true work of art carries its verification within itself: Artificial and forced concepts do not survive their trial by images; both image and concept crumble and turn out feeble, pale, and unconvincing. However, works which have drawn on the truth and which have presented it to us in concentrated and vibrant form seize us, attract us to themselves powerfully, and no one ever—even centuries later—will step forth to deny them.

So perhaps the old trinity of Truth, Goodness, and Beauty is not simply the decorous and antiquated formula it seemed to us at the time of our self-confident materialistic youth. If the tops of these three trees do converge, as thinkers used to claim, and if the all too obvious and the overly straight sprouts of Truth and Goodness have been crushed, cut down, or not permitted to grow, then perhaps the whimsical, unpredictable, and ever surprising shoots of Beauty will force their way through and soar up to *that very spot*, thereby fulfilling the task of all three.

And then no slip of the tongue but a prophecy would be contained in Dostoyevsky's words: "Beauty will save the world." For it was given to him to see many things; he had astonishing flashes of insight.

Could not then art and literature in a very real way offer succor to the modern world?

Today I shall attempt to set forth those few aspects of this problem which I have been able to discern over the years.

THREE

To have mounted this rostrum from which the Nobel lecture is delivered—a platform placed at the disposal of but few writers and then only once in a lifetime—I have climbed not the three or four attached steps, but hundreds and even thousands of them, with almost no toehold, steep, and covered with ice, leading out of the darkness and cold where it had been my fate to survive while others—perhaps more gifted and stronger than I—perished. Only a few of them did I meet in the "Gulag Archipelago," scattered as it was into a multitude of islands. But under the burden of surveillance and mistrust I could not say much to most of them; of some I only heard; of still others I could only guess. Those who vanished into this abyss when they had already earned a literary reputation are at least known; but how many there were who had not yet been recognized, who had never been publicly named! And almost no one managed to return. An entire national literature remains there, buried without a coffin, even without underwear—naked, with only an identifying tag on one toe. Not for a moment did Russian literature cease! Yet from the outside it seemed a wasteland. Where a congenial forest might have stood, there remained after all the felling but two or three trees overlooked by chance.

And today, accompanied by the shades of the fallen, as with bowed head I permit others who were worthy earlier to precede me to this platform—how am I today to surmise and to express what *they* would have wished to say?

This duty has long weighed upon us and we knew it all along. In the words of Vladimir Soloviev:

> Even in chains we must ourselves complete
> That orbit which the gods have traced for us.

In the midst of exhausting prison camp relocations, marching in a column of prisoners in the gloom of bitterly cold evenings, with strings of camp lights glimmering through the darkness, we would often feel rising in our breast what we would have wanted to shout out to the whole world—if only the whole world could have heard any one of us. It all seemed very clear then: just what our fortunate messenger would say and how the world would at once respond in turn. Our field of vision was then filled with distinct physical objects and clear psychological motivations; an unambiguous world seemed to contain nothing which could prevail against this vision. These thoughts came not from books and were not borrowed for their appearance's sake: They were forged in prison cells and around bonfires in the forest, in conversation with people now dead; they were tested by *that* life and it is *from there* that they arose.

But when the external pressures had fallen off, our field of vision grew broader, and gradually, even if only through a tiny crack, that "whole world" became visible and understandable. To our amazement the "whole world" turned out to be quite different from what we had hoped, it was not living by the "right" values, nor was it headed in the "right" direction; it was a world which upon seeing a slimy bog exclaimed: "What a charming meadow!" and of a concrete pillory said: "What an exquisite necklace!" Where some were shedding tears that could not be wiped away, there others danced to the tune of a carefree musical.

How did this happen? Why this yawning chasm? Were we insensible? Or is the world? Or is this due to a difference in languages? Why are people who address each other sometimes incapable of making out distinct speech? Words ring out and fade away, they flow off like water—leaving no taste, no color, no smell. No trace.

As I came to understand this more and more over the years, a succession of changes was introduced into the structure, meaning, and tone of my projected speech. Today's speech.

And it now bears little resemblance to the one first conceived on those icy evenings in the prison camp.

FOUR

Man has from the beginning been so constituted that his view of the world (if it is not induced by hypnosis), his motivations and scale of values, his actions and his intentions, are all defined by his experience as an individual and as a member of a group. In the words of the Russian proverb: "Your brother, he might lie; trust instead your own bad eye." This is the soundest of bases for understanding one's environment and for acting in it. And for many long centuries, while our world was completely and mysteriously dispersed— before it was interlaced by unbroken lines of communication and turned into a single feverishly throbbing mass—people were unfailingly guided by their own experience within their own circumscribed locality, within their community, within their society, and finally within their national territory. At that time it was possible for the individual human eye to see and accept a certain common scale of values: what was considered average, what unbelievable; what was cruel, what was beyond villainy; what constituted honesty, and what deceit. And even though the scattered nations lived quite differently, and the scales of their social values could diverge as strikingly as their systems of measurement, these discrepancies astonished only the infrequent wayfarer or turned up as curiosities in magazines. They held no danger for humanity, which was not yet united.

But in the course of the last few decades, humanity has imperceptibly and suddenly become united—a unity fraught with hope and with danger— so that shocks or inflammations in one part are instantly passed on to the other portions—some of which may well lack the appropriate immunity. Humanity has become one, but it is not the stable undividedness of a former community or even that of a nation. It is a unity achieved not by means of gradually acquired experience, not from the eye, affably referred to as "bad" in the proverb, not even through a common native language; but rather— surmounting all barriers—this is unity brought about by international radio and the press. Onrushing waves of events bear down upon us: Half the world learns in one minute of what is splashed ashore. But lacking are the scales or yardsticks to measure these events and to evaluate them according to the laws of the parts of the world unfamiliar to us. Such scales are not, nor can they be, carried to us through the ether or on sheets of newsprint: These scales of values have been settling into place and have been assimilated for too long a time and in too unique a fashion in the particular lives of specific countries and societies; they cannot be transmitted on the wing. In each region men apply to events their own particular hard-won scale of values; intransigently and self-confidently, they judge by their own scale and by no other.

There are perhaps not multitudes of such different yardsticks in the world, but certainly several: a scale for close-by events and a scale for far-off ones; the scale used by old societies and that used by new ones; the scale of the well off and that of the unfortunate. The gradations on the various scales diverge drastically, their kaleidoscopic variety makes our eyes smart. To prevent discomfort, we dismiss all alien scales out of hand, as if they were madness and error, and we confidently judge the whole world according to our own homegrown scale. Thus we perceive as more significant, more painful, and more intolerable not those conditions which are indeed all these things— but those which are closer to us. But everything that is far away and does not threaten, today, to surge up to our doorsill, we accept—with all its groans, stifled shouts, destroyed lives, and even its millions of victims—as being on the whole quite bearable and of tolerable dimensions.

In one region not so long ago hundreds of thousands of voiceless Christians laid down their lives for their faith in God amid a persecution that yielded nothing to that of ancient Rome. In another hemisphere a certain madman (and he is undoubtedly not alone) speeds across an ocean in order to *free* us from religion with a blade-thrust aimed at the Pontiff.[1] He deduced this from his own scale of values for the benefit of us all.

What according to one scale—from afar—seems an enviable and contented freedom is perceived according to another scale—close at hand—as galling coercion which calls for buses to be overturned. What in one land would be dreamed of as an improbable level of well-being, in another land provokes resentment as a barbaric exploitation demanding an immediate strike. Different also are the scales for evaluating natural disasters: A flood with two hundred thousand victims seems less important than a minor incident in our home town. There are different scales for assessing personal insult: In one place an ironical smile or a disdainful gesture can humiliate, in others even a cruel beating can be forgiven as a bad joke. There are different scales for punishment and for wrongdoing: According to one, a month-long detention, a banishment to the countryside, or "solitary" with white rolls and milk, all stagger the imagination and fill columns of newsprint with wrath. But according to another scale it is both commonplace and forgivable to have prison sentences of twenty-five years, punishment cells with ice on the walls where the prisoners are stripped to their underwear, insane asylums for normal persons, and shootings at the border of countless unreasonable people who for some reason keep trying to flee somewhere. Our heart is especially at ease about that exotic land about which we know nothing whatsoever, from which no tidings ever reach our ears

---

[1] In November 1970, Pope Paul VI was attacked at the Manila airport by a knife-wielding man.

with the exception of some belated and hackneyed conjectures from a few correspondents.

This double vision, this torpid inability to understand someone else's distant grief, should not be blamed on human eyesight: Man is simply built that way. But for mankind as a whole, compressed as it is into a single mass, such a mutual lack of understanding threatens to bring on quick and violent extinction. Given six, four, or even two scales of values, there cannot be a unified world, a united humanity. We shall be torn apart by this difference in rhythm, the divergence in frequency of oscillation. We could not manage to survive on one earth, just as a man with two hearts is not long for this world.

FIVE

But who will reconcile these scales of values and how? Who is going to give mankind a single system of evaluation for evil deeds and for good ones, for unbearable things and for tolerable ones—as we differentiate them today? Who will elucidate for mankind what really is burdensome and unbearable and what merely chafes the skin due to its proximity? Who will direct man's anger toward that which is more fearsome rather than toward that which is closer at hand? Who could convey this understanding across the barriers of his own human experience? Who could impress upon a sluggish and obstinate human being someone else's far off sorrows or joys, who could give him an insight into magnitudes of events and into delusions which he has never himself experienced? Propaganda, coercion, and scientific proof are all equally powerless here. But fortunately there does exist a means to this end in the world! It is art. It is literature.

They both hold the key to a miracle: to overcome man's ruinous habit of learning only from his own experience, so that the experience of others passes him by without profit. Making up for man's scant time on earth, art transmits between men the entire accumulated load of another being's life experience, with all its hardships, colors, and juices. It recreates—lifelike—the experience of other men, so that we can assimilate it as our own.

But even more, much more than this: Countries and entire continents continually repeat each other's mistakes with a time lag—occasionally one of centuries—when, it would seem, everything is so very clear. But no: What one people has already endured, appraised, and rejected suddenly emerges among another people as the very latest word. Here once again the sole substitute for an experience which we have not ourselves lived through is art and literature. Both are endowed with the miraculous power to communicate—despite differences in language, custom, and social structure—the experience of the entire nation to another nation which has not undergone such a difficult decades-long collective experience. In a fortunate instance, this could save an entire nation from a redundant, or erroneous, or even destructive course, thereby shortening the tortuous paths of human history.

It is this great and blessed property of art to which I resolutely wish to call attention today from this Nobel platform.

There is one other invaluable direction in which literature transmits incontrovertible condensed experience: from generation to generation. In this way literature becomes the living memory of a nation. It sustains within itself and safeguards a nation's bygone history—in a form which cannot be distorted or falsified. In this way does literature together with language preserve the national soul.

(It has lately been fashionable to speak of the leveling of nations, of the disappearance of individual peoples in the melting pot of modern civilization. I disagree, but a discussion of this problem would be a theme in itself. It is here appropriate to say only that the disappearance of nations would impoverish us not less than if all men should become alike, with one personality and one face. Nations are the wealth of mankind, its generalized personalities; the least among them has its own unique coloration and harbors within itself a unique facet of God's design.)

But woe to that nation whose literature is cut short by the intrusion of force. This is not merely interference with "freedom of the press" but the sealing up of a nation's heart, the excision of its memory. A nation can no longer remember itself, it loses its spiritual unity, and despite their seemingly common language, countrymen cease to understand one another. Mute generations live out their lives and die, without giving an account of their experiences either to themselves or to their descendants. When such literary masters as Akhmatova or Zamyatin are walled up for their entire lives, condemned till the grave to create in silence and unable to hear any echoes to their work—then this is not only their personal misfortune, but a calamity for the whole nation, a menace to it.

And in some cases this could even be a grievous misfortune for the whole of humanity: whenever such silence causes all of *history* to become incomprehensible.

SIX

At various times and in various countries there have been heated, angry, and refined polemics about whether art and the artist should live for their own sake or whether they must always keep in mind their duty toward society and serve it, albeit without bias. For me the answer is obvious, but I shall not once again rehearse the long train of arguments. One of the most brilliant statements on this theme was Albert Camus's Nobel lecture, and I happily join in his conclusions. Indeed, Russian literature has for decades been disinclined to engage in excessive self-contemplation, or in flitting about in too carefree a manner—and I am not ashamed to continue this tradition to the best of my ability. Through Russian literature we have long ago grown familiar with the concept that a writer can do much among his people—and that he must.

We shall not trample on the *right* of an artist to express nothing but his personal experiences and his self-observations while disregarding all that occurs in the rest of the world. We shall not make *demands* on him—but surely we can be permitted to reproach him, beg him, call him, or beckon to him. After all, an artist develops his gift only partially by himself; the greater part has been breathed into him ready-made at birth. And together with this talent, a responsibility has been imposed upon his free will. Granted, an artist does not *owe* anything to anyone, but it is painful to see how, by withdrawing into self-created worlds or into the realms of subjective whim, he *can* surrender the real world into the hands of profit-seekers, of nonentities, or even of madmen.

This twentieth century of ours has proved to be crueler than its predecessors, and its horrors have not been exhausted with the end of its first half. The same old atavistic urges—greed, envy, unrestrained passion, and mutual hostility—readily picking up respectable pseudonyms like class, race, mass, or trade union struggle, claw at and tear apart our world. A primitive rejection of all compromise is given the status of a theoretical principle and is regarded as the high virtue which accompanies doctrinal purity. This attitude creates millions of victims in ceaseless civil wars, it drones into our souls that there exist no lasting concepts of good and justice valid for all mankind, that all such concepts are fluid and ever changing—which is why you should always act in a way that benefits your party. Any professional group, at the first opportunity to *get their hand on something extra*—though unearned and even unneeded—grabs it, and the rest of society be damned. As seen from the outside, the careening fluctuations of Western society seem to be approaching that amplitude beyond which a system becomes metastable and must disintegrate. Less and less restrained by the confines of long-established legality, violence strides brazenly and triumphantly through the world, unconcerned that its futility has already been demonstrated and proven many times in history. It is not even brute force alone that is victorious, but also its clamorous justification: The world is being flooded by the brazen conviction that force can do all, and righteousness—nothing. Dostoyevsky's *Devils*, who had seemed part of a provincial nightmarish fantasy of the last century, are now infesting the world before our eyes, reaching lands where they could not earlier have even been imagined. And now, by the hijacking of airplanes, by the seizing of hostages, by the explosions and conflagrations of recent years, they signal their determination to shake civilization to its roots and to bring it down. And they may well succeed. Today's youth, at an age when they have not yet had any experience except sex, before they have lived through their own years of suffering and reached their own personal understanding—these young people enthusiastically mouth the discredited clichés of the Russian nineteenth century, thinking that they are uncovering something new. The recently manifested degradation of human beings into nonentities as practiced by the Chinese Red Guards is taken as a joyous model by the young. What shallow lack of understanding of timeless human nature, what naïve confidence of inexperienced hearts: "We'll just oust *these* vicious, greedy oppressors and rulers, and those next in charge (that's us!), having put aside grenades and submachine guns, will be compassionate and just." Some chance indeed! . . . And yet among those who have seen life, who do understand, and who could refute these young people—many *do not dare* to do so. They even assume fawning attitudes, just so as not to seem "conservative." This once again is a Russian nineteenth-century phenomenon; Dostoyevsky called it *subservience to progressive little notions.*

The spirit of Munich has by no means retreated into the past, it was no short-lived episode. I would even dare to claim that the spirit of Munich dominates the twentieth century. A timorous civilized world, faced with the onslaught of a suddenly revived and snarling barbarism, has found nothing to oppose it with except concessions and smiles. The spirit of Munich is a malady of the will of affluent people; it is the chronic state of those who have abandoned themselves to a pursuit of prosperity at any price, who have succumbed to a belief in material well-being as the principal goal of life on earth. Such people—and there are many in today's world—choose passivity and retreat, just so long as their accustomed life can be made to last a little longer, just so long as the transition to hardship can be put off for another day; and tomorrow —who knows?—everything may turn out to be all right. (But it never will! The price paid for cowardice will only be the more exorbitant. Courage and victory come to us only when we are resolved to make sacrifices.)

We are also threatened by destruction from another quarter: Our physically compressed and cramped world is restrained from merging spiritually; molecules of knowledge and sympathy are prevented from leaping from one half to the other. This *blockage of information flow* between parts of the planet is a mortal danger. Modern science knows that the blockage of information is the way of entropy and of general destruction. Information blockage renders illusory international agreements and treaties: Within the *isolated* zone there is nothing easier than to reinterpret any treaty or simply to forget it as if it had never existed (Orwell understood this well). This isolated zone seems to be inhabited not by earthlings but by some expeditionary force from Mars; these people know nothing about the rest of the earth and are ready to trample it underfoot in the solemn belief that they are "liberating" it.

A quarter of a century ago the United Nations Organization was born amid the great hopes of mankind. But alas, in an immoral world it too grew up without morality. It is not a United Nations Organization but a United Governments Organization, where governments freely elected are equated with regimes imposed by force or with those that have gained control by an armed seizure of power. By dint of the self-interested bias of the majority of its members, the UN jealously guards the freedom of certain peoples and completely neglects the freedom of others. Through an obeisant vote it has rejected the investigation of *private grievances*—the moans, cries, and entreaties of humble individual *mere people*, who were judged entities just too minuscule for such a great organization. Its best document in the twenty-five years of its existence—the Universal Declaration of Human Rights—the UN has not taken the trouble to make *mandatory* for its member governments, a *condition* of membership, and has thereby abandoned little people to the mercy of governments they did not elect.

One might have thought that the structure of the modern world would be entirely in the hands of scientists, since it is they who decide all the technical steps of mankind. One might have thought that the direction in which the world is to move would be determined by a worldwide concord of scientists, not of politicians. All the more so since the example of individuals demonstrates how much ground they could gain if only they joined forces. But no: Scientists have made no explicit attempts to become an important, independently motivated force within mankind. Entire congresses of them back away from the suffering of others: It is cozier to remain within the limits of science. The same spirit of Munich has spread its enervating wings over them.

What, then—in this cruel, dynamic, explosive world which totters on the brink of destruction—what *is* the place and role of the writer? We do not, after all, send up rockets, we don't even push the meanest of supply carts. Indeed, we are held in total contempt by those who respect material might alone. Would it not be natural for us also to retreat, to lose faith in the unshakable nature of goodness, in the indivisible nature of truth? Should not we merely recite to the world our bitter but detached observations about how hopelessly warped mankind is, how shallow people have become, and how burdensome it is for a lone refined and beautiful soul to dwell among them?

But even this escape is not open to us. Once we have taken up the word, it is thereafter impossible to turn away: A writer is no detached judge of his countrymen and contemporaries; he is an accomplice to all the evil committed in his country or by his people. And if the tanks of his fatherland have bloodied the pavement of a foreign capital, then rust-colored stains have forever bespattered the writer's face. And if on some fateful night a trusting friend is strangled in his sleep—then the palms of the writer bear the bruises from that rope. And if his youthful fellow citizens nonchalantly proclaim the advantages of debauchery over humble toil, if they abandon themselves to drugs, or seize hostages—then this stench too is mingled with the breath of the writer.

Have we the insolence to declare that we do not answer for the evils of today's world?

SEVEN

But I am encouraged by a vivid sense of *world literature* as one great heart which beats for the cares and woes of our world, though each of these is manifested and perceived in its own way in its separate corner of the globe.

Apart from the well-established tradition of national literatures, there has long existed the concept of world literature. It was traditionally seen as a curve enveloping the peaks of the national literatures and as the sum total of all literary influences. But there were time lags: Readers and writers discovered foreign authors with a delay, occasionally one of centuries. As a result, mutual influences were held back and the curve encompassing the national literary high points was discerned only by posterity, not by contemporaries.

But today there exists an interaction between the writers of one land and the writers and readers of other lands which, though not immediate, is close to it; I can vouch for this myself. My books—unpublished, alas, in my own country—have in spite of hasty and often poor translations rapidly acquired a responsive world readership. Outstanding Western writers such as Heinrich Böll have devoted critical analyses to them. Throughout these last years, when my work and my freedom did not collapse, when they seemed to hang in midair in violation of the laws of gravity, seemingly supported by *nothing at all*—except the invisible and mute tension of the cohesive film of public sympathy—all those years I have gratefully and quite unexpectedly come to know the support of the worldwide brotherhood of writers. On my fiftieth birthday I was astounded to receive congratulations from well-known European writers. No pressure upon me could any longer pass unnoticed. In the hazardous weeks when I was being expelled from the Union of Writers, the *protective wall* erected by the writers of the world saved me from worse persecution, while Norwegian writers and artists hospitably readied a shelter for me in case the threatened banishment from my homeland should occur. Finally, my very nomination for the Nobel Prize was initiated not in the country where I live and work, but by François Mauriac and his colleagues. And more recently still, entire organizations of national writers have expressed their support for me.

And so I came to understand through my own experience that world literature is no longer an abstract enveloping curve, no longer a generalization coined by literary scholars, but a kind of collective body and a common spirit, a living unity of the heart which reflects the growing spiritual unity of mankind. Borders of states continue to turn crimson, heated to a red glow by electrified wire and by bursts of machine-gun fire. Certain ministries of internal affairs continue to believe that literature too is an "internal affair" of the countries over which they claim jurisdiction. Newspapers continue to display banner headlines: "They have no right to interfere in our internal affairs!" But in the meantime—all *internal affairs* have ceased to exist on our crowded earth! The salvation of mankind lies only in making everything the concern of all. People in the East should without exception be concerned with what people are thinking in the West; people in the West should without exception care about what is happening in the East. Literature, one of the most sophisticated and sensitive instruments available to human beings, has been one of the first to pick up, to assimilate, and to join in expressing this feeling of the growing unity of mankind. And I here confidently address myself to the world literature of today—to the hundreds of friends whom I have never met in person and whom I perhaps may never see.

Friends! Let us try to help if we are worth anything at all! Who in our various countries—torn as they are by the tumultuous discord of parties, movements, castes, and groups—who is it that from the beginning has not been a divisive force but a unifying one? That, in essence, is the role of writers: They are the articulators of the national tongue (that main tie which holds a nation together) and of the very land inhabited by a people; in fortunate instances, they give expression to the national soul.

I believe that world literature is fully capable of helping a troubled humanity to recognize its true self in spite of what is advocated by biased individuals and parties. World literature is capable of transmitting the concentrated experience of a particular region to other lands so that we can overcome double vision and kaleidoscopic variety, so that one people can discover, accurately and concisely, the true history of another people, with all the force of recognition and the pain that comes from actual experience—and can thus be safeguarded from belated errors. And at the same time we ourselves shall perhaps be able to develop a *world vision*. Focusing on what is close at hand with the center of our eye—just like everyone else—we shall begin to use our peripheral vision to take in what occurs in the rest of the world. And we shall proceed to make correlations, adhering to a worldwide standard.

Who else but writers shall condemn their incompetent rulers (in some states this is in fact the easiest way to earn a living; it is done by anyone who feels the urge), who else shall censure their respective societies—be it for cowardly submission or for self-satisfied weakness—as well as the witless excesses of the young and the youthful pirates with knives upraised?

We shall be told: What can literature do in the face of a remorseless assault of open violence? But let us not forget that violence does not and cannot exist by itself: It is invariably intertwined with *the lie*. They are linked in the most intimate, most organic and profound fashion: Violence cannot conceal itself behind anything except lies, and lies have nothing to maintain them save violence. Anyone who has once proclaimed violence as his *method* must inexorably choose the lie as his *principle*. At birth, violence acts openly and even takes pride in itself. But as soon as it gains strength and becomes firmly established, it begins to sense the air around it growing thinner; it can no longer exist without veiling itself in a mist of lies, without concealing itself behind the sugary words of falsehood. No longer does violence always and necessarily lunge straight for your throat; more often than not it demands of its subjects only that they pledge allegiance to lies, that they participate in falsehood.

The simple act of an ordinary brave man is not to participate in lies, not to support false actions! His rule: Let *that* come into the world, let it even reign supreme—only not through me. But it is within the power of writers and artists to do much more: *to defeat the lie!* For in the struggle with lies art has always triumphed and shall always triumph! Visibly, irrefutably for all! Lies can prevail against much in this world, but never against art.

And no sooner will the lies be dispersed than the repulsive nakedness of violence will be exposed—and age-old violence will topple in defeat.

This is why I believe, my friends, that we are capable of helping the world in its hour of crisis. We should not seek to justify our unwillingness by our lack of weapons, nor should we give ourselves up to a life of comfort. We must come out and join the battle!

The favorite proverbs in Russian are about *truth*. They forcefully express a long and difficult national experience, sometimes in striking fashion:

> *One word of truth shall outweigh the whole world.*

It is on such a seemingly fantastic violation of the law of conservation of mass and energy that my own activity is based, and my appeal to the writers of the world.

Repentance and Self-Limitation
in the Life of Nations

Solzhenitsyn has repeatedly cautioned against an inordinate concentration on the specifically political dimensions of his work. He has also insisted that politics must ultimately be subordinated to higher spiritual and ethical concerns. But there is no doubt that politics in the noble sense of the term remains an enduring preoccupation of Solzhenitsyn's. If the pursuit of truth and the spiritual progress of the individual human soul rightly take precedence over the proper structuring of social institutions, there can be few prospects for either without thoughtful attention to the moral foundations of political life. This problem is particularly pressing as Solzhenitsyn's beloved Russia desperately struggles to find her way toward a humane and viable post-totalitarian future.

In "Repentance and Self-Limitation in the Life of Nations" (one of three essays he contributed to the 1974 collection *From Under the Rubble*), Solzhenitsyn challenges the positivist dogma that ethical considerations are inapplicable to actions by states and cannot be subject to rational discussion or analysis. In a deeply personal essay studded with penetrating philosophical and historical insights, Solzhenitsyn defends the "transference" of individual moral qualities and judgments to society as a whole. In particular, he argues that "repentance" and "self-limitation" are qualities of heart and soul that are indispensable for building a balanced future for both Russia and the West, one that judiciously combines "external" technological and economic development with precious "inner development."

This essay powerfully illustrates the essentially humane and moderate character of Solzhenitsyn's patriotism. In it, the Russian writer articulates a principled middle way between cosmo-

politan elites who freely disparage Russian "national consciousness" and unsavory "National Bolsheviks" who uncritically defend the full range of crimes and injustices that marked the "Petersburg" and especially the Bolshevik periods of Russian national
life. Solzhenitsyn makes clear that there can be no authentic patriotism without a people's willingness to come to terms with its
"internal" and "external sins." Solzhenitsyn's model of patriotism
also requires a just and generous recognition of the legitimate
claims and admirable spiritual qualities of other nations and
peoples.

ONE

The Blessed Augustine once wrote: "What is the state without justice? A
band of robbers." Even now, fifteen centuries later, many people will, I think,
readily recognize the force and accuracy of this judgment. But let us note
what he is about: An ethical judgment about a small group of people is applied by extension to the state.

It is in our human nature to make such judgments: to apply ordinary,
individual, human values and standards to larger social phenomena and associations of people, up to and including the nation and the state as a whole.
And many instances of this transference can be found in writers through the
ages.

The social sciences, however, and particularly the more modern of them,
strictly forbid such extensions of meaning. Only economic, statistical, demographic, ideological, to a lesser extent geographical, and—very dubiously—psychological procedures are held to guarantee the serious scientific character of research into society and the state, while the evaluation of
political life by ethical yardsticks is considered totally provincial.

Yet people do not cease to be people just because they live in social ag-
glomerations, nor do they lose the age-old human impulses and feelings—
we all know the spectrum; all they do is express them more crudely, sometimes keeping them in check, sometimes giving them free rein. It is hard to
understand the arrogant insensitivity of the modern trend in the social sciences: Why are the standards and demands so necessarily and readily applied
to individuals, families, small groups, and personal relations, rejected out of
hand and utterly prohibited when we go on to deal with thousands and millions of people in association? The arguments in favor of such an extension are
certainly no weaker than those for deducing the complex psychological delu-

sions of societies from crude economic processes. The barrier against trans-ference of values is in any case lower where the principle itself undergoes no transformation, where we are not being asked to beget the living upon the dead, but only to project the self onto larger quantities of human beings.

The transference of values is entirely natural to the religious cast of mind: Human society cannot be exempted from the laws and demands which constitute the aim and meaning of individual human lives. But even without a religious foundation, this sort of transference is readily and naturally made. It is very human to apply even to the biggest social events or human organizations, including whole states and the United Nations, our spiritual values: noble, base, courageous, cowardly, hypocritical, false, cruel, magnanimous, just, unjust, and so on. Indeed, everybody writes this way, even the most extreme economic materialists, since they remain after all human beings. And clearly, whatever feelings predominate in the members of a given society at a given moment in time, they will serve to color the whole of that society and determine its moral character. And if there is nothing good there to pervade that society, it will destroy itself, or be brutalized by the triumph of evil instincts, no matter where the pointer of the great economic laws may turn.

And it is open to every one of us, whether learned or not, to choose—and profitably choose—not to evade the examination of social phenomena with reference to the categories of individual spiritual life and individual ethics.

We shall try to do this here with reference to only two such categories: repentance and self-limitation.

Two

Whether the transference of individual human qualities to society is easy or difficult in a general way, it is immensely difficult when the desired moral quality has been almost completely rejected by individual human beings themselves. This is the case with repentance. The gift of repentance, which perhaps more than anything else distinguishes man from the animal world, is particularly difficult for modern man to recover. We have, every last one of us, grown ashamed of this feeling; and its effect on social life anywhere on earth is less and less easy to discern. The habit of repentance is lost to our whole callous and chaotic age.

How then can we transfer to society and the nation that which does not exist on the individual level? Perhaps this article is premature or altogether pointless? We start, however, from what seems to us beyond doubt: that true repentance and self-limitation will shortly reappear in the personal and the social sphere, that a hollow place in modern man is ready to receive them. Obviously then the time has come to consider this as a path for whole nations to follow. Our understanding of it must not lag behind the inevitable development of self-generating governmental policies.

We have so bedeviled the world, brought it so close to self-destruction, that repentance is now a matter of life and death—not for the sake of a life beyond the grave (which is thought merely comic nowadays), but for the sake of our life here and now and our very survival on this earth. The *end of the world,* so often foretold by the prophets only to be postponed, has ceased to be the particular property of mystics and confronts us as sober reality, scientifically, technically, and psychologically warranted. It is no longer just the danger of a nuclear world war—we have grown used to that and can take it in our stride. But the calculations of the ecologists show us that we are caught in a trap: Either we change our ways and abandon our destructively greedy pursuit of progress, or else in the twenty-first century, whatever the pace of man's development, we will perish as a result of the total exhaustion, barrenness, and pollution of the planet.

Add to this the white-hot tension between nations and races and we can say without suspicion of overstatement that without *repentance* it is in any case doubtful if we can survive.

It is by now only too obvious how dearly mankind has paid for the fact that we have all throughout the ages preferred to censure, denounce, and hate *others,* instead of censuring, denouncing, and hating ourselves. But obvious though it may be, we are even now, with the twentieth century on its way out, reluctant to recognize that the universal dividing line between good and evil runs not between countries, not between nations, not between parties, not between classes, not even between good and bad men: The dividing line cuts across nations and parties, shifting constantly, yielding now to the pressure of light, now to the pressure of darkness. It divides the heart of every man, and there too it is not a ditch dug once and for all, but fluctuates with the passage of time and according to a man's behavior.

If we accept just this one fact, which has been made plain, especially by art, a thousand times before, what way out remains to us? Not the embittered strife of parties or nations, not the struggle to win some delusive *victory*—for all the ferocious causes already in being—but simply *repentance* and the search for *our own* errors and sins. We must stop blaming everyone else—our neighbors and more distant peoples, our geographical, economic, or ideological rivals, always claiming that we alone are in the right.

Repentance is the first bit of firm ground underfoot, the only one from which we can go forward not to fresh hatreds but to concord. Repentance is the only starting point for spiritual growth.

For each and every individual.

And every trend of social thought.

True, repentant political parties are about as frequently encountered in history as tiger doves. (Politicians of course can still repent—many of them do not lose their human qualities. But *parties* are obviously utterly inhuman formations, and the very object of their existence precludes repentance.)

Nations, on the other hand, are very vital formations, susceptible to all moral feelings, including—however painful a step it may be—repentance. "An ethical idea has always preceded the birth of a nation," says Dostoyevsky (in his *Diary of a Writer*). The examples he gives are those of the Hebrew nation, founded only after Moses; and the several Moslem nations founded after the appearance of the Koran. "And when with the passage of time a nation's spiritual ideal is sapped, that nation falls, together with all its civil statutes and ideals." How then can a nation be defrauded of its right to repent?

But here certain doubts at once arise, if only the following:

(1) Is it not senseless to expect repentance from a whole nation—does this not assume that the sin, the vice, the defect is that of the whole nation? But this way of thinking—judging nations as a whole, talking about the qualities or traits of a whole nation—has been strictly forbidden to us for at least a hundred years.

(2) The mass of the nation as a whole does not perform united actions. Indeed, under many systems of government, the mass can neither obstruct nor contribute to the decisions of its leaders. *What* should it repent of?

And finally, even if we dismiss the first two points:

(3) How can the nation as a whole express its repentance? Surely only through the mouths and by the pens of individuals?

Let us try to answer these questions.

THREE

(1) Those who set the highest value on the existence of the nation, who see in it not the ephemeral fruit of social formations but a complex, vivid, unrepeatable organism not invented by man, recognize that nations have a full spiritual life, that they can soar to the heights and plunge to the depths, run the whole gamut from saintliness to utter wickedness (although only individuals ever reach the extremes). Of course, great changes occur with the passage of time and the movement of history. That shifting boundary between good and evil, of which we spoke, oscillates continuously in the consciousness of a nation, sometimes very violently, so that judgments, reproaches, self-reproaches, and even repentance itself are bound up with a specific time and pass away with it, leaving only vestigial contours behind to remind history of their existence.

But then, individuals too change beyond recognition in the course of their lives, under the influence of events and of their own spiritual endeavors (and man's hope, salvation, and punishment lie in this, that we are capable of change, and that we ourselves, not our birth or our environment, are responsible for our souls!). Yet we venture to label people "good" or "bad," and our right to do so is not usually questioned.

The profoundest similarity between the individual and the nation lies in the mystical nature of their "givenness." And human logic can show no cause why, if we permit value judgments on the one mutable entity, we should forbid them in the case of the other. To do so is a mere face-saving convention, or perhaps a precaution against their careless misapplication.

If we continue to base ourselves on intuitive perceptions, to consult our feelings and not the dictates of positivist knowledge, we shall find that national sympathies and antipathies *do exist* in the vast majority of people. Sometimes they are shared only by a particular circle, large or small, and can only be uttered there (not too loudly for fear of offending against the spirit of the times), but sometimes these feelings (of love, or alas more often than not of hate) are so strong that they overwhelm whole nations and are boldly, even aggressively, trumpeted abroad. Often such feelings arise from fallacious or superficial experience. They are always relatively short-lived, flaring up and dying down again from time to time, but they *do exist*, and very emphatically. Everyone knows it is so, and only hypocrisy forbids us to talk about it.

The changing conditions of its life, and changing external circumstances, determine whether a nation has anything to repent of *today*. Perhaps it has not. But because of the mutability of all existence, a nation can no more live without sin than can an individual. It is impossible to imagine a nation which throughout the course of its whole existence has no cause for repentance. *Every* nation without exception, however persecuted, however cheated, however flawlessly righteous it feels itself to be today, has certainly at one time or another contributed its share of inhumanity, injustice, and arrogance.

There are only too many examples, hosts of them, and this article is not a historical inquiry. It is a matter for special consideration in each particular case how much time must elapse before a sin ceases to weigh on the national conscience. Turkey bears the still-fresh guilt of the Armenian massacres, yet for centuries before that she persecuted the Balkan Slavs—is the guilt for the latter still a living thing, or a thing of the past? (Let the impatient reader not rebuke me for not beginning immediately with Russia. Russia's turn of course will come soon enough—what else would you expect from a Russian?)

(2) No one would now dispute that the British, French, and Dutch peoples as a whole bear the guilt (and marks on their souls) for the colonial policies of their governments. *Their* system of government allowed for considerable ob-struction to be placed in the way of colonialism by society. But there was little obstruction of this sort, and the nation was drawn into this seductive enterprise, with some individuals participating, others supporting and others merely accepting it.

Here is a case much nearer to hand, from the middle of the twentieth century, when public opinion in Western countries practically determines government behavior. After the Second World War the British and American authorities made a deal with their Soviet counterparts and systematically handed over in southern Europe (Austria and Italy) *hundreds of thousands* of civilian refugees from the USSR (over and above repatriated troops) who had no desire to return to their native land, handed them over deceitfully, with-out warning, contrary to their expectations and wishes, and in effect sent them to their death—probably half of them were destroyed by the camps. The relevant documents have been carefully concealed up to now. But there were living witnesses, knowledge of these events filtered out to the British and Americans, and during the past quarter of a century there have been plenty of opportunities in those countries to make inquiries, raise an outcry, bring the guilty to judgment. But no one has raised a finger. The reason is that the West today sees the sufferings of Eastern Europe in a distant haze. Com-placency, however, has never purged anyone of guilt. It is just because of this complacent silence that the vile treachery of the military authorities has seeped into and stained the national conscience of those countries. Yet the voice of repentance has still not been heard.

In Uganda today the meddlesome General Amin expels Asians suppos-edly on his own personal responsibility, but there is no doubt that he has the self-interested approval of a population which battens on the spoils of the deported. This is how the Ugandans have set out on the path of nationhood, and, as in all countries which previously suffered oppression and now franti-cally aspire to physical might, repentance is the very last feeling they are about to experience.

It would be much less simple to demonstrate the responsibility of the Albanians for the behavior of their fanatical ruler, whose own country bears the full brunt of his tyranny only because he lacks the strength to turn upon others. But the enthusiastic layer of the population which keeps him in orbit must surely have been recruited from ordinary Albanian families?

This is the peculiar feature of integrated organisms—that all their parts benefit and suffer alike from the activity of each organ. Even when the major-ity of the population is quite powerless to obstruct its political leaders, it is fated to answer for their sins and their mistakes. Even in the most totalitarian states, whose subjects have no rights at all, we all bear responsibility—not only for the quality of our government, but also for the campaigns of our military leaders, for the deeds of our soldiers in the line of duty, for the shots fired by our frontier guards, for the songs of our young people.

"For the sins of the fathers"—the saying is thousands of years old. How, you may ask, can we repent on their behalf—we weren't even alive at the time! We are even less responsible than the subjects of a totalitarian regime! But the saying is not an idle one, and we have only too often seen and still see children *paying* for the fathers.

The nation is mystically welded together in a community of guilt, and its inescapable destiny is common repentance.

(3) Individual expressions of this common repentance are dubiously representative, for we cannot know whether those who make them speak with authority. And they are extremely difficult for the people who make them. Individual repentance is one thing: The counsels of outsiders, or even of those close to you, carry no weight once you have wholeheartedly committed yourself. But the man who takes it upon himself to express the repentance of a nation, on the other hand, will always be exposed to weighty dissuasions, reproaches, and warnings not to bring shame upon his country or give comfort to its enemies. Moreover, if in your own person you pronounce words of repentance on behalf of society as a whole, you must inevitably *distribute* the blame, indicating the various degrees of culpability of various groups—and that necessarily changes the spirit and tone of repentance and casts a shadow on it. It is only at a historical distance that we can unerringly judge to what degree one man has expressed a genuine change of heart in his nation.

But it can happen—and Russia is a striking example of this—that repentance is expressed not just once and momentarily by a single writer or orator, but becomes the normal mood of all thinking society. Thus in the nineteenth century a repentant mood spread among the Russian upper-class intelligentsia (and so overwhelmed them that the penitents ceased to acknowledge any good in themselves or any sin in the common people), then gathered force, took in the middle-class intelligentsia as well, and, translating itself into action, became a historical movement with incalculable—and even counterproductive—consequences.

The repentance of a nation expresses itself most surely and palpably in its *actions*. In its finite actions.

Even in our own calculating and impenitent age we see a powerful movement of repentance in the country which bears the guilt for two world wars. Not, alas, in the whole nation. Only in that half (or three-quarters) where the ideology of hate does not stand like an impregnable concrete wall in the way of repentance.

This repentance, not just in words, in protestations, but in real actions, in large *concessions*, was dramatically manifested to us in Chancellor Brandt's "*Canossa-Reise*" to Warsaw, to Auschwitz, and then to Israel, and found further expression in his whole *Ost-Politik*. From a practical point of view, this policy seems less carefully weighed and balanced than "policies" generally are. It was born, perhaps, of moral imperatives, in the cloudy atmosphere of penitence which hung over Germany after the Second World War. This is what makes it remarkable—that an ethical impulse, rather than political calculation, lies behind it—and it is just the sort of noble and generous impulse which one longs to see today in other nations and countries (and above all in our own!). It would have vindicated itself in practical terms too if it had met with a similar spiritual response from the East European partners, instead of grasping political greed.

It is, however, only fitting that a Russian author, writing for Russia, should turn to the question of Russia's need to repent. This article is written with faith in the natural proclivity of Russians to repent, in our ability even as things are now to find the penitential impulse in ourselves and set the whole world an example.

Significantly, one of the fundamental proverbs expressing the Russian view of the world was (at any rate before the revolution) "*God is not in might but in right.*" This belief may be partly natural to us, but was powerfully reinforced by the Orthodox faith, which was once sincerely embraced by the whole mass of the people. (It is only nowadays that we are persuaded, almost to a man, that "might is right," and act accordingly.)

We were generously endowed with the gift of repentance: At one time it irrigated a broad tract of the Russian character. Not for nothing was the "day of forgiveness" such a high point in our calendar. In the distant past (until the seventeenth century) Russia was so rich in penitential movements that repentance was among the most prominent Russian national characteristics. Upsurges of repentance, or rather of religious penitence on a mass scale, were in the spirit of pre-Petrine Russia: It would begin separately, in many hearts, and merge into a powerful current. This is probably the noblest and only true way of broad, popular repentance. Klyuchevsky, studying the economic documents on ancient Russia, found many cases of Russians moved by repentance to forgive debts, to cancel debt-slavery or set their bondsmen free, and this did much to soften the force of cruel laws. Inordinate accumulations of wealth were mitigated by lavish bequests to charity. We know how very many penitents retired to religious settlements, hermits' cells, and monasteries. The chronicles and ancient Russian literature alike abound in examples of repentance. And Ivan the Terrible's terror never became so all-embracing or systematic as Stalin's, largely because the tsar repented and came to his senses.

But with the soulless reforms of Nikon[1] and Peter the Great began the extirpation and suppression of the Russian national spirit, and our capacity for repentance also began to wither and dry up. The monstrous punishment of the Old Believers—the burnings at the stake, the red-hot pincers, the impalements on meat hooks, the dungeons—followed for two and a half centuries by the senseless repression of twelve million meek and defenseless fellow countrymen, and their dispersal to the most uninhabitable regions of the country or even expulsion from the country—all this is a sin for which the established Church has never proclaimed its repentance. This was bound to weigh heavily on the whole future of Russia. Yet all that happened was that in 1905 the persecuted were forgiven (too late, far too late, to save the persecutors).

The whole Petersburg period of our history—a period of external greatness, of imperial conceit—drew the Russian spirit even farther from repentance. So far that we managed to preserve serfdom for a century or more after it had become unthinkable, keeping the greater part of our own people in a slavery which robbed them of all human dignity. So far that even the upsurge of repentance on the part of thinking society came too late to appease angry minds, but engulfed us in the clouds of a new savagery, brought a pitiless rain of vengeful blows on our heads, an unprecedented terror, and the return, after seventy years, of serfdom in a still worse form.

In the twentieth century the blessed dews of repentance could no longer soften the parched Russian soil, baked hard by doctrines of hate. In the past sixty years we have not merely lost the gift of repentance in our public life but have ridiculed it. This feeling was precipitately abandoned and made an object of contempt, the place in the soul where repentance once dwelt was laid waste. For half a century now we have acted on the conviction that the *guilty* ones were the tsarist establishment, the bourgeois patriots, social democrats, White Guards, priests, émigrés, subversives, kulaks, henchmen of kulaks, engineers, "wreckers,"[2] oppositionists, enemies of the people, nationalists, Zionists, imperialists, militarists, even modernists—anyone and everyone except you and me! Obviously it was *they*, not we, who had to reform. But they dug their heels in and refused to. So how could they be made to reform, except by bayonets (revolvers, barbed wire, starvation)?

---

[1] Patriarch Nikon: Patriarch of the Russian Orthodox Church in the seventeenth century. The "Old Believers" clung to old customs and rites.

[2] The name applied to alleged industrial saboteurs in the twenties.

One of the peculiarities of Russian history is that our evildoing has always, even up to the present day, taken the same direction: We have done evil on a massive scale and mainly in our own country, not abroad, not to *others*, but at home to our own people, to ourselves. No one has borne so much of the suffering as the Russians, Ukrainians, and Byelorussians. So that as we awaken to repentance we shall have to remember much that concerns only us, and for which outsiders will not reproach us.

Will it be easy for us honestly to remember it all, when we have lost all feeling for truth? We, the present older and middle generations, have spent our whole lives floundering and wallowing in the stinking swamp of a society based on force and fraud—how could we escape defilement? Are there naturally angelic characters—gliding as it were weightlessly above the slime without ever sinking into it, even when their feet touch its surface? We have all met such people—Russia is not so short of them as all that. They are the "just," we have all seen them and marveled ("such funny people"), profited from their goodness, repaid them in kind in our better moments, for we can't help liking them, and then plunged back into the depths to which we are doomed. We have floundered, some (the lucky ones) ankle-deep, some knee-deep, some waist-deep, some up to our necks, according to the changing circumstances and our peculiarities of character, while some were totally immersed and only occasional bubbles from a not quite dead soul reached the surface to remind us of their existence.

But who, if not we ourselves, constitutes *society*? This realm of darkness, of falsehood, of brute force, of justice denied and distrust of the good, this slimy swamp was formed by *us*, and no one else. We grew used to the idea that we must submit and lie in order to survive, and we brought up our children to do so. Each of us, if he honestly reviews the life he has led, without special pleading or concealment, will recall more than one occasion on which he pretended not to hear a cry for help, averted his indifferent eyes from an imploring gaze, burned letters and photographs which it was his duty to keep, forgot someone's name or dropped certain widows, turned his back on prisoners under escort, and—but of course—always voted, rose to his feet, and applauded obscenities (even though he felt obscene while he was doing it)—how, otherwise, could we survive? How, moreover, could the great Archipelago have endured in our midst for fifty years unnoticed?

Need I mention the common or garden informers, traitors, and sadists of whom there must surely have been more than one million, or how could such an Archipelago have been managed?

And if we now long—and there is a glimmer of hope that we do—to go forward at last into a just, clean, honest society—how else can we do so except by shedding the burden of our past, except by repentance, for we are all guilty, all besmirched? We cannot convert the kingdom of universal false-hood into a kingdom of universal truth by even the cleverest and most skill-fully contrived economic and social reforms: these are the wrong building bricks.[3]

But if millions pour out their repentance, their confessions, their con-trite sorrow—not all of them perhaps publicly, but among friends and people who know them —what could all this together be called except "the repen-tance of the nation"?

But here our endeavor, like any attempt to summon a nation to repen-tance, runs into objections from within: Russia has suffered so much that she cannot be asked to repent as well, she must be pitied, not tormented with reminders of her sins.

And it is true. No country in the twentieth century has suffered like ours, which within its own borders has destroyed as many as seventy million people over and above those lost in the world wars—no one in modern history has experienced such destruction. And it is true: It is painful to chide where one must pity. But repentance is always painful, otherwise it would have no moral value. Those people were not the victims of flood or earthquake. There were innocent victims and guilty victims, but they would never have reached such a terrifying total if they had suffered only at the hands of others: *We, all of us,* Russia herself, were the necessary accomplices.

An even harsher, colder point of view, or rather current of opinion, has become discernible of late. Stripped to essentials, but not distorted, it goes like this: The Russian people is the noblest in the world; its ancient and its modern history are alike unblemished; tsarism and Bolshevism are equally

---

[3] The line of repentance becomes easier and clearer to follow if it is compared with the line traced by the defense of civil rights. Here is a fresh recent example that puts the whole thing in a nutshell. Some years ago a now well-known dissident wrote a film script in the course of his normal, officially approved artistic career which was highly thought of and allowed onto the country's cinema screens— which means it is not difficult to guess at its spiritual value. On the occasion of some recent diplomatic triumph it was thought appropriate to exhibit this film once more, but the name of the now offending scriptwriter was cut out. And what was the scriptwriter's reaction? What would have been the most natural thing to do? The line of repentance would have indicated joy and satisfaction that he had, as it were, been automatically relieved of the disgrace of this former spiritual compromise and reprieved of an ancient sin. Might he not even have made a public statement about his feelings of absolution? Well, the scriptwriter certainly made a public statement, but it was a protest, asserting his right to have his name on the film. The infringement of his civil rights struck him as more important than the opportunity to purge himself of a previous sin. [Author's note, 1974.]

irreproachable; the nation neither erred nor sinned either before 1917 or after; we have suffered no loss of moral stature and therefore have no need of self-improvement; there are no nationality problems in relations with the border republics—Lenin's and Stalin's solution was ideal; communism is in fact unthinkable without patriotism; the prospects of Russia-USSR are brilliant; blood alone determines whether one is Russian or non-Russian. As for things spiritual, all trends are admissible. Orthodoxy is not the least bit more Russian than Marxism, atheism, the scientific outlook, or, shall we say, Hinduism. God need not be written with a capital letter, but Government must be.

Their general name for all this is "the Russian idea." (A more precise name for this trend would be "National Bolshevism.")

"We are Russians, what rapture," cried Suvorov.[4] "And how fraught with danger to the soul," added F. Stepun[5] after our revolutionary experiences.

As we understand it patriotism means unqualified and unwavering love for the nation, which implies not uncritical eagerness to serve, not support for unjust claims, but frank assessment of its vices and sins, and penitence for them. We ought to get used to the idea that no people is eternally great or eternally noble (such titles are hard won and easily lost); that the greatness of a people is to be sought not in the blare of trumpets—physical might is purchased at a spiritual price beyond our means—but in the level of its *inner* development, in its breadth of soul (fortunately one of nature's gifts to us), in unarmed moral steadfastness (in which the Czechs and Slovaks recently gave Europe a lesson, without however troubling its conscience more than briefly).

In what we may call the neo-Muscovite period the conceit of the preceding Petersburg period has become grosser and blinder. And this has led us even farther from a penitential state of mind, so that it is not easy to convince our fellow-countrymen, to force on them an awareness that we Russians are not traversing the heavens in a blaze of glory but sitting forlornly on a heap of spiritual cinders. And unless we recover the gift of repentance, our country will perish and will drag down the whole world with it.

Only through the repentance of a multitude of people can the air and the soil of Russia be cleansed so that a new, healthy, national life can grow up. We cannot raise a clean crop on a false, unsound, obdurate soil.

---

[4] Alexander Suvorov (1730–1800), Russia's most famous military leader.
[5] Fyodor Stepun: Russian philosopher expelled from the Soviet Union in 1922.

FOUR

If we try to make an act of national repentance we must be ready for hostility and resistance on the one hand, and impassioned efforts to lead us astray on the other. S. Bulgakov[6] has written that "only suffering love gives one the right to chastise one's own nation." You would think it was impossible to take it upon oneself to "repent" on behalf of a nation to which one felt alien or even hostile. Yet people eager to do just this have already come forward. Given the obscurity of our recent history, the destruction of archives, the disappearance of evidence, our defenselessness against all sorts of presumptuous and unproven judgments and all sorts of galling distortions, we can probably expect many such attempts. And we already have the first of them, a fairly resolute effort which claims to be nothing less than an act of "national repentance."

We cannot pass it by unexamined. I am speaking of articles in the *Vestnik RSKD*[7] No. 97, and particularly "Metanoia" (self-condemnation, self-examination—a term taken from the same Bulgakov writing in 1910) by the anonymous NN, and "Russian Messianism" by the pseudonymous Gorsky.

Even the boldest works of *samizdat* always have an eye to the surrounding *circumstances*. But here, writing in a foreign publication and anonymously, the authors have absolutely no apprehension either for themselves or for their readers and therefore seize the chance to pour out their hearts for just once in their lives—an urge entirely understandable to any Soviet person. Their tone could not be sharper, and the style becomes informal, even impertinent. The authors fear neither the authorities nor the critical reader: They are will-o'-the-wisps, safe from discovery; there is no arguing with them. This makes them still more uncompromising in their conduct of the case against Russia. There is not the slightest hint that the authors share any complicity with their countrymen, with the rest of us; there is nothing but denunciation of the irredeemably vicious Russian people and a tone of contempt for those who have been led astray. Nowhere do we feel that the authors think of themselves and their readers as "we." Living among us, they call on us to repent, while they themselves remain unassailable and guiltless. (The punishment for this alienness extends even to their language, which is quite un-Russian and in the tradition of those instant translations from Western philosophy which people were forever rushing out in the nineteenth century.)

---

[6] Sergei Bulgakov: After abandoning Marxism, he became a prolific, influential author of philosophical and theological works; expelled from the Soviet Union in 1922.

[7] Published in Russian by the YMCA Press in Paris.

These articles solemnly bury Russia, with a bayonet thrust just in case—just as prisoners in the camps are buried: It's too much trouble to make sure whether the man's dead, just bayonet him and sling him in the burial trench.

Here are a few of their statements.

"When it began its revolt against God, the Russian people knew that the socialist religion could be made a reality only through despotism!" (Gorsky).

When were we, in our birchbark sandals, so mature and perceptive? The revolt was started by the intelligentsia, but it too *did not know* what can be so effortlessly formulated in the seventies of the twentieth century.

"More Evil has been brought into the world by Russia than by any other country" (NN).

We shall not say that Russia has brought little evil into the world. But did the so-called Great French Revolution, did France, that is, bring less? Is there any way of calculating? What of the Third Reich? Or Marxism as such? Not to go any further. . . . And there is another side to the question: Perhaps our inhuman experience, paid for mainly with our own blood and that of the peoples nearest akin to us, has even benefited some of earth's more distant inhabitants? Perhaps in some places it has taught the obtuse ruling classes to make a few concessions? Perhaps the liberation of the colonial world was not entirely uninfluenced by the October revolution—as a reaction to it, to prevent a repetition of what happened to us—God alone can know, and it is not for us to judge which country has done most evil.

"In the revolution the people proved to be an imaginary quantity. . . . Its own national culture is completely alien to the Russian people." The proof: "In the first years of the revolution icons were found useful for firewood, and churches for building material" (Gorsky).

There you have it: Anybody who feels like it can come along with a snap judgment, because our chronicles have been obliterated. If the people proved to be an imaginary quantity—how can it be blamed for the revolution, whatever other charges are brought against it? If it proved to be an imaginary quantity—who was resisting the revolution in the peasant risings which inundated Tambov and Siberia? The people had to be reduced to "imaginary" status by long years of destruction, oppression, and seduction—and this destruction is just what Gorsky appears not to know about. It was a complicated process—and how simple he has made it. In 1918 Russian peasants rose in defense of the Church—*several hundred* such risings were put down by Red arms. Of course, after the clergy had been destroyed, after defenders of the faith among the peasantry and in urban parishes had been massacred and all the rest terrorized—while the Komsomols[8] and Communist youth organizations grew up in the meantime—after all this they did indeed go and wreck the churches with crowbars (but even then it was mainly the work of Komsomol members who were specially hired for this purpose). Ever since, in the northern regions, icons have been, not "sold for a song" to treasure hunters from Moscow, as our well-informed author writes (true, they sometimes change hands for a bottle), but *given away.* It is considered a sin to take money for them. Whereas the progressive young intellectuals who receive such a gift quite often do a profitable trade with foreigners.

But most of the heat and space in this bulky publication is devoted to the denunciation of *Russian messianism.*

"Overcoming the national messianic delusion is Russia's most urgent task." Russian messianism is more tenacious of life than Russia itself: Russia, we are told, is dead, of "archaeological" interest, like Byzantium, but its messianism is not dead, it has simply been reborn as Soviet messianism (Gorsky).

This cunning perversion of our history comes as such a surprise that it is not immediately discernible. The author begins by tracing in exaggeratedly academic fashion the "history" of our ill-starred and deathless messianism, which however was for some reason not always discernible in Russia: For two centuries (the fifteenth to the seventeenth) it was in evidence, then missing for the next two, then it reemerged in the nineteenth century (apparently the intelligentsia was "carried away" by it—does anyone remember anything of the kind?), it disguised itself during the revolution as "proletarian messianism," and in recent decades has torn off its mask and once more revealed itself as Russian messianism. So, traveling via dotted lines, sophistries, and abrupt transitions, the idea of the Third Rome suddenly surfaces again in the guise of the Third International![9] With the obsessive thoroughness of hate, our whole history is arbitrarily distorted for some never quite graspable purpose—and all this is speciously represented as an act of *repentance!* The blows seem to be aimed only at the Third Rome and messianism—then suddenly we discover that the breaker's hammer is not smashing dilapidated walls but pounding the last spark of life out of the long dormant, barely surviving Russian national consciousness. See how keen his aim is:

---

[8] Komsomol: The League of Young Communists, the youth arm of the Communist Party.

[9] Third Rome: Refers to the medieval Russian religious belief that after the fall of Constantinople (the "second Rome") in 1453, Moscow would become the center of Christendom and a "third Rome." The "Third International," or Comintern, was a world organization of Communist parties that existed from 1919 to 1943 with the aim of conquering the world for communism.

"The Russian idea is the main content of Bolshevism"! "The crisis of the Communist idea is the crisis of that source of faith by which Russia lived so long" ("for centuries," according to the context).

See how they turn us inside out and trample us. Russia "lived so long" by the Orthodox faith, as everybody knows. But the main content of Bolshevism is unbridled militant atheism and class hatred. Still, according to our neo-Christian authors, it all comes to the same thing. The tradition of fanatical atheism is received into the tradition of ancient Orthodoxy. Is the "Russian idea," then, the "main content" of an international doctrine which came to us from the West? When Marat called for "a million heads" and asserted that the hungry have the right to *eat* the well-fed (how well we know such situations!)—was this also the "Russian messianic consciousness" at work? Sixteenth-century Germany seethed with communistic movements—so why, when this "Russian idea" was about, did nothing similar happen during the Time of Troubles in seventeenth-century Russia?

"Revolution could exercise its fatal fascination only because of Russia's ecumenical pride" (NN).

How can we tie these loose ends together? If tsarism rested on "Russia's ecumenical pride," how can revolution, which brought down the tsarist structure in ruins, also *originate* in "Russian pride"?

"Proletarian messianism is taking on a blatantly Russophile character" (Chelnov).

This is in our own day, when half the Russian people live like serfs, without internal passports. Have we memory and courage enough to recall the first fifteen years after the revolution, when "proletarian messianism took on a blatantly" *Russophobe* character? The years from 1918 to 1933, when "proletarian messianism" destroyed the flower of the Russian people, the flower of the old classes—gentry, merchants, clergy—then the flower of the intelligentsia, then the flower of the peasantry? What shall we say of the time *before* it acquired its "blatantly Russophile character," and had a blatantly Russophobe character?

"Bolshevism is an organic outgrowth of Russian life" (NN and Chelnov).

Whether this is so or not will be much debated for a long time to come. And it cannot be decided in heated polemics, but only by detailed and carefully documented research. *Quiet Flows the Don*[10]—the authentic version, undistorted by illiterate interpolations—offers more useful evidence than a dozen modern publicists. Our scholars and artists will long be debating whether the Russian revolution was the consequence of a moral upheaval

---

[10] The epic novel about the Russian Revolution and Civil War was published in installments between 1928 and 1940 by Mikhail Sholokhov. Solzhenitsyn, for one, has challenged Sholokhov's claim of authorship.

that had already taken place among the people, or vice versa. And when they do, let none of the circumstances passed over here be forgotten.

Of course, once it was victorious on Russian soil the movement was bound to draw Russian forces in its wake and acquire Russian features! But let us remember the international forces of the revolution too! Did not the revolution throughout its early years have some of the characteristics of a foreign invasion? When in a foraging party, or the punitive detachment which came down to destroy a rural district, there would be Finns and there would be Austrians, but hardly anyone who spoke Russian? When the organs of the Cheka[11] teemed with Latvians, Poles, Jews, Hungarians, Chinese? When in the critical early phases of the civil war it was foreign and especially Latvian bayonets that turned the scales and kept the Bolsheviks in power? (At the time this was not a matter for shame or concealment.) Or later, throughout the twenties, when the Russian tradition and all trace of Russian history were systematically ferreted out in all fields of culture, eliminated even from place names, in a way seen only under enemy occupation—was this self-destructive urge also a manifestation of the "Russian idea"? Gorsky notes that in 1919 the borders of Soviet Russia roughly corresponded with those of the Muscovite state—ergo Bolshevism was supported mainly by Russians. But this geographical fact could equally well be interpreted to mean simply that it was mainly Russians who were forced to shoulder the burden of Bolshevism. And can we think of any people on earth in the twentieth century which when trapped by the incoming tide of communism has pulled itself together and stood firm? So far there is not a single example of this, except South Korea, where the United Nations came to the rescue. South Vietnam might have been another case, but has apparently been thrown off balance. And right now, are we to say that communism in Cuba or in Vietnam "is an organic outgrowth of Russian life"? Is "Marxism one of the forms taken by the populist-messianic mentality" in France too? Or in Latin America? Or in Tanzania? And does all this come from the unwashed monk Filofei?[12]

What a state of disrepair twentieth-century Russian history is in, how grotesquely distorted and full of obscurities, if people so self-confidently ignorant of it can offer us their services as judges. Because of our complacency we may live to see the day when fifty or a hundred years of Russian history will have sunk into oblivion, and nobody will be able to establish any reliable record of them—it will be too late.

The publication of these articles is not fortuitous—the idea is perhaps to take advantage of our helplessness, turn recent Russian history inside out,

---

[11] Cheka: The original name of the Soviet secret police (1917–22).

[12] Filofei: Sixteenth-century Russian monk who popularized the concept of Russia as the "Third Rome."

blame *us* Russians *alone* not only for our own misfortunes but also for those of our erstwhile tormentors and nowadays pretty well the whole planet. These accusations are typical of their authors, plucked out of thin air and shamelessly fabricated, and it is easy to foresee already how they intend to go on searing our wounds with them.

This article has not been written to minimize the guilt of the Russian people. Nor, however, to scrape all the guilt from mother earth and load it onto ourselves. True, we were not vaccinated against the plague. True, we lost our heads. True, we gave way, and then caved in altogether. All true. But we have not been the first and only begetters in all this time since the fifteenth century!

We are not the only ones; there are many others. Indeed, almost everyone when the time comes gives way, gives up, sometimes under less pressure than we succumbed to, and at times even eagerly. (The brief period of our history from February to October 1917 has turned out to be a compressed résumé of the later and present history of the West.)

Thus, at the very beginning of our repentance we have been warned: The path ahead will bristle with such insults and slanders. If you are the first to repent, earlier and more fully than others, you must expect predators in the guise of penitents to flock around and pick your liver.

Nonetheless, there is no way out, except that of repentance.

FIVE

It may turn out that we are already incapable of following the path of our dreams, reaching out and acknowledging our mistakes, our sins, our crimes. In that case there is no moral escape route from the pit into which we have fallen. And every other way out is illusory, no more than a short-lived social delusion.

But if it turns out that we are still not utterly lost and can find in ourselves the strength to pass through this burning zone of general national repentance, of *internal* repentance, for the harm which we have done here in our own country, to ourselves, will it be possible for Russia to stop at that? No, we shall have to find in ourselves the resolve to take the next step: to acknowledge our *external* sins, those against other peoples.

There are plenty of them. To clear the international air and convince others of our sincere goodwill, we must not conceal these sins, not tuck them away nor slur over them in our remembrance. My view is that if we err in our repentance, it should be on the side of exaggeration, giving others the benefit of the doubt. We should accept in advance that there is no neighbor toward whom we bear no guilt. Let us behave as people do on the day of forgiveness, and ask forgiveness of all around us.

The scope of our repentance must be infinite. We cannot run away even from ancient sins; we may write off other people's sins as ancient history, but we have no right to do it for ourselves. A few pages further on I shall be talking about the future of Siberia—and whenever I do so my heart sinks at the thought of our age-old sin in oppressing and destroying the indigenous peoples. And is this really ancient history? If Siberia today were densely populated by the original national groups the only step we could ethically take would be to cede their land to them and not stand in the way of their freedom. But since there is only a faint sprinkling of them on the Siberian continent, it is permissible for us to seek our future there, so long as we show a tender fraternal concern for the natives, help them in their daily lives, educate them, and do not forcibly impose our ways on them.

A historical survey would be out of place in this article—and besides, space does not permit it. It would contain crimes enough—as for instance those we committed against the mountain peoples of the Caucasus: the Russian military encroachment in the nineteenth century (condemned at the proper time by the great Russian writers) and the deportations of the twentieth century (which Caucasian writers themselves dare not deal with).

Repentance is always difficult. And not only because we must cross the threshold of self-love, but also because our own sins are not so easily visible to us.

If we take the Russo-Polish theme—here too there is an endless tangle of crimes. To unravel it would teach us much about human relations in the broadest sense. (Today, when both the Poles and we ourselves are crushed by brute force, such a historical inquiry may seem inappropriate. But I write for posterity. Someday it may seem appropriate.)

So much has been said about our guilt toward Poland that it has left a deposit on our memory, and we need no more persuasion. The three Partitions. The suppression of the 1830 and 1863 risings. After that, Russification: Polish-speaking elementary schools were completely forbidden, in high schools even the Polish language was taught in Russian (as an obligatory subject) and pupils were forbidden to speak Polish among themselves in their living quarters! In the twentieth century there was the stubborn struggle to deny Poland its independence, and the crafty ambiguities of Russia's leaders in 1914–1916.

At the same time, how frequent were the expressions of penitence from the Russian side, from Herzen[13] onward, how unanimous was the sympathy of all educated Russian society for the Poles, so much so that in the councils of the Progressive Bloc, Polish independence was regarded as a war aim no less important than Russian victory.

---

[13] Alexander Herzen: Famous nineteenth-century Russian political figure and thinker.

If the most recent happenings have inspired no such cry of repentance in Russia, it is only because we are so crushed, but we all remember, and there will yet be occasion to say it out loud: the noble stab in the back for dying Poland on 17 September 1939; the destruction of the flower of the Polish people in our camps, Katyn in particular; and our gloating, heartless immobility on the bank of the Vistula in August 1944, whence we gazed through our binoculars at Hitler crushing the rising of the nationalist forces in Warsaw—no need for them to get big ideas, we will find the right people to put in the government. (I was nearby, and I speak with certainty: The impetus of our advance was such that the forcing of the Vistula would have been no problem, and it would have changed the fate of Warsaw.)

But just as some individuals more readily open their hearts of repentance, and others are more resistant and offer not a single chink, so, I think, with nations—some are more and some less inclined to repent.

In previous centuries Poland in its prime, strong and self-confident, was busy just as long and just as energetically annexing our territory and oppressing us. (Galician Ruthenia and Podolia in the fourteenth to sixteenth centuries; then Polesia, Volynia, and the Ukraine were incorporated under the Union of Lublin in 1569. In the sixteenth century came Stefan Batory's campaign against Russia, and the siege of Pskov. At the end of the sixteenth century the Poles put down the Cossack rising under Nalivaiko. At the beginning of the seventeenth century—the wars of Zygmunt III, the two false claimants to the Russian throne, the occupation of Smolensk, the temporary occupation of Moscow, the campaign of Wladyslaw IV. At that point the Poles almost deprived us of our national independence, and the danger for us was no less serious than that of the Tartar invasion, since the Poles were out to destroy the Orthodox faith. In their own country they systematically oppressed the Orthodox, and forced them into the Uniate church. In the mid-seventeenth century came the repression of Bogdan Khmelnitsky, and even in the middle of the eighteenth the crushing of the peasant rising at Uman.) Well then, has any wave of regret rolled over educated Polish society, any wave of repentance surged through Polish literature? Never. Even the Arians, who were opposed to war in general, had nothing special to say about the subjugation of the Ukraine and Byelorussia. During our Time of Troubles, the eastward expansion of Poland was accepted by Polish society as a normal and even praiseworthy policy. The Poles thought of themselves as God's chosen people, the bastion of Christianity to the "semipagan" Orthodox of savage Muscovy, and to be the propagators of Renaissance university culture. And when some people openly voiced their second thoughts and regrets about this when Poland went into decline in the second half of the eighteenth century, they were of a political and never of an ethical nature.

True, one cannot always draw the line between a general national characteristic and the imprint of a particular social order. The Polish social order, with its weak elected kings, its all-powerful magnates, and the utterly undisciplined selfishness of the gentry, led to the noisy self-assertion of nationhood, which ruled out self-limitation and made repentance seem inappropriate. In such a society educated Poles felt themselves to be participants and authors of all that was done, and not detached observers, whereas repentance was made easier for Russians in the nineteenth and early twentieth century by the fact that those who condemned official policy could consider themselves uninvolved: It was all *their* doing, the tsar did not consult society.

But perhaps Polish penitence expressed itself in deeds? For more than a century Poland experienced the misery of dismemberment, but then under the Versailles treaty gained independence and a great deal of territory (once more at the expense of the Ukraine and Byelorussia). Poland's first action in its relations with the outside world was to attack Soviet Russia in 1920—it attacked energetically, and took Kiev with the object of breaking through to the Black Sea. We are taught at school—to make it seem more awful—that this was the "Third Campaign of the Entente" and that Poland concerted its actions with the White generals in order to restore tsarism. This is rubbish. It was an *independent* act on the part of Poland, which waited for the rout of all the main White forces so as *not* to be their involuntary ally and so that it could plunder and carve up Russia for itself while the latter was most helplessly fragmented. This did not quite come off (though Poland did extract an indemnity from the Soviets). Then in 1921 came its second foreign policy initiative: the illegal detachment of Vilnius and the surrounding area from a weak Lithuania. And neither the League of Nations, nor all the admonitions and appeals to the Polish conscience, had any effect: Poland still clung to the piece it had grabbed to the very day of its collapse. Can anyone remember the nation repenting in this connection? (Poland's aggressive acts, incidentally, were carried out by the socialist Pilsudski, one of Alexander Ulyanov's[14] codefendants.) In the Ukrainian and Byelorussian lands annexed under the treaty of 1921, a policy of relentless Polonization was carried out; even Orthodox sermons and scripture lessons had a Polish accent. And in the infamous year of 1937, Orthodox churches were demolished (more than a hundred of them, including Warsaw Cathedral) on the Polish side of the frontier too, and priests and parishioners were arrested.

How can we possibly rise above all this, except by mutual repentance?

And is it not true that the degree of our repentance, individual or national, is very much influenced by an awareness of guilt on the other side? If those whom we hurt have previously hurt us, our guilt feelings are not so

---

[14] Alexander Ulyanov: Lenin's elder brother.

hysterical, their guilt modifies and mutes our own. The memory of the Tartar yoke in Russia must always dull our possible sense of guilt toward the remnants of the Golden Horde. Our guilt feelings toward the Estonians and Lithuanians are always more painful and shameful than any we have toward the Latvians or Hungarians, whose rifles barked often enough in the cellars of the Cheka and the backyards of Russian villages. (I ignore the inevitable noisy protests that these were "not the same people," that one cannot transfer the blame from one set of people to another. *We* are not the same people either. But we must all answer for everything.)

This is yet another argument in favor of general repentance. What relief, what rapturous relief it gives us when our enemies acknowledge their guilt toward us! How gratefully eager we are to outstrip them in repentance, to surpass them in magnanimity!

But repentance loses all sense if it goes no farther: if we have a good cry and then go on as before. Repentance opens up the path to a new relationship. Between nations as between individuals.

The repentance of a nation, like any other kind, assumes the possibility of *forgiveness* on the part of the injured. But it is impossible to expect forgiveness before you yourself have made up your mind to forgive. The path of mutual repentance and mutual forgiveness is one and the same.

Who has no guilt? We are all guilty. But at some point the endless account must be closed; we must stop discussing whose crimes are more recent, more serious, and affect most victims. It is useless for even the closest neighbors to compare the duration and gravity of their grievances against each other. But feelings of penitence can be compared.

This picture does not seem to me an idyll, unreal, and irrelevant to our modern situation. On the contrary. Just as it is impossible to build a good society when relations between people are bad, there will never be a good world while nations are on bad terms and secretly cherish the desire for revenge. Neither a "positive" foreign policy nor yet the most skillful efforts on the part of diplomats to draw up tactfully incomplete treaties so that each side can find some balm for its national pride—none of this can smother the seeds of discord and prevent even more conflicts from arising.

At present the whole atmosphere of the United Nations is saturated with hatred and spite—remember how the Assembly went wild with joy (some uninhibited members are said to have jumped up on the benches) when ten million Chinese in Taiwan were thrown out of the human family for refusing to submit to totalitarian aggression.

Without the establishment of radically *new*, really good relations between nations the entire quest for "world peace" is either utopian or a precarious balancing act.

The stock of mutual guilt mounts especially high in multinational states and federations, like Austria-Hungary in the past, or the USSR, Yugoslavia, Nigeria, and other African states with a multiplicity of tribes and races today. If such states are to achieve internal stability and be held together by something other than coercion, the peoples who live in them cannot possibly manage without a highly developed capacity for repentance. Otherwise the fires will smolder forever beneath the ashes and flare up again and again, and these countries will never know stability. The West Pakistanis were ruthless toward those of the East—and the country collapsed, but still the hatred did not die down. On the contrary, northern Nigeria, with the help of British and Soviet arms and with the whole world indifferently looking on, took cruel revenge on the eastern regions and preserved the unity of the country, but unless this wrong is righted by repentance and kindness on the part of the victors, that country will not enjoy stability and health.

Repentance is only a clearing of the ground, the establishment of a clean basis in preparation for further moral actions—what in the life of the individual is called "reform." And if in private life what has been done must be put right by deeds, not words, this is all the more true in the life of a nation. Its repentance must be expressed not so much in articles, books, and broadcasts as in national *actions*.

With regard to all the peoples in and beyond our borders forcibly drawn into our orbit, we can fully purge our guilt by giving them genuine freedom to decide their future for themselves.

After repentance, and once we renounce the use of force, *self-limitation* comes into its own as the most natural principle to live by. Repentance creates the atmosphere for self-limitation.

Self-limitation on the part of individuals has often been observed and described, and is well known to us all. (Quite apart from the pleasure it gives to those around us in our everyday lives, it can be universally helpful to men in *all* areas of their activity.) But so far as I know, no state has ever carried through a deliberate policy of self-limitation or set itself such a task in a general form—though when it has done so at difficult moments in some particular sector (food rationing, fuel rationing, and so on) self-limitation has paid off handsomely.

Every trade union and every corporation strives by all possible means to win the most advantageous position in the economy, every firm aims at uninterrupted expansion, every party wants to run its country, medium-sized states want to become great ones, and great ones to rule the world.

We are always very ready to limit *others*—this is what all politicians are engaged in—but nowadays the man who suggests that a state or party, without coercion and simply in answer to a moral call, should limit *itself*, invites ridicule. We are always anxiously on the lookout for ways of curbing the inordinate greed of the *other man*, but no one is heard renouncing his *own* inordinate greed. History knows of several occasions on which the greed of a minority was curbed, with much bloodshed, but who is to curb the inflamed greed of the *majority*, and how? That is something it can only do for itself.

The idea of self-limitation in society is not a new one. We find it a century ago in such thoroughgoing Christians as the Russian Old Believers. In the journal *Istina* (No. 1, 1807), in an article by K. Golubov, who corresponded with Ogarev and Herzen, we read:

"A people subjects itself to great suffering by its immoral acquisitiveness. That which is obtained by revolt and sequestration can have no true value. These are rather the fruits of the overweening behavior of a corrupt conscience: The true and lasting good is that which is attained by *farsighted self-limitation*" (emphasis added).

And elsewhere: "Save through self-restriction, there is no other true freedom for mankind."

After the Western ideal of unlimited freedom, after the Marxist concept of freedom as acceptance of the yoke of necessity—here is the true Christian definition of freedom. Freedom is *self-restriction!* Restriction of the self for the sake of others!

Once understood and adopted, this principle diverts us—as individuals, in all forms of human association, societies, and nations—from *outward* to *inward* development, thereby giving us greater spiritual depth.

The turn toward *inward* development, the triumph of inwardness over outwardness, if it ever happens, will be a great turning point in the history of mankind, comparable to the transition from the Middle Ages to the Renaissance. There will be a complete change not only in the direction of our interests and activities but in the very nature of human beings (a change from spiritual dispersal to spiritual concentration), and a greater change still in the character of human societies. If in some places this is destined to be a revolutionary process, these revolutions will not be like earlier ones—physical, bloody, and never beneficial—but will be *moral revolutions*, requiring both courage and sacrifice, though not cruelty—a new phenomenon in human history, of which little is yet known and which as yet no one has prophetically described in clear and precise forms. The examination of all this does not lie within the scope of our present article.

But in the material sphere this change will also have conspicuous results. The individual will not flog himself to death in his greed for bigger earnings, but will spend what he has economically, rationally, and calmly. The state will not, as it does now, use its strength—sometimes even with no particular end in view—simply on the principle that where something will give, one must exert pressure, if a barrier can be moved, move it—no, among states too the moral rule for individuals will be adopted—do not unto others as you would not have done unto you: Instead, learn to use to the full what you have. Only thus can a well-ordered life be created on our planet.

The concept of unlimited freedom is connected in its origin with the concept of *infinite progress*, which we now recognize as false. Progress in this sense is impossible on our earth with its limited surface area and resources. We shall in any case inevitably have to stop jostling each other and show self-restraint: With the population rapidly soaring, mother earth herself will shortly force us to do so. It would be spiritually so much more valuable, and psychologically so much easier, to adopt the principle of self-limitation— and to achieve it through *prudent self-restriction.*

Such a change will not be easy for the free economy of the West. It is a revolutionary demolition and total reconstruction of all our ideas and aims. We must go over from uninterrupted progress to a *stable economy*, with *nil growth* in territory, parameters, and tempo, developing only through im- proved technology (and even technical successes must be critically screened). This means that we must abjure the plague of expansion beyond our bor- ders, the continual scramble after new markets and sources of raw material, increases in our industrial territory or the volume of production, the whole insane pursuit of wealth, fame, and change. No incentive to self-limitation has ever existed in bourgeois economics, yet the formula would so easily and so long ago have been derived from moral considerations. The funda- mental concepts of private property and private economic initiative are part of man's nature, and necessary for his personal freedom and his sense of normal well-being. They would be beneficial to society *if only*... if only the carriers of these ideas on the very threshold of development had *limited themselves,* and not allowed the size of their property and thrust of their avarice to become a social evil, which provoked so much justifiable anger, not tried to purchase power and subjugate the press. It was as a reply to the shamelessness of unlimited money-grubbing that socialism in all its forms developed.

But a Russian author today need not rack his brains for an answer to these worries. Self-limitation has countless aspects—international, politi- cal, cultural, national, social, and party-political. We Russians should sort out those which concern us.

And show an example of spiritual breadth. Show that repentance is not fruitless.

It is in this hope and faith that I am writing this article.

Our native land, after centuries of misapplying its might (both in the Pe- tersburg and the neo-Muscovite periods), after making so many useless acqui- sitions abroad and causing so much destruction at home, now, before the chance is lost forever, is perhaps more than any other country in need of comprehensive *inward* development—both spiritual, and the ensuing geographical, economic, and social development that will occur as a consequence.

Our foreign policy in recent decades might have been deliberately devised in defiance of the true interests of our people. We have taken on ourselves a responsibility for the fate of Eastern Europe incommensurable with our present level of spiritual development and our ability to understand European needs and ways. We are ready in our conceit to extend our responsibility to any other country, however distant, even on the other side of the globe, provided it declares its intent to nationalize the means of production and centralize power. (These, according to our theory, are the primary features, and all the rest—national peculiarities, way of life, thousand-year-old cultural traditions—are secondary. We meddle indefatigably in conflicts on every continent, lay down the law, shove people into quarrels, shamelessly push arms till they have become our most important item of export. We are what Soviet newspapers until the forties called "traders in blood.") In pursuit of all these artificial aims, which are of no use to our nation, we have exhausted our strength and wrecked several of our generations—mainly physically in the past, but now mainly spiritually.

All these world tasks, which have been of no use at all to us, have left us *tired*. We need to get away from the hurly-burly of world rivalries. And from the exhibitionistic space race, which is useless to us: What is the point of our painful efforts to erect villages on the moon when our Russian villages have become dilapidated and unfit for habitation? In our insane industrial drive we have drawn inordinate masses of people into unnatural towns and absurd, hastily erected buildings, where they are poisoned, collapse under nervous strain, and start degenerating in early youth. Sweated female labor instead of sex equality, the neglect of parental duty, drunkenness, loss of appetite for work, the decline of the school, the decadence of our native language—whole spiritual deserts are eating into our life and laying waste to great patches of it, and it is only in overcoming *these* that we can win for ourselves true and not bogus prestige. Should we be struggling for warm seas far away, or ensuring that warmth rather than enmity flows between our own citizens?

And as if this were not enough, we who boast so much about our lead over others have slavishly copied Western technical progress and unthinkingly become jammed in a blind alley, finding ourselves together with the West in a crisis which threatens the existence of all mankind.

A family which has suffered a great misfortune or disgrace tries to withdraw into itself for a time to get over its grief by itself. This is what the Russian people must do: spend most of its time alone with itself, without neighbors and guests. It must concentrate on its inner tasks: on healing its soul, educating its children, putting its own house in order.

The healing of our souls! Nothing now is more important to us after all that we have lived through, after our long complicity in lies and even crimes. It may be too late for the older generations, but this only means that we must work with even greater zeal and selflessness to bring up our children, so that when they grow up they will be incomparably purer than our fallen society. The *school*—that is the key to the future of Russia! But it is a complicated and contradictory problem: Bad parents and teachers must rear better people to follow them. It cannot be solved in one generation. It will require immense efforts. The whole public educational system must be created anew, and not with rejects but with the people's best forces. It will cost billions and we should take them from our vainglorious and unnecessary foreign expenditure. We must stop running out into the street to join every brawl and instead retire virtuously into our own home so long as we are in such a state of disorder and confusion.

Fortunately we have such a home, a spacious and unsullied home preserved for us by history—the Russian Northeast. Let us give up trying to restore order overseas, keep our grabbing imperial hands off neighbors who want to live their own lives in freedom—and turn our national and political zeal toward the untamed expanses of the Northeast, whose emptiness is becoming intolerable to our neighbors now that life on earth is so tight packed.

The *Northeast* means the north of European Russia—Pinega, Mezen, Pechora—it means too the Lena and the whole central zone of Siberia north of the railway line, which is to this day deserted, in places virgin territory and unknown—there are hardly any open spaces like it left on the civilized earth. And then too the tundra and permafrost of the Lower Ob, Yamal, Taimyr, Khatango, Indigirka, Kolyma, Chukotka, and Kamchatka cannot be abandoned in despair, given the technological skills—and the population problems—of the twenty-first century.

The Northeast is the wind in our faces described by Voloshin: "In that wind is the whole destiny of Russia." The Northeast is the outward vector, which has long indicated the direction of Russia's natural movement and development. It was appreciated by Novgorod, but neglected by Muscovite Russia, partly opened up by a spontaneous movement that took place without state encouragement, then by the forced flight of the Old Believers. Peter the Great failed to see its significance, and in the last half century it has in effect been overlooked, despite all the sensational plans.

The Northeast is a reminder that Russia is the northeast of the planet, that our ocean is the Arctic, not the Indian Ocean, that we are not the Mediterranean nor Africa and that we have no business there! These boundless expanses, senselessly left stagnant and icily barren for four centuries, await our hands, our sacrifices, our zeal, and our love. But it may be that we have only two or three decades left for this work: Otherwise the imminent world population explosion will take these expanses away from us.

The Northeast is also the key to many apparently intricate Russian problems. Instead of casting greedy eyes on lands which do not really belong to us, or in which we are not in the majority, we should be directing our forces and urging our young people toward the Northeast—that is the far sighted solution. Its great expanses offer us a way out of the worldwide technological crisis. They offer us plenty of room in which to correct all our idiocies in building towns, industrial enterprises, power stations, and roads. Its cold and in places permanently frozen soil is still not ready for cultivation, it will require enormous inputs of energy—but the energy lies hidden in the depths of the Northeast itself, since we have not yet had time to squander it.

The Northeast could not be brought to life by camp watchtowers, the yells of armed guards and the barking of man-eating dogs. Only free people with a free understanding of our national mission can resurrect these great spaces, awaken them, heal them, beautify them with feats of engineering.

The Northeast—more than just a musical sound and more than just a geographical concept—will signify that Russia has resolutely opted for self-limitation, for turning inward rather than outward. In its whole future life—national, social, personal, in the schools, and in the family—it will concentrate its efforts on inward, not outward, growth.

This does not mean that we shall shut ourselves up within ourselves forever. This would not be in accordance with the outgoing Russian character. When we have recovered our health and put our house in order we shall undoubtedly want to help poor and backward peoples, and succeed in doing so. But not out of political self-interest, not to make them live as we do or serve us.

Some may wonder how far a nation, society, or state can go in self-limitation. Unlike the individual, a whole people cannot afford the luxury of impulsive and totally self-sacrificing decisions. If a people has gone over to self-limitation, but its neighbors have not, must it be ready to resist aggression?

Yes, of course. Defense forces must be retained, but only for genuinely defensive purposes, only on a scale adequate to real and not imaginary threats, not as an end in themselves, not as a self-perpetuating tradition, not to maintain the size and glamour of the high command. They will be retained in the hope that the whole atmosphere of mankind will soon begin to change.

And if it does not change, the Club of Rome has done the arithmetic: We have less than a hundred years to live.

November 1973

555

Live Not by Lies!

On the day Solzhenitsyn was arrested, February, 12, 1974, he released the text of "Live Not by Lies!" The next day, he was exiled to the West, where he received a hero's welcome. This moment marks the peak of his fame. Solzhenitsyn equates "lies" with ideology, the illusion that human nature and society can be reshaped to predetermined specifications. And his last word before leaving his homeland urges Soviet citizens as individuals to refrain from cooperating with the regime's lies. Even the most timid can take this least demanding step toward spiritual independence. If many march together on this path of passive resistance, the whole inhuman system will totter and collapse.

There was a time when we dared not rustle a whisper. But now we write and read samizdat and, congregating in the smoking rooms of research institutes, heartily complain to each other of all *they* are muddling up, of all *they* are dragging us into! There's that unnecessary bravado around our ventures into space, against the backdrop of ruin and poverty at home; and the buttressing of distant savage regimes; and the kindling of civil wars; and the ill-thought-out cultivation of Mao Zedong (at our expense to boot)—in the end we'll be the ones sent out against him, and we'll have to go, what other option will there be? And they put whomever they want on trial, and brand the healthy as mentally ill—and it is always "they," while *we* are—helpless.

We are approaching the brink; already a universal spiritual demise is upon us; a physical one is about to flare up and engulf us and our children, while we continue to smile sheepishly and babble:

"But what can we do to stop it? We haven't the strength."

We have so hopelessly ceded our humanity that for the modest handouts of today we are ready to surrender up all principles, our soul, all the labors of our ancestors, all the prospects of our descendants—anything to avoid disrupting our meager existence. We have lost our strength, our pride, our passion. We do not even fear a common nuclear death, do not fear a third world war (perhaps we'll hide away in some crevice), but fear only to take a civic stance! We hope only not to stray from the herd, not to set out on our own, and risk suddenly having to make do without the white bread, the hot water heater, a Moscow residency permit.

We have internalized well the lessons drummed into us by the state; we are forever content and comfortable with its premise: we cannot escape the *environment*, the social conditions; they shape us, "being determines consciousness." What have we to do with this? We can do nothing.

But we can do—everything!—even if we comfort and lie to ourselves that this is not so. It is not "they" who are guilty of everything, but *we ourselves*, only *we!*

Some will counter: But really, there is nothing to be done! Our mouths are gagged, no one listens to us, no one asks us. How can we make *them* listen to us?

To make them reconsider—is impossible.

The natural thing would be simply not to reelect them, but there are no re-elections in our country.

In the West they have strikes, protest marches, but we are too cowed, too scared: How does one just give up one's job, just go out onto the street?

All the other fateful means resorted to over the last century of Russia's bitter history are even less fitting for us today—true, let's not fall back on them! Today, when all the axes have hewn what they hacked, when all that was sown has borne fruit, we can see how lost, how drugged were those conceited youths who sought, through terror, bloody uprising, and civil war, to make the country just and content. No thank you, fathers of enlightenment! We now know that the vileness of the means begets the vileness of the result. Let our hands be clean!

So has the circle closed? So is there indeed no way out? So the only thing left to do is wait inertly: What if something just happens *by itself*?

But it will never come unstuck *by itself*, if we all, every day, continue to acknowledge, glorify, and strengthen it, if we do not, at the least, recoil from its most vulnerable point.

From lies.

When violence bursts onto the peaceful human condition, its face is flush with self-assurance, it displays on its banner and proclaims: "I am Violence! Make way, step aside, I will crush you!" But violence ages swiftly, a few years pass—and it is no longer sure of itself. To prop itself up, to appear decent, it will without fail call forth its ally—Lies. For violence has nothing to cover itself with but lies, and lies can only persist through violence. And it is not every day and not on every shoulder that violence brings down its heavy hand: It demands of us only a submission to lies, a daily participation in deceit—and this suffices as our fealty.

And therein we find, neglected by us, the simplest, the most accessible key to our liberation: a *personal nonparticipation in lies!* Even if all is covered by lies, even if all is under their rule, let us resist in the smallest way: Let their rule hold *not through me!*

And this is the way to break out of the imaginary encirclement of our inertness, the easiest way for us and the most devastating for the lies. For when people renounce lies, lies simply cease to exist. Like parasites, they can only survive when attached to a person.

We are not called upon to step out onto the square and shout out the truth, to say out loud what we think—this is scary, we are not ready. But let us at least refuse to say what we *do not* think!

This is the way, then, the easiest and most accessible for us given our deep-seated organic cowardice, much easier than (it's scary even to utter the words) civil disobedience à la Gandhi.

Our way must be: *Never knowingly support lies!* Having understood where the lies begin (and many see this line differently)—step back from that gangrenous edge! Let us not glue back the flaking scales of the Ideology, not gather back its crumbling bones, nor patch together its decomposing garb, and we will be amazed how swiftly and helplessly the lies will fall away, and that which is destined to be naked will be exposed as such to the world.

And thus, overcoming our temerity, let each man choose: Will he remain a witting servant of the lies (needless to say, not due to natural predisposition, but in order to provide a living for the family, to rear the children in the spirit of lies!), or has the time come for him to stand straight as an honest man, worthy of the respect of his children and contemporaries? And from that day onward he:

- Will not write, sign, nor publish in any way, a single line distorting, so far as he can see, the truth;
- Will not utter such a line in private or in public conversation, nor read it from a crib sheet, nor speak it in the role of educator, canvasser, teacher, actor;
- Will not in painting, sculpture, photograph, technology, or music depict, support, or broadcast a single false thought, a single distortion of the truth as he discerns it;
- Will not cite in writing or in speech a single "guiding" quote for gratification, insurance, for his success at work, unless he fully shares the cited thought and believes that it fits the context precisely;

- Will not be forced to a demonstration or a rally if it runs counter to his desire and his will; will not take up and raise a banner or slogan in which he does not fully believe;

- Will not raise a hand in vote for a proposal which he does not sincerely support; will not vote openly or in secret ballot for a candidate whom he deems dubious or unworthy;

- Will not be impelled to a meeting where a forced and distorted discussion is expected to take place;

- Will at once walk out from a session, meeting, lecture, play, or film as soon as he hears the speaker utter a lie, ideological drivel, or shameless propaganda;

- Will not subscribe to, nor buy in retail, a newspaper or journal that distorts or hides the underlying facts.

This is by no means an exhaustive list of the possible and necessary ways of evading lies. But he who begins to cleanse himself will, with a cleansed eye, easily discern yet other opportunities.

Yes, at first it will not be fair. Someone will have to temporarily lose his job. For the young who seek to live by truth, this will at first severely complicate life, for their tests and quizzes, too, are stuffed with lies, and so choices will have to be made. But there is no loophole left for anyone who seeks to be honest: Not even for a day, not even in the safest technical occupations can he avoid even a single one of the listed choices—to be made in favor of either truth or lies, in favor of spiritual independence or spiritual servility. And as for him who lacks the courage to defend even his own soul: Let him not brag of his progressive views, boast of his status as an academician or a recognized artist, a distinguished citizen or general. Let him say to himself plainly: I am cattle, I am a coward, I seek only warmth and to eat my fill.

For us, who have grown staid over time, even this most moderate path of resistance will be not be easy to set out upon. But how much easier it is than self-immolation or even a hunger strike: Flames will not engulf your body, your eyes will not pop out from the heat, and your family will always have at least a piece of black bread to wash down with a glass of clear water.

Betrayed and deceived by us, did not a great European people—the Czechoslovaks—show us how one can stand down the tanks with bared chest alone, as long as inside it beats a worthy heart?

It will not be an easy path, perhaps, but it is the easiest among those that lie before us. Not an easy choice for the body, but the only one for the soul. No, not an easy path, but then we already have among us people, dozens even, who have for years abided by all these rules, who live by the truth.

And so: We need not be the first to set out on this path, Ours is but to join! The more of us set out together, the thicker our ranks, the easier and shorter will this path be for us all! If we become thousands—they will not cope, they will be unable to touch us. If we will grow to tens of thousands—we will not recognize our country!

But if we shrink away, then let us cease complaining that someone does not let us draw breath—we do it to ourselves! Let us then cower and hunker down, while our comrades the biologists bring closer the day when our thoughts can be read and our genes altered.

And if from *this also* we shrink away, then we are worthless, hopeless, and it is of us that Pushkin asks with scorn:

> Why offer herds their liberation?
> . . . .
> Their heritage each generation
> The yoke with jingles, and the whip.

February 12, 1974

Harvard Address

June 8, 1978

Solzhenitsyn's June 8, 1978, commencement address at Harvard was the most controversial and commented upon public speech he delivered during his twenty-year exile in the West. His remarks on that occasion challenged many of the pieties that were dear to the contemporary intellectual clerisy. Like Tocqueville, Solzhenitsyn insisted that he spoke as a "friend, not as an adversary," of American democracy. He defended liberty under God and the law even as he criticized soulless legalism and lamented the growing "tilt of freedom toward evil" in the contemporary world. Far from defending political authoritarianism, as his critics sometimes claimed, Solzhenitsyn recommended "freely accepted and serene self-restraint" as the wisest and most prudent course for both individuals and societies. At the conclusion of his searching diagnosis of the modern crisis, Solzhenitsyn announced that the world had reached a "major watershed in history," one that required nothing less than an ascent to a new "anthropological stage" that would reconcile the legitimate claims of the human soul and the physical nature of man.

Solzhenitsyn's first tentative effort to sketch a morally serious and politically responsible "postmodernism" obviously has nothing in common with the nihilist currents that typically claim that name. In fact, Solzhenitsyn pointed out how vulnerable liberal humanism is to cooptation by more consistent and radical currents of modern thought. Moderate liberalism gave way to radicalism, radicalism to socialism, and socialism soon found itself powerless before communism's claim to embody the "full logic of materialistic development." For Solzhenitsyn, the inherent vulnerability of humanism to "the current which is farthest to the Left" goes some way toward explaining the shameful indulgence of many intellectuals to communism in the twentieth century.

In 1978 Solzhenitsyn's philosophical reflections on the crisis of modernity were overshadowed by his warnings about the imminent global threat posed by totalitarian communism. But now that Solzhenitsyn's principled opposition to totalitarianism has been fully vindicated, it is easier to embrace his claim that human freedom needs sturdier foundations than those provided by an "anthropocentric humanism" that refuses to defer to a "Superior Spirit" above Man. There was indeed a "measure of bitter truth" contained in Solzhenitsyn's powerful 1978 address. But far from being inspired by hostility to the West, Solzhenitsyn refuses to break faith with a civilization still capable of drawing intellectual and spiritual sustenance from "the moral heritage of Christian centuries with their rich reserves of mercy and sacrifice."

I am sincerely happy to be here with you on the occasion of the 327th commencement of this old and illustrious university. My congratulations and best wishes to all of today's graduates.

Harvard's motto is "Veritas." Many of you have already found out and others will find out in the course of their lives that truth eludes us as soon as our concentration begins to flag, all the while leaving the illusion that we are continuing to pursue it. This is the source of much discord. Also, truth seldom is sweet; it is almost invariably bitter. A measure of bitter truth is included in my speech today, but I offer it as a friend, not as an adversary.

Three years ago in the United States I said certain things that were rejected and appeared unacceptable. Today, however, many people agree with what I then said....

The split in today's world is perceptible even to a hasty glance. Any of our contemporaries readily identifies two world powers, each of them already capable of utterly destroying the other. However, the understanding of the split too often is limited to this political conception: the illusion according to which danger may be abolished through successful diplomatic negotiations or by achieving a balance of armed forces. The truth is that the split is both more profound and more alienating, that the rifts are more numerous than one can see at first glance. These deep manifold splits bear the danger of equally manifold disaster for all of us, in accordance with the ancient truth that a kingdom—in this case, our Earth—divided against itself cannot stand.

Contemporary Worlds

There is the concept of the Third World: Thus, we already have three worlds. Undoubtedly, however, the number is even greater; we are just too far away to see. Every ancient and deeply rooted self-contained culture, especially if it is spread over a wide part of the earth's surface, constitutes a self-contained world, full of riddles and surprises to Western thinking. As a minimum, we must include in this category China, India, the Muslim world, and Africa, if indeed we accept the approximation of viewing the latter two as uniform. For one thousand years Russia belonged to such a category, although Western thinking systematically committed the mistake of denying its special character and therefore never understood it, just as today the West does not understand Russia in Communist captivity. And while it may be that in past years Japan has increasingly become, in effect, a Far West, drawing ever closer to Western ways (I am no judge here), Israel, I think, should not be reckoned as part of the West, if only because of the decisive circumstance that its state system is fundamentally linked to religion.

How short a time ago, relatively, the small world of modern Europe was easily seizing colonies all over the globe, not only without anticipating any real resistance, but usually with contempt for any possible values in the conquered peoples' approach to life. It all seemed an overwhelming success, with no geographic limits. Western society expanded in a triumph of human independence and power. And all of a sudden the twentieth century brought the clear realization of this society's fragility. We now see that the conquests proved to be short-lived and precarious (and this, in turn, points to defects in the Western view of the world which led to these conquests). Relations with the former colonial world now have switched to the opposite extreme and the Western world often exhibits an excess of obsequiousness, but it is difficult yet to estimate the size of the bill which former colonial countries will present to the West and it is difficult to predict whether the surrender not only of its last colonies, but of everything it owns, will be sufficient for the West to clear this account.

Convergence

But the persisting blindness of superiority continues to hold the belief that all the vast regions of our planet should develop and mature to the level of contemporary Western systems, the best in theory and the most attractive in practice; that all those other worlds are but temporarily prevented (by wicked leaders or by severe crises or by their own barbarity and incomprehension) from pursuing Western pluralistic democracy and adopting the Western way of life. Countries are judged on the merit of their progress in that direction.

But in fact such a conception is a fruit of Western incomprehension of the essence of other worlds, a result of mistakenly measuring them all with a Western yardstick. The real picture of our planet's development bears little resemblance to all this.

The anguish of a divided world gave birth to the theory of convergence between the leading Western countries and the Soviet Union. It is a soothing theory which overlooks the fact that these worlds are not at all evolving toward each other and that neither one can be transformed into the other without violence. Besides, convergence inevitably means acceptance of the other side's defects, too, and this can hardly suit anyone.

If I were today addressing an audience in my country, in my examination of the overall pattern of the world's rifts I would have concentrated on the calamities of the East. But since my forced exile in the West has now lasted four years and since my audience is a Western one, I think it may be of greater interest to concentrate on certain aspects of the contemporary West, such as I see them.

A Decline in Courage

A decline in courage may be the most striking feature that an outside observer notices in the West today. The Western world has lost its civic courage, both as a whole and separately, in each country, in each government, in each political party, and, of course, in the United Nations. Such a decline in courage is particularly noticeable among the ruling and intellectual elites, causing an impression of a loss of courage by the entire society. There remain many courageous individuals, but they have no determining influence on public life. Political and intellectual functionaries exhibit this depression, passivity, and perplexity in their actions and in their statements, and even more so in their self-serving rationales as to how realistic, reasonable, and intellectually and even morally justified it is to base state policies on weakness and cowardice. And the decline in courage, at times attaining what could be termed a lack of manhood, is ironically emphasized by occasional outbursts of boldness and inflexibility on the part of those same functionaries when dealing with weak governments and with countries that lack support, or with doomed currents which clearly cannot offer any resistance. But they get tongue-tied and paralyzed when they deal with powerful governments and threatening forces, with aggressors and international terrorists.

Must one point out that from ancient times a decline in courage has been considered the first symptom of the end?

Well-Being

When the modern Western states were being formed, it was proclaimed as a principle that governments are meant to serve man and that man lives in order to be free and pursue happiness. (See, for example, the American Declaration of Independence.) Now at last during past decades technical and social progress has permitted the realization of such aspirations: the welfare state. Every citizen has been granted the desired freedom and material goods in such quantity and of such quality as to guarantee in theory the achievement of happiness, in the debased sense of the word which has come into being during those same decades. (In the process, however, one psychological detail has been overlooked: The constant desire to have still more things and a still better life and the struggle to this end imprint many Western faces with worry and even depression, though it is customary to carefully conceal such feelings. This active and tense competition comes to dominate all human thought and does not in the least open a way to free spiritual development.) The individual's independence from many types of state pressure has been guaranteed; the majority of the people have been granted well-being to an extent their fathers and grandfathers could not even dream about; it has become possible to raise young people according to these ideals, preparing them for and summoning them toward physical bloom, happiness, the possession of material goods, money, and leisure, toward an almost unlimited freedom in the choice of pleasures. So who should now renounce all this, why and for the sake of what should one risk one's precious life in defense of the common good and particularly in the nebulous case when the security of one's nation must be defended in an as yet distant land?

Even biology tells us that a high degree of habitual well-being is not advantageous to a living organism. Today, well-being in the life of Western society has begun to take off its pernicious mask.

Legalistic Life

Western society has chosen for itself the organization best suited to its purposes and one I might call legalistic. The limits of human rights and rightness are determined by a system of laws; such limits are very broad. People in the West have acquired considerable skill in using, interpreting, and manipulating law (though laws tend to be too complicated for an average person to understand without the help of an expert). Every conflict is solved according to the letter of the law and this is considered to be the ultimate solution. If one is right from a legal point of view, nothing more is required, nobody may mention that one could still not be entirely right, and urge self-restraint or a renunciation of these rights, call for sacrifice and selfless risk:

This would simply sound absurd. Voluntary self-restraint is almost unheard of: Everybody strives toward further expansion to the extreme limit of the legal frames. (An oil company is legally blameless when it buys up an invention of a new type of energy in order to prevent its use. A food product manufacturer is legally blameless when he poisons his produce to make it last longer: After all, people are free not to purchase it.)

I have spent all my life under a Communist regime and I will tell you that a society without any objective legal scale is a terrible one indeed. But a society with no other scale but the legal one is also less than worthy of man. A society based on the letter of the law and never reaching any higher fails to take advantage of the full range of human possibilities. The letter of the law is too cold and formal to have a beneficial influence on society. Whenever the tissue of life is woven of legalistic relationships, this creates an atmosphere of spiritual mediocrity that paralyzes man's noblest impulses.

And it will be simply impossible to bear up to the trials of this threatening century with nothing but the supports of a legalistic structure.

THE DIRECTION OF FREEDOM

Today's Western society has revealed the inequality between the freedom for good deeds and the freedom for evil deeds. A statesman who wants to achieve something important and highly constructive for his country has to move cautiously and even timidly; thousands of hasty (and irresponsible) critics cling to him at all times; he is constantly rebuffed by parliament and the press. He has to prove that his every step is well-founded and absolutely flawless. Indeed, an outstanding, truly great person who has unusual and unexpected initiatives in mind does not get any chance to assert himself; dozens of traps will be set for him from the beginning. Thus mediocrity triumphs under the guise of democratic restraints.

It is feasible and easy everywhere to undermine administrative power and it has in fact been drastically weakened in all Western countries. The defense of individual rights has reached such extremes as to make society as a whole defenseless against certain individuals. It is time, in the West, to defend not so much human rights as human obligations.

On the other hand, destructive and irresponsible freedom has been granted boundless space. Society has turned out to have scarce defense against the abyss of human decadence, for example against the misuse of liberty for moral violence against young people, such as motion pictures full of pornography, crime, and horror. This is all considered to be part of freedom and to be counterbalanced, in theory, by the young people's right not to look and not to accept. Life organized legalistically has thus shown its inability to defend itself against the corrosion of evil.

And what shall we say about the dark realms of overt criminality? Legal limits (especially in the United States) are broad enough to encourage not only individual freedom but also some misuse of such freedom. The culprit can go unpunished or obtain undeserved leniency—all with the support of thousands of defenders in the society. When a government earnestly undertakes to root out terrorism, public opinion immediately accuses it of violating the terrorists' civil rights. There are quite a number of such cases.

This tilt of freedom toward evil has come about gradually, but it evidently stems from a humanistic and benevolent concept according to which man—the master of this world—does not bear any evil within himself, and all the defects of life are caused by misguided social systems, which must therefore be corrected. Yet strangely enough, though the best social conditions have been achieved in the West, there still remains a great deal of crime; there even is considerably more of it than in the destitute and lawless Soviet society. (There is a multitude of prisoners in our camps who are termed criminals, but most of them never committed any crime; they merely tried to defend themselves against a lawless state by resorting to means outside the legal framework.)

THE DIRECTION OF THE PRESS

The press, too, of course, enjoys the widest freedom. (I shall be using the word "press" to include all the media.) But what use does it make of it?

Here again, the overriding concern is not to infringe the letter of the law. There is no true moral responsibility for distortion or disproportion. What sort of responsibility does a journalist or a newspaper have to the readership or to history? If they have misled public opinion by inaccurate information or wrong conclusions, even if they have contributed to mistakes on a state level, do we know of any case of open regret voiced by the same journalist or the same newspaper? No; this would damage sales. A nation may be the worse for such a mistake, but the journalist always gets away with it. It is most likely that he will start writing the exact opposite to his previous statements with renewed aplomb.

Because instant and credible information is required, it becomes necessary to resort to guesswork, rumors, and suppositions to fill in the voids, and none of them will ever be refuted; they settle into the readers' memory. How many hasty, immature, superficial, and misleading judgments are expressed every day, confusing readers, and are then left hanging? The press can act the role of public opinion or miseducate it. Thus we may see terrorists heroized, or secret matters pertaining to the nation's defense publicly revealed, or we may witness shameless intrusion into the privacy of well-known people according to the slogan "Everyone is entitled to know everything."

(But this is a false slogan of a false era; far greater in value is the forfeited right of people *not to know*, not to have their divine souls stuffed with gossip, nonsense, vain talk. A person who works and leads a meaningful life has no need for this excessive and burdening flow of information.)

Hastiness and superficiality—these are the psychic diseases of the twentieth century and more than anywhere else this is manifested in the press. In-depth analysis of a problem is anathema to the press; it is contrary to its nature. The press merely picks out sensational formulas.

Such as it is, however, the press has become the greatest power within the Western countries, exceeding that of the legislature, the executive, and the judiciary. Yet one would like to ask: According to what law has it been elected and to whom is it responsible? In the Communist East, a journalist is frankly appointed as a state official. But who has voted Western journalists into their positions of power, for how long a time, and with what prerogatives?

There is yet another surprise for someone coming from the totalitarian East with its rigorously unified press: One discovers a common trend of preferences within the Western press as a whole (the spirit of the time), generally accepted patterns of judgment, and maybe common corporate interests, the sum effect being not competition but unification. Unrestrained freedom exists for the press, but not for the readership, because newspapers mostly transmit in a forceful and emphatic way those opinions which do not too openly contradict their own and that general trend.

A Fashion in Thinking

Without any censorship in the West, fashionable trends of thought and ideas are fastidiously separated from those that are not fashionable, and the latter, without ever being forbidden, have little chance of finding their way into periodicals or books or being heard in colleges. Your scholars are free in the legal sense, but they are hemmed in by the idols of the prevailing fad. There is no open violence, as in the East; however, a selection dictated by fashion and the need to accommodate mass standards frequently prevents the most independent-minded persons from contributing to public life and gives rise to dangerous herd instincts that block successful development. In America, I have received letters from highly intelligent persons—maybe a teacher in a faraway small college who could do much for the renewal and salvation of his country, but the country cannot hear him because the media will not provide him with a forum. This gives birth to strong mass prejudices, to a blindness which is perilous in our dynamic era. An example is the self-deluding interpretation of the state of affairs in the contemporary world that functions as a sort of a petrified armor around people's minds, to such a degree that human voices from seventeen countries of Eastern Europe and

Eastern Asia cannot pierce it. It will be broken only by the inexorable crowbar of events.

I have mentioned a few traits of Western life which surprise and shock a new arrival to this world. The purpose and scope of this speech will not allow me to continue such a survey, in particular to look into the impact of these characteristics on important aspects of a nation's life, such as elementary education, advanced education in the humanities, and art.

Socialism

It is almost universally recognized that the West shows all the world the way to successful economic development, even though in past years it has been sharply offset by chaotic inflation. However, many people living in the West are dissatisfied with their own society. They despise it or accuse it of no longer being up to the level of maturity attained by mankind. And this causes many to sway toward socialism, which is a false and dangerous current.

I hope that no one present will suspect me of expressing my partial criticism of the Western system in order to suggest socialism as an alternative. No; with the experience of a country where socialism has been realized, I shall certainly not speak for such an alternative. The mathematician Igor Shafarevich, a member of the Soviet Academy of Science, has written a brilliantly argued book entitled *Socialism;* this is a penetrating historical analysis demonstrating that socialism of any type and shade leads to a total destruction of the human spirit and to a leveling of mankind into death. Shafarevich's book was published in France almost two years ago and so far no one has been found to refute it. It will shortly be published in English in the US.

Not a Model

But should I be asked, instead, whether I would propose the West, such as it is today, as a model to my country, I would frankly have to answer negatively. No, I could not recommend your society as an ideal for the transformation of ours. Through deep suffering, people in our country have now achieved a spiritual development of such intensity that the Western system in its present state of spiritual exhaustion does not look attractive. Even those characteristics of your life which I have just enumerated are extremely saddening.

A fact which cannot be disputed is the weakening of human personality in the West while in the East it has become firmer and stronger. Six decades for our people and three decades for the people of Eastern Europe; during that time we have been through a spiritual training far in advance of Western experience. The complex and deadly crush of life has produced stronger, deeper, and more interesting personalities than those generated by standardized Western well-being. Therefore, if our society were to be transformed into yours, it would mean an improvement in certain aspects, but also a change for the worse on some particularly significant points. Of course, a society cannot remain in an abyss of lawlessness, as is the case in our country. But it is also demeaning for it to stay on such a soulless and smooth plane of legalism, as is the case in yours. After the suffering of decades of violence and oppression, the human soul longs for things higher, warmer, and purer than those offered by today's mass living habits, introduced as by a calling card by the revolting invasion of commercial advertising, by TV stupor, and by intolerable music.

All this is visible to numerous observers from all the worlds of our planet. The Western way of life is less and less likely to become the leading model.

There are telltale symptoms by which history gives warning to a threatened or perishing society. Such are, for instance, a decline of the arts or a lack of great statesmen. Indeed, sometimes the warnings are quite explicit and concrete. The center of your democracy and of your culture is left without electric power for a few hours only, and all of a sudden crowds of American citizens start looting and creating havoc. The smooth surface film must be very thin, then, the social system quite unstable and unhealthy.

But the fight for our planet, physical and spiritual, a fight of cosmic proportions, is not a vague matter of the future; it has already started. The forces of Evil have begun their decisive offensive. You can feel their pressure, yet your screens and publications are full of prescribed smiles and raised glasses. What is the joy about?

SHORT-SIGHTEDNESS

Very well known representatives of your society, such as George Kennan, say: "We cannot apply moral criteria to politics." Thus we mix good and evil, right and wrong, and make space for the absolute triumph of absolute evil in the world. Only moral criteria can help the West against communism's well-planned world strategy. There are no other criteria. Practical or occasional considerations of any kind will inevitably be swept away by strategy. After a certain level of the problem has been reached, legalistic thinking induces paralysis; it prevents one from seeing the scale and the meaning of events.

In spite of the abundance of information, or maybe partly because of it, the West has great difficulty in finding its bearings amid contemporary events. There have been naïve predictions by some American experts who believed that Angola would become the Soviet Union's Vietnam or that the impudent Cuban expeditions in Africa would best be stopped by special US courtesy to Cuba. Kennan's advice to his own country—to begin unilateral disarmament—belongs to the same category. If you only knew how the youngest of the officials in Moscow's Old Square[1] roar with laughter at your political wizards! As to Fidel Castro, he openly scorns the United States, boldly sending his troops to distant adventures from his country right next to yours.

However, the most cruel mistake occurred with the failure to understand the Vietnam war. Some people sincerely wanted all wars to stop just as soon as possible; others believed that the way should be left open for national, or Communist, self-determination in Vietnam (or in Cambodia, as we see today with particular clarity). But in fact, members of the US antiwar movement became accomplices in the betrayal of Far Eastern nations, in the genocide and the suffering today imposed on thirty million people there. Do these convinced pacifists now hear the moans coming from there? Do they understand their responsibility today? Or do they prefer not to hear? The American intelligentsia lost its nerve and as a consequence the danger has come much closer to the United States. But there is no awareness of this. Your short-sighted politician who signed the hasty Vietnam capitulation seemingly gave America a carefree breathing pause; however, a hundredfold Vietnam now looms over you. Small Vietnam had been a warning and an occasion to mobilize the nation's courage. But if the full might of America suffered a full-fledged defeat at the hands of a small Communist half-country, how can the West hope to stand firm in the future?

I have said on another occasion that in the twentieth-century Western democracy has not won any major war by itself; each time it shielded itself with an ally possessing a powerful land army, whose philosophy it did not question. In World War II against Hitler, instead of winning the conflict with its own forces, which would certainly have been sufficient, Western democracy raised up another enemy, one that would prove worse and more powerful, since Hitler had neither the resources nor the people, nor the ideas with broad appeal, nor such a large number of supporters in the West—a fifth column—as the Soviet Union possessed. Some Western voices already have spoken of the need of a protective screen against hostile forces in the next world conflict; in this case, the shield would be China. But I would not wish such an outcome to any country in the world. First of all, it is again a doomed alliance with evil; it would grant the United States a respite, but when at a later date China with its billion people would turn around armed with American weapons, America itself would fall victim to a Cambodia-style genocide.

---

[1] The Old Square in Moscow (*Staraia ploshchad*) is the place where the headquarters of the Central Committee of the CPSU was located; it is the real name of what in the West is conventionally referred to as the Kremlin.

LOSS OF WILL

And yet, no weapons, no matter how powerful, can help the West until it overcomes its loss of willpower. In a state of psychological weakness, weapons even become a burden for the capitulating side. To defend oneself, one must also be ready to die; there is little such readiness in a society raised in the cult of material well-being. Nothing is left, in this case, but concessions, attempts to gain time, and betrayal. Thus at the shameful Belgrade conference, free Western diplomats in their weakness surrendered the line of defense for which enslaved members of the Helsinki Watch Groups are sacrificing their lives.

Western thinking has become conservative: The world situation must stay as it is at any cost; there must be no changes. This debilitating dream of a status quo is the symptom of a society that has ceased to develop. But one must be blind in order not to see that the oceans no longer belong to the West, while the land under its domination keeps shrinking. The two so-called world wars (they were by far not on a world scale, not yet) constituted the internal self-destruction of the small progressive West which has thus prepared its own end. The next war (which does not have to be an atomic one; I do not believe it will be) may well bury Western civilization forever.

In the face of such a danger, with such historical values in your past, with such a high level of attained freedom and, apparently, of devotion to it, how is it possible to lose to such an extent the will to defend oneself?

HUMANISM AND ITS CONSEQUENCES

How has this unfavorable relation of forces come about? How did the West decline from its triumphal march to its present debility? Have there been fatal turns and losses of direction in its development? It does not seem so. The West kept advancing steadily in accordance with its proclaimed social intentions, hand in hand with a dazzling progress in technology. And all of a sudden it found itself in its present state of weakness.

This means that the mistake must be at the root, at the very foundation of thought in modern times. I refer to the prevailing Western view of the world which was born in the Renaissance and has found political expression since the Age of Enlightenment. It became the basis for political and social doctrine and could be called rationalistic humanism or humanistic autonomy: the proclaimed and practiced autonomy of man from any higher force above him. It could also be called anthropocentricity, with man seen as the center of all.

The turn introduced by the Renaissance was probably inevitable historically: The Middle Ages had come to a natural end by exhaustion, having become an intolerable despotic repression of man's physical nature in favor of the spiritual one. But then we recoiled from the spirit and embraced all that is material, excessively and incommensurately. The humanistic way of thinking, which had proclaimed itself our guide, did not admit the existence of intrinsic evil in man, nor did it see any task higher than the attainment of happiness on earth. It started modern Western civilization on the dangerous trend of worshiping man and his material needs. Everything beyond physical well-being and the accumulation of material goods, all other human requirements and characteristics of a subtler and higher nature, were left outside the area of attention of state and social systems, as if human life did not have any higher meaning. Thus gaps were left open for evil, and its drafts blow freely today. Mere freedom per se does not in the least solve all the problems of human life and even adds a number of new ones.

And yet in early democracies, as in American democracy at the time of its birth, all individual human rights were granted on the ground that man is God's creature. That is, freedom was given to the individual conditionally, in the assumption of his constant religious responsibility. Such was the heritage of the preceding one thousand years. Two hundred or even fifty years ago, it would have seemed quite impossible, in America, that an individual be granted boundless freedom with no purpose, simply for the satisfaction of his whims. Subsequently, however, all such limitations were eroded everywhere in the West; a total emancipation occurred from the moral heritage of Christian centuries with their great reserves of mercy and sacrifice. State systems were becoming ever more materialistic. The West has finally achieved the rights of man, and even to excess, but man's sense of responsibility to God and society has grown dimmer and dimmer. In the past decades, the legalistic selfishness of the Western approach to the world has reached its peak and the world has found itself in a harsh spiritual crisis and a political impasse. All the celebrated technological achievements of progress, including the conquest of outer space, do not redeem the twentieth century's moral poverty, which no one could have imagined even as late as the nineteenth century.

An Unexpected Kinship

As humanism in its development was becoming more and more materialistic, it also increasingly allowed its concepts to be used first by socialism and then by communism. So that Karl Marx was able to say, in 1844, that "communism is naturalized humanism."

This statement has proved to be not entirely unreasonable. One does see the same stones in the foundations of an eroded humanism and of any type of socialism: boundless materialism; freedom from religion and religious responsibility (which under Communist regimes attains the stage of antireligious dictatorship); concentration on social structures with an allegedly scientific approach. (This last is typical of both the Age of Enlightenment and of Marxism.) It is no accident that all of communism's rhetorical vows revolve around Man (with a capital *M*) and his earthly happiness. At first glance it seems an ugly parallel: common traits in the thinking and way of life of today's West and today's East? But such is the logic of materialistic development.

The interrelationship is such, moreover, that the current of materialism which is farthest to the left, and is hence the most consistent, always proves to be stronger, more attractive, and victorious. Humanism which has lost its Christian heritage cannot prevail in this competition. Thus during the past centuries and especially in recent decades, as the process became more acute, the alignment of forces was as follows: Liberalism was inevitably pushed aside by radicalism, radicalism had to surrender to socialism, and socialism could not stand up to communism. The Communist regime in the East could endure and grow due to the enthusiastic support from an enormous number of Western intellectuals who (feeling the kinship!) refused to see communism's crimes, and when they no longer could do so, they tried to justify these crimes. The problem persists: In our Eastern countries, communism has suffered a complete ideological defeat; it is zero and less than zero. And yet Western intellectuals still look at it with considerable interest and empathy, and this is precisely what makes it so immensely difficult for the West to withstand the East.

BEFORE THE TURN

I am not examining the case of a disaster brought on by a world war and the changes which it would produce in society. But as long as we wake up every morning under a peaceful sun, we must lead an everyday life. Yet there is a disaster which is already very much with us. I am referring to the calamity of an autonomous, irreligious humanistic consciousness.

It has made man the measure of all things on earth—imperfect man, who is never free of pride, self-interest, envy, vanity, and dozens of other defects. We are now paying for the mistakes which were not properly appraised at the beginning of the journey. On the way from the Renaissance to our days we have enriched our experience, but we have lost the concept of a Supreme Complete Entity which used to restrain our passions and our irresponsibility. We have placed too much hope in politics and social reforms, only to find out that we were being deprived of our most precious possession: our spiritual life. It is trampled by the party mob in the East, by the commercial one in the West. This is the essence of the crisis: The split in the world is less terrifying than the similarity of the disease afflicting its main sections.

If, as claimed by humanism, man were born only to be happy, he would not be born to die. Since his body is doomed to death, his task on earth evidently must be more spiritual: not a total engrossment in everyday life, not the search for the best ways to obtain material goods and then their care-free consumption. It has to be the fulfillment of a permanent, earnest duty so that one's life journey may become above all an experience of moral growth: to leave life a better human being than one started it. It is imperative to reappraise the scale of the usual human values; its present incorrectness is astounding. It is not possible that assessment of the president's performance should be reduced to the question of how much money one makes or to the availability of gasoline. Only by the voluntary nurturing in ourselves of freely accepted and serene self-restraint can mankind rise above the world stream of materialism.

Today it would be retrogressive to hold on to the ossified formulas of the Enlightenment. Such social dogmatism leaves us helpless before the trials of our times.

Even if we are spared destruction by war, life will have to change in order not to perish on its own. We cannot avoid reassessing the fundamental definitions of human life and human society. Is it true that man is above everything? Is there no Superior Spirit above him? Is it right that man's life and society's activities should be ruled by material expansion above all? Is it permissible to promote such expansion to the detriment of our integral spiritual life?

If the world has not approached its end, it has reached a major watershed in history, equal in importance to the turn from the Middle Ages to the Renaissance. It will demand from us a spiritual blaze; we shall have to rise to a new height of vision, to a new level of life, where our physical nature will not be cursed, as in the Middle Ages, but even more importantly, our spiritual being will not be trampled upon, as in the Modern Era.

This ascension is similar to climbing onto the next anthropological stage. No one on earth has any other way left but—upward.

Templeton Lecture

LONDON, GUILDHALL, MAY 10, 1983

In 1983 in London, Solzhenitsyn received the Templeton Prize for Progress in Religion. As he explains in *The Little Grain*, memoirs of his years in exile, the Templeton Foundation's invitation had impressed him by citing passages from his works that were appropriate to this award. Although his habit had been to let his faith "flow silently but incontrovertibly," the nature of this occasion prompted him to lower his reserve and speak directly about his deepest beliefs. The process of writing about religion, he reports, became "a step toward greater understanding for myself." The result was his most explicit, sustained statement of his Christian commitment. Even so, attention remains fixed on the beliefs, rather than on the self in testimonial mode. He had experienced a similar increment of self-knowledge when he read a 1970 essay by Father Alexander Schmemann, who had observed that Solzhenitsyn's writings incorporated "intuitions" of the central Christian doctrines of creation, fall, and redemption. Solzhenitsyn testified that this essay "explained me to myself" and "formulated important traits of Christianity which I could not have formulated myself."

In the memorable opening lines of this lecture, Solzhenitsyn recalls that as a boy he had heard his elders' simple explanation for the calamities visited upon Russia: "Men have forgotten God." Then, however, he quickly turns these pithy words to the purpose of historical analysis. They remain, a half century later, his best explanation for what unfolded in his homeland, where hatred of God provided the primary motive force for the officially atheist Soviet regime. The same plain words summarize what happened in the West as well, where God-consciousness withered from neglect. Forgetting God has opened the door to the twentieth century's incalculable crimes and horrors. Although he dwells longest on Soviet examples, which he knows best and feels most deeply, the evil he beholds is elemental in character and global in scope.

The last five paragraphs of this speech, which in their richness repay slow reading and rereading, bring together broad themes that underlie all of Solzhenitsyn's writings. The key battleground in the conflict between good and evil is the individual human heart. Human beings are called to return to their Creator in repentance. God is personal, and his providential activity operates in individual lives. It also extends to the world as a whole. Solzhenitsyn's works characteristically end on the note of hope, and the conclusion of this speech makes clear that the ultimate source of his hope is God.

More than half a century ago, while I was still a child, I recall hearing a number of older people offer the following explanation for the great disasters that had befallen Russia: "Men have forgotten God; that's why all this has happened."

Since then I have spent well-nigh fifty years working on the history of our Revolution; in the process I have read hundreds of books, collected hundreds of personal testimonies, and have already contributed eight volumes of my own toward the effort of clearing away the rubble left by that upheaval. But if I were asked today to formulate as concisely as possible the main cause of the ruinous Revolution that swallowed up some sixty million of our people, I could not put it more accurately than to repeat: "Men have forgotten God; that's why all this has happened."

What is more, the events of the Russian Revolution can only be understood now, at the end of the century, against the background of what has since occurred in the rest of the world. What emerges here is a process of universal significance. And if I were called upon to identify briefly the principal trait of the *entire* twentieth century, here too I would be unable to find anything more precise and pithy than to repeat once again: "Men have forgotten God." The failings of human consciousness, deprived of its divine dimension, have been a determining factor in all the major crimes of this century. The first of these was World War I, and much of our present predicament can be traced back to it. That war (the memory of which seems to be fading) took place when Europe, bursting with health and abundance, fell into a rage of self-mutilation that could not but sap its strength for a century or more, and perhaps forever. The only possible explanation for this war is a mental eclipse among the leaders of Europe due to their lost awareness of a Supreme Power above them. Only a godless embitterment could have moved ostensibly Christian states to employ poison gas, a weapon so obviously beyond the limits of humanity.

The same kind of defect, the flaw of a consciousness lacking all divine dimension, was manifested after World War II when the West yielded to the satanic temptation of the nuclear umbrella. It was equivalent to saying: Let's cast off our worries, let's free the younger generation from its duties and obligations, let's make no effort to defend ourselves, to say nothing of defending others—let's stop our ears to the groans emanating from the East, and let us live instead in the pursuit of happiness. If danger should threaten us, we shall be protected by the nuclear bomb; if not, then let the world be burned in Hell for all we care. The pitifully helpless state to which the contemporary West has sunk is in large measure due to this fatal error: the belief that the defense of peace depends not on stout hearts and steadfast men, but solely on the nuclear bomb.

Only the loss of that higher intuition which comes from God could have allowed the West to accept calmly, after World War I, the protracted agony of Russia as she was being torn apart by a band of cannibals, or to accept, after World War II, the similar dismemberment of Eastern Europe. The West did not perceive that this was in fact the beginning of a lengthy process that spells disaster for the whole world; indeed the West has done a good deal to help the process along. Only once in this century did the West gather its strength—for the battle against Hitler. But the fruits of that victory have long since been lost. Faced with cannibalism, our godless age has discovered the perfect anaesthetic—trade! Such is the pathetic pinnacle of contemporary wisdom.

Today's world has reached a stage that, if it had been described to preceding centuries, would have called forth the cry: "This is the Apocalypse!"

Yet we have grown used to this kind of world; we even feel at home in it.

Dostoevsky warned that "great events could come upon us and catch us intellectually unprepared." That is precisely what has happened. And he predicted that "the world will be saved only after a visitation by the demon of evil." Whether it really will be saved we shall have to wait and see; this will depend on our conscience, on our spiritual lucidity, on our individual and combined efforts in the face of catastrophic circumstances. But it has already come to pass that the demon of evil, like a whirlwind, triumphantly circles all five continents of the earth.

We are witnesses to the devastation of the world, be it imposed or voluntarily undergone. The entire twentieth century is being sucked into the vortex of atheism and self-destruction. This plunge into the abyss has aspects that are unquestionably global, dependent neither on political systems, nor on levels of economic and cultural development, nor yet on national peculiarities. And present-day Europe, seemingly so unlike the Russia of 1913, is today on the verge of the same collapse, for all that it has been reached by a different route. Different parts of the world have followed different paths, but today they are all approaching the threshold of a common ruin.

In its past, Russia did know a time when the social ideal was not fame, or riches, or material success, but a pious way of life. Russia was then steeped in an Orthodox Christianity that remained true to the Church of the first centuries. The Orthodoxy of that time knew how to safeguard its people under the yoke of a foreign occupation that lasted more than two centuries, while at the same time fending off iniquitous blows from the swords of Western crusaders. During those centuries the Orthodox faith in our country became part of the very patterns of thought and the personality of our people, the forms of daily life, the work calendar, the priorities in every undertaking, the organization of the week and of the year. Faith was the shaping and unifying force of the nation.

But in the seventeenth century Russian Orthodoxy was gravely weakened by an internal schism. In the eighteenth, the country was shaken by Peter's forcibly imposed transformations, which favored the economy, the state, and the military at the expense of the religious spirit and national life. And along with this lopsided Petrine enlightenment, Russia felt the first whiff of secularism; its subtle poisons permeated the educated classes in the course of the nineteenth century and opened the path to Marxism. By the time of the Revolution, faith had virtually disappeared in Russian educated circles; among the uneducated, too, faith had declined.

It was Dostoevsky, once again, who drew from the French Revolution and its seething hatred of the Church the lesson that "revolution must necessarily begin with atheism." That is absolutely true. But the world had never before known a godlessness as organized, militarized, and tenaciously malevolent as that practiced by Marxism. Within the philosophical system of Marx and Lenin, and at the heart of their psychology, hatred of God is the principal driving force, more fundamental than all their political and economic pretensions. Militant atheism is not merely incidental or marginal to Communist policy; it is not a side effect, but the central pivot. To achieve its diabolical ends, Communism needs to control a population devoid of religious and national feeling, and this entails the destruction of faith and nationhood. Communists proclaim both of these objectives openly, and just as openly go about carrying them out. The degree to which the atheistic world longs to annihilate religion, the extent to which religion sticks in its throat, was demonstrated by the web of intrigue surrounding the recent attempts on the life of the Pope.

The 1920s in the USSR witnessed an uninterrupted procession of victims and martyrs among the Orthodox clergy. Two metropolitans were shot, one of whom, Veniamin of Petrograd, had been elected by the popular vote of his diocese. Patriarch Tikhon himself passed through the hands of the Cheka-GPU and then died under suspicious circumstances. Scores of archbishops and bishops perished. Tens of thousands of priests, monks, and nuns, pressured by the Chekists to renounce the word of God, were tortured, shot in cellars, sent to camps, exiled to the desolate tundra of the far north, or turned out into the streets in their old age without food or shelter. All these Christian martyrs went unswervingly to their deaths for the faith; instances of apostasy were few and far between.

For tens of millions of laymen access to the Church was blocked, and they were forbidden to bring up their children in the faith: Religious parents were wrenched from their children and thrown into prison, while the children were turned from the faith by threats and lies. One could argue that the pointless destruction of Russia's rural economy in the 1930s—the so-called de-kulakization and collectivization, which brought death to 15 million peasants while making no economic sense at all—was enforced with such cruelty, first and foremost, for the purpose of destroying our national way of life and of extirpating religion from the countryside. The same policy of spiritual perversion operated throughout the brutal world of the Gulag Archipelago, where men were encouraged to survive at the cost of the lives of others. And only atheists bereft of reason could have decided upon the ultimate brutality—against the Russian land itself—that is being planned in the USSR today: The Russian north is to be flooded, the flow of the northern rivers reversed, the life of the Arctic Ocean disrupted, and the water channeled southward, toward lands already devastated by earlier, equally foolhardy "feats of Communist construction."

For a short period of time, when he needed to gather strength for the struggle against Hitler, Stalin cynically adopted a friendly posture toward the Church. This deceptive game, continued in later years by Brezhnev with the help of showcase publications and other window dressing, has unfortunately tended to be taken at face value in the West. Yet the tenacity with which hatred of religion is rooted in Communism may be judged by the example of its most liberal leader, Khrushchev: For though he undertook a number of significant steps to extend freedom, Khrushchev simultaneously rekindled the frenzied Leninist obsession with destroying religion.

But there is something they did not expect: that in a land where churches have been leveled, where a triumphant atheism has rampaged uncontrolled for two-thirds of a century, where the clergy is utterly humiliated and deprived of all independence, where what remains of the Church as an institution is tolerated only for the sake of propaganda directed at the West, where even today people are sent to labor camps for their faith and where, within the camps themselves, those who gather to pray at Easter are clapped in punishment cells—they could not suppose that beneath this Communist steamroller the Christian tradition would survive in Russia. It is true that millions of our countrymen have been corrupted and spiritually devastated by an officially imposed atheism, yet there remain many millions of believers: It is only external pressures that keep them from speaking out, but, as is always the case in times of persecution and suffering, the awareness of God in my country has attained great acuteness and profundity.

It is here that we see the dawn of hope: For no matter how formidably Communism bristles with tanks and rockets, no matter what successes it attains in seizing the planet, it is doomed never to vanquish Christianity.

The West has yet to experience a Communist invasion; religion here remains free. But the West's own historical evolution has been such that today it too is experiencing a drying up of religious consciousness. It too has witnessed racking schisms, bloody religious wars, and rancor, to say nothing of the tide of secularism that, from the late Middle Ages onward, has progressively inundated the West. This gradual sapping of strength from within is a threat to faith that is perhaps even more dangerous than any attempt to assault religion violently from without.

Imperceptibly, through decades of gradual erosion, the meaning of life in the West has ceased to be seen as anything more lofty than the "pursuit of happiness," a goal that has even been solemnly guaranteed by constitutions. The concepts of good and evil have been ridiculed for several centuries; banished from common use, they have been replaced by political or class considerations of short-lived value. It has become embarrassing to appeal to eternal concepts, embarrassing to state that evil makes its home in the individual human heart before it enters a political system. Yet it is not considered shameful to make daily concessions to an integral evil. Judging by the continuing landslide of concessions made before the eyes of our own generation alone, the West is ineluctably slipping toward the abyss. Western societies are losing more and more of their religious essence as they thoughtlessly yield up their younger generation to atheism. If a blasphemous film about Jesus[1] is shown throughout the United States, reputedly one of the most religious countries in the world, or a major newspaper publishes a shameless caricature of the Virgin Mary, what further evidence of godlessness does one need? When external rights are completely unrestricted, why should one make an inner effort to restrain oneself from ignoble acts?

---

[1] *Life of Brian*, a British film of 1979 by Monty Python.

Or why should one refrain from burning hatred, whatever its basis—race, class, or ideology? Such hatred is in fact corroding many hearts today. Atheist teachers in the West are bringing up a younger generation in a spirit of hatred of their own society. Amid all the vituperation we forget that the defects of capitalism represent the basic flaws of human nature, allowed un-limited freedom together with the various human rights; we forget that un-der Communism (and Communism is breathing down the neck of all mod-erate forms of socialism, which are unstable) the identical flaws run riot in any person with the least degree of authority; while everyone else under that system does indeed attain "equality"—the equality of destitute slaves.

This eager fanning of the flames of hatred is becoming the mark of today's free world. Indeed, the broader the personal freedoms are, the higher the level of prosperity or even of abundance—the more vehement, paradoxi-cally, does this blind hatred become. The contemporary developed West thus demonstrates by its own example that human salvation can be found neither in the profusion of material goods nor in merely making money.

This deliberately nurtured hatred then spreads to all that is alive, to life itself, to the world with its colors, sounds, and shapes, to the human body. The embittered art of the twentieth century is perishing as a result of this ugly hate, for art is fruitless without love. In the East art has collapsed be-cause it has been knocked down and trampled upon, but in the West the fall has been voluntary, a decline into a contrived and pretentious quest where the artist, instead of attempting to reveal the divine plan, tries to put himself in the place of God.

Here again we witness the single outcome of a worldwide process, with East and West yielding the same results, and once again for the same reason: Men have forgotten God.

Confronted by the onslaught of worldwide atheism, believers are dis-united and frequently bewildered. And yet the Christian (or post-Christian) world would do well to note the example of the Far East. I have recently had an opportunity to observe in Free China and in Japan how, despite their apparently less clearly defined religious concepts, and despite the same un-assailable "freedom of choice" that exists in the West, both the younger gen-eration and society as a whole have preserved their moral sensibility to a greater degree than the West has, and have been less affected by the destruc-tive spirit of secularism.

What can one say about the lack of unity among the various religions, if Christianity has itself become so fragmented? In recent years the major Chris-tian churches have taken steps toward reconciliation. But these measures are far too slow; the world is perishing a hundred times more quickly. No one expects the churches to merge or to revise all their doctrines, but only to present a common front against atheism. Yet even for such a purpose the steps taken are much too slow.

There does exist an organized movement for the unification of the churches, but it presents an odd picture. The World Council of Churches seems to care more for the success of revolutionary movements in the Third World, all the while remaining blind and deaf to the persecution of religion where this is carried through most consistently—in the USSR. No one can fail to see the facts; must one conclude, then, that it is deemed expedient not to see, not to get involved? But if that is the case, what remains of Christianity?

It is with profound regret that I must note here something which I cannot pass over in silence. My predecessor in the receipt of this prize last year[2]— in the very month that the award was made—lent public support to Communist lies by his deplorable statement that he had not noticed the persecution of religion in the USSR. Before the multitude of those who have perished and who are oppressed today, may God be his judge.

It seems more and more apparent that even with the most sophisticated of political maneuvers, the noose around the neck of mankind draws tighter and more hopeless with every passing decade, and there seems to be no way out for anyone—neither nuclear, nor political, nor economic, nor ecological. That is indeed the way things appear to be.

With such global events looming over us like mountains, nay, like entire mountain ranges, it may seem incongruous and inappropriate to recall that the primary key to our being or non-being resides in each individual human heart, in the heart's preference for specific good or evil. Yet this remains true even today, and it is, in fact, the most reliable key we have. The social theories that promised so much have demonstrated their bankruptcy, leaving us at a dead end. The free people of the West could reasonably have been expected to realize that they are beset by numerous freely nurtured falsehoods, and not to allow lies to be foisted upon them so easily. All attempts to find a way out of the plight of today's world are fruitless unless we redirect our consciousness, in repentance, to the Creator of all: Without this, no exit will be illumined, and we shall seek it in vain. The resources we have set aside for ourselves are too impoverished for the task. We must first recognize the horror perpetrated not by some outside force, not by class or national enemies, but within each of us individually, and within every society. This is especially true of a free and highly developed society, for here in particular we have surely brought everything upon ourselves, of our own free will. We ourselves, in our daily unthinking selfishness, are pulling tight that noose.

---

[2] The American evangelist Billy Graham.

Let us ask ourselves: Are not the ideals of our century false? And is not our glib and fashionable terminology just as unsound, a terminology that offers superficial remedies for every difficulty? Each of them, in whatever sphere, must be subjected to a clear-eyed scrutiny while there is still time. The solution of the crisis will not be found along the well-trodden paths of conventional thinking.

Our life consists not in the pursuit of material success but in the quest for worthy spiritual growth. Our entire earthly existence is but a transitional stage in the movement toward something higher, one rung of the ladder. Material laws alone do not explain our life or give it direction. The laws of physics and physiology will never reveal the indisputable manner in which the Creator constantly, day in and day out, participates in the life of each of us, unfailingly granting us the energy of existence; when this assistance leaves us, we die. And in the life of our entire planet the Divine Spirit surely moves with no less force: This we must grasp in our dark and terrible hour.

To the ill-considered hopes of the last two centuries, which have reduced us to insignificance and brought us to the brink of nuclear and non-nuclear death, we can propose only a determined quest for the warm hand of God, which we have so rashly and self-confidently spurned. Only in this way can our eyes be opened to the errors of this unfortunate twentieth century and our hands be directed to setting them right. There is nothing else to cling to in the landslide: The combined vision of all the thinkers of the Enlightenment amounts to nothing.

Our five continents are caught in a whirlwind. But it is during trials such as these that the highest gifts of the human spirit are manifested. If we perish and lose this world, the fault will be ours alone.

Playing Upon the Strings of Emptiness
In Acceptance of the National Arts Club
Medal of Honor for Literature
NEW YORK, JANUARY 19, 1993

In January 1993, the storied National Arts Club of New York City awarded Solzhenitsyn its medal of honor for literature. His acceptance speech, delivered by his son Ignat, extends the literary theorizing in his *Nobel Lecture* and examines contemporary literature's malaise. The radical relativism of postmodernism yields nihilistic literature that discards God, truth, an ordered universe, and a moral compass. Such literature has destructive effects on society. The "healthy conservatism" that he recommends promotes creativity without jettisoning tradition. In spirit this approach is akin to T. S. Eliot's literary theory and parallels Solzhenitsyn's middle way in politics. The *New York Times* pasted onto this essay the crude title "The Relentless Cult of Novelty and How It Wrecked the Century."

There is a long-accepted truth about art that "style is the man" (*le style est l'homme*). This means that every work of a skilled musician, artist, or writer is shaped by an absolutely unique combination of personality traits, creative abilities, and individual, as well as national, experience. And since such a combination can never be repeated, art (but I shall here speak primarily of literature) possesses infinite variety across the ages and among different peoples. The divine plan is such that there is no limit to the appearance of ever new and dazzling creative talents, none of whom, however, negate in any way the works of their outstanding predecessors, even though they may be five hundred or two thousand years removed. The unending quest for what is new and fresh is never closed to us, but this does not deprive our grateful memory of all that came before.

No new work of art comes into existence (whether consciously or unconsciously) without an organic link to what was created earlier. But it is equally true that a healthy conservatism must be flexible both in terms of creation and perception, remaining equally sensitive to the old and to the new, to venerable and worthy traditions, and to the freedom to explore, without which no future can ever be born. At the same time the artist must not forget that creative freedom can be dangerous, for the fewer artistic limitations he imposes on his own work, the less chance he has for artistic success. The loss of a responsible organizing force weakens or even ruins the structure, the meaning, and the ultimate value of a work of art.

Every age and every form of creative endeavor owes much to those outstanding artists whose untiring labors brought forth new meanings and new rhythms. But in the twentieth century the necessary equilibrium between tradition and the search for the new has been repeatedly upset by a falsely understood "avant-gardism"—a raucous, impatient "avant-gardism" at any cost. Dating from before World War I, this movement undertook to destroy all commonly accepted art—its forms, language, features, and properties—in its drive to build a kind of "superart," which would then supposedly spawn the New Life itself. It was suggested that literature should start anew "on a blank sheet of paper." (Indeed, some never went much beyond this stage.) Destruction, thus, became the apotheosis of this belligerent avant-gardism. It aimed to tear down the entire centuries long cultural tradition, to break and disrupt the natural flow of artistic development by a sudden leap forward. This goal was to be achieved through an empty pursuit of novel forms as an end in itself, all the while lowering the standards of craftsmanship for oneself to the point of slovenliness and artistic crudity, at times combined with a meaning so obscured as to shade into unintelligibility.

This aggressive impulse might be interpreted as a mere product of personal ambition, were it not for the fact that in Russia (and I apologize to those gathered here for speaking mostly of Russia, but in our time it is impossible to bypass the harsh and extensive experience of my country), in Russia this impulse and its manifestations preceded and foretold the most *physically* destructive revolution of the twentieth century. Before erupting on the streets of Petrograd, this cataclysmic revolution erupted on the pages of the artistic and literary journals of the capital's bohemian circles. It is there that we first heard scathing imprecations against the entire Russian and European way of life, the calls to sweep away all religions or ethical codes, to tear down, overthrow, and trample all existing traditional culture, along with the self-extolment of the desperate innovators themselves, innovators who never did succeed in producing anything of worth. Some of these appeals literally called for the destruction of the Racines, the Murillos, and the Raphaels, "so that bullets would bounce off museum walls." As for the classics of Russian literature, they were to be "thrown overboard from the ship of modernity." Cultural history would have to begin anew. The cry was "Forward, forward!"—its authors already called themselves "futurists," as though they had now stepped over and beyond the present, and were bestowing upon us what was undoubtedly the genuine art of the Future.

But no sooner did the revolution explode in the streets, than those "futurists" who only recently, in their manifesto entitled *A Slap in the Face of Public Taste,* had preached an "insurmountable hatred toward the existing language"— these same "futurists" changed their name to the "Left Front," now directly joining the revolution at its left-most flank. It thus became clear that the earlier outbursts of this "avant-gardism" were no mere literary froth, but had very real embodiment in life. Beyond their intent to overturn the entire culture, they aimed to uproot life itself. And when the Communists gained unlimited power (their own battle cry called for tearing the existing world "down to its foundations," so as to build a new Unknown Beautiful World in its stead, with equally unlimited brutality) they not only opened wide the gates of publicity and popularity to this horde of so-called "avant-gardists," but even gave some of them, as to faithful allies, power to administrate over culture.

Granted, neither the ragings of this pseudo-"avant-garde" nor its power over culture lasted long; there followed a general coma of all culture. We in the USSR began to trudge, downcast, through a seventy-year-long ice age, under whose heavy glacial cover one could barely discern the secret heartbeat of a handful of great poets and writers. These were almost entirely unknown to their own country, not to mention the rest of the world, until much later. With the ossification of the totalitarian Soviet regime, its inflated pseudo-culture ossified as well, turning into the loathsome ceremonial forms of so-called "socialist realism." Some individuals have been eager to devote numerous critical analyses to the essence and significance of this phenomenon. I would not have written a single one, for it is outside the bounds of art altogether: The *object* of study, the style of "socialist realism," never existed. One does not need to be an expert to see that it consisted of nothing more than servility, a style defined by "What would you care for?" or "Write whatever the Party commands." What scholarly discussion can possibly take place here?

And now, having lived through these seventy lethal years inside Communism's iron shell, we are crawling out, though barely alive. A new age has clearly begun, both for Russia and for the whole world. Russia lies utterly ravaged and poisoned; its people are in a state of unprecedented humiliation, and are on the brink of perishing physically, perhaps even biologically.

Given the current conditions of national life, and the sudden exposure and ulceration of the wounds amassed over the years, it is only natural that literature should experience a pause. The voices that bring forth the nation's literature need time before they can begin to sound once again.

However, some writers have emerged who appreciate the removal of censorship and the new, unlimited artistic freedom mostly in one sense: for allowing uninhibited "self-expression." The point is to *express* one's own perception of one's surroundings, often with no sensitivity toward today's ills and scars, and with a visible emptiness of heart; to express the personality of an author, whether it is significant or not; to express it with no sense of responsibility toward the morals of the public, and especially of the young; and at times thickly lacing the language with obscenities which for hundreds of years were considered unthinkable to put in print, but now seem to be almost in vogue.

The confusion of minds after seventy years of total oppression is more than understandable. The artistic perception of the younger generations finds itself in shock, humiliation, resentment, and amnesia. Unable to find in themselves the strength fully to withstand and refute Soviet dogma in the past, many young writers have now given in to the more accessible path of pessimistic relativism. Yes, they say, Communist doctrines were a great lie; but then again, absolute truths do not exist anyhow, and trying to find them is pointless. Nor is it worth the trouble to strive for some kind of higher meaning.

And in one sweeping gesture of vexation, classical Russian literature—which never disdained reality and sought the truth—is dismissed as next to worthless. Denigrating the past is deemed to be the key to progress. And so it has once again become fashionable in Russia to ridicule, debunk, and toss overboard the great Russian literature, steeped as it is in love and compassion toward all human beings, and especially toward those who suffer. And in order to facilitate this operation of discarding, it is announced that the lifeless and servile "socialist realism" had in fact been an organic continuation of full-blooded Russian literature.

Thus we witness, through history's various thresholds, a recurrence of one and the same perilous anti-cultural phenomenon, with its rejection of and contempt for all foregoing tradition, and with its mandatory hostility toward whatever is universally accepted. Before, it burst in upon us with the fanfares and gaudy flags of "futurism"; today the term "post-modernism" is applied. (Whatever the meaning intended for this term, its lexical makeup involves an incongruity: the seeming claim that a person can think and experience after the period in which he is destined to live.)

For a post-modernist, the world does not possess values that have reality. He even has an expression for this: "the world as text," as something secondary, as the text of an author's work, wherein the primary object of interest is the author himself in his relationship to the work, his own introspection. Culture, in this view, ought to be directed inward at itself (which is why these works are so full of reminiscences, to the point of tastelessness); it alone is valuable and real. For this reason the concept of play acquires a heightened importance—not the Mozartian playfulness of a Universe overflowing with joy—but a forced playing upon the strings of emptiness, where an author need have no responsibility to anyone. A denial of any and all ideals is considered courageous. And in this voluntary self-delusion, "post-modernism" sees itself as the crowning achievement of all previous culture, the final link in its chain. (A rash hope, for already there is talk of the birth of "conceptualism," a term that has yet to be convincingly defined in terms of its relationship to *art*, though no doubt this too will duly be attempted. And then there is already "post-avant-gardism"; and it would be no surprise if we were to witness the appearance of a "post-post-modernism," or of a "post-futurism.") We could have sympathy for this constant searching, but only as we have sympathy for the suffering of a sick man. The search is doomed by its theoretical premises to forever remaining a secondary or ternary exercise, devoid of life or of a future.

But let us shift our attention to the more complex flow of this process. Even though the twentieth century has seen the more bitter and disheartening lot fall to the peoples under Communist domination, our whole world is living through a century of spiritual illness, which could not but give rise to a similar ubiquitous illness in art. Although for other reasons, a similar "post-modernist" sense of confusion about the world has also arisen in the West.

Alas, at a time of an unprecedented rise in the material benefits of civilization and ever-improving standards of living, the West, too, has been undergoing an erosion and obscuring of high moral and ethical ideals. The spiritual axis of life has grown dim, and to some lost artists the world has now appeared in seeming senselessness, as an absurd conglomeration of debris.

Yes, world culture today is of course in crisis, a crisis of great severity. The newest directions in art seek to outpace this crisis on the wooden horse of clever stratagems—on the assumption that if one invents deft, resourceful new methods, it will be as though the crisis never was. Vain hopes. Nothing worthy can be built on a neglect of higher meanings and on a relativistic view of concepts and culture as a whole. Indeed, something greater than a phenomenon confined to art can be discerned shimmering here beneath the surface—shimmering not with light but with an ominous crimson glow.

Looking intently, we can see that behind these ubiquitous and seemingly innocent experiments of rejecting "antiquated" tradition there lies a deep-seated hostility toward any spirituality. This relentless cult of novelty, with its assertion that art need not be good or pure, just so long as it is new, newer, and newer still, conceals an unyielding and long-sustained attempt to undermine, ridicule and uproot all moral precepts. There is no God, there is no truth, the universe is chaotic, all is relative, "the world as text," a text any post-modernist is willing to compose. How clamorous it all is, but also—how helpless.

For several decades now, world literature, music, painting, and sculpture have exhibited a stubborn tendency to grow not higher, but to the side, not toward the highest achievements of craftsmanship and of the human spirit, but toward their disintegration into a frantic and insidious "novelty." To decorate public spaces we put up sculptures that aestheticize pure ugliness—but we no longer register surprise. And if visitors from outer space were to pick up our music over the airwaves, how could they ever guess that earthlings once had a Bach, a Beethoven, and a Schubert, now abandoned as out of date and obsolete?

If we, the creators of art, will obediently submit to this downward slide, if we cease to hold dear the great cultural tradition of the foregoing centuries together with the spiritual foundations from which it grew—we will be contributing to a highly dangerous fall of the human spirit on earth, to a degeneration of mankind into some kind of lower state, closer to the animal world.

And yet, it is hard to believe that we will allow this to occur. Even in Russia, so terribly ill right now—we wait and hope that after the coma and a period of silence, we shall feel the breath of a reawakening Russian literature, and that we shall witness the arrival of the fresh new forces of our younger brothers.

This address was delivered orally by Ignat Solzhenitsyn, acting for the author, in New York City on January 19, 1993. The text was published in the New York Times Book Review *of February 7, 1993.*

We have ceased to see the Purpose

Address to the International Academy of Philosophy

LIECHTENSTEIN, SEPTEMBER 14, 1993

On September 14, 1993, Aleksandr Solzhenitsyn delivered his valedictory address to the Western world. Speaking to a receptive audience of conservative-minded Catholics in the tiny principality of Liechtenstein, Solzhenitsyn reprises the principal themes of his controversial 1978 Harvard address. He highlights "the justifiable and necessary share of morality in politics" and appeals to voluntary self-limitation as the wisest means for directing modern Progress ("which cannot be stopped by anyone or anything") towards the "perpetration of good." The Liechtenstein address can even be read as a salutary self-correction. While Solzhenitsyn could not recommend the West as a model for Russia in every respect, he emphatically praises "its historically unique stability of civic life under the rule of law." This speech is strikingly more restrained than its 1978 predecessor. Solzhenitsyn fixes his gaze more intently on "eternal questions" such as the problem of death and the underlying purpose of things that have lost none of their importance in our contemporary world.

Above all, the Liechtenstein address clarifies Solzhenitsyn's relationship to the "modern world." It shows that the Nobel laureate does not so much reject modernity as refuse its willful identification of moral progress with technological progress. With characteristic lucidity, Solzhenitsyn defends the "one true Progress: the sum total of the spiritual progresses of individuals; the degree of self-perfection in the course of their lives." Without ignoring pressing political matters, Solzhenitsyn remains focused on the permanent things, the things of the spirit that ultimately endure.

Each time I arrive in the principality of Liechtenstein, I recall with emotion that outstanding lesson in courage which this tiny country and its esteemed prince, the late Franz Joseph II, presented to the world in 1945: Standing up to the relentless menace of the Soviet military machine, they did not hesitate to shelter a detachment of Russian anti-Communists seeking refuge from Stalin's tyranny.

This example is all the more instructive because in those same months the mighty democratic powers, authors of the Atlantic Charter, with its ringing promise of freedom for all the oppressed of the earth, sought to ingratiate themselves with the victorious Stalin by yielding up into slavery all of Eastern Europe, and turning over—from the West's own territory!—hundreds upon hundreds of thousands of Soviet citizens, against their expressed will, disregarding the suicides of some right there on the spot. With base force, these people were literally prodded with bayonets into Stalin's murderous reach, towards the torments of concentration camp and death. It was appropriate that the Soviet people lay down their lives by the millions for the common victory with the West, but, it turned out, they themselves did not have the right to freedom. (And it is astonishing that the free Western press helped to cover up this crime for twenty-five years. No one, either at the time or later, has called those British and American generals and administrators *war criminals* for their deeds, much less brought them to trial.)

POLITICS AND ETHICS

This contrast between the courageous act of little Liechtenstein and the act of betrayal in the halls of the Great Powers naturally leads us further: What is the role, the justifiable and necessary share of morality in politics?

Erasmus believed politics to be an ethical category, and called on it to manifest ethical impulses. But that, of course, was in the sixteenth century.

And then came our Enlightenment, and by the eighteenth century we had learned from John Locke that it is inconceivable to apply moral terms to the State and its actions. Politicians, who throughout history were so often free of burdensome moral constraints, had thus obtained something of an added theoretical justification. Moral impulses among statesmen have always been weaker than political ones, but in our time the consequences of their decisions have grown in scale.

Moral criteria applicable to the behavior of individuals, families, and small circles certainly cannot be transferred on a one-to-one basis to the behavior of states and politicians; there is no exact equivalence, as the scale, the momentum, and the tasks of governmental structures introduce a certain deformation. States, however, are led by politicians, and politicians are ordinary people, whose actions have an impact on other ordinary people. Moreover, the fluctuations of political behavior are often quite removed from the imperatives of State. Therefore, any moral demands we impose on individuals, such as understanding the difference between honesty, baseness, and deception, between magnanimity, goodness, avarice, and evil, must to a large degree be applied to the politics of countries, governments, parliaments, and parties.

In fact, if state, party, and social policy are not based on morality, then mankind has no future to speak of. The converse is true: If the politics of a state or the conduct of an individual is guided by a moral compass, this turns out to be not only the most humane but, in the long run, the most prudent behavior for one's own future.

Among the Russian people, for one, this concept—understood as an ideal to be aimed for, and expressed by the word *truth (pravda)* and the phrase *to live by the truth (zhit' po pravde)*—has never been extinguished. And even at the murky end of the nineteenth century, the Russian philosopher Vladimir Solovyov insisted that, from a Christian point of view, moral and political activity are tightly linked, that political activity must a priori be *moral service,* whereas politics motivated by the mere pursuit of interests lacks any Christian content whatsoever.

Alas, in my homeland today these moral axes have fallen into even greater disuse than in the West, and I recognize the present vulnerability of my position in passing such judgments. When, in what had been the USSR, seven decades of appalling pressure were followed by the sudden and wide-open unchecked freedom to act, in circumstances of all-around poverty, the result was that many were swept down the path of shamelessness, unrestrainedly adopting the worst features of human behavior. It must be noted here that, for seventy years, annihilation was visited upon people in our country not in a purely random fashion but was directed at those with outstanding mental and moral qualities. And so the picture in Russia today is bleaker and more savage than if it were simply the result of the general shortcomings of our human nature.

But let us not partition the misfortune between countries and nations: The misfortune is for all of us to share, as we stand at the end of Christianity's second millennium. Moreover, should we so lightly fling about this term—morality?

BENTHAM'S BEHEST

The eighteenth century left us the precept of Jeremy Bentham: Morality is that which gives pleasure to the greatest number of persons; man can never desire anything except that which favors the preservation of his own existence. And the eagerness with which the civilized world took up so convenient and precious an advice was astonishing! Cold calculation holds sway in business relations, and has even become accepted as normal behavior. To yield in some way to an opponent or competitor is considered an unforgivable blunder for the party having an advantage in position, power, or wealth. The ultimate measure of every event, action, or intention is a purely legalistic one. This was designed as an obstacle to immoral behavior, and it is often successful; but sometimes, in the form of "legal realism," it facilitates precisely such behavior.

We can only be grateful that human nature resists this legalistic hypnosis, that it does not allow itself to be lulled into spiritual lethargy and apathy towards the misfortunes of others: For many in the well-to-do West respond with spirit and warmth to far-off pain and suffering by donating goods, money, and not infrequently expending significant personal effort.

INFINITE PROGRESS

Human knowledge and human abilities continue to be perfected; they cannot, and must not, be brought to a halt. By the eighteenth century this process began to accelerate and grew more apparent. Anne-Robert-Jacques-Turgot gave it the sonorous title of Progress, meaning that Progress based on economic development would inevitably and directly lead to a general mollification of the human temperament.

This resonant label was widely adopted and grew into something of a universal and proud philosophy of life: we are *progressing!* Educated mankind readily put its faith in this Progress. And yet somehow no one pressed the issue: progress yes, but *in what?* And *of what?* And might we not lose something in the course of this Progress? It was enthusiastically assumed that Progress would engulf all aspects of existence and mankind in its entirety. It was from this intense optimism of Progress that Marx, for one, concluded that history will lead us to justice without the help of God.

Time passed, and it turned out that Progress is *indeed* marching on, and is even stunningly surpassing expectations, but it is doing so only in the field of technological civilization (with especial success in creature comforts and military innovations).

Progress has indeed proceeded magnificently, but has led to consequences which the previous generations could not have foreseen.

PROGRESS IN CRISIS

The first trifle which we overlooked and only recently discovered is that unlimited Progress cannot occur within the limited resources of our planet; that nature needs to be supported rather than conquered; that we are successfully *eating up* the environment allotted to us. (Thank heaven the alarm has been sounded, especially in developed countries, and rescue operations have begun, although on much too small a scale. And one of the most positive consequences of Communism's collapse is the disintegration of the world's most senseless, recklessly wasteful economy, a tempting model for so many nations.)

The second misjudgment turned out to be that human nature did not become gentler with Progress, as was promised. All we had forgotten was the human soul.

We have allowed our wants to grow unchecked, and are now at a loss where to direct them. And with the obliging assistance of commercial enterprises, newer and yet newer wants are concocted, some wholly artificial; and we chase after them *en masse*, but find no fulfillment. And we never shall.

The endless accumulation of possessions? That will not bring fulfillment either. (Discerning individuals have long since understood that possessions must be subordinated to other, higher principles, that they must have a spiritual justification, a mission; otherwise, as Nikolai Berdyaev put it, they bring ruin to human life, becoming the tools of avarice and oppression.)

Modern transportation has flung the world wide open to people in the West. Even without it, modern man can all but leap out beyond the confines of his being; through the eyes of television he is present throughout the whole planet all at the same time. Yet it turns out that from this spasmodic pace of technocentric Progress, from the oceans of superficial information and cheap spectacles, the human soul does not grow, but instead grows more shallow, and spiritual life is only reduced. Our culture, accordingly, grows poorer and dimmer, no matter how it tries to drown out its decline with the din of empty novelties. As creature comforts continue to improve for the average person, so spiritual development grows stagnant. Surfeit brings with it a nagging sadness of the heart, as we sense that the whirlpool of pleasures does not bring satisfaction, and that, before long, it may suffocate us.

No, all hope cannot be pinned on science, technology, or economic growth. The victory of technological civilization has also instilled in us a spiritual insecurity. Its gifts enrich, but enslave us as well. All is *interests*, we must not neglect our *interests*, all is a struggle for material things; but an inner voice tells us that we have lost something pure, elevated, and fragile. We have ceased to see *the purpose*.

Let us admit, even if in a whisper and only to ourselves: In this hustle of life at breakneck speed—*what* are we living for?

THE ETERNAL QUESTIONS REMAIN

It is up to us to stop seeing Progress (which cannot be stopped by anyone or anything) as a stream of unlimited blessings, and to view it rather as a gift from on high, sent down for an extremely intricate trial of our free will.

The gifts of the telephone and television, for instance, when used without moderation, fragment the wholeness of our time, jerking us from the natural flow of our life. The gift of lengthened life expectancy has, as one of its consequences, made the elder generation into a burden for its children, while dooming the former to a lingering loneliness, to abandonment in old age by loved ones, and to an irreparable rift from the joy of passing on their experience to the young.

Horizontal ties between people are being severed as well. With all the seeming effervescence of political and social life, alienation and apathy towards others have grown stronger in human relations. Consumed in their pursuit of material interests, people find only an overwhelming loneliness. (It is this that gave rise to the howl of existentialism.)

We must not simply lose ourselves in the mechanical flow of Progress, but strive to harness it in the interests of the human spirit; not to become the mere playthings of Progress, but rather to seek or expand ways of directing its might towards the perpetration of good.

Progress was understood to be a shining and unswerving vector, but it turned out to be a complex and twisted curve, which has once more brought us back to the very same eternal questions which loomed in earlier times, except that facing these questions then was easier for a less distracted, less disconnected mankind.

We have lost the harmony with which we were created, the internal harmony between our spiritual and physical being. We have lost that clarity of spirit which was ours when the concepts of Good and Evil had yet to become a subject of ridicule, shoved aside by the principle of fifty-fifty.

And nothing so bespeaks the current helplessness of our spirit, our intellectual disarray, as the loss of a clear and calm attitude towards *death*. The greater his well-being, the deeper the chilling fear of death cuts into the soul of modern man. This mass fear, a fear the ancients did not know, was born of our insatiable, loud, and bustling life. Man has lost the sense of himself as a limited point in the universe, albeit one possessed of free will. He began to deem himself the center of his surroundings, adapting not himself to the world but the world to himself. And then, of course, the thought of death becomes unbearable: It is the extinction of the entire universe at a stroke.

Having refused to recognize the unchanging Higher Power above us, we have filled that space with personal imperatives, and suddenly life has become a harrowing prospect indeed.

AFTER THE COLD WAR

The middle of the twentieth century passed for all of us under the cloud of the nuclear threat, a menace fierce beyond the limits of imagination. It seemed to blot out all the vices of life. Everything else seemed insignificant: We are lost for anyhow, so why not live as we please? And this great Threat also served both to halt the development of the human spirit and to postpone our reflection on the meaning of our life.

But paradoxically, this same danger temporarily gave Western society something of a unifying purpose of existence: to withstand the lethal menace of Communism. By no means did all fully understand this threat, and in no sense was this firmness equally absorbed by all in the West; there appeared not a few faint hearts thoughtlessly undermining the West's stand. But the preponderance of responsible people in government preserved the West and allowed for victory in the struggles for Berlin and Korea, for the survival of Greece and Portugal. (Yet there was a time when the Communist chieftains could have delivered a lightning blow, probably without receiving a nuclear one in return. It may be that only the hedonism of those decrepit chieftains served to postpone their scheme, until President Reagan derailed them with a new, spiraling, and ultimately unbearable arms race.)

And so, at the end of the twentieth century there burst forth a sequence of events, expected by many of my countrymen but catching many in the West by surprise: Communism collapsed due to its inherent lack of viability and from the weight of the accumulated rot within. It collapsed with incredible speed, and in a dozen countries at once. The nuclear threat suddenly was no more.

And then? A few short months of joyful relief swept over the world (while some bemoaned the death of the earthly Utopia, of the Socialist Paradise on Earth). It passed, but somehow the planet did not grow calmer; it seems instead that with a greater frequency something flares up here or explodes there; even scraping together enough UN forces for peacekeeping has become no easy task.

Besides, Communism is far from dead on the territory of the former USSR. In some republics, its institutional structures have survived in their entirety, while in all of them millions of Communist cadres remain in reserve, and its roots remain embedded in the consciousness and the daily life of the people. At the same time, under the nascent savage nonproducing capitalism, ugly new ulcers have surfaced from years of torment, ushering in such repulsive forms of behavior and such plunder of the nation's wealth as the West has not known. This, in turn, has even brought an unprepared and unprotected populace to a nostalgia for the "equality in poverty" of the past.

Although the earthly ideal of Socialism-Communism has collapsed, the problems which it purported to solve remain: the brazen use of social advantage and the inordinate power of money, which often direct the very course of events. And if the global lesson of the twentieth century does not serve as a healing inoculation, then the vast red whirlwind may repeat itself in its entirety.

The cold war is over, but the problems of modern life have been laid bare as immensely more complex than what had hitherto seemed to fit into the two dimensions of the political plane. That earlier crisis of the meaning of life and that same spiritual vacuum (which during the nuclear decades had even deepened from neglect) stand out all the more. In the era of the balance of nuclear terror this vacuum was somehow obscured by the illusion of attained stability on the planet, a stability which has proved only transitory. But now the former implacable question looms all the clearer: What is our destination?

ON THE EVE OF THE TWENTY-FIRST CENTURY

Today we are approaching a symbolic boundary between centuries, and even millennia: Less than eight years separate us from this momentous juncture (which, in the restless spirit of modern times, will be proclaimed a year early, not waiting until the year 2001).

Who among us does not wish to meet this solemn divide with exultation and in a ferment of hope? Many thus greeted the twentieth, as a century of elevated reason, in no way imagining the cannibalistic horrors that it would bring. Only Dostoyevsky, it seems, foresaw the coming of totalitarianism.

The twentieth century did not witness a growth of morality in mankind. Exterminations, on the other hand, were carried out on an unprecedented scale, culture declined sharply, the human spirit waned. (The nineteenth century, of course, did much to prepare this outcome.) So what reason have we to expect that the twenty-first century, one bristling with first-class weaponry on all sides, will be kinder to us?

And then there is environmental ruin. And the global population explosion. And the colossal problem of the Third World, still called so in quite an inadequate generalization. It constitutes four-fifths of modern mankind, and soon will make up five-sixths, thus becoming the most important component of the twenty-first century. Drowning in poverty and misery, it will, no doubt, soon step forward with an ever-growing list of demands to the advanced nations. (Such thoughts were in the air as far back as the dawn of Soviet Communism. It is little known, for example, that in 1921 the Tatar nationalist and Communist Sultan Galiev called for the creation of an International of colonial and semicolonial nations, and for the establishment of its dictatorship over the advanced industrial states.) Today, looking at the growing stream of refugees bursting through all European borders, it is difficult for the West not to see itself as something of a fortress—a secure one for the time being, but clearly one besieged. And in the future, the growing ecological crisis may alter the climatic zones—leading to shortages of fresh water and arable land in places where they were once plentiful. This, in turn, may give rise to new and menacing conflicts on the planet, wars for survival.

A complex balancing act thus arises before the West. While maintaining full respect for the entire precious pluralism of world cultures and for their search for distinct social solutions, the West cannot at the same time lose sight of its own values, its historically unique stability of civic life under the rule of law—a hard-won stability which grants independence and space to every private citizen.

Self-Limitation

The time is urgently upon us to limit our wants. It is difficult to bring ourselves to sacrifice and self-denial, because in political, public, and private life we have long since dropped the golden key of self-restraint to the ocean floor. But self-limitation is the fundamental and wisest step of a man who has obtained his freedom. It is also the surest path towards its attainment. We must not wait for external events to press harshly upon us or even topple us; we must take a conciliatory stance and through prudent self-restraint learn to accept the inevitable course of events.

Only our conscience, and those close to us, know how we deviate from this rule in our personal lives. Examples of deviations from this course by larger entities—parties and governments—are in full view of all.

When a conference of the alarmed peoples of the earth convenes in the face of the unquestionable and imminent threat to the planet's environment and atmosphere, a mighty power (one consuming not much less than half of the earth's currently available resources and emitting half of its pollution) insists, because of its present-day internal interests, on lowering the demands of a sensible international agreement, as though it does not itself live on the same earth. Then other leading countries shirk from fulfilling even these reduced demands. Thus, in an economic race, we are poisoning ourselves.

Similarly, the breakup of the USSR along the fallacious Lenin-drawn borders has provided striking examples of newborn formations, which, in the pursuit of great-power imagery, rush to occupy extensive territories that are historically and ethnically alien to them—territories containing tens of thousands, or in some cases millions, of ethnically different people—giving no thought to the future, imprudently forgetting that taking never brings one to any good.

It goes without saying that the application of the principle of self-restraint to groups, professions, parties, or entire countries raises difficult questions which outnumber the answers already found. On this scale, all commitments to sacrifice and self-denial will have repercussions for multitudes of people who are perhaps unprepared for or opposed to them. (And even the personal self-restraint of a consumer will have an effect on producers somewhere.)

And yet, if we do not learn to limit firmly our desires and demands, to subordinate our interests to moral criteria—we, humankind, will simply be torn apart, as the worst aspects of human nature bare their teeth.

It has been pointed out by various thinkers many times (and I quote here the words of the twentieth century Russian philosopher Nikolai Lossky): If a personality is not directed at values higher than the self, corruption, and decay inevitably take hold. Or, if you will permit me to share a personal observation: We can only experience true spiritual satisfaction not in seizing, but in refusing to seize. In other words: in self-limitation.

Today it appears to us as something wholly unacceptable, constraining, and even repulsive, because we have over the centuries grown unaccustomed to what for our ancestors had been a habit born of necessity. They lived with far greater external constraints, and had far fewer opportunities. The paramount importance of self-restraint has only in this century arisen in its pressing entirety before mankind. Yet, taking into account even the various mutual links running through contemporary life, it is nonetheless only through self-restraint that we can gradually cure both our economic and political life, albeit with much difficulty.

Today, not many will readily accept this principle for themselves. However, in the increasingly complex circumstances of our modernity, to limit ourselves is the only true path of preservation for us all.

And it helps bring back the awareness of a Whole and Higher Authority above us—and the altogether forgotten sense of humility before this Entity.

There can be only one true Progress: the sum total of the spiritual progresses of individuals; the degree of self-perfection in the course of their lives.

We were recently entertained by a naïve fable of the happy arrival at the "end of history,"[1] of the overflowing triumph of an all-democratic bliss; the ultimate global arrangement had supposedly been attained.

But we all see and sense that something very different is coming, something new, and perhaps quite stern. No, tranquility does not promise to descend upon our planet, and will not be granted us so easily.

And yet, surely, we have not experienced the trials of the twentieth century in vain. Let us hope: We have, after all, been tempered by these trials, and our hard-won firmness will in some fashion be passed on to the following generations.

---

[1] Solzhenitsyn is referring to Francis Fukuyama's famous claim (in a widely discussed 1989 article in the *National Interest* and in his 1992 book *The End of History and the Last Man*) that the end of the Cold War had brought an end to the rivalry of regimes and ideologies and that, henceforth, liberal democracy was the only legitimate and credible political arrangement in the world.

A Reflection on the Vendée Uprising

Delivered at the dedication of a memorial in

Lucs-sur-Boulogne, France

SEPTEMBER 25, 1993

In the fall of 1993 Solzhenitsyn traveled to Western Europe to say his final goodbyes before his imminent return to Russia. On September 25 he delivered the principal address at the dedication of a memorial to the tens of thousands of Frenchmen who perished between 1793 and 1795 during the Vendée uprising in western France.

It is not surprising that this dramatic uprising would capture the imagination of the Russian Nobel laureate. Ordinary French peasants, loyal to king, country, and their ancestral faith, rose up to defend their traditional way of life against the forced imposition of revolutionary despotism. Solzhenitsyn could not help noticing the direct parallel between the desperate heroism of the Catholic peasants of the Vendée and that of those ordinary Russian peasants who refused to submit to the Bolshevik yoke and were ground down mercilessly during the early years of the Leninist regime. In his remarks on the Vendée uprising, Solzhenitsyn honors "the resistance and the sacrifice" of both sets of heroes and warns against the revolutionary illusion that human nature can be transformed at a stroke. His eloquent defense of evolutionary social change and his identification of terror with an ideology of inexorable Progress are central to his political reflection as a whole.

Mr. President of the General Council of the Vendée, Respected Vendéans:

Two thirds of a century ago, while still a boy, I read with admiration about the courageous and desperate uprising of the Vendée. But never could I have even dreamed that in my later years I would have the honor of dedicating a memorial to the heroes and victims of that uprising.

Twenty decades have now passed, and throughout that period the Vendée uprising and its bloody suppression have been viewed in ever new ways, in France and elsewhere. Indeed, historical events are never fully understood in the heat of their own time, but only at a great distance, after a cooling of passions. For all too long, we did not want to hear or admit what *cried out* with the voices of those who perished, or were burned alive: that the peasants of a hard-working region, driven to the extremes of oppression and humiliation by a revolution supposedly carried out for their sake—that these peasants had risen up *against* the revolution!

That revolution brings out instincts of primordial barbarism, the sinister forces of envy, greed, and hatred—this even its contemporaries could see all too well. They paid a terrible enough price for the mass psychosis of the day, when merely *moderate* behavior, or even the perception of such, already appeared to be a crime. But the twentieth century has done especially much to tarnish the romantic luster of revolution which still prevailed in the eighteenth century. As half-centuries and centuries have passed, people have learned from their own misfortunes that revolutions demolish the organic structures of society, disrupt the natural flow of life, destroy the best elements of the population and give free rein to the worst; that a revolution never brings prosperity to a nation, but benefits only a few shameless opportunists, while to the country as a whole it heralds countless deaths, widespread impoverishment, and, in the gravest cases, a long-lasting degeneration of the people.

The very word "revolution" (from the Latin *revolvo*) means "to roll back," "to go back," "to experience anew," "to re-ignite," or at best "to turn over"—hardly a promising list. Today, if the attribute "great" is ever attached to a revolution, this is done very cautiously, and not infrequently with much bitterness.

It is now better and better understood that the social improvements which we all so passionately desire can be achieved through normal evolutionary development—with immeasurably fewer losses and without all-encompassing decay. We must be able to improve, patiently, that which we have in any given "today."

It would be vain to hope that revolution can improve human nature, yet your revolution, and especially our Russian Revolution, hoped for this very effect. The French Revolution unfolded under the banner of a self-contradictory and unrealizable slogan, "liberty, equality, fraternity." But in the life of society, liberty, and equality are mutually exclusive, even hostile concepts. Liberty, by its very nature, undermines social equality, and equality suppresses liberty—for how else could it be attained? Fraternity, meanwhile, is of entirely different stock; in this instance it is merely a catchy addition to the slogan. True fraternity is achieved by means not social but spiritual. Furthermore, the ominous words "or death!" were added to the threefold slogan, thereby effectively destroying its meaning.

I would not wish a "great revolution" upon any nation. Only the arrival of Thermidor[1] prevented the eighteenth-century revolution from destroying France. But the revolution in Russia was not restrained by any Thermidor as it drove our people on the straight path to a bitter end, to an abyss, to the depths of ruin.

It is a pity that there is no one here today who could speak of the suffering endured in the depths of China, Cambodia, or Vietnam, and could describe the price they had to pay for revolution.

One might have thought that the experience of the French revolution would have provided enough of a lesson for the rationalist builders of "the people's happiness" in Russia. But no, the events in Russia were grimmer yet, and incomparably more enormous in scale. Lenin's Communists and International Socialists studiously reenacted on the body of Russia many of the French revolution's cruelest methods—only they possessed a much greater and more systematic level of organizational control than the Jacobins.

We had no Thermidor, but to our spiritual credit we did have our Vendée, in fact more than one. These were the large peasant uprisings: Tambov (1920–21), western Siberia (1921). We know of the following episode: Crowds of peasants in handmade shoes, armed with clubs and pitchforks, converged on Tambov, summoned by church bells in the surrounding villages—and were cut down by machine-gun fire. For eleven months the Tambov uprising held out, despite the Communists' effort to crush it with armored trucks, armored trains, and airplanes, as well as by taking families of the rebels hostage. They were even preparing to use poison gas. The Cossacks, too—from the Ural, the Don, the Kuban, the Terek—met Bolshevism with intransigent resistance that finally drowned in the blood of genocide.

And so, in dedicating this memorial to your heroic Vendée, I see double in my mind's eye—for I can also visualize the memorials which will one day rise in Russia, monuments to our Russian resistance against the onslaught of Communism and its atrocities.

---

[1] A reference to the relative normalization of French politics and society that followed the overthrow of Robespierre and the Jacobin "reign of terror" on the 9th of Thermidor (July 27, 1794).

We all have lived through the twentieth century, a century of terror, the chilling culmination of that Progress about which so many dreamed in the eighteenth century. And now, I think, more and more citizens of France, with increasing understanding and pride, will remember and value the resistance and the sacrifice of the Vendée.

Cavendish Farewell

FEBRUARY 28, 1994

Shortly after Solzhenitsyn and his family took up residence at Cavendish, Vermont, in 1976, he appeared at a town meeting to introduce himself. Confidently predicting that "the day will come when [my people] will be cured of this disease" which is the Communist system, he vowed, "On that day I will thank you for your friendly neighborliness and your goodwill—and will go home to my motherland!" The local citizens stood and applauded. In 1994, "that day" came, and he again attended a town meeting to say thanks and goodbye. Another hearty ovation ensued.

Truly, these townspeople deserved Solzhenitsyn's gratitude. They had greeted him amiably whenever they saw him but otherwise had left him alone and shielded him from prying outsiders. The only sign in town mentioning his name was outside the general store: "No directions to the Solzhenitsyn home." His happiest years of writing unhindered were those passed at Cavendish. He left behind autographed copies of his books for the local public library and special friends. His matter-of-fact praise for the "grassroots democracy" practiced at New England town-hall meetings undercuts the allegation that he is antidemocratic. As he says in *Rebuilding Russia* and elsewhere, post-Soviet Russia, too, needs to develop democracy from the bottom up.

Citizens of Cavendish, our dear neighbors,

At the town meeting seventeen years ago I told you about my exile and explained the steps which I took to ensure a peaceful working environment, without the burden of constant visitors.

You were very understanding; you forgave me my unusual way of life, and even took it upon yourselves to protect my privacy. For this, I have been truly grateful throughout all these years; and now, as my stay here comes to an end, I thank you. Your kindness and cooperation helped to create the best possible conditions for my work.

I have worked here for almost eighteen years. It has been the most productive period in my life. I have done all that I wanted to do. Today, I offer those of my books that have been translated well into English to the town library.

Our children grew up and went to school here, alongside your children. For them, Vermont is home. Indeed, our whole family has felt at home among you. Exile is always difficult, and yet I could not imagine a better place to live, and wait, and wait for my return home, than Cavendish, Vermont.

Now, at the end of May, my wife and I will go back to Russia, which is going through one of the most difficult periods in its history—a period in which the majority of the population lives in poverty, and standards of human decency have fallen, a period of lawlessness and economic chaos. That is the painful price we have had to pay to rid ourselves of communism, during whose seventy-year reign of terror we lost up to sixty million people, just from the regime's war on its own nation. I hope that I can be of at least some help to my tortured nation, although it is impossible to predict how successful my efforts will be. Besides, I am not young.

Here in Cavendish, and in the surrounding towns, I have observed the sensible and sure process of grassroots democracy, in which the local population solves most of its problems on its own, not waiting for the decisions of higher authorities. Unfortunately, we do not have this in Russia, and that is still our greatest shortcoming.

My sons will complete their education in America, and the house in Cavendish will remain their home.

Lately, while walking on the nearby roads, taking in the surroundings with a farewell glance, I have found every meeting with any neighbor to be warm and friendly.

And so today, both to those of you whom I have met over these years, and to those whom I haven't met, I say: Thank you and farewell. I wish all the best to Cavendish. God bless you all.

Greeting at Vladivostok

MAY 27, 1994

On May 27, 1994, Solzhenitsyn returned home in the flesh, thus fulfilling his longstanding, improbable prediction. His three prerequisites had, also improbably, been met: citizenship restored, treason charges dropped, and all his writings published in Russia. He sprang a surprise by entering Russia through the Pacific coast's "back door," so to speak. He landed at Magadan, capital of Kolyma, where the harshest Soviet prison camps had been located. Having thereby identified himself symbolically with his "*zek* [prisoner] nation," he proceeded to Vladivostok, where four thousand citizens had braved hours of rain to welcome him. Though later speeches would call people to repent for their individual and collective guilt in the Soviet tragedy, the main theme of this first speech is commiseration.

After addressing a thousand cheering university students, Solzhenitsyn launched a two-month cross-country train trip to Moscow. As a writer rather than a politician, he took copious notes of citizens' concerns at each whistle stop; and, as promised, he transmitted them to the leaders. All along, he conceded uncertainty about what he could accomplish—and with good reason. His views appealed to ordinary people more than to Moscow's elites. As the novelty of his return wore off, the public spotlight turned elsewhere.

Dear countrymen! Through all the years of my exile, I have followed intensively the life of our nation. I never doubted that communism was doomed to collapse, but I was always fearful that our exit from it, the price of it, would be terribly painful. And now, I feel the doubled pain for Russia's last two years, which have been so very trying for people's lives and spirits.

I know that your present life is extremely and unusually harsh, entangled in a myriad of mishaps, and that there is no clear future for you or for your children.

I know that I am returning to a Russia tortured, stunned, altered beyond recognition, convulsively searching for itself, for its own true identity.

Everywhere I go, I hope to meet and listen to local residents, to test or revise my own judgments. I am eager to understand truly and accurately your conditions, to enter into and share your worries and your fears, and to search together for the surest path out of our seventy-five-year quagmire.

My heart longs for the day when our country's long-suffering people might finally find a ray of light ahead. I bow to you in respect and admiration.

Message at the Opening of the Center for Russian Culture Abroad

SEPTEMBER 2, 2005

Solzhenitsyn lived in involuntary exile for twenty years after his expulsion from the Soviet Union in February 1974. He never considered himself an émigré, since he had made no "spiritual decision" to leave his homeland and start his life elsewhere. But as the following text makes clear, Solzhenitsyn had nothing but admiration and respect for the "first wave" of refugees who streamed out of Russia after the Revolution and Civil War. As he put it in an interview with the BBC in 1979, they had a "historical mission" of the first order: "to help [Russians] preserve a historical memory of the pre-revolutionary and revolutionary years when everything in the Soviet Union was being trampled underfoot."

To aid this endeavor, Solzhenitsyn established the Russian Memoir Library in 1977 and helped arrange the publication of a series of memoirs of émigrés, as well as historical investigations under the title *Studies in Modern Russian History.* The opening in Moscow of the Center for Russian Culture Abroad on September 2, 2005, is the culmination of this work of nearly thirty years and guarantees that the "pride and flower of Russian thought and creativity" will be available for future generations.

Following the Catastrophe of 1917 and the Civil War, there rushed out of Russia and beyond her borders a wave not so much of émigrés as of three million refugees. They came from the most varied strata of society—from simple Cossacks and common soldiers of the Volunteer Army to the wealthy and aristocratic set—and they encompassed the most elite and refined intellectuals: scientists, philosophers, and artists of all disciplines. Thus formed a diaspora lasting three-quarters of the twentieth century, unprecedented both in its size and in its spiritual qualities; a diaspora that drew into its ranks the pride and flower of Russian thought and creativity.

For three-quarters of a century this diaspora was cut off from the Homeland by an impregnable fence. For many, this separation lasted until their deaths. More than anything else, the communist government feared their ideas, their thought, the harsh truth that they spoke about what exactly transpired in Russia's revolutionary period, and how it transpired. Thus, the greatest works born of the Russian émigré spirit were denied access to the homeland, and the worthiest émigré names remained obscure and unknown to the new Soviet generations.

Thirty years ago, calling on Russian emigrants to write their memoirs for future's sake, and promising them that my heirs would faithfully preserve their manuscripts and one day deliver them to a free Russia, I could not have much hoped to live to see that moment myself.

Yet the moment has now arrived. Through the resources and efforts of the Moscow authorities, with the impassioned participation and assistance of Mayor Yuri Luzhkov, there now stands—outfitted, completed, and working—that promised place, of which the Russian emigration dreamed for eighty-five years. That place in the homeland where all emigrants can grant and entrust for safekeeping the history of their lives—lives without shelter, full of wandering and calamitous poverty—as well as the spiritual fruits of those lives, their historical memory, the creative bursts of their quills. Now, too, all our countrymen who never left Russia can deposit at our All-Russia Memoir Library the story of their own lives, full of events and calamities of a different kind, of oppression, of the complete uprooting of their very existence.

And so these manuscripts—letters and tales for our successors—have acquired their home.

Today we welcome and thank all those who have gathered to share in our celebration.

12

MINIATURES

Solzhenitsyn's miniatures provide the strongest reminder that his literary output is not restricted to the long works on which his acclaim primarily rests. And the label of prophet is too one-sided to capture the range of his genres. Although initially known in English as prose poems, these *Krokhotki* (the Russian title) are literally "tinies," or miniatures. Solzhenitsyn composed a series of them in 1958–60. A couple of years later, he penned "A Prayer," which he views as belonging to the same genre. Then, as he has remarked, he simply could not write in this genre again until after he returned to his native soil in the mid-1990s.

These miniatures take their inspiration from Russia, but they invite universal application. Typically, they begin with a single observation or experience and end in thematic elucidation. In contrast to Solzhenitsyn's fiction, the miniatures have mood and tone as their controlling and unifying literary elements. Their mood is pensive, often melancholy, sometimes nostalgic; their tone is usually gentle, with affirmations outweighing reproaches. Setting, especially rural landscape, also is prominent. Solzhenitsyn contrasts, as dark background and bright foreground, the soulless sterility of modern, particularly Soviet, life and the spiritual sustenance available from nature and the past. Human beings once lived in respectful harmony with nature, accepting with equanimity the all-encompassing rhythms of life and death. The affirming attitudes that modernity has mutilated can be renovated.

Of the various recurring themes, the most basic is the embrace of the life force as such. Ex-prisoners feel revived in the sheer act of breathing freely. The mystery of life and the authority of nature are on display in the freely frolicking puppy, the insubstantial duckling that scientists are powerless to recreate, the felled elm tree that sends out a new shoot, the lightning bolt that cleaves a tree down to its roots. Contemplative observations of nature disclose parallels to human traits; ants return home to a burning log as patriots are drawn to their suffering homeland, and the personified larch tree symbolizes the human virtues of solidarity, soft-heartedness, and inner toughness. By contrast, the Soviets show no respect for the fittingness between man and nature; they expropriate the lovely Lake Segden for the ruling class's private indulgence. Even more vehemently they attack the past as a source of spiritual support. They desecrate the old churches that punctuated the countryside and the church bells that kept time and souls in tune. Churches, when not destroyed, are converted into cowsheds, tractor garages, clubhouses. A dammed river destroys a cathedral and part of the town that had survived marauding foreigners over eight centuries, though the partially submerged bell tower with a cross on top juts straight up toward heaven as a sign, despite all, of enduring hope. Shorn of belief, modern man can act only as if "we" will never die and starts the day not with spiritual devotions but with bodily exercises.

Although the two cycles of miniatures are bound together in continuity, the second set inclines toward greater explicitness in stating moral themes. In one new subset Solzhenitsyn searchingly addresses Russia's third—and current—"Time of Troubles" as it emerges from communism. Another subset introduces reflections on death and dying, as befits the author in old age. All these exquisite gems reward unhurried, meditative reading.

The two prayers that Solzhenitsyn places among the miniatures deserve special notes. In "A Prayer," composed shortly after *One Day in the Life of Ivan Denisovich* made him famous, he serenely acknowledges that God's gracious providence governs his ongoing career; thus, it shows better than anything else his personal relationship with God. The behind-the-scenes story is fascinating. One of his helpers, Elizaveta Voronyanskaya, released this text without permission. Although he scolded her at the time, the widely reproduced prayer elicited many grateful reactions. Moreover, it was a key factor in his being awarded the Templeton Prize, and he recounts that composing the "Templeton Lecture" deepened his understanding of himself. Voronyanskaya played a similar role in the appearance of *The Gulag Archipelago* by disregarding Solzhenitsyn's instruction to destroy her copy, which the KGB then located. With his hand forced, Solzhenitsyn ordered the work published, and it went on to exert its world-historical influence. About Voronyanskaya, he concludes, "For both willful acts I can only be grateful to her—she had served as an instrument of God's will." After Solzhenitsyn returned to Russia in 1994, he wrote "A Prayer for Russia"; he felt a need for such a prayer, and he prays it every day.

1958–63

BREATHING

There was rain in the night, clouds are drifting over the sky, and there is still an occasional sprinkle.

I stand under an apple tree that is losing its blossom—and I breathe. The apple tree and the grass around it are saturated with moisture, and there is no name for the sweet and heady smell that intoxicates the air. I draw it deep, deep into my lungs, my whole chest tingles with the fragrance. I breathe and breathe again, shutting my eyes, opening my eyes—I don't know which way is best.

This perhaps is the freedom, the only freedom but the most precious one, of which prison deprives us: the freedom to breathe like this, to breathe in this place. No food on earth, no wine, not even a woman's kiss is sweeter to me than this air, this heady, blossom-scented, rain-fresh air.

So what if it is only a tiny garden hemmed in by five-storied buildings like cages in a zoo? I no longer hear the backfiring motorcycles, the howling radiograms, the crackling loudspeakers. So long as I can stand under an apple tree after rain and just breathe—it is possible to live.

LAKE SEGDEN

No one ever writes about the lake or mentions it aloud. All roads to it are blocked, as though it were some enchanted castle, and over all of them hangs a sign, a single mute mark of prohibition. When you see that mark over your path, whether you are man or beast—turn back! It has been put up by the earthly power that rules here. The mark means: no riding and no flying, no walking and no crawling.

And by the roadside, in the pine forest, sentries with muskets and pistols lie in wait.

Round and round you wander in the silent woods looking for a way through to the lake. But you won't find it, and there is nobody to ask. People have been frightened off and no one ever comes into the wood. All you can do is to follow the muffled tinkle of a cowbell and pick your way along a cattle track at noontide on a rainy day. Suddenly that great stretch of water will flash upon you from between the trees, and while you are still running you know that this of all earth's places you will love for the rest of your days.

Lake Segden is a circle, as if cut out with a compass. If you stand on one bank and shout—but you won't shout in case someone notices you—only a tired echo will reach the other side. It's a long long way. Along the shoreline woods lap the lake in a close embrace. An even, matching row of trees, without a gap. When you get down to the edge you can see all round the enclosed shore: a yellow strip of sand, a fuzz of gray reeds, a flat patch of green grass. The water is so smooth, calm, and unruffled. There is duckweed here and there near the shore, but elsewhere the water is transparent white, for the bottom is white.

Secluded water. Secluded woods. The lake looks at the sky, the sky at the lake. There may be other things on earth, but who knows—nothing can be seen over the trees. And if there is anything else, it isn't wanted and will never be missed here.

This is a place to settle down for good. . . . Your soul would flow, like the quivering air, between water and sky, and your thoughts would run pure and deep.

It cannot be. A wicked prince, a cross-eyed villain holds sway over the lake: There is his summer house, there his bathing place. His villainous children fish and shoot ducks from a boat. First a wisp of blue smoke over the lake, after a while the sound of a shot.

Out there, beyond the woods, the countryside toils and moils. But, so that no one can disturb them, all the roads here are barred, the fishing and the game are kept up for them alone. Here are the traces of a campfire that someone tried to light: they put it out, then drove him away.

Dear, deserted lake.

Home. . . .

The Duckling

A comical yellow duckling, wobbling on its thin little legs, its whitish belly bobbing up and down in the wet grass, runs in front of me and cheeps: "Where is my mama? Where are all my family?"

It isn't really his mama at all. They put some duck eggs under a hen, and she sat on them together with her own and warmed them all alike. Now it looks like rain and their little house—an upturned basket with no bottom—has been carried under shelter and covered with sacking. The others are all there, but this one has got lost. Come on then, little thing, come into my hand.

What keeps body and soul together in this tiny creature? He weighs nothing at all, his little black eyes are like beads, his feet are like a sparrow's, just one little squeeze and there would be nothing. And yet—how warm he is. His little beak, pale pink as a lacquered fingernail, is already shovel-flat. His feet are already webbed, he is as yellow as all his kind, his downy wings are already sprouting. And look how different he is in character from his brothers.

We are the ones who will shortly be flying to Venus. Even now, if we all worked together with a will, we could plow up the whole earth in twenty minutes.

But, with all our atomic might, never, never shall we be able to synthesize in our retorts, nor even to assemble from bones and feathers ready-made—a weightless, puny, and pathetic little yellow duckling. . . .

A POET'S ASHES

What is now the village of Lgovo, and was formerly the ancient town of Olgov, stands on a cliff high over the river Oka: The Russians of those distant times valued natural beauty a close second behind water that was fast-running and good to drink. Ingvar Igorevich, who was delivered miraculously from the knives of his brothers, built here, for his soul's sake, the monastery of the Assumption. On a clear day you can see a long way from here, over the rolling water-meadows, and more than twenty miles away on a hill as high as this stands the tall belltower in the monastery of St. John the Divine.

Batu Khan was superstitious and spared them both.

This place took the eye of Yakov Petrovich Polonsky. He liked it more than any other, and gave orders that he should be buried here. We cannot help imagining that our souls will hover over our graves and gaze on the broad and peaceful countryside.

But the domes have gone, the churches have gone, only half of the stone wall is left, and the holes have been stopped with board fence and barbed wire. Looming over the ancient ruins there are watchtowers, those hideous scarecrows that we know so well . . . and in the gateway of the monastery—a guardhouse. A poster with the caption "Peace among the Nations" shows a Russian worker with an African child in his arms.

We pretend to know nothing, and one of the warders, off-duty and wearing a singlet, explains to us, amidst the guard huts:

"Used to be a monastery here. Number two in the world. Number one was in Rome, I think. Moscow had but number three. The place was a children's settlement once, and the boys, of course they know no better. They made a mess of all the walls and smashed the icons. Then a collective farm bought the two churches for forty thousand rubles—for bricks, to build a six-row cowshed. I got taken on myself. They paid fifty kopecks for whole bricks and twenty for halves. Only the bricks weren't easy to pick out—it was all chunks of brick and mortar. A vault was found under the church, and there was a bishop lying there. Nothing left of him but his skull. But his robe was still in one piece. Two of us tried to tear it off, but we couldn't . . ."

"Yes. Well, according to the map, the poet Polonsky's grave should be somewhere here. Can you tell me where it is?"

"You can't get to Polonsky. He's in the *zone*.[1] You can't get to him. And anyway, what's there to see? Just a broken-down memorial. Wait a bit though." The camp-guard turned to his wife—"Didn't they dig Polonsky up?"

His wife, cracking sunflower seeds on the porch, nodded: "Of course. He was taken off to Ryazan."

The camp-guard couldn't help laughing. "Got his release, eh. . . ."

THE ELM LOG

We were sawing firewood, picked up an elm log, and cried out in surprise—all that time since the trunk had been trimmed, and uprooted by a tractor, and sawn into pieces, and the pieces flung into barges and on to trucks, and stacked and tipped out on to the ground—and still the elm log had not given up! It had put out a new shoot, which might become an elm itself, or a leafy rustling branch.

We had already placed the log on the sawhorse—as though on the headsman's block—but we could not bring ourselves to cut into it. How could we saw it? It wants to live too! Just look how much it wants to live—more than we ourselves!

---

[1] *Zone*: the fenced-in portion of a labor camp to which inmates return after work.

REFLECTION IN WATER

On the surface of swift-running water you cannot make out the reflections of objects near or distant. Even if it is not muddy, even if it is free of foam, reflections in the ceaselessly wavering ripples, the boisterously shifting race are deceptive, vague, incomprehensible.

Only when, from stream to stream, the current has reached a placid estuary, or in still backwaters, or in small lakes with never a tremulous wave, can we see in the mirror-smooth surface the smallest leaf of a tree on the bank, every fiber of a fine-combed cloud, and the intense blue depths of the sky.

So it is with you and me. If, try as we may, we never have been and never shall be able to see, to reflect the truth in all its eternal fresh-minted clarity, is it not simply because we are still in motion, still living? . . .

A STORM IN THE MOUNTAINS

It caught us on a pitch-black night on the mountainside. We crawled out of our tents—and were speechless.

It was coming towards us from over the Ridge.

There was nothing in the world but darkness—no above, no beneath, no horizon. Then there was a rending flash of lightning, the darkness was divided from the light, the gigantic mountains of Belala-Kai and Djuguturlyuchat stood out, and the black pines towering around us looked as high as the mountains. Just for a moment we half-believed that land already existed, then once more all was darkness and the abyss.

The flashes were coming closer, darkness alternated with blinding light, a white glow, a pink glow, a mauve glow, and time and time again the mountains and the pine trees appeared, just where they were before, awed us with their majestic size, yet when they vanished again it was impossible to believe that they existed.

The voice of the thunder filled the ravines and the ceaseless roar of rivers could no longer be heard. Like the arrows of the Lord of Hosts the lightning flashes fell from on high upon the Ridge and split into wriggles and dribbles of light, and smashed into the face of the cliffs as though slaying some living thing.

And we forgot our fear of the lightning, the thunder, and the downpour, for a drop in the ocean does not fear the hurricane. We became insignificant and grateful particles of that world. A world created today, from nothing, right before our eyes.

The City on the Neva

Angels, lamp in hand, bow down around the Byzantine dome of St. Isaac's. Three fluted golden spires greet each other across the Neva and the Moika. Here and there lions, griffins, and sphinxes keep watch over treasures, or doze and dream. Victory's team of six leap over Rossi's cunning crooked arch. There are hundreds of porticos, thousands of columns, horses rearing, bulls straining. . . .

How fortunate that nothing else can be built here!—no wedding-cake skyscraper wedged into the Nevski, no five-storied box slapped down by the Griboyedov Canal. The most eminent and incompetent architect of the lot could not with all his influence get a construction site closer than the Chyornaya Rechka or the Okhta.

So alien to us—and yet our greatest glory—this magnificence. How delightful it is now to stroll along these avenues! But other Russians, clenching their teeth and cursing, rotted in the sunless bog to build all this beauty. The bones of our forefathers caked and fused and petrified into palaces—yellowish, reddish, chocolate, green.

It is awesome to contemplate: our own ungainly and wretched lives, our explosive disagreements, the groans of the executed and the tears of their wives—will all this, too, be clean forgotten? Will from this, too, come such perfect and undying beauty? . . .

Sharik

A boy in our yard keeps a little dog called Sharik on a chain. They tied him up when he was just a puppy.

One day I took him some chicken bones while they were warm and smelt good. But the boy had just let the poor creature off his chain for a run. The snow in the yard lay thick and fluffy. Sharik bounded about like a hare, on his back legs one minute and his front legs the next, rushing from corner to corner of the yard and back again, with snow on his muzzle.

He ran to me, the shaggy creature, and jumped all over me, sniffed the bones—and off he went again, up to his belly in snow.

"I don't want your bones," he seemed to say, "just give me my freedom. . . ."

Means of Locomotion

Take, say, the horse—prancing with arched back, stomping its hooves, with its sprawling mane and lucid warm eye. Or, take the camel—that two-humped swan, that languid sage with a smirk of cognition on its round lips. Take, even, the homely donkey—with its patient fortitude and lively, caressive ears.

And we chose? . . . —this most unsightly of the Earth's creatures, on fast rubber paws, with dead, glassy eyes and a blunt, ribbed snout, with an iron box for a hump. It will never neigh of the joy of the steppe, of the smells of the pastures, of its love for the mare or the master. Incessantly it grates its iron and spits, spits its violet fetid fume.

Well, as we are—such also is our means of locomotion.

THE OLD BUCKET

Oh, how depressing for a former front-liner to roam Kartun Forest. Somehow the earth here has almost perfectly preserved, for eighteen years already, not only the trench lines, not only the firing positions of field guns, but even a distinct small weapon pit, where an unknown Ivan sheltered his large body in a short, threadbare greatcoat. Over the years the roof-beams of the dugout have been pilfered, of course, but the trenches are still plain to see.

Although I did not fight right here, I was in action in another wood like it nearby. I walk from dugout to dugout, trying to reconstruct the position. Suddenly, coming out of one dugout, I stumble upon an old bucket which had already seen better days when it had been left lying there eighteen years ago.

Even then, in that first wartime winter, it was shabby. Maybe some quick-witted soldier had picked it up in a burnt-down village, had battered the lower half of the sides into a cone, and had used it to connect his tin stove to a flue. Here, in this same dugout, during that anxious winter, for the ninety or perhaps hundred and fifty days that the front line was stabilized in this sector, smoke had been driven through this shabby bucket. It had glowed hellishly hot; men had warmed their hands over it; you could light a cigarette on it and toast bread in front of it. As much smoke had passed through that bucket as all the unspoken thoughts and unwritten letters of the men there—men, perhaps, long since dead.

Then one fine morning, by cheery sunshine, the tactical position changed, the dugout was abandoned, and as the officer urged them on—"Come on, get moving!"—an orderly doused the stove and jammed it onto the truck until everything was stowed away, even the pipe elbows, except that no room could be found for the shabby bucket. "Chuck the filthy thing away!" shouted the sergeant-major. "You'll find another one in the new place." They had a long way to go, and in any case the warmer spring weather was not far off; the orderly stood there with the shabby bucket, sighed—and set it down by the entrance.

Everybody laughed.

Since then the logs have been pulled off the roof, the bunks and the table removed from the inside, but that shabby faithful bucket has stayed right there by its dugout.

As I stand over it, tears flood my eyes. My good chaps, my friends from the front! The spirit that kept us going, our hopes, even that selfless friendship of ours—it has all vanished like smoke and there will never again be a use for that rusty, forgotten. . . .

YESENIN'S BIRTHPLACE

Four villages, one after another, stretch monotonously along one street. Dust. There are no orchards, and no nearby woods, only rickety fences and garishly painted window frames. A filthy pig scratches itself against the pump in the middle of the road. An orderly procession of geese turns in unison to send a martial challenge after the fleeting shadow of a bicycle. Busy hens scratch up the roadway and the back yards, searching for food.

The village shop at Konstantinovo is in a hut like a rickety henhouse. There are herrings. All sorts of vodka. There are sweets, a sticky mass of those satin cushions that people everywhere stopped eating fifteen years ago. And there are black loaves the size of hefty cobblestones, twice heavier than in the cities, loaves that need an axe, not a knife.

Flimsy partitions divide the Yesenin house into cubbyholes and hutches—there's nothing you could call a room. In the garden there is a windowless shed, and there used to be a bathhouse. Sergei crept out there in the dark to write his first verses. Beyond the stick fence there is a little field.

I walk round this village which is like so many, many others, where everybody is preoccupied with getting a living, making money, keeping up with the neighbors . . . and I am excited. A heavenly fire once scorched this neighborhood, and it still makes my cheeks burn now. I come out on the sloping bank of the Oka, gaze into the distance and marvel: Can he have been looking at that dim strip of scrubby forest in the distance when he said mysteriously: "The pinewoods ring with the weeping of woodcocks. . . ," and did he think of these meadows along the bends of the quiet Oka when he wrote about "stooks of sun in the lap of the water . . ."?

What an astounding nugget of talent did the Creator fling here, into this hut, into the heart of this rowdy peasant lad, so that he, stunned, could find so much raw beauty—at the stove, in the pens, on the threshing-floor, beyond the village outskirts—beauty which people have been treading, unawares, for a thousand years. . . .

THE KOLKHOZ[2] RUCKSACK

When you're traveling on a country bus and somebody gives you a painful jab in the chest or the ribs with its sharp corners—don't start a row, but take a good look at it, that basket of plaited bast on its broad strap of frayed canvas. A woman takes milk and cottage cheese and tomatoes to market in it, for herself and two neighbors, and brings four dozen loaves from town to feed three families.

It is roomy, stout, and cheap, this countrywoman's rucksack; its gaudy sporting brethren, all side-pockets and shining buckles, cannot compare with it. It holds so much weight that even over a jerkin its strap is too much for a practiced peasant shoulder.

So the women have made it the fashion to swing the plaited basket on to the small of the back and pass the strap over their heads like a horse-collar. Then the weight is evenly distributed over shoulders and breast.

Brother writers! I don't ask you to try one of these baskets on your own backs. But if you get jostled—just travel by taxi.

THE FIRE AND THE ANTS

I tossed a rotten log on the fire without noticing that it housed a dense colony of ants.

As the wood began to crackle the ants poured out and ran around in despair. They ran about the surface of the log, shriveling and burning to death in the blaze. I took a grip on the log and rolled it to one side. Many of the ants escaped now, running on to the sand and the pine needles. But strangely enough they did not run right away from the fire. Barely had they mastered their dread when they turned back, ran around in circles, as though some force was drawing them back to their abandoned homeland—and there were many who even swarmed back on to the burning log and scurried about on it until they perished. . . .

WE SHALL NEVER DIE

Above all things we have begun to fear death and the dead.

If we hear of someone dying, we avoid writing to the family or visiting them: We don't know what to say about it, about death.

We're ashamed even to mention a cemetery seriously. You wouldn't tell them at work that "I can't come in on Sunday, I have to go and visit my folks

---

[2] *Kolkhoz*: a Soviet collective farm.

in the cemetery." What sort of nonsense is that—visiting people who don't need to be fed?

You want to move a dead man from one town to another? You must be crazy—nobody will give you room on a train for that. And the dead are no longer borne slowly through the town with music, but rushed away in trucks.

At one time they used to go round our cemeteries on Sundays singing joyously and swinging sweet-smelling censers. The heart was at peace, and the scar which inevitable death had left on it throbbed less painfully. It was as though the dead were looking at us from under their little green mounds with a slight smile and saying: "It's all right. It's all right. . . ."

But nowadays, if the cemetery is kept up at all, there are notice-boards saying: "Grave owners! You are liable to a fine if you fail to remove last year's litter!" And more often than not they roll the ground flat and level it with bulldozers to make room for a stadium or an amusement park.

And then there are those who have died for their country, as you and I may yet have to die. Our Church used to set aside a day for them—for remembering warriors fallen on the field of battle. Britain remembers them on Poppy Day. Every nation does the same—sets aside a day for thinking about those who gave their lives for us.

For us in this country more lives were given than anywhere else, yet we have no such day. If we keep looking back at all those who perished . . . who will do the brick-laying? We have lost husbands, sons, sweethearts in three wars—well, get lost, you pests, under your painted wooden obelisks, don't hamper our lives! *We*, after all, shall never die.

Approaching the Day

At sunrise, thirty young people ran out into the clearing, lined up facing the sun, and started bending, squatting, bowing, lying face downwards, stretching their arms outwards, raising their arms about their heads, and rocking backwards and forwards on their knees. This went on for a quarter of an hour.

From a distance you might imagine that they were praying.

No one in our time finds it surprising if a man gives careful and patient daily attention to his body.

But people would be outraged if he gave the same attention to his soul.

No, they weren't saying their prayers. They were doing their morning exercises.

ALONG THE OKA

When you travel the byroads of Central Russia you begin to understand the secret of the pacifying Russian countryside.

It is in the churches. They trip up the slopes, ascend the high hills, come down to the broad rivers like princesses in white and red, they lift their belltowers—graceful, shapely, lovingly carved—high over mundane timber and thatch, they nod to each other from afar, from villages that are cut off and invisible to each other, they soar to the same heaven.

And wherever you wander in the fields or meadows, however far from habitation, you are never alone: From over the hayricks, the wall of trees, and the very curvature of the earth, the head of some belltower will beckon to you from Borki Lovetskie, or from Lyubichi, or from Gavrilovskoye.

But when you get into the village you find that not the living but the dead greeted you from afar. The crosses were knocked off the roof or twisted out of place long ago. The dome has been stripped, and there are gaping holes between its rusty ribs. Weeds grow on the roofs and in the cracks in the walls. usually the graveyard has not been kept up, the crosses have been flattened and the graves churned. The icons over the altar have been smeared by the rains of decades and defaced by obscene inscriptions.

On the porch there are barrels of lubricating oil and a tractor is turning towards them. Or else a truck has backed into the church doorway to pick up some sacks. In one church there is the shudder of lathes. Another is locked up and silent. In another and another there are clubs. "Let us Attain High Milk Yields!" "A Poem About the Sea." "A Heroic Deed."

People were always selfish and often unkind. But the evening chimes used to ring out, floating over villages, fields, and woods. Reminding men that they must abandon the trivial concerns of this world, and give time and thought to eternity. These chimes, now preserved for us just in the olden chants, raised people up and prevented them from sinking down onto all fours.

Our forefathers put all that was finest in themselves, all their understanding of life, into these stones, into these belltowers.

Ram it in, Vitka, give it a bash, don't be shy! Film-show at six o'clock, dancing at eight. . . .

A PRAYER

How easy for me to live with you, Lord!
How easy to believe in you!

When my mind casts about
or flags in bewilderment,
when the cleverest among us
cannot see past the present evening,
not knowing what to do tomorrow—
you send me the clarity to know
that you exist
and will take care
that not all paths of goodness should be barred.
At the crest of earthly fame
I look back in wonderment
at the journey beyond hope—to this place,
from which I was able to send mankind
a reflection of your rays.
And however long the time
that I must yet reflect them
you will give it me.
And whatever I fail to accomplish
you surely have allotted unto others.

1996–99

THE LARCH

What an extraordinary tree this is!

All we see when we look at her are needles and more needles. Obviously another conifer then? But not so fast! As autumn sets in, the deciduous trees around her start to shed their leaves, almost as if death were upon them. And then—is she commiserating? I won't desert you! the rest of my kind can winter safely here without me—she too begins to shed. And how suddenly her needles shower down—in festive, glinting sparks of sunlight.

Do we conclude that there is a softness at her very heart? Wrong again! The texture of her wood is among the toughest in the world—not every axe can get the better of it, it is too dense to drag and float downstream, and, far from rotting when abandoned in the water, it draws ever closer to the eternal strength of stone.

But when the gentle warmth of spring creeps back, a gift that each year takes us by surprise . . . it seems another year of life has been bestowed upon us, then why not spread our foliage anew, why not rejoin our kin, arrayed in needles soft as silk?

One could point to people who share those same qualities.

LIGHTNING

Only in books had I read of lightning splitting a tree in two; it was not something I had ever seen.

But I have now! It came from a thunderstorm passing overhead in broad daylight—a blinding flash of lightning that bathed our windows in coruscating gold, followed, a split second later—by an almighty clap of thunder—it couldn't have been more than two or three hundred yards from the house.

The storm passed. And sure enough—there it was, in a patch of trees close by. Why, among all those towering pines, should the lightning have singled out a lime tree—and not even the tallest one? From just below its crown the bolt had coursed downwards—down the length of the trunk, slicing through its core, its vitality and self-assurance. But for all the lightning's power, it had not reached the very bottom—had it glanced off to one side? or simply exhausted itself? . . . All one could see was the gouged-up earth near the scorched roots and the coarse wood-chips, hurled fifty yards in every direction.

One section of trunk, reaching midway down the tree itself, had split off and toppled over to one side, coming to rest against the branches of its blameless neighbors. The other half lingered on for another day, though with such a gaping hole torn clean through it that who can say what force sustained it? Finally, it too heeled over to be welcomed into the forked arms of another of its tall sisters.

And so it is with some of us: when conscience does hurl its chastening bolt, it strikes through our inmost being and down the length of our days. And after such a blow there is no telling who of us will remain standing, and who will not.

THE BELL AT UGLICH

What Russian has not heard of the bizarre punishment meted out to this bell? How its tongue was plucked out, how they broke off one of the lugs by which it hung so that it should never again grace a belltower and how, for good measure, they whipped it, then exiled it twelve hundred jolting miles by cart to Tobolsk, drawn not by horses—no, this accursed load was hauled every inch of the way by condemned townsfolk of Uglich—over and above the two hundred already put to death for tearing apart "the Tsar's retainers" (sent to murder Dmitri, the young heir to the throne)—and their tongues were sliced off lest they tell their own tale of what really happened that day at Uglich.

Returning to Russia by way of Siberia, I chanced upon the traces left behind by this former exile in the Tobolsk Kremlin: I stood in the tiny chapel where it had served out its three-hundred-year solitary confinement before being pardoned and allowed to go home. And now here I am in Uglich itself, in the Church of Dmitri-on-the-Blood. And the bell, only half a man's height for all its seven hundred weight, hangs here in a place of honor. Long suffering has dulled its bronze to gray. Its clapper hangs idle. And I am invited to ring it.

I strike just once. And a marvelous deep boom resounds through the church! How richly evocative these intermingling bass tones, appealing from the distant past to our foolishly bustling, turbid souls! A single blow—yet for half a minute it reverberates, then lingers a full minute more before dying away in slow and solemn majesty, preserving to the last its rich palate of sounds. How well our forebears knew the secrets of metal!

Within minutes of learning that Prince Dmitri had been butchered, the sexton of the cathedral church had raced into the bell-loft—he had the foresight to bolt the door behind him—and however hard the scoundrels battered at the door, he rang and rang, sounding the tocsin on this very bell. In the horror and lamentation of the townspeople of Uglich the bell proclaimed its fear for the very survival of Russia.

Those rolling peals, signaling a great calamity, heralded Russia's first Time of Troubles. And now it has fallen to me to ring this bell, so steeped in suffering, amidst the clinging, lingering decay of a third Time of Troubles. There is no escaping the comparison: The prophetic alarm of the people is but a pinprick to the throne and to the thick-skinned nobles clustered round it. This is as true today as it was four hundred years ago.[1]

---

[1] Historians are divided in their interpretation of this event, but popular tradition holds firmly to the view that Dmitri, the young son of Tsar Ivan IV of Russia, was murdered in Uglich in 1591. Boris Godunov, who succeeded to the throne in 1598 upon the death of Fyodor I, Ivan's other surviving son, was immediately suspected of complicity. The end of Boris's reign inaugurated a period of unrest and civil war, known as the "Time of Troubles" (1605–13), which ended with the accession of Mikhail Romanov. Solzhenitsyn sees the revolution and Civil War which brought the Romanov dynasty to a close as a second Time of Troubles, and the period since the end of the 1980s as a third.

THE BELLTOWER

Whoever seeks to grasp, to compass at a glance our Russian land before it is finally submerged—should take the time to look upon the belltower of Kalyazin.

It once stood hard by the cathedral in the thick of a flourishing trading town near the covered market of the Gostinyi dvor, and streets of two-story merchant houses ran down onto the square at its feet. And no prophet could then have foretold that in its eighth century of life this ancient town, survivor of successive onslaughts by marauding Tatars and Poles, would be deliberately submerged at the ignorant behest of petty tyrants, leaving two-thirds of the town beneath the Volga—the Bolsheviks begrudged the money for a second dam, which would have saved it. (Two-thirds submerged? Why, the entire town of Mologa is lying down at the bottom of the river too.) Kalyazin, swallowed up like the fabled town of Kitezh, lies in ten fathoms of water, and if you stand today at the river's edge no effort of the imagination can raise this reluctant Atlantis from the abyss.

But what survives of the drowned town is its tall, graceful belltower. The cathedral was blasted apart or dismantled to provide the building bricks for our radiant future, yet for some reason they didn't get around to flattening the belltower, didn't lay a finger on it—you'd think it was a protected building! And here it stands, jutting out of the water, its white brickwork built to last, its six tiers tapering as they rise (one and a half of them submerged)—in the last few years they have been tipping rubble against her sides to form a protective platform round the base—here it stands with no sign of a tilt or twist, thrusting heavenward the open-work pattern of its five visible tiers, surmounted by an onion-dome and spire. And on the spire—what miracle is this?—the cross survives intact! Bulky Volga steamers forge by—yet when viewed from afar they reach barely halfway up the first of the belltower's exposed tiers—and their wake sends the waves slapping against its white walls, while from the decks Soviet passengers gape at the tower, just as they have these fifty years.

You roam the surviving little streets—dismal, mutilated, and still showing here and there the buckled hovels of those first, hastily resettled flood victims. Along the false new embankment the women of Kalyazin, devoted as ever to the renowned gentleness and purity of the Volga water, are trying to rinse out their linen. The ravaged town lingers on, a broken stump, more dead than alive, with but a handful of its once splendid buildings left intact. Yet even amidst this desolation, cheated and abandoned as they are, people have no choice but to go on living. And where are they to live but—here?

And still, for them, as for all who have once beheld this marvel—the belltower stands! Like the hope we cherish. Like the prayer we raise on high. No, the Lord will not permit *all* of Russia to be plunged beneath the waves. . . . .

GROWING OLD

For all that has been written about death's horrors, what an organic link death is in the chain of life, when it comes without violence!

I remember a Greek poet I knew in the labor camps: He was still in his thirties but not long for this world. Yet his gentle, wistful smile betrayed no fear of death. This amazed me. But, he told me, "Before the onset of death we go through an inner process of preparation; we grow and mature to meet it—and then it no longer holds any terror for us."

Barely a year was to pass before—at thirty-four years of age—I experienced the same thing at first hand. Month by month, week by week, as I drew ever nearer to death and adapted to it—my readiness and resignation outstripped that of my own body.

How much easier it is, then, how much more receptive we are to death, when advancing years guide us softly to our end. Aging thus is in no sense a punishment from on high, but brings its own blessings and a warmth of colors all its own.

There is warmth in watching little children at play, seeing them gain in strength and character. There is even warmth to be drawn from the waning of your own strength compared with the past—just to think how sturdy I once used to be! You can no longer get through a whole day's work at a stretch, but how good it is to slip into the brief oblivion of sleep, and what a gift to wake once more to the clarity of your second or third morning of the day. And your spirit can find delight in limiting your intake of food, in abandoning the pursuit of novel flavors. You are still of this life, yet you are rising above the material plane. The shrill cry of the tomtits in a snow-clad wood in early spring holds twice the charm, for soon you will hear it no more—so listen to your heart's content! And what an inalienable treasure your memories prove! This is something the young are denied, but you carry them all with you, unfailingly, and a living portion of them calls upon you each day— during the infinitely slow transition from night to day, and again from day to night.

Growing old serenely is not a downhill path, but an ascent.

But, Lord, spare us from an old age racked by poverty and cold.

The fate to which we have consigned so very, very many. . . .

SHAME

How agonizing it is to feel ashamed for your own Motherland!

Whose callous hands are these, whose scheming hands that rule Her life so rashly and corruptly? What faces these—haughty, cunning, or void of character—that represent Her to the world? What rancid swill is She now served in place of wholesome spiritual fare? To what depths of ruin and penury are Her people reduced, powerless to clamber from the pit?

The sense of humiliation is unremitting. It has none of the transience of those everyday personal emotions, which change readily to match the fleeting play of circumstance. No, it oppresses you constantly, dogs your every step—it is with you when you wake, with you as you drag out each hour of the day, and with you as you sink back into night. And even death, which sets us free from personal afflictions, can offer no escape from this shame—it will simply continue to hang over the heads of the living, and you, after all, are a particle of their being.

You peruse the depths of Russia's past in search of encouraging precedents. And yet you know equally well the implacable truth—that nations of the earth have sometimes perished utterly. This would not be the first time.

But no, there are other depths to draw upon—those two dozen regions of the Russian heartland that I visited on my travels—it is they that whisper words of hope to me. There I saw aspirations still untarnished, a questing spirit as yet uncrushed, and living, generous-hearted countrymen of mine. Can it be that they will never break out of this pale of doom? No—they *shall* break free! It is yet within their power.

But day after day the shame hangs over us, like a pinkish-yellow cloud of poison gas, corroding our lungs. And even when at last it is dispersed, the blot upon our history will never be erased.

ILL WEEDS

To think of the labor expended by the tiller of the soil in preserving the seed grain until its time, sowing it to best advantage and lovingly tending the good plants until they bear fruit! Yet weeds spring up with a savage exuberance, knowing neither care nor nurture, but thriving in scornful defiance of them. That is what the proverb has in mind when it says: "Ill weeds are slow to wither."

But why should the good plants always be the weaker ones?

Looking back over the clinging morass of human history—from the dimmest recesses of the past to the vivid freshness of the present moment—we bow our heads despondently: Yes, this seems to be a universal law. And for all our well-meaning contrivances and all our earthly schemes, we shall never, ever escape its dictates.

Not till the end of humankind.

And to each of the living is granted nothing more than his labor—and his soul.

MORNING

What happens to our soul in the course of the night? Amidst the numb inertia of sleep it seems to detach itself from this body, to soar free through vast, pure expanses, stripping away the petty, murky accretions of the past day, and even of whole years. It returns, in pristine snowy whiteness, to open up for us the boundless, calm lucidity of our morning state of mind.

What better moments than these for thought and reflection! Your perceptions seem unexpectedly heightened, as if you were on the brink of grasping something which you have never before . . . something which. . . .

You pause, motionless. Something seems poised to burst into growth within you, something hitherto unknown and unsuspected. Scarcely daring to breathe, you summon forth this radiant shoot—the white tip of a tiny lily, soon to pierce the smooth unbroken surface of the eternal waters.

These are moments of grace! Moments which raise you high above yourself. There is something incomparably precious that you are capable of discovering, resolving, conceiving—if only you do not ruffle, or let others disturb the glassy calm of this lake that lies within you. . . .

But all too soon something comes along to unsettle and disrupt that heightened sensibility, whether it be another person's word or deed, or some petty thought of your own. And at once the spell is broken. That wondrous glassy stillness and the lake itself have vanished in a trice.

And all through the day, try as you might, you will not retrieve it.

Nor will every new morning bring it back to you.

THE CURTAIN

Heart disease can serve as an image of life itself—darkness shrouds its future course, we never know just when our end will come: Is that it lurking at our door, or might it still be a long way off?

When a tumor swells ominously within you, at least you can face the implacable truth and work out how long there is to go. But heart disease plays cunning tricks: At times you seem quite healthy—so you're not doomed after all! Why, it's as if you'd never been ill!

Blissful ignorance. What a merciful gift!

But in its acute phase heart disease is like being on death row. Each evening you sit and wait—is that the sound of footsteps? Are they coming for *me*? But then, each morning—what relief! and what a blessing! God has granted me a whole new day. One can live and do so very much in the space of but a single day.

IN TWILIGHT

I well remember the very widespread custom, back in the South, of "twilighting." Carried over from before the Revolution, it might have also been fortified by the meager, perilous years of the Civil War. Yet this practice had come about much earlier. Was it born of the months-long warmness of the Southern dusk? Many became accustomed never to rush lighting their lamps; yet, having completed their chores (or tended to the livestock) before nightfall, they were in no hurry to get to bed. Instead, they emerged outside to sit on dirt ledges, or benches, or just lounged inside with the windows wide open—no light to draw in bugs. One after another they would sit softly down, as if lost in thought. And long remained silent.

If someone did speak, it was quietly, delicately, unobtrusively. Somehow, in those exchanges, no one got fired up to argue, or to reproach spitefully, or to quarrel. Faces could barely be made out, then not at all; and, lo, one began to discern in them, and their voices, something unfamiliar, something one failed to observe through the prior course of years.

A feeling would take hold of everyone, of something impalpable and unseen that descended gently from the dimming after-sunset sky, dissolved in the air, streamed in through the windows: that profound seriousness of life, its unfragmented meaning, that goes ignored in the bustle of day. Our brush with the enigma that we let flit away.

ROOSTER SONG

With the depopulation, abandonment, and extinction of our villages, we have forgotten, and younger generations have never even heard, the many-voiced rooster roll call of midday. In sunny summertime, from one yard to the next, across the street, and farther, beyond the village outskirts, how marvelous is this chorus of triumphant life.

Little else can bestow such tranquility upon the soul. Not drowned out by any noisy bustle, this vivid, vibrant, succulent, stalwart cry conveys to us that throughout these parts there reigns a blessed peace, an untroubled calm. That's how today has unfolded so far, and why shouldn't it continue? Carry on, everyone, your benign pursuits.

Right here, somewhere, he saunters about proudly, all white and orange, with his sumptuous, knightly scarlet comb.

Comports himself gloomlessly.

If only *we* could.

NOCTURNAL THOUGHTS

It's one thing in a labor camp: You break your back the livelong day and, just you lay your head on a straw pillow, you hear: "U-u-u-up you get!" No nocturnal thoughts here.

But in the merry-go-round of our modern life, so frayed and fragmented, thoughts have no chance to ripen and settle during the day, and are abandoned. It is at night that they return to claim their due. No sooner does your mind's fog begin to lift, they lunge, they flood your flattened consciousness, jostling with each other. And one of the more caustic and audacious of the lot coils in front, ready to sting.

But your resistance, your dignity—is not to give yourself up to these gusts, but to master the dark torrent and guide it toward that which heals. For there is always a thought, often more than one, that introduces a tiny element of tranquility, like those control rods inserted into a nuclear reactor to impede a meltdown. Just learn to find this element, this saving ray of God—or even have it on the ready—and hold on to it.

Then your soul and reason are cleansed, those gusts disperse, and into the troubled world of insomnia step beneficent, spacious thoughts—ones you could never have approached in the bustle of day.

And thank insomnia: From this lookout even the insoluble can be solved. Power over self.

REMEMBRANCE OF THE DEPARTED

It is an act bequeathed to us in deep wisdom, by men of holiness.

We come to understand its purpose not in vigorous youth, amidst the company of loved ones, family, friends; but with age.

Parents have passed; peers now pass as well. Where go they? It seems unguessable, unfathomable, beyond our grasp. Yet as with some foreordained clarity, it dawns for us, it glimmers—no, they have not vanished.

And no more shall we learn of it, while we live. But a prayer for their souls—it casts from us to them, from them to us, an impalpable arch of measureless breadth yet effortless proximity. Why, here they are, you can almost touch them. Both unknowable are they and, as ever, so familiar. Except, they have fallen back in years: Some were older than we, but now are younger.

Focusing, you even inhale their answer, their hesitation, their warning. In exchange, you send them your own earthly warmth: Perhaps we too can help somehow? And a promise: We shall meet.

A PRAYER FOR RUSSIA

Our Father All-Merciful!
Don't abandon your own long-suffering Russia
In her present daze,
In her woundedness,
Impoverishment,
And confusion of spirit.
Lord Omnipotent!
Don't let, don't let her be cut short,
To no longer be.
So many forthright hearts
And so many talents
You have lodged among Russians.
Do not let them perish or sink into darkness
Without having served in Your name.
Out of the depths of Calamity
Save your disordered people.

About the Author
and Editors

Aleksandr I. Solzhenitsyn was born on December 11, 1918, in Kislovodsk, Russia. He returned to his homeland in 1994 after twenty years of involuntary exile in the West. He lived in Moscow until his death on August 3, 2008.

Edward E. Ericson, Jr., is Professor Emeritus of English at Calvin College. He abridged *The Gulag Archipelago* with Solzhenitsyn's cooperation and is co-author with Alexis Klimoff of *The Soul and Barbed Wire: An Introduction to Solzhenitsyn.*

Daniel J. Mahoney is Professor of Politics at Assumption College. An expert on French political philosophy and on antitotalitarian thought, his books include the critically acclaimed *Aleksandr Solzhenitsyn: The Ascent from Ideology* and *Bertrand de Jouvenel: The Conservative Liberal and the Illusions of Modernity.*